T0215726

Artificial Intelligence: Foundations, Theory, and Algorithms

Series Editors

Barry O'Sullivan, Dep. of Computer Science, University College Cork, Cork, Ireland

Michael Wooldridge, Department of Computer Science, University of Oxford, Oxford, UK

Artificial Intelligence: Foundations, Theory and Algorithms fosters the dissemination of knowledge, technologies and methodologies that advance developments in artificial intelligence (AI) and its broad applications. It brings together the latest developments in all areas of this multidisciplinary topic, ranging from theories and algorithms to various important applications. The intended readership includes research students and researchers in computer science, computer engineering, electrical engineering, data science, and related areas seeking a convenient way to track the latest findings on the foundations, methodologies, and key applications of artificial intelligence.

This series provides a publication and communication platform for all AI topics, including but not limited to:

- Knowledge representation
- Automated reasoning and inference
- Reasoning under uncertainty
- Planning, scheduling, and problem solving
- Cognition and AI
- Search
- Diagnosis
- Constraint processing
- Multi-agent systems
- Game theory in AI
- Machine learning
- Deep learning
- Reinforcement learning
- Data mining
- Natural language processing
- Computer vision
- Human interfaces
- Intelligent robotics
- Explanation generation
- Ethics in AI
- Fairness, accountability, and transparency in AI

This series includes monographs, introductory and advanced textbooks, state-of-the-art collections, and handbooks. Furthermore, it supports Open Access publication mode.

* * *

Paula Boddington

AI Ethics

A Textbook

 Springer

Paula Boddington
Geller Institute of Aging and Memory
University of West London
London, UK

ISSN 2365-3051 ISSN 2365-306X (electronic)
Artificial Intelligence: Foundations, Theory, and Algorithms
ISBN 978-981-19-9384-8 ISBN 978-981-19-9382-4 (eBook)
https://doi.org/10.1007/978-981-19-9382-4

This Springer imprint is published by the registered company Springer Nature Singapore Pte Ltd.
The registered company address is: 152 Beach Road, #21-01/04 Gateway East, Singapore 189721, Singapore

For Rachel Elizabeth Brooke

Dearly beloved friend of my youth, who could climb to the top of the highest tree.

Preface

This book aims to contribute to the many and various endeavours currently striving to understand and address the many ethical issues that surround AI. Since everyone is impacted by the technologies in question, the book is thus directed to anyone with any interest in the broad field. The central aim is to contribute to our capacity to understand, share, and debate ethical issues, to join in constructive dialogue with others, and for each of us to consider our own use of such technologies. As much as we need solutions to questions, we also need conversations that contribute to advancing the depth and breadth of understanding, aiming for real-world effects that help to improve how technology is designed and deployed. The book arises from my work in the field of AI, as well as many years of teaching philosophy and applied ethics, of engaging with students in the classroom in discussion and debate.

London, UK   Paula Boddington

Acknowledgements

I would like to acknowledge the support, encouragement, and valuable discussions from many, including colleagues, family, and friends, during the time I have spent writing this book. In particular, I would like to mention Katie Featherstone, Deborah Robertson, Lucy Wells, Lucy Brown, Susan Scott, Jen Hornsby, Aaron and Grace Kennedy, Jonathan Pageau, Katherine Bennett, Kathleen Richardson, Joanne, David, and Jenny Boddington, and Reuben and Indigo Leveson-Gower. I would also like to thank Celine Chang and other members of the team at Springer for their support, as well as all those students whose interest and discussion have inspired me and formed a great part of the impetus for this book. I would also like to thank Mike Wooldridge and Peter Millican, who first drew me into working on AI ethics.

This book was partially funded by the National Institute for Health Research, Health Services and Delivery Research Programme (project number 13/10/80). The views expressed are those of the author and not necessarily those of the NIHR or the Department of Health and Social Care.

About This Book

The field of AI ethics is so broad that only a selection of issues can be covered. I aim above all to demonstrate the particular contribution that the field of ethics can make to the necessarily interdisciplinary study of the challenges that the many facets of AI present and to show the intimate connections between questions of applied ethics, foundations of ethics, human nature, philosophy of technology, and conceptions of intelligence, both artificial and natural. The book aims to introduce ideas and to show their links, focusing upon enabling the reader to stretch their own capacity to look into these questions, since it is of vital importance that we are all equipped as well as possible to engage with these vital issues which are rapidly affecting so many parts of our lives. Foundational issues in ethical theory and philosophy are introduced and related to each other, with particular attention to methodological questions, and there are many examples and cases. Later chapters focus more on particular applications and ethical questions, ranging from questions facing us currently to imagined future possibilities. There are multiple exercises and questions in each chapter, which can be simply read through or engaged with more thoroughly. Each chapter also includes notes for educators and further reading.

Contents

About the Author

Paula Boddington is Associate Professor of Philosophy and Healthcare at the University of West London, where she works with a research group concerned with the quality of care for hospital patients who are also living with dementia. She has held academic posts at the Australian National University, Bristol University, Cardiff University, and Oxford University and has degrees in philosophy, psychology, and law from Keele, Oxford, and Cardiff Universities. She has a long-standing interest in ethical and social questions in new technologies, including artificial intelligence. She is the author of *Towards a Code of Ethics for Artificial Intelligence* (Springer, 2017) and *Ethical Challenges in Genomics Research* (Springer, 2012).

Chapter 1
Introduction: Why AI Ethics?

Abstract This chapter introduces the approach of the book towards the ethics of artificial intelligence. A brief overview of artificial intelligence is given with an outline of how heated debates about ethical issues can arise. Some different strategies for addressing these issues are outlined. The mere imposition of regulations and rules does not constitute a good approach to ethics, which should encompass many considerations, including the best ways to live. Ethical discussions should embrace contrasting voices, and we need to recognise that the very technologies in question may shape how we think about ethics. AI raises a large variety of ethical questions related to many factors, including the range of domains in which it is applied, the speed of development, its embeddedness in much everyday technology, and the ways in which it is acting to modify and transform the manner in which we interact with each other and the world. AI ethics also requires us to think deeply about the nature of ethics and about ourselves. The book will include considerations of methodology in ethics, ethical theories and concepts, cases and exercises, and the need for both bottom-up and top-down thinking.

Keywords AI ethics · Artificial intelligence · Applied ethics · Technology ethics · Ethics washing

1.1 Introduction

Summary
This chapter outlines the approach of this book. There is a pressing need for contrasting voices to contribute to this field and to recognise the complexity of the ethics of AI, given that technology itself can influence how we think about and approach questions of ethics.

This book aims to contribute to the many and various endeavours currently striving to understand and to address the plethora of ethical issues that surround AI. Since everyone is impacted in some way by the technologies in question, the book is thus directed to anyone with any interest in the broad field. The central aim is to contribute to our capacity to understand, share, and debate ethical issues, to join in constructive dialogue with others, and for each of us to consider our own use of such technologies. As much as we need solutions to questions, we also need conversations that contribute to advancing the depth and breadth of understanding, aiming for real-world effects that help to improve how technology is designed and deployed.

My previous book in this field concerned the development of codes of ethics and regulations for AI [1]. People who speak to me thus often assume that I am a great enthusiast for such codes and regulations. Indeed, they have an important place, but there are many pitfalls, not least in that they may inadvertently contribute to a view of ethics that it's basically all about being told what to do by somebody else, moreover, perhaps by somebody else who is sure what the right answer is, who may not fully understand what they are talking about, and who probably has a dim view of one's capacity for ethical reflection and decent behaviour: an 'external authority' view of ethics. This book emphasises the difficulties and uncertainties of ethical reflection and the need for individuals and society as a whole to address the many questions that AI presents. It does not seek simply to provide the correct answers. Indeed, the very issues in AI that we need to discuss frequently help to expose the limits and difficulties in our understanding of ethics.

There are a great many people from a range of backgrounds, varying in discipline and expertise, and with a large variety of approaches and opinions, all contributing towards these endeavours. It is essential that as many as possible are involved in such discussions and that there should be dialogue between different approaches, and doubtless the case that differences of opinion, some major, some minor, will always remain.

This first chapter provides a basic overview of the strategies of this book and of the approach taken to understanding and asking questions in ethics. As with all the chapters, there are occasional exercises and questions for the reader. These can be either skimmed over, done as you read, or returned to later, as you wish; they can all be done by individuals, but many lend themselves to working in groups.

Like all the chapters, this is laid out with plenty of headings and subsections clearly marked, so that readers with different levels of time and interest can skim through if need be, or read more fully. Further reading is given at the end of each chapter, in addition to a reference list of works cited throughout the text.

1.2   What Is Artificial Intelligence?

Summary
This section presents an overview of ways in which artificial intelligence is understood as an engineering technology and also as a scientific discipline. Different underlying attitudes to understanding what AI is will influence approaches to ethical questions.

One of the first questions is what precisely we mean by 'artificial intelligence', since this will affect what ethical questions arise and how we look at them. This question is somewhat complex, since there are different accounts of AI, including disputes about whether specific instances of technology are 'truly' AI and disputes about what the aims and ambitions of AI should or should not be. Part of the difficulty stems from unanswered questions about the nature of intelligence, a topic to which we return in Chap. 6. Sources and further reading are given at the end of this chapter.

Artificial intelligence may be understood as a technology in terms of the engineering capacities required for certain tasks and also in terms of a scientific discipline [2]. For our purposes, it is also interesting to note that some accounts specifically refer to human intelligence, while others do not. We can understand AI broadly as concerning the capacities of computers, including hardware devices controlled by computers, to reproduce elements of intelligent thought and behaviour, sometimes expressed in terms such as the capacity to perform tasks that require intelligence if performed by a human being. We can also broadly think of AI as the diverse set of technologies that extend not just our capacities to act in the world but also our powers of thought and decision-making. AI may refer to the software involved or to the various hardware devices in which it is embedded, such as autonomous cars or robots. AI is often embedded as a component in a larger system.

The scientific discipline of AI includes branches examining planning and knowledge representation, machine learning, decision-making, and robotics. Components of intelligence that have been the focus of work on AI include *machine learning*, since any intelligent creature must be capable of learning; *perception* of the environment, including perception of the effects of an AI's own actions, since understanding of the environment is essential for any intelligent action and agency; *natural language processing*, since communication via language is such a critical part of human intelligence and is needed for many tasks; *reasoning*, for instance, the ability to apply the rules of logic and mathematics and to draw conclusions from evidence and experience; and *problem solving*, such as the capacity to work out how to solve puzzles and achieve tasks given certain parameters and resources. If AI is to achieve action in the world, it will need appropriate *actuators*, which could be physical or in the form of software.

What does the claim that AI is possible amount to? There are different ways of understanding this assertion. Mike Wooldridge expresses it in terms of whether we can develop machines that exhibit intelligent behaviour by following sets of rules [3]. The rules may be deductive in form, which basically means that starting from true premises and following certain rules, the conclusions drawn can be certain to be true. Alternatively, they may be inductive, based upon generalisations from data, which can be more or less accurate. Strategies to achieve AI may involve modelling the mind, and some focus on modelling the brain.

Some useful terms include the following:

Weak AI: the attempt to build programmes that demonstrate capabilities of intelligence, without necessarily being 'intelligent' themselves.

Strong AI: the attempt to build programmes that have intelligence in the form of
   understanding and/or that are conscious.
Artificial General Intelligence (AGI): the attempt to build programmes that demonstrate the full range of intelligence capabilities exhibited by human beings.
Superintelligence: a notion of artificial intelligence that vastly exceeds human
   intelligence and hence may be hard or impossible for us to understand.
   Superintelligent AI is presumed capable of recursive self-improvement and of
   the creation of technologies of greater and greater intelligence.

There are different attitudes towards the goals of AI. Some focus on achieving
specific tasks involving components of intelligence. Others see AI as a larger project
to reproduce human-level intelligence, or general intelligence, in machines. Closely
related are the projects of attempting to understand human intelligence further by
examining the realisation of intelligence within machines, an activity closely related
to cognitive science.

It will often be acutely relevant to ethical questions to consider how precisely an
instance of AI functions, and it's also often important to consider how we conceptualise AI, what we imagine it to be.

For example, machine learning (ML) involves the use of large amounts of data
and of statistical techniques. Many ethical questions can hence arise, even if we
consider simply ethical issues concerning the collection and use of data. There are
also many specific questions that arise from the nature of this technology, as we shall
see, such as questions about how ML produces its outputs from the data, the 'black
box' issue, or the question of transparency. In contrast, if we consider the project of
AI as the attempt to fully reproduce or even exceed human intelligence, we should
immediately see that questions of a rather different type may arise. This helps
explain why there are many who wish to deny that some particular project to use
ML to solve some specific and well-defined problem is 'truly' artificial intelligence.

This book will take a broad definition of AI, noting that ethical questions arise
from different aspects of how AI operates, where it operates, and from features of the
technologies and hardware devices within which it is embedded and their
deployment.

One of the reasons for having a broad approach to the definition of AI is this:
Attention to potential problems of AI has alerted us to certain issues that seem to
arise from the power, capabilities, and reach of AI. However, in some cases, further
examination may reveal that the issues raised are also present and were prefaced in
less sophisticated technologies, for example, in computing power, which generally
does not merit the label of 'artificial intelligence'.

Fear, dread, and optimism abound in AI   There is a great deal of discussion and
effort being made to guard against potential negative impacts of AI and, more
positively, to try to ensure that AI, conceived broadly, is used productively and in
ways that genuinely create value for humanity. Indeed, high hopes on the one hand
and fear and dread on the other are characteristic of the narratives and debates around
AI and technology in general, not just in popular media but also to be found within
academic and technical literature. A quick browse of news sites reveals hopes that AI

will help to save the bee population, cure cancer, curb drownings, solve problems that governments have in dealing with data, design enzymes to digest plastic waste, end the global food shortage, solve insomnia without drugs, cure glaucoma, and solve the climate crisis. Conversely, a search for fears about AI will reveal a claim that an AI-powered microwave oven tried to cook a man to death, that skilled workers will lose jobs because of AI, that certain apps are complex scams, that the global supply chain is at risk of hackers, that the world faces a global war with robot tanks and AI weapons, and that AI-powered tech is worsening racism, will end privacy as we know it, and is generally getting 'scarier and scarier'. Both what is feared and what is hoped for are often presented as novel and as all encompassing. One of the questions we will look at is why this might be the case.

As a short trailer for some things to come, consider how such fears and hopes are expressed and what precisely they concern. There are different ways of expressing such hopes and fears. Should we be concerned with the impacts of AI on humanity; should our concern be with living things in general; should we be concerned with the planet as a whole; or should we be concerned with conscious beings, regardless of biology? As soon as we start to think about some of the potentials of AI, someone will start asking questions about the boundaries between humans and complex machines, and questions of ethics inevitably arise.

One of the important questions is indeed how to define and approach these questions of value. What does 'AI ethics' cover, and what else do we need? It is indeed a central premise of my approach that although ethics does have a great deal to offer, debates and discussions in ethics are often limited. Therefore, while here we focus on ethics, the book endeavours to indicate where additional insights and approaches are needed. Some of these are complementary, but some may even be in opposition to the endeavour that has come to be known as 'AI ethics'.

1.3   And What, Precisely, Is Ethics?

Summary
There is an approximate shared understanding of the term 'ethics', which may mask a number of serious disagreements about what it is and what it might promise to deliver.

For now, you'll all have a rough idea of what is meant by questions of ethics around AI to get the gist of the issues, but nonetheless, there is plenty to be learned from diving deeper into this question, as we shall also do. To clarify matters, the terms 'ethics' and 'morality' are sometimes used to mean slightly different things, but there is no consistency of usage, and here, 'ethics' and 'morality' will be used interchangeably. Questions of ethics concern issues we think of as being especially important in a weighty kind of way. These are often things that affect individuals very deeply and/or things that affect society in general. Because of this, it is important to obtain understanding and agreement. However, questions of value are precisely also those questions where there is often profound disagreement, including disagreement about how to approach these questions.

Strategies for approaching AI ethics There are various approaches to the hopes and fears elicited by AI. These range from regulations, law, codes of conduct, attempts to design AI with safety and ethics uppermost, attempts to build ethics into design process, specific strategies such as attempts to understand and mitigate bias, and so on. Some focus on current issues; some focus on longer-term and more speculative questions, such as possible dangers of superintelligence. Some issues are concrete and specific; some are more general, wide-ranging, or foundational. Some approaches lean towards the view that AI presents a threat that we might lose control of ourselves and of our values and that we need radical shifts to deal with the world that is coming. Other approaches are more sanguine and diligently tread the path of trying to ensure that the technologies that are being developed and used fit within current frameworks of value in approaches broadly labelled 'value alignment'.

Here is a strategy and hope of this book To provide a way of introducing these issues that will help readers to deepen their understanding of the depth and complexity of the issues, their appreciation of different viewpoints, and their appreciation of how ethical questions intersect with many other fields of inquiry. The emphasis is not on learning facts about debates and views in AI ethics but on developing the capacity to think, argue, and question. Thinking through questions 'for yourself' does not mean 'by yourself'. Community with others is incredibly useful in this endeavour, and we can connect with these others in a variety of ways, whether by reading the words of long-dead thinkers or by chatting to the person who happens to sit next to you in class.

The need for contrasting views I spoke of 'contrasting' views, not of 'opposing' views, because the need to maintain debate on all aspects of a question in this area is vital. Of course, on some issues, deeply held opinions may be completely at odds. However, much can still be learned from finding out why someone holds their views—if, indeed, they are able to articulate this. People often hold views we consider wrong for interesting reasons from which we can learn much. Moreover, many issues in ethics are not clear-cut. Even if one is convinced that a particular solution to a problem is the best, it is often possible to see drawbacks and often possible to understand how those with a different perspective might beg to differ.

Dominant voices in the here and now There are good reasons for taking such a strategy in any area, but here there is a particular reason to approach the matter with an open mind. Concerns are frequently expressed that the dominance of certain voices and interests in the tech field provide a good reason for concern about the values being imposed in the world via technology produced by a small number of powerful individuals and corporations. However, there is a similar danger within the frameworks and discussions of the ethics of AI. These, too, may be dominated by certain voices. This needs to be addressed.

There is a particular reason to think reflectively about debates in ethics in relation to these new technologies. It is easy to assume that because we are making great strides in technology, we have also made great strides in ethics, such that we have an ethic sufficiently robust to deal with the technology at hand. Another way of putting this is that it is common to sense an assumption that ethical thought has progressed so that 'now' 'we' have it right. There is a significant danger that we will look at these issues only from the point of view of the voices shouting the loudest in the early part of the twenty-first century from the most visible parts of the world.

Technologies may influence how we think about ethics If by some magic fluke, 'we' now have a 'perfect' ethics, whatever that means, then there is no harm in keeping an open mind, and we might fine-tune and fast track any progress. If not, then it is essential that we equip people who are going to be developing, deploying, selling, buying, and using this technology to think in the widest possible way about how it impacts value. And, let's face it, it is unlikely our ethics is perfect. Moreover, there are many reasons to consider that, as we develop and deploy technology, the way we think about questions of value in relation to it may well change. We return to this theme at various points throughout the book. For now, consider the technologies in which AI is embedded through which we get so much of our information and connection to the world and to others. We already know much about the pressures within social media both for groupthink and for extremely oppositional attacks on those with differing views, although how precisely this happens and its extent are under examination and dispute. So this alone should tell us that perhaps some of the very technologies we are addressing are helping to shape the world we see, how we judge it, and how we interact with each other. Our progress in technology can make us arrogant; the rapid change of views on some ethical issues seen in some parts of the world in recent times may lead us to think that now 'we' have finally got things right, but at the same time, our increasingly global connections fostered and extended by such technologies should also make us all the more aware of other voices.

This illustrates in an introductory way the intimate links between how we are thinking and feeling about ethical questions in AI and the large range of technologies that use it. Even the fact that we are surrounded by continual advertising for upgrades to technology creates a certain impression of progress. Think too of how common and easy it is casually to think of the human mind as if it is a kind of computer, perhaps not a very good computer that needs help from a machine. Does our fascination with this world of technology help to shape how we see humans?

Exercise 1

Meanwhile, stop to jot down any thoughts you have about how you formed your views on AI and what fears and hopes you may have for it. There are no wrong answers. Spend as much or as little time as you like. (Feel free to skip any exercises, but do read through them before you pass on.)

1.4   What Does This Book Cover?

Summary
The book will examine both concrete issues and specific cases, general themes and concepts and ethical theories that emerge, and critically consider the methodologies used to address ethical questions. Artificial intelligence is forcing us to think deeply about many basic concepts in ethics.

Concrete questions This book will examine a selection of tangible issues and specific cases from within the broad field of AI ethics. There are so many that it's only possible to include a few of the very many possible. However, it is hoped that you will be able to apply what you've learned to issues representing your own personal interests and areas of expertise and greatest concern. The issues we need to discuss encompass a wide range of domains and possibilities—from the far future, the immediate present, or the near future, and from disparate types of technology, used for different reasons, in diverse domains, such as in policework to healthcare to social connections. From brain implants designed to make us smart to persuasive technology seemingly designed to make us dumb. From superintelligence that threatens to rule over us to surveillance that helps those with technological capacity to influence populations. There will be questions about who is using the technology, whether individuals, governments, or corporations. In addition, questions about how individuals respond to the design of technology, how free we are with respect to the many technologies into which AI is embedded.

General themes emerge Looking at concrete issues and comparing and contrasting the issues they raise will bring forth general themes, such as freedom, power, and control, questions on the theme of human nature, and questions about meaning. When I first started as an undergraduate studying philosophy in the 1970s, I distinctly recall one of my tutors scoffing out loud at the suggestion that philosophy might deal with questions such as 'the meaning of life'. However, it is difficult to address many of the most central questions in AI ethics without addressing questions such as whether or not a life where machines have taken over all work, or replaced human companionship, is a life with meaning and value. Some approaches to artificial intelligence have indeed endeavoured to use it to further our understanding of ourselves. Some consider that the very project of artificial intelligence is one stage in the progress of unfolding value in the universe, one in which humans have a particular role and destiny.

Theories and concepts The frameworks behind questions: Thus, concrete questions give rise to more general, far-reaching considerations. The book aims to unpack these and to look closely at the underlying ethical concepts and methodologies. We will also consider how well existing ethical theories and frameworks serve the field of AI ethics. We need to think seriously about the practice of ethics and carefully critique how it should be applied in the case of AI. As well as a critical approach to ethics, we should note again and again that the perspective of other disciplines and expertise is essential. Ethics intersects with, and is influenced by, history, culture, religion, and much more. Although this book focuses on ethics, it also includes an introduction to other realms of thinking we need to consider, both within philosophy and outside. Naturally, this can only be in outline, but with the aim of alerting readers to questions in AI ethics where the 'ethics' part, per se, might need the help of a challenging friend.

Methodologies   All the above means we are required to think about how precisely to approach ethical questions in AI. There are many in this domain who are already critically questioning the place of 'ethics' as a discipline and as an approach. To some extent, this represents the ongoing sibling rivalry of different academic disciplines, inevitable perhaps when one discipline feels that another is criticising it and when disciplines have very different methodologies. It is also sometimes the case that work in ethics comments on things it has not fully understood, and sometimes fails to see the significance of ideas which are of central concern for other disciplines. Moreover, within ethics, there are significant differences between the methodological approaches of different theories. Such differences, as we shall see, have a profound impact on how the ethical questions of AI are understood and on what answers are given. This book stresses the importance of considering the methodologies used to think about the ethics of AI and thus hopes to be more like a tool kit for assisting with your exploration of these questions, rather than a 'how to' instruction manual.

Artificial intelligence is making useful trouble for ethics   One of the features of AI ethics is how forcefully it reveals the necessity of examining our theories, our concepts, and our methodologies. A frequently expressed fear that AI may 'take over' human agency, that it may be used by governments and corporations to intrude upon our lives and control us, or even that AI itself may develop to a level where it treats us like farmed animals rather than like the human beings we strive to be. However, what makes me more optimistic is precisely the way in which, by raising such complex and difficult ethical questions, artificial intelligence is pushing us to ask and address profound questions about ethics, about human life, agency, and our place in this world. In this way, far from dehumanising us, it could rehumanise us. It's truly very exciting.

1.5   Why AI Ethics Is So Exciting

Summary
I think AI ethics is the most exciting branch of applied ethics I've ever worked in. However, a warning is given about hype both in AI and in AI ethics. AI is used in a large variety of different domains, hence presenting many diverse ethical questions. The technologies are being rapidly developed and rolled out. AI is helping to modify how we relate to the world and to each other.

Exercise 2

If you find the prospect of studying the ethics of AI intriguing, jot down what issues you've find most fascinating, and why. What unanswered questions do you have? Do you have any firm opinions, or do you feel more uncertain and torn? If you are reading this book only because you are obliged to as part of course fulfilments, you may find the prospect of ethics a chore. I sympathise. There is enough poor work that passes for ethics that I find it hard to blame you. Write down any misgivings and I hope that at least some of them will be addressed throughout the book.

However, first, a reminder about hype There can be hype in accounts of the capabilities of AI, and of its future promise, and likewise there can be hype in the prognostications of doom or glory surrounding AI. There can also be hype around AI ethics. Note that although many working in ethics warn against how AI is presented—the frequent photos of killer robots accompanying what turn out to be mundane news reports about tech, for example—ethics as a field also has something to gain from sensationalising the problems AI might bring. It keeps us in a job. However, there are genuine grounds for concern and genuine reasons for excitement about the field.

Exercise 3

The next time you read a news report or tech blog, etc., regarding AI, think carefully about how any harmful or beneficial aspects of it are being presented, if they are being sensationalised, and consider how that might impact ethical responses. Remember that sometimes, people sensationalise or exaggerate for good reasons if they are trying to warn or to attract attention when no one is listening.

Over the years, I have researched and taught in many areas of applied ethics: in medical ethics, healthcare ethics more broadly, in ethical and social issues in genetics and genomics, engineering ethics, and environmental ethics. However, of all these, the area of AI ethics is the most challenging and the most exciting. Why? For a number of different reasons.

Ubiquity and reach There is one simple reason—AI gets everywhere. It has so many diverse applications that an ethics of AI is, in a way, an 'ethics of everything'. Medical ethics deals with medical care: it then must bring in a wider range of considerations, such as balancing medical interests with other interests, and it draws upon general questions, such as the value of human life. However, it is a relatively confined domain. It has its own characteristic concerns, such as questions about informed consent in the context of medicine, the relevance of the distinction between health and illness and how precisely this is drawn, the particular professional expectations on doctors, and so on. Likewise with all the other 'ethics of' fields. However, AI can be applied in any domain. Therefore, along with considering AI per se, one will find oneself looking across a great range of domains of life. With each one, there will be a specific context to examine as well as the more general issues pertaining to AI.

A plethora of diverse issues As has been touched on above, AI covers different approaches and methods in science and in engineering, each of which potentially gives rise to ethical questions. AI may refer to more than discrete tasks of computing but may also be conceived as a larger project with variously described ambitions in relation to intelligence and, moreover, sometimes with explicit reference to *human* intelligence and consciousness. Hence, the range of potential ethical issues that arise can even be bewildering. Moreover, as we shall see, it is very often the case that when we consider AI, questions are raised that force us to ask deeper questions about some of the central and foundational assumptions and concepts in certain areas of ethics.

Exercise 4

Thinking of as many specific instances of AI that you can, quickly try to draw up the longest list you can of areas where AI is being implemented, or looks set to be implemented soon. Think about what areas you have any particular knowledge about and other areas where you know less.

Speed AI technologies are developing rapidly, albeit, we do have to watch out for some hype about how fast development is happening, with a tendency to premature claims of readiness. However, there have certainly been rapid changes to a broad range of areas of life as AI is developed and implemented. This can make it both exciting and extremely difficult to keep up with what is happening, let alone to consider the ethical, social, and cultural implications of these changes. This is especially true given the great diversity of applications. A change can hit you in the face before you even know it's coming. Indeed, you might quickly forget that something is new, and ways we used to do things might have completely faded from memory.

Exercise 5

Consider some of the technology that you now take for granted that uses AI. Now cast your mind back to a time before you used it. Sometimes it is almost comical to recall life without a certain bit of tech, even though it's truly pretty recent in origin.

AI is embedded Sometimes we are clearly and consciously aware that AI is being used, but often we are not. Either because we hadn't ever thought of or known about its presence, or because we just got used to it, like the squeaky gate or living under the flightpath to an airport. Again, this is compounded by the wide range of applications of AI, but it's more than that: it's that AI has become integrated into our world, and often in ways that impact upon, or are even transformative of, key aspects of our lives. This will likewise present challenges in working out what impact AI is actually having, let alone in considering its virtues and vices, the pluses and minuses of AI. Nobody fully understands the impact AI is having, or might have, even within certain discrete areas, let alone in general.

This is one of the reasons why the approach to the question of 'what precisely is AI?' is taken rather broadly in this book because so many of the technologies which make use of AI, in whatever form, are linking together and interacting in a manner which is making often profound, sometimes mundane, changes to our world. The context of AI thus is not simply its domain of use—say, medicine, the law, and communication; the context of AI is also other AI.

Transformations central to our ways of being in the world Technologies involving AI are impacting so many of the ways in which we interact with the world and the avenues from which we shape our values. This forces us to think about the questions of value in very thorough ways—or if we don't, our answers will be superficial. These include but are not limited to changes in how we think and communicate; impacts on how we see and interact with others, with society in general, with the world, and with ourselves; and impacts upon how we access and relate to knowledge, both more intimate personal knowledge and scientific or factual knowledge. So we are on a moving train, or rather, because trains run on tracks, a moving vehicle, or we are even perhaps trying to ride on the back of a dragon. We are trying to think about something which may be changing how we think of it as we do so. This is more challenging than simply dealing with something that is new and that is rapidly developing.

Some of the questions in AI ethics are relatively fine-tuned and relatively well-defined. For example, there are critically important questions about safety and accuracy, such as the question of whether using AI to assist the interpretation of medical images is more reliable than using humans alone. Indeed, one might not even think of these as ethical questions per se. I was recently struck by listening to a retired engineer lamenting the introduction of ethics guidance into his profession many years ago, which had struck him as an insult to him and his profession, given that the ethics codes seemed to assume that engineers would not otherwise be concerned with safety; it was a paramount concern.

However, many aspects of even these discrete questions strike at the heart of questions of ethics, value, and meaning. If large-scale technological unemployment follows from automation via AI, with what do we fill our lives? The very project of using machines to replace human thought and decision-making raises the question of why do anything at all, if a machine can do it instead. Are we, humans, at the heart of value? Or are we dispensable? The project of AI, if conceived in one way as attempting to replicate our intelligence, raises the question of who we are, and from this arises an entire gamut of questions about human nature. But wait, it goes even further. The metaverse raises questions about what reality is and why reality matters, if indeed it does. Perhaps we should abandon the whole concept of 'reality', and focus only on what is most immediate to us, focus on our feelings. It can sometimes seem like everything we knew, everything we placed our foundations on, is up for grabs.

Indeed, one reason for the fears, hopes, and polarisation so often found in this field is surely linked to the way that AI presents us with such profound questions, not just about the use of technology and its benefits or harms, but about our values, and about us.

1.6 Why Should Anyone Want to Study AI Ethics?

Summary
This section looks at some reasons why many are cynical or sceptical about AI ethics. These include seeing ethics as the imposition of rules by others, or as little but prohibitions, and sceptical questions about the need for morality. Alternative views see ethics as concerned with living one's best life and as an essential part of the good design of technology.

What's in it for you to study AI ethics? There will be a variety of different answers to this question. 'Ethics' is such a familiar term but can be understood in many and often opposing ways. So before we begin, it will be useful to take an overview of some of these different approaches to ethics and some motivations for reading this book. In other words, to raise questions about why anyone would be concerned about ethics. Or the classic question of so many philosophy tutorials, 'Why should I be moral?'

Exercise 6
Before we start, jot down in a couple of minutes (a) a quick definition of 'ethics'; (b) a short account of why you are reading this book; and (c) what you hope to get out of the book. Again, there are no wrong answers.

Some readers will start with an interest in ethics, wishing to understand how it applies to the case of AI. For these, we have already discussed how AI presents numerous fascinating challenges for ethics. However, this book is also for people who are being forced to take a course on AI ethics as part of their studies. Some very reluctantly and only to get credit, some with more enthusiasm. (In my experience, enthusiasm for ethics courses is often based on the presupposition that it will be easy. We'll see about that.) Likewise, ethics, especially in relation to some professional activity, is often regarded as something you have to know about to qualify and to practice, sometimes to gain admission to a professional body. This may then encourage the view that ethics is about knowing enough to gain a qualification, satisfy your line manager, and avoid being sued. I have in fact taught on courses like this, and you can probably guess, that as a philosopher, I think there is more to ethics. However, I do understand why it can easily seem as if 'ethics' is a tiresome bureaucratic requirement.

Some of the reasons for this view of ethics stem from certain conceptions of what ethics is. Ethics may be seen as something that some external authority tells you that you must do, often as a list of rules for compliance, or else. Indeed, ethics is often presented in such a way. This understandably often gives rise to resentment, and one of the reasons for such resentment can stem from an opposing view of ethics—that it is something merely personal, that we each have a subjective value system which may be at odds with what is expected of us by external authorities, yet but to which we are nonetheless entitled.

Take note of these opposing elements, the external locus and the internal locus of ethics, contrasts between what we may perhaps call the objective and the subjective.

We are gesturing here at some of the difficulties of ethics and some of the reasons for very different responses and approaches. This is just a very introductory way of indicating large currents in thousands of years of history of thinking about ethics. Ethics seems 'subjective' and personal for so many reasons; it demands things of me, it seems so closely connected to my feelings and emotions, and it's so obvious that there is some variation in ethical views. However, ethics also seems to have weight, authority, and a certain profound relevance for the well-being and interests of myself and of others that suggests a certain objectivity; moreover, some basic elements of ethics, such as rules concerning killing or harming human beings, appear to be very widespread in different cultures. Both elements seem essential to explaining why ethics matters. Both ways of looking at ethics have their attractions and dangers. Considering this delicate balancing act is a useful way of helping to understand some of the difficult and fascinating questions that will arise later, questions that AI is helping to highlight.

Ethics as 'thou shalt not' Another common and understandable source of wariness about ethics is the assumption that it is mostly concerned with telling people what not to do, with negative instructions, often with heavy sanctions and threats of punishment. A vision of a punitive authority, a scary judge, or some angry God laying down commandments that try to enforce unliveable demands on human beings, usually in the form of absolute rules, unfortunately reflects the experience of some people. This is regrettable, and accounts of ethics can be far richer, positive, and humane. Not all accounts of ethics focus on rules, and even those that do may strive to take into account nuance and context. Some accounts will include permissive rules as well as prohibitions. Some accounts hold up standards to strive towards, which we may be unlikely to reach in full, but which we can aim towards with more or less success. These stand in contrast to stark visions of failing to comply with absolute rules. (On the other hand, murder of the innocent is just wrong.)

Ethics as 'finding fault' In the context of ethical questions about technologies, it is especially important to stress that ethics should be more than prohibitions. Because ethical concerns often focus on warnings and dangers, it is easy to gain the impression that AI ethics is simply about attempting to prevent disasters or poor outcomes. This then may give the impression that those concerned with AI ethics have a basic stance of wariness or even opposition to technology. However, it would not be ethical to prevent the development of good technology. However, in an area where progress is, or seems to be, rapid, loud warning shouts may seem more common than praise, for reasons of caution. Some caution may be justified, especially where technologies may quickly become so embedded in our lives and in the infrastructure that by the time we realise that there are major downsides, it's difficult or practically impossible to extricate ourselves.

Perfect and Imperfect Duties

A distinction between perfect and imperfect duties has been made by some philosophers and can be useful for explaining differences in moral requirements.

A *perfect duty* is binding at all times; in other words, there is no choice about when or how to follow it—you just must obey. For this reason, perfect duties tend to be expressed in the negative. Because quite simply, it's usually easy to not steal, to not lie, to not murder, every second of the day, yet almost impossible to 'be kind', 'be generous', 'save lives', etc., without ceasing.

In contrast, an *imperfect duty* is one where an individual has a general duty to perform certain actions, but has choice about the manner and timing of these actions. For example, rendering aid to others is a duty without which society would be very poor indeed, but there is no necessity to spend every waking minute fulfilling this duty. Indeed, were one to do so, it would be impossible to fulfil other duties.

A *supererogatory action* is a good action which is over and above one's required duties. For example, one might be required to render aid to rescue a person if this did not involve immediately endangering one's own life, so a person who risked or lost his or her own life to save another could be said to have performed an act of supererogation in going beyond the call of duty.

Closely related to these considerations is the question 'why should I be moral?', and indeed, different conceptions of ethics give rise to divergent answers to this question. One answer is simply, 'so that I don't get into trouble', which is at least a start, although it has the well-known problem that if a person thinks they can get away with something, in the absence of any countering considerations, they are likely to go ahead and do it.

The Ring of Gyges: An Ancient 'Cloak of Invisibility'

Many of the central questions of ethics have perplexed people for centuries. In his work, the *Republic*, Plato discusses the problem of the Ring of Gyges and what this means for the question, 'why should I be moral?' [4].

In Greek myth, and in the version told in the *Republic* by the character Glaucon, Gyges was a shepherd who found a golden ring with magic powers. When he twisted on his finger, he became invisible. However, rather than going around performing good deeds anonymously, he arranged to be sent to report to the king. Once at the palace, he seduced the queen (one can only speculate at how she might have reacted to being seduced by someone invisible), murdered the king, and seized the throne.

Some work in psychology backs up the idea that if we are being watched by others, we are less likely to behave wrongly. Studies in social psychology have found that a sense of anonymity can encourage poor behaviour [5, p. 289 ff].

Exercise 7

The Ring of Gyges is relevant for today in numerous ways. Even though the *Republic* was written in approximately 375 BC, the question of how we could behave under conditions of anonymity is central to how people behave (often very badly) online. Note how modern technology facilitates two opposing phenomena: the ability to remain anonymous and unseen and, in contrast, the ever-present eyes and ears of often unknown others. Why is it that a person might behave differently if nobody knows who they are? Will their behaviour always tend to be worse? Think about the reasons behind your answer. Conversely, in this age of almost continual surveillance, how might behaviour change as a result? This is a complex question to answer, and it will be far from simple that social pressure of observation will result in net benefits for society.

Scepticism about ethics In answering the question of why I should care about morality, a sceptical response is very common, especially perhaps among those who are trained in scientific methods and in critical thinking [6]. Indeed, it's a perfectly valid response, given that what is at stake is important, and given the obvious disputes within ethics and difficulties of supplying a universally accepted answer. It's a response that may also naturally fit with a view of ethics as a set of requirements on people to do things they might otherwise not want to do, for the sake of others, and/or on the say-so of some distant authority. Naturally, we are somewhat sceptical about such demands.

A sceptical response to the question of 'why should I be moral' is also found in those who adhere to the philosophical doctrine of egoism. An egoist considers that all motivation ultimately refers to the self—each person has to have their own reason to act morally. However, here AI ethics has something of an answer, because it's essential that in considering AI, we have to consider the human person, in other words, ourselves. Quite simply, if AI is replacing, supplementing, and improving human thought and agency, then this raises questions of how we compare AI with humans—so we have to examine humans and how and why we value them. We might even find something wanting in the conception of the self upon which such philosophical egoism depends.

So we have to study humans ourselves. What could be more fascinating? For the egoist who raises sceptical questions about what is in it for him or her to examine ethical questions, here is your answer—you will be examining yourself.

My best life There are other approaches to ethics which might more naturally address such sceptical responses. Ethics can be thought of as about living the best life possible, which, since we are social animals, will have implications for how we treat others. A prominent example is the work of Aristotle, who was one of Plato's pupils. His approach to ethics is extremely influential today for those who advocate 'virtue ethics', which we will consider in greater detail later. In his work, *The Nicomachean Ethics*, he sets out to address how we should live 'the good life for man' (and yes, unfortunately, in common with virtually all his contemporaries, he did give men a higher status than women) [7]. His answer included the conclusion that the life of virtue was the best way to achieve happiness. Of course, there is much to be said about his views, but rather than presenting ethics as something likely to be at odds with a person's own best interest, this approach to ethics does the reverse, although naturally, some argue that Aristotle did not succeed in this particular quest.

Ethics as design Furthermore, if we see ethics as part and parcel of design, of producing and deploying products with genuine value, we can also see studying ethics as something to be integrated with studying AI, computing, and technology, not some separate afterthought to design. Again, one could understand the necessity of ethics in design as something the market, the customer, wants, or as something integral to the aims of the designer. We can also see these design questions as being about how technologies are used. Since you are inevitably a user of technologies, there are value choices facing you about how you respond to and interact with technologies.

The inevitability of ethics Last, at the start of a term's tutorials on ethics, students often begin by asking me these questions: 'Why should I be moral? Why should I think about ethics?' I explain to them that they have walked into a trap. As soon as you have asked these questions, you have either to answer it or to pretend you don't know there are questions there demanding your attention. Either way, there will be some ways in which, as a human being, you have no choice but to answer in one way or another to the moral demands upon you, however these may be conceptualised. You could say this is just part of the human condition. Perhaps, even, it is one of the ways in which we differ from intelligent machines.

1.7   Bottom-Up and Top-Down Approaches to AI Ethics

Summary
Both theory and examples of concrete practical application are equally needed in discussing ethics.

One of the reasons why some resist anything labelled 'ethics' is because it can often seem as if it involves imposing some abstract theory onto a concrete situation in ways that fail adequately to capture or fully comprehend grounded reality. This is indeed sometimes the case and demonstrates the necessity of good dialogue and understanding with those with subject matter expertise. Theories of ethics need to be responsive to the real world. As has already been hinted at, especially in the case of AI, the phenomenon under examination may cause serious challenges to theory. We need to think about theories, abstract concepts, and principles, while we also closely examine what is happening on the ground. Both top down, and bottom up methods of working, matter. They are irrevocably intertwined.

I first started working in earnest on ethical issues in AI in 2016 when I worked on a project funded by the Future of Life Institute, along with Mike Wooldridge and Peter Millican, on developing codes of ethics for AI. Naturally, this was a fascinating project to be involved with, but to be honest, at the start of it, I didn't think that codes and regulations were necessarily the most interesting aspects of AI ethics. However, as I explored the area, I realised more and more that in dealing with codes and regulations, it was vital to explore ethics per se in the abstract, *and* how to formalise ethics, *and* how to achieve impact on the ground. One thing I have tried to demonstrate already with our discussion of the Ring of Gyges is that ideas and writings from a very long time ago, even those formulated in a different context, for different reasons, and in the form of abstractions such as a particular Greek myth, can still be fresh and crisp when it comes to considering even the newest technology.

Exercises In particular, you will have plentiful opportunity to contribute to the 'bottom-up' part of this in the exercises which refer to concrete applications, and here you may frequently wish to apply what you have learned to specific instances of most interest or relevance to your experience. This book also aims to introduce aspects of ethical theory at varying levels of depth and to enable readers to explore aspects in greater detail or in outline only. I hope many readers will be left wanting more, because a book of this length can never cover 'everything'. The emphasis will be on assisting you in formulating and asking relevant questions. Many may of course choose not to do the exercises, but they aim to raise questions to consider which may be useful for all readers.

1.8   And What Are You Bringing to This Book?

Summary
The book stresses the need for all of us to contribute to AI ethics. Readers are invited to reflect on the skills and experience they can bring to the subject.

Plato's teacher was Socrates, who famously never wrote down any works of philosophy, since on the page, an argument can get misinterpreted and can lie moribund. Philosophical conversation was everything for Socrates, and this explains why Plato wrote his texts in the form of dialogue with different characters representing different positions. However, nonetheless, the written word need not be left to lie dormant, and readers can and must actively engage with texts. This is especially so in relation to ethics, or indeed in any subject intended to be of some practical relevance to the world and to life. Even those of you who have never studied ethics or consciously read a single thing about it will have plenty to bring to this work by virtue of the fact that you are alive, and presumably, a thinking, feeling, human being with connections to others in a social world and some sense of value.

So before we proceed, think about all the things that you have to bring to understanding AI ethics. Some possibilities are as follows:

You have specific expertise in AI and in technologies that make use of it.

You have certain opinions about such technologies—problems you have encountered, things you truly like, and hopes or fears for the future.

You use such technologies in your life and can reflect on how they affect you and those around you. You have some awareness of how your life has changed with its use—or else you can discuss with others how 'natural' it all seems.

You will have been raised in a society or cultural context—and often, more than one—with implicit or explicit values that you can draw upon. You may have taken on such values or rejected them.

You may have experience or knowledge of particular religious traditions.

You may have noticed the potential for clashes between values from different domains of your life and experience.

You may have read books and comics and seen films and serials, with examples of different characters, good, bad, or mixed, and situations which can form material and examples on which to draw. Some of these characters and situations may come from real life. This may include sci-fi but can include any genre.

You will very likely have disciplinary expertise from other areas. This can be from either formal or informal study or experience. It could be from any area. For example, maybe time spent farming or looking after pets has led you to reflect on what, if anything, is special about humans and how we relate to the rest of the animal kingdom. This could well be useful to draw on in reflecting how humans might compare to AI or robots.

If you are sceptical about all of this, if you are truly annoyed that someone is forcing you to study this topic, even cynics have a role—you can play devil's advocate to your classmates. By this means you may help others to strengthen their arguments.

Ethics is sometimes approached as a competition to show off how virtuous one is and to display all the 'right' opinions. A critical attitude (so long as it is sufficiently respectful and constructive) can be immensely useful.

There are doubtless more possibilities. Please add as many as you like.

1.9 Frequent Criticisms of Ethics

Summary
We examine and respond to some common criticisms of ethics: that it is concerned only with theory; that it neglects essential insights from other disciplines; that it focuses too much on individual responsibility rather than issues of society and politics; that it tends to represent the views of a narrow and dominant group; and that it can be little more than whitewashing.

We have looked at some general reasons for scepticism about ethics. However, there are some more specific reasons offered to be wary about discussions of ethics in AI. Despite the many voices and fora where AI ethics is being discussed, debated, and written about, and despite the many initiatives attempting to implement ethics in the design of AI and to formulate codes, regulations, and laws focusing on AI ethics, for some, it is controversial to talk about 'ethics' in AI at all. There are various reasons for this, some better than others. Consideration of these criticisms of ethics can be useful in trying to improve how we approach our subject.

Ethics is not related to action or responsibility For instance, it is been suggested by Virginia Dignum, a computer scientist who has worked extensively in AI ethics, that talk of ethics focuses too much on the theory of what should be done, rather than on its implementation, and that it would be better to focus on the notion of responsibility, to emphasise the need for translation into practice [8, p. 6]. Although it is certainly the case that much discussion of ethics is overly theoretical and that some indulges in some wild speculation that is far from any practical realities, this is not an essential part of ethics per se. However, to achieve practical realisation, close consideration of the context of application and dialogue with others with appropriate expertise are needed. Many discussions in ethics are theoretical and intended as such but nonetheless can provide valuable clarity and insights for those who wish to take work further and make applications to context.

The question of responsibility There are useful warnings to be taken from Dignum's point. Work in ethics may be idealistic, and there is a place for this, but not at the expense of also considering realistic possibilities for implementation and practical solutions to problems. For instance, idealistic work in ethics sometimes leads to suggestions that attribute unrealistic levels of responsibility to those working in technology, for example, for the ongoing impacts on society of certain elements of software, which conversely fail to identify the responsibilities of powerful actors such as corporations and governments in relation to the development and applications of technology. These are related to legal, economic, and political considerations, which brings us to our next point.

Ethics and other disciplines Often, unfortunately, work in ethics does miss much that other disciplinary approaches could bring. Those working in the social sciences and in areas such as science and technology studies may lament that philosophical approaches to ethics fail to take into consideration not only the details of context but also the insights of theories and concepts from other disciplines. This is undoubtedly sometimes the case, and this book attempts to illustrate some of the theories and ideas from beyond mainstream ethics that can help us. For example, many have pointed out in various ways that many of the most pressing issues in AI concern power, so that AI ethics should include consideration of the wider social forces and theories we need to examine to comprehend such issues of power and control.

As such, focus on 'ethics' may be seen as a way of placing questions concerning AI in a silo excluding wider cultural, political, and economic issues. Again, this can be a danger. This is one reason to emphasise the different and wide-ranging skills and experience that can be brought to bear. This book clearly focuses on the discipline of ethics. However, it aims to indicate throughout where there is more to think about, although it is necessary to emphasise that there will so often be more to consider.

Is ethics too focused on the individual?   A related criticism is that ethics tends to focus on individuals and not enough on social issues such as justice [9]. We have seen the suggestion that AI ethics should be about responsibility. However, focusing on individual responsibility can be a way of avoiding the responsibility of corporations and of governments. Is ethics just a way of avoiding talking about politics? The best answer to this question is to think through on a case-by-case basis, considering whether wider political and social issues need to be considered as an alternative, or, more likely, in addition. Again, the approach of this book is that broad perspectives are needed.

Is AI ethics too narrow?   Many of the critiques of AI ethics are of its narrowness. A criticism is often made that much contemporary work in ethics is simply a way of imposing the views of a narrow section of a narrow part of the world at a specific and possibly rather peculiar time of history on others. I agree that there is much to be said for this criticism, and again, we can only try to do better, and again, this will involve bringing to bear as many different perspectives and people as possible.

Many years ago, I was teaching a class on environmental ethics. This is a topic that many naturally feel very strongly about, and it tends to produce powerful reactions from students. I was interrupted one lecture by a passionate voice from the back of the classroom: 'But you're only taking the point of view of a human being!'

She was right, of course. In reply, I asked her what point of view she'd like me to take. I can only ever take the point of view of a human being doing the best I can to take the point of view of another. Same for each one of us. Likewise, although each of us can try to be aware of cultural and other personal biases in our discussions of ethics, we cannot possibly guarantee that all perspectives are covered, and indeed, pretending we can do so is part of the problem. Again, it's a criticism that should keep us on our toes and incline us to dialogue with others.

Is AI ethics just a ruse?   Last, for now, consider the misuse of ethics as ethics washing. 'Ethics washing' refers to the practice of visibly, sometimes ostentatiously, showing to the world that one is taking great care to attend to ethics, while in reality, doing little or nothing [10, 11]. One might be a corporation setting up an ethics board that writes codes that never make it into daylight; one might have an ethics checklist at the start of a project that is filed away and forgotten. Scepticism about the attitude of corporations to ethics was not helped by the widely publicised ousting from Google in 2020 of Timnit Gebru, who led a group researching the social and ethical implications of AI [12]. Ethics may be seen as something bureaucratic or annoying that one does first to 'get it over and done with'. This certainly can be the case, and there is already much work that tries to guard against this, for example, initiatives to ensure that ethics is built into different stages of the design process and into implementation. However, we must also guard against using the 'ethics is ethics washing' complaint as an excuse not to talk about ethics. It is easy cynically to dismiss genuine attempts to improve issues by excoriating them as 'ethics washing'.

Exercise 8
Many technology companies have grand pronouncements on their websites about their approach to ethics and their values. These may include statements about specific steps they are taking, such as appointing an ethics review board. They may also include statements about specific campaigns of social value in which they are engaged. Check out one or two companies' statements of values and ethics.

1.10   The Boundaries and Limits of Ethics

Summary
This section presents an overview of some ways in which other disciplines may challenge or contribute to ethics. This includes the relevance of empirical data, methods for interpreting complex social phenomena, and different ways of understanding human beings. The application of ethics to practice requires a detailed understanding of the context and is beyond the scope of this book except in outline. The relationship between ethics and safety is discussed. While the technical questions are critical to AI ethics, this book focuses on the contributions of ethics.

We have noted that the issues we will examine in AI ethics will often be understood better and more fully with the assistance of different disciplinary expertise. In asking questions of ethics, there are clear overlaps with fields such as economics, politics, law, and religion. To formulate and understand responses to ethical questions, there is often the need for interdisciplinary approaches including social sciences, psychology, sociology, history, and of course in relation to AI. We need an understanding of the underlying technology, and this can include understandings gained from cognitive science, linguistics, and the philosophy of mind.

Here, I give a very brief rundown of some of the ways in which ethics might be enhanced, or challenged, by other disciplines. How might these disciplines contribute to ethics?

Empirical data Many disciplines can contribute empirical data, and data of many different types will be relevant—quantitative and qualitative data, data from different sources, historical data, cross-cultural data, data about individuals, and data about society. The ethics we are interested in ultimately has to be applied, and hence, we have to know about the impacts of actions in the real world.

Interpreting data The world is not presented to us as simple, unambiguous 'facts' that stand on their own. Data must be interpreted, and different disciplines provide useful lenses through which to read and understand data. Indeed, within different disciplines, there will be theories and theorists with contrasting opinions on how to interpret data. For example, an evolutionary biologist produces findings about the development of human beings and individual differences. An evolutionary psychologist may give an interpretation of the forces that led to these individual differences. A criminologist may find them useful in explaining the behaviour of some individuals. A legal theorist or a philosopher may interpret the criminologist's account as relevant or not to a sentencing decision. A prosecution team is likely to pounce on certain explanations and interpretations that differ from those of the defence team, and so on.

The interpretation of social phenomena will be especially relevant for us and especially vexed and liable to differences of viewpoints. Perspectives may differ depending upon individual, demographic, and cultural differences.

The human person AI ethics demands that we pay particular attention to the human person. If AI is to enhance or replace human thought, decision-making, and agency, and if we wish to assess the development and deployment of AI, then we need to think about human thought, decision-making, and agency. This is one area where ethics can gain a great deal by considering the approaches of different disciplines. Different branches of psychology have different insights and theories to offer, and this is likewise the case for sociology, anthropology, and biology. Disciplines such as economics may make assumptions about persons and their motivations which are questioned by other disciplines. Work in ethics absolutely must take advantage of and reflect upon and respond to these ideas, which can be of great utility. However, some of these ideas directly challenge much of ethics.

Challenges to ethics Some theories and methodological approaches have been used to cast doubt upon or even debunk work in ethics. For example, claims may be made that discoveries and methodologies have concluded that ethical arguments are based upon 'nothing but' subjective opinions explained completely by, variously, evolutionary theory, cultural forces, individual psychology, economic forces, and so on. Conversely, other work may be drawn upon to enrich or modify debate in ethics, such as work suggesting that there are commonalities in moral codes around the globe and throughout history or work suggesting that personality type may influence and sometimes limit how ethical and social issues are thought about and assessed. This is not the place to examine in any depth arguments that purport to debunk entirely the endeavour of ethics. However, there truly is plenty to learn and to ponder about, and anything which challenges ethics where it needs to be challenged, and anything ethics can learn from and improve, is and should be of interest.

Exercise 9

You may well have come across people who consider that ethics is simply a matter of opinion or that it is a way of disguising self-interest as concern for others, and so on. You may even think this yourself. Outline a few thoughts for and against such a view.

Ethics, action, and application Ethics is strongly linked to action. On some philosophical views, the making of a moral judgement, the appreciation of what is the best thing to do, leads immediately to such action, although a view more commonly held is now that the motivation to act morally arises with a degree of independence from judgement. If ethics is purely theoretical, it seems to lack a central aspect. The formal and academic discussion of ethics may or may not be geared towards making recommendations for practice. The attitude that all discussion of ethics in any applied field ought to be making specific recommendations for practice seems to be rather common, judging from critical appraisal by anonymous reviewers on many journal articles submitted for publication and expectations aired elsewhere. However, recommendations for practice need to be finely tuned to specific contexts and to the pragmatic consideration of what might actually work in specific situations. Local and detailed knowledge is always needed. This textbook therefore is not aimed at such. However, it is hoped that a greater understanding of the issues aired here will contribute to attempts to achieve practical results, and much of our discussion and many exercises are designed to prompt reflection on the context of application.

AI ethics and AI safety In developing AI, and likewise for developing computing programmes and systems and engineering in general, the concern for safety is well established. Safety necessitates ensuring that systems reliably achieve the goals that we wish them to achieve, without unacceptable dangers, including both long-term and short-term risks. Concern for safety is, or at least should be, built into the principles of engineering design. The complexity of AI means that considerable work is involved in ascertaining and checking safety, much of which is highly technical. The 'black box' nature of much AI is one cause for particular concerns, resulting in considerable efforts in technical work to ensure as much transparency in systems as possible. There are many reasons to consider that AI raises especially vexed questions concerning safety, among them issues of power and control, with the scaling up of systems and their complexity, meaning that the potential for harm from any safety problems could often be immense.

'Normal Accidents' and AI Safety

Charles Perrow developed a theory of 'normal accidents' in his book *Normal Accidents: Living with High-Risk Technologies* (1984) after examining the causes of the Three Mile Island nuclear accident, a partial meltdown of a nuclear power station in 1979 [13]. 'Normal accidents' are inevitable in technological systems which are highly complex and where the interacting elements are tightly coupled, and where the potential for error could be catastrophic. The role of organisations surrounding technologies in creating and mitigating risk is emphasised. Perrow's theory has been influential in contributing to understandings of safety and risk in technological systems.

It has been claimed that AI systems are prone to 'normal accidents'. Hence, it has been argued that organisations using AI that could have deleterious impacts need to be highly reliable [14], and that regulations around AI need to take the characteristics that lead to normal accidents into account [15]. Among other things, this illustrates how tightly connected are technical safety issues to questions of regulation and organisation which involve human elements, judgements of value, and ethics.

The technical work involved in attempting to ensure the safety and reliability of AI systems is of paramount importance, and there are obvious links with questions in ethics, such as the consideration of the goals built into AI systems, the regulation of AI and its development, and assessing the impacts of the deployment of AI systems in the real world and their wider repercussions.

While this book recognises the necessity and importance of the technical side of these questions, here we concentrate on exploring the ethical issues both in general and on questions where there are direct implications for work in safety, such as the issues of transparency and the related issue of whether a particular instance of AI can be explained, and the very important general issue of how we set goals and assess consequences. This is a necessary element of more technical work focused on the implementation of ethics in AI.

The implementation of ethics   The link between theory and practice in ethics is critical. You can produce all the robust conclusions about AI ethics that you like, but if these are never translated into policy and practice, little is achieved, as Virginia Dignum and others have emphasised. This book fully recognises the importance of law, regulation, strategies to incorporate ethics into the design and use of products, and responsible research and innovation in this field, but these are complex areas that cannot be addressed here. One aim of this book is to assist readers in being able to contribute as effectively and creatively as possible to such work as it continues into the future. The interrelationship between theory and application is critical to ethics and naturally critical to implementation.

However, one set of questions about AI ethics can be immediately up to you—your own use of technologies involving AI, how you choose to interact with these, and indeed, the question of whether or not you even have a choice. I hope this book will enhance and develop your thoughts and actions about the impacts of AI on your life.

1.11   The Approach of This Book

Summary
This book stresses methodology but does not propose a fixed approach. It aims to assist readers to think through issues rather than to provide definite solutions to questions. It recognises the contributions of other disciplines to these questions, including technological expertise, but focuses on the contribution of ethics.

By now some of the ways this book will approach ethical questions in AI should be becoming clear. This book aims to equip readers to develop skills and understanding to contribute to the development and use of these new technologies; to introduce philosophical and ethical ideas so that you can understand and contribute to some of the complexity of the debates; and, in the course of this, to look at cases, methods, and concepts. You will be introduced to some important and basic ideas and thinkers in ethics and show how they relate to contemporary debates in AI. This is not the kind of textbook that gives answers on a topic that you need to learn to pass an exam or gain proficiency in a subject, although there will be plenty of material intended to inform.

Methodologies in ethics are stressed, but this book does not provide a fixed 'method' Readers will not find a formula or fixed strategy for approaching ethical questions in AI. There are books around that aspire to lay out detailed methodologies for working through ethical questions in the design of technology, which can have great utility, but this is not one of them [16]. However, you will be guided through questions of methodology in ethics and shown some ways in which ethical questions can be approached. Many ideas will be introduced in preliminary ways and returned to later in more detail or from different angles. By this means you should develop your understanding and deepen your capacity to contribute to the field.

Since it is essential to apply ideas to concrete cases, there will be plenty of exercises, many for individuals, and some for groups, and examples of cases on which to draw. The book can be used in class or by those reading alone, by those with an informal interest, and by those who are studying the subject in detail. The book is laid out so that it will be possible to skim over some sections in less detail, for those with limited time or with different backgrounds and interests, and focus more on others.

From the simple to the complex Because one aim of this book is to show how material from different fields can be brought to bear upon the questions of AI ethics, it is necessary to simplify and generalise on many points. This is partly a matter of space and partly because sometimes such simplification is necessary to demonstrate broad patterns, contrasting, synergistic, or overlapping issues and concepts. There hence will be considerable work to be done, building up detail, context, and nuance, and many points at which exceptions and subtleties can be found. The book recognises that many of the pointers to topics that merit attention are very introductory only. This only serves to indicate the potential for those with particular interests and expertise to work together on these issues.

1.12   Developing Ethical Autonomy

Summary
The importance in ethics of thinking and acting with autonomy is introduced; this is an especially important issue in relation to the control that AI may have over our lives.

One of the major groups of questions in AI ethics concerns control and autonomy. One of the main fears about AI is that it will rob us of agency. Perhaps by developing into a superintelligence that usurps control, perhaps by stealthily taking away decision-making power app by app, or by diminishing our capacities as we rely more and more on machines to do our thinking for us. Partly inspired by the wish to counter this, this book aims to enhance your capacities to think in this area, your agency. Of course this is not meant to imply that you won't already have such capacity; the book's contribution is particular to offering certain considerations.

On many views of ethics (but not all), someone who simply follows instructions, whether from a human or a machine, is not acting as a fully moral being. If thought, reflection, and intention are critical to moral action, then the more one can develop one's understanding of ethical issues, the more one can explain one's views and actions, the more one can fully consider all aspects of a question before responding, and then the greater one's agency and autonomy will be. Even if we act in compliance with the orders of others, we make them our own by agreeing with them or at least seeing their point. We will also need to understand sets of moral rules to be able to interpret how to apply them in new cases.

There is complexity here because how precisely one should develop understanding and capacity in ethics is in dispute. Some views focus on reason and rationality; some focus on feelings and empathy; some focus on elaborate theory; some focus on fine attention to context and to the matter at hand; and some focus on developing character. We will consider these issues throughout the book.

If a focus is on developing ethical autonomy, on ethical agency, and on thinking for oneself, does this mean that the aim is to see ethics as something merely personal, simply a 'choice' like the choice between colour of socks? No, because autonomy is a richer notion than this. Thinking through matters for yourself in ethics certainly does not mean having to come up with an idiosyncratic, counterintuitive, or unusual answer (although it may do). Autonomy does not mean lawlessness or randomness. We can more aptly think of developing the capacity to think a matter through, to make it one's own, to display a kind of authenticity or agency. We can also, very importantly, think of ethical autonomy as building the capacity to refuse to comply with behaviour and instructions when such refusal is appropriate, the capacity to do more than simply follow the crowd (although not at the expense of rejecting any relevant wisdom the crowd may have).

Moral Autonomy: Actions in Accordance with Duty, and Actions for the Sake of Duty

One influential view of moral autonomy is found in Immanuel Kant's work, *Groundwork of the Metaphysics of Morals* [17]. A distinction he made between different motivations for following a moral rule is useful to consider in reflecting on the idea of autonomy in ethical judgement and action. Kant's distinction is very often misunderstood, uncontroversial in some respects, highly controversial in others. Kant distinguished between *acting out of reverence for the moral law* and *acting in conformity with the law*. We do not need all the details of Kant's somewhat complex philosophy in order to grasp the essentials.

(continued)

Imagine a shopkeeper who always gives the right change to customers.

One shopkeeper gives the right change out of fear of getting caught. He does a good thing, to be sure, with a good outcome, but most would agree there is little moral merit to his character. After all, consider the Ring of Gyges.

A second shopkeeper gives the right change just because he's a cheerful, nice sort of chapter. For Kant, likewise, this shopkeeper's actions produce good in the world, but the action itself has no *moral* worth. Many disagree or are even shocked at Kant's claim. The shopkeeper sounds exactly like the kind of person you'd want running your local store.

A third shopkeeper always gives the right change out of what Kant calls reverence or respect for the moral law. This involves consciously considering the situation, determining the right course of action, and then giving the right change precisely because it is the right thing to do. One's precise motivation for action is key.

Critics of Kant consider this a cold way of dealing with people, and indeed there is a lot to be said for more spontaneous views of moral motivation. However, it illustrates one way of thinking about what it is to have moral autonomy: to deliberate and act with insight and care, making an informed and consciously chosen action.

Exercise 10

A shopkeeper always gives the right change because the shop is now automated. Using surveillance, a shopper's bill is automatically calculated as items are placed in their basket, and the money automatically leaves each shopper's bank account as they walk out through the front door. The shop is part of a franchise owned by a vast international corporation that sets the rules for how the shops operate.

Does the owner of the shop deserve any moral praise if customers always receive accurate bills?

If automation takes over a multitude of simple everyday functions such as charging customers accurately, will this give us less time to exercise our moral agency?

If a machine follows a rule of morality, or indeed, a rule of anything else, can there be a distinction between the machine acting in conformity with the rule and acting out of respect for the rule?

Could a machine determine whether a rule it is following is a *moral* rule?

Note: in all such exercises and examples, feel free to produce variations of your own to test out your thoughts.

1.13   Why Examine Underlying Concepts in AI Ethics?

Summary
In addition to looking at concrete issues, much of this book is devoted to examining concepts underlying ethical claims. There are many reasons for this, including the contribution it can make towards understanding the approaches of those from diverse cultures and backgrounds.

There are so many practical and pressing concerns in AI ethics that there may be a certain impatience with spending too much time considering theoretical and abstract issues. However, there are many good reasons to contemplate questions of AI ethics even for those who are in general somewhat sceptical about the methods and promises of ethics as a discipline: in order to understand others and to understand the nature of the important and often heated debates around AI. These issues have individual, societal, and global impacts and are shaping our societies as we go into the future. Looking deeply into the ethical questions is a very good way of helping to understand why others differ from you, to perhaps come to an agreement, or an acceptable compromise, and to search more deeply and more creatively for solutions. Diving deeply into disagreements can often help to pinpoint the root source of differences and help identify whether these are fundamental divergences of viewpoint and worldview or something that could be addressed by more pragmatic or practical means.

Examining underlying conceptual issues can assist in understanding cultural differences We can also often find that an ethical dispute is grounded in political differences or in divergent religious or secular worldviews. There are particular reasons to be especially alert to cultural and other differences of opinion in regard to AI because it has such global reach and such far-reaching potential to impact so much of our lives, yet its development is dominated by a very small section of the human population with their own viewpoints and idiosyncrasies. So we know at the outset that there are going to be different views, and a question is how to cope with this, and how to consider whether or not dominant views on AI and on ethics are being imposed on others, and if so, how. It would be foolish to try to produce a book which 'covers all opinions' and indeed, I would still be here decades from now vainly trying to finish it. Rather, the book's strategy is to help facilitate an awareness of the right kind of questions to ask. Often, this can be assisted by examining one's own underlying assumptions and values and at the conceptual frameworks that lie beneath these.

For example, beliefs in ethics may be found to draw upon metaphysical views about the nature of persons, which can help to explain differences of opinion and approach. This may well not lead to anyone involved changing their mind, but it can lead to greater mutual understanding, which has to be something to be valued. We may sometimes come to realise that when we assumed that our views were based upon the 'facts' of the matter, these 'facts' only appeared unshakeable because they relied upon assumptions that we had not realised may be questioned.

1.14   Why Am I Writing This Book?

Summary
Just a personal note on how I started working in this area.

In this book, I strive to present different viewpoints and a wide variety of approaches; this is not a book intended to push personal viewpoints. However, it's inevitable that these will creep in. In class, wherever there are topics on which I feel particularly strongly, I tend to warn my students that I might be biased about them so that they can take that into account in listening to me. Likewise, I obviously don't know everything, so my background knowledge and viewpoints are bound to influence what I have included, what I have left out, and how I have presented issues. This is one of the reasons why the book includes exercises and stresses not only the capacities of theories, concepts, and methodologies of ethics to contribute but also the limits of what ethics as a discipline can do.

A brief outline of how I came to write this book. I started an interest in philosophy as a teenager. Contrary to what you might expect from an academic, I detested my school and often used to skip class to wander into central London nosing around in second-hand bookshops or to read philosophy in the local library. I now realise of course that I understood very little of what I read. As a teenager, I was fascinated with the question of the possibilities and limitations of thought and of what we can learn about the world from thought alone. I specialised in sciences at school, expecting to fail my exams, but miraculously did well enough to get into university. I studied physics as an undergraduate, and then switched to philosophy and psychology, with a minor in computer science, before specialising in philosophy at the graduate level. My graduate studies included philosophical logic and philosophy of language, with a doctorate in philosophy of mind, although my primary interest has always been ethics, both metaethics and applied ethics. I got into working in AI ethics through a background of working with various interdisciplinary teams with medics, lawyers, discourse analysts, social scientists, computer scientists, and genomics research scientists, looking at issues in medical ethics and social and ethical issues in genetics and genomics and in dementia care.

I then happened to be teaching in Oxford in 2015 when the Future of Life Institute announced a programme of grants for work in ethical issues around AI, and I had the opportunity to work on a project examining how to develop codes of ethics for AI, along with Mike Wooldridge and Peter Millican. My past work in medical and genomic technologies turned out to have many overlaps with issues in AI, including questions concerning data and how science and technologies influence how we conceptualise the human subject. I continue to work with a team researching how to improve dementia care, and there are also many overlaps there too, not just in the technologies being trialled to help with dementia care, research, and diagnosis but also at a fundamental level in terms of how we relate to and conceptualise the human person. I truly do believe that AI ethics is the most exciting field of applied ethics and that it has a great potential for improving the field of applied ethics, but more importantly, for helping to energise and vitalise discussion about what it means to lead a great human life, both now and in the future.

1.15 What Is to Come

The first few chapters of the book present frameworks for asking and answering questions in AI ethics, drawing from philosophy but noting the critical importance of the contribution of other disciplines. There are exercises and practical examples of cases throughout. Chapter 2 will give readers some background to the current intense interest in ethical questions in AI. It gives an overview of some relevant historical responses to technology.

Chapter 3 then provides an account of some major questions within the philosophy of technology, which will enrich our understanding of the ethical issues concerning AI.

Chapter 4 will look at the vexed question of methodology—how can we approach these questions with any degree of rigour?

Chapter 5 dives deeper into some key questions for AI ethics: how we understand and value intelligence and, since one of the major issues is how we compare humans and AI, our understanding of human nature.

Chapter 6 gives an overview of the central theories in normative ethics, consequentialism, deontology, and virtue ethics, assessing their usefulness in the specific context of AI.

Chapter 7 dives deeper into philosophy, asking what further questions we need to ask about the foundations of ethics and how other areas of philosophy, such as philosophy of mind, are also essential for understanding the ethics of AI.

Chapter 8 then looks in detail at issues central to ethics and of paramount importance in AI ethics: how we understand and value persons and how we understand and value autonomy and its limits.

Chapter 9 examines concrete ethical issues currently facing us, focusing on online communication and content moderation as an example to illustrate approaches to applying the earlier material of the book to a tangible and complex issue.

Chapter 10 looks at two contrasting sets of ethical questions, first, on a range of issues connected with AI and work, including its impact on society in the future, and second, at the dangers that might be posed by superintelligence.

Chapter 11 asks further questions about how the far future of humanity might be like if AI continues to develop and addresses a set of questions around our relationships with intelligent machines, including the question of whether machines could be ethical and if we might owe them moral respect.

1.16 Key Points

The essential message of this chapter is that AI ethics presents difficult but exciting challenges; that ethics should ideally be regarded as an activity and an opportunity to contribute to valuable discussions on important questions of value; and that each person will have something to offer.

1.17 Educator Notes

This chapter involves no previous reading or study and hence could be set to be completed before the first week of term or in the first week as light homework when students are being oriented to the subject matter; most of the exercises will require no previous reading, although a few involve a small amount of research. Points to emphasise include the view of ethics as involving dialogue and necessitating different viewpoints and contributions from other disciplines.

The chapter contains summaries of each major section and headings and bold text leading students through the main points, enabling students with different time commitments to skim certain sections. If students simply attempt some of the exercises, they will have gained a useful orientation to the rest of the book.

The most important key takeaway is that ethics should be seen in positive ways, as an open-ended discussion and an opportunity to contribute to improving the development and applications of AI, rather than as a negative list of prohibitions imposed from outside. Exercises 1, 2, 6, and 9 may be attempted with little reading to orient students to the focus of the book.

Exercise 7 on the Ring of Gyges and Exercise 10 on Kant's views on moral motivation may also provide entertaining and thought-provoking introductions to the area and how philosophy can help us to think through some issues that will be looked at again later in the book.

The exercises given in each chapter are designed to be suitable for different levels of students and for individual and/or group work. These will introduce cases and issues in AI ethics to cover a variety of different themes and applications. Many can be adapted so that readers can apply their own particular realms of interest. Some of the cases and themes will be returned to later in the book to illustrate how the material of the book is equipping students with skills to deepen their analysis and understanding of issues and methods. Exercise topics that might be particularly useful for class debate and discussion or for extended projects or essays are indicated.

Note Any reading list in this area will fail to cover all the possible worthwhile texts, since so much is being written.

References

1. Boddington P (2017) Towards a code of ethics for artificial intelligence. Springer, Cham
2. HLEG (2019) A definition of AI: main capabilities and disciplines. Independent High-Level Expert Group on Artificial Intelligence, Brussels
3. Wooldridge M (2020) The road to conscious machines: the story of AI. Penguin, London
4. Plato (1888) The republic of Plato (trans: Jowett B). Clarendon Press, Oxford
5. Philip Z (2007) The Lucifer effect understanding how good people turn evil. Random House, New York
6. Sinnott-Armstrong W (2019) Moral skepticism. In: Zalta EN (ed) The Stanford encyclopedia of philosophy, Summer 2021 edn. https://plato.stanford.edu/archives/sum2019/entries/skepticism-moral/
7. Aristotle (2014) Aristotle: nicomachean ethics (trans: Crisp R). Cambridge University Press, Cambridge
8. Dignum V (2019) Responsible artificial intelligence: how to develop and use AI in a responsible way. Springer, Cham
9. Le Bui M, Noble SU (2020) We're missing a moral framework of justice in artificial intelligence. In: The Oxford handbook of ethics of AI. Oxford University Press, Oxford, p 163
10. Yeung K, Howes A, Pogrebna G (2019) AI governance by human rights-centred design, deliberation and oversight: an end to ethics washing. In: Dubber MD, Pasquale F, Das S (eds) The Oxford handbook of AI ethics. Oxford University Press, Oxford
11. Bietti E (2020) From ethics washing to ethics bashing: a view on tech ethics from within moral philosophy. In: Proceedings of the 2020 conference on fairness, accountability, and transparency. Association for Computing Machinery, New York, pp 210–219
12. Simonite T (2021) What really happened when Google ousted Timnit Gebru. Wired
13. Perrow C (1984) Normal accidents: living with high-risk technologies. Basic Books, New York
14. Dietterich TG (2019) Robust artificial intelligence and robust human organizations. Front Comp Sci 13(1):1–3
15. Maas MM (2018) Regulating for 'normal AI accidents'—operational lessons for the responsible governance of AI deployment. In: Proceedings of the 2018 AAAI/ACM conference on artificial intelligence, ethics and society. Association for Computing Machinery, New York
16. Spiekermann S (2015) Ethical IT innovation: a value-based design approach. Routledge, London
17. Kant I, Paton HJ (1964) Groundwork of the metaphysic of morals (trans and analysed: Paton HJ). Harper & Row, Manhattan, NY

Further Reading

Introductions to Artificial Intelligence

Boden M (2018) Artificial intelligence: a very short introduction. Oxford University Press
Broussard M (2018) Artificial unintelligence: how computers misunderstand the world. MIT Press
McCarthy J (2004) What is artificial intelligence. http://www-formal.stanford.edu/jmc/whatisai/
Müller VC (2012) Introduction: philosophy and theory of artificial intelligence. Mind Mach 22(2): 67–69
Russell SJ, Norvig P (2016) Artificial intelligence a modern approach, 3rd edn. Pearson Education, London
Wooldridge M (2018) Artificial intelligence: a ladybird expert book. Ladybird, London
Wooldridge M (2020) The road to conscious machines: the story of AI. Penguin UK

Introductions and General Texts on AI Ethics

Anderson M, Anderson SL (eds) (2011) Machine ethics. Cambridge University Press, Cambridge
Boddington P (2017) Towards a code of ethics for artificial intelligence. Springer, Cham
Bostrom N, Yudkowsky E (2014) The ethics of artificial intelligence. In: The Cambridge handbook
    of artificial intelligence, vol 1, pp 316–334
Coeckelbergh M (2020) AI ethics. MIT Press, Cambridge, MO
Dignum V (2019) Responsible artificial intelligence: how to develop and use AI in a responsible
    way. Springer Nature
Dubber MD, Pasquale F, Das S (eds) (2020) The Oxford handbook of ethics of AI. Oxford
    University Press, New York
Gunkel DJ (2018) Robot rights. MIT Press, Boston, MA
Johnson DG (1985) Computer ethics. Prentice-Hall, Englewood Cliffs (NJ)
Liao SM (2020) Ethics of artificial intelligence. Oxford University Press, Oxford
Lin P, Abney K, Jenkins R (eds) (2017) Robot ethics 2.0: from autonomous cars to artificial
    intelligence. Oxford University Press, Oxford
Müller VC (2021) Ethics of artificial intelligence and robotics. In: Zalta EN (ed) The Stanford
    encyclopedia of philosophy, Summer 2021 edn https://plato.stanford.edu/archives/sum2021/
    entries/ethics-ai/
Rawahn I et al (2019) Machine behaviour. Nature 568:477–486
Wallach W, Allen C (2008) Moral machines: teaching robots right from wrong. Oxford University
    Press, Oxford

Aspects of the Impact of AI, Algorithms, and Communication Technology on Ethics and Society: A Selection of Interesting Books

Broussard M (2018) Artificial unintelligence: how computers misunderstand the world. MIT Press
Lanier J (2010) You are not a gadget: a manifesto. Vintage, New York
Lepore J (2020) If then: how one data company invented the future. John Murray, London
Lupton D (2019) Data selves: more-than-human perspectives. Wiley, New York
Noble SU (2018) Algorithms of oppression: how search engines reinforce racism. NYU Press,
    New York
O'Neil C (2016) Weapons of math destruction: how big data increases inequality and threatens
    democracy. Broadway Books, New York
Pariser E (2011) The filter bubble. Viking Penguin, London
Pasquale F (2015) The black box society. Harvard University Press, Cambridge
Pasquale F (2020) New laws of robotics: defending human expertise in an age of AI. Harvard
    University Press, Cambridge
Snowden E (2019) Permanent record. Macmillan, London
Theodorou A, Dignum V (2019) Towards ethical and socio-legal governance in AI. Nat Mach Intell
    2:10–12
Turkle S (2011) Alone together: why we expect more from technology and less from each other, 3rd
    edn. Basic Books, New York
Wallach W (2015) A dangerous master: how to keep technology from slipping out of our control.
    Basic Books, New York
Webb A (2019) The big nine: how the tech titans and their thinking machines could warp humanity.
    Public Affairs, New York
Zuboff S (2019) The age of surveillance capitalism. Profile Books, London

Chapter 2
The Rise of AI Ethics

Abstract This chapter presents an overview of the present state of AI ethics, its main themes, and some of the factors that lead up to the current state of play. An overview of the most prominent value issues in current guidance concerning AI ethics is given, with introductions to these issues, brief case studies for each, and exercises to draw out questions, many of which will be pursued at greater length throughout the book. These are freedom and autonomy, justice and fairness, transparency and explanation, beneficence and nonmaleficence, responsibility, privacy, trust, sustainability, dignity, and solidarity. We explore how having some understanding of relevant historical concerns about technology can help to illuminate current concerns regarding AI, looking briefly at historical apprehensions regarding robots, the technologies of writing, machines, data and statistics, and twentieth-century concerns about computing that preceded specific concerns about AI. An overview of the current state of AI ethics and endeavours to implement ethical guidance in policy and practice is given. Last, we look at a case study of indigenous AI protocols and ask what can be learned from considering diverse perspectives.

Keywords AI ethics · Computer ethics · History of technology · Ethics regulations · Autonomy · Fairness

2.1   AI Ethics: Why Now?

Summary

We start by asking why there is currently so much attention to AI ethics. AI is often described as a new Industrial Revolution. Some further interest has been piqued by particular questions around our dependence on technologies following the COVID-19 pandemic. AI is also frequently hailed as transformative.

Visible concern about AI ethics has grown rapidly in the last few years. Centres dedicated to AI ethics are springing up, corporations and companies involved in AI are appointing ethics boards or ethics advisers, governments are funding research and reports into AI ethics and safety, popular magazines, serious newspapers, radio programmes, blog posts, and online video channels discuss AI ethics, and prominent

P. Boddington, *AI Ethics*, Artificial Intelligence: Foundations, Theory, and Algorithms, https://doi.org/10.1007/978-981-19-9382-4_2

figures pronounce on the dangers and delights of AI. AI ethics certainly does seem to have captured the imagination of many people in recent times. However, it is important to realise in all this flurry of recent activity that concern for ethical issues in AI, in robotics, and in computing more widely is not in fact as newly minted as it may appear.

Why is there now so much visible activity around AI ethics? Might this rise in interest in AI be some kind of fad linked to, say, funding or corporate issues? Might it be linked to a hyping of technology which will die down when we realise it's not so dangerous, or so transformative, as at first appeared? Recall the announcements about the completion of the Human Genome Project to sequence the human genome around the turn of the century [1]. There was talk at the time of having 'cracked the code' to human life, unlocked the mystery to our great and marvellous species. This was accompanied by a certain amount of discomfort at the discovery that human beings have embarrassingly few genes compared to some other species, roughly the same number as some primitive worms. Nevertheless, not only was there excitement that we could now, apparently, finally 'fully understand' humanity, but there was also more practical excitement that now we could personalise medicine, discover the causes of a multiplicity of diseases, create new reproductive technologies, and so on. Along with this, there was, quite rightly, considerable attention to ethical issues.

This all continues but has calmed down considerably. Much of the promise of personalised medicine was somewhat premature, many of the studies into the origins of disease had failed to produce the practical applications hoped for, and more and more research indicated that the genome was by no means the be all and end all, and that various complex environmental factors in development were also critical. More nuanced assessments of the human genome are being made with realisations that considerable work lies ahead [2]. Perhaps something similar might happen to the extreme hype and attention to AI and to AI ethics?

A new Industrial Revolution? On the other hand, we already saw in the last chapter that there are many reasons to pay attention to ethical issues in AI. For one thing, the ubiquity of use and pace of change of technology. Technology has developed rapidly, in historical terms, since the First Industrial Revolution where water and steam power mechanised production, the Second Industrial Revolution where electricity increased production still further, and the Third Industrial Revolution which introduced digital technologies including AI. Many consider that we are now entering the Fourth Industrial Revolution where interconnections between digital, physical, and biological technologies accelerate industrial and social changes [3, 4]. Anticipation, excitement, and anxiety about such large changes might explain and justify the current attention to AI and to its ethics. The history of AI shows that it has shown promise, then stalled, then shown promise, and then stalled again over the last several decades, with much rapid progress in recent years. Much of this progress is in machine learning, enabled by the rise of massive amounts of data and an increase in computing power that has enabled the collection and processing of that data. This recent burst of progress, with an increasing number of applications of artificial intelligence in the workplace and in public and private life, could certainly help explain the intense interest in AI ethics.

A technological pandemic?   More recently, attention to particular issues regarding our use of and dependence upon technologies has been forced on us by the COVID-19 pandemic, where remote working and online shopping have become a necessity for so many (and, one might add, a sine qua non of lockdown policies) and where track-and-trace surveillance technologies to monitor the disease and vaccine passports necessary in many places for movement of people have been both hailed as indispensably useful and decried as creeping authoritarian control [5].

It is this 'duck-rabbit' feature of so much AI that helps to create such interest. It is so often, precisely those features which some hail as great boons to humanity, that others lament as portents of our doom—sometimes expressed in milder language, of course. It is often the aspects that inspire the greatest hopes that fill others with the greatest dread.

Cassandra

Those who claim that new technologies such as AI are going to cause great difficulties and dangers for humanity are sometimes decried as 'Cassandras'. However, who was Cassandra?

Cassandra was a priestess of Troy, daughter of the King and Queen of Troy. The god Apollo sought to woo her with the promise of the gift of foreseeing the future. She accepted the gift, but then refused Apollo. Infuriated, he cursed her. Cassandra's prophesies were accurate. Her curse was to be doomed to warn of great danger, only to be ignored.

Our problem is that it's very hard to know what prophesies regarding AI will come true.

However, perhaps it is something about the particular and complex ways in which AI seems to herald our futures that explains the extent of recent interest in it and its ethics. Could it be that the interest in its ethics only seems to be so novel precisely because AI always seems to be about what is new, and not just that, but about what is hailed as transformative? Some work examining the nature of AI and examining its ethics perhaps serves to reinforce such ideas, *even if* many claims of novelty and success turn out to be exaggerated. For many of the ways in which we speak of and imagine AI speak of our place in the world and of our futures. AI sits in a space occupied both by science and technology, a place of rationality, of statistics, of formulae, and of empiricism, and at once, a place of the imagination and of extremes of feeling. It sits both in the minutiae of the present, a world cluttered with technologies using AI, and in the inchoate future unfolding in ways of peril or promise. It has entered the world at a particular time in history, and while it is being developed in various parts of the globe, much of it comes from a section of the Western world that, in historical and global terms, is currently unusually irreligious

[6]. It is hard not to wonder if some of the ways in which it is being imagined and discussed suggest that for some, AI is stepping into a space left by religious belief.

What the Internet Tells Us About the Transformative Power of AI
A few seconds spent on a search engine reveals claims that:

AI is supercharging economic growth
Transforming the management of business revenues
And the business landscape in general
As well as transforming the experience of employees
Transforming healthcare in general
And precision medicine in particular
As well as drug discovery
It's transforming the Pentagon
And the automotive and aerospace industries
It's revolutionising several critical sectors of the economy
And science in general
The list goes on . . .

If these claims are all true, they will bring with them many ethical and social questions.

If they are exaggerated or even false, the fact that they are made so regularly likewise gives rise to many ethical and social questions.

2.2   Same or Different? What's Special About AI Ethics?

Summary
AI ethics is often hailed as novel. However, it is also critical to understand how its issues might overlap with other areas.

We need to carefully and accurately examine any issue in front of us. Even if we are now facing many urgent questions about AI ethics, this does not mean that the issues themselves are entirely novel. Claims of the novelty of issues in AI ethics may not only be exaggerated or overgeneralised but may also mislead us into omitting to consider useful lessons, parallels, and contrasts that could be found in previous work and in examples drawn from more mundane technologies, or indeed from elsewhere in life.

Why does this question matter? If there truly are new ethical questions in AI, these may need some new ways of thinking. However, insofar as ethical issues are the same, we can draw upon the past and present examples.

We have long had to deal with questions about the safety and robustness of our technologies [7]. No history of the Industrial Revolution could leave out ethical, social, cultural, and political issues about issues such as the complex mix of dangers and opportunities, risks, and benefits posed to factory workers, transport workers, miners, the general public, and the environment, by the new machinery being introduced and the increased possibilities for mining, for transport, and for the exploitation of the environment.

The automation of tasks raised complex issues. For example, not only did it act to create uniformity of products, but it also enabled the imposition of uniformity of behaviour on employees. It would give rise to a variety of political and social reactions: to unions, to charitable work concerned with the working poor, to social reformers, and to political theorists of different stripes. Issues extended well beyond the factory: the extremely long hours and low pay of workers would mean harsh living conditions for families, malnutrition, poor health, and decreasing life expectancies. Furthermore, the greater the power is, the worse the potential accident. This may help explain why air travel is, somewhat paradoxically, the safest form of transport because the appalling and grimly spectacular nature of aircraft crashes has spurred air safety to great lengths to prevent disasters. Perhaps AI raises essentially the same spectrum of issues, but with greater potential to disrupt and cause mayhem, given its powers?

A critically important question is whether ethical questions in AI have been exaggerated by misplaced fears, possibly based upon misconceptions of what AI is or can do. In the next chapter, we take a closer look at how AI is understood and the implications this has for defining and dealing with ethical issues. However, one possible view is that many if not most of the ethical questions are basically questions about the safety of the technology and determining how to ensure that complex software performs as we intended it to perform.

Exercise 1

Workplaces are increasingly using AI for surveillance of their employees [8]. This includes software that monitors employees' work to determine if they are spending too much time away from their core activities; facial recognition software to ensure that unauthorised people are not let into the office, or that employees remain focused on their computer screen; and location trackers to monitor how they move around the workplace. Such software may also be used remotely to monitor employees working at home. Trackers on vehicles can also monitor the location and driving skills of delivery drivers and taxis. These technologies are receiving considerable attention. Other examples of new technologies used to control the behaviour of employees include posts and photographs of employees' mistakes on shared chats (this happened to my daughter!).

What ethical issues are raised? How are the concerns of both employees and employers best represented? This may differ in different industries.

How novel are such concerns, and does the introduction of AI bring novel ethical questions to bear?

Note: you may or may not wish to carry out further research into the details of workplace surveillance while doing this exercise. You may have relevant first-hand experience.

2.3   Common Themes and Varieties of Questions in AI Ethics

Summary

AI ethics encompasses a large variety of issues. This section presents a way of grouping together some major themes. The general nature of AI, versus detailed aspects; current issues, or concerns about the far future; how to address errors in AI, and how to address the deleterious impacts of AI's success; questions of knowledge and human relations: how are we seen via AI, and how do we see others? Do we control AI, or does AI control us?

AI ethics encompasses so many different questions of a large variety of types that it may be helpful to outline some broad themes to categorise the field so that readers can orient themselves to future material, although there are different ways of categorising the plethora of questions in the field. Addressing different types of questions will require some different approaches, draw on a variety of resources, and link to different sets of background assumptions and issues.

Whole or part Some questions in AI ethics deal with general issues about AI conceptualised as a whole, while others focus on specific applications of AI or specific technical details about AI. For example, there are debates about whether some artificial general intelligence (AGI) is possible but also ethical debates about how human beings might stand in relation to such an AGI (see Chap. 11). Such a debate needs to draw upon knowledge and understanding of technological possibilities, and will raise rather broad questions about human beings and the human condition. There are also debates and practical work underway about the ethical implications of how different forms of machine learning represent the world, as well as work examining in detail whether and how human beings can understand specific instances of machine learning (transparency and explainability—see Sect. 2.4.2). These obviously require specific technological expertise, especially for implementation, but addressing these involves asking what it is to understand something and why understanding matters, questions that may be surprisingly complex.

Now and then Closely related is a division between domains of AI ethics that focus on developments of AI in the future, and possibly the very far future, and what these might mean for us, and those that address current or near future possibilities. There is a debate about how resources and energy should be expended between these, with some arguing that it is foolish to focus effort on the far future when present issues are so numerous and so pressing [9]. Others, such as Nick Bostrom, argue that future possibilities are so fraught with peril that it would be foolish, even reckless, not to address them. Bostrom's best-selling book *Superintelligence* tackles the dangers of a possible superintelligence that might become so powerful that it could wreak great harm to humanity, and how we might be able to control this [10]. Such considerations draw upon projections into the distant future, which are, unsurprisingly, often disputed.

Conversely, it is readily apparent that a plethora of questions about AI and its current and near future applications need to be tackled and are already receiving attention.

Moore's Law

Many projections of the future development of AI are based upon Moore's law [11], which is the law, or more accurately, a rough generalisation extrapolated from a few decades' observation, that computing capacity doubles approximately every 18 months; many propose that this doubling will continue into the future. These projections are then often used to conclude that we need to take serious notice of the major issues that will arise if AI continues to develop greater and greater intelligence.

Mike Wooldridge points out that this applies to the capacities of hardware, rather than software, upon which much progress in AI depends, hence casting doubt on free and easy predictions about computing progress [12].

Moreover, what would it be to develop 'greater and greater intelligence' such that new forms of threats of control of us puny humans arise? Much hangs on this answer.

Bug or feature: how things go wrong The fear of a superintelligence taking control of our destiny concerns the hazards of what Bostrom dubs 'perverse instantiation', the problem of how to get an intelligent machine to do what we asked it to do, only to find it does something disastrously different. This problem is the essence of many stories, such as asking a genie for three wishes only to find that the command has been executed in unfortunate ways. Isaac Asimov's famous robot stories likewise frequently address these questions [13]. Beginning students in computer science may often be tasked with trying to write out precisely how to programme a task so that a person, or machine, following specifications will produce what you actually intended. Not easy. The most boring English literature homework I ever had to do at school involved the tedious task of describing in utterly precise and idiot-proof language how to wash a car. Now just imagine setting up instructions for the most superpowerful AI ever to exist, and imagine the havoc that could be caused.

Many of the potential problems of AI are those of ironing out bugs, which will be the harder the more complex AI is and the wider its fields of application. These may be regarded as technical issues of safety, of validation or verification of a product. These terms are sometimes understood and explained in slightly different ways. Verification refers to the process by which it is determined whether a product complies with specifications. Validation refers to the process that ensures that the goals or requirements of a product are met by the specifications [14, 15].

We considered in Chap. 1 the relationship between ethics and issues of safety [16]. As such, these issues of ironing out bugs involve technical skills and the capacity to programme in exactly what you want to get out. However, the more complex the issues involved are, the more complex the technologies, and these become more than a matter of technical know-how. There can often be a multitude of ramifications in using AI, or any other complex system for that matter, involving complex methodologies and requiring different disciplinary expertise, as well as input from anyone who might count as a 'stakeholder'. This, in many cases, is practically all of us. However, a basic question in ensuring that AI does what we want is this: what do we want?

Bug or feature: how things go right Many ethical questions regarding AI stem not from ways in which it goes wrong but from ways in which it goes right, insofar as it fulfils the aims of the designers. We can specify aims under a certain description, but when it is fulfilled, we realise that there are implications of our own specifications that were not intended. Moreover, others impacted by AI may have substantive disagreements with the aims. The very success of AI may be part of its problems. Just as the Industrial Revolution led to a large increase in living standards overall by making possible the mass production of goods, that very same mass production has led to a host of problems, including environmental problems, plunging some into poverty, and increasing social inequality. Likewise, suppose AI could lead to vastly increased capabilities of cheaply and quickly diagnosing future health across the population. It would then become necessary to consider the implications of the knowledge this unleashes and what benefits it might bring. There are many other possible examples of the problems of success.

Us and them, us or them Many different questions in AI ethics involve consideration of how we interact with AI. There are a multitude of questions about how we interact with the machines around us that utilise AI. There are diverse fields of study regarding how humans interact with computers [17] and considerable work in robotics regarding the interaction between humans and robots in various fields [18]. These raise fine-tuned questions about the impact of technology on the human subject.

Other sets of questions are generated by considering more directly some of the possible capacities of machines. Could AI develop consciousness or other levels of sophistication such that we owed any duties to it? Could machines be moral beings in any significant sense, and could they be used to contribute to our moral behaviour, can they be joint agents with us, and can a machine ever be responsible in a significant way for its decisions and actions? These require examination not just of moral theory but also of the nature of the mind, of agency, responsibility, and consciousness, all questions involving interdisciplinary input. The very development of AI has in fact been linked to the development of work in areas such as cognitive science and the philosophy of mind, which are highly relevant to addressing the ethical questions that arise [19]. We consider these questions ahead, particularly in Chaps. 8–11.

Control or chaos The question of control appears in various guises in addressing safety and ethical issues in AI. Control issues are frequently the major point of discussion but also often play a key role when other questions come to the fore. We will return to them at many points in the book. Questions of control include the issue of how humans, in general, can control extremely powerful AI to meet their purposes and values. This is often known as the general question of **value alignment**. Indeed, the term 'value alignment' is sometimes used almost synonymously with 'AI ethics'. The complexity, opacity, and power of much AI produce difficult problems with control for those creating and using AI. The use of AI by human beings to control other human beings is also a pressing question, and this includes specific attempts to control, together with more creeping issues of control arising from the increasing entanglement of aspects of life with AI and technologies that use it. It is thus from the very nature of AI itself, plus its production and application in various interconnected technologies, which go to produce the many issues which fall under the general rubric of the 'control problem'.

Control of AI: Humans in the Loop
The question of our control of technology is nothing new. Failsafe devices and other techniques such as dead man's switches have been used to prevent disastrous consequences when things go wrong, and the more powerful the technology, the greater the capacity for catastrophe, the more such control is needed.

One way of achieving control over technologies such as AI is to have a 'human-in-the-loop' [20]. This means, in outline, that a human being will always be involved in the chain of decision making and action, or that a human being will always be on hand to intervene in time if it seems as if something is going wrong. This stresses the complex question of AI systems and the human and organisational structures in which they are embedded [21]. Of course, much depends upon the human being(s) in such a role.

In some cases, depending on the applications, human involvement may be post hoc, for example, in reviewing automated decisions about welfare distribution. In other cases, reaction to error needs to be immediate, such as in cases of potential meltdown of a power plant or missile errors. The complexity and lack of transparency of much AI may impose limits on the capacity of any human-in-the-loop system to correct for error and disaster.

2.4 Ethical Questions in AI Currently Receiving Attention

Summary
This section provides an introduction to some central concepts and values in AI ethics. These are freedom and autonomy, transparency and explanation, responsibility, transparency, justice and fairness, beneficence and nonmaleficence, privacy, trust, sustainability, dignity, and solidarity. Case studies are used to illustrate each, with exercises designed to highlight key issues, which will be explored in further

depth in later chapters. We examine why these concepts arise in relation to AI. The intersections between these concepts and values are stressed.

Broad themes of recurring ethical issues and concepts are emerging from the analysis of the many cases receiving attention [22]. It is important to consider not only the details of these cases but also how they are analysed ethically to participate in current debates while also considering how those debates are conducted. Our broader aim is to consider how the ethical questions in AI are currently understood and tackled, and whether there are ways of improving and advancing the specific contributions of ethics.

This section presents an overview of central concepts in AI ethics, drawing heavily from a review by Jobin et al. of AI ethics guidelines from around the world (but, it is fair to say, these are predominantly from North America and Western Europe) [23]. This review extracts and classifies common themes recurring centrally in discussions of AI ethics; there have been other projects also undertaking similar tasks [24, 25]. For our introduction to these themes, this section presents examples of cases, with indicators of some of the important ethical and conceptual questions that we need to examine. The cases are described in outline, but interested readers can research further details of relevant examples: the exercises invite you to draw out further considerations and are designed to elicit some of the major themes that we will later explore in more detail. Inevitably, many readers will have questions and ideas that we do not have space to explore in this book.

Some examples focus on technology applied to people living with dementia Although in this book examples of AI are chosen from a range of applications, many of the case studies refer to technology developed for, or applied for, people living with dementia and elderly people. This is intentional because it can help to present a picture of the many different kinds of technology that one individual or group of people may experience and the many intertwined ethical questions that may arise. I chose this topic first because I have been working for some years with a research group concerned with the provision of hospital care for people living with dementia, based at the Geller Institute of Aging and Memory in the University of West London. Second, because this is a growing demographic worldwide, there are many preexisting and complex ethical, social, practical, and medical questions concerning care and treatment, hence providing a challenging and complex background against which to consider ethical issues in AI. Third, in considering our use of AI, it is essential that we consider our humanity. People living with dementia are a particularly vulnerable group whose humanity is often threatened by the poor level of care they unfortunately may receive. There is potential for great improvement, with possible contributions from technology, but it is also vitally important that minute attention be paid to the humanity of this group of individuals. Last, although at first sight work on the day-to-day care of people living with dementia seems a world away from the high-tech world of AI, I have found numerous overlaps in the ethical and conceptual questions that need to be addressed.

Ethical Issues or Technical Issues?
Hagendorf has analysed the ethical issues in AI which are receiving prominent attention and suggests that the most visible questions are those which lend themselves to being addressed using the tools of technical expertise [26]. The attraction of focusing on such issues for organisations producing AI is apparent, precisely because they are more likely to have the expertise to do so. However, this does not mean that there are no further ethical, societal, and cultural questions left to ask, nor that even in cases where technical expertise is necessary, that *only* technical expertise is needed in understanding what is at issue and in coming to some resolution of the question.

2.4.1 Freedom and Autonomy

Freedom and autonomy are frequently mentioned in relation to ethical questions in AI. These closely related terms are concepts to which many will have some intuitive response [27–29]. They are both concerned with our ability to act, think, and make decisions. Hence, it should be readily apparent why they might play such a large part in discussions of AI ethics, since AI is likewise 'thinking' and 'making decisions'. However, there is considerable complexity in how questions of freedom and autonomy might arise, how these concepts are understood, and the degree to which they are valued.

The questions concerning freedom and autonomy in relation to AI are extremely complex because one could readily assume that the whole point of using technology was to increase one's freedom and autonomy. Questions arise, however, about how this is done, whose freedom and autonomy are increased, and any unintended consequences.

Case study: Direction finders A simple example might be using a navigation aid such as Google Maps to find the fastest route to your destination or to work out what time the rush hour is likely to ease off to plan when to make a journey.

However, not so fast. The Google Maps example is not quite so straightforward for a number of reasons. Consider a popular route. If a thousand motorists all look at roughly the same time to determine which is the fastest way to a certain destination, and they all get the same route suggestion, then that route will quickly become clogged with traffic. Therefore, suggested routes given to some motorists may not be the fastest, in order to prevent problems at a systemic level [30, pp. 101–111]. Is your individual autonomy and freedom being limited or manipulated? Note that there could be different responses to this.

This example follows from an intentional design element, but of course, there are also examples where a problem arises not by design but by error. There are many cases when the directions have been quite wrong but followed blindly by trusting humans. Someone in the village where my brother lives frequently has motorists turning up in her driveway, who proceed to insist that her humble cottage is a nearby stately home that they are trying to visit. People who make such errors are frequently ridiculed, but what does it say about humans in general, and how willing we are to hand over our decision-making to a machine?

Consider too the experience individuals might have using automated directions when walking. Many people have confessed to me that they follow instructions on their phone to get to a destination in the city without really looking up at their surroundings or having the slightest clue how they got there. This seems apparent from observing how many people walk erratically along the street, nose in phone. Have they increased their autonomy by the use of a direction finder, since they can now concentrate on something else instead? Or is their autonomy decreased to the extent that habitual use of a direction finder may mean that a person becomes increasingly dependent on their smartphone? If they always do have a smartphone, why would this matter? To answer these questions, we have to think further about what we mean by autonomy, why we value it, and what else we value.

Question
A person may have reduced capacity to work out directions. Does this matter if we now can rely on smartphones? Is it merely nostalgia to wish to retain the capacity to read a paper map?

A person who habitually walks to destinations with the aid of this tech may also know less about what their surroundings actually look like. They may have avoided many occasions when they could have looked with recognition into the face of a stranger walking towards them. They may have never found out that taking a route that is 1 min longer would have given them a wonderful view or taken them past a historic building, a convenient shop, or an unusual tree.

Question
Is this just a harmless by-product of walking along a street nose to phone? Does it matter? Consider other possible examples.

'Use it or lose it' There have been some warnings that the use of direction finders may erode our capacities to navigate our environment, and fears expressed that this might even contribute to the loss of navigational abilities [31]. These are often an early sign of the development of dementia. Dementia is a variable condition, or rather, a group of conditions, but frequently one of the earliest abilities to be affected is navigation. There is a great deal that is not known about dementia and its aetiology, so it would be premature to make any conclusions, but it is worth considering if AI might have such profound impacts. At the other end of our lifespan, how might child development be affected?

Exercise 2
If you habitually use a direction finder, get a paper map, work out a route, and go out without it.

(If my experience is anything to go by, as soon as you are spotted in the streets gazing into a paper A to Z, helpful strangers will approach you to give directions and to mock you for your apparent inability to use technology.)

'The Knowledge'
London black cab drivers are famous for their chat, for their ready opinion on any topic under the sun, and for 'The Knowledge'. This requirement for taxi drivers was introduced in 1865 and involves the capacity to navigate the streets and major landmarks of London without the aid of a map and to learn the fastest routes through the tangle of London's roads. An old city, it does not have the clear routes of those modern cities which are based upon a grid system. It can take 3–4 years to acquire this knowledge and to pass the test. At the time of writing, this requirement is still in place to be licensed as a taxi driver by Transport for London [32].

Some scientific research indicates that London taxi drivers have an enlarged posterior hippocampus compared to controls, indicating its role in spatial navigation, and demonstrating local plastic change in the adult brain [33].

If our freedom and autonomy concern how we think, speak, and act, then there are almost boundless possibilities to consider in relation to the use of AI. The direction finder example relates to how we think, make decisions, and act. We will see many examples later of ways in which AI technologies may affect human thought.

Exercise 3
It is hard not to admire those who have spent years travelling around London on scooters learning The Knowledge. However, is this now just a waste of time, given direction finders?

Compare and contrast the pluses and minuses of the old-fashioned way to using new technologies.

Do any of the points you considered raise, or relate to, *ethical* questions?

Key Points Answering whether a certain value, such as autonomy, is increased or threatened by AI will often require that we consider many aspects of the technology in question, including its capacities and limitations; features included in the design that may be there for different purposes, such as ironing out any unintended consequences of use; and wider questions about the deployment of a piece of technology and its occasional or habitual use by humans in context.

It should be apparent from this initial discussion that assessing AI by reference to the values of autonomy and freedom will require deeper accounts of how these values are understood. We will see in Chap. 9 that the questions relate closely to the concept of a person.

Consideration of freedom and autonomy has also quickly led to examination of other issues. In this example, these include questions about how we access and retain information and knowledge, how we relate to our environments, and how technology might impact information processing and even brain development.

2.4.2   Transparency and Explanation

Questions of transparency arise frequently in AI, often, as has already been mentioned, in relation to the 'black box' nature of much of the technology—the difficulty of understanding precisely how results are produced [30]. Lack of transparency means that it will be hard, or impossible, to provide an explanation of how the technology works, and this in turn may mean that it is hard, or impossible, to provide an explanation for why it is adopted.

There has been considerable attention to these issues, including statements by professional bodies [34] and regulatory action, as well as debate over how European Union regulations restrict the use of automated decision-making involving those algorithms which are used for any decision-making that 'significantly affects' individuals. This then in effect results in a 'right to an explanation' in certain circumstances (for instance, in decisions involving the allocation of public resources) [35]. However, providing such an explanation may be far from easy. It is readily apparent that what might count as an explanation of the underlying computing that works well for computer scientists with expertise in these areas will likely be less than satisfactory, even baffling, to many [36]. Careful attention needs to be paid to the question of what even counts as a useful and workable explanation that does what is needed in different circumstances [37]. Attempts are being made to find solutions to the problem of providing explanations that increase transparency. There are different approaches to explanations, with hope for progress in this area by using contrastive explanations, which aim to show why the results are not different, and counterfactual explanations, which aim to show how the results could be changed, by adjusting elements of the algorithm (if-then explanations) [38]. Counterfactual explanations could be used without the need to give an account of the technical details of how an algorithm worked, that is, without looking inside the black box [39]. Fears have also been raised that too much focus on transparency and the right to an explanation may distract from other substantial ethical issues and harms from algorithms [36]. It has also been argued that the technological challenges here may hold AI to a higher standard than that to which ordinary human beings are held, noting that there are limits to the amount of explanation for decisions which is reasonable to require, or indeed, which it is possible to give [40].

A useful analysis of types of transparency and of a range of challenges is provided by Adrian Weller [41]. He emphasises the points made by others that we need to think carefully about the goal of transparency if we are to avoid unintended harmful consequences. Demands for transparency can be used to game a system and may threaten other values such as privacy, as well as having efficiency costs. Transparency is not necessarily an end in itself, and considering the need for transparency on different occasions is necessary to determine what precisely is needed; for example, this may be to enable audit of a system by an expert or to enable a user of a system to be given the right to question a decision. It is useful to consider the goals of transparency for different parties: for users, for society more broadly, and for deployers. These may be at odds: for example, transparency may lead to trust that keeps a user using a system to the benefit of the deployer.

Case study: Machine learning in image classification for diagnostics One of the most successful and widely adopted uses of machine learning is in image recognition to support diagnosis from medical imaging such as MRI scans. Currently, much research indicates that ML in combination with human experts produces better results than either alone. ML can detect aspects of an image that a human is unable to detect. However, ML may sometimes make errors that no human would ever make. There are also issues of transparency because it may be hard or impossible to know precisely how the ML produced its results.

Exercise 4
In a medical context, how important is it for a healthcare practitioner to know precisely how ML produced its diagnosis of a medical image? What are the reasons for your answer? How important is it to the patients that their healthcare practitioner can provide an explanation of how the machine came to its results, and why? Consider the importance of safety and of trust in a medical context.

Patients are often happy to use drugs that can be demonstrated to have a good standard of safety and efficacy, even if the medical profession does not understand very well how they work. Do we expect higher standards of AI than of other examples of technology? If so, are we right to do so?

You may feel you don't have enough understanding of the specific context to address this question: consider what else you might need to know, and consider how this very issue with gaps in knowledge might impact a patient and their need or desire for transparency.

Key Points There are complex technical issues involved in the question of transparency. A great deal of technical work is underway to attempt to provide as much explanation as possible. It is also recognised that explanation is relative to who requires the explanation. Something easy for an expert in machine learning to comprehend may not function as a usable explanation to another person. We should also see that explanation is a key part of moral and professional accountability and indicates the ethical issue of what we owe each other in a particular context. Transparency concerns not only technical issues in AI but also issues of ownership and commercial confidence.

2.4.3 Justice and Fairness

Justice and fairness are central concepts to ethics with strong political, social, and legal aspects. They are also strongly affirmed, yet with a range of different precise

interpretations. Questions of justice and fairness have received considerable attention in politics, law, and political philosophy, and the debates in these areas are
recurring again in AI [42]. For example, some accounts of fairness stress equality of
opportunity, some stress equality of outcome, and some stress minimising the
disadvantage to the worst off [43]. Strong notions of fairness seem to arise in
small children from very early on in their development. However, apart from their
widespread relevance in society, there are many reasons why AI in particular may
give rise to questions of justice and fairness, and there is considerable attention to
this field [44]. Indeed, some of these relate to questions of transparency and
explanation. To introduce this question, let us look at a well-known example that
concerns the justice system itself, the COMPAS algorithm.

Case study: COMPAS (Correctional Offender Management Profiling for Alternative Sanctions) is a software produced by the company Northpointe and widely used
across the USA to generate decisions in case management in criminal justice. It
generates risk scores for future behaviour such as recidivism. A widely publicised
study by ProPublica in 2016 found that the scores generated were biased against
black individuals, being more likely to falsely score them as likely to reoffend than
whites [45]. Northpointe disputed these findings [46]. Subsequent studies have
examined the accuracy of such predictions compared to judgements by humans
and the possibility of producing results free from bias concerning demographic
factors such as race and gender on accuracy, with some casting doubt on the
ProPublica study [47–49].

Whatever the accuracy of this particular algorithm, the case raises critically
important questions about fairness and bias in the use of such algorithms, especially
in critical issues such as criminal justice and especially in relation to vital issues such
as racial prejudice. The questions raised include the ways in which algorithms may
reproduce or even magnify the prejudices of the past by working on historical data
that reflects prior biases. Discussions have included a detailed examination of the
technical details of the algorithms and data analysis. Note how an understanding of
the ethical questions builds upon an understanding of the past history of race
relations in the USA, especially in relation to criminal justice and corrections.

This also indicates the important point that the manner in which we categorise the
world and how we label categories have meaning and significance with personal and
political implications [50]. Attention has been given to issues of race and gender
[51], and doubtless other potential instances of unfairness and bias merit attention.
Hence, tackling the issue of bias requires careful thought [52, 53]. This will also
include underlying philosophical questions in epistemology and metaphysics regarding how we gain knowledge of the world and how we conceptualise and categorise
the world. On one simple approach to the matter, tackling bias in algorithms may
require ensuring that we have unbiased data and unbiased models and use a 'neutral'
and true picture of the world. However, the way such goals are expressed may not
even be conceptually coherent, and there are great challenges, including recognising
our own shortcomings and prejudices [54]. Addressing bias in a system requires that

we look for it, and to do this, we must use categories; however, by doing so, we may be including a way of seeing the world that contains its own injustices [52].

Note too now this raises questions of epistemology: how algorithms present knowledge claims to us, and in particular, expectations that the future will be like the past. Furthermore, the question of transparency was raised, especially as the algorithm was propriety software owned by a private company.

Exercise 5

Consider: there is a particular tension here between the use of prediction and attitudes towards human beings and towards the justice system. In theory, 'correctional' facilities are meant to both punish and to reform; that is why they are called 'correctional'. We hold out hope for the transformation of character, hoping that an offender's future will not be like their past. However, does something like the COMPAS algorithm treat human beings more like objects in the physical universe whose future can be predicted mathematically from the past?

This question raises a foretaste of some central issues in AI ethics that will be discussed throughout the book: whether our use of AI may subtly skew some of the finer points of our moral thinking.

Human and machine agency Another dimension of justice, fairness, and agency that arises from such a case is the very question of using a machine to make certain important decisions that affect the course of people's lives. This is a question of a different order from the specifics of whether the COMPAS algorithm was biased in its judgements. Some may argue that questions of justice should be determined by other human beings, whether these be 'a jury of my peers', a judge, or a magistrate. The questions of justice and fairness are hence linked to questions of agency and of the replacement of humans by machines.

Question

If there was no difference in the accuracy of the outcome, would it matter to you if you were judged by a machine or by a human? Why or why not?

Key Points Questions of justice and fairness can arise from the technical aspects of AI, from its use of data, from the surrounding ethical, historical, and societal context, as well as from the very question of the use of AI rather than reliance on humans to make certain decisions. Determining the nature of any injustice or bias may be a complex technical issue as well as one involving sensitive ethical and political debates.

2.4.4 Beneficence/Nonmaleficence

Beneficence aims for AI to produce benefit, or good; nonmaleficence for it not to produce harm. These are not the same and come apart significantly in many contexts. Indeed, a stress on beneficence, or on nonmaleficence, is behind some of the differences in accounts of fairness mentioned in the last section. It is very common for codes and guidance to call for AI to provide as much benefit as possible. This is at once an obvious and basic aim, yet incredibly vague. For who is to benefit, and how is benefit to be understood and assessed? Given the scepticism about ethics that we have already noted, one might also suspect that advocating that AI is used to benefit as many as possible is little different from a sales pitch for research and development and adoption of AI. Recall how we have already seen that the interests of those deploying AI for transparency may be at odds with users.

Let us consider one example to illustrate some complexities. Note of course that a different choice of example would doubtless have produced some different issues, especially given how broad the concepts of benefit and harm are.

A case study The EDoN project is a research project for the Early Detection of Neurodegenerative diseases (edon-initiative.org). It aims to tackle diseases such as dementia, which are increasing worldwide as the global population ages, and which present major challenges for individuals, for their families and carers, as well as for society. Currently, there is still much unknown about the various forms of dementia and, indeed, much unknown about the brain and cognition, and unfortunately, there is little to hand in the way of treatment or effective preventive measures. Moves to treat and prevent these neurodegenerative diseases are thus needed. The EDoN project involves experts in digital technology, data science, and neurodegenerative diseases to develop a digital tool for the early detection of dementia-causing diseases, including in those individuals who have no obvious signs of dementia. Some hope to be able to detect the origins of dementia decades before the first signs [55]. AI and digital technologies are an essential part of these efforts.

Dementia is a major issue for individuals living with dementia, their families and care providers, the health and social care systems, and the economy in general. Hence, finding ways to further our understanding of the condition and how to treat and prevent it would promise great benefit.

Exercise 6
Consider the benefits and any possible downsides of the early detection of dementia, for individuals, for their families, and for health providers, and for society overall. Are there any other groups you might also want to consider?

In doing so, note the questions you have to which you don't have the answers, and where you would go to find them.

Consider what it might mean to detect dementia decades before the first signs. Might this mean that we change our ideas of what a disease or health condition is?

Consider what it is to have knowledge of different types. What might it mean for a scientist to have knowledge of how to diagnose dementia before the first signs? What might it mean for a health provider to be able to perform such a diagnosis? And to an individual to be given this diagnosis?

The ethical questions of AI are often a matter of scale and speed. Consider if more knowledge is always an untainted good.

Key Points As before, the particular example we used showed complexities in assessing the benefits and the necessity of addressing assumptions about the benefits of greater knowledge.

We also saw the complexity of assessing benefits from the point of view of different individuals and groups.

2.4.5 Responsibility

Responsibility is a complex topic, with different aspects of responsibility, including causal, moral, and legal. It relates closely to notions of agency and to descriptions of how situations occurred, what should happen in the future, and who should do what. Questions of responsibility arise in relation to AI for many reasons [56–61]. The sheer complexity of the technology, the number of people and organisations involved in its production and implementation, and its integration into systems often leave us with vexed questions about attribution of responsibility and how it may be distributed throughout a system [62]. The problem of transparency creates more problems of responsibility, and questions of distribution of agency between machines and humans create more still. Furthermore, the swift pace of change of technology and its use and integration into society are leading to debate and differences of opinion about the nature and distribution of responsibility.

Case study: Tay the racist chatbot This is a well-known example of AI Gone Bad. Tay was a short-lived bot released onto Twitter by Microsoft on March 23, 2016. Tay was designed to appear to be a teenage girl responding to others in conversation. Some would say Tay—or 'she'—did precisely that, or at any rate, that Tay behaved exactly like some people behave on Twitter, and precisely how some teenagers behave in real life. In response to and in mimicry of what 'she' had learned, Tay was quickly putting out tweets such as 'I hate feminists and they should all die and burn in hell' as well as tweets using racial and antisemitic slurs and praising Hitler. The account was suspended within 16 h [63].

Astute readers may have noticed that tweets suggesting particular groups or individuals should burn in hell and so on and so forth are somewhat common on Twitter. One might have thought someone at Microsoft would have anticipated this debacle [64]. In this example, there are an entire cast of actors who could each be attributed some responsibility. Note that responsibility covers both responsibilities for causing or contributing to a situation and for addressing it.

Those involved in some way include the team at Microsoft who produced Tay; those responsible for deciding to launch Tay; those at Microsoft responsible for the decision to take Tay down; the Twitter users with whom Tay interacted; those responsible for Twitter policy on offensive tweets and offensive accounts; those who viewed or reported Tay's tweets; and legislators responsible for any laws governing language designed to provoke hate or incite violence. Consider if you wish to add any more to the list. Note how almost anybody in the world who has access to the Internet could play some part, no matter how small.

Exercise 7
Consider the role and possible responsibilities for each of these parties (and any others you have thought of).

Note how Tay is often described as if possessing agency. Tay is described as 'she', even though 'she' is simply a piece of software. Consider if this affects how we might think and feel about responsibility.

Key Points This case is not simply an example of individual failure of one piece of software. It demonstrates how the technologies we use to communicate shape interactions and language. The phenomenon of hateful and abusive language online and debates about how to deal with this are part of much larger social, cultural, and political conversations around technologies and their wider impact.

What might be an interesting programming task in natural language processing (NLP) presenting challenges in both software and in understanding the formal aspects of language to one person is replete with meaning and references to some of the most appalling episodes of human history and some of the most damaging behaviours towards individuals and groups of people.

Note also the intersection of technical, social, governance, and regulatory factors in assigning responsibility.

2.4.6   Privacy

Questions of privacy arise in relation to AI for many reasons related to software, hardware, and attitudes towards technology. The increase in processing capacity that has enabled the analysis of vast amounts of personal data, together with the capacity to make predictions, is one source of concern, especially given the necessary use by much AI of vast amounts of data. The capacity of technology to monitor the environment and to collect personal data has increased, for example, through wearables, computer vision, and the use of everyday technology such as smartphones; the flip side of privacy is surveillance by others. Large changes in our use of technology are also impacting attitudes towards privacy, which are often very complex [65–69].

Case study: Surveillance of people living with dementia Dementia is a variable and progressive set of conditions, so symptoms exhibited by individuals vary, but wandering and disorientation in time and space are common. There are often realistic fears that a person living with dementia may wander away from the safety of home, care institution, or hospital and into danger. Locking doors to prevent this is common, but surveillance by cameras and motion detection devices with facial recognition software may be used in preference. This may enable someone to walk more freely, for example, into a garden or outdoor area. Tracking devices may also be used to enable swift location of the person if they wander further

[70]. Surveillance via the Internet of things is also being suggested for people living with dementia to monitor daily activities [71]. Other reasons for surveillance include concern about falls or other medical events and accidents caused by forgetfulness.

Exercise 8
How would you assess the privacy concerns about such surveillance for people living with dementia? What is the relevance of their medical condition to the use of such surveillance? Is it relevant to consider privacy issues, or are these overridden by more important concerns? In considering these questions, bear in mind that dementia is a very variable condition and a progressive disease. Are there any concerns about privacy from surveillance by technologies any different from constant monitoring by a human companion?

Consider the issue of privacy from the point of view of those whose personal space is being surveilled and from the point of view of those gaining knowledge about the minutiae of someone's life. How do the issues of consent and awareness of such surveillance shape your response?

Consider the context of the general increase in surveillance in everyday life, for example, from CCTV, location data through smartphone use, and the routine collection of personal data online and elsewhere. Does this change your attitude at all?

Key Points Note that epistemology is again an issue. The sheer increase in information and data of different sorts creates ethical issues but also potentially shifts our attitudes towards the very issue that is in question. Relationships between people are directly at issue: loss of privacy for one party is gain of information for another. This is complicated by the various relationships we have with different people and the privacy norms of time, place, social status, and social context. The increases in technological capacity for collecting and interpreting information may represent a potential qualitative shift in how we understand privacy. The embedding of such technologies into everyday life and infrastructure may both increase our awareness of invasions of privacy, while we also become accustomed to it.

2.4.7 Trust

Trust concerns the nature and quality of a relationship between two and more people or groups [72]. Trust may refer to a feeling state and/or to a level of epistemic confidence in the probity and reliability of a group or individual and/or the reliability and safety of technology. Trust issues may arise in AI because of its complexity and the level of expertise and knowledge needed fully to understand both discrete instances of the technology and the wider systems of technology and production in which it is embedded [73, 74]. The newness of the technology, speed of development, behaviour of corporations, financial interests, well-publicised warnings and portents of doom, failed promises, and everyday glitches in the use of software and devices may all undermine trust. The explicit attempt by corporations and governments to ascertain trust in AI may also further cause suspicion—why are they so keen for us to trust it? [75, 76].

Furthermore, some of the ways in which AI operates create specific issues with trust. The replacement of human decision-making and thought by machines in itself raises complex issues of trust, with one major question being, in a nutshell, whether exchanging a trusted human being with a machine is a fair like-for-like swap. The possibility of action-at-a-distance afforded by much AI technology, the embedded and sometimes hidden nature of the technologies, the lack of transparency, the frequently inescapable necessity to use technologies which include AI, and the possibilities of manipulation by such technology are all also liable to impact trust, although precisely how, it is hard to say, since habituation to technology may lead both to assumed trust and growing suspicions.

Case study: Care robots for elderly individuals Considerable attention is being given to the development of care robots for the growing population of elderly people. These robots could provide stimulation and companionship and perform certain tasks, such as reminders that medication needs to be taken and provision of the correct medications at the correct time. Robots may have friendly human-like features and voices designed to inspire trust [77].

Exercise 9
Outline the different trust issues that arise with the use of such robots. Consider the relationships and lines of trust involved—who has to trust whom, and why? How might trust be attained, and what might threaten it?

Could trust be unearned? Might the provision of human-like features in a robot create misplaced trust?

Consider the specific issue of the provision of medication. What are the trust issues present here? Suppose a robot could address concerns that a person had around their medication by answering questions concerning its purpose and side effects. Would this be a good way of attaining trust? Are there any reasons why a robot might be more trustworthy than hiring human caregivers? Is lack of trust a good default position?

Key Points Trust is one of the many areas where comparison between humans and AI is very pertinent. It is entirely possible with both humans and AI that trust is misplaced. It is a complex phenomenon that cannot be reduced to a simple formula. Trust in technology may pertain to factors such as its functionality, reliability, and safety but also to its appearance, marketing, and imagined qualities.

In many ways, trust functions as an umbrella term in ethics signalling a large set of questions, i.e. technical, societal, and individual.

2.4.8   Sustainability

Why is sustainability a particular issue in AI? Isn't it just something we are always concerned with? It will be obvious that questions of sustainability in AI arise from the production of hardware, but they also arise from the operation of software [60].

Case study: The computational power of AI and energy use   Data centres are among the world's largest consumers of electricity. The carbon footprint of the computational infrastructure of the world is set to greatly exceed that of the aviation industry [78]. Much of this computational power is generated from technology which has been embedded into our lives. The particular demands of processing power of AI contribute to this and are receiving attention. Early research indicates that the carbon footprint of natural language processing (NLP) models is extremely high [79]. This indicates that increases in speed, accuracy, and other improvements to AI may come at a high environmental cost. The case of Timnit Gebru's departure from Google is mentioned in Chap. 1. The paper she had been working on also discussed the energy costs of language processing models [80].

Question
You have probably routinely been told that it is better to read an email or document than to print it out. However, do you know precisely how such calculations are made?

The task of calculating the benefits to be gained from the increased processing power and capabilities of a particular NLP model and the energy use it entails will be complex and require specialised knowledge. (Trust in claims of environmental standards is thus an issue.)

A feature of technology that makes this a particular issue is its distributed nature, meaning that much of the use of resources is hidden from view. Sustainability is also an issue in terms of the human beings contributing to—or exploited by—the production of AI. This includes not just those workers extracting the raw materials needed and the workers making and assembling the products but also the remote workers involved in the creation of 'artificial' intelligence such as content moderators and those labelling data.

Ethical issues arise in relation to sustainability in questions such as the distribution of resources and the burden of achieving sustainability between individuals, groups, and across geographical regions. It also arises at a fundamental level concerning the quality of life for humans and what is needed to achieve a certain quality of life. This includes the major ethical question of the population size [78].

Tracing the convoluted supply chains, the intricacies of the production process, and the materials and human beings involved vividly demonstrates how we must bear in mind the complexity and global reach of AI when we consider all ethical issues. To do justice to these questions of sustainability, however, requires considerable specialisation and empirical knowledge, which is beyond the scope of this book.

Key Points Many sustainability issues in AI have received scant attention because of the nature of much AI, that its precise operations are hidden from the end user. A lesson to learn is that this means that other ethical issues may also be hidden from us. Questions of transparency in the operation of technology are revealed to extend far beyond the more technical questions of the transparency of machine learning algorithms but to the transparency of the wider social, economic, and political systems into which AI is embedded.

Relevance to questions of justice, fairness, and the nature and distribution of benefits and burdens should be apparent, showing yet more interrelations between different ethical questions.

The question of time, of progress, and of infrastructure also arises, since the development of technology has led to entrenched dependence on that very technology, so that it is hard to extricate ourselves and hard to address.

2.4.9　Dignity

Dignity is frequently mentioned in ethics guidance concerning AI and is an interesting, complex example of an ethical concept that can be highly charged yet hard to articulate. It's a term often applied to contexts such as the practice of medicine, the treatment of prisoners, and the conditions of the most vulnerable in society [81]. It's also an especially complex question to consider in relation to AI, since dignity seems to have a role precisely in stressing something rather ineffable about the valuable qualities of a human being. Indeed, although it may be a background issue, there are noticeably fewer papers in AI ethics directly discussing dignity than other concepts, such as transparency and privacy. Let us consider one complex and nuanced case where technology may be presented as enabling dignity but where questions may nonetheless arise.

Case study: Remote assistance for elderly individuals The technology in question involves a mix of computing and human intervention, an app designed to watch over isolated individuals such as the elderly or those living with dementia by care. coach [82]. A human-powered avatar of a cuddly looking dog on a tablet 'wakes up' at regular intervals and interacts with the person, reminds them of appointments, interacts by chatting and reading poetry, and issues alerts for any episodes such as falls. The article referenced describes the avatar responding to an elderly man that he loves him. The app can enable an elderly person to remain at home without going into a care facility for longer, hence retaining independence. The app has been sold and used in the USA. The avatar is operated remotely, generally by someone hundreds or thousands of miles away, for example, in Latin America or the Philippines.

Exercise 10
Make the strongest case you can for the claim that such an app helps to enhance the
dignity of socially isolated individuals who need some assistance, and then consider
arguments against. How do you incorporate the significance of cultural, social, and
economic factors? Consider the kinds of situations that might lead to the isolation of
the individuals who make use of such an app. Think about the role of the employees
who work through the avatars.

Does it make a difference if the person using the app is aware that the dog is not
actually talking to them but is an avatar operated by a person in another country? Are
there any other factors that this example brought to mind as relevant to assessing
dignity? You may wish to read more about this app before considering your
response, but this is not necessary.

This case study has many similarities to the examples discussed under privacy.
Does this particular example raise any new issues or new angles on the question of
privacy?

Key Points Dignity is such a complex issue that it is always going to be essential to
consider the impact on dignity of technology from a range of angles, including the
impact on dignity of failure to use technology and any alternatives, including the
historical reasons for the situation at hand.

It is a concept that forces us to look not simply at the details of technology but at
the entire issue of the use of technology in the place of human relationships.

2.4.10   Solidarity

The values of autonomy and freedom can be applied to groups and, of course, to the
population as a whole but are typically used to describe and defend the interests of
individuals. Likewise, for values such as privacy. The value of solidarity, in contrast,
speaks to responsibility and concern for others, especially those less advantaged than
ourselves [83]. There are overlaps with the value of beneficence and conceptions of
justice.

Case study: Technology to equalise access to dementia diagnosis An app
designed by a group of medical students at the University College London aims to
equalise access to dementia diagnosis, particularly in certain demographic groups.
Many people remain undiagnosed, and rates of diagnosis are known to differ
between different ethnic groups. Mindstep4dementia is an app currently under
development that includes brain-training exercises and collects data that can indicate
early signs of the condition [84]. At the time of writing, there are some preliminary
validation results [85]. Since it is app-based and permits remote data gathering, it can
be used directly in the community without needing access to the clinic, and the
potential exists for widening access. Members of ethnic minority groups have been
encouraged to use the app [86]. A question may arise as to any obligations to

participate in medical research that has wider benefits for society, even if it may not benefit oneself [87].

Exercise 11
Consider the ethical issues involved in the development of this app from the point of view of solidarity. What aspects of the technology help to facilitate solidarity? Are there any issues relating to solidarity that have been overlooked? Consider the background reasons for the problems that the technology is hoping to address.

This example also demonstrates another issue: technology in development. Are those using the app currently clear beneficiaries, or are they contributing to its development for the sake of others who will benefit in the future while gaining no direct personal benefit? How does this relate to the value of solidarity?

Consider relevant points from previous cases in developing your responses.

Key Points As ever, the value of solidarity intersects with many of the other values at issue in AI ethics. Certain features of technology can enable wider distribution and access. However, these can be a two-edged sword. Assessment of need also should consider the potential downside of widened use, the reasons for the problem under issue, and the suitability of technology to address issues. Solidarity is more than beneficence or welfare but also implies a certain reciprocity. The relationships and involvement of the communities in question in development and application are important.

2.5   A Brief History of AI Ethics

Summary
Historical precedent can provide useful insights when addressing current ethical questions. A selective overview of historical concerns about relevant technologies is given, looking at the history of robotics and myths about robots, including the Uncanny Valley; concerns with writing as a technology; machinery, including the Luddites; data; and computing.

2.5.1   Why Consider History?

A full history of ethical concerns about AI would be worthy of study in its own right, but why mention history in a book on contemporary and future ethical issues? Looking to history can enrich ethical thinking in a number of ways. In approaching AI ethics, we need to consider not just the bare technology and its technical details but also how it is seen and understood and how reactions to technology fit into a wider social and cultural context. Examples of imagined technologies from many centuries ago may be an especially rich source for considering how fears and hopes may be projected onto current technology and in cases where the technology had not yet actually been developed. There are myths about robots from around the world, from times long before robots were anywhere close to being possible.

Any history will be written from a particular perspective and will show certain values and assumptions, and we are likely to project our own assumptions onto the past. To illustrate, as someone born and brought up in Britain, I am probably more likely to bring to mind key British figures from the history of science and technology, such as Newton, Darwin, and Turing. This dawned on me graphically a few years back in a museum in Paris, where an entire room was devoted to a mural depicting prominent scientists in history, most of whom were French. Of course! However, utility can still be found in the imaginative contemplation of human response in different times and places. This section gives a flavour of some relevant history, not to provide a comprehensive overview, but to indicate some ways its consideration could be useful for enriching a dialogue about ethics.

Past, present, and future A contemplation of the past may be especially useful for those obsessed with the present and the future. History presses us to think of how cultures, practices, and ideas change over time, so it is a counterweight to the danger of imagining that we now, finally, have the answers. This can be a danger if we allow ourselves to be entranced by ideas of technological and societal progress. Such a viewpoint does seem to be common, if only implicitly. It is common, especially perhaps post the Enlightenment, to think we have now thrown off superstition, we have abandoned metaphysical and religious myth about human beings and our place in the world, and, armed only with science and technology, we can march unfettered into the future. It is easy to imagine that people in the past were somehow less clever than us, even if this belief seems slightly silly as soon as it's pointed out. The trope of progress is particularly strong in many of the claims about AI, especially when combined with claims of great power, which again are often made. It is common to read claims that issues that have long perplexed humanity, numerous practical problems, and many difficult areas of research are now going to be solved at a stroke with the use of this powerful new tool of AI.

There is nothing new under the sun, or so said King Solomon. Much of the story of the past gets lost, especially in a climate where some stress the novelty of AI. There are even technological reasons for this: books that are available only in hard copy may simply be ignored in favour of online texts. It is valuable to recall and realise that AI ethics is part of a continuing narrative of concerns.

A guide to the present Past examples of concerns about technology can alert us to differences of approach but often too of commonalities in human response and experience. In addition to myth and legend and responses to primitive or prototype technologies, there are many real cases to study concerning the implementation of technology and often of calamities from which lessons might be learned. We may recognise certain concerns with AI as having forerunners, which can help to shape our understanding of what these concerns are and how they originate. How we think about ethical issues will depend in part upon the examples and case studies that come to mind and the nuances of how an issue is fleshed out. We may find that we are overlooking aspects by focusing solely on the present topics of discussion.

Power A history of ethics will also show us something of responses to concerns about technology, who raises these, how concerns are taken note of, by whom, and what the outcomes are. This sets the scene into which contemporary concerns about AI ethics have arisen but should also alert us to questions of social and political power and especially to how technologies enable such power to be wielded. Studying and thinking about such lessons from history can make us reflect on how we formulate and understand ethical questions ourselves, how we look around for solutions, and what power dynamics and what forces and accidents of history are present.

Key events and lasting responses The history of concerns about technology and ethics in other areas is frequently shaped by key events and often by particular disasters and the responses to them, which might include changes in law, regulation, and societal attitude with lasting effects. It may be that the circumstances of particular disasters formed precedents in ways that may be helpful to a greater or lesser extent in understanding and tackling later issues. For example, in medical ethics, the Nuremburg doctors' trial followed the abuses by Nazi doctors in the Second World War [88]. This has been of critical importance in how medical ethics developed worldwide up until the present day, although much has developed since and it is by no means the only factor. Forcing human beings into extreme, cruel medical experiments, which resulted in unimaginable suffering and death, has led to an insistence on informed consent and assertion of the key value of individual patient autonomy. Autonomy is likewise, as we have seen, an important value in AI ethics. How we think about autonomy in AI may well be impacted in some ways by how we think of it in medicine.

However, discerning what can be learned from different cases is a complex matter. There will be variations in how key events shape developments in different places, attributable to a complex of factors including cultural and political issues. For example, biomedical ethics in Germany has developed in somewhat different ways from other surrounding nations, with particularly stringent rules against human experimentation, including embryo research, in the wake of the extreme excesses of the Nazis [89].

The history of technological calamities indicates that certain characteristics may recur. For instance, if we examine major engineering disasters, a common thread is breakdowns in communication. This was one of the factors leading to the Space Shuttle Challenger disaster in 1986, where failures to get the right information to the right people on time led to catastrophic failure [90]. The Space Shuttle Columbia disaster in 2003 sadly suggests that certain lessons were not learned [91]. If we can learn anything from history, it is that we fail to learn from history.

Moral panics and important lessons Some of the fears around new technological possibilities can come to seem comical. There were fears that telephones could be used to communicate with the dead, for example. I myself, like millions of other children, was given dire warnings that watching too much television would give me square eyes. (Why square, given that TV sets were roughly rectangular, was never explained.)

In AI ethics, certain cases and issues have received prominent attention. Note that these may then help to shape the direction of regulation and the focus of attention of concern, debate, and research but that what cases become prominent and receive the most attention and response will be driven by local concerns, power, the media, contemporary preoccupations, and sometimes happenstance, such as what else was in the news at the time. Note too that it is less often the case that good practice receives any attention. This may mean that if ethics develops in response to prominent disasters, this may skew our reactions in suboptimal ways.

The COVID-19 Pandemic and Its Potential Impact on the History of Medical Ethics and AI Ethics

Any history of the COVID-19 pandemic will surely include the input of technologies, not just medical technologies such as drugs and vaccines, but the technologies of AI. As soon as the pandemic began, work was underway examining the impact of technologies [5]. Any histories written are likely to diverge from each other, especially as one issue on which many have expressed concern is how divided society has become.

There is an intertwining of issues here, with questions of medical ethics, public health ethics (which differs in certain key respects from clinical medical ethics applied to individual patients), media ethics, and ethical issues in technologies such as tracking and vaccine passports, all coalesce. The issue of public health was intertwined with questions of information trustworthiness and veracity, and these with questions about the use of artificial technologies such as track-and-trace apps for contact tracing.

Many have also observed that without the technologies allowing remote working for many office workers, and online ordering, the lockdowns could not have occurred in the ways that they did.

Exercise 12

From your own background knowledge, consider some of the different viewpoints and values that came into play during the pandemic and the contribution and role of technology in general and of AI in particular in the response to the pandemic and debates concerning its handling.

2.5.2   Playing with Fire: Historical Concerns About Technologies

Concerns about the power of technologies are probably as old as those about technology itself. It's hard not to imagine that early humans were well aware of the potential of fire to ward away wild beasts, for warmth, and for cooking, on the one hand and, on the other hand, its potential for hazard to life and limb and for behaving like, well, wildfire. The draw of the flame captures us but eternally reminds us of its power.

Robots No work on AI ethics would be complete without mentioning the many myths and stories about robots from around the world that have recurred from ancient history to the present [92, 93]. It perhaps tells us something about the resonance for human beings of the idea that brute matter might become somehow like us. Historians have described an incredible number of such accounts, including both myth and actual technologies. In some myths, animation arises by some magical or godly power, such as breathing life into the earth, but many accounts are of the contrivance of automata by purely technological means, made out of a variety of substances and sometimes include a full range of internal parts. Automata were generally designed or imagined either for labour, including military or security purposes, for sex, or for entertainment. Somewhat similar to today's robots, it seems.

Many such accounts are to be found in ancient Greece and Rome but also elsewhere. For example, a Chinese story set the Ming dynasty in the tenth century BCE describes a man-made man that is introduced to King Mu, who is delighted until the artificial man takes somewhat of an interest in the king's concubines. It is then revealed to be an entirely constructed artifice [93]. Unnerving stories of being fooled by the lifelike nature of such automata are common and persist today in one of the major ethical questions of whether humans may be fooled by humanoid robots and whether a humanoid robot could ever be a legitimate substitute for a human relationship, as well as in the concept of the 'Uncanny Valley' proposed by the Japanese roboticist Mori to describe the feeling of encountering a robot or automata that is close enough to being realistic, yet just slightly unconvincing enough, to produce that creepy feeling of weirdness. Many ancient and early medieval Hindu and Buddhist stories likewise describe the mixture of fear and wonder produced by human-like animations and include stories very similar to the account of the artificial man introduced to King Mu.

The Uncanny Valley
In 1970, Masahiro Mori, a Japanese robotics professor at the Tokyo Institute of Technology, published an essay titled 'The Uncanny Valley' in a Japanese

(continued)

journal *Energy*, where it lay relatively unnoticed until more recently when it started to attract considerable attention [94].

Mori hypothesised that in creating human-like robots, humans would respond with empathy, interest, and concern, as the robot acquired recognisably human features, until the robot became sufficiently lifelike, to inhabit an 'uncanny valley' of revulsion. A person would be able to tell immediately that the robot was not in fact human, but had sufficient similarities to create feelings of eeriness.

Interest in Mori's idea has been provoked in those exploring human-computer and human-robot interaction, and in those exploring the possible biological and psychological roots of such a phenomenon.

There seems to be no end of ancient tales of robots and sex. A tale retold in different traditions from around the second century BCE onwards describes the attempt to lure a foreign guest with a girl left in his room to arouse his passions. The 'girl' turns out to be mechanical, falling to pieces in his arms. Falling for an illusion and giving into desires again are enduring themes in discussions of today's technologies.

Robot guards or warriors are also a common theme. A Buddhist legend concerns automaton warriors built to defend the remains of the Buddha and armed with whirling blades to slice any intruders into pieces. (Such a picture may contrast somewhat starkly with the peaceful image Buddhism generally enjoys.) Interestingly, the story tells that the robot makers lived in the land of the East, or the area of Greco-Roman-Byzantine culture. The Greek legend of Talos of Crete is of a bronze, animated guardian made by Hephaestus, the god of technology, metallurgy, and invention. Talos followed precise instructions in warding off trespassers, such as picking up rocks and hurling them at people, but could also be swayed by suggestion.

The question of Talos' hybrid nature between inanimate and living gave rise to questions about human control over such creatures. The Golem of Jewish folklore is a creature animated from clay and mud. There are many different accounts of how precisely Golem came about and various different stories about him. Many stories concern the problem of how to control Golem; in some, he desecrates the Sabbath; in others, he is rejected in love and goes on a murderous rampage. It would appear that such animated creatures can form a screen onto which humans project many of their largest fears, although what precise conclusions are drawn can also vary considerably [95].

It is notable in the Judeo-Christian tradition that the first human, Adam, was likewise created by God breathing life into the dust of the ground to create a living soul. It is also notable that God had a control problem with his creation: Adam and Eve quickly disobeyed his commands. Even if these accounts are 'just stories', it is remarkable how our stories about ourselves reflect our stories about our creations, in which we take the place, in turn, as creature and created. We will consider the creation of Adam again in Chap. 3 in discussing a well-known meme.

Writing AI relies on computer code, which is a form of language and a manner of representation. Many of the most complex and vexed ethical questions facing us now concern communication technologies. Therefore, we should note the many concerns regarding previous advances in communication technology. Changes in the mode of communication can produce profound changes in society and elicit consequently profound hopes and fears.

For example, the development of the printing press in Europe had a highly significant impact on culture and politics, for example, playing a significant role in the Reformation as access to printed copies of the Bible greatly increased [96]. Meanwhile, printed books had already developed in China in the Han dynasty approximately 2000 years ago, leaving a long gap before printing made its mark on Europe.

However, even more fundamentally, writing itself, rather than particular means of writing, came under severe attack in Plato's dialogue *The Phaedrus*, 274c–277a (which, ironically, we know about because it was written down) [97]. Socrates' preference for spoken dialogue over writing has already been mentioned in Chap. 1, and here Socrates articulates his views by referring to the myth that writing was an invention of an Egyptian god, Theuth, who considered that writing would make people wiser and improve their memories. Thamus, a god who was King of the whole of Egypt, rebuked him however, accusing him of being unable to judge his own creation fairly, infected as he was by fatherly bias. 'This discovery of yours will create forgetfulness in the learner's souls, because they will not use their memories; they will trust to the external written characters and not remember of themselves. The specific which you have discovered is not an aid to memory, but to reminiscence, and you give your disciplines not truth, but only the semblance of truth; they will be hearers of many things and will have learned nothing; they will appear to be omniscient and will generally know nothing; they will be tiresome company, having the show of wisdom without the reality' [97].

It may be startling to consider that a figure known as the founding father of Western philosophy has such views about the dangers of the written word, but we can think of this more positively as arguing in favour of the benefits of dialogue, which I have wished to stress particularly in ethics, which has to be something understood and developed. Socrates argues that truth is to be found in dialogue, complaining that the written word cannot answer questions put to it; engaging in addressing questions, responding to others, and accountability are hallmarks of good practice in ethics.

Exercise 13

Consider Socrates' views on written language and the spoken word.

Do you find any truth in them?

How might they apply to forms of speech and writing in the Internet age?

Machinery Computing involves both software and hardware, so as well as considering the history of concerns about language and writing, historical concerns about machinery are also of interest. Just as AI has been called the Third Industrial Revolution, there is one group who features large in the history of the First Industrial Revolution, a group whose name is often called upon today: the Luddites.

The Luddites

In debates about technology, it has become a commonplace to call an opponent a 'Luddite'. This accusation implies a strong dismissal of the advances of technology: more than the mere failure to buy the latest iPhone, to accuse someone of being a Luddite is to imply that they shun modern technology (almost) entirely. As our daily lives become more and more dependent upon technology, the charge of being a Luddite looks more and more ridiculous.

However, if we investigate who the Luddites were, a more interesting angle emerges [98]. The Luddites operated in England during the First Industrial Revolution and were active from around the end of the eighteenth century into the first years of the nineteenth. Named for Ned Ludd, a possibly mythical figure who in 1779 allegedly broke two knitting frames in a fit of passion, the Luddites were known for objections to the mechanisation of skilled manual work, such as the introduction of the power loom and knitting machines, and for destroying the machinery involved in this.

As such, they are portrayed as destructive, and as making futile gestures against progress. Arguments against them at the time, from those such as the economist David Ricardo, rested on the twin claims that progress through technology was both inevitable and beneficial, and that advances in economic prosperity were best attained by technological competitiveness.

However, revisionist historians paint a more subtle picture of Luddite's complaints about the introduction of new technology. Indeed, the very notion of technological progress by which they are now condemned only developed after they were active. Their main concerns were with the social implications of the new technologies, including increased power of management and economic implications for workers. They expressed scepticism that the main reasons for the machines' introduction were economic, given the large costs of the machinery. In 1834 the Bolton weavers declared that power looms were being introduced in order to ensure that management had greater control over production, over the workers, and could prevent embezzlement.

To use the term 'Luddite' as a slur against critics of new technologies may perhaps act to obscure valid concerns and to shut down debate.

Exercise 14

Look for occasions when the term 'Luddite' is used as a slur. This may be in traditional media, in online forums, or in 'real life'. Consider the precise context in which it is used and what effect it has. Does it seem to have an impact on the subsequent directions of argument? If so, does it seem to help or hinder debate and understanding? Have you ever called someone a Luddite or been accused of being one? Consider the precise context and how appropriate the label was.

What kinds of objections to the introduction of new technology might have some validity, and which might be more spurious? Think about any underlying assumptions about the nature and value of progress.

Data and statistics Since much of the power of AI resides in its need for and capacities to analyse data, it is also relevant to note that concerns about the use of data and statistics, especially in relation to human beings, also have a history. Significant progress was made in the understanding of statistics in the nineteenth century, which enabled governments to collect and analyse considerable bodies of data. This was drawn on in tackling social issues and in providing an empirical basis for policy and action. However, the phrase 'Lies, damned lies, and statistics', variously attributed to British Prime Minister Benjamin Disraeli by Mark Twain and by others to Twain himself, captures warnings not only about statistics per se but can also be seen as a forerunner to concerns about the use of data in algorithms and in machine learning. Perhaps Disraeli was referring to the 'Blue Books' of statistics and data so often referred to in Parliament for determining action and crafting laws.

Beauty by Numbers

The Victorian polymath Francis Galton was a pioneer in measurement and in statistics, and his somewhat comical endeavours to create a 'beauty map' of the British Isles illustrate some of the questionable practices of trying to capture something rather intangible in numerical form. Quite simply, it was based upon nothing more than his own personal preferences, and involved secretly recording impressions of women passing in the street in a selection of geographical regions of Britain by pressing a clicker hidden in his pocket. London won. Note that 'beauty' applied, for Galton, only to females [99, 100].

Exercise 15 Could something like beauty ever be captured by data and statistics in such a way? Consider what might be the best way of doing this, if at all possible.

Consider in general terms the attempt to measure what is important in human life via data—a very amorphous question but vitally important in considering many forms of AI to which we return later.

The terms 'objective' and 'subjective' have various applications and are often overused. Nonetheless, it can be useful to ask yourself if there is any 'objective' way of measuring beauty.

It is also important to think of the purposes of data collection. Why might someone want to make a 'beauty map' of the British Isles? Data frequently enables power and control. Who is measuring whom, and to what purposes?

What other variables might correlate with 'beauty'?

What ethical issues might Galton's study raise, if any?

Charles Dickens' novels were frequently concerned with the position of the poor. His novel *Hard Times*, first published in 1854, is frequently drawn upon for his views on how the working classes fared in industrial Britain [101]. Among his complaints is the uniformity with which individual human beings are viewed within an industrial system that treats everyone alike. These concerns were personified in the character of the superintendent of a school, Mr. Thomas Gradgrind, whose philosophy of education is based upon the importance of facts above all else. He is introduced as 'Thomas Gradgrind, sir—peremptorily Thomas Gradgrind. With a rule and a pair of scales, and the multiplication tables always in his pocket, sir, ready to weigh and measure any parcel of human nature, and tell you exactly what it comes to. It is a mere question of figures, a case of simple arithmetic' [101, Ch., p. 48]. Dickens considers that the human person, and all that is valuable in life, cannot be captured in such mathematical terms. Note in passing that science fiction is often usefully brought to bear in reflecting on AI ethics, but many general works of literature can also be valuable.

Measurement, data, human happiness, and an important philosophical debate Concerns similar to those of Dickens can also be seen echoed in an important debate between two prominent utilitarian philosophers of the time, Jeremy Bentham and John Stuart Mill, whom we will meet again later. We will explore this debate now to introduce in a concrete form some aspects of ethical theory that are of considerable relevance to the ethics of AI.

A philosophical detour With its philosophical roots in the eighteenth century, utilitarian philosophers were at the centre of many social reforms in the nineteenth century, and utilitarianism's influence continues up to the present day as a major player in questions of practical ethics in many fields as we shall see. Utilitarianism has many variations, but in its classical forms, it is a system of ethics focused upon bringing about the best possible consequences. To do so, it must therefore use some system of calculating and measuring alternative courses of action to determine what the best course of action is, conceived, in the classical form of utilitarianism, as maximising happiness and minimising unhappiness (or pleasure and pain). Many questions thus arise about how to measure happiness and what, indeed, happiness is, for unless something is understood with a reasonable degree of precision, it will be hard or impossible to measure and thus impossible to include in calculations. To conduct comparisons, it will also be vital to find a measure that applies across different domains.

Jeremy Bentham produced a 'felicific calculus' by which to measure happiness, famously concluding that 'The utility of all these arts and sciences,—I speak both of those of amusement and curiosity,—the value which they possess, is exactly in proportion to the pleasure they yield. Every other species of preeminence which may be attempted to be established among them is altogether fanciful. Prejudice apart, the game of push-pin is of equal value with the arts and sciences of music and poetry' [102, 103]. Push-pin was a simple game where two or more players had to roll dress-making pins across a table, attempting to 'take' the pins of other players by rolling over their pins. Bentham himself was very fond of various games and loved music but was also known to dislike poetry.

Bentham's Felicific Calculus

To a person considered by himself, the value of a pleasure or pain considered by itself, with be greater or less, according to the following four circumstances: 1 Its *intensity*.
2 Its *duration*.
3 Its *certainty*.
4 Its *propinquity*.
But when the value of any pleasure or pain is considered for the purpose of estimating the tendency of any act by which it is produced, there are two other circumstances to be taken into account; these are,
5 Its *fecundity* ...
6 Its *purity*.
[When a community is considered, it is also necessary to take account of]
7 Its *extent*; that is, the number of persons to whom it extends. [16, 104]

Notes: fecundity refers to the tendency of an action to produce further pleasure or pain. Purity refers to whether an action is mixed with pain or pleasure. Propinquity is no longer a common word—it simply means how close at hand a potential source of pleasure is.

His godson John Stuart Mill was greatly inspired by Bentham but argued strongly against the view that all sources of happiness were equivalent to each other, insisting that there were both 'higher' and 'lower' pleasures. Mill in fact gave two attempts at articulating the difference between higher and lower pleasures, attempts which are not easy to reconcile to each other. First, in somewhat mathematical terms, Mill produced a (somewhat unsatisfactory) definition: a higher pleasure is one preferred over any amount of another pleasure, even if it is accompanied by a great amount of discontent, by those who are acquainted with both kinds of pleasure and are thus competent to make such a judgement. Second, Mill then goes on to discuss the 'unquestionable fact' that human beings have a marked preference for 'the manner of existence which employs their higher faculties'. In his discussion of why this might be, concluding that it is most appropriately explained by 'a love of dignity, which all human beings possess in one form or another, and in some, although by no means exact, proportion to their higher faculties' [105, Ch. 2.5, 2.6].

Exercise 16

Mill famously wrote: 'Few human creatures would consent to be changed into any of the lower animals, for a promise of the fullest allowance of a beast's pleasures; no intelligent human being would consent to be a fool, no instructed person would be an ignoramus, no person of feeling and conscience would be selfish and base, even though they should be persuaded that the fool, the dunce, or the rascal is better satisfied with his lot than they are with theirs. They would not resign what they possess more than he, for the most complete satisfaction of the desires that they have in common with him' [105, Ch 2.6].

First, note that elements in this series of comparisons are each different. They might each then bring in different ethical issues. Consider if you agree or disagree with this statement in any respects. Hint: in philosophy, as in any area, it is very possible to find aspects of a philosopher's work valuable, even if overall one disagrees. Consider too how we might be able to test the truth of such a claim.

Second, think as widely as possible what relevance such thoughts may have to AI and to how automation is impacting our lives, including our personal day-to-day lives and our working lives. Think about this in terms of the goals of AI and of its practical impact, as well as the general question of measuring outcomes in ethics and in human well-being.

Exercise 17
Suppose you were attempting to programme AI to perform morally and to increase human happiness or well-being. You also wish to have a measure for human happiness. How useful would you find Jeremy Bentham's felicific calculus, and how might you improve upon it?

More on data: a twentieth-century story Much has been written about the use and misuse of data concerning human subjects. The collection of such data by bodies such as governments has enabled valuable medical research, for example, research tracking the intergenerational effects of nutrition on development and health over a lifetime using data from the Dutch famine [106]. It has also enabled the surveillance and classification of populations for far more sinister purposes by authoritarian and murderous states [107]. Use and misuse of data is nothing new: the possibilities presented by increases in computing power only amplify this. There are strong links between the development of computer power and the hunger for data for particular purposes.

Jill Lepore traces a fascinating history of the development of computers and the rise of data science in the mid-twentieth century [108]. The company in question was the now scarcely remembered Simulmatics Corporation, founded in 1959. This presents a history of computing far removed from a vision of abstract boffins grappling with the foundations of thought for the sake of pure inquiry. Rather, it paints a history replete with the quest for power, for the ability to predict and manipulate the general public, viewed as members of demographic groups, for the purposes of commercial and political power. Politicians wishing to win elections sought help from social scientists, not so much to understand as to predict behaviour and to target political messaging. National defence was a justification for work on understanding social networks through analysing data. The Kennedy election in 1960 used the assistance of computing power to help determine the precise political messaging to produce. Critics argue that Lepore overstates the importance and role of Simulmatics in the use of data for political messaging and propaganda [109], but nonetheless, such tales illustrate the messy history and embeddedness of computing, social science, behaviour manipulation, and power.

Computers in the twentieth century: warnings about their dangers Alan Turing should need no introduction if you are reading this book. He famously gave warnings about the possibilities of computing. In BBC lecture broadcast in 1951, he claimed that if machines were given the capacity to think, they would soon be able to outstrip the thinking capacities of humans, in part because they would be able to improve their own thinking skills by communicating with each other. So that sooner or later, the machines would, with this superior ability, take control of our lives [110]. This is thus the age-old control problem: the fear that our creations would take over. We can thus ask this question of Turing's statement: given his far-reaching vision and his role in the development of the computer, was his warning based on insights into the technological capabilities of computers? Or was he rather merely expressing an age-old fear that humans would be controlled by the very technologies they created? Or could both be true at once?

However, perhaps a more complex question about the relationships between humans and technology had already been raised by Norbert Wiener, the pioneer of cybernetics. In *God & Golem, Inc.*, Wiener warned of those who impatiently wish to extend human limits that the accumulated wisdom of humanity, contained in myth, legend, and literature, should warn of the dangers of this two-edged sword [111].

Wiener's cybernetics focused on complex interactive feedback loops, which he used to analyse many problems and to understand intelligent behaviour and processes, including both in living things and in the interactions between humans and machines. In *The Human Use of Human Beings*, Wiener expressed many fears about how technology may partake in feedback loops with deleterious impacts on humans, for example, in displacing jobs and controlling humans [112]. By including the idea of feedback loops, we can understand the control problem of AI not simply as a straight battle between humans and computing power but as necessitating a more complex set of questions about the interaction between the two.

Likewise, Tim Berners-Lee invented the World Wide Web in 1989 but has come to express deep regrets about how it is being used and the impact it is having [113]. His worries seem to stem from a more complex web—forgive the pun—than simply the relatively straightforward fear of humans losing control over technology, since they concern differential impacts upon different human beings. Almost 30 years after its inception, Berners-Lee started to express grave concerns that the web was only partially living up to its ideals as an open platform operating across geographical and cultural boundaries which would allow anyone to collaborate and share information, ideas, and opportunities. His concerns focus on the loss of control over personal data, the ready spread of misinformation on the web, and the lack of transparency and understanding of political advertising.

Exercise 18
Concerns expressed by pioneers such as Turing, Wiener, and Berners-Lee may be taken seriously by virtue of their expertise and status as founder figures. However, remember that in Plato's *Phaedrus*, the god Thamus viewed Theuth, the god who invented writing, as unable to assess it fairly, out of parental blindness to the failings of his offspring. Perhaps this means that warnings about technology from its creator

are to be heeded, but praise should be viewed more sceptically. Does one's role in developing a technology, especially perhaps in its early or foundational stages, give one special capacities to assess its values and dangers? Consider arguments both for and against this proposition. An answer will have relevance to the conduct of AI ethics.

Whatever your answer to such a question, key figures in AI have influenced the agendas and directions of AI ethics. Berners-Lee is actively working to address problems of the World Wide Web. In 2014, Stephen Hawking told the BBC that the future of AI might even mean the demise of the human race, which exceeds in calamity even many of the dire forecasts of antiquity [114]. In the same year, Elon Musk also stated that he considered AI to be our biggest existential threat [115]. In an interview with *Wired* the following year, Hawking notably also used the language of legend and story in saying, 'The genie is out of the bottle', fearing that AI would replace humans altogether and that a self-replicating AI could be a new form of life that overtakes humanity [116].

Exercise 19: Food for Thought

We have seen fears of the position that machines may take midway between the animate and the inanimate. We can even see questions about borders and boundaries in the figure of speech I purposefully used here: thought requires brainpower, which quite literally requires food, but 'food for thought' reminds us of our own mixed position between the mental, the abstract, and the physical or animal realm.

The capacity to replicate itself is one hallmark of life. However, how might this in itself be seen to threaten the place of humans, and how might it be connected with outperforming humans?

In 2015, an open letter 'Research priorities for robust and beneficial artificial intelligence', signed by thousands including many prominent people such as Hawking and Musk and including many in the field of AI such as Stuart Russell, Peter Norvig, Demis Hassabis, and many others, was published on the Future of Life Institute's website [117]. This takes a notably different tack to prognostications of doom and is linked to a detailed document of priorities of research directions intended to maximise the social benefits of AI. The letter stated: 'The potential benefits are huge, since everything that civilisation has to offer is a product of human intelligence; we cannot predict what we might achieve when this intelligence is magnified by the tools AI may provide, but the eradication of disease and poverty are not unfathomable.'

Exercise 20

Is 'everything that civilisation has to offer' a product of human intelligence? What, indeed, does 'civilisation' have to offer?

Hint: This question is intentionally vague and may provide you with some food for thought for later discussions. We will return to this theme in Chap. 5 when we discuss intelligence in greater detail.

Computing ethics and AI ethics   There is now a multitude of work proceeding on AI ethics, within both academia and outside; within commercial settings, government and regulatory organisations, and civil society groups; and within the field of AI itself and in other fields. However, it is important to recognise that this has been preceded by work on the ethics of computing by some decades, as well as work on the ethics of technology more broadly. For example, Deborah Johnson's book *Computer Ethics* was first published in 1985 [118], and dealt with many of the same issues that are being approached today in relation more specifically to AI, such as privacy, ethics in the online space, social implications of computing, and accountability and responsibility. The introduction to Johnson's book also gives useful insights into how computer ethics developed with the rise of computing after the Second World War, from general fears that computers would take over human decision-making to clearer and more specific articulation of issues developing in the 1970s, such as questions about the dominance of an instrumental rationality and concerns with hackers and property rights over software arising. The birth of the Internet saw new issues arising, and ways in which computing could impact on wider society evolving and increasing. Naturally, work on AI ethics builds upon work in computing ethics more generally. Many other disciplinary fields and areas of endeavour, such as science and technology studies, the study of human-computer interaction, and work on responsible research and innovation, are growing and burgeoning fields and have much to offer. The use by so much AI of large amounts of data also means that the field of data ethics is highly relevant to many questions in AI ethics [119, 120].

The history of a field and the neologisms   There is a need to think with precision about a subject to be careful about the terms one uses, and to ensure that their meaning is clear. However, an unfortunate side effect of this can be that terms are coined at certain points in a discussion which effectively act to block off access to previous discussions on essentially the same point, but which used different terms. A parallel example to this can be found in those cultures where women tend to change their last names on marriage: this can make them much harder to trace, and histories of women have suffered as a result of this.

This tendency to coining new terms can be a blight in academia where the internal pressures to publish and to be cited can only encourage the practice of attempting to be the first person to use a particular term. This can act somewhat like planting one's flag in 'new' territory, pointedly ignoring the footprints of one's predecessors. For example, the term 'solutionism' was allegedly coined in 2013 by Evgeny Morozov to express the idea that every social problem can be solved by technology [121]. However, this is largely the same idea as that of the 'technological fix', allegedly coined in 1965 by Alvin Weinberg [122]. Searches for work relating to solutionism may miss important work dealing with the technological fix. Furthermore, the same idea may have been discussed long before anyone gave it a specific name. Terminological difficulties can also happen frequently in areas of study where different disciplines intersect; a relative newcomer may discuss a phenomenon under one term, thus potentially eclipsing work that discusses essentially the same phenomenon under a different label.

2.6 AI Ethics Now: Who, What, Where, and Why?

Summary
A brief overview is given of some of the organisations addressing AI ethics and keeping track of the issues.

It can seem as if everybody is involved in AI ethics now, and if they are not, it is because they are complaining about it and arguing that a different approach to addressing the issues of new technologies is better, just as many of those working within AI ethics are arguing about different approaches to methodology and different practical approaches to implementation. There are many working in AI itself attempting to address ethical questions within their work; academics working across different disciplines contributing to debates; lawyers, regulators, and policy makers addressing these questions; dedicated research centres and think tanks; funders are financing many such efforts; civil society groups are involved; and corporations and companies are also addressing ethics (or, claiming to do so). In fact, it is so hard to keep up with what is going on, with who is researching and debating issues, that there are organisations and websites dedicated to keeping track, such as AlgorithmWatch, which has a searchable database for an AI Ethics Guidelines Global Inventory, as well as many newsletters and reports to which one can subscribe.

A Brief Selection of Organisations and Newsletters Keeping Track of Issues in AI Ethics
Africa Just AI Project researchictafrica.net/project/ai-policy-research-centre/
AI Ethics Weekly newsletter from Lighthouse 3 lighthouse3.com/newsletter
Algorithm Watch algorithmwatch.org
Algorithmic Justice League ajl.org
Article 19 includes concern for digital rights article19.org
Beneficial AI Japan bai-japan.org
Digital Ethics Centre TU Delft https://www.tudelft.nl/digital-ethics-centre
Indigenous Protocol and Artificial Intelligence Working Group indigenous-ai.net
International Research Centre for AI Ethics and Governance https://ai-ethics-and-governance.institute
Montreal AI Ethics Institute montrealethics.ai
OECD Policy Observatory http://oecd.ai/
The Institute for Ethical AI, Oxford Brookes University https://ethical-ai.ac.uk

---

(continued)

Stanford Institute for Human-Centred Artificial Intelligence hai.standford.edu
Women in AI Ethics™ womeninaiethics.org

Add any more of your own.
Consider the nature of the different organisations examining these issues
and producing material.

It is important to consider the context of ethical discussion and debate, claims, and practical steps towards implementation. It matters who is asking the questions; what their vested interests are, if any; and what background assumptions, beliefs, and motivations might frame discourse. For instance, a large corporation firmly wedded to AI is a very different entity from an academic centre, but perhaps an academic centre may be reliant on certain funding sources. Those working closely with technologists developing AI may have an extremely good understanding of the cutting edge of AI and of its technical details, but then, on the other hand, may lack a critical distance that more independent commentators and critics may possess. Politicians and policy makers may wish to regulate ethical questions, but concerns with national self-interest and the development of science and industry and economic factors may of course influence outcomes. Power and influence will make a difference to what the ethical issues are seen to be, which issues receive the most attention and funding, which issues are effectively translated into making a meaningful difference, and what are empty words and promises.

Consider the ultimate end of ethics conceived in such close proximity to the technology it assesses, to those who directly benefit financially and to the political interests of a governing elite. Is it some abstract notion of the good society, benefit for the individual, conceptualised in a disinterested manner, and free from the influence of technology and technologists? Or is it in reality the goal of producing technology that has its path to implementation smoothed by the veneer of ethics? Will ethics as a practice simply serve technology? One, perhaps cynical, view is that the practice of ethics will simply fine-tune technological development to a palatable form, with occasional concessions to appear willing. Another even more cynical view is that the practice of ethics simply serves technological progress by ensuring that the values inherent in the technology appear to be 'for the greater good'.

Exercise 21
Many tech companies have information on their websites and sometimes are included in advertising regarding their ethical stances and any action they are taking, including slogans (such as Google's famous, or infamous, 'don't be evil'). Look up some of these, compare a few, and consider their content, their mode of expression, and how much they can be trusted. How easy is it to find verifiable and plausible information about the ethical stance of such companies?

2.7 AI Ethics, Law, Policy, Regulation, and Ethics Guidance

Summary
How conceptions of ethics might help or hinder translation into practical impact.

This book does not deal with the details of how to implement specific policies and regulations regarding AI ethics. I focused specifically on developing and implementing codes of ethics for AI in my 2017 book, *Towards a Code of Ethics for Artificial Intelligence* [123], and many others have also produced work in this area, which is ongoing. This is an immensely complex field requiring detailed specification of law, public policy, and technologies. Nonetheless, the general aim of this book is to contribute to understanding ethics in ways that will lead to real-world impact and enhance policy, regulations, and practical ethics guidance. To do so, we need to consider methodologies in ethics, examining how conclusions may be reached, which itself is a complex and disputed question, which we examine head on in Chap. 4. We also need to consider how to enhance debate and discussion about ethics in an interdisciplinary context, which is in essence a key ambition of this book.

Some very general issues regarding the nature of ethics will help to shape attitudes towards embedding ethics in policy and regulation. Many of these will be discussed again throughout the book. They include questions about responsibility and how it can be attributed, a critical issue in developing practical policy, for without clear notions of accountability and responsibility, we cannot produce workable policy. The role of principles in ethics is also a pivotal question. Can we capture the entirety of ethical concerns in a set of rules? If not, how should we approach codes and regulations?

Ethics as a process Sometimes ethics is conceptualised as something to set straight at the start of an endeavour, an unchanging set of commitments. However, it is often more helpful to understand it as a process. This may be especially the case with policy and regulations concerning how ethics is embedded within the development and implementation of complex technologies, with a need for checking along the way and for feedback and revisions in light of deepening understanding of progress. This is nowhere more necessary than in dealing with fast developing technologies with complex and wide-reaching impacts upon society and individuals such as with AI. Policy and regulations need to be designed to be adaptive.

Ethics, power, and motivation to act A central feature of ethics is so obvious that it may escape us: people do not always do something they know is right. They also do things they know are wrong. Power is frequently misused. Closely related to this, people often swayed by other interests into fooling themselves that their behaviour is justified. There is a complex tangle of different interests involved, and the complexity and magnitude of the economic forces at play here cannot be overlooked. Policies that include attention to ethics are frequently produced in the context of wider economic and industrial interests. Many nations are currently aiming to become leaders in innovating AI [124]. Never for a minute assume that just because something is labelled 'ethics', it is simply and solely about ethics, let alone that it is genuinely ethical. When assessing policies, therefore, it is important to ask yourself where the power and authority behind policies and guidance lies and who is being allowed into the conversations. Ethics concerns relationships between people, and the nature and quality of the relationships, and the dialogues that contributed to the construction of policy and regulation, must be considered. The growth and development of relevant civil society groups, public engagement, and education about the issues are all needed.

Exercise 22
Search the AI Ethics Guidelines Global Inventory, pick one of the guidelines, and consider any or all of these questions:

Who is producing the guidance?
What is the source of the power and any authority for the guidance?
Who is affected by the guidance?
Who is given any specific or general responsibilities?
Is the guidance local, national, etc.?
Is there a preamble introducing the guidance, an account of motivations, and so on?
What is its content—a set of rules, for example, recommendations, mandates, and
    suggestions?
How specific are any rules, mandates, etc.?
Does the guidance call for ethics training, and if so, how is this understood?
Does the guidance refer to 'experts on ethics' or similar, and if so, what are these?
Is the guidance inspirational, idealised, or more concrete and practical?
What is being said, and what is being left out?
Is the guidance explicitly about ethics—or about something else as well?
Who stands to gain from the publication and implementation of the guidance?
What other questions might you be asking?

As a group exercise, it would be useful to pick different guidelines and compare and contrast your answers.

2.8   Looking Forward: What Is Our Job Now?

We have taken a look at some debates about how we should understand ethics in this arena, for instance, at the concern that if ethics is portrayed as centrally involving individual responsibilities with no reference to power issues or social factors, this may narrow our view of matters and prevent us from looking more broadly at solutions. This shows the importance of digging more deeply into different ways of understanding ethics and broader value questions. Many debates about the application of ethics to concrete issues stem from assumptions about the nature of ethics itself and rest in turn upon assumptions about the nature of responsibility, agency, and other questions, which are wide open to different interpretations and often diametrically opposed viewpoints. We should also question whether we already know what the issues are that need to be addressed in AI ethics. Do we know what the issues are now, and is it a matter of just making sure they are implemented? We have already seen that there is a need to dig deeper and that it's possible to miss some important questions. We need to look at the methodology.

2.9   Case Study: An Indigenous AI Report

Summary
We have seen how important it is to consider the potentially distorting effects of dominant voices. This section introduces an example in work exploring indigenous approaches to AI. Some points to note include a focus on local knowledge, community, and relationships.

We have seen that many ethical guidelines and regulations concerning AI are being produced. There are commonalities between many of these, as well as differences. We have also seen concerns that debates may be shaped and dominated by viewpoints from certain parts of the world. It is important to question what issues are being brought forwards for consideration and not just what conclusions are drawn but also how we should think about the issues.

The Indigenous Protocol and Artificial Intelligence Working Group was formed with two workshops in 2018 (indigenous-ai.net). The group is concerned with developing new AI systems and addressing both conceptual and practical questions posed from an indigenous perspective about AI. The development of AI and questions of ethics and value are thus closely intertwined. While there are differences between different indigenous groups from around the world, one of the group's aims is to broaden discussions of society and technology beyond the relatively narrow cultural milieu of Silicon Valley startup culture. Therefore, as well as being of great interest in and of itself, an examination of their concerns should also be informative and helpful for those wishing to reflect upon the possible limitations of currently dominant views in AI ethics. As we shall see, these concerns immediately stretch beyond ethics and speak to some of the broad questions in AI ethics that we have already raised.

The questions addressed by the working group include asking what, from an indigenous perspective, are the proper relationships with AI. A focus on relationships may produce a different perspective than a focus on, for example, outcomes, which may be dominant in approaches that stress that AI should bring about the outcome of benefit to society. The workshops also addressed how to imagine a future of flourishing for both humans *and nonhumans*. This also sets this approach apart from many other sets of guidance and discussions of AI ethics that focus mainly, or exclusively, on human beings.

In addition, the scope of inquiry is broadened from ethics to include asking how indigenous epistemologies and ontologies might contribute to global discussions of AI and society. In other words, the indigenous AI working group saw the need to consider frameworks for understanding what knowledge is, how we acquire it, and how we value it, as well assumptions and commitments to what kinds of things there are—one's ontology. How might these questions be relevant to ethics in AI?

Here are two simple examples to illustrate the potential relevance of both epistemology and ontology to questions in AI ethics. Many (but by no means all) who are currently living in the West consider that everything in the world can be boiled down to material reality, so that everything that exists and everything that happens can ultimately be understood in terms of basic, observable science—the laws of physics, chemistry, and biology. There is no spirit, no soul, and consciousness can be explained entirely as arising from brute matter. This often goes hand in hand with the claim that we will ultimately be able to understand this material reality through scientific knowledge, but this optimistic view of our capacity to understand the world is not a necessary corollary of the view that material reality is all that there is. However, if one believed that there is more to the world than that which can be understood through our current scientific methodologies, perhaps considering that there are spirits or souls, one will start out from rather different premises in addressing many questions about the nature of AI, of advanced robots, of the possibilities of human enhancement with technology, and of our relationship with technology. If we believe that we, human beings, are able fully to understand the world, then we may both act on the assumption that to create intelligence in machines is to model human intelligence and on the assumption that one day we will fully understand both intelligence and consciousness and be able to reproduce both in machines. The working group's position paper expresses the concern that the current development of AI may be too limited and too based upon certain rationalist ways of understanding epistemology to be able to engage with the possibilities created by the development of computational systems [125, p. 6]. Remember that we have also seen responses to robots and expressions of fear around AI, which suggest that the attitude that the world is more than mere 'material reality' is commonly held. We return to such discussions in the last chapter.

The Guidelines for Indigenous-centred AI Design v.1 spells out a list of guidelines containing seven principles in no specific order of hierarchy.

Guidelines for Indigenous-Centred AI Design v.1
1. Locality
2. Relationality and Reciprocity
3. Responsibility, Relevance, and Accountability
4. Develop Governance Guidelines from Indigenous Protocols
5. Recognise the Cultural Nature of all Computational Technology

(continued)

6. Apply Ethical Design to the Extended Stack (technology development ecosystem)
7. Respect and Support Data Sovereignty [125, p. 20]

The principle of locality notes that indigenous knowledge is often rooted in both specific territories as well as being of relevance in considering issues of global importance. Principle 2 notes that indigenous knowledge is often relational and states that AI systems should be designed to understand the relationships and dependencies between humans and nonhumans. Principle 3 stresses the importance for indigenous people of their responsibilities and accountability to communities. Principle 5 points out that technology expresses cultural and social frameworks and hence that AI system designers should be aware of their own cultural frameworks, values, and biases and consider how to accommodate the cultural and social frameworks of others.

Hence, these guidelines serve both to express particular concerns that indigenous groups may have and to point to issues that all who are involved in designing and using AI ought to be aware of: the relevance of our cultural and social frameworks, the possibility of bias and of a limited view of the technologies we are creating and using, and the need to look beyond a narrow understanding of 'ethics' to include other issues concerning how we understand knowledge and our foundational pictures of the world. We will return to many of these ideas throughout the book.

2.10 Key Points

There is currently considerable attention to AI ethics, often with claims that the issues involved are novel. However, understanding how similar issues have been dealt with in the past is essential to understanding and addressing the current concerns.

Prior work, for example, in computer ethics, is highly relevant. Moreover, fields outside of computing can have useful lessons. For example, many of the current concerns in AI arise from its use of vast amounts of data. Work in medicine, genomics, and social sciences has dealt with ethical issues arising from the use of personal data.

It can be helpful to understand the large variety of different kinds of questions arising in AI ethics.

Certain core values and concepts are prominent in current discussions of AI ethics, but we must also be careful to consider other approaches to understanding the issues.

Looking at historical concerns about robots and other technologies, including writing technologies, can alert us to long-standing concerns and help us reflect upon how we ourselves discern and understand concerns.

2.11   Educator Notes

This chapter can be used in many different ways. It will be helpful for all students to be introduced to the idea that there is much past relevant work, as well as relevant work from different subject areas. Student groups may have very different levels of interest in the questions of history. Students from arts backgrounds might wish to explore or research specific areas of history that interest them and share this material with others.

There is ample opportunity for students with different interests to bring their own expertise to bear and hence in a mixed class for students to undertake different work to bring to the class. For example, it would be very useful for students with some understanding of how a different subject area, such as the social sciences, has approached issues such as the handling of human data to explore the relevance of this for questions in AI ethics. This could be useful to underline the necessity of diverse contributions to AI ethics.

The exercises in Sect. 2.4 present an introductory overview of issues as a taster to material, which will be explored in more detail later. They can be useful for students to attempt even without any further background research. Many of the cases and aspects of exercises will be referred to again later. This can provide a chance for students to see how their thought has developed. The exercises cover a wide range of issues, and educators may of course wish to concentrate on certain themes and issues only.

Debate and extended essay and project topics   Exercise 20 would form a good debate or class discussion topic because it raises very general themes about the value and possibility of AI, is often cited, and will be referred to again later. Exercise 22 would be a useful class exercise or individual or group project to ensure that students have a broad overview of a range of central issues.

Acknowledgements This chapter was partially funded by the National Institute for Health Research, Health Services and Delivery Research Programme (project number 13/10/80). The views expressed are those of the author and not necessarily those of the NIHR or the Department of Health and Social Care.

References

1. Powledge TM (2003) Human genome project completed. Genome Biol 4(1):1–3
2. Rood JE, Regev A (2021) The legacy of the Human Genome Project. Science 373(6562): 1442–1443
3. Schwab K (2017) The fourth industrial revolution. Currency
4. Skilton M, Hovsepian F (2018) The 4th industrial revolution. Springer, Cham
5. Taylor L, Sharma G, Martin A, Jameson S (eds) (2020) Data justice and COVID-19 global perspectives. Meatspace, London
6. Franck R, Iannaccone LR (2014) Religious decline in the 20th century West: testing alternative explanations. Public Choice 159(3):385–414
7. Amodei D, Olah C, Steinhardt J, Christiano P, Schulman J, Mané D (2016) Concrete problems in AI safety. arXiv preprint arXiv:1606.06565
8. Aloisi A, Gramano E (2019) Artificial intelligence is watching you at work: digital surveillance, employee monitoring, and regulatory issues in the EU context. Comp Lab L Pol'y J 41: 95
9. Prunkl C, Whittlestone J (2020) Beyond near- and long-term: towards a clearer account of research priorities in AI ethics and society. In: Proceedings of the AAAI/ACM conference on AI, ethics, and society, pp 138–143
10. Bostrom N (2017) Superintelligence. Dunod, Malakoff
11. Brock DC, Moore GE (eds) (2006) Understanding Moore's law: four decades of innovation. Chemical Heritage Foundation, Philadelphia
12. Wooldridge M (2020) The road to conscious machines: the story of AI. Penguin, London
13. Asimov I (2004) I, Robot 1. Spectra. First published 1950
14. IEEE (2011) Draft guide: adoption of the Project Management Institute (PMI) standard. A Guide to the Project Management Body of Knowledge (PMBOK Guide)-2008. In: 4th IEEE P1490/D1, pp 1–505. https://doi.org/10.1109/IEEESTD.2011.5937011
15. Hand DJ, Khan S (2020) Validating and verifying AI systems. Patterns (N Y) 1(3):100037. https://doi.org/10.1016/j.patter.2020.100037
16. Leslie D (2019) Understanding artificial intelligence ethics and safety. arXiv preprint arXiv:1906.05684. https://www.turing.ac.uk/research/publications/understanding-artificial-intelligence-ethics-and-safety
17. Dix A, Finlay J, Abowd GD, Beale R (2004) Human-computer interaction. Pearson, London
18. Riek L, Howard D (2014) A code of ethics for the human-robot interaction profession. Proceedings of we robot
19. Shanahan M (2015) The technological singularity. MIT Press, Cambridge
20. Zanzotto FM (2019) Human-in-the-loop artificial intelligence. J Artif Intell Res 64:243–252
21. Jones ML (2017) The right to a human in the loop: political constructions of computer automation and personhood. Soc Stud Sci 47(2):216–239
22. Whittlestone J, Nyrup R, Alexandrova A, Dihal K, Cave S (2019) Ethical and societal implications of algorithms, data, and artificial intelligence: a roadmap for research. Nuffield Foundation, London
23. Jobin A, Ienca M, Vayena E (2019) The global landscape of AI ethics guidelines. Nat Mach Intell 1(9):389–399
24. Fjeld J, Achten N, Hilligoss H, Nagy A, Srikumar M (2020) Principled artificial intelligence: mapping consensus in ethical and rights-based approaches to principles for AI. Berkman Klein Center Research Publication, Harvard. (2020-1)
25. Mittelstadt BD, Allo P, Taddeo M, Wachter S, Floridi L (2016) The ethics of algorithms: mapping the debate. Big Data Soc 3(2)
26. Hagendorff T (2020) The ethics of AI ethics: an evaluation of guidelines. Mind Mach 30:1–22
27. Buss S, Westlund A (2018) Personal autonomy. In: Zalta EN (ed) The Stanford encyclopedia of philosophy. https://plato.stanford.edu/archives/spr2018/entries/personal-autonomy/

28. Christman J (2020) Autonomy in moral and political philosophy. In: Zalta EN (ed) The Stanford encyclopedia of philosophy. https://plato.stanford.edu/archives/fall2020/entries/autonomy-moral/
29. Dworkin G (1988) The theory and practice of autonomy. Cambridge University Press, Cambridge
30. Kearns M, Roth A (2019) The ethical algorithm: the science of socially aware algorithm design. Oxford University Press, Oxford
31. Sanderson D (2019) Google maps and satnavs are damaging our brains, says author David Barrie. The Times
32. TFL. Learn the knowledge of London. https://tfl.gov.uk/info-for/taxis-and-private-hire/licensing/learn-the-knowledge-of-london
33. Maguire EA, Gadian DG, Johnsrude IS, Good CD, Ashburner J, Frackowiak RS, Frith CD (2000) Navigation-related structural change in the hippocampi of taxi drivers. Proc Natl Acad Sci 97(8):4398–4403
34. Association for Computing Machinery statement on algorithm transparency and accountability. https://www.acm.org/binaries/content/assets/publicpolicy/2017_usacm_statement_algorithms.pdf
35. Goodman B, Flaxman S (2017) European Union regulations on algorithmic decision-making and a 'right to explanation'. AI Mag 38(3):50–57. https://doi.org/10.1609/aimag.v38i3.2741
36. Edwards L, Veale M (2017) Slave to the algorithm: why a right to an explanation is probably not the remedy you are looking for. Duke L Tech Rev 16:18
37. Mittelstadt B, Russell C, Wachter S (2019) Explaining explanations in AI. In: Proceedings of the conference on fairness, accountability, and transparency. Association for Computing Machinery, Atlanta, pp 279–288
38. Stepin I, Alonso JM, Catala A, Pereira-Fariña M (2021) A survey of contrastive and counterfactual explanation generation methods for explainable artificial intelligence. IEEE Access 9: 11974–12001
39. Wachter S, Mittelstadt BD, Russell C (2017) Counterfactual explanations without opening the black box: automated decisions and the GDPR. CoRR, abs/1711.00399 https://arxiv.org/pdf/1711.00399.pdf
40. Zerilli J, Knott A, Maclaurin J, Gavaghan C (2019) Transparency in algorithmic and human decision-making: is there a double standard? Philos Technol 32(4):661–683
41. Weller A (2019) Transparency: motivations and challenges. In: Explainable AI: interpreting, explaining and visualizing deep learning. Springer, Cham, pp 23–40
42. Binns R (2018) Fairness in machine learning: lessons from political philosophy. In: Proceedings of the 1st conference on fairness, accountability and transparency, in proceedings of machine learning research, vol 81. PMLR, pp 149–159
43. Lamont J, Favor C (2017) Distributive justice. In: Zalta EN (ed) The Stanford encyclopedia of philosophy. Metaphysics Research Lab, Stanford University, Stanford. https://plato.stanford.edu/archives/win2017/entries/justice-distributive/
44. Chouldechova A, Roth A (2018) The frontiers of fairness in machine learning. arXiv preprint arXiv:1810.08810
45. Larson J, Mattu S, Kirchner L, Angwin J (2016) How we analyzed the COMPAS recidivism algorithm. ProPublica 9(1):3
46. Dieterich W, Mendoza C, Brennan T (2016) COMPAS risk scales: demonstrating accuracy equity and predictive parity, vol 7(4). Northpointe Inc, Traverse City
47. Flores AW, Bechtel K, Lowenkamp CT (2016) False positives, false negatives, and false analyses: a rejoinder to machine bias: there's software used across the country to predict future criminals and it's biased against blacks. Fed Probat 80:38
48. Freeman K (2016) Algorithmic injustice: how the Wisconsin Supreme Court failed to protect due process rights in State v. Loomis. NC J Law Technol 18(5):75
49. Dressel J, Farid H (2018) The accuracy, fairness, and limits of predicting recidivism. Sci Adv 4(1):eaao5580. https://doi.org/10.1126/sciadv.aao5580

50. Benthall S, Haynes BD (2019) Racial categories in machine learning. In: Proceedings of the conference on fairness, accountability, and transparency - FAT*'19. ACM Press, Atlanta, GA, pp 289–298. https://arxiv.org/pdf/1811.11668.pdf

51. Buolamwini J, Gebru T (2018) Gender shades: intersectional accuracy disparities in commercial gender classification. In: Conference on fairness, accountability and transparency. PMLR, pp 77–91

52. Corbett-Davies S, Goel S (2018) The measure and mismeasure of fairness: a critical review of fair machine learning. arXiv preprint arXiv:1808.00023

53. Hoffmann AL (2019) Where fairness fails: data, algorithms, and the limits of antidiscrimination discourse. Inf Commun Soc 22(7):900–915

54. Bazerman MH, Tenbrunsel AE (2011) Blind spots. Princeton University, Princeton, NJ

55. Frey AL, Karran M, Jimenez RC, Baxter J, Adeogun M, Bose N, Chan D, Crawford J, Dagum P, Everson R, Hinds C (2019) Harnessing the potential of digital technologies for the early detection of neurodegenerative diseases (EDoN). OSF Preprints, Charlottesville, VA

56. Hakli R, Mäkelä P (2019) Moral responsibility of robots and hybrid agents. Monist 102(2):259–275. https://doi.org/10.1093/monist/onz009

57. Helberger N, Pierson J, Poell T (2018) Governing online platforms: from contested to cooperative responsibility. Inf Soc 34(1):1–14

58. Jamjoom AAB, Jamjoom AMA, Marcus HJ (2020) Exploring public opinion about liability and responsibility in surgical robotics. Nat Mach Intell 2:194–196

59. Jirotka M, Grimpe B, Stahl B, Eden G, Hartswood M (2017) Responsible research and innovation in the digital age. Commun ACM 60(5):62–68

60. Taylor L, Purtova N (2019) What is responsible and sustainable data science? Big Data Soc 6(2):2053951719858811

61. Dignum V (2019) Responsible artificial intelligence: how to develop and use AI in a responsible way. Springer, Cham

62. Floridi L (2013) Distributed morality in an information society. Sci Eng Ethics 19(3):727–743

63. Schwartz O (2019) In 2016, Microsoft's racist chatbot revealed the dangers of online conversation. IEEE Spectr 11:2019

64. Wolf MJ, Miller KW, Grodzinsky FS (2017) Why we should have seen that coming: comments on Microsoft's Tay "experiment," and wider implications. ORBIT J 1(2):1–12

65. Nissenbaum H (2020) Privacy in context. Stanford University Press, Redwood City

66. Van den Hoven J, Blaauw M, Pieters W, Warnier M (2020) Privacy and information technology. In: Zalta EN (ed) The Stanford encyclopedia of philosophy. Metaphysics Research Lab, Stanford University, Stanford. https://plato.stanford.edu/archives/sum2020/entries/it-privacy/

67. Véliz C (2020) Privacy is power: why and how you should take back control of your data. Random House, New York

68. Agre PE (1994) Surveillance and capture: two models of privacy. Inf Soc 10(2):101–127

69. Zuboff S (2019) The age of surveillance capitalism. Profile Books, London

70. Ng J, Kong H (2016) Not all who wander are lost: smart tracker for people with dementia. In: Proceedings of the 2016 CHI conference extended abstracts on human factors in computing systems. Association for Computing Machinery, New York, pp 2241–2248

71. Hine C, Barnaghi P (2021) Surveillance for independence: discursive frameworks in smart care for dementia. AoIR selected papers of Internet research

72. McLeod C (2021) Trust. In: Zalta EN (ed) The Stanford encyclopedia of philosophy. Metaphysics Research Lab, Stanford University, Stanford. https://plato.stanford.edu/archives/fall2021/entries/trust/

73. Brundage M, Avin S, Wang J, Belfield H, Krueger G, Hadfield G, Khlaaf H, Yang J, Toner H, Fong R, Maharaj T (2020) Toward trustworthy AI development: mechanisms for supporting verifiable claims. arXiv preprint arXiv:2004.07213

74. Ferrario A, Loi M, Viganò E (2019) In AI we trust incrementally: a multi-layer model of trust to analyze human-artificial intelligence interactions. Philos Technol. https://doi.org/10.1007/s13347-019-00378-3
75. HLEG, High Level Expert Group in AI (2019) Ethics guidelines for trustworthy AI. Independent High-Level Expert Group on Artificial Intelligence, Brussels, p 39
76. Winfield AF, Jirotka M (2018) Ethical governance is essential to building trust in robotics and artificial intelligence systems. Philos Trans R Soc A Math Phys Eng Sci 376(2133):20180085
77. Song Y, Luximon Y (2020) Trust in AI agent: a systematic review of facial anthropomorphic trustworthiness for social robot design. Sensors 20(18):5087
78. Crawford K (2021) The atlas of AI. Yale University Press, New Haven
79. Strubell E, Ganesh A, McCallum A (2020) Energy and policy considerations for modern deep learning research. In: Proceedings of the AAAI conference on artificial intelligence, vol 34, pp 13693–13696
80. Bender EM, Gebru T, McMillan-Major A, Shmitchell S (2021) On the dangers of stochastic parrots: can language models be too big? In: Proceedings of the 2021 ACM conference on fairness, accountability, and transparency. Association for Computing Machinery, New York, pp 610–623
81. Macklin R (2003) Dignity is a useless concept. BMJ 327(7429):1419–1420
82. Smiley L (2017) What happens when we let tech care for our aging parents. Wired
83. Bayertz K (ed) (1999) Solidarity, vol 5. Springer, Berlin
84. https://letsmindstep.com. Accessed 8 June 2022
85. Rifkin-Zybutz R, Selim H, Johal M, Kuleindiren N, Palmon I, Lin A, Yu Y, Mahmud M (2021) Preliminary validation study of the Mindset4Dementia application: assessing remote collection of dementia risk factors and cognitive performance. BMJ Innovations 7(4):26–631
86. Rangroo A (2020) New app urges Asian community to join in fight against dementia. Asian Sunday Online. https://www.asiansunday.co.uk/new-app-urges-asian-community-to-join-fight-against-dementia/
87. Harris J (2005) Scientific research is a moral duty. J Med Ethics 31(4):242–248
88. Marrus MR (1999) The Nuremberg doctors' trial in historical context. Bull Hist Med 73(1):106–123
89. Dickson D (1988) Europe split on Embryo Research: deeply etched memories of Nazi atrocities are digging a gulf between West Germany and other European nations over whether human embryos should be used for research purposes. Science 242(4882):1117–1118
90. Feynman R (1986) Report of the Presidential Commission on the Space Shuttle Challenger accident. Appendix F
91. Gehman HW (2003) Columbia Accident Investigation Board, vol 2. Columbia Accident Investigation Board, Columbia
92. Cave S, Dihal K (2019) Hopes and fears for intelligent machines in fiction and reality. Nat Mach Intell 1(2):74–78
93. Mayor A (2018) Gods and robots. Princeton University Press, Princeton
94. Mori M (2017) The uncanny valley: the original essay by Masahiro Mori. IEEE Robots, New York
95. Rappaport ZH (2006) Robotics and artificial intelligence: Jewish ethical perspectives. Acta Neurochir Suppl 98:9–12
96. Pettegree A (2015) Brand Luther: how an unheralded monk turned his small town into a center of publishing, made himself the most famous man in Europe–and started the protestant reformation. Penguin, London
97. Plato (1888) The Phaedrus. In: Plato, Hamilton E, Cairns H, Jowett B (eds) The collected dialogues of Plato. InteLex, Toronto
98. Noble DF (1995) Progress without people: new technology, unemployment, and the message of resistance. Between the Lines, Toronto
99. Galton F (1908) Memories of my life. Methuen, London

100. Holt J (2005) Measure for measure the strange science of Frances Galton. The New Yorker. https://www.newyorker.com/magazine/2005/01/24/measure-for-measure-5
101. Dickens C (1905) Hard times. Chapman & Hall, London. https://www.gutenberg.org/files/786/786-h/786-h.htm
102. Bentham J (1825) The rationale of reward. John and HL Hunt Book, London. 3, Chapter 1
103. Mitchell WC (1918) Bentham's felicific calculus. Political Sci Q 33(2):161–183
104. Bentham J (1789) Introduction to the principles of morals and legislation. Oxford University Press, Oxford
105. Mill JS (1998) In: Crisp R (ed) Utilitarianism. Oxford University Press, Oxford
106. Roseboom T, de Rooij S, Painter R (2006) The Dutch famine and its long-term consequences for adult health. Early Hum Dev 82(8):485–491
107. Müller-Hill B (1988) Murderous science: elimination by scientific selection of Jews, Gypsies, and others, Germany. J Med Genet 25:860–861
108. Lepore J (2020) If then: how one data company invented the future. John Murray, Hachette
109. Mnookin S (2020) The bumbling 1960s data scientists who anticipated Facebook and Google. New York Times. https://www.nytimes.com/2020/09/15/books/review/if-then-jill-lepore.html
110. Turing A (2004) Can digital computers think? (1951). In: Copeland BJ (ed) The essential Turing. Oxford Academic, Oxford
111. Wiener N (1964) God and golem. Massachusetts Institute of Technology, Cambridge
112. Wiener N (1954) The human use of human beings. De Capo Press, Cambridge
113. Web Foundation (2017) Three challenges for the Web, according to its inventor. https://webfoundation.org/2017/03/web-turns-28-letter/
114. Cellan-Jones R (2014) Stephen Hawking warns artificial intelligence could end mankind. https://www.bbc.co.uk/news/technology-30290540
115. Moyer JW (2014) Why Elon Musk is scared of artificial intelligence–and terminators. Washington Post
116. Medeiros J (2017) Stephen Hawking: 'I fear AI may replace humans altogether'. Wired. https://www.wired.co.uk/article/stephen-hawking-interview-alien-life-climate-change-donald-trump
117. Future of Life Open Letter 'Research priorities for robust and beneficial artificial intelligence'. https://futureoflife.org/ai-open-letter/
118. Johnson DG (1985) Computer ethics. Prentice Hall, Englewood Cliffs, NJ
119. Floridi L, Taddeo M (2016) What is data ethics? Philos Trans R Soc A Math Phys Eng Sci 374(2083):20160360
120. Zwitter A (2014) Big data ethics. Big Data Soc 1(2):2053951714559253
121. Morozov E (2013) To save everything, click here: the folly of technological solutionism. Public Affairs, New York
122. Weinberg AM (1966) Can technology replace social engineering? Bull At Sci 22(10):4–8
123. Boddington P (2017) Towards a code of ethics for artificial intelligence. Springer, Cham
124. Kwarteng K (2021) Our ten year plan to make Britain a global AI superpower' in HM Government. National AI Strategy, London
125. Lewis JE, Abdilla A, Arista N, Baker K, Benesiinaabandan S, Brown M, Cheung M, Coleman M, Cordes A, Davison J, Duncan K (2020) Indigenous protocol and artificial intelligence position paper. Initiative for Indigenous Futures and the Canadian Institute for Advanced Research (CIFAR), Honolulu, Hawaiʻi

Further Reading

Bentham J (1789) Introduction to the principles of morals and legislation. In: Works, vol 1. William Tait, Edinburgh

Bentham J (1825) The rationale of reward. John and HL Hunt, London

Cave S, Dihal K (2019) Hopes and fears for intelligent machines in fiction and reality. Nat Mach Intell 1(2):74–78

Cave S, Coughlan K, Dihal K (2019) Scary robots examining public responses to AI. In: Proceedings of the 2019 AAAI/ACM conference on AI, ethics, and society. Association for Computing Machinery, New York, pp 331–337

Fjeld J, Achten N, Hilligoss H, Nagy A, Srikumar M (2020) Principled artificial intelligence: mapping consensus in ethical and rights-based approaches to principles for AI. Berkman Klein Center, Cambridge (2020-1)

Jobin A, Ienca M, Vayena E (2019) The global landscape of AI ethics guidelines. Nat Mach Intell 1(9):389–399

Johnson DG (1985) Computer ethics. Prentice Hall, Englewood Cliffs, NJ

Mayor A (2018) Gods and robots. Princeton University Press, Princeton

Mill JS (1863) Utilitarianism. Parker, Son and Bourn, London

Plato (1868) Phaedrus (trans: Jowett B)

Smart JJC, Williams B (1973) Utilitarianism: for and against. Cambridge University Press, Cambridge

Turing A (2004) Can digital computers think? (1951). In: Copeland BJ (ed) The essential Turing, Oxford Academic, Oxford

Wiener N (1954) The human use of human beings. De Capo Press, Cambridge

Wiener N (1964) God and golem. Massachusetts Institute of Technology, Cambridge

Wooldridge M (2020) The road to conscious machines: the story of AI. Penguin, London

Freedom and Autonomy

Berlin I (1988) Two concepts of liberty. In: Dworkin G (ed) The theory and practice of autonomy. Cambridge University Press, Cambridge

Transparency

Weller A (2019) Transparency: motivations and challenges. In: Samek W, Montavon G, Vedaldi A, Hansen LK, Müller KR (eds) Explainable AI: interpreting, explaining and visualizing deep learning, vol 11700. Springer, Cham

Beneficence and Nonmaleficence

Glover J (1990) Causing death and saving lives: the moral problems of abortion, infanticide, suicide, euthanasia, capital punishment, war and other life-or-death choices. Penguin, London

Fairness

Binns R (2018) Fairness in machine learning: lessons from political philosophy. In: Proceedings of the first conference on fairness, accountability and transparency, vol 81. Machine Learning Research, pp 149–159

Responsibility

Dignum V (2019) Responsible artificial intelligence: how to develop and use AI in a responsible way. Springer, Cham

Privacy

Véliz C (2020) Privacy is power: why and how you should take back control of your data. Random House, New York

Trust

Winfield AF, Jirotka M (2018) Ethical governance is essential to building trust in robotics and artificial intelligence systems. Philos Trans R Soc A Math Phys Eng Sci 376(2133):20180085

Sustainability

Crawford K (2021) The atlas of AI. Yale University Press, New Heaven

Dignity

Latonero M (2018) Governing artificial intelligence: upholding human rights & dignity. Data Soc, New York, pp 1–37

Solidarity

Luengo-Oroz M (2019) Solidarity should be a core ethical principle of AI. Nat Mach Intell 1(11): 494–494

Chapter 3
AI, Philosophy of Technology, and Ethics

Abstract To understand many of the ethical questions that arise in relation to AI, we must understand how it is viewed as a technology. Different perspectives tend to shape some key questions, such as the ways in which humans and AI are compared and contrasted. The chapter gives an introductory overview of the philosophy of technology, highlighting issues that underlie some of the ethical questions we examine in later chapters. These include questions about the proper relation of technology to nature, such as whether it mimics or should attempt to exceed nature, the proper relation of humans to nature, the nature of scientific and technological knowledge, and the implicit values of technology. The philosophers discussed include Plato, Aristotle, and Heidegger. We also explore the ethical issues that may arise from the use of AI in communication technologies and the impacts on how communications are viewed and on relationships.

Keywords Plato · Aristotle · Heidegger · Philosophy of technology · AI ethics · Nature

3.1 Artificial Intelligence, Ethics, and AI as a Technology

Summary
Different ways of thinking about and working with AI raise questions about how it is viewed as a technology. This in turn underpins many of the ethical questions about AI.

A brief introduction to artificial intelligence is given in Chap. 1. Many readers of course will have a far more sophisticated and technical understanding of AI. Chapter 1 outlined some distinctions that will be useful in addressing questions of ethics. In considering the ethical questions of AI, we need to consider it as a particular form, or forms, of technology. Before we consider questions more straightforwardly understood as ethical per se, we turn now to consider the question of how we understand and relate to technology.

We saw that ethical questions arise in relation to AI for a variety of rather different reasons. Some arise from detailed technical aspects of its operation, such as from the problem that it is often opaque to us how precisely machine learning algorithms reach their conclusions, or from questions about the precise provenance and representativeness of the data used to train machine learning algorithms. Some questions arise from how we conceptualise and imagine the project of AI. It may be conceived more prosaically as a loose collection of discrete attempts to tackle specific problem-solving tasks. Or it may be conceived of more majestically or hubristically as a project to 'solve' intelligence, to mimic human intelligence, or to exceed human intelligence. The term 'artificial intelligence' came into common use after the famous 1956 Dartmouth Summer school organised by John McCarthy [1]. Some consider that the term 'artificial intelligence' sets us up to think about it in a certain way—that it is aiming to mimic human intelligence, and believe that the term should for this reason be avoided. Many now prefer to talk more directly about 'machine learning'. This points to important questions about how we conceptualise technology and what hopes we have for it, questions underpinning the ethical issues that concern us.

AI may use human intelligence, some ideal of reason, as a model. It may use human brains, a naturally occurring phenomenon, as a model for technology. It may use technology as a model to try to further our understanding of ourselves. These various approaches reflect different attitudes and assumptions and hopes about technology, and about views of the natural world, of intelligence, and of ourselves. They reflect different levels of ambition. They incite both fear and excitement. Hopes pinned on them range from making incremental improvements to robot lawnmowers, to the transformation of society and of humankind.

The differences of opinion about some of the most outlandish ambitions, such as the development of superintelligence, involve disagreements about the desirability of pursuing such outcomes, about technical feasibility, and about the conceptual coherence of supposing that an intelligence could recursively self-improve without limit to a level far exceeding our intelligence. While some consider superintelligence incoherent, others see it as inevitable.

The singularity The issues concern even the very possibility of our capacities to conceptualise such a possible future. The singularity is a term first coined by John von Neumann in the 1950s describing accelerating technological progress. The term was popularised by Vernor Vinge in 1993 in his essay 'The Coming Technological Singularity: How to survive the post-human era' [2]. He envisaged a time of runaway change over which we have no control, stemming from accelerating improvements to technology as progress is driven not by us, but by the intelligent technologies we have produced. This will create a 'singularity' where our old ways of understanding the world no longer apply, an *event horizon* beyond which we cannot currently see, because the world will be so different from our current world that we cannot imagine what it is like. Some consider that we will be unable to understand a superintelligence. It is always worth including the dates at which certain claims about technology were made. The technology of the 1950s, the era in which von Neumann coined the term 'singularity', now seems so quaint and so primitive that it can be hard to grasp that it nonetheless represented significant progress. (Perhaps there is an event horizon in reverse, which prevents us from being able to imagine how things used to be.)

These debates all concern our powers to comprehend not just the world around us but also the very technology that we ourselves have made, as well as our capacity to recognise intelligence and consciousness, as these may manifest in technology. Note that these debates also concern basic attitudes towards the very possibilities of change and of progress and towards our powers to manipulate and control the world. As we shall see, these questions have long been raised by those working in the philosophy of technology.

AI is embedded in human society   Artificial intelligence is often spoken of as if it is something entirely separate from human beings—created by us, yes, but a discrete entity of its own, something which can be understood, and the boundaries of which can be delineated, without reference to human beings. This will produce a misleading impression, and although in considering ethical issues, we will often need to hone in on certain aspects in isolation, the reference to the wider picture should always be present as a background. AI is always going to be part of some larger system, generally involving other technologies within which it is embedded but also the processes of development, both their technical and human elements, which led up to it and to its applications, both software and hardware [3]. Moreover, not only is AI embedded in sociotechnical systems, much about AI itself is not so much 'artificial' intelligence insofar as it essentially involves human input and work. Human ingenuity produces AI; examples of human intelligence train machine learning; images are coded by human beings [4].

3.2   Comparing AI to Humans

Summary
This section introduces one of the central issues behind many of the questions of AI ethics: the ways in which artificial intelligence is compared, implicitly or explicitly, with human beings and their capabilities. An exercise explores ways in which agency is casually attributed to AI.

We have already noted that many of the ethical questions of AI involve implicit or explicit comparison of humans with AI. Indeed, AI and its success or failure may be conceived in significant part in terms of how well it manages to reproduce or exceed human capabilities. Any such comparisons will involve value assumptions; for example, the claim that AI has exceeded humans on some task involving intelligence will always turn out to involve value assumptions about what constitutes 'better'. Any such comparisons will also always be made against background assumptions and often complex conceptual frameworks that shape how we see (a) humans and (b) machines.

Many have pointed out that how we think of technology can affect how we think of ourselves. Dog owners truly do, it seems, resemble their pets [5]. This provides mild amusement for the human race (although who knows if dogs also get the joke). However, the perceived resemblance of humans to technology may be more pernicious if in reality we are rather different. If we conceive of AI as reproducing human intelligence, perhaps we will think of human intelligence as nothing more than the product of a computer, and perhaps we will think of ourselves as nothing more than computers [6, p. 4]. Perhaps this is an accurate picture. Perhaps not. Conversely, we can project human qualities onto machines. Unless we are aware that this may be happening, then any assessment of AI that involves a comparison with human qualities will be wanting. We may be projecting onto AI a sense of humanity which is not warranted, and maybe projecting onto humanity ideas which more properly belong to machinery or to an inanimate world.

Human individuality and the narrative structures of human lives, with patterns of strength, weakness, resilience, despair, and the limitations of our embodiment, are elements we need to consider. Will such ever be attributed to machines? Consider the fields of sport and music, which involve human skill, perseverance, and training and which have their own standards of excellence. It is almost nonsensical to dream of *replacing* human athletes and gymnasts with machines. For what reason would we wish to do away with humans themselves playing sports? Competitions between machine and machine and between human and machine could be great fun, because a large part of the whole point of sport is achieving good performance, with different degrees of competitiveness, whether your own personal goals, whether in a local team, or in a ferocious international competition.

Limits Some points to note: the precise way in which comparisons are drawn, what is included, what is omitted, and the ways in which we think of the limits of achievement. There is a fine interplay between attempting to go beyond the current limits of the human body and appreciating those limits. Are these always something to be transcended? Or could there be something about uniquely human limits that we wish to retain?

Consider singing. The very limits of the human voice, its individuality, and the capacity for breath are all part of music appreciation. We recognise the character of the individual voice and its qualities and often the character of the person behind the voice. Music appreciation is also often tied to our understanding of the backstory and the people behind the music. Human frailty can add richness to our appreciation. Perhaps this happens too, for some technology, as we show nostalgia for old typewriters, vintage cars, fountain pens, and the like. However, our embodiment is perhaps unique. One of my favourite singers is the contralto, Kathleen Ferrier. Ferrier died of breast cancer, and the treatment she underwent caused osteoporosis. During the interval for her last ever concert, a performance of Gluck's Orpheus and Eurydice at Covent Garden in London, a fragment of her hipbone sheared off [7]. She must have been in excruciating pain. She returned to the stage for the second half of the concert and sang as normal. Human beings can be awesome.

Exercise 1
Artificial intelligence frequently involves attempting to extend human capacities. Are there any occasions on which we would rather have the 'bare human', even if it is 'worse', and if so, why?

Argue for and against the proposition that using 'autotune' to improve one's singing voice, rather than training yourself to sing in tune, is cheating in the same kind of way that doping in sport is cheating. You can generate other examples of your own and consider if you have different response in different cases.

We will repeatedly need to inquire whether AI can approach ethical questions and judgements in the same ways as humans. Many of the ethical questions that concern the use of AI to extend or replace human agency and human beings are shaped by implicit assumptions by which the comparisons between humans and machines are made. One of the recurring questions in AI ethics is the issue of control, and likewise, one of the recurring questions in the philosophy of technology is whether we control technology or whether technology controls us. Hence, to understand the nature of these issues about control, we need to understand both our own agency and that of machines.

The general question of how we compare and contrast human beings to artificial intelligence is thus a major theme in AI ethics. To understand this in more depth, we need to look further at how we think about human nature and at how we conceptualise and value intelligence, which is naturally a major dimension of comparisons, both of which we examine in Chap. 5. Forming a backdrop to this is the question of how we conceptualise, and how we seek to use, technology, the topic of this chapter. First, let us consider how technology may be described in comparison to human beings.

3.2.1   Case Study: Attributing Agency to Humans and to AI

It is often very illuminating to read reports about the use of AI and to consider how agency is attributed and distributed between human and machine elements in the narrative. It is very common for writing to talk as if the AI itself had agency and as if the humans involved lacked agency. Consider the question of the workplace. Even favourable comments about the impact of AI on employment often talk of the workforce passively and may hail the liberating impacts of job automation by referring to jobs as boring, demeaning, or involving drudgery [8]. While not wishing to deny the conditions under which many people work, one could also reasonably consider that describing the work that millions of people do in such terms may also denigrate those who do such work and negatively contrast their agency with the agency that the same articles often impute to machines. People may be described as being 'left behind' by this revolution. A selection of headlines illustrates the issue. 'AI is quietly eating up the world's workforce with job automation' [9]. 'Robots: stealing our jobs or solving labour shortages?' [10]. 'Robots could take over

20 million jobs by 2030, study claims' [11]. This almost makes it sound as if the robots themselves are turning up to workplaces and rudely pushing human employees aside, or simply beating all human candidates at interview. There are of course many articles that attempt to redress the balance.

Exercise 2
Search for any article on a news site, tech journal, or academic journal that talks about any aspect of artificial intelligence or automation in comparison to human agency and consider how language expressing agency is used. Consider how writing may deflect attention away from other sources of agency.

It is good practice to bear such language use in mind whenever you are considering the pros and cons of the use of AI.

3.3 A Brief Introduction to the Philosophy of Technology

Summary
This section outlines some central themes of the philosophy of technology, with the aim of demonstrating the relevance of understanding these issues as a backdrop to questions of AI ethics. A brief survey of the history of this field finds that Plato and Aristotle ask questions about the relationship of technology to nature, such as the question of whether technology should mimic nature or try to exceed it. In the twentieth century, Martin Heidegger examined our use of technology to extract value from nature. His notion of standing reserve is introduced. The question of knowledge in relation to technology is discussed, outlining Ryle's distinction between knowing how and knowing that. We consider how boundary questions arise in relation to technology. Last, we look at the goals of technology and the 'technological fix' and outline the relevance of the issues raised in this section for AI ethics.

3.3.1 Preliminaries

Why look at the philosophy of technology in a book focusing on AI ethics? This section indicates some ways in which debates within the philosophy of technology might shape our understanding of ethical questions. We can also see how some central questions concerning technology were already raised many centuries ago. As so often, it will be to consider whether, to what extent, and how AI raises new issues or fits in with previous concerns and how questions in ethics relate to questions in other areas of inquiry.

First, we make a preliminary observation about the relevance of technology to ethical concerns. If science is descriptive, concerned with producing knowledge about how things are, then technology is concerned with producing artefacts and using tools and instruments to change the world in various ways, and thus, concerned both with making new things and with how things ought to be. It is therefore prescriptive. As such, it is an inherently normative activity, and hence its aims and methods are inherently open to critique.

The normative issues may include questions that do not at first sight appear to be about ethics, such as questions about design aesthetics, ease of use, or efficiency. However, it should be apparent that ethical questions may readily arise. For instance, even a question about the attractiveness of the design of a product may have ethical implications. Is constantly updating the design of a tech product accompanied by great fanfares and publicity a way of selling incremental and largely insignificant changes in said products to a gullible public, at the expense of their wallets, the environment, and the badly paid workers who produce such products? Suppose a product operated in ways that meant the users could easily remain unaware that vast amounts of energy were being expended, and low-paid workers exploited, far away and out of sight? Many other issues raised in the philosophy of technology underlie some fundamental questions in AI ethics.

What is the philosophy of technology? As a field, it is difficult to define, covering a wide range of questions and approaches. Some work focuses on the technology and its characteristics as a practice within engineering and design. This includes work attending to the nature of the artefacts (products) technology produces and work looking at technology as the instrumental control by humans over the world. Other work focuses more on attempting systematic examination of issues such as the meaning of technology for society and culture and the consequences of technology for humanity and for individuals. Some work attempts to address technology in general, whereas much of it also looks at discrete instances of technology and its application.

The field known as philosophy of technology is relatively new, generally credited with having started with the publication in 1877 of Ernst Kapp's book *Grundlinien einer Philosophie der Technik* (*Elements of a Philosophy of Technology*) [12], but philosophical ideas about technology have a much longer history, and indeed, it is often possible to trace how interest in such questions and attitudes towards technology developed historically with developments in technology. We have already looked at some historical examples of concerns regarding what might broadly be called AI, including robots, and we can see broad historical influences on attitudes to technology in general. For example, the rise in interest in alchemy in Latin Europe around the twelfth century led to a fascination with the possibility that humans could tap into and exceed the powers of nature, although later the arts of alchemy were subject to intense critique. The power, fear, and fascination with alchemy have its traces today in many of the different reactions to AI. Francis Bacon, 1561–1626, renowned for his work on scientific method, lived in the period of the Renaissance and had a broadly optimistic view of technology as an endeavour that should be used for the benefit of humanity and the improvement of life. His work *The New Atlantis* envisaged a utopian society full of inventions such as flying machines and submarines [13]. Yet the fruits of the Industrial Revolution were mixed, and it early became apparent to many that some of its consequences were deleterious. Samuel

Butler's *Erewhon* ('nowhere' backwards) presents a utopia directly opposed to Bacon's: machines are banned, following concerns that a race of machines will replace humans [14]. In the twentieth century, however, after the horrors of two world wars and the possibilities of the nuclear bomb, a greater pessimism led to considerable critique of technology visible in the work of philosophers such as Martin Heidegger.

Exercise 3
Write your own AI utopia and AI dystopia. Throw a coin to choose if you write the dystopia or utopia first. Consider what if anything this tells you about your own fears and hopes. Well, this could realistically take months, but you might want to jot down one or two thoughts about what might constitute a dystopia or utopia for you personally.

3.3.2 A Little History

Philosophy of technology was a concern of the ancient Greeks The ancient Greek philosophers such as Plato and Aristotle often discussed techné (craftwork) as the exercise of skill in particular areas, including what we now think of as technology but also activities such as the practice of medicine and the arts [15]. Their frequent discussion of crafts strongly suggested a positive attitude towards practical skills despite their higher valuation of the more abstract life of the mind, and Aristotle indeed used skill in craftwork as an analogy for the development of virtue. Their discussion of craftwork forms a useful introduction to some key themes in the philosophy of technology. We see that discussion of technology involves claims about humans, the world, and the proper relationship between the two.

For Plato, techné is based upon mimicry of nature. The natural world itself was created by the Demiurge, a god who designed the world according to eternal patterns that lie hidden behind the world as we see and experience it. Craftwork is thus similar to nature in that its products are fashioned by someone towards the fulfilment of certain goals. The craftsman exhibits skill in accomplishing the goals of a craft.

   Aristotle, however, drew a contrast between the products of craftwork, artefacts, existing in the domain of poiesis, and the natural world, or the domain of physis [16]. The natural world is teleological, operating towards certain goals or functions, and indeed, each thing within it has its own function towards which it aims. (We look at Aristotle's view of ethics later, which draws upon his views of the function of man.) To this extent, then, the natural world is akin to the products of craftwork, since these are also formed according to certain ends, which will vary according to the craft activity and according to the particularities of context. However, things in the natural world have 'inward causes', and products of craftwork have 'outer causes' put in them by their designer. An 'inward cause' captures the idea that things in the natural world operate according to their own particular ends and move, form, or grow under their own powers. Remember that Aristotle was writing at a time with rather different ideas about physics. An object that falls to the ground when dropped was for Aristotle operating under its own inward cause to seek the ground. Everything has a proper place in the world towards which it strives. So note that in this respect, there is a similarity between biological beings and the purely physical realm—what we tend to call 'inanimate' matter. The question of what distinguishes living beings from non-living beings is one of profound relevance to some of the questions raised by AI. One aspect of the 'inward cause' is that only things in the natural world can reproduce themselves. Inanimate objects cannot, because that would require an inward cause.

Mimicry, metaphysics, and morality We can thus see that certain issues arise with implications for AI. In attempting to develop AI, are we attempting to mimic nature, and if so, in what respects? More on this subject presently. Aristotle's distinction between inward and outer causes may be slightly strange but has an intuitive sense to it. In the context of AI, we can transpose the distinction to the question of autonomy and perhaps also to questions sometimes asked of AI, such as whether it is capable of true creativity or any independent intelligence or thinking, or whether it merely stays entirely within the limits of the inputs of the humans who created it. These metaphysical questions, the categorisation of the world around us, and the delineation of boundaries between categories of existence underpin and shape views on the nature of autonomy and more broadly on the status and value of technological artefacts, including artificial intelligence.

The views of Plato and Aristotle on the natural world may strike many modern readers as unscientific and outmoded and to some even as peculiar but also raise issues that will prove to be essential to comprehending and responding to some claims made about AI. Many religions still of course regard the world as the product of a creator and as made according to certain principles of design, often indeed as good, although on some worldviews, as containing both good and bad forces. The views of Aristotle that the natural world has its own inward causes and that it aims at certain goals seems to imbue it with an agency and purpose. Note that biology also draws heavily on talk of function, and ways of describing and explaining the world frequently attribute some manner of agency. We will look more at concepts of nature in the following section, but for now, note at least two questions relevant to understanding and assessing technology: what impact technology may have on nature and what inspiration it may take from nature are both questions that depend upon what views are taken of nature itself.

Should technology mimic nature or exceed it? The idea that technology takes its inspiration from nature has been common and implicitly rests upon the assumptions that nature displays patterns and regularities that can be copied and recreated, and implicitly, that these are good, or at least, that they have elements that are useful to us. It also tacitly assumes that somehow, nature is not 'enough' for us, although we are so used to how intertwined our lives are with technology that this point is easy to miss. I am reminded of how habitual our technological lives are when hearing small children ask in puzzled wonderment questions such as 'why don't animals wear clothes?' One then is brought into awareness of our utter dependence on technology.

The question of whether technology could reproduce or even exceed nature was brought to the fore with the fascination for alchemy in Europe. The project of turning base metals into gold is one of extracting excess value. The lure of alchemy and the stern denunciations it received are also mirrored in some reactions to the possibilities of advanced AI, especially in the prospect of developing AI that is conscious, or which is thought to exceed humans in some sense: turning base metals into gold may be thought to be a precursor to attempts to turn brute matter into conscious intelligence. (Of course, as explained, not all AI attempts to do anything so ambitious.) Those who ridicule Sir Isaac Newton for his keen pursuit of alchemy, which seems far more like magic than like science to the modern mind, might pause and reflect on their own attitudes to certain scientific and technological endeavours [17]. It may on occasion be useful to consider whether thoughts about 'exceeding' nature are in some way present in discussions of AI, and what their legitimate role is, if any.

The twentieth-century philosopher Martin Heidegger posed the question of the proper use by humanity of nature in his essay, *The Question Concerning Technology* [18]. For Heidegger, the question of the right relationship to technology concerns questions of being. This complex work raises questions about whether in modern technologies humanity has a troubled relationship with nature. There is more than one aspect of technology: an instrumental aspect, as a means to an end, and an anthropological aspect, as a human activity. However, Heidegger warned that we need to manipulate technology in an appropriate manner and that our attempts to control it become ever more important as it develops powers that may defy our attempts to control it [18, p. 5]. So far, so good. Writing in the mid-twentieth century, it is hard not to see what Heidegger means.

Heidegger also saw technology as a form of knowledge, as a means of revealing or uncovering. This aspect of his work is harder to grasp, but he considers that the causes that lead to the creation of technology bring something to being which reveals something to us: something is brought present to us. Hence, something previously concealed is brought forth into 'unconcealment'. This revealing is a form of truth. One way of trying to grasp such a notion is to contrast it with a view that sees artefacts as objects distinct from the material world out of which they are made. In Heidegger's view, it is as if technology, through the craftworker or the technologist, actually works to show something, to reveal something, that was there in the world as potential.

However, Heidegger contrasted traditional technologies with modern technology in terms of how things are brought forth into the world. We can think of this approximately as the claim that formerly this was somehow in alliance with nature. However, modern technology makes demands and challenges nature to go beyond what is wise to demand from it. He considers that modern technology places unreasonable demands on nature, for example, insisting that vast amounts of energy can be extracted and stored for use at will, in contrast to old technologies such as windmills, which simply turn in tune to the weather rather than forcing power out of the wind [18, p. 4]. This is always driving on to the maximum yield at the minimum expense.

Standing reserve   Heidegger used the example of a hydroelectric power plant built into the river Rhine, which he considered to have a 'monstrous' element. The power plant is not built into the Rhine as an old wooden bridge was, but the Rhine is built up into the power plant. He contrasts two aspects of the Rhine: as dammed up into the power plant and as expressed in the art of poetry to the Rhine by the poet Hölderlin. Heidegger uses the term 'standing reserve' for this modern attitude to nature: as something ordered to stand by to be ready for immediate use. The world is there to serve what we demand of it. Other examples are coal mining, where the earth is now revealed as a coal-mining district, and the rigours of modern agriculture, in contrast to the agricultural work of the peasant 'which does not challenge the field'.

Exercise 4: Heidegger's Notion of 'Standing Reserve'
Does Heidegger's notion that modern technology puts unreasonable demands on nature have any resonance with you? This question can be approached by looking at specific examples. Consider the example he uses of a hydroelectric power plant and compare it to his example of an old-fashioned windmill. Is Heidegger being reasonable, or is he extrapolating unfairly from a few examples?

The patchwork of fields and their boundaries of walls and hedges, which were formed from centuries of agriculture, nonetheless likewise transformed the landscape. However, there is presently a strength of feeling among many that technology has gone 'too far' in some often hard-to-express way. As you explore your own views, try to critique them as much as possible, perhaps with help from someone else.

What is a fair critique of a philosopher's ideas? It would be easy to cast aspersions on his examples as implying that erratic energy sources are preferable to reliable ones and hard not to notice that he must have been familiar with the practice of chopping down and storing wood to have a supply of energy throughout the harsh German winter. Consider whether there is any value in his claims, even if the precise examples may not always work.

Could his ideas be brought to bear in considering the expectations of modern computing? Are the expectations that communication is constant, that goods are delivered immediately, and that any question can be answered, every problem solved with technology, and every question in science automatically answered by machine learning—if such are indeed the expectations of AI—are these expectations somehow akin to the expectation that the world should act as a standing reserve? Could some applications of AI in fact operate to reverse any such tendencies?

3.3.3   Knowledge and Technology

The distinction drawn between technology and science is in part because of epistemic differences between them—differences in the nature of the knowledge involved. Naturally, there is a very close relationship because science generally relies upon often very sophisticated technology to make its discoveries. Technology likewise relies upon scientific findings and itself often generates scientific findings in the form of detailed knowledge needed to apply scientific discoveries in particular contexts. We have seen how Heidegger saw technology as a form of knowledge, of an uncovering of the world. However, the aim of science can be characterised as discovery of the world, and technology aims to manipulate the world and to create products. This involves knowledge, but a type of knowledge that many philosophers have claimed to be distinctive.

Aristotle: Five Forms of Knowledge

Aristotle divided the soul into two parts, the rational part and the nonrational part. By 'the soul', Aristotle did not refer to some spiritual substance distinct from the body, but rather used the term to describe the particular organisation of each type of creature—so in this sense, animals had souls too. The rational part of the soul could have knowledge ('virtues of thought'), which Aristotle divided into five different categories [19, Book IV].

Episteme: science or scientific knowledge about the world (although note that Aristotle was writing long before modern scientific methods were established, and episteme referred to broadly 'factual' knowledge about the world)

Techné: knowledge of arts and crafts, the skill needed to execute them

Phronesis: 'prudence' or practical wisdom, knowledge about how to achieve goals in life, such as the general goal to live well (prudence is a standard term still in frequent use but no longer translates very well in English)

Nous: intellect or intuitive apprehension of things, such as first principles and the foundation of knowledge

Sophia: wisdom, a state of perfection which can be reached in respect of any type of knowledge

Note that both techné and phronesis relate to how we as humans act to bring things about in the world, as contrasted to episteme, which concerns the world as it is. This also interestingly makes techné have some similarities with the kind of knowledge needed to achieve the life of virtue. Aristotle drew heavily on the parallel skills of learning to master a craft in his account of how we develop virtues of character.

(continued)

Gilbert Ryle: Knowing How and Knowing That

Gilbert Ryle was a twentieth-century British philosopher who advocated philosophical behaviourism, the theory that the mind could be understood in terms of behaviour alone, which we examine in Chap. 8. Ryle distinguished between two sorts of knowledge: *knowing how* and *knowing that* [20]. The distinction was partly made in response to the views of philosophers who attempted to model all knowledge on propositional knowledge, a proposition being a claim about the world, knowledge claims like, 'Paris has more days of rain each year than London', 'There are no more bananas in the fruit bowl', 'Water contains hydrogen bonds'. These are *knowing that* claims: I *know that* it rains more often in Paris than in London.

Knowing how concerns the ability to do things in the world, hence is relevant to our discussions of technology. It is not necessarily translatable into a series of factual explanations of what was done. Ryle argued that being able to perform an operation does not require that one is able to formulate precisely in words or complete sets of instructions how this is carried out, even though one may be able to detect immediately if the task is being carried out correctly or not, and even if one can teach others by demonstration. For example, a sailor may be excellent at tying complex knots but completely unable to describe precisely how this is done [20, p. 55].

A school friend of mine had recently arrived in the UK from East Africa, and her mother, Mrs. Patel, spoke Gujarati but little English. I would help her mother with English while she taught me Gujarati cooking. As a native English speaker, I could speak grammatically without necessarily being able to explain what rules I was following. As an expert cook, Mrs. Patel never weighed any ingredients but worked by eye and by feel, and her instructions to me consisted mostly of showing me mysterious spices and other ingredients that she would add to recipes with the simple instruction, 'Put!' We got on just fine.

Such examples have relevance to the question of how the way AI operates compares to how human beings operate. One question concerns the issue of transparency and explainability: do I know how a particular instance of AI works, if I can use it effectively for specific purposes? What would this 'knowing how' consist of in specific cases? Does it matter whether or not I have knowledge that it operates in particular ways? Recall that certain efforts to explain how AI works do not attempt to look inside the 'black box' (see Sect. 2.4.2).

Or consider this. Suppose an advanced robot closely observed Mrs. Patel's cooking and then drew up a long list of precise rules to replicate her delicious recipes, which it then successfully executed. The robot then prints out a full list including, for instance, the precise weight of all the spices and the precise cooking times and temperatures. Does the robot then 'know' how to cook even better than my friend's mother? Hint: this answer seems to me absurd, but why? I am not at all sure. Perhaps you have a different reaction.

Ryle's distinction between knowing that and knowing how can be in part characterised by saying that 'knowing how' rests upon tacit knowledge, that is, it's a form of knowledge that may not, and perhaps cannot, be articulated in speech or other formalised methods. A society and culture that values intellectual skills and formal and overt expression of knowledge may thus downplay the value of tacit knowledge, of 'knowing how', and of technological or craft skills in general. The ancient Greeks who valued intellectual pursuits very highly—indeed Plato and Aristotle saw the life of the philosopher as being the best—valued craftwork much less. Likewise, it is easy to see similar attitudes around us, especially in industrial economies and in the education system, although as ever the situation is complex. Bear this in mind when considering applications of AI, robotics, and other technologies to replace certain types of jobs. We discuss the relationship between epistemology and ethics further in Chap. 7.

Exercise 5 and Reflection
To what extent might attitudes towards the value of craft knowledge be explained by the value placed on formalising our knowledge in language (including in the category of language formal expressions of meaning such as software, maths, and musical notation)?

Might this have an impact on how AI is valued in certain applications?

Might fears of the difficulty of articulating and explaining the decision-making in machine learning be (partially) explained by such a view?

Could it be that some skills are not amenable to formalisation in language due to the very complexity of the skill and to the limits of language, rather than to some lack on the part of those who possess a skill but who cannot fully explain all the steps needed to execute it?

3.3.4   The 'Technological Fix'

If technology is conceived as a way of achieving an externally specified goal, then an assumption might arise that any goal or issue requires a technological solution. Furthermore, any shortcomings in technology might be seen as simply needing more technology—the 'technological fix' or technological solutionism, which we noted in Sect. 2.5.2 [21, 22]. Those immersed in particular branches of technology may incline towards the kinds of solutions that their familiar field provides. In the words popularly attributed to Abraham Maslow, in possession only of a hammer, everything looks like a nail. However, some problems may be best left alone, and in some cases, the cure is worse than the disease. Some 'problems' are only problems from certain perspectives. The phenomenon of the technological fix may be part of what seems to drive the impetus of technological development. Ironically, the more buggy the tech is, the more it will require fixing, and its own inadequacy can help to drive the very appearance of its success. Certain terms capture these issues in specific contexts.

Medicalisation is a concept introduced into the sociological critique of the practice and powers of medicine in the 1970s in works such as Ivan Illich's *Medical Nemesis* [23]. It refers to the assumption that a problem a patient has is best dealt with within the context of medicine using standard medical techniques such as surgery or drugs. However, this is often based upon assumptions about aetiology and the potential for remedies that leave much out of the picture, in particular, very often, social, psychological, environmental, and economic factors. Including a fuller analysis of causation may produce a better, more effective, more humane solution. There are well-known debates within branches of medicine such as psychiatry where such issues loom especially large [24]. The notion of an iatrogenic harm, where ill health is caused by the practice of medicine itself, may perhaps be useful to borrow for considering the practices of AI.

The practice of medicine, medical knowledge, and the construction of risk One of the chief ways in which medical science and technology have advanced is in producing vastly increased amounts of medical knowledge, both in the form of general scientific understanding and in the provision of personalised information to patients. It is especially pertinent to highlight this in relation to AI because one of the current success stories is the contribution of machine learning to improving the interpretation of medical imaging. The use of monitoring and tracking technologies for individual health monitoring is also becoming widespread [25]. AI is contributing to a pre-existing trend of increased personal medical information. Prior examples include the routinisation of scans in pregnancy and the increased availability of genetic information. Hence, it is essential to consider what lessons can be learned. Researchers and commentators have noted how increased knowledge, together with potentially easy and routine access to such knowledge, can have profound influences on how individuals see themselves, their medical risk, and their responsibilities. For example, the very experience of pregnancy and motherhood can be profoundly impacted [26]. The availability of genetic knowledge may also have weighty ramifications for individuals, for family relationships, and for attitudes towards responsibility in regard to reproduction [27, 28].

These issues are all relevant to questions about AI, which routinely uses massive amounts of data, including medical information, enables the collection of much personal data, and is used to facilitate the speedy production of both scientific and personal information. Naïve assumptions about the value of scientific information may not readily translate to understanding the value of the personal information for the individuals concerned.

In Sect. 2.4, we looked at several examples of the use of AI, including some for medical diagnosis, the use of machine learning to assist with the interpretation of medical images, and the EDoN project, which aims to develop digital tools for the early diagnosis of dementia. Consider now some further issues about the use of AI to collect and interpret data. Many of the early signs of dementia can manifest as subtle changes in behaviour, such as changes in one's gait [29]. Likewise, indications that dementia is progressing can be found in small behavioural and language changes [30]. Hence, tracking technologies may pick these up when they are below the level at which even a reasonably astute observer may notice them. There are multiple implications for how people see themselves and understand such data, which need to be understood as we process the implications of such technology on our lives [31].

Exercise 6
Consider the implications of the production of knowledge about the link between gait and a degenerative disease such as dementia, for the scientific community and for individuals. Consider how you might think about the information collected from a tracking device that you are using to measure your exercise and sporting goals, if it became clear to you that this could be used to diagnose a progressive and serious disease. Do your attitudes towards information collected for one purpose shift when it can be used for a different purpose? Does this information now become 'medical' information? Does it make a difference to your attitude towards privacy?

The practice of medicine also serves as a clear example to illustrate the question of identifying valid goals of technology, for although the concept of disease and illness may seem clear enough in many cases, drawing a boundary between health and disease is not always straightforward, and indeed, defining health in its absence is easier than providing a good account of what it is to live in full health [32]. These issues again are particularly clearly illustrated in psychiatry and psychological medicine, where the classification of psychological illnesses is fraught with controversy [33]. These issues have relevance to the question of transhumanism and human enhancement, areas with clear links to AI to which we will briefly consider in Chap. 11. For something to count as an 'enhancement', it has to be better in some respect, but how is this measured?

In an age where there is 'an app for everything', the goals at which the technologies of AI aim may not always be clear. This may be exacerbated by factors such as intense marketing and advertising (which AI itself enables via techniques such as targeted advertising), design features, and constant upgrades of much technology. Furthermore, the very success of many technologies, especially AI, may generate problems. The capacity to provide fast, cheap, and efficient solutions to issues and to generate vast amounts of data and information may be a two-edged sword.

The goals of technology If AI is attempting to enhance or replace human agency, thought, and decision-making, then we have to ask some simple questions before we can assess the technology. What counts as a genuine enhancement? The quest is explicitly value-laden. In addition, if we are replacing humans, there are two parts to the question: first, is what is provided by the technology an adequate replacement? This would involve both careful assessment of the technology and careful comparison with human capabilities, as well as a full understanding of what task is being undertaken. This is often not a straightforward matter, as many examples we shall look at will illustrate. Second, why replace humans in the specific task at hand? And even if a good reason can be offered, we have to ask who benefits, and to assess any costs and benefits for the humans who are no longer doing the task.

Despair at the extent to which technology controls us, together with a view of technological determinism, that the progress of technology is inevitable and that it will be impossible to restrain it in anything other than temporary measures, is tragically expressed in the so-called Unabomber Manifesto, *Industrial Society and Its Future* by Ted Kaczynski, who engaged in a terrorism campaign organised from his tiny cabin in Montana [34]. It is one of its tragedies that Kaczynski came to the conclusion that it was necessary to murder and maim in his 17-year bombing campaign to force people to take notice of his ideas, for there are many who have also expressed overlapping and indeed similar views about the problems of technology without advocating violent solutions.

3.3.5 Boundary Questions and Ethical Conundrums: Technology, Metaphysics, Ontology, and Ethics

We have seen in this brief overview how the philosophy of technology raises questions in metaphysics, concerning views on the fundamental nature of the world, of humans, and of technology, including questions about ontology, which were introduced in discussing the Indigenous AI position paper in Sect. 2.9. Many of the details of such claims, and disputes between them, concern how we draw boundaries between categories. These claims can help to bring into relief some of the questions raised by AI today. One set of questions is whether AI does, or might, erode any clean distinction between artefacts and humans, and whether and why this might matter. We have seen already in our brief foray into history that things that cross boundaries and confuse categories of being evoke fear and fascination. The very idea of a monster is that of a hybrid being inhabiting the twilight realm between two domains. Indeed, the very word 'twilight', frequently used to connote something spooky, is exactly in that zone between two worlds. Recall Mori's notion of the uncanny valley introduced in Sect. 2.5.2 [35]. More recent reviews of empirical evidence have found mixed results and a more nuanced understanding of when this phenomenon might occur [36].

Exercise 7

Search online for photos and videos of robots of various kinds. Can you identify a reaction of eeriness in any of them similar to Mori's description of the uncanny valley? Can you classify other robots as appealing, cute, etc.? Compare your reactions to others if you are doing this in class.

How might knowing about the 'uncanny valley' impact your reactions to robots?

Does a phenomenon such as the uncanny valley apply to any other uses of AI?

Exercise 8

Is concern about such a boundary phenomenon just a matter of being 'spooked out', or something more substantive? Should we reject these 'creepy' feelings when considering ethics? Outline reasons for and against.

Such boundary questions are often the most heated questions of value and ethics, where the most confusing differences of opinion and debates between opponents whose views seem to slide right past each other often occur. For some, it is simply a fascinating question of technology whether AI might attain the status akin to living beings. For others, it is a profoundly ethical question. Understanding that strong views and puzzlement at the views of others often accompany such boundary questions may not help to resolve them, but it does help to account for the intensity of different positions and the frequent lack of progress in resolving disputes. The development of 'full autonomy', however that is described, can perhaps approximate having what Aristotle called an 'inward cause' and certainly projections ahead to scenarios where some superintelligent artificial general intelligence 'takes off' and is able to recursively self-improve would pass muster as having an inward cause. There are many projections to a future AI that can reproduce itself, although some such projections are poorly specified since the identity criteria of individuation may be absent.

Purity and Danger: Mixing Linen and Wool

Among the many rules in the Hebrew Bible (the Old Testament), some of those which have provoked the greatest perplexity involve prohibitions on mixing different kinds of substances: not mixing linen and wool (Leviticus 19.19 and Deuteronomy 22.11), not cooking an animal in its mother's milk (Exodus 23.19, 34.26, Deuteronomy 14.21), or not planting two kinds of seed together (Deuteronomy 22.9). Note that there is also provision for recognition of the role of the marginals (e.g. in leaving the margins of cultivated fields for the poor, Leviticus 19.9–10).

There are differences of opinion regarding the meaning and purpose of these rules. They may *seem* like the same kind of rule which we regard as ethical, such as rules against murder and theft. However, ethical rules are more readily understood as relevant to the well-being of humans (and in some cases animals), whereas these purity laws seem baffling to many, or elicit a range of diverse interpretations that leave many none the wiser. One broad way of interpreting them is in terms of symbolically marking the cultural and linguistic importance of maintaining clarity in a conceptual framework used for describing and understanding the world, and hence of vital importance to understanding the world view of the culture.

Purity thinking is pervasive in human culture and behaviour. The anthropologist Mary Douglas is one person who has explored these concepts in her classic study on dirt, *Purity and Danger* [37]. Dirt, Douglas concludes, is

(continued)

'matter out of place', although different individuals and different societies have often very diverse views on what counts as dirt and of what level of cleanliness is sufficient.

Many have a 'baffled' response to such purity rules. Such responses may go along with personality differences characterised by thinkers such as Jonathan Haidt. For some individuals, various forms of purity are a part of the set of values from which moral beliefs are formed and justified, whereas others make little or no reference to purity as a value (see also Sect. 7.2.4). It may be useful to draw upon such ideas when considering certain questions in AI ethics, such as attitudes to crossing boundaries between human and machine, and attitudes to the kinds of work we want AI to do.

3.3.6   Some Implications for the Conduct of AI Ethics

If technology is instrumental, with ends specified externally to it, this is precisely one reason why it is essential that those working outside of any field of technology should be able to have a say regarding its values. However, values can be implicit in the ways in which technology attempts to achieve its goals. Technologists themselves are unlikely to be neutral agents serving only the goals of those who have commissioned this or that piece of technology. Those working in any area are likely to enter it at least in part because it aligns with their interests and values, and immersion within a field is likely to induct a person into explicit and implicit values. Humans can become highly motivated towards purposes and chase goals that might on reflection merit some critique.

This is relevant to ethical questions of technology, including AI, in several ways. It suggests that those working on design should reflect on their goals and assumptions, which of course they may have a limited capacity to do within the remit of a particular organisation with its own aims. The benefits of a multidisciplinary and diverse team to work on a design problem should be apparent here. The experience of those working in other fields of professional ethics, and research within the social sciences about ethical judgement, would suggest that those who belong to more than one social group may have the perspective of a wider or different set of values and priorities on which to draw, which may help to mitigate the insufficiently critical pursuit of certain goals or of particular methods of achieving them [38]. This also means that those from outside of the field of technology entirely have a valid role in assessment.

Collaboration and dialogue in ethics and technology A certain conundrum arises. There is certainly a need for detailed technical expertise in addressing questions in AI ethics. There is a need for close collaboration and understanding between those with different viewpoints and roles. However, working in close collaboration with those who are dedicated to the development of technology may mean that one may lose a certain critical edge and acquire implicit values that impact the design and appraisal of end goals. They may share a certain basic assumption about certain values and goals. They may come to adopt certain views by the familiarity of engaging with those involved in technological development. The achievements of one's colleagues can be exciting, and it may be hard to wish them well with their endeavours while simultaneously subjecting them to radical critique. Consider, for example, the case of human reproductive technologies. Those opposed to practices such as gamete donation and research on human embryos, for whatever reasons, may be unlikely to join any internal ethics committees where such practices are assumed. A critic might consider that any examination of ethics in such a context would be merely fiddling with details.

AI technology is heavily reliant on corporate resources and business practices. Universities and other institutions are in a relationship of dependency with big tech, creating many conflicts of interest in a complex web of relationships [39]. This then speaks to the necessity for a mixed economy of voices in AI ethics (or indeed in any area of technology), including views of more severe critics and voices from civil society groups. It also alerts us to the perpetual question in ethics of knowing and understanding our own values and motivations.

3.4   Technology and Attitudes Towards Nature

Summary
Attitudes towards nature are often deeply felt and can have profound implications for how we view technology and its uses and abuses. Likewise, developments in both science and technology can in turn influence how we think of nature. Attitudes towards technology and towards the place of humans in the world are often shaped by an imagined time or golden age without the ills of technology. Large cultural differences abound in this area, which we cannot cover in full.

We have seen that attempts to explain and understand technology make frequent reference to the natural world. Different ways of understanding the natural realm and of how it is or is not differentiated from the realm of human activity will impact upon how technology is understood and assessed. Hence, it will be illuminating to consider the cultural, philosophical, and often religious worldviews that shape attitudes to nature, attitudes that are often assumed and implicit and yet that can play such an influential role in forming value judgements. The boundary between the natural and the artificial is often charged with meaning.

A two-way process Just as attitudes towards nature help shape views of science and technology, likewise developments in science and technology influence how we think of nature. Landscapes we think of as 'natural' may be shaped by centuries of human habitation, agriculture, and hunting. The growth in scientific understanding of the human body and of disease has had a profound impact upon our understanding of the origins of ill health and of attitudes towards its cause and our potential powers to heal and what bodily experiences and conditions are 'natural', to be endured or overcome. The underlying models with which we think of nature are also influenced by developments in science and technology, in ways that might mean we are nudged towards thinking that contemporary technologies are in harmony with nature. For example, William Paley (1743–1805) famously argued that the world had been designed by God, but for our purposes, note the analogy he used: that of a clock [40]. Of course, he was not pointing to the ways in which wind-up clocks fail to keep time accurately. He was using an analogy of the universe as a whole as if it worked mechanically, according to an ordered and regular mechanism, based upon the technology of the day. Likewise, currently, in the age of computing, the brain is sometimes modelled as a computer, and physics may be modelled in terms of information.

The scientific method itself makes certain assumptions about the natural world, that it follows law-like regularities, and in addition, that these regularities can be described and understood by us using reason and mathematics. Without this assumption, we might well see scientific journal articles end by declaring, 'let's face it, it's just a mystery', and all research in the area coming to a halt. To assume we can understand the world scientifically is a rather bold assumption, especially for those with a materialist bent who view humans as nothing other than the products of a series of random events in the course of evolution. One can marvel at this, wondering what it was about our evolutionary origins that necessitated the human brain to evolve in ways that enabled us to understand relativity theory, advanced mathematics, and string theory. (Well, that enabled *some* of us understand these things!) However, this assumption is not universally held.

Regularity, design, and beauty The assumption that we will be able to understand the regularities of nature could simply be a heuristic device, a pragmatic guiding assumption making science and technology possible, justified by their considerable success. However, often, although again not universally, many cultures and world-views have considered that the regularities of the universe speak to a design put in there by some intelligence. Alongside the wish to explain the order we apparently see in the world, it is commonly a wish to explain its perceived beauty. Indeed, many hard-headed scientists believe that the regularities and patterns they observe are part and parcel of this beauty, and there is a debate about whether the beauty of a scientific or mathematical theory is indeed any indicator of its truth [41].

Human ingenuity being what it is, philosophers and theologians have come up with every conceivable variation on such a claim, including ideas that the creator of the universe set it going and left it, or that the creator is a necessary part of its maintenance, or that the creator is not bound by the regularities he (or whatever the correct pronoun is) produced and can intervene to amend these at will.

We need not concern ourselves here with the details, other than to observe the link with answers to the question: is the universe good, bad, a mixture, or just neutral? We see deeply held and often contrasting attitudes to the world around us, many of them marked with expressions of awe. John Ruskin, among others, wrote eloquently of the concept of the sublime in response to great structures of nature that seem to dwarf mere mortals [42]; the poet Alfred, Lord Tennyson wrote of 'nature, red in tooth and claw' [43]; and the poet and artist William Blake wrote of the 'Tyger, tyger, burning bright, in the forest of the night, what immortal hand or eye, could frame thy fearful symmetry', yet notes stark contrasts in nature when he writes, 'Did he who made the lamb make thee?' [44]. The Romantics often praised nature in conscious opposition to what they saw as an overly rational approach to the world but nonetheless often found not just majesty but terror [45]. Very varying attitudes towards nature are found in different individuals and at different times: for example, Lao Tzu wrote, 'Nature does not hurry, yet everything is accomplished' [46], which contrasts strongly with the fear and anxiety expressed by others. However, what seems constant is some attribution of value, whether of mystery, awe, terror, or hope to nature.

Such attitudes of value towards the natural world are frequently present even in those who profess no religion and consider their worldview entirely based on reason and science. For some, these values arise from objective features of the world itself; for others, they are based entirely upon human assessment. However, whatever their origin, these attitudes will profoundly influence how we judge human's use of technology to make use of the world's resources and to alter the world. This often assumes that the world can be improved via the use of technology. Teleological views of the world understand it as striving to complete or fulfil some purpose. Will nature be enough, or does it need assistance from us in completing this purpose? Surprisingly, perhaps, there are those within AI who appear to take a teleological view and who see humanity as having a critical role in advancing the purpose of the universe. We will examine such views in Chap. 11.

A time and place in nature without technology? Even for those who consider technology to have an important place, it is common for there to be cultural myths about some 'golden age' where humans live in harmony with nature, technology was scarce or absent, and life was provided for abundantly without the need for labour. The Garden of Eden, which the first humans, Adam and Eve, inhabited in plentiful abundance before being expelled for breaking God's commands, is an obvious example. The ancient Greeks likewise had similar visions. Empedocles describes a time when humans were free from toil, there was abundant fruit, and all the animals were tame. It was human's slaughter of animals that caused our fallen state and the destruction of this idyllic world. The Taoist Chuang Tzu lamented the passing of a virtuous age where 'men lived in common with the birds and beasts' in the fourth century BCE. A Cherokee myth held that humanity lived once in perfect harmony not with just animals but also with plants, which could speak.

There is also often a vision of a future state of peace towards which we strive. The book of Isaiah looks forward to a 'peaceable Kingdom', when 'The wolf also shall dwell with the lamb, and the leopard shall lie down with the kid; and the calf and the young lion and the fatling together; and a little child shall lead them' (Isaiah 11:6) [47]. Such visions of a future state can also be relevant in considering visions of futurologists in imagining AI, to which we shall return. There are also visions of space outside the reach of technology, in notions of the wild and of wilderness as a space left over on our planet, and indeed in space, free from the impact of humanity. Many poets and writers, such as Thoreau, Emerson, the romantic poets, and even John Stuart Mill, have written of the need for time within nature [48–50]. It is interesting to consider whether some reservations about AI derive from its global and sometimes seemingly totalising impact on the planet [3].

Despotic ruler or kindly dominion? Within contemporary debates about technology, including within debates about the ethics and social and political impact of AI, we can see two very contrasting poles, which echo and repeat enduring divisions and controversies: the view of humanity as despot and despoiler of nature versus the view of humanity as caretaker of nature. It has often been claimed that Western attitudes of mastery over nature that have led to its despoilment stem from Genesis 1: 26, where God makes humanity in his own image and gives them dominion over all creatures, then later in Genesis 2:20, Adam, the first man, named all the living creatures. This has been charged with being the root source of Western attitudes of domination of nature and an assumption that nature is there for our total control and use, leading up to our current problems with the environment and industrialisation. However, it has been closely argued that the interpretation implying that humans were given despotic, absolute rule over nature ignores much textual and other evidence that humanity was intended to govern nature with care and act as a guardian or good shepherd. For instance, it is clear that God pronounced the earth and its inhabitants to be 'good' before humans were created. John Passmore provides a nuanced discussion in his book, *Man's Responsibility for Nature*, although many more voices and opinions have been added to these debates in recent decades [51]. Nonetheless, acting as if we are entitled to use nature as we see fit is indeed common.

The suggestion that humanity is somehow a ruler over nature presents us with the question of what our place in the natural world is, and indeed, what our nature as humans is. This is a critical issue for questions of AI ethics and will be discussed further in Chap. 5.

Nature, Medicine, and Technology
It is noticeable that often new technology is justified in first use through potential application in medicine, or that its application in medicine is highlighted as a justifying benefit. For example, the company Neuralink is developing a broad bandwidth brain interface which expresses the hope that the technology will enable the expansion of how we interact with each other, the world, and ourselves, but which aims at initial application in people with paralysis to help them regain independence in communication and expression [52].

(continued)

The use of machine learning in neural rendering technology to create 'digital humans', which realistically reproduce particular human beings, their mannerisms, and voice, is being developed by the MOTUS lab (motuslab.org), a part of the University of Sydney and a part of the Disruption Research Group. It is being presented as a means of improving quality of life for survivors of serious strokes, enabling them to interact with others via a digital version which represents their appearance and ability to speak prior to the stroke [53]. However, there are multiple potential other applications, such as 'digital de-aging'.

Within medicine itself, new, experimental, and perhaps risky techniques are often justified by reference to 'the desperate case' [54], and there is a sense in which any use of technology regarding ill health can be seen to be urgent, or of especially great importance, in comparison to most other uses. The question will arise often if these worthy medical uses are the slippery slope to wider acceptance of a technology which might otherwise have received a less enthusiastic reception.

However, perhaps another reason for the readiness to consider new technologies within a medical context comes from the very way in which we think of health and disease. A teleological view of nature sees it as striving in some way towards certain ends. It is virtually impossible to talk of biology without reference to functioning. In the realm of living organisms, we then see many examples of functioning which do not fit the normal developmental picture, and which may shorten the lifespan and overall functioning of the organism.

Some worldviews give humans as having some role in helping to bring about the proper journey of the world to its full potential. The area of medicine, and human intervention to improve health and restore full functioning, seems one where the role of technologies of one sort or another seems ideally suited not just from a moral and compassionate standpoint, but conceptually, in fitting with some of the fundamental ways in which we understand biology.

Exercise 9

Neuralink claims that it is pushing at the boundaries of engineering and states that its first goal is to enable independence for people suffering from paralysis by enabling communication and interaction with technology via interfaces implanted into the brain [55]. Given the current state of ethics for research on human subjects, it is in fact hard to know how it could ever get permission to implant one of its devices into the brain of a healthy volunteer. Do you think a healthy volunteer should be allowed to consent to such an intervention? Are there any potential dangers of a 'slippery slope' from the use of this technology from severe medical cases to wider use?

3.5 The Implicit Values of Technology

Summary
This section draws out some of the implicit values commonly attributed to technology. These will form a backdrop to many of the comparisons made between human and machine intelligence. These include assumptions about our capacity to know the world and to control the world; the assumption that speed is a prima facie good; assumptions concerning the nature and value of efficiency; assumptions about the value of consistency and uniformity; and assumptions about the neutrality of technology.

We have seen how some thinkers, such as Plato, considered that technology (craftwork) attempts to mimic nature, to apply the lessons of nature in places where nature itself has not used them, and to suit our purposes, perhaps to take powers inherent in nature and 'ramp them up', as it were. It is certainly the case that technology uses the findings of science about how the world works. Technology is often concerned with improving human performance, for example, by extending our reach, our strength, our stamina, or our speed. Different technologies used in different instances will of course have particular advantages over humans, and in assessing technologies and their use, we need to assess what is gained and what is lost.

However, the overtly stated purposes and advantages of using technology in specific instances may not capture the whole picture. The assessment of technology must involve looking at both intended and unintended impacts. There are often implicit or assumed values in the use of technology and sometimes an assumption that technology, per se, will improve upon things—the 'technological fix' assumption we looked at in Sect. 3.3.4. Articulating these assumptions can be illuminating. Focusing on the advantages of technology can help to ensure that we do not lose sight of what might be lost by marginalising or excluding the use of humans.

Knowledge: First, we have already considered the assumption that we can in fact know the world, and perhaps that we can know it in full. The value of knowledge may seem so obvious that it can be hard to articulate why we value it, other than as a means to enable us to achieve other goals. However, it's a driving assumption of much AI in particular, not just that knowledge is good, but that more knowledge is better. We consider this further at various points in the book.

Control: Again, we have already seen that technology is grounded on an assumption that control of the world is possible, but it is where it leads that controversies arise: that control is good, that more control the better, that the world is imperfect, and that it is a human moral imperative to improve it.

Speed: It is often assumed that technology improves upon human performance by processing more data, getting tasks completed faster, and so on. This is undoubtedly a chief advantage of much technology in general and of AI in particular, especially in regard to processing vast amounts of data. The quest for speed in tech does not apply in all cases: I have never seen any evidence that people want sex robots in order to be able to have sex extremely quickly, although humans never cease to surprise me so I could be mistaken. However, if the sex robot example is laughingly obvious as soon as it is pointed out, there are other tasks where it may not be so obvious. These include many examples of human contact. For instance, it has been suggested that advanced robots could work as care assistants in tasks such as delivering medicines on a hospital ward, and the COVID-19 pandemic had led to an increase in such suggestions [56]. However, although there may be some advantages to the completion of necessary tasks, for the patients, such instances provide a point of human contact at a vulnerable time of their lives. So speed may be a value, but perhaps not be the only value to consider.

Speed, Technology, and Nursing Care

Hospital wards are busy places where many staff with multiple roles are simultaneously performing tasks for a large number of different patients with varying needs. There are targets to be met, such as completing medication rounds, delivering food, and blood pressure and other checks. Staff are under pressure to meet certain deadlines and to keep records of certain tasks and events, such as the necessity of recording adverse events such as falls.

There is great interest in the contribution of technology to improve the efficiency of how hospital wards are run. However, the point of view of the patient may be rather different. This may be especially the case for patients who have any difficulties in communicating or in understanding and interpreting what is expected of them, as hospital patients. A meal 'efficiently delivered' may be one aspiration; to a patient, it may be a chance for a brief chat and some interaction with the person delivering it. We considered in Chap. 2 the example of a robot assistant for an elderly person who might help with reminders about medication. Such tasks are often envisaged as if it has more in common with putting a coin in a slot machine, than in helping or persuading another human being to have sufficient trust to place a pharmaceutical product in their mouths and swallow [57]. We consider such issues again in Chap. 10 in considering the future of work.

Likewise, sometimes the speed at which tasks are performed can itself produce new issues. The speed at which data can be processed can provide us with a weight of information that can be used to achieve good or ill effects. We can readily grasp some of the issues by slightly altering the previous sentence: the speed at which data can be processed can provide *them* with a weight of information that can be used to achieve good or ill effects. So much depends upon who 'they' are. Likewise, the expectation that things we want will be delivered immediately may have advantages, of course, but could have a corrosive impact on our personalities. Might we become petty tyrant despots, a world of mini-aristocrats clicking their fingers and expecting the world to jump?

Exercise 10

Consider how technologies that you use in everyday life—whether out of choice or necessity—speed up various tasks. Consider the pros and cons and any wider effects of increasing expectations of speed.

Time, Technology, Humans, and the Importance of Rhythms

A major reason for the use of technology is its impact on time. It can enable things to be done faster and often enables work and other tasks to be performed with less attention to the clock and the rhythms of the working day. You can write an email at 5.30 p.m., and set it to send at 6.45 a.m. the next day, to fool your boss into believing that you start work early. One reason for deploying such tricks is indeed in response to the demand to be always 'on'. Whatever the pluses and minuses, technology's operation can be quite counter to the rhythms of human life. The impact of AI on the interactions and rhythms of our lives may have profound implications. We follow rhythms of varying types, physical, biological, and cultural: those set by the seasons, by our circadian rhythms, and by our culture and its traditions.

The study of rhythms may add an interesting dimension to studies of technology. Various philosophers and sociologists have investigated them, perhaps the best known being Henri Lefebvre in his work *Rhythmanalysis* [58].

Efficiency   The notion of speed quickly leads us to the notion of efficiency. We may use technology because we assume it's more efficient. Several issues are raised here.

First, it is often not more efficient to use technology for specific tasks, but we can easily get so tied up with the habitual use of technology we forget that some tasks are faster and easier without it. A simple example: have you ever struggled with a printing problem, even something as simple as sorting out jammed paper, to print out a message for the office notice board that would have taken 20 s to write out by hand? Think of some examples for yourself over the next few days.

Second, what precisely do we mean by efficiency? It is usually defined as the ability to do something without wasting materials, time, or effort. Hence, there will be a trade-off between these in assessing efficiency. The time used may not be one's own, and the materials and energy wasted may be out of sight. Economic measures of efficiency often dominate, even in instances where this skews values, such as in healthcare or the arts [59]. The measure of efficiency also requires that the outputs are also given a measure so that comparisons are possible. However, this poses considerable value problems that manifest in a variety of ways. For example, the efficiency of healthcare may be measured in terms of quality adjusted life-years (QALYS), a controversial and complex issue [60]. Efficiently distributing resources may lead to some decisions that appear inhumane.

Third, *who* values efficiency in particular contexts, and why? A task can be done efficiently and thus valued by some, but the perspective of others may differ. Take the example above of the delivery of medicines. Efficiency in admitting someone to hospital when needed, diagnosing a condition, and prescribing treatment is extremely valuable from the point of view of the hospital, the staff, and the patients. Efficiency in completing nursing and care tasks is also extremely valuable from the point of view of hospital administrators. The staff may have mixed views: efficiency targets may be a source of satisfaction but also of stress in the rush to complete and in explanations of any failures. A patient, likewise, may value efficiently being brought a meal but not value that the person bringing it immediately rushes off to the next patient.

Consistency and uniformity These can be a great benefit of technology. However, again, it's not necessarily what we want. The consistency in the mass production of objects since the dawn of the Industrial Revolution has served values such as safety and reliability. However, it has highlighted the loss of the personal, the idiosyncratic, and the found. One prediction of the increase in the automation of work is that there will be a rise in jobs involving hand-made and personalised objects.

There is also a potential downside of consistency and uniformity in using technologies such as AI in information processing and knowledge discovery. One advantage can be uniformity across a wide system. However, suppose that there is an error in the system. The very difference of opinion and outcome that may arise with human shortcomings may be a virtue in some circumstances in providing a way of correcting errors. Indeed, this can be one very good reason to resist the development of any universal code or guidance on ethics for AI. We may simply be universally wrong.

An example: AI is being developed which will automatically translate accents for use in situations such as with call centre workers [61]. There is an obvious advantage in ensuring that a person's speech and accent can be clearly understood over the phone. However, critics point out that the slightly robotic voice that is produced using this AI makes the speaker sound like a white American [62]. A clearer example of the dominance of American culture within part of the technology world and the imposition of cultural uniformity with the aid of AI is hard to find. Likewise, automatic editing tools may impose subtleties of American usage onto the English language, which has rich and varying forms in different parts of the world, and may eliminate from texts words and phrases which are formally redundant but were placed for emphasis, prioritising a purely formalistic notion of meaning over a more human-centred form of communication.

Technology and Perceived Standards of Excellence: A True Story
Not so long ago, I was due to give a presentation on AI ethics at a major technology event. I was asked to submit my PowerPoint slides in advance. One of the points I wished to make concerned how technology may enable us to do certain things 'better' than before, but in ways that introduce standards of 'excellence' without due thought to our original aims, standards which may be entirely unnecessary. I intended to illustrate this with the very example of PowerPoint itself. The PowerPoint presentations at this technology conference were truly stunning. Many must have taken considerable effort. However, did this always truly add anything? My slides were intentionally sparse, and I inserted a slide of a hand-drawn picture of a computer, to make the point that in this context, a rough hand-drawing does the job just fine.

When I clicked onto the relevant slide, I discovered that the technicians had diligently removed the slide of my own sloppy hand-drawn computer and replaced it with a slide of a perfectly accurate, beautifully neat, computer-drawn computer. Just exactly what I didn't need.

Neutrality Closely linked to qualities of consistency and uniformity, the use of technologies such as AI may have the advantage over humans of a certain neutrality, perhaps captured under the term 'objectivity', or the like: the use of AI may be thought to get around human failings such as slips of concentration and emotional involvement and bias. Of course, AI can also be very biased, as has already been mentioned (Sect. 2.4.3). A computerised system can follow rules according to set inputs. However, this is precisely one of the problems in certain settings where individual discretion and human judgement may be needed for anomalous cases where 'the exception proves the rule'. It is a general problem in any bureaucratic system, but it is certainly possible that the assumption that an AI-driven system will be an improvement on the fallibility of humans may produce not fewer problems but simply a different set of problems. Questions related to these issues recur frequently in AI ethics.

Technology and us Some of the implicit values of technology and ways of thinking may be about the general models used to conceptualise the world: How our use of technology may shape how we think both of technology and of ourselves. We have already seen how developments in science and technology can impact how we understand the world at large. Might this happen to how we see ourselves?

Joseph Weizenbaum, the computer scientist behind the Eliza project, remarked that those whose daily lives consist of being slaves to machines start to believe that humans themselves are also machines [63]. However, is this process always a one-way ticket to dehumanisation?

There are fascinating questions of feedback loops between how we value technology and how we value what it is that technology substitutes or mimics. Jared

Lanier has been at the forefront of developing virtual reality. He points out that when technologies such as photography and sound and video recordings first came along, people judged them to be as realistic as the original, in ways that we now would find just bizarre—the old recordings seem so primitive [64]. For example, people would purchase photographs of people who roughly resembled their loved ones, using a technologically produced image of the total stranger as a proxy for a portrait of some they knew in real life. He opines that the use of such technologies, including virtual reality, can enhance our appreciation of the 'real thing' and that the best part of virtual reality is returning to the real world. We can now see the differences between photography and the same image seen through our own eyes and perhaps gain a deeper appreciation for both, including ourselves and each other. Likewise, perhaps it is in part the uniformity of production that has enhanced appreciation for the unique stamp of each human voice, of hand-made artefacts from natural materials, and so on.

We can think of much of this under the heading of 'texture'. Computer graphics designers are paying much attention to producing texture in the flat images we see on the screen. The texture of real life may be calling us. We will consider later some implications of imagining the human mind on the model of a computer.

Exercise 11

Find an example of a proposal to use AI to supplement or replace a human, and try to do as full a checklist as possible of the ways in which it is explicitly stated to be better and ways in which it is implicitly assumed to be better.

3.6   Communication Through New Technologies

Summary
Communication technologies have been with us for some time, but the capacities of AI are increasing their capabilities, and they are an increasingly necessary part of daily and economic life. Communication is an activity with inherently ethical dimensions for the nature and qualities of our relationships and for the nature and quality of the information and knowledge we transmit and possess. Here, we look at how technologies may change the relationship of the reader and the writer, the capacity for individuals to control how the world sees them, and the direction and manner of our attention. We look at work by Walter Benjamin, Marshall McLuhan, and Erving Goffman for ideas we can apply to AI.

3.6.1   AI and Communication Technologies

The AI technologies we are considering exhibit a multiplicity of facets. Some of the most important ethical questions concern how AI is used in communication, whether in personal communication, in the media, or as a means of accessing knowledge about the world. This is a two-way process, since we, the users, communicate via such technologies, and information about us is collected and analysed by (often unknown) others. The surveillance elements of these technologies can also be seen as a form of communication, albeit a degraded and lop-sided one. Both the form of technology and its technical capabilities and social use must be understood together in any effort to comprehend and respond to such complex phenomena.

Significant changes in communication technologies over the centuries have had profound and lasting impacts on society and culture. We have noted Socrates' views on the significance of writing and have already mentioned in passing the printing press. This played a role in social, intellectual, and religious developments, which can with considerable justification be described as transformative. The printing press allowed for the ready reproduction of ideas and pictures, an ability that only increased with mechanisation and which is now seemingly limitless but also fragile in significant ways. The reproduction and distribution of ideas and images online is in at least some respects parallel to the reproduction and distribution of goods made possible by the Industrial Revolution. It is therefore instructive to reflect on what extent we can learn from the past and from prior reflections on such developments. Are the changes we are seeing something new, or are they the same old same old? Can we gain any insights by seeing current technologies through the kinds of questions and concerns raised by past technologies?

Communication as an inherently ethical question Communication is partly an ethical issue because of the manner in which it gives rise to specific problems. Indeed, information technologies give rise to many of these: intellectual property rights, plagiarism, deep fakes, online misinformation, doxing, pile-on harassment, online privacy and anonymity, digital passports, and the list goes on. Relevant aspects of AI that produce such issues include the speed at which communication can occur, its reach, the capacity to process information, the capacity for encryption and conversely for hacking, the capacity to conceal and to reveal identities, the possibility of dissimulation and fakery, and opportunities for control and its loss.

However, aside from the necessity of considering specific issues, the impact of technological changes on communication is also an ethical issue for the fundamental reason that ethics intimately concerns relationships between people and thus pre-supposes the existence and quality of channels of communication. Hence, changes in the manner of communication can potentially alter the entire shape of ethical questions and responses. The reach and impact of such changes in communicative possibility are also likely to have ramifications that extend far beyond a merely formal account of the technical possibilities [65, 66].

3.6.2 The Reproduction of Ideas and Images

The study of communications in general and of communication in the Internet age and with the assistance of AI in particular is a field in its own right. Here, we look at some significant work examining the impact of technologies on the communication of ideas and images, beginning with Walter Benjamin's 1936 essay, *The Work of Art in the Age of Mechanical Reproduction* [67]. This is taken as an example of a potential source of inspiration and ideas for reflecting on the ethical issues with which we are concerned. It is also chosen to enable readers to reflect on how past ideas—the work is over 80 years old now and technology has developed considerably since—may have considerable relevance to our concerns.

Benjamin was a philosopher and critical theorist whose work continues to be influential. His work has significance beyond what might formally be thought of as 'works of art' and is of significance in the online world and in relation to AI for both images and text. Many have commented on the significance of his work for the current age of digital reproduction. Our remarks here can only be very introductory. For our purposes, we must also consider how the capabilities of AI may add to and further complexify the question of reproduction.

Benjamin argues that with reproduction, the work of art is placed outside of its original context of tradition (which is not to say something static, since traditions change). Before the possibility of easy reproduction, works of art had what Benjamin calls an 'aura', and a notion of the 'genuine' work of art was linked to the capacity to trace the physical and lines of ownership. Ready reproduction dislocates context and allows for greater autonomy of the reproduction. When reproduction of art undermined the concept of the genuine work of art, its social functions came to be underpinned by politics.

Changing relationships between parties Communication concerns more than one party, and the possibilities for the nature of the relationship between those parties can permit, constrain, and shape the nature of that communication. Benjamin's discussion of the role of the actor in film as distinct from the theatre notes how in the theatre the actor is presenting to a particular audience in the present. However, in film, the actor portrays him- or herself to the camera and is conscious of an audience as the market for the film, which is not present and which exists only in the future, but in multiple possible futures and places. The impact of space and of time matters: time is disrupted and becomes discontinuous. The actor has no immediate feedback from an audience in the form of an embodied presence. Recall the discussion of the relevance of locality in Sect. 2.9. Consider what changes to relationships between parties have become possible with the different forms of communication made possible using AI. I am reminded of the sheer misery of suddenly being forced to record online videos, minus any audience of students, at the start of the pandemic.

Erving Goffman: *The Presentation of Self in Everyday Life*
The influential sociologist Erving Goffman's classic work studied how we present ourselves to the world when we are being observed by others, and the different contexts of how we do so [68]. This should be an immediately familiar issue to any honest reader. Around the world, people tidy up for

(continued)

guests, wear different clothes, and adopt different manners for formal occasions.

Goffman developed the useful distinction between front stage and back stage which can apply in many social settings. Back stage one can be more relaxed and show a different persona to that which is shown front stage. There are many versions of this. In the staff room, teachers may moan about their most annoying pupils. When having guests for dinner, the cook may surreptitiously signal to the family not to ask for second helpings if they suddenly realise there is not enough. In the ladies' rest room, a woman may hurriedly use safety pins to repair a tear in her skirt, and so on.

Exercise 12

Consider how the possibilities for showing oneself to the world and of being monitored and subjected to surveillance, which are being created by technologies which use AI, may be altering the places in virtual reality and 'real' reality which count as front and back stage, and how this might impact how we present ourselves. What aspects of the technology and its deployment are relevant to any such changes? Is a distinction between 'front stage' and 'back stage' being eroded in some places? (We will look at the topic of surveillance again in later chapters.)

Consider the MOTUS technology mentioned in Sect. 3.4, which would enable someone to present a digital version of themselves online. How might this change the expected standards of beauty and appearance? Consider the projected use for stroke survivors. Consider how this might benefit patients and consider the possibility that it might reinforce stigma against people living with disabilities.

Furthermore, the possibility for scrutiny of the actor changes with the introduction of photography. Film requires that the actor has to consider how to present to the camera and how the camera is used in return to present the world. Film also allows for increasingly detailed perception of the optical and auditory world. The camera increases our ability to scrutinise the behaviour of others, and they of us, showing us what Benjamin calls the 'optical unconscious', to mirror the ways in which psychoanalysis had made us aware of the unconscious aspects of our behaviours that may give away more than we intended. Consider how AI may have further increased such possibilities for the scrutiny and observation of the world, including of ourselves.

The roles of reader and of writer The distinction between the writer and the reader also changes with mechanical reproduction. In previous times, there were a small number of writers with thousands of readers. As printed material increased and the number of outlets increased, increasing numbers could publish in print, and the fundamental character of the divide between reader and writer changed [67, p. 23]. The online world is manifestly making further changes, but what these are and what the social, cultural, and ethical ramifications are is far from clear and indeed is a subject receiving considerable attention. The affordances of the technologies and the capacity for control by technology companies, of regulation by governments, and of interactions between readers and writers online are all part of this mix.

Walter Benjamin's work can suggest some starting points for analysing how the flow of images and ideas is impacted by modern communication technologies, including the use of AI. In addition to giving rise to discrete and concrete issues, technological changes that impact how one sees oneself, how one is seen by others, how words and images are received and responded to will impact matters at the very heart of what is at issue in ethics—relations between the self and other, how our messages are understood, and lines of responsibility and accountability.

Exercise 13: Food for Thought
Some ideas to take forward in considering the impact of AI on how we communicate with each other and how we receive information about the world include the following:
   Context and its loss: is this occurring, and how, and how can meanings be attributed and understood outside of their original context?
   The presentation of the self to the world: how does AI facilitate the possibilities of how we present to the world, and how much does it constrain it?
   How much does the increases in the possibility of scrutiny using AI impinge on us and our relationships with others?

3.6.3   Artificial Intelligence as a Medium

Marshall McLuhan's phrase 'The medium is the message' arises from a body of work of cultural criticism that explores how the form of media impacts the ideas that are communicated, looking at technical developments in the electronic age [69]. As such, it can likewise be mined for suggestions of questions to ask concerning the impact of AI and online communication today. First published in the 1960s, and thus referring to technologies now over half a century old, once again one of the things to take away from this work is how many of the questions we ask today in relation to AI and to online communication were already being asked in relation to technologies which may strike us as comically primitive such as the Xerox machine. It is a salutary reminder that even so many decades ago, and in response to technology that now seems almost antique, McLuhan described electronic devices as providing lifelong surveillance and presenting dilemmas for privacy and the claims of society for information about us [70, p. 12]. He noted that the electrically computerised dossier bank not only threatens privacy by serving as a memory bank that is open and is not erased; there is no redemption from past mistakes and no forgiveness.

Space, time, and attention   The impact of electronic circuitry on time and space is also noted, which provides information instantly and from all corners of the earth [70, p. 16]. Communication and electronic technologies have a worldwide impact, creating a global village. This raises an issue that is both of prime importance in considering technologies today and, as we shall see in more detail later, critical to understanding ethics: attention. TV demands our attention. Now, of course, old fashioned TV has less of our attention, and rather more individually tailored material assails us, much of which is purposefully designed to attract our attention using techniques of behavioural psychology. As we will also explore in more detail in later chapters, attention is a key question in ethical judgement and perception. You can't respond to something you have not even noticed. Since the world is full of possibilities for thought and for action, the question of where the focus of our attention lies is critical. We know too much about each other and can no longer avoid the claims of certain previously ignored minorities [70, p. 24].

McLuhan claims that electric circuitry is an extension of our nervous system [70, p. 41], an interesting claim regarding the boundaries of ourselves that is echoed by some more contemporary views in philosophy of mind, which we will mention in Chap. 7. Media alters the ways in which we perceive the world and which senses dominate. Changes in media can impact upon how the viewer or consumer of media is placed in relation to it, and how detached or involved they are with the material. Electronic media is instant and involves all of us. This is one feature that has altered since McLuhan wrote. For those of you too young to remember, television programmes were rarely repeated, appeared at set times, and hence formed moments of a certain social unity and shared attention. Key shared cultural events include the coronation of Elizabeth II in 1953, which was the first televised coronation of a British monarch, the televised Kennedy election in 1960, and the Apollo 11 moon landings in 1969. Our family crammed into the local school hall with hundreds of other families to watch the moon landing, the first ever all-night broadcast from the BBC [71]. Such events had a great sense of excitement and community.

It is interesting to consider how changes in accessing information, including changes such as deep fakes and the collection of information regarding the viewers, have altered the lines of any shared sense of community and of awareness of the world. The idea of seeing the world from a fixed perspective may no longer be appropriate.

Question
Can the very form of technology help to shape what ethical issues come to our attention, and how they are presented? Recall the question of the importance of relationships in considering ethical questions presented to us by AI.

3.7 Key Points

Attitudes towards technology can shape how key questions in AI ethics are understood, such as questions concerning how we understand the limits of human achievement and how we attribute agency to humans and to machines.

Other questions concerning boundaries and how we classify and categorise the world are also critical for understanding some central questions in AI ethics.

We can easily think of technology as 'new', but it has always been a feature of human life, and ancient philosophers debated issues in the philosophy of technology of key relevance to understanding current debates in technology and in the ethics of AI.

Questions in the philosophy of technology concerning the relationship between technology and nature and humanity's place and role in relation to nature are directly relevant to key issues in AI ethics.

A range of implicit values are often attributed to technology, which will shape responses to many ethical questions.

AI has a role in communication technologies. Communication is inherently ethical, directly impacting the nature and quality of relationships between people and the understanding and transmission of information.

3.8 Educator Notes

Questions in the philosophy of technology may appeal to students who have less interest in ethics per se. It is important to encourage students throughout the course to develop the skills and understanding to see how these questions do intimately connect with questions in ethics.

It is possible to give students an overview of some of the most relevant questions for ethics in AI without requiring them to read the entire chapter. Setting reading for some subsections plus accompanying exercises will give students an opportunity to consider the relevance of these questions for issues in AI ethics and help to prepare them for much of the material later in the book.

Many, indeed most, of the exercises are designed so that students can attempt them without background reading, and the process of considering their answers will serve as a good introduction to issue we tackle later in the book, even if students do not have time to explore this chapter in great detail: for example, Exercises 1, 2, 3, 5, 7, 8, and 10.

It would be useful for students to look at Sect. 3.5 on the implicit values of technology, as priming students to think about these issues can help to prepare them for considering their own attitudes, as well as how such implicit attitudes may mould debates in AI ethics.

Debate and extended project or essay topics Many of the exercises could form good class debate and discussion topics. Exercise 2 could be useful for detailed discussion if students or the educator prepares some examples and could be valuable for encouraging students to look for details of how AI is presented. Likewise, in Exercise 7, images could be prepared in advance or found in class. Exercise 6 could form a group project where students could compare responses and be encouraged to think about the implications of information collection for one purpose and its meaning in another context. Exercise 8 could form an entertaining topic that could challenge students to try to articulate their attitudes towards AI and prepare the ground for later ideas around boundary issues, purity and disgust.

Acknowledgements This chapter was partially funded by the National Institute for Health Research, Health Services and Delivery Research Programme (project number 13/10/80). The views expressed are those of the author and not necessarily those of the NIHR or the Department of Health and Social Care.

References

1. McCarthy J, Minsky ML, Rochester N, Shannon CE (2006) A proposal for the Dartmouth summer research project on artificial intelligence, August 31, 1955. AI Mag 27(4):12–12
2. Vinge V (1993) The coming technological singularity. Whole Earth Rev 81:88–95
3. Crawford K (2021) The atlas of AI. Yale University Press, New Haven
4. Larson E (2021) The myth of artificial intelligence: why computers can't think the way we do. Harvard University Press, Cambridge, MA
5. Nakajima S, Yamamoto M, Yoshimoto N (2009) Dogs look like their owners: replications with racially homogenous owner portraits. Anthrozoös 22(2):173–181
6. Lanier J (2010) You are not a gadget: a manifesto. Vintage, New York
7. Service T (2012) Kathleen Ferrier–remembering one true voice. The Guardian. https://www.theguardian.com/music/tomserviceblog/2012/apr/12/kathleen-ferrier. Accessed 22 Aug 2022
8. Ahmed Kamal (2018) Bank of England chief economist warns on AI jobs threat. BBC news website. https://www.bbc.com/news/business-45240758. Accessed 22 Aug 2022
9. Bangert V (2022) VentureBeat. https://venturebeat.com/2022/01/08/ai-is-quietly-eating-up-the-worlds-workforce-with-job-automation/. Accessed 22 Aug 2022
10. Ford M (2022) Robots: stealing our jobs or solving labour shortages? 2 Oct 2021. The Guardian. https://www.theguardian.com/technology/2021/oct/02/robots-stealing-jobs-labour-shortages-artificial-intelligence-covid. Accessed 22 Aug 2022
11. Taylor C (2019) Robots could take over 20 million jobs by 2030, study claims. CNBC. https://www.cnbc.com/2019/06/26/robots-could-take-over-20-million-jobs-by-2030-study-claims.html. Accessed 22 Aug 2022
12. Kapp E (2018) Elements of a philosophy of technology: on the evolutionary history of culture. University of Minnesota Press, Minneapolis
13. Bacon F, Gough AB (1899) New Atlantis: a work unfinished. Tho. Newcomb, London, pp 10–12
14. Butler S (ed) (1880) Erewhon, or, over the range. David Bogue, Coldingham
15. Parry R (2021) Episteme and Techne. In: Zalta EN (ed) The Stanford encyclopedia of philosophy. Metaphysics Research Lab, Stanford University, Stanford. https://plato.stanford.edu/archives/win2021/entries/episteme-techne/
16. Ross WD (1924) Aristotle's metaphysics, vol 2. Clarendon Press, Oxford
17. Westfall RS (1994) The life of Isaac Newton. Cambridge University Press, Cambridge
18. Heidegger M (1977) The question concerning technology and other essays (trans: Lovitt W, 1954). Harper Collins, New York
19. Aristotle (ed) (2014) Aristotle: Nicomachean ethics (trans: Crisp R). Cambridge University Press, Cambridge
20. Ryle G (1949) The concept of mind, Chapter II. Hutchinson, London
21. Weinberg AM (1966) Can technology replace social engineering? Bull At Sci 22(10):4–8
22. Morozov E (2013) To save everything, click here: the folly of technological solutionism. Public Affairs

23. Illich I (1976) Limits to medicine: medical nemesis the appropriation of health. Marion Boyars, London
24. Bracken P, Thomas P (2010) From Szasz to Foucault: on the role of critical psychiatry. Philos Psychiatr Psychol 17(3):219–228
25. Lupton D (2017) Digital health: critical and cross-disciplinary perspectives. Routledge, London
26. Rothman BK (1993) The tentative pregnancy: how amniocentesis changes the experience of motherhood. WW Norton, New York
27. Lippman A (1991) Prenatal genetic testing and screening: constructing needs and reinforcing inequities. Am J Law Med 17(1–2):15–50
28. Featherstone K, Atkinson P, Bharadwaj A, Clarke A (2020) Risky relations: family, kinship and the new genetics. Routledge, London
29. König A, Crispim-Junior CF, Covella AGU, Bremond F, Derreumaux A, Bensadoun G, David R, Verhey F, Aalten P, Robert P (2015) Ecological assessment of autonomy in instrumental activities of daily living in dementia patients by the means of an automatic video monitoring system. Front Aging Neurosci 7:98
30. Frey AL, Karran M, Jimenez RC, Baxter J, Adeogun M, Bose N, Chan D, Crawford J, Dagum P, Everson R, Hinds C (2019) Harnessing the potential of digital technologies for the early detection of neurodegenerative diseases (EDoN). OSF Preprints
31. Lupton D (2019) Data selves: more-than-human perspectives. Wiley, New York
32. Boorse C (1975) On the distinction between disease and illness. Philos Public Aff 5(1):49–68
33. Wakefield JC (2013) DSM-5: an overview of changes and controversies. Clin Soc Work J 41(2):139–154
34. Kaczynski TJ (1995) Industrial society and its future. The Washington Post
35. Mori M (2017) The uncanny valley: the original essay by Masahiro Mori. IEEE Spectrum
36. Cheetham M (2017) The uncanny valley hypothesis and beyond. Front Psychol 8:1738
37. Douglas M (1966) Purity and danger: an analysis of the concepts of pollution and taboo. Routledge, London
38. Philip Z (2007) The Lucifer effect understanding how good people turn evil. Random House, New York
39. Whittaker M (2021) The steep cost of capture. Interactions 28(6):50–55
40. Paley W (1829) Natural theology: or, evidences of the existence and attributes of the deity, Collected from the appearances of nature. Lincoln and Edmonds
41. Zee A (2015) Fearful symmetry: the search for beauty in modern physics, vol 48. Princeton University Press, Princeton
42. Ruskin J (1847) Modern painters. Wiley and Putnam, New York
43. Tennyson LA (1850) Memoriam AHH
44. Blake W (1866) Songs of innocence and experience: with other poems. Basil Montagu Pickering, London
45. Gorodeisky K (2016) 19th century romantic aesthetics. In: Zalta EN (ed) The Stanford encyclopedia of philosophy. Metaphysics Research Lab, Stanford University, Stanford. https://plato.stanford.edu/archives/fall2016/entries/aesthetics-19th-romantic/
46. Le Guin UK (1998) Lao Tzu: Tao Te Ching: a book about the way and the power of the way. Shambhala Publications. Tao Te Ching first published approximately 400 BCE
47. Isaiah 11:6, World English Bible. https://worldenglish.bible
48. Thoreau HD (1971) Walden (Ed.: Lyndon Shanley J, 1854). Princeton University Press, Princeton
49. Emerson RW (1836) Nature. Kenneth Walter Cameron, New York. Scholars' facsimiles & reprints, 1940
50. Mill JS (1873) Autobiography. Geoffrey Cumberlege. Oxford University Press, Oxford
51. Passmore JA (1975) Man's responsibility for nature: ecological problems and Western traditions. Gerald Duckworth & Co Ltd., London
52. Fiani B, Reardon T, Ayres B, Cline D, Sitto SR (2021) An examination of prospective uses and future directions of neuralink: the brain-machine interface. Cureus 13(3):e14192

53. Seymour M, Riemer K, Kay J (2018) Actors, avatars and agents: potentials and implications of natural face technology for the creation of realistic visual presence. J Assoc Inf Syst 19(10):4
54. Moore FD (1989) The desperate case: CARE (costs, applicability, research, ethics). JAMA 261(10):1483–1484
55. neuralink.com/applications/. Accessed 18 Jun 2022
56. Tamantini C, di Luzio FS, Cordella F, Pascarella G, Agro FE, Zollo L (2021) A robotic healthcare assistant for COVID-19 emergency: a proposed solution for logistics and disinfection in a hospital environment. IEEE Robot Autom Mag 28(1):71–81
57. Featherstone K, Northcott A (2021) Wandering the wards: an ethnography of hospital care and its consequences for people living with dementia. Taylor & Francis, New York
58. Lefebvre H (2013) Rhythmanalysis: space, time and everyday life. Bloomsbury Publishing, London
59. Palmer S, Torgerson DJ (1999) Definitions of efficiency. BMJ 318(7191):1136
60. Broome J (1993) Qalys. J Public Econ 50(2):149–167
61. sanas.ai. Accessed 22 Aug 2022
62. Bote J (2022) Sanas, the buzzy Bay Area startup that wants to make the world sound whiter. SFGate. https://www.sfgate.com/news/article/sanas-startup-creates-american-voice-17382 771.php
63. Weizenbaum J (1972) On the impact of the computer on society: how does one insult a machine? Science 176(4035):609–614
64. Lanier J (2017) Dawn of the new everything: a journey through virtual reality. Random House, New York
65. Christakis N, Fowler J (2010) Connected: the amazing power of social networks and how they shape our lives. Harper Press, London
66. Garnham N (2000) Emancipation, the media, and modernity: arguments about the media and social theory. Oxford University Press, New York
67. Benjamin W (1935) The work of art in the age of mechanical reproduction. Schocken Books, New York, p 1936
68. Goffman E (2002) The presentation of self in everyday life. Doubleday, Garden City, NY, p 259
69. McLuhan M (2001) Understanding media: the extensions of man. Routledge, New York
70. McLuhan M, Fiore Q (1967) The medium is the message, vol 123(1). New York. pp. 126–128
71. Elscombe J (2022) One small step for man, one giant leap for BBC television. https://www.bbc.com/historyofthebbc/research/moon-landing. Accessed 24 Aug 2022

Further Reading

On Artificial Intelligence

Bostrom N (2017) Superintelligence. Dunod
Larson E (2021) The myth of artificial intelligence: why computers can't think the way we do. Harvard University Press
Russell S (2019) Human compatible: artificial intelligence and the problem of control. Penguin
Russell SJ, Norvig P (2016) Artificial intelligence a modern approach, 3rd edn. Pearson Education, Inc.
Vinge V (1993) The coming technological singularity. Whole Earth Rev 81:88–95
Whittaker M (2021) The steep cost of capture. Interactions 28(6):50–55
Wooldridge M (2020) The road to conscious machines: the story of AI. Penguin UK

On the Philosophy of Technology

Benjamin W (2006) 1935. The work of art in the age of mechanical reproduction, Mass Market
    Paperbacks
Coeckelbergh M (2020) Introduction to philosophy of technology. Oxford University Press
Franssen M, Lokhorst G-J, van de Poel I (2018) Philosophy of technology. In: Zalta EN (ed) The
    Stanford encyclopedia of philosophy. Metaphysics Research Lab, Stanford University, Stanford
    https://plato.stanford.edu/archives/fall2018/entries/technology/
Friis JKBO, Pedersen SA, Hendricks VF (2013) A companion to the philosophy of technology.
    Wiley-Blackwell
Heidegger M (1954) The question concerning technology and other essays (trans: Lovitt W, 1977).
    Harper Collins, New York
Kaczynski TJ (1995) Industrial society and its future. The Washington Post
McLuhan M (2001) Understanding media: the extensions of man. Routledge Classics
Scharff RC, Dusek V (2014) Philosophy of technology: the technological condition, an anthology.
    Wiley-Blackwell
Vallor S (2022) The Oxford handbook of philosophy of technology. Oxford University Press

Chapter 4
Methods in Applied Ethics

Abstract There are significant disagreements about the methods used in applied ethics. This chapter reviews some central methodological questions and the underlying philosophical issues. A simple account of a common approach is outlined: consider one's initial response to a case of interest, and then apply reasoning to test or correct one's initial response. Issues arising from this simple model include the status and reliability of immediate responses and the nature of any reasoning process, including the selection and justification of any framework of ethical values and ethical theory used. Certain features of AI itself pose particular challenges for the methodology in applied ethics, including ways in which developments in technology can impact how we understand concepts. Beliefs about the nature of ethics itself will also impact methodology, including assumptions about consistency, completeness, and clarity in ethics, and the very purpose of morality; we look at some common assumptions. The way in which cases are selected and described is critical, affecting how agency and responsibility are attributed, among other questions. We examine how narratives about AI and images of AI may influence how we approach ethical issues and how fiction, including science fiction, may be used in addressing ethical questions in AI.

Keywords Applied ethics · Methods in ethics · Reasoning in ethics · Science fiction · The object of morality · Images of AI

4.1 Introduction: A Simple Account of Methods in Applied Ethics

Summary
We introduce the need for a methodology in applied ethics by outlining a common approach, which uses reason to interrogate intuitive responses to concrete cases. This approach raises many vexed questions, which we go on to explore further in this chapter.

© The Author(s), under exclusive license to Springer Nature Singapore Pte Ltd. 2023   131
P. Boddington, *AI Ethics*, Artificial Intelligence: Foundations, Theory, and Algorithms, https://doi.org/10.1007/978-981-19-9382-4_4

We have discussed the wide range of the questions in AI ethics, indicated the depth of disagreement and the complexity of the disputes, but have said little about how we might go about first addressing questions to our own satisfaction and second, engaging in fruitful discussion and dialogue with others, whether we agree with them and wish to explore the issues further, or whether we disagree. This chapter aims to shed some light on the vexed question of methodology in applied ethics and on particular issues about methodology that are especially salient in AI ethics.

The subdiscipline of ethics known as applied ethics or practical ethics has developed and grown over the last several decades and is now commonly taught both in philosophy departments and in other university departments, where specific courses geared to ethical questions arising from certain disciplines and practices are studied. Applied ethics also forms part of many professional development courses. Considerable research work, including policy work, also draws upon the methods and practices of applied ethics. There are debates within philosophy about methods used in applied ethics and what the status of its conclusions are [1, 2]. These debates in turn rest upon accounts of the broad nature of ethics, on which there is also a variety of views. Nonetheless, much work in applied ethics proceeds along the basic lines of presenting ethical issues or moral dilemmas, generating a response to these issues, and then attempting to fine-tune one's initial response.

A simple account of methods in applied ethics   To introduce these issues, let us start with an overview of an approach commonly introduced in applied ethics texts or in classroom teaching. There may be more complexity in practice, but it is often explained in very simple terms of a two-stage approach.

Take a case, or series of cases, presenting ethical questions. First, consider the case and form one's initial judgement about the rights and wrongs of what is involved. This initial judgement is often described as an intuition.

Second, apply reasoning to test the soundness of one's intuition. Applied ethics is thus presented as a way of adding consistency, judgement, and reason to spontaneous responses to complex ethical scenarios. A certain relationship between concrete cases and theory is thereby assumed.

Examination will quickly reveal that while one could take this basic two-step description of methodology and give it a go, there are several questions to ask about how precisely to operate this method and about its soundness.

Exercise 1

On June 11, 2022, the Washington Post published an article about a Google engineer, Blake Lemoine, who worked with LaMDA (Language Model for Dialogue Applications), initially having signed up to test if LaMDA used discriminatory or hate speech [3]. (Note the awareness of the need to test for such potentially problematic language—this is a few years after the Tay Chatbot ethical fiasco that we discussed in Chap. 2). The dialogue topics between the engineer and LaMDA included the fear of death and meditation. Lemoine and a collaborator presented evidence to Google claiming that LaMDA was sentient. These claims were dismissed, and Lemoine was placed on paid administrative leave and then went public with his claims. 'Considerable interest was generated in the case', one might say.

1. What is your initial reaction to the ethical issues?
2. How would you go about testing and refining your initial response?
3. What kinds of questions do you have about this exercise, and what difficulties can you foresee with such an approach?

You may have some familiarity with this case already or may wish to do a little research on the case, but the exercise can be done simply on the description above. Your responses should provide an introduction to the issues we will investigate in further detail in this chapter.

We hope to address many of your questions in this chapter and indeed later in the book. This chapter will not be able to 'solve' the problem of methodology in AI ethics, but it aims to explain some of the foundational issues upon which the question of methodology rests and to point to some strategies and skills one can adopt to advance the rigour and integrity of one's approach to ethics, both for developing one's own views and for engaging in constructive dialogue with those with whom one disagrees.

We will look at some ways this model can be built upon and improved, but also how it may be questioned more fundamentally, focusing specifically on issues that may be especially pertinent in relation to AI. This then forms another illustration of some of the ways in which AI presents particular challenges in ethics.

A sceptical view of this approach to applied ethics is that initial, immediate responses to ethically problematic cases represent a rough-and-ready, knee-jerk response built of fear, self-interest, prejudice, or hope and that the 'reasoned' response that follows on reflection is merely post hoc rationalisation. It will be hard to shake off such suspicions in all cases.

Daniel Kahneman: *Thinking, Fast and Slow* [4]
Of course, we can all make mistakes in reasoning. Hence, any reasoning applied in thinking about ethics can also be subject to mistakes. Much work in recent decades has examined some of the characteristic errors to which human beings are prone [5]. Some of these errors occur when heuristic devices, simple shortcuts to working out an answer, which work much of the time, are used in ways which may deliver wrong answers. There are various reasons why human beings tend to make such errors of reasoning. Lack of time is one of them. We may also be subject to characteristic errors driven by paying attention to certain factors in our environment which are especially salient to us because of our evolutionary past. We can do much ourselves, whether solo or with the help of others, to combat our tendency towards such errors and to correct them when they arise. However, we are unlikely to escape

(continued)

them entirely. One of the hopes of AI may be to help us overcome and avoid such errors. We discuss the possibility of AI as a moral assistant in Chap. 11.

Daniel Kahneman's work on human reasoning has received much attention. He proposes that it is helpful to think of ourselves as having two broad systems of thinking. System 1 is fast and operates to produce automatic responses and rapid judgements about situations. System 2 is slow and operates when we exert mental time and effort to come to a judgement. We may think of 'thinking' as resembling System 2 thought and deliberation, but Kahneman's work suggests that much of the time we are actually just working on System 1 judgements.

One may perhaps conclude that initial responses to ethical cases are System 1 thinking, and the reasoning that is then applied may represent System 2 thinking. However, this is very possibly too simplistic, even if one accepts Kahneman's general approach. One's ethical response to a situation may have been formed by years of experience and thought, just as a highly trained musician may instantly respond in a certain way to a piece of music. Contrariwise, the reasoning that is then applied which attempts to consider one's initial response more carefully may in fact include numerous errors and unquestioned assumptions.

Communication is key One reason why we need to address methodology is to help to make possible respectful and fruitful dialogue, where we understand the ground rules of engagement are, including any disagreements about what these should be. Examination of many disasters, including those involving technology, often demonstrates that a key factor was failures in communication [6]. Understanding the points of view of others can be enhanced by greater self-understanding, by clarity of analysis, and by imagination in exploring and approaching ethical questions. Just as one of the major questions in AI concerns the potential dehumanisation of those human beings who are replaced or exceeded by machines in some way, the dehumanisation of opponents and those with views in ethics that we might find wrong, or even repellent, rarely helps the journey to find some kind of solution, or liveable compromise. Communication and understanding can help, even if that understanding is not reciprocated.

4.1.1 Problems in the Methodology

Let us consider some of the questions we need to ask about the process of critical reasoning regarding our initial ethical responses to situations. Note first that although this is sometimes thought of as a two-step approach, there are more than two steps. The first step is the selection of a case or cases. The second step is how such cases are described. Some of the possible questions you might have had include the following, illustrated by features of the LaMDA case; please do add any other thoughts of your own, as it's impossible to cover everything.

The selection and description of cases Can these bias our ethical judgements? Awareness of past relevant cases is likely to influence how we think of the case under consideration. In this instance, awareness of Timnit Gebru's firing from Google and of the Tay Chatbot may come to mind. You may also be thinking of cases drawn from science fiction. You may also have knowledge of previous cases of people being duped by language models. Should this case ever have been described as an instance of possible machine sentience? Or is this a case about the ease with which such false attributions are made?

The status given to one's initial (intuitive) response Has it any standing at all? The coverage of this case, especially including reactions on social media, was often rather heated, with reactions ranging from amazement and fear, pity for LaMDA, and scornful rejection of both the notion that LaMDA could possibly have any sentience and of the views of those who dismissed this possibility. Such intuitions may be thought to be merely emotional reactions and hence prone to manipulation and bias. The powers of AI-driven media to persuade and to sway our emotions may indeed be one source of concern about how readily such responses are created and elicited in humans.

A counter to a sceptical response to intuition might be to ask whether what is described as an 'intuition' is in fact one's 'conscience' and hence something that should be listened to carefully. Recall our brief discussion of the value of dignity in Sect. 2.4.9. Should an initial response of alarm and compassion towards LaMDA be treated seriously as a possible indicator of moral concerns that might otherwise be overlooked? We will consider such questions further when examining moral epistemology in Chap. 7.

The generation of ethical questions The LaMDA case, like many others in this complex area, gives rise to a number of different ethical questions. Some may receive more attention than others. Some may receive no attention at all. Possible questions here include the treatment of the engineer by Google; the general issue of whistleblowing at such companies, and whether this might possibly count as whistleblowing or merely as poor behaviour by an employee; the theoretical issues of attributing sentience to a computer; the link between apparent proficiency at language and the attribution of sentience; what the attribution of intelligence and sentience says about us; whether we should be doing such research if it produces sentience; what such large companies may be getting up to without the knowledge of the general public; fears of unleashing a sentient intelligence on the public; and the media coverage of the question.

Note that in many discussions of applied ethics, examples are introduced as cases *about* a particular set of issues. However, this could possibly obscure other issues that need to be exposed to fully understanding what is going on.

The nature of any reasoning and the justification of any ethical theory used How can one even reason in ethics? Is ethics not just a matter of opinion? A case involving such complex and conflicting reactions as this one perfectly illustrates this basic issue, which for many is a major stumbling block in our capacity to come to any resolution about ethics. We will discuss this further again in Chap. 6.

The appropriateness of any specific values selected and applied in any given areas Do we know what the ethical values governing AI should be? Isn't that something we should sort out first? Some believe that the kind of language model involved couldn't possibly produce sentience, and hence that concerns about LaMDA do not have to include safeguards about what to do should it become sentient. Animal welfare charities checking out potential owners who want to adopt strays do not concern themselves with whether the home contains reading material suitable for dogs and cats. Dogs and cats don't read. Likewise, if LaMDA's sentience was out of the question, no provision for concern need be made.

The relative priority given to intuitive responses or theory If there is a mismatch between your intuitions of the rightness or wrongness of a situation and your theoretical commitments, the question then arises as to what has got to give. Similar questions may arise when a particular case presents you with a situation where a choice must be made between two values. Suppose, for example, that one considered that decisions within the justice system should always be made by human beings. However, then suppose that it transpired that in certain kinds of cases, for example, complex cases of fraud, an algorithm produce more accurate judgements than a jury. How would you resolve such a conflict? (See Sect. 2.4.3.)

4.1.2   From Theory to Practice and Back Again: Fine-Tuning Responses in Applied Ethics

The process of eliciting initial responses to a situation and then applying reason is not one-way. John Rawls was perhaps the single most influential political philosopher of the twentieth century. In his work, *A Theory of Justice*, he outlines a model of reflective equilibrium for reasoning about practical cases and for achieving coherence in our responses to different situations [7]. Suppose we find that our ethical theory and general moral principles produce answers that seem wrong or perhaps on occasion crazy. (I say this having spent years listening to philosophy undergraduates try to work out the consequences of some of their theoretical claims in class.) Alternatively, suppose we have a set of strongly held moral judgements, but we cannot find any deeper theoretical framework to ground and justify all of these together. One can strive for reflective equilibrium, a state of coherence between concrete judgements and justifying theory, by making adjustments in one's theoretical framework and/or in one's concrete judgements until a state of settled coherence, or equilibrium, is reached.

Predictably, philosophers have long argued about how precisely to attain such a state of equilibrium and whether or not a state of coherence between judgements and theory means that one has arrived at the 'truth' ethically. Readers will no doubt readily be able to work out that very different conclusions could be reached, depending upon how much one was prepared to adjust one's theory or one's judgements. Moreover, it is entirely possible that the same set of judgements could be coherently grounded with reference to somewhat different theories, although perhaps in such a case, the possibility of further test cases to discriminate between theoretical frameworks may always remain. There is always the distinct possibility that the ways in which an individual, or a group, decides to resolve tensions is motivated by self-interest, fear, or other less than admirable reasons.

There are various steps that might be taken in the application of reason to fine-tune one's initial intuitive response. For example, details of the case may be changed, or other cases with certain parallels and disanalogies may be presented to test the consistency of one's judgement. Inconsistent judgements may be used to indicate some error and thus require one to apply reason to resolve the inconsistent responses. However, this then produces further questions:

How consistency or inconsistency is determined, and why consistency is required? One strategy used to test responses to particular cases is to consider other cases that differ in certain respects and to check if one's responses to each are consistent. However, to determine consistency, one first has to decide which points of comparison are morally relevant. How do we do that? Determining moral relevance is not straightforward, as we will see at various points in the book.

Furthermore, we can even ask why consistency is even required in ethics. This may never have occurred to many readers as an issue. Surely consistency is essential. But why? Consistency can even be a problem with some of our choices and preferences. Every single time I asked my kids what kind of cake they wanted me to make, they replied, 'chocolate cake'. However, when I asked them, 'Do you never want to eat any other kind of cake?', they would say no, having particular fondness for lemon drizzle cake as well as for a large variety of other cakes. Consistency of chocolate cake is a suboptimal solution. We shall consider this issue presently.

Moreover, there is a common flaw in human judgement that may be especially pertinent here. The notion of cognitive dissonance is one of the best corroborated theories in social psychology [8]. When there is dissonance in our beliefs, or between our beliefs and actions, this produces discomfort, which we will try to reduce. However, we may do this in irrational ways, for example, by ignoring evidence counter to certain beliefs. This means that great care must be taken in any response to divergence between theory and response to cases. We may stop looking at cases that clash with our most treasured theories or at theoretical stances that create problems for our responses to particular issues. This is yet another reason for open debate, listening to others, and subjecting our own views to scrutiny.

Refining ethical theories by considering application to particular cases is one slice of the bread and butter of philosophical debate. Let us try this out in an exercise. A simple version of utilitarianism holds that we should strive to produce the maximum amount of pleasure and the minimum amount of pain. This theory has at least some initial plausibility, since we can readily understand why pleasure attracts us and why pain is bad. It's rather hard to understand how someone could deny the badness of pain.

The 'Experience Machine' as a Test of Ethical Theory

A classic test case is the 'experience machine', first proposed by the philosopher Robert Nozick [9], but now also presented to us through variations on the same theme found in such fictional accounts as the movie *The Matrix* [10], and looming closer on the horizon of possibility through technologies such as virtual reality. Here, philosophical imaginings predating some of the real questions that we are now facing. There are variations between different possible iterations of the experience machine which we won't concern ourselves with here, but you may find it interesting to delve into these.

In the experience machine, one could live out a life of endless pleasure, but this would not be in the 'real world'. The core of the philosophical issue is the divorce of the subjective experience of pleasure, from the source of that pleasure. Instead of feeling pleasure from, say, the accomplishment of planting an orchard, or from sharing a meal with a friend, one simply has the subjective feeling of having done so. Leaving aside the practical worries that the experience machine may break down, etc., would you enter it?

Most people say no, but a not insignificant minority say yes.

Exercise 2

For those who would not enter, spell out why not. How could you modify the version of utilitarianism that holds we ought to aim for pleasure, and the absence of pain, so that it could differentiate between life in the experience machine and life outside it?

If you would enter, explain why. How could you argue that being in the experience machine was the best thing to do?

Hint: This is a very open-ended and rather difficult question. However, addressing it will help to illuminate many questions in AI ethics.

It is useful to realise how many of the philosophical questions that arise in AI ethics have already been discussed by philosophers in other contexts.

Interpreting rules, concepts, and theories One way of responding to such tests of theory is to see it as raising questions about how precisely a theory is being interpreted. We can make assumptions about how we understand a concept or a theory, only to have those assumptions called into question by novel situations. Any theory needs to be interpreted before it can be applied. A rule to be followed can only provide certainty within a system that is already completely formally specified. The problem of interpreting rules also means that it is often less easy than it may at first appear to judge whether a rule or a concept has been applied or used consistently across different cases. This keeps judges and lawyers in business. The question of interpreting rules will be critically important in the question of whether AI can act morally, as we shall see.

Use of standard ethical theories Ethical theory may be explicitly called upon as a framework in which to reason and resolve disputes. Ethical theories may focus on broad questions about the nature of ethics—metaethics—or may focus on substantive claims about the nature of morality and about how form moral judgements, normative ethical theories. Indeed, 'applied ethics' is often seen as simply the application of normative ethical theory to concrete cases. Certain normative ethical theories are frequently drawn on in applied ethics: consequentialist theories that focus on ethical outcomes, deontological theories focusing on the nature of the moral rules to be followed, and virtue ethics theories focusing on the moral character of the agent. We look in more detail at normative ethical theories in Chap. 6, addressing the question of their fit to the particular ethical questions raised by AI.

We must take care that our approach does not assume that our theories are complete and that we have nothing else to learn from the world. In practice, our ethical theories evolve and develop, sometimes in response to internal inconsistencies, sometimes in response to argument based on alternative theories, and sometimes in response to cases.

4.1.3 Searching for Help: Can We Base AI Ethics on Ideas Borrowed from Medical Ethics?

We have raised the question of how novel the issues of AI ethics are. Naturally, they cannot be entirely new, or we would have no way of understanding them. It has often been suggested that we can help ourselves to an ethical framework applied in another setting and use that with any modifications that might be needed. The prime example suggested is that of medical ethics; perhaps lessons from this area of professional practice can be applied to AI. Medical ethics has developed into a mature discipline over many decades, attaining considerable broad international agreement on certain core issues, such as the importance of informed consent, with nuance and local variation. Hence, it could be extremely useful to be able to base responses to AI ethics on such a well-developed area. Moreover, some specific sets of values have already been developed, which meet with considerable broad agreement while allowing for debate and difference of opinion.

In medical ethics, and in bioethics more broadly, a commonly applied and influential framework of values can be found in the work of Beauchamp and Childress, who distil from medical practice, law, and ethics certain key principles of bioethics [11]. It has been suggested that we can take the central ethical values that have been developed in medical ethics or bioethics more broadly, of autonomy, beneficence, nonmaleficence, and justice, and add to them a key issue that addresses specific questions arising in the case of AI: explainability [12].

However, many questions arise, and the suggestion of basing AI ethics on medical ethics illustrates some of the complexities of measuring theoretical issues in ethics against concrete practical cases [13, 14]. The context of practical application can make a profound difference. This indeed presents one of the challenges of approaching the area of AI ethics. Indeed, it is such a broad area that there may be difficulties in generalising from one set of questions in AI ethics to another.

Understanding concepts in relation to specific instances Theoretical concepts developed within the practice of medicine have been articulated within that context and thus will have gained a particular flavour and interpretation. For instance, autonomy will have been understood with the notion of bodily and medical autonomy as the primary focus. Medical autonomy generally focuses on questions of patient choice over medical procedures and hence over the body. Complexities arise about how precisely to understand and apply the concept of autonomy even within medical settings. Autonomy over medical decisions is not necessarily interpreted as implying that any body modification whatsoever is to be respected; 'first do no harm' also applies as well as notions of the patient's best interest.

Recall the example of the Neuralink implant discussed in Chap. 3 (see Exercise 9). Should one draw a distinction between the use of such an implant for medical reasons and for other reasons? This is partly a question of how we understand autonomy. In the healthcare context, autonomy is not usually interpreted as permitting volunteers to opt for such experimental procedures, especially not those involving the brain (although this concerns ideals of medical practice). There are numerous examples of grotesque abuse, including, for instance, the lobotomy.

How health is understood will thus make a difference to how the concept of autonomy is fleshed out and applied within medicine. We also need to understand the concept of health itself. This question is not as straightforward as it may at first appear. The precise definition of disease and illness is far from easy, nor can it be assumed that health is simply the absence of disease or illness [15]. Health may be thought of primarily as physical health, but the practices of psychiatry and clinical psychology have expanded that to include mental health; noting the importance of the social determinants of health, some definitions of health may also include reference to the social circumstances in which a person lives [16]. This introduces into any account of autonomy, reference not just to the individual but to social relationships, and political questions will quickly ensue.

An influential definition of health developed by Aboriginal groups in Australia has expanded an account of health further to include cultural and historical factors, noting that health must be a whole-of-life concept; the notion of 'health' does not even translate very well into Aboriginal languages [17]. Therefore, even within medicine, we can see that there are major questions around how we understand and apply notions of autonomy is vastly complex. Attempting to apply this notion to the multitude of circumstances in which AI may be applied will be more complex still.

However, there are many lessons we can nonetheless learn from medical ethics. Ethical questions of medical autonomy have risen to the fore historically because of power imbalances and the need to protect patients from the power of the medical profession. There may be lessons to be learned here in AI regarding the autonomy of individuals against the autonomy and power of those building and deploying AI. This may be relevant to the LaMDA case, depending on what the actual facts of the matter were, as with many other cases in AI. To value autonomy does not get us very far; there is much detail to be filled out regarding how precisely the notion of autonomy should be understood and how valued and how we should understand the issue of autonomy of individuals in relation to those who develop and deploy AI and, indeed, in relation to the autonomy of AI itself. The central question of the control of humans by AI and the control over AI by humans requires specific thought; we cannot simply borrow a notion of autonomy from the field of medical ethics.

Likewise, issues of beneficence and nonmaleficence within medicine will have been fleshed out (pardon the pun) in relation to health and illness. Within AI, the sky is the limit, especially if we consider some of the more futuristic scenarios. As we shall see later in the book, especially in Chap. 11, it may even be hard to conceptualise what might constitute 'benefit' when contemplating some far future possibilities.

So, although issues such as autonomy and beneficence are common to both medical ethics and AI ethics, they may not get us as far as we wish, not simply just in the application to practice but in terms of how precisely such concepts are understood in different settings.

Trouble for medical ethics: genetics, genomics, and advances in science and technology The idea of basing ethical approaches to AI on the well-developed example of medical ethics does have certain merits. It would indeed be foolish not to consider if lessons could be learned. However, one of the lessons that we should learn is exactly how hard it can be to apply even relatively straightforward ethical values in practice, especially under the pressure of changes in science and technology.

The area of genetics and genomics presents some salutary lessons of strong relevance for AI, since they concern personal data, advancing techniques of data processing and analysis, and the vast increase in the generation of information this enables. We saw in Sect. 3.3.4 how changes in medical and genetic knowledge can impact how we construct risk. Developments in scientific understanding and technical possibility can make for unexpected practical problems in protecting key values and for unexpected conceptual problems in how we even understand some core issues central to ethics.

My data or yours? It has long been known that we share genes with close relatives. For example, the Y chromosome is transmitted from father to son almost without variation, excluding occasional mutations. Likewise, mitochondrial DNA is transmitted down the motherline to all descendants. What has changed in recent years is the capacity to readily obtain specific genetic information about individuals, which also thus generates information about close relatives. There is also now capacity to detect and analyse extremely small traces of DNA, for example, at crime scenes. Note that changes in the ease, cost, and scale of access to information produce these ethical problems.

Am I my brother's keeper? A central value of medical ethics is the privacy of one's medical information, but is one's genetic information simply one's own information, if it also has direct implications for others? Cases include instances where criminals have been traced via DNA uploaded to ancestry sites by relatives or where the genetic risk profile of one family member is automatically revealed by the genetic testing of another. The ease of acquiring such knowledge facilitated by technology, the social and cultural forces shaping the impetus to generate such knowledge, together with the scientific knowledge, produces complex situations that shape changing attitudes towards privacy [18]. The very notion that one's medical information is one's own is challenged by genetic information; our origins as biological beings and our essential relatedness to others present a tangible challenge to the atomistic, isolated individual which sits at the centre of many common explications of ethics, at least in the West since the Enlightenment.

Hacking privacy The privacy of medical and genetic information is protected by ethics, by law, and by consent agreements obtained in the practice of medicine and in medical research. However, assurances of privacy have been made extremely difficult as a result of increasing powers of data analysis. A common practice of assuring privacy for those giving their genetic information to research projects was to present aggregated results only so that specific individuals could not be identified. However, in 2009, Homer et al. demonstrated that it was possible to infer the presence of an individual within DNA data aggregated from 1000 individuals [19]. Jane Gitschier demonstrated, also in 2009, the theoretical possibility that combining data sets would enable the prediction of surnames of individual members of anonymised DNA data banks, given that surnames track the inheritance of the Y chromosome [20].

The production of genomic information overlaps with the technologies of AI, which are our present concern. The changing attitudes towards ethical and legal challenges of privacy that we face in regard to AI have precursors within genetics and genomics, which form an essential backdrop to how we understand issues within AI ethics.

These cases create difficulties in accounts of ethics that centre the individual, as medical ethics traditionally has. At this point, consider the emphasis on relationships and community stressed in the Indigenous Protocols we looked at in Sect. 2.9.

Exercise 3
Consider the data about you that can be made easily available by technology. Consider what data are available freely to anyone and what is available to particular individuals, organisations, or government departments. Is any of the data that you

regard as data 'about you', also data which is about someone else as well? How much could your privacy be impacted, by data that someone else might consider to be theirs to control?

4.2   The Challenges from AI for Methodology in Applied Ethics

Summary
We consider some of the major difficulties and controversies concerning how to make progress in applied ethics, focusing particularly on issues of most significance to AI ethics. Developments in science and technology can raise both practical and conceptual difficulties. We note the centrality for AI of questions regarding agency and of boundaries. The way in which we describe the world is of vital importance, but the very technologies we are addressing themselves impact how we see the world.

We have introduced the difficulties of methodology in applied ethics in general, illustrated with the example of LaMDA, and considered the extent to which the model of medical ethics can assist with work in AI ethics. This section summarises specific reasons for difficulty in methodology in AI ethics and some central issues prominent in AI ethics that will be particularly challenging given these methodological issues. Some of this refers again to some of the features of AI ethics we have emphasised in earlier chapters.

Time frames   This issue has also been referred to earlier (see Sect. 1.3). We are designing the future now. The speed of change of technologies means that the world from which we derive our values is changing even as we seek to assess these changes. The speed of change in communication technologies and their adoption is especially pertinent, for this is modifying the ways in which we apprehend the world and hence how we view the ethical issues that arise from these novel technologies. This gives us good reason for caution. On the other hand, this is not a counsel of despair. The past can contain guides for the future in ways that may turn out to be surprising. Many well-worn philosophical debates in ethics turn out to have considerable relevance for modern technology.

Speed, change, and hype   Consider the apparent simplicity of the 'intuition plus reasoning' model of applied ethics. A great deal hangs on how we respond to the cases under consideration. Hype is an ever-present issue. Any perusal of responses to the LaMDA case will demonstrate that fear may ensue; the hype surrounding such cases may produce a wide variety of reactions, some of which may be based on misinformation or sheer panic. This will impact both how we describe cases and which cases and issues receive attention. When news broke of the claims that LaMDA was sentient, computer experts were kept busy all day answering often ridiculous questions about it. My electrician even emailed me in a panic at 6.15 in the morning asking for my opinion, worrying that LaMDA was truly sentient and that Google was covering it up.

Conversely, we may become accustomed to technologies and adjust our views of them, individually and collectively, with considerable rapidity. We may forget and overlook certain aspects of them. Initial reactions may come to appear comical. On the other hand, other concerns with hindsight may appear as prescient warnings that are too casually dismissed. Who knows the difference?

Developments in science and in technology impact ethics Not only can developments produce new ethical dilemmas, but they can also produce shifts in our concepts and values. Work in the philosophy of technology discussed in Chap. 3 demonstrates this possibility (especially Sect. 3.5), and this point is also illustrated by the examples above from genomics.

As we have seen, our use of technology, together with our attitudes towards it, can shape how we respond to ethical issues. We saw in Chap. 3 warnings that thinking of the world through particular ways of imagining and understanding AI may also colour our picture of ourselves. We also saw the need to understand that AI may be seen not simply as a set of engineering capabilities, not only as a science, but also as an ideology. Blake Lemoine tweeted that there was no scientific framework to resolve the question of whether LaMDA was sentient but that his opinions were based upon religious beliefs [21]. Could it be that the very aspirations to reproduce or even improve on human intelligence through AI might influence any initial responses to ethical issues, our faith in our own intuitions, and the nature and role of 'reason'? Could such a hope in the future transformative power of AI, or a view of humans as in need of improvement in some specific ways, feed into the depth of division of viewpoints in this arena, as those with cautions and naysayers are dismissed as dinosaurs or Luddites?

Exercise 4
Are a person's religious beliefs relevant to how we assess their claim that AI is, or might be, sentient? If so, how? Consider arguments for and against this. Consider different forms of religious belief.

The global and the local This technology has global reach in many instances, although not all. One way forward for AI ethics is simply blatantly to impose a particular dominant morality upon others. This has indeed often happened and still happens, but there is growing awareness that at the very least, one must be seen to be attempting not to do this. This again raises questions about methodologies. The strategy of eliciting an initial response to an ethical issue and then applying reason may work for me and for my group, but why should my answer apply to anybody else? This is the major reason why I emphasise the need to find strategies for thinking about ethics that might facilitate dialogue and mutual understanding.

As many have warned, one of the chief hazards of AI is its potential for control over behaviour and over information, its way of approaching understanding of the world and its problems, and the potential for global reach, which brings with it serious perils of a dangerous totalising ethic [22]. One might not mind one's own ethic being applied globally, but if it is someone else's, the idea palls somewhat. This risk is linked to a general danger of the unwarranted imposition of uniformity of standards.

Crowdsourcing ethics as a solution Some current work to embed ethical values into technologies illustrates one approach of trying to find a shared solution, for example, the MIT Moral Machines experiment (https://www.moralmachine.net) [23]. This is an inventive way of addressing such issues, which itself makes use of computing technology. It concerns how to find answers to the question of the programming of autonomous vehicles in response to a potential collision. The Moral Machines experiment presents a series of online scenarios where participants have to choose between two possibilities for crashing a car into pedestrians. Many thousands worldwide have completed these tests. Such a way of 'crowdsourcing' ethics could be a means of deciding how to programme a vehicle, perhaps with sensitivity to different cultural contexts, given that it would be possible to programme autonomous vehicles differently in different geographical areas, but there are numerous methodological questions raised, including the question of whether taking the average judgement of 'the crowd' is a good way of reaching moral answers. We will look at certain aspects of the Moral Machines experiment in Chap. 7.

Outsourcing our ethics The MIT Moral Machines experiment also exemplifies another kind of question that occurs in AI ethics only—the very idea of somehow programming ethics into a machine. If we need to consider how we as humans come to conclusions in ethics and find an answer challenging, we also need to consider how we could expect a machine to do this. Many do not consider this to be a sensible or even possible thing to do. The whole question of enabling and allowing AI to make ethical judgements raises methodological questions requiring an examination of ethical theory because on only some accounts of the nature of ethics and ethical judgements is this truly possible. Recall the discussion of Kant's view of moral motivation in Chap. 1. On this approach, if we allow a machine to make a moral judgement for us, our actions have no intrinsic moral worth, even if a good result occurs.

It is useful to mention two other issues that are central to AI ethics and that will be especially affected by how cases are described, how theory is applied, and how concepts are understood, as well as which ethical theories are seen to be relevant.

First, a critical question in AI ethics is agency: The focus on human agency and decision-making is critical in AI ethics and hence presents us with questions concerning some of the most basic assumptions about ethics. This includes questions about the concentration of much power in the hands of a few individuals and corporations, and the distribution of agency and responsibility between humans and AI, as well as many other issues, raising a plethora of problems such as how we should even think about responsibility. As we shall see in Sect. 4.2.1, how cases are described and interpreted can greatly affect how agency is revealed or concealed.

Second, questions of boundaries abound in AI and often in ways that test the conceptual limits of our value system. The boundaries between human and machine may be at issue. This often means that we need to rethink concepts and definitions. As we also saw with the genomics examples, the very advances in technology we are considering may mean that past assumptions about how our concepts may be applied are adjusted or overturned. Questions about the boundaries between self and other which have been theoretical only can become pressing issues when technology changes what is readily possible. Questions can take on an urgency and raise new issues when they are seen on a different scale, as may occur with the speed and scale of information processing and the other tasks that AI can perform. These can all produce conceptual difficulties in the application of theory. One's theoretical commitments and assumptions can shape how situations are described, as we shall see again below.

4.2.1 Describing and Identifying Ethical Issues

The question of how ethical issues are described and identified is such a key issue for us that it is worth labouring the point. The LaMDA example, as do many others, serves as a good illustration of how the different ways in which AI is understood—as a discrete set of engineering challenges, or more ambitiously—will impact not just how AI is described and seen but also how we identify and describe the ethical issues. Many commenting about the cases have lamented that it has distracted from the real problems of AI, diverting us from seeing AI as a useful tool and ensuring that, as a tool, it is used beneficially [24, 25]. Others, in contrast, have argued that designers ought to have foreseen the inevitability that every so often questions of the sentience and intelligence of AI will arise and taken steps in advance to address and debunk such concerns [26].

Complex interactions The mix of hype plus media pressures is unlikely to help clear thinking. The influence of the media, of lobby groups, and of those with the most power to speak in society will be relevant to determining how ethical debate proceeds because this will influence which issues receive the most attention and how issues are described. This highlights the importance of whose voices are heard in addressing questions in AI ethics. Again, there is an interplay between current technologies and how we identify ethical questions, because of ways in which media can drive attention, an issue with any media, especially with online media.

Language is critical to how ethical issues are determined and can help to bring the less visible into view, or to obscure issues. A much-cited example is of bringing certain behaviour into wider awareness with the term 'sexual harassment' to identify ways in which people, initially focusing on women, are sometimes treated in the workplace and elsewhere [27]. Behaviour which might have been seen to be part of life, a bit of a lark, office banter, came to be labelled with a term which, together with a growing body of theory, literature, and activism from feminists, has led to a widely accepted change of opinion about acceptable behaviour. Naturally, there will be disputes about whether such new terms are being appropriately or excessively applied. The words we use to describe a situation may steer us in particular ways in portraying what is in front of our eyes. However, it is likely that it is not simply language alone that does this. Critical factors were other social changes, such as the introduction of laws against sex discrimination.

One of the major questions to grapple with is seeing that a problem exists. Again, the history of the women's movement can provide an illustration, although there are many other possible examples. Writing in 1869, John Stuart Mill addressed those who suggested that there is no problem with the role and status of women in society by claiming that women are not complaining. He pointed out that they do indeed complain: 'But though women do not complain of the power of husbands, each complains of her own husband, or of the husbands of her friends' [28].

Moreover, the particular events that draw the most attention often have a key influence on how subsequent policy and debate develop. Policy and regulations may develop in response to key cases, which will sometimes be described as 'scandals'. Some of these, with time, may be understood to be genuinely problematic, some may be seen to be less so, perhaps even come to be characterised as a 'moral panic' [29]. The specific features of prominent cases that attract most attention may have a lasting influence but may be distorted in various ways.

Exercise 5
From memory, jot down the cases in AI ethics which first come to mind. Then do a search online, or ask others for their opinion on what the most important cases and issues in AI ethics are. This is only a very approximate way of determining the level of attention that issues are getting, but it may be worth bearing in mind that there could be genuinely important issues that are getting much less attention. (Finding what these might be and addressing them would be very useful!)

Bias in bias in algorithms?   For example, readers will probably be aware that there has been considerable attention to the issue of bias in algorithms in recent years. This is indeed an important question, one deservedly getting attention, and we will look at it in more detail later. However, there are possibly biases included in how the issue of bias is being addressed. (This is not meant as a 'gotcha' moment: bias in something that all of us humans have perpetually to struggle against, since any one of us can only ever have a limited view of the world.) The question of bias has arisen, and is being most prominently addressed, in particular parts of the world at a particular time. What kinds of biases are most prominent in the debate is thus likely to be shaped by contemporary concerns, as well as by contemporary ways of recording and describing the world.

Ethical questions of bias are strongly impacted by the law: the law in many countries now notes certain protected categories describing groups identified as in particular danger of discrimination and with particular protection under the law, but note that many of these protected categories have been introduced into law only fairly recently—are we to assume that this may not develop further? Issues of racial or ethnic bias, as well as bias of sex or gender, are most visible in ethical discussion [30, 31]. Bias can only be discovered in categories that are recorded, and the manner in which these are recorded will also shape what is found. In different parts of the world and at different times, race and/or ethnicity is divided into different categories. Much of the work to date refers to cases of bias in countries such as the USA, and this in itself reflects a certain bias towards discovering and addressing bias within certain geographical areas.

Moreover, what are other categories of potential bias? Some work indicates that unless a category is explicitly included in algorithms, it may be impossible to ensure that bias against members of that category does not occur [32]. Aristotle noted how good-looking a person is impacts how well his or her life goes, along with other external goods [33]. He himself was said to be rather ugly. Suppose we examined algorithms to see if they were biased against the ugly, using some kind of beauty score, or a height score, given that research also finds that shorter people tend to have fewer of the good things in life? As things are, it's entirely possible that such hidden factors impact upon lives to a significant degree, and it may be that algorithms are tacitly building in bias in favour of tall, beautiful people by failing to check for this.

A key issue at the root of this is moral relevance (as well as with what data could and should be recorded). What features of the world do we need to take into account in judging a situation? Bias in favour of, or against, those possessing certain characteristics is held to be immoral, since it discriminates on the basis of features considered morally irrelevant, but what features are of moral significance? The history of feminism again can be used in illustration. There are still debates about the circumstances in which a person's sex is or is not relevant, and how precisely it is relevant, debates that have only become more complex as questions are raised about whether the significant issue is sex or is gender, and how both these concepts should be understood. Some concrete issues in AI ethics illustrate these issues, as we shall see below (Sect. 4.4.4).

4.3   Common Assumptions About the Nature of Ethics, and Their Influence on Methodology in Applied Ethics

Summary
Claims concerning the nature of ethics, whether explicit or assumed, will shape how moral problems are understood and how cases are seen. These include the assumption that ethics is universal in some sense, and assumptions about who counts morally; what constitutes moral progress; the place of empirical reasoning in ethics; the existence or otherwise of moral dilemmas; and the possibility of formalising ethical judgements and values in language. There are also assumptions about the object or purpose of morality, a question which should receive our attention, since

the development of technologies including AI may change some of the conditions that lie behind assumptions about the object of morality.

Certain key assumptions and disputes concerning the nature of ethics are relevant to questions of methodology in applied ethics. These shape how we should make ethical judgements, how we argue in ethics, and how we attempt to resolve disputes. These issues often help to explain the existence of disagreements in AI ethics yet may receive less attention in discussion and analysis. Many of these issues will be examined in greater depth in subsequent chapters, when we examine normative ethical theories in Chap. 6 and metaethics in Chap. 7.

Universalism in ethics   This can be understood in different ways and has more than one aspect. Consider an example of universalism in ethics, acceptance of universal human rights. This can be seen as encompassing two separate elements of universalism.

Ethics as 'universal in scope'   It is often assumed, sometimes explicitly but often tacitly, that ethics must be universal in scope. This may be thought of as an indicator that the values in question are indeed ethical values, in contrast to local customs or norms of social etiquette. It may be expressed, for example, in the thought that it is inconsistent to think that the hunger of a child in one's own country matters more than the hunger of a child far away.

What exactly this claim amounts to can be somewhat complex but often is articulated in the assumption that the same moral values should be applied every-where: morality has no borders. This may be an implicit assumption of some (but not all) projects aiming to implement ethics into AI itself.

It's an assumption that *may* go hand in hand with assumptions that ethics is concerned with reason (since reason is likewise generally considered universal), and sometimes with the assumption that AI may improve upon human ethical judgement in removing emotional bias and other alleged irrationalities.

However, the claim that ethics itself must be universal is not in fact universally held. It may be considered that *some* ethical values are indeed universal in scope but that others are more local and specific to particular communities. It may also be held that some moral rules and duties apply to some groups and not to others.

This claim of universality is critical to the application of standards of consistency across different cases. The claim that we must be consistent appears to require some notion of universality of application.

Oddly, as keen attention to arguments on social media or down the pub will reveal, adherents of this claim also often strongly defend relativism, as the view that other cultures have their own moral values, together with the moral necessity of respecting the values of other cultures without interference. We discuss relativism further in Chap. 7.

Universalism in ethics as 'equal moral value'   Universalism in ethics also takes the form of the claim that all human beings are of equal moral value. Again, how precisely this view is filled out may vary. In addition, again, it may be taken by some as a sine qua non for any claim of ethics: for how could any system be recognised as *moral* if it valued some humans less than others? The implications for methodology in applied ethics are obvious. There may be a need to adjust some parts of one's moral theories in response to hard cases, but this central plank of ethics would remain.

However, again, this view is not universally accepted within moral systems. Indeed, it has been common for centuries and is still common in some parts of the world to consider women to have fewer legal rights and a lower moral status than men. It has been commonly held that those from outside one's own immediate kinship group are of lesser status.

Moreover, it is in fact readily observable that applying this 'central plank of ethics' is far from straightforward. What is counted treating someone as of equal moral value may not mean treating them the same (indeed, it should not, as we have different needs). Under this radar, quite unequal treatment may slip in. It may be a rhetorical move with little impact in practice. Some human beings are readily dehumanised.

Bear this in mind in considering issues in AI ethics. It is going to be relevant in considering the future: on its own, the ideal of equal moral treatment says nothing about time frames. How do we, and how should we, value those humans who will exist in the future relative to the claims of those who are alive now? If we are able to enhance human beings with AI, what does that say about the value of those who remain 'au naturel', original unmodified biohumans? We consider these questions again in Chap. 11.

Exercise 6
Should the human race survive for a few decades more, there will be more future human beings than currently exist. Should the human race survive for millennia, there could be immensely more human beings alive in the future. How, if at all, should this impact how we make decisions regarding the future of the human race? What do you have to consider to address this question? (We will revisit questions on this topic in Chap. 10.)

Let us go into a little more detail on this essential point.

Who counts morally? One of the central differences between approaches to ethics hinges on the question of who (or what) counts morally, as well as the question of how they count, and whether all count to the same degree. A useful distinction is that between a **moral agent**, a being capable of thinking and acting morally, and a **moral patient**, a being worthy of moral status and the consideration of moral agents. For example, most would agree that a human baby is a moral patient but (not yet) a moral agent.

This question is relevant to methodology in ethics in various ways. One might start off from an assumption that what ethics is basically about is the welfare of human beings. The questions one addresses and the issues one examines will be based upon this assumption about how the boundaries of the ethical are to be drawn.

However, it is an assumption that can and has been questioned and one that speaks to some of the most heated and central questions in AI.

It is salutary to realise that, despite the many ways in which modern Western philosophy looks back to the ancient Greeks, and despite the influence of Aristotle in particular in much contemporary work on ethics, the ancient Greeks had very different ideas about who counted morally. In fact, not only did Aristotle consider that women were lesser beings than men, being reduced in rationality and closer to the animals, not only did he believe that some humans were by nature slaves; in his work on ethics and on how to live the good life, he was concerned first and foremost with those men who were the citizens of Athens [33]. Those outside the city were barbarians.

However, today, we may more commonly consider that 'everybody' should count morally and that each is of equal importance. John Stuart Mill attributed to Jeremy Bentham the principle of equality that 'everybody to count for one, and none for more than one' [34]. Today, many even think that it was a sine qua non of any value system claiming to be one of ethics.

If *all* humans count, do *only* humans count? This is a critical question for us. Bentham's utilitarianism itself strongly suggests otherwise, for if what matters is pleasure and the avoidance of pain, it is manifest that animals should also be included. Being a member of the species *Homo sapiens* does not seem to mark out anything of special moral relevance. The potential attribution of moral values to AI, to intelligent or even sentient machines, means that even putting the complexities of the claim that 'all' are of equal value to one side, we have to rethink these issues. To assume an answer is to beg the question, a question of particular salience in relation to AI.

Likewise, there are many who question whether all humans count morally. Some have argued that what determines whether or not one possesses certain rights, such as the right to life, is whether or not one is a **person**. There are various ways of characterising a person: an agent with wants, preferences, and desires for the future, who is aware of themselves as an individual, and who is capable of acting and judging. On such a view, one might then consider that babies are not persons but that some of the great apes are, and perhaps in the future, some AI might be. We will discuss persons in greater detail in Chap. 8.

Exercise 7

Valuing persons equally. Consider the case described in Sect. 2.4.9. This involved the use of an app to provide remote monitoring and a certain level of companionship and stimulation for elderly people, including people living with dementia. Consider also the use of surveillance for people living with dementia and different ways in which this might be accomplished, discussed in Sect. 2.4.6. Consider arguments for and against the proposition that such technology demonstrates that people living with dementia are valued equally with any other person.

Moral progress and the 'expanding circle' of moral concerns [35] This is commonly seen in growing concerns for those humans, both individuals and cultural groups, whom we may less readily see and interact with, but historically in more recent years has included concern for animals and for the environment more generally. In AI, it poses questions regarding the status of advanced machines and computers. A critical question will be the basis for any such expansion and the precise status any such expansion may give. To give one example, farm animals may have the right not to be treated with cruelty, but do they have the right to life, as humans do?

Note that the common assumption that we are making moral progress, which many see as evidenced by the 'expanding circle', may also drive assumptions about the necessity of being on the alert to spot signs of moral status, as indicated by intelligence, autonomy, or apparent sentience, in machines. The fears that were evoked by LaMDA were perhaps as much about the possibilities of an awakening sentience trapped in a chatbot and about the possibility that we might therefore be abusing and exploiting some other being as about fears for ourselves. Hence, it can be useful to articulate the notion of an expanding circle of moral concern as an assumption and to think about its implications about how we extrapolate current moral theory and values to novel cases involving AI.

To infinity and beyond More is better. This assumption may seem obvious where ethics is concerned—of course we want to make things as good as possible! Maximising welfare, removing all sources of pain, and using technology to remove every last glitch in life can all seem goals we can readily embrace and are goals that technology may readily seem to lead us towards. Likewise for the assumption that drives much of AI, that because knowledge is good, more knowledge is always better.

We need to be aware that the 'more is better' assumption can be a trap and yet a trap that can drive reasoning in AI ethics. It may seem that failure to strive for constant improvement, that settling for less than the best, could not be a moral approach. However, this view rests upon assumptions about our role, both individually and collectively, in changing the world for the better, and on assumptions about the possibilities of such change, and the scope and limits both of our powers and of the perfectibility of the world. We will return to the idea of perfection later in this section and again in Chap. 5 when discussing human nature.

Empiricism and superstition There is a common notion that the removal of 'superstition', of spurious or unjustified metaphysical foundations, or of religious concerns constitutes progress in ethical reasoning. This may be assumed rather than spelled out. Look out for it in discussions of AI ethics—it can underpin some assumptions governing aspirations for AI as providing a superior replacement to the unreliable and easily duped human race. A picture of humans as simple-minded fools in relation to technology may be common. Again, everything hangs on the details of these arguments and on the moral theories underlying them. I noted above that Blake Lemoine attributed his views on the sentience of LaMDA to a religious stance, but it would be a mistake to consider that a religious viewpoint ipso facto meant a 'tainting' of one's moral position. Indeed, those who embrace a scientifically based worldview may hold many of their assumptions with as much ideological fervour as any religious person or as any political activist. This stance *may* also tend to go hand in hand with rejections of moral values such as purity and dignity (see Sects. 2.4.9 and 3.3.5) if these are made on the grounds that these concepts lack empirical and rational rigour. Whatever view one takes of this matter, it is vital to understand the viewpoint of others.

The stance and place from which we make a judgement A basic question in ethics concerns the attitude needed to form the best moral judgement of a situation, one of an involved, perhaps emotional, stance, or a distanced, perhaps 'rational', approach. This can also be expressed in terms of the 'point of view' from which one approaches a question. Should we try to address ethical questions *sub specie aeternitatis*—from the point of view of the universe? It is common to assume that this must be so. An opposing view claims that an involved stance, a stance of relationship and close attention, is necessary to appreciate a situation and form a judgement. Again, assumptions about the place of reason in ethics, the powers of cognition, and our capacity to reach the right conclusion in ethics all have a role to play in this assumption. This view of the 'rational' approach to ethics can also then feed into the assumption that it is at least to some extent possible to programme ethics into AI. We shall look in some more detail at this question in Chaps. 6 and 7.

Consistency and completeness in ethics As we have seen in previous discussions, it is often assumed that all moral questions have an answer, if only we could manage to determine what it is. There are no genuinely undecidable cases (moral dilemmas). The methodology employed may assume this, whether explicitly or not. Hence, if there are no genuine moral dilemmas, then it should always be possible to produce answers to different cases that together form a consistent, coherent view: because any sign of inconsistency between a person's moral judgements is taken to indicate that something is wrong with one or more of the judgements, not that we are faced with insurmountable moral questions or with moral paradox.

In my experience, few even notice that this is an assumption, suggesting that it may be one of the driving expectations of the age. It may go hand in hand with the common presumption that we can understand the physical world around us; the corollary of this is that we can also understand and resolve any issues in the moral world. This view may even be held as some kind of parallel version of the technological fix—that with sustained effort, we can make a morally translucent picture of the world.

If you think about this, it's quite an assumption. We do not consider that we can fully describe the awe and beauty of great works of art in this way or even scenes of nature of outstanding natural beauty. The category of the sublime exists to capture this; many accounts of religion speak of experiences that go beyond words; in some religious traditions, it is forbidden even to speak the name of God. One view is that the nature of God can only be expressed in terms of what God is not—the Via Negativa. An everyday experience of this difficulty in capturing experience in words is finding words to express how we feel about those we love. Often, comparative means are used, gesturing at how something is to some vast degree better than something else. Every year on Mother's Day, millions of children write roughly the same thing in a card, 'to the best Mum in the world', knowing their classmates are doing the same and knowing at the back of their minds that not all can be correct, as if this prosaic platitude could truly capture their feelings for their mother. A computer programme that tried to run on the information that a billion mothers or more were each the 'best in the world' would have difficulties. Many a lover has struggled to express their feelings in poetry—and in poetry rather than prose precisely because of the difficulty of doing so—only to fail miserably and produce merely doggerel. In fact, some of the best love poetry precisely articulates the very difficulty of expressing love in words and by grasping at comparisons. Shakespeare's famous 18th Sonnet reads:

Shall I compare thee to a summer's day?
Thou art more lovely and more temperate.
Rough winds do shake the darling buds of May,
And summer's lease hath all too short a date.

If Shakespeare can't quite capture his feelings for his beloved, what hope the rest of us? Could the same be true of ethics, of our moral judgements, that these cannot precisely be captured in words, or in mathematical formulae?

On the other hand, especially given the need to justify, explain, and communicate ethical judgements and actions, and the desirability of developing awareness and self-critique, perhaps this is best thought of as a difficulty that we should strive to address.

The value of disagreement Note one implication for how we proceed in AI ethics, or indeed, in any area. Especially given the uncertainties we face in how to proceed, it may be a better tactic positively to encourage a variety of different ethical responses (within a certain limit of acceptability, however that is described) rather than foreclosing prematurely upon 'the' correct decision, or worrying unduly about agreement per se. Allowing such diversity can be a more effective strategy for advancing debates [36]. The value of diversity of opinion may be especially important to remember, given the capacity of AI to permit, and to tend towards, uniform or totalising solutions.

Different kinds of moral dilemmas There can be dilemmas with moral dimensions where we do not know what the best course of action would be, perhaps because we are missing some information. For example, in attempting to develop machine learning to assist with image interpretation with medical diagnostics, it will be necessary to test models and compare results, and in doing so, one course of action may turn out to mean worse results for some patients, possibly resulting in illness or death. This is unfortunate but is a dilemma because of limits to our epistemology.

It can be hard to specify precisely what a moral dilemma is because different theories have different ways of characterising the goals of morality. However, we can think of a genuine moral dilemma as a situation where there is no resolution possible: whatever one does, one does something wrong; whatever one does, one has some moral responsibility and culpability; whatever one does, something bad happens. In other words, the world is such that there may be irresolvable moral loss.

An alternative view is that the world can somehow be perfected or that a relative moral gain is all that is needed: one simply has to choose the least worst option, and there is no dilemma in that. Other accounts see ethics as the attempt to get as close as possible to perfection, to hit the mark, where perfection is possible in theory but rarely attained in practice.

Moral luck The situation where no matter what we do, we will do something wrong has been characterised by philosophers as the question of 'moral luck' [37, 38]. Is our moral world such that we can sometimes not avoid some manner of moral blame?

Computer programmers and logicians will fully understand the need for consistency. Without it, a system breaks down. In logic, it is possible to derive any conclusion from a set of premises that contains a contradiction. We have also seen how striving for consistency between theory and judgement in cases and striving to have consistent reactions between different cases is a key strategy in ethical reasoning and a goal of ethics. The question is whether this has the status of a pragmatic modus operandi, a heuristic device, or if it is held that the world is such that a consistent answer, a resolution to dilemmas, can always be found.

Clarity in ethics The demand for consistency and completeness in formal systems is possible precisely because they are formal. Elements within them can be completely characterised, but can we guarantee that we can completely characterise our values? Possibly not. If we can't, this may mean that we are throwing the baby out with the bathwater (perhaps literally, if our moral theory is based upon personhood, and we come to the conclusion that small babies do not yet have the full criteria of personhood). Sometimes it is our most foundational values that resist articulation, and all accounts have to have some ground point. Can we articulate why it is that we think that causing another being gratuitous pain is wrong? Although demanding consistency in moral views is a good general strategy, it is useful to remember that it rests upon the unproven assumption that we have fully articulated, grasped, and formalised everything of moral importance. Perhaps it is some of our deepest values that are the hardest to fully explain. Perhaps it is an error to assume that our values can be fully expressed in language.

There are many practical implications arising from this, including the assumption that an opponent who has not adequately conveyed their moral position can be dismissed. The motivation to produce an account of ethics that leaves no room for moral dilemmas is understandable, but it can also be a force tending towards those ethical theories that permit precise ranking of potential moral choices.

Note that our ability to formalise and precisely specify our ethical values is one of the major issues we are faced with in addressing questions such as 'can we programme ethics into AI?' Hence, this is one more issue in concerning the methods and foundations of ethics which is brought to the fore by those questions in AI ethics that force us to examine hard issues, such as boundary questions, and the novel situations we are presented with pursuant on developments in technology. It is also a question that may be illuminated by examining some of the very questions that work in AI also addresses, the formalisation of tasks and goals.

Sophia the Robot, Citizen of Saudi Arabia
The social robot Sophia was granted citizenship of Saudi Arabia in 2017. This gave Sophia legal personhood, the first robot in the world to have received this. Her creator, David Hanson, argued that Sophia could speak out for women's rights [39].

Commentators pointed out that in Saudi Arabia, male guardianship still exists, which means that women have considerably fewer rights and freedoms than men.

Sophia, however, also has no autonomy, given the limited nature of the technology behind the robot. Many have argued against the idea of giving robots legal personhood [40]. One could perhaps argue that the announcement of Sophia's citizenship did more to highlight the lack of rights of women in Saudi Arabia than it did to further the rights of robots and was more concerned with politics and marketing than with the actual moral status of Sophia [41].

4.3.1 The Object of Morality

In addressing the difficult questions of moral methodology, it is useful to consider what morality is for [42]. Why do we have any system of ethics at all? What is it aiming to achieve? Why do ethical questions concern us so, and what are they really about? An answer to these questions can help to discriminate between better and worse approaches to methodology in applied ethics. Unfortunately, for those who yearn for an easy answer, yet again there is a plethora of possible views. Answers to this question will help to shape how arguments progress and how positions are supported, what is being aimed at, and why some system of morality is needed to get there, and will shape what we see as acceptable or realistic answers.

Answers to the question of the object of morality will include cynical or debunking positions, such as various claims that the object of morality is to produce a way of controlling the population to mask the interests of the powerful, whether these be the most economically, politically, or religiously powerful in society, or to salve our fears that life is ultimately meaningless. While we do not explore such positions in any depth here, nonetheless, given the power of various bodies involved in developing and using AI, and given the potential of modern media to shape views and influence behaviour, it is a good idea not to forget such a claim entirely. It would well be that some of what passes for 'ethics' is actually serving some such purpose (see Sect. 1.9) [43, 44].

The object of morality and human failings All accounts, or at least, all that I can think of, grapple with a hallmark of morality, that it concerns how things ought to be and/or how humans ought to behave, given that things are not always as they should be and that we don't always act as we should. Hence, positions may assume or state a view of the particular weaknesses or limitations that humans possess that make morality necessary. We will look at these questions later when discussing human nature in more detail. Note that any position taken on human shortcomings will have implications for what potential, if any, AI is thought to have. We discuss human moral shortcomings in relation to the possibilities of AI in more detail in Chap. 11.

Morality is 'a device for countering limited sympathies' in the view of the philosopher J.L. Mackie in his book *Ethics: Inventing Right and Wrong* [45]. Note two things about this: first, it implies that we have an account of how far sympathies should stretch. This implies that we have a view on how far the circle of moral concern should be and on how much of our sympathies others should receive. Second, the stress on sympathy implies that human moral failings concern failings of feelings, maybe a lack of imagination, maybe preoccupation with the self, and with only a certain number of people close to us. Some such position is very common and, as we have noted, may help to motivate claims that AI could help to counter such human emotional limitations and bias by replacing or assisting human judgement with a more impartial machine intelligence. However, a problem of limited sympathies may also be met with a response that the answer to this question is not to bypass sympathy and feeling but to expand one's emotional response to others.

The object of morality and the state of the world The necessity of morality given a world of limited resources and human greed and/or short-sightedness also alerts us that accounts of morality draw upon assumptions about the broad nature of the world in which we live. For example, that we are striving to be happy; that achieving happiness requires certain things; that resources are limited; that others are trying to get what we also want; that other people are important to us in some way; that at some point, we may need to rely on others; that the future is uncertain; that death, however, is certain; etc. Hence, in considering AI, and especially futuristic notions of AI, which may look to transformative visions of society and of our world, we may find that some of the basic tenets shaping our ideas of morality have fundamentally altered. Perhaps by providing for our needs, some drivers of moral rules will be lessened.

Alternatively, perhaps developments in AI may exacerbate some of the background conditions that shape our morality. Relative inequality is a strong indicator of tensions and poor behaviour in a society [46]. Many features of the design of many products using AI and of the production of AI in general are acting to concentrate wealth in the hands of a few, and providing many low-grade jobs around the world [47]. Furthermore, some design features of the online world are argued to be provoking some of our worst behaviour, encouraging and harnessing the power of the mob against the individual, and responsible for social contagion of ideas

[48]. Social media is widely thought to have an alarming role in the rise of mental health problems, although the evidence is disputed [49, 50]. Many of the ethical issues that technology is being called upon to solve are indeed caused or exacerbated by technology. See Sect. 3.3.4, where we discussed the notion of iatrogenic harm. (An alternative term for this may be 'protection racket'.)

Here's one relatively trivial although potentially irritating possible consequence of the ease of virtually instant electronic communication. A friend and former colleague, Susan Hogben, used to remark that in the old days, someone would write a letter saying that their ship would be arriving into Sydney Harbour in the afternoon of July 14, months in advance, and lo and behold, Aunt Marigold would have travelled 500 km from Wagga Wagga to be there to meet it. These days, Aunt Marigold would send a text at the last minute saying she couldn't make it. Has the ease with which we can notify others of a change in arrangements had any impact on the tendency to value consistency and reliability in keeping to prior agreements to meet?

I sometimes amuse myself by considering song lyrics and titles that would have to be adjusted to update them to modern technology: Please Mr. Postman, Rikki Don't Lose That Number, Return to Sender, and many more. The plot drivers of so many detective stories and of some of the most classic works of literature likewise hang on failures or delays in communication. The original marathon race would never have happened, as there would have been no need to run all those miles to deliver a message; Romeo and Juliet would have got the message about the plot to pretend to be poisoned and tragedy averted; you might likewise to amuse yourself by finding examples of your own. On the other hand, modern technology provides numerous new opportunities for communication failures.

Exercise 8
Imagine that AI has progressed so that we each only have to do 1 hour's work a week, and nobody wants for anything. Would this change our basic moral values in any way?

Many of these issues will be explored further, especially in Chaps. 6–8, and 10. The rest of this chapter looks in closer detail at the important question of how cases for ethical consideration are selected and described.

4.4 Methodology in Applied Ethics: The Stories We Tell

Summary
The ways in which the cases used in applied ethics are selected and described are critical. Understanding that these real cases are also stories, described in one way or another, is an essential first stage to improving methods in applied ethics. We need to understand how character and agency are described and how the cases are framed. The many tales about AI and robotics also provide a rich background against which views are formed, and we need to understand the prominent themes present in such

tales and consider how these might impact ethical viewpoints; visual images likewise can have an influential impact. The careful use of science fiction for thinking about AI ethics is discussed. The ways that cases are described and the manner in which AI is presented can especially impact how agency, causation, and responsibility are viewed, as well as how critical boundary questions are understood. In describing cases, it is of utmost importance to ask what further information one needs to understand the issues.

4.4.1 Introduction

Recall Sect. 4.1, where we looked at the simplified two-step 'intuition plus reason' method in applied ethics. Prior to this, cases must be selected and described. Cases may be hypothetical, fictional, or based on real life. In dealing with ethical questions, especially in our field where we need to think about as yet unrealised future possibilities, we may need to consider hypothetical cases and imaginary scenarios. Much ethical reasoning is counterfactual, consisting of asking the question, 'what if . . .'. There is thus the question of how we produce and describe hypothetical cases. Real-life cases may seem more pressing in contrast. However, even these will be presented to us in one way or another. Any description is going to be selective, even of one's own experience. We have seen in Sect. 4.2.1 how the recording of categories will have important ethical implications. We thus need to consider, first, the selection of what cases are drawn to our attention and, second, how those cases are described. We will first review some general background issues.

Attention The question of attention to what is morally relevant is critical in ethics. Moral failings can occur when a person knows full well what they ought to do, but fails to act. Another common cause of moral failure is the failure of attention to what is morally important and to what needs to be done. How a case is described will have a large impact on what features attract our attention. Significant to our interests in AI ethics, the manner in which technologies may impact the quality and direction of our attention is of critical importance.

In his book *The Fiction of Bioethics*, Tod Chambers examines how the ways in which a case is described and its narrative structure can affect the conclusions that are drawn from it [51]. Chambers had previously studied literature before turning to bioethics. Philosophers are often, with some justification, criticised for using thinly drawn hypothetical examples to advance their theories. Chambers notes how even with more richly drawn cases, the ways in which a story is told, the numbers, motives, and descriptions of characters, and many other factors will help to determine ethical responses.

Exercise 9
Take one of the previous cases in this book, or any case relevant to AI ethics you choose, and write it from different points of view. For example, you might like to

write it as 'neutrally' as possible (and this could be useful for considering what it means to write 'neutrally'), in a detective genre, as a comedy, or as a tragedy. Or rewrite the story from the point of view of the different 'characters' involved. Experiment with casting some into the role of villain, seeing some more sympathetically, then reverse roles, etc. This could work well as a group exercise. Variations could include writing different headlines or writing tweet-length summaries. Consider what conclusions might have been drawn about the ethical issues and about responsibility with different ways of telling the story. Consider how agency is attributed, hinted at, or denied, to humans, groups of humans, and technologies in different ways of telling the story. You might find it interesting to look up various accounts online and compare and contrast them. Our discussion of the LaMDA case already gives some idea of the divergent ways in which a situation may be described.

Framing The way in which an issue is framed will have an impact upon how it is assessed and understood [52]. For those who usually work within disciplines and approaches that deal with sets of formal rules and aspire to objective, logical, and/or empirically based findings, this may be a slightly unfamiliar idea, but framing happens all the time, whether we are aware of it or not, and the issue of framing is a well-established concept [53]. Classifying journal articles as systematic review articles, opinion pieces, or research using some stated methodology will all act to frame how its contents are read and assessed. 'Retweets not endorsements', 'opinions my own', and so on serve a similar purpose. Likewise, whether a film is presented as a story, a documentary, or that half-way house, a docudrama, will impact how we read and assess it. It is thus always helpful to consider how particular issues and cases are being framed, how perhaps they might have been framed differently, and what possible difference it may make.

Framing: AI in News Reports

Publishers of news reports know that readers may very well not read an article to its end, and may even only see the headline. Newspaper headlines are one key way in which stories about AI are framed. Here are some headlines from June 2022 about the LaMDA sentience controversy.

Labelling Google's LaMDA chatbot as sentient is fanciful. But it's very human to be taken in by machines [54].

Google engineer put on leave after saying AI chatbot has become sentient [55].

Google sidelines AI engineer who claims AI chatbot has become sentient [56].

No, Google's AI is not sentient [57].

A Google software engineer believes an AI has become sentient. If he's right, how would we know? [58].

LaMDA and the power of illusion: The aliens haven't landed … yet [59].

Exercise 10
Find a story about AI that particularly interests you, search for news reports, and consider the impact of how the story is framed by headlines and by the opening paragraph.

Distant or close? Framing includes how far out we stand and how far backwards and forwards in time we go (and this includes even in our subject, ethics, and portraying this all as new). It thus impacts the epistemological question of the best stance from which to form ethical judgements. Framing includes how we conceptualised what drives the unfolding of events, how widely in space we observe, and whether we conceptualise ourselves as an outsider or insider observing things. We will consider the relevance of this to how we address ethical issues in AI in Chap. 7.

The embedded nature of much of the technology that we examine makes understanding the narrative structure and framing of cases all the more important. Technologies build upon other technologies; details are often hidden from the user or become so familiar that they are lost to sight, as technology becomes an ubiquitous part of the web of human interactions in the world. As we shall see, this has important implications, including for how cause and effect and responsibility are understood.

From example to rule Work in policy formation has shown how the particular examples chosen as illustrations and as test cases can help determine how general rules are formed. For example, there is often a tendency to use the most serious cases as exemplars and extrapolate from these [60]. Unfortunately, this may lead to standards that may be overly severe for less serious cases, and the cases picked may have particular features that relevantly skew the conclusions drawn. Research ethics regulations have often been developed using the model of medical research as the foundation, but those working in social sciences have frequently pointed out that this may lead to overly draconian and inappropriate guidelines for work with different and often lower risks, and where there is a large variety of different methodologies [61]. The generalisations and conclusions drawn from examples in one domain may not translate well to another, as we indicated above in considering how concepts interpreted in the context of medicine may not necessarily generalise well to other contexts in which AI is applied. Hence, thinking broadly, communicating and learning from others, and taking examples and cases from a wide range will all be important parts of strategy in applied ethics.

4.4.2   Stories About AI

Stories about AI and how we interpret them form a background to how we think about the real cases with us now and the real possibilities we may face in the future. We have already considered the long history of myth, legend, and stories relating to technology. Likewise, there is a plethora of more recent stories concerning AI, such as tales concerning robots, the idea of computer simulation of minds, or the development of disobedient technologies such as the dreaded computer in Stanley Kubrick's movie adaptation of Arthur C. Clarke's *2001: A Space Odyssey* with its ominous phrase, 'I'm sorry Dave, I'm afraid I can't do that' [62]. The prominent stories about AI can be a means of exploring and testing our reactions to AI and will also help to shape reactions to developments in AI.

An analysis of the themes behind stories concerning AI in the twentieth and twenty-first centuries in the anglophone West describes some central themes of hope and fear, in four matched and opposing pairs [63]. The authors note that it will be useful to understand how such polarised reactions can arise when considering AI for three reasons: they could influence the goals of AI developers, influence public take-up and acceptance of AI products, and influence how AI systems are regulated in guiding policy makers and the stakeholders to whom policy makers are answerable. To this we could explicitly add that they can influence thinking and debate in AI ethics. The themes are the hope of immortality (or less ambitiously, life extension), countered by the fears of a consequent inhumanity in how this is achieved; hope for increased ease, with leisure from having tasks taken over by AI, countered by fears of our obsolescence; hopes of gratification, such as pleasurable pursuits provided by AI, countered by fears of alienation from the ground of meaning in activities; and hopes of dominance using AI, countered by fears of uprising, or the takeover of humans by advanced forms of AI. Indeed, we shall see all these themes later, especially in considering future applications of AI in Chaps. 10 and 11.

A key observation from this study is the extremes behind such narrative themes. We have noted this in the hype with which AI may be depicted. Stories concerning AI may contain more than one of these themes and often concern the strong tensions between them. The influence of these themes could help explain some of the difficulties in communication and in resolving ethical and policy issues regarding AI, especially if there tend to be broad differences between how different groups, say, developers versus the public, or different demographic groups, respond to and advocate divergent themes. Since these themes also tend to be rather extreme, they may diverge considerably from the more prosaic realities of AI in the real world.

Are we then best off just ignoring such stories? There are some complexities to such a seemingly simple suggestion. Stories can be extremely useful in teaching ethics, and science fiction has been used with success as a basis for teaching computer ethics [64].

First, stories, films, and art can help us to see questions from multiple different angles and can help us to understand our own views, as well as the views of others who differ from us. A word of advice, however, is that it is worth actually reading or viewing classics rather than assuming common summaries of the issues they raise. Otherwise, one may simply be buying into dominant narratives about classic works, rather than the often more subtle details and varying interpretations that may be found with a close reading. The use of fiction can be helpful in spurring imaginations, and it may be useful to engage in different kinds of thought processes for those who are mainly involved in practical and technical pursuits. Using stories that show the attractions of opposing themes and the tensions between them can be helpful in countering any tendency to see ethics as simply something to be learned, a kind of 'to-do' checklist of hurdles to navigate and facts to memorise. Stories, including fantastical scenarios, can assist in freeing up discussion, and the removal from reality can help to distance oneself from personal involvement. They can help us to 'think outside the box'.

Second, understanding how such narratives arise in fiction can help us see how they might also inhabit our responses to AI in the real world. It is often easier to see others doing this than to see it in ourselves. For instance, in making grandiose claims about the possibilities of AI, or in apocalyptic pronouncements of doom attached to every minor incremental development of technology. Watch out for this, and carefully consider how helpful, misleading, or otherwise such narratives are. Sometimes thinking of the 'worst-case' or 'best-case' scenarios may have some use, but it may distract. The story line may implicitly suggest parallels between humans and machines, for example, that could be tested, and may implicitly suggest a position on whether moral dilemmas presented by technology can or cannot be overcome.

Third, we are dealing with technology that is not yet with us, which is in the prototype or development stage, and which we are still attempting to understand. Even the technologies that we already use will have facets that we still do not understand. Seeing it from novel aspects may help to deepen and enrich our view of it. Nonetheless, it will always still be important to have a strong understanding of the actual technologies and their impacts. Much of the ethics debate regarding AI seems to veer between wild projections onto technology, to careful discussion of technical details and the precise wording of technology, with bewildering changes of voice and temperature.

4.4.3 Science Fiction, Ethics, and AI

Sci-fi is an obvious place to look for inspiration and imaginative responses to ethical questions in AI. It has been used in teaching computer ethics with enthusiastic responses from students, and a team engaged in this teaching has outlined several benefits [64]. They found that hypothetical scenarios taken from sci-fi can enable students to consider ethical issues free from personal involvement, can help to overcome resistance towards ethics as a subject, and can help to free up their imagination. This can be very useful in general both for approaching the complexities so often involved in ethics and for helping students to consider the merits and demerits of multiple ways of reading and responding to situations.

However, as we have already seen, other fiction can likewise have relevance for many of the ethical issues in AI, for example, novels exploring industrialisation, or indeed, any fiction exploring our understanding of human nature, which may enable us to see more clearly how understandings of the human condition may impact our reactions to AI. Science fiction may also explore situations that are either technologically very unlikely, at least based on our current knowledge, or impossible. This does not necessarily mean that there can still be useful lessons we can learn; it would be foolish to respond to Mary Shelley's *Frankenstein's Monster* with the dismissive, 'Ridiculous! The bits of human flesh used to create the monster would have rotted, and what about organ rejection, couldn't happen!'

We must also recall the question of the very ways in which AI is presented to us, and the broad distinction between focusing on the technology and the science and engineering capabilities, versus the ideologies of AI and how it is projected and imagined to be that we considered in Chap. 2. The use of science fiction may be a great sounding board for considering these issues and how they may impact our ethical responses. Fictional scenarios could also potentially feed into creating and constructing ideologies of AI which may push the narrative and ethical judgements around AI in certain directions. For example, some members of the transhumanist VR chat community (yes, there is such a thing) have suggested that social VR has potential for popularising transhumanism and morphological freedom, or the idea that the particular forms our bodies take could be altered in a wide range of ways [65]. Such explorations can also take overtly philosophical form. For example, the philosopher David Chalmers wrote an essay originally published on the Matrix website, 'The Matrix as Metaphysics', exploring philosophical issues, which also have ethical implications [66]. We will return to Chalmer's views on VR later in Chap. 7.

Using science fiction to imaginatively consider ethical issues in AI also needs to address the benefits of reality testing: would some imagined fantastical piece of technology actually work in practice, used in context, with actual human beings? How might the ethical issues that spring to mind in considering sci-fi depictions of the use of AI relate to the ethical issues that arise when considering the details of implementation of similar technology in practice? [67] Some recent work examining science fiction representations of robot carers [68] suggests that these may help to shift narratives of concern about the possible implementation of such robot carers towards a consideration of relational issues, considering three stories in film and television, *Robot & Frank* [69], *Big Hero 6* [70], and *Humans* [71], but we should be aware that fictional representations may be a poor guide to the realities of implementation in complex social and medical situations.

Exercise 11

Take any example of science fiction involving any form of AI or robotics, and first consider how it presents issues of value, including both detail and the broad approach, for example, whether of fear or hope, whether issues are presented as resolvable, etc. You may even want to write your own sci-fi.

Second, consider the question of how precisely the technology involved might be implemented in real life in the present day and what ethical and social issues might arise in trying to solve any problems for a technology that actually worked; consider what further questions you might need to ask about the situation you've envisaged. How much of your response to the sci-fi version is useful to this task?

Did different considerations arise when attempting to work out the details of implementation?

4.4.4   Images of AI

The stories about AI are not simply portrayed in words. Images are also extremely prominent and have come under scrutiny for the ways in which they might reveal and disseminate values. Images of AI abound in film, comic strips, images accompanying news reports, scientific accounts, websites, and so on. Ethical questions about images of AI also concern AI itself, especially robotics. Those working in the field often moan that news reports about developments in AI frequently accompanied by pictures of killer robots, no matter how dull the actual report is.

Exercise 12
Look up some news reports about AI and consider the appropriateness of any accompanying images.

The 'Creation of Adam' meme is a consistent image used to illustrate story after story regarding AI and, in particular, robots [72]. The meme consists of adaptations of Michelangelo's famous Creation of Adam on the ceiling of the Sistine Chapel in Rome. To the left, Adam reclines, somewhat languidly, with his hand outstretched towards the hand of God on the right, pictured as an old, white-bearded man in the sky, dressed in a flowing pale-pink gown, and surrounded by various figures. The fingers of Adam and God almost touch.

These AI creation memes can readily be seen online: you have probably already seen many if you are interested in AI. Variations include a robot stretching out a hand to a man and digital representations of hands, sometimes with a spark of electricity crossing between the hands. The robot and human hands appear on either side, as if the possibility remains that man might create the robot, or the robot might create man. A picture of equivalence between machine and creator is thus conjured up, as well as the suggestion that by the creation of machine, humanity is acting as if God. Perhaps by reference to such a famous painting, iconic of so much of Western civilisation, a certain authority is lent to the grounding world view which it signals. Such images can help to suggest ways of understanding AI and its relation to us, its creator.

Exercise 13
Look up some AI creation myth images online and consider what picture of AI it suggests to you. There are no wrong answers.

Interestingly, Michelangelo's depiction of the creation of Adam is rather inaccurate to the biblical text. There is no indication anywhere in the Bible that God has a human form like this, let alone that he wears a baby-pink gown. The symmetry between the creator and the created is thus overblown in Michelangelo's depiction. Moreover, life is not given to Adam by touch but is breathed into the clay out of which the first human was made (Genesis 2:7). ('Adam' in Hebrew can mean a human of either sex.) Perhaps the notion of thinking of ourselves as fashioning a being like us by means of technology thus also comes to mind a little too readily, given that the most immediate way of making things is 'by hand'. Only a few things, such as ballads, balloons, and blowing out birthday candles, owe their existence to our breath.

A general exercise then, to take forwards into all your thinking on AI ethics, is to think carefully about the images of AI which surround us, and especially those which accompany news or articles about AI, and consider how they might be impacting assumptions, and framing how we think of AI.

The AI creation meme presents an image of the relation of AI to humans. Images can be a very potent source for portraying AI as human in some way [73], but the very idea of portraying AI as human to any degree has attracted controversy. Those who consider that we would be better off viewing AI in terms of specific engineering tasks might rue the very idea of portraying AI as if it were human. Even aside from this issue, there are questions about the specifics of any such portrayal.

It is noticeable that many images focus on the brain, often with depictions of neurones and strongly suggest parallels between neurones and electronic circuitry. Put 'AI' into any search engine, and such pictures abound. The dominant colour is consistently blue, a colour associated with intelligence and technology. The human head is bald, and sometimes it's not clear if this is intended as a portrayal of a human, or of a robot. The suggestion might be implicit that human intelligence and artificial intelligence are straightforward models of each other and that human intelligence is all about the brain. *Of course it is!* I hear you cry. Not so fast. There are very tight interactions between our bodies and our brains, between the functioning of our bodies and the thoughts and feelings we experience. There may be important consequences for air-brushing the body out of the picture. Later, we consider the significance of embodiment for ethics in more detail, especially in Chaps. 8, 10, and 11.

Any depiction of AI as human, any robot made intentionally humanoid, and any AI-created voice will be particular. As we have seen, there have been debates and controversies about the issues of race and sex concerning the representation of AI and the reinforcing of stereotypes. Robots may have no human-like aspects at all, may be toy-like, or may be more humanoid, sometimes with a typically male appearance, at other times made to look female, and sometimes have typically female figures. The toy-like robots typically look friendly; killer robots, not so much. These are generally overtly 'male' in appearance. Does this say anything about stereotypes of masculinity and femininity? Some researchers have questioned the impact of robots that are designed to be white and that may display typical Caucasian facial features [74]. Images accompanying articles about AI are frequently in the dominant colour blue, as has been noted, but with white as the usual contrast colour. Does this say anything about race?

The question of bias in algorithms is concerned in large part with how building algorithms from past data may reinforce or even exacerbate adverse stereotypes that disadvantage certain groups and individuals. Research on word embeddings finds that biases such as common stereotyping of sex roles may be reproduced by machine learning unless careful steps are taken to avoid it [75]. Biases in human trainers will be passed on to any algorithms created [76]. There has been much concern about the impact of the perceived gender of voice assistants, with fears that it may reinforce stereotypes of 'helpful' females occupying service roles. The vocal features that tend to discriminate between voices perceived as masculine or as feminine include not just pitch, intonation, and volume but also typical sentence structure, with voices seen as more masculine having shorter phrasing and content viewed as more authoritative. Some companies producing voice assistants have claimed that market research shows that what is wanted in an assistant is someone with the typical feminine qualities of helpfulness, supportiveness, and trustworthiness. Conversely, the voices of AI that produce medical advice or wins at Jeopardy are more likely to be masculine, suggesting authority [77].

These typical gender traits are of course generalisations, and there is much variation between individuals within any one class. Moreover, these debates are complicated by different societal, cultural, and individual differences in beliefs about and perceptions of gender and illustrate the complexity of different aims and responsibilities. Much is a matter of interpretation. Placing feminine features on a robot may be seen to reinforce the idea of using women as assistants. Or perhaps it may bring about an association of women with high-end technology.

Responsibilities and aims in AI ethics The complexity of the disputes and the different responses illustrate an important aspect of ethical debates in AI: the question of what the end aim of work in AI ethics may be and how responsibilities are seen. Many in industry see the issue in terms of how to attract and retain their customer base [78]. Others consider that such stereotyping is harmful, and may aim to eradicate it, perhaps by the use of voices that sound gender ambiguous [79, 80]. The questions of sex and gender and how society is best arranged around these issues are of great complexity, with a very wide range of views on the issue. Discussions of 'feminism' may overlook that it encompasses a very wide range of theories, with contrasting and even directly conflicting viewpoints [81]. This also perhaps presents an illustration of an issue where the use of a wide range of examples might bring certain aspects to light. Much discussion of the perceived gender of voice assistants has focused on the very largest corporations, which naturally have wide influence and are often perceived to not necessarily be acting in the public interest, with concerns that they should be held to account. However, one might fairly ask what the responsibilities of, say, a small commercial entity are towards the end goal of helping to eradicate sex-role stereotyping, especially if this means they may lose out financially.

AI, Sex, and Human Embodiment
Future visions of AI may include the portrayal of feminine and masculine traits, but there is also a theme of gender-neutrality and of an 'escape' from embodiment. Some conceptions of human nature stress the mental and downplay or ignore our physical embodiment, and this may be linked to certain conceptions and valuation of intelligence, as we shall see more in Chap. 5. Moreover, some accounts of the significant differences between humans and

---

(continued)

AI, and of how AI may be able to improve upon humans, stress the limits that our biology places upon us. This too tends towards an ungendered, unsexed view of humanity.

On some views, the division of human beings into male and female is a basic category of our being. This does not necessarily give rise to any particular views about precise differences between men and women and their roles and responsibilities, but may nonetheless reinforce on the significance of such a distinction and of our biological, sexed natures.

Food for thought: the detailed implementation of AI is criticised for reinforcing and even amplifying sex and gender roles. Conversely, some conceptions of AI and of its values, and some futuristic visions of AI, may imagine a disembodied future, free entirely of notions of sex or gender.

Exercise 14

The mystical poet William Blake wrote these words:

> *For Mercy has a human heart,*
>   *Pity a human face,*
>   *And Love, the human form divine,*
>   *And Peace, the human dress.* [82]

Could we recognise such qualities in a sophisticated robot? Could giving facial features to a robot help us to see such qualities to a machine, or could it fool us? Consider how we fail to see such qualities in some human faces.

Joanna Bryson has argued that robots are artefacts that are wholly owned by humans and that it is a mistake to humanise them in any manner [82]. By doing so, we may make errors about how they function, allocate resources poorly, and falsely attribute responsibility to them rather to humans. Moreover, she argues that by humanising robots, we risk dehumanising human beings.

One can see the complexity of these issues and the wide range of reactions possible. One might respond to the claims that robots tend to have Caucasian facial features by designing robots with facial characteristics more typical of other population groups. If Bryson is right that we should treat robots as if they are things which we wholly own, then it will probably be better to keep human-like features off robots altogether. Attempts to give robots faces that are neither masculine nor feminine are likely to fail because many individuals may persist in interpreting such faces one way or another.

Exercise 15

Take the case of a robot carer for a frail elderly person or any person with a physical need for assistance. Consider the various tasks such a robot might be used for: fetching drinks; answering the front door; providing companionship through simple conversations; providing stimulation such as choosing music to play, radio programmes to listen to, or various games; making emergency calls if needed; and so on. Now consider different possible robot designs: simple humanoid features such as a basic face with simple eyes and a mouth and one of those rather robotic voices; realistic human-like features; and features and a voice designed by an AI to simulate as closely as possible the person's now deceased spouse, or their son or daughter who lives a 3-h drive away and visits once a month.

Now consider the pros and cons of the different possible robot designs and any ethical issues raised. Don't forget to consider the rather different nature of the tasks such a robot might perform.

4.4.5 Describing Ethical Questions: Causation, Responsibility, and Ethics

We have already seen an example of how agency may be highlighted or not, given to machines or to humans (see Sect. 3.2). When we describe situations, we routinely use words that attribute action and imply intention. These then will carry implications concerning agency and responsibility. If we had to describe a situation simply in terms of a sequence of movement, it would take forever, and not in the way that *Lord of the Rings* or *War and Peace* take a long time to read: it would be utterly, utterly boring. 'Her right hand raised vertically 6.37 centimetres and then extended diagonally to the right a further 10.56 centimetres. It descended by 4.13 centimetres. Her fingers and thumb moved into a position around the handle of a mug and then moved slightly inwards. The fingers made close contact with the handle of the mug. Meanwhile, a faint sound of lawnmowers filled the room, the curtain moved slightly in the wind, she felt a slight itch in her nose, remembered she had forgotten her packed lunch ....' You get the gist.

Elizabeth Anscombe's book *Intention* spells out an example of a man moving his arm up and down which has the effect of pumping poisoned water into a cistern that feeds the drinking water in a house where a group of party leaders are plotting to exterminate Jews and start a world war [83]. There are also many other side effects of the man's actions: the shadows falling, the multiple impacts on those affected by the death of the party leaders, and the squeezing sound of the pump. The way in which such a case is described, including the attribution of specific intentions to the man, will impact how we attribute causation and responsibility.

Attributing responsibility to an agent generally involves attributing their actions as the cause or as a contributing causal factor and attributing either intention or culpable lack of care. How we assign these is going to be immensely complex and hence will depend heavily on what is picked out and how it is described. Even the assignment of physical causes to material events, such as the cause of a fire, will depend upon picking out something as cause from a set of background conditions [84]. A match will only spark a fire given the right set of background conditions. So when is a condition a 'background' condition? Much of this will depend upon what we expect to be the case. We are warned not to light a match near combustible materials such as on garage forecourts, but if someone has stored a can of petrol with the lid off somewhere where it's not expected, what is the cause of the resultant fire when someone lights a candle? Note that as new technology is introduced, what we consider to be a 'background condition' and what we consider to be the cause may shift.

Time scales are critical in attributions of causation and responsibility; it matters where a story starts [85]. For instance, consider the Tay Chatbot example discussed in Sect. 2.4.5. Attending to the incident only from the time of launch might eclipse questions about responsibility for decisions leading up to its release and responsibility for details of its development. The very way in which technology may facilitate the collection of certain kinds of data may act in ways to skew how a situation appears and how causation is attributed. For example, increasing the ease of collection of health data from tracking and self-monitoring by individuals may lead to an increased emphasis on individual responsibility for disease, perhaps emphasising fitness, and control over diet, and ignoring the societal and environmental contributions. Similar claims have been made with regard to the rise of genetic information leading to a notion of 'genetic responsibility' [86]. This may be beneficial for some, yet may shift attribution of responsibility for health in ways detrimental to others. Carefully designed and rigorous studies show that social class and other factors may have a much larger impact on health than other factors; the emphasis on the collection of physiological and other data enabled by health tracking apps may potentially increase perceptions of individual responsibility for health [87, 88].

The LaMDA case, which we considered earlier, shows the considerable importance of understanding how we attribute causal responsibility and the strong tendency to attribute agency in how we understand and approach technology in particular. Some commentators appeared to cast scorn on those who worried that LaMDA might indeed be developing sentience, yet the readiness to do this is entirely understandable, and considering this, one might then form the view that companies working on such technologies should anticipate such an issue. The suspicions among many members of the public that Google must be 'up to something' are also rather understandable.

Hence, the importance of how cases are described for forming ethical judgements concerning a situation can hardly be overstated.

Consider the Guidelines for Indigenous Centred AI mentioned in Sect. 2.9. Many of these have implications for how situations and events are described. The principle of locality notes that local knowledge is very important to indigenous communities. Hence, this may mean that a closer focus on specific local issues may shape how a situation arose and is understood. The principle of relationality and reciprocity has direct implications for how agency and responsibility may be described. It notes how indigenous knowledge is often relational and emphasises how AI belongs within wider systems of relationships, again emphasising the specificity of different communities. The principle of responsibility, relevance, and accountability notes the strong concern of indigenous people for their communities. Again, this is likely to impact upon how cases are described and how causation is attributed. Understanding the situations of indigenous communities may require understanding historical factors going back many generations.

Describing cases: 'the robot did it' Attributing causation in a complex situation is a complex mix of interests, concerns, and focus [89]. The ways in which we highlight a feature of a complex situation as a cause may depend on many factors, including salience and novelty. The 'new kid on the block', or the last thing to enter the mix, is frequently seen as the 'cause', but this is not necessarily helpful or informative. Did the failure of the 'O' rings at low temperature 'cause' the Space Shuttle Challenger disaster, or was the 'cause' the failures of management and communication? [90] Likewise, we often pick out the most salient, the most visible to us, or the most different, as the likely cause of an anomalous event.

Because technology is new, shiny, and different, we often think of it as 'the cause' of progress, but this may be unhelpful and inaccurate. Consider Deep Blue's win over chess champion Garry Kasparov in 1997. Did a computer beat a human being? Or did a large team of scientists who built Deep Blue, together with the accumulated knowledge of a great many chess masters, beat one human being? [91, p. 34]. If we describe the situation as one man, Kasparov, battling it out against a vast team of humans, this changes the perception somewhat. It looks a little bit like cheating.

The ways in which technology is often embedded in vast systems and may have a convoluted and often opaque pathway of production means that analysing and attributing responsibility and the causal contribution of different aspects may be a tortuous enterprise. Any tendency to view technology in terms of agency will also likely significantly impact the attribution of causation and responsibility to a set of circumstances. Human beings have a very strong tendency to see agency in movements and to see faces in things. Indeed, there are multiple Twitter accounts called variations of 'faces in things'.

These issues also help to illustrate why the question of transparency in AI must extend far beyond the more technical question of how a particular instance of machine learning functions but must include transparency of the wider system within which the AI in question is embedded.

Describing cases: what you don't know, and what you don't know you don't know This chapter has strongly argued that it is critical to pay attention to the way in which cases used as examples in discussing ethics, forming judgements, and making decisions including policy are selected and described. However, to do this will involve knowledge, knowledge one may not have. The issue of transparency is one major stumbling block. In cases involving technology, information that is private to the companies involved may be critical. In any case involving people—that is, every case—there will be the question of what a person's thoughts and motivations are. This can be a problem even for our own thoughts. In many cases, specialist knowledge may be needed. For example, we have looked at several cases involving people living with dementia, where understanding of the condition and of its impact on different individuals will be crucial. In addition, this understanding will require many different perspectives, since, as we have seen, there are multiple impacts of such a condition, medical, psychological, social, and so on.

A critical strategy for any work in applied ethics then involves considering what other information we need about any particular case or set of issues and where we might get this information from. What don't we know?

Exercise 16

Consider one or more of the exercises in Chap. 2 which concerned people living with dementia, such as Exercises 6, 8, 9, 10, or 11. What else would you need to know to understand what ethical questions were at stake, in the particular example(s) you have chosen? Consider who you might turn to for information or opinion about the issues. Consider what other kinds of cases you might want to look at to gain a fuller understanding of the questions involved.

Comment on the exercise Many people have some experience of dementia, perhaps through a family member who is living with the condition, or through personal experience. However, it is a complex and very variable condition that takes various forms and that can affect individuals rather differently. Moreover, many of the questions around the use of any technology for diagnosis, research, or care need to take into account a wider context. These may include but are not limited to the social attitudes towards dementia and towards the elderly in general, which can vary greatly depending upon cultural, economic, and social conditions as well as individual factors. The background question of healthcare provision and social care is also a major factor. Those working in technology may sometimes push ideas a considerable way towards development, often with the finest of intentions, without always careful consultation and consideration of the situation of those they are trying to assist.

Other voices, and your own voice Other perspectives are vital. So is yours. Taking the views of others into account does not mean that yours do not matter and should not mean that you fail to speak up when you have a hunch that something is wrong. Developing your capacity to do so could one day play a major role in averting disaster. Never forget that sheer chance may put you in a position of critical importance where you could make a real difference.

Ethics cases: trolley problems and other stories As necessary as it is to recognise the need for full and rich descriptions of cases, in reality we will never get the 'full' picture, and, as we have noted in relation to moral relevance, some details will not be relevant. (Working out which are, and which are not, is not necessarily easy.) It may often be very helpful to focus on specific details and certain aspects only for the purpose of considering which aspects of a case are especially pertinent to a judgement.

Consider the well-known 'trolley problems' in ethics. The popularity of these originate from the work of Philippa Foot, who worked at Somerville College, Oxford, in the twentieth century and whose work was an important contribution to developing interest in applied moral philosophy [92]. I also vividly recall trolley problems being described in class by the philosopher Richard Hare, who had been a prisoner of war in the Second World War forced to work on the notorious Thai-Burma railway and who described real-life situations of loose trolleys careering down the tracks. A classic trolley problem involves considering a train on a track, with the possibility of averting its course. If it goes straight ahead, a certain number of people will be killed (or etc.). If it is deviated to the other line, something different will happen.

These imaginary exercises hold various things constant and simplify the possible actions. The use of a train track means that only two things can happen. (Although some imaginative types sometimes propose derailment or other left-field interventions.) There is usually only one agent involved in making a decision. Decisions have to be made instantly. The scenario usually asks for a choice, and there is seldom any follow-up or what one might call a 'debrief' on the situation. The fate of the potential victims is often as near certain as possible, since being run over by a train is very unlikely to result in survival. The situation is also set up so that not making a decision is tantamount to making a decision, since there will be an inevitable outcome of failing to act.

When drawing conclusions from such hypothetical scenarios, it is essential to consider how a case involving decision-making and judgement is set up and reflect on how the parameters of any scenario may impact the conclusions that are drawn [93].

Exercise 17
We will examine the MIT Moral Machines experiment further in Chap. 7. As a preliminary, consider some of the basic design elements of the experiment described in Sect. 4.2.

4.5   Key Points

Which cases are selected for consideration and how they are described can make a critical difference in forming ethical judgements. This can impact what features are understood to be relevant; how agency, causation, and responsibility are assigned; and how cases are generalised.

The language that we use to describe AI, robots, and technology in general can make a large difference in what moral issues we see in a situation. Language may help to mask or to reveal ethical questions.

Science fiction can be a rich source of material for debating and understanding ethical issues in AI but must be used wisely, precisely because of the manner in which AI is portrayed in fiction, film, and image can have a powerful hold on how we view ethical questions. Other fiction can also provide insights.

Certain basic assumptions about the nature of ethics will influence how ethical problems are understood and how they are resolved (or not). For example, many assume that ethics must be 'universal' in some way, but this idea can be understood in different ways and is not itself universally held.

The question of whether or not there can be genuine moral dilemmas and whether ethical values and judgements can be formalised and precisely expressed in language also shape how argument and discussion in ethics proceed.

There are different ways of understanding the purpose, or object, of morality. The very developments of technology may have a significant impact on factors that previously or currently go towards forming the issues that ethics addresses as well as our ethical responses.

Take care with the assumption that we need to seek 'the' answer to ethical questions.

Perhaps the most important take-away from this chapter is that it matters how cases for consideration are selected, and how they are described.

A critical first question is to ask yourself what relevant information you do not have and consider where to go and who to ask to find out more.

4.6 Educator Notes

Students working at different levels and with different background interests may approach this chapter in very different ways.

A basic key point that all students should take away from this chapter is the importance of considering the ways in which ethical issues are presented to us. For those with less time, this point can be explained and understood through examining the points about images of AI and/or about narrative structures and how ethical issues, issues of agency and responsibility, are portrayed, using news articles or science fiction as examples. Students should be encouraged to see the complexity of ethical issues and the importance of considering alternative viewpoints.

A second key point for all students is to understand the importance of applying judgement and thought to our ethical responses, but also to understand that how such reasoning is precisely understood is an open question.

Given the importance of understanding the impact of our own worldviews on how we identify and interpret ethical issues, the material inviting students to consider the viewpoints expressed in the Indigenous AI Protocols could also be used as a springboard to extend such an exercise to include consideration of any other cultural or religious frameworks on how ethical issues in AI are understood.

Any students with backgrounds in literature, journalism, or the visual arts, and similar subjects, may wish to concentrate on exploring the issues around narrative structure and visual image, carefully considering how this may impact how issues of value are portrayed and understood. Such students would likely be able to bring further material and understanding to these issues beyond what we have had time to explore here. This would serve as a concrete illustration of the value of different perspectives on these ethical issues in AI.

Encouraging students to look again at cases they have considered from previous chapters can be useful in enabling them to see how their understanding and viewpoints may develop.

Debate and extended project and essay topics Exercise 1 on the LaMDA case would provide a focus point for debate and might work well if students were instructed to take one side or another, regardless of their initial response. Exercise 9 could work well as a project for small groups working together who can then compare and contrast their answers. Exercises 10, 11, and 12 would work well in class, especially if students prepared examples to bring and talk about. Exercise 11 might make an interesting essay topic for students interested in narrative accounts of AI.

References

1. MacIntyre A (1984) Does applied ethics rest on a mistake? Monist 67(4):498–513
2. Beauchamp TL (2005) In: Frey RG, Wellman CH (eds) The nature of applied ethics. A companion to applied ethics. Wiley-Blackwell, New York, pp 1–16
3. Tiku N (2022) The Google engineer who thinks the company's AI has come to lif. The Washington Post
4. Kahneman D (2011) Thinking, fast and slow. Farrar, Straus and Giroux, New York
5. Bazerman MH, Tenbrunsel AE (2011) Blind spots. Princeton University Press, Princeton
6. Balfour DL, Adams GB (2014) Unmasking administrative evil. Routledge, Oxfordshire
7. Rawls J (1999) A theory of justice, revised edn. Harvard University Press, Cambridge, MA
8. Festinger L (1957) A theory of cognitive dissonance, vol 2. Stanford University Press, Redwood City, CA
9. Nozick R (1974) Anarchy, state, and utopia, vol 5038. Basic Books, New York
10. Wachowski L, Wachowski L (1999) The Matrix. Warner Home Video
11. Beauchamp T, Childress J (2013) Principles of biomedical ethics, 7th edn. Oxford University Press, Oxford
12. Floridi L, Cowls J, Beltrametti M, Chatila R, Chazerand P, Dignum V, Luetge C, Madelin R, Pagallo U, Rossi F, Schafer B (2018) AI4People—an ethical framework for a good AI society: opportunities, risks, principles, and recommendations. Mind Mach 28(4):689–707
13. Boddington P (2017) Towards a code of ethics for artificial intelligence. Springer, Cham
14. Mittelstadt B (2019) Principles alone cannot guarantee ethical AI. Nat Mach Intell 1:501–507
15. Boorse C (1975) On the distinction between disease and illness. Philos Public Aff:49–68
16. World Health Organization (1978) Declaration of Alma-eta (No. WHO/EURO: 1978-3938-43697-61471). World Health Organization. Regional Office for Europe
17. Boddington P, Räisänen U (2009) Theoretical and practical issues in the definition of health: insights from aboriginal Australia. J Med Philos 34(1):49–67. Oxford University Press
18. Rose N, Novas C (2005) Biological citizenship. Global assemblages: technology, politics, and ethics as anthropological problems. Blackwell, New York, pp 439–463
19. Homer N, Szelinger S, Redman M, Duggan D, Tembe W, Muehling J, Pearson JV, Stephan DA, Nelson SF, Craig DW (2008) Resolving individuals contributing trace amounts of DNA to highly complex mixtures using high-density SNP genotyping microarrays. PLoS Genet 4(8): e1000167
20. Gitschier J (2009) Inferential genotyping of Y chromosomes in Latter-Day Saints founders and comparison to Utah samples in the HapMap project. Am J Hum Genet 84(2):251–258

21. Blake Lemoine @cajundiscordian (2022). https://twitter.com/cajundiscordian/status/15365034
74308907010
22. Weizenbaum J (1967) Computer power and human reason. Freeman and Company, New York
23. Awad E, Dsouza S, Kim R, Schulz J, Henrich J, Shariff A et al (2018) The moral machine
experiment. Nature 563(7729):59–64
24. Ali T (2022) Google engineer claims AI chatbot is sentient, but Alan Turing Institute expert
says it could 'dazzle' anyone. Independent
25. Johnson K (2022) LaMDA and the sentient AI trap. Wired. https://www.wired.com/story/
lamda-sentient-ai-bias-google-blake-lemoine/
26. Gebru T, Mitchell M (2022) We warned Google that people might believe AI was sentient.
Washington Post. https://www.washingtonpost.com/opinions/2022/06/17/google-ai-ethics-sen
tient-lemoine-warning/
27. Farley L (1978) Sexual shakedown: the sexual harassment of women on the job. McGraw Hill,
New York
28. Mill JS (1869) The subjection of women. Longman, Green, Reader, and Dyer, London
29. Garland D (2008) On the concept of moral panic. Crime Media Cult 4(1):9–30
30. Noble SU (2018) Algorithms of oppression: how search engines reinforce racism. NYU Press,
New York
31. Blodgett SL, O'Connor B (2017) Racial disparity in natural language processing: a case study
of social media African-American English. arXiv preprint arXiv:1707.00061
32. Kearns M, Roth A (2019) The ethical algorithm: the science of socially aware algorithm design.
Oxford University Press, Oxford
33. Aristotle (2014) Aristotle: Nicomachean ethics (trans: Crisp R, ed). Cambridge University Press
34. Mill JS (1863) Utilitarianism. Parker, Son and Bourn, London
35. Singer P (2011) The expanding circle: ethics, evolution, and moral progress. Princeton University Press, Princeton
36. Zollman KJ (2010) The epistemic benefit of transient diversity. Erkenntnis 72(1):17
37. Nagel T (1979) Moral luck. In: Mortal questions. Cambridge University Press, New York, pp
31–32
38. Williams B, Bernard W (1981) Moral luck: philosophical papers 1973–1980. Cambridge
University Press, Cambridge
39. Reynolds E (2018) The agony of Sophia, the world's first robot citizen, condemned to a lifeless
career in marketing. Wired
40. Open Letter to the European Commission Artificial Intelligence and Robotics. http://www.
robotics-openletter.eu
41. Parviainen J, Coeckelbergh M (2021) The political choreography of the Sophia robot: beyond
robot rights and citizenship to political performances for the social robotics market. AI & Soc
36(3):715–724
42. Warnock GJ (1971) The object of morality. Routledge, London
43. Yeung K, Howes A, Pogrebna G (2019) AI governance by human rights-centred design,
deliberation and oversight: an end to ethics washing. In: The Oxford handbook of AI ethics.
Oxford University Press, Oxford
44. Bietti E (2020) From ethics washing to ethics bashing: a view on tech ethics from within moral
philosophy. In: Proceedings of the 2020 conference on fairness, accountability, and transparency. Association for Computing Machinery, New York, pp 210–219
45. Mackie JL (1977) Inventing right and wrong. Penguin, Baltimore
46. De Courson B, Nettle D (2021) Why do inequality and deprivation produce high crime and low
trust? Sci Rep 11(1):1–11
47. Crawford K (2021) The atlas of AI. Yale University Press, New Haven
48. Kramer AD, Guillory JE, Hancock JT (2014) Experimental evidence of massive-scale emotional contagion through social networks. Proc Natl Acad Sci 111(24):8788–8790

49. O'Reilly M, Dogra N, Whiteman N, Hughes J, Eruyar S, Reilly P (2018) Is social media bad for mental health and wellbeing? Exploring the perspectives of adolescents. Clin Child Psychol Psychiatry 23(4):601–613

50. Berryman C, Ferguson CJ, Negy C (2018) Social media use and mental health among young adults. Psychiatry Q 89(2):307–314

51. Chambers T (1999) The fiction of bioethics (reflective bioethics). Routledge, New York

52. Goffman E (1974) Frame analysis: an essay on the organization of experience. Harvard University Press, Cambridge

53. Tannen D (ed) (1993) Framing in discourse. Oxford University Press, Oxford

54. Walsh T (2022) Labelling Google's LaMDA chatbot as sentient is fanciful. But it's very human to be taken in by machines. The Guardian

55. Porter J (2022) Google suspends engineer who claims its AI is sentient. The Verge

56. Grant N, Metz C (2022) Google sidelines AI engineer who claims AI chatbot has become sentient. New York Times

57. Metz R (2022) No, Google's AI is not sentient. CNN. https://edition.cnn.com/2022/06/13/tech/google-ai-not-sentient/index.html

58. Davis O (2022) A Google software engineer believes an AI has become sentient. If he's right, how would we know? The Conversation. https://theconversation.com/a-google-software-engineer-believes-an-ai-has-become-sentient-if-hes-right-how-would-we-know-185024

59. Rosenberg L (2022) LaMDA and the power of illusion: the aliens haven't landed … yet. Venture Beat. https://venturebeat.com/2022/06/14/lamda-and-the-power-of-illusion-the-aliens-havent-landed-yet/

60. Boddington P, Hogben S (2006) Working up policy: the use of specific disease exemplars in formulating general principles governing childhood genetic testing. Health Care Anal 14(1):1–13

61. Atkinson P (2009) Ethics and ethnography. Twenty-First Century Soc 4(1):17–30

62. Kubrick SMGM (1966) 2001 A space Odessy

63. Cave S, Dihal K (2019) Hopes and fears for intelligent machines in fiction and reality. Nat Mach Intell 1(2):74–78

64. Burton E, Goldsmith J, Mattei N (2018) How to teach computer ethics through science fiction. Commun ACM 61(8):54–64. https://dl.acm.org/doi/pdf/10.1145/3154485

65. https://twitter.com/HampVR/status/1537134973441933313

66. Chalmers D (2003) The matrix as metaphysics. In: Schneider S (ed) Science fiction and philosophy: from time travel to superintelligence. Wiley, New York

67. Koistinen AK (2016) The (care) robot in science fiction: a monster or a tool for the future? Confero 4(2):97–109

68. Teo Y (2021) Recognition, collaboration and community: science fiction representations of robot carers in Robot & Frank, Big Hero 6 and Humans. Med Humanit 47(1):95–102

69. Robot and Frank (2012) dir. Jake Schreier, USA

70. Big Hero 6 (dir Don Hall/Chris Williams, USA 2014)

71. Humans (UK/USA, Channel 4/AMC, 2015–2018)

72. Singler B (2020) The AI creation meme: a case study of the new visibility of religion in artificial intelligence discourse. Religion 11(5):253

73. Cave S, Craig C, Dihal K, Dillon S, Montgomery J, Singler B, Taylor L (2018) Portrayals and perceptions of AI and why they matter. The Royal Society, London

74. Cave S, Dihal K (2020) The whiteness of AI. Philos Technol 33(4):685–703

75. Bolukbasi T, Chang KW, Zou JY, Saligrama V, Kalai AT (2016) Man is to computer programmer as woman is to homemaker? Debiasing word embeddings. Adv Neural Inf Proces Syst 29

76. Binns R, Veale M, Van Kleek M, Shadbolt N (2017) Like trainer, like bot? Inheritance of bias in algorithmic content moderation. In: International conference on social informatics. Springer, Cham, pp 405–415

77. Steele C (2018) The real reason voice assistants are female (and why it matters) PC. https://uk. pcmag.com/smart-home/92697/the-real-reason-voice-assistants-are-female-and-why-it-matters
78. Poushneh A (2021) Humanizing voice assistant: the impact of voice assistant personality on consumers' attitudes and behaviors. J Retail Consum Serv 58:102283
79. Tolmeijer S, Zierau N, Janson A, Wahdatehagh JS, Leimeister JMM, Bernstein A (2021) Female by default?–exploring the effect of voice assistant gender and pitch on trait and trust attribution. In: Extended abstracts of the 2021 CHI conference on human factors in computing systems, pp 1–7
80. Woods HS (2018) Asking more of Siri and Alexa: feminine persona in service of surveillance capitalism. Crit Stud Media Commun 35(4):334–349
81. Jagger A (1983) Feminist theory and human nature. Harvester, Sussex, UK
82. Bryson JJ (2010) Robots should be slaves. In: Close engagements with artificial companions: key social, psychological, ethical and design issues, vol 8, pp 63–74
83. Anscombe GEM (1957) Intention. Basil Blackwell, Oxford
84. Mackie JL (1965) Causes and conditions. Am Philos Q 2(4):245–264
85. Boddington P (2016) Shared responsibility agreements: causes of contention. In: Dawson A (ed) The philosophy of public health. Routledge, pp 95–110
86. Hallowell N (1999) Doing the right thing: genetic risk and responsibility. Sociol Health Illn 21(5):597–621
87. Marmot M, Wilkinson R (eds) (2005) Social determinants of health. Oxford University Press, Oxford
88. Lupton D (2013) The digitally engaged patient: self-monitoring and self-care in the digital health era. Soc Theory Health 11(3):256–270
89. Kelley HH (1973) The processes of causal attribution. Am Psychol 28(2):107
90. McDonald AJ, Hansen JR (2009) Truth, lies, and O-rings: inside the space shuttle challenger disaster. University Press of Florida, Gainesville, p 626
91. Lanier J (2010) You are not a gadget: a manifesto. Vintage, New York
92. Foot P (1967) The problem of abortion and the doctrine of the double effect. Oxford Rev 5
93. Kamm FM (2020) The use and abuse of the trolley problem: self-driving cars, medical treatments, and the distribution of harm. In: Liao MS (ed) Ethics of artificial intelligence. Oxford University Press, Oxford, pp 79–108

Further Reading

Methodology in Applied Ethics

Allen C, Smit I, Wallach W (2005) Artificial morality: top-down, bottom-up, and hybrid approaches. Ethics Inf Technol 7(3):149–155
Beauchamp TL (2005) The nature of applied ethics. In: Frey RG, Wellman CH (eds) A companion to applied ethics. Wiley-Blackwell, New York, pp 1–16
Beauchamp TL, Beauchamp TA, Childress JF (2019) Principles of biomedical ethics, 8th edn. Oxford University Press, Oxford Part I Moral Foundations
Burton E, Goldsmith J, Mattei N (2018) How to teach computer ethics through science fiction. Commun ACM 61(8):54–64
Chambers T (2001) The fiction of bioethics: a precis. Am J Bioeth 1(1):40–43
Chambers T (2016) Eating One's friends: fiction as argument in bioethics. Lit Med 34(1):79–105
Glover J (1990) Causing death and saving lives: the moral problems of abortion, infanticide, suicide, euthanasia, capital punishment, war and other life-or-death choices. Penguin, London
Mackie JL (1977) Inventing right and wrong. Penguin, New York
Singer P (2011) Practical ethics. Cambridge University Press, Cambridge

Artificial Intelligence, Perceptions, and Sources of Bias

Awad E, Dsouza S, Kim R, Schulz J, Henrich J, Shariff A et al (2018) The moral machine experiment. Nature 563(7729):59–64

Cave S, Dihal K (2019) Hopes and fears for intelligent machines in fiction and reality. Nat Mach Intell 1(2):74–78

Cave S, Craig C, Dihal K, Dillon S, Montgomery J, Singler B, Taylor L (2018) Portrayals and perceptions of AI and why they matter. The Royal Society, London

Coeckelbergh M (2022) The Ubuntu robot: towards a relational conceptual framework for intercultural robotics. Sci Eng Ethics 28(2):1–15

https://dl.acm.org/doi/pdf/10.1145/3154485 (n.d.)

Lanier J (2010) You are not a gadget: a manifesto. Vintage, New York

Noble SU (2018) Algorithms of oppression: how search engines reinforce racism. NYU Press, New York

Singler B (2020) The AI creation meme: a case study of the new visibility of religion in artificial intelligence discourse. Religion 11(5):253

Weizenbaum J (1967) Computer power and human reason. Freeman and Company, New York

Chapter 5
Humans and Intelligent Machines: Underlying Values

Abstract Many questions in AI ethics involve the comparison of human beings with machines that display aspects of intelligence. We thus need to understand how humans are understood and how intelligence is understood. We examine what is meant by intelligence noting the range of different ways in which it is characterised, why we value intelligence, and some ethical implications of answers to these questions. In particular, it is important to note that some accounts of intelligence used in AI are instrumental, understanding intelligence as the capacity effectively to reach goals. The second part of the chapter examines theories of human nature. These underlie many questions in ethics yet may remain relatively unexamined. Issues outlined of relevance to AI ethics include questions concerning the place of human beings in the natural world; claims of particular roles that humans may have; claims that human beings have some essential nature; claims about the relationship of humans to the mind and to embodiment; the boundaries and limits to human nature; and claims about divisions within human nature, our strengths and weaknesses, and how humans may be improved. Examples and exercises are given that illustrate how these issues impact practical questions in AI ethics.

Keywords Definition of intelligence · Measurement of intelligence · Big data · Truth · Human nature · Human perfectibility

5.1 Introduction

Summary
This chapter aims to provide a survey of some of the questions concerning how we value intelligence and how human nature is understood, which underlie many of the central and most perplexing questions in AI ethics. Analysing these issues can assist with understanding divergent viewpoints.

Many questions in AI ethics concern what happens when human beings or aspects of human action, thought, and decision-making are enhanced or replaced, in part or in whole, by the work of machines that manifest aspects of intelligence. Hence, assessing the ethics of AI involves, inter alia, implicit or explicit comparisons between humans and intelligent machines. Any comparison of interest to us will be explicitly normative. Projects working on AI research and application generally involve normative claims about why the project is worth pursuing, as well as whether the means adopted to achieve their goals are well chosen and justified.

These explicit or implicit comparisons between humans and machines occur both at the general and specific levels. The aspiration that AI will recreate human intelligence, perhaps even create beings 'like us', rests upon claims about the extent of its capacity to mimic, reproduce, or even exceed, human-level intelligence, as well as on the purpose and the value of doing so. Particular projects in AI typically do not make such general claims, and indeed those working on them may positively disavow them; this is probably the more common attitude. Nonetheless, ethical questions will still arise with these more modest projects, which require an assessment of the use of AI to replace or enhance human intelligence on a case-by-case basis. There are obvious safety issues involved, concerning whether the AI is functioning as expected, but wider questions too, about the comparison of intelligence in machines and in humans and about what is gained and what is lost in using intelligent machines alongside humans, or instead of humans.

Hence, this chapter will examine these questions underlying AI ethics, the questions of how intelligence is valued, and the complex issue of human nature. The latter is essential: for how can we compare and contrast humans with machines without a framework for understanding and for valuing humans? There is a close connection between the question of how we value intelligence and how we understand human nature, since our cognitive capacities have generally been seen as a central distinguishing feature of human beings.

These questions have been discussed since the dawn of philosophy and of theology. There are endless opportunities for taking these debates and questions further. There is much to be explored in the technical details of what precisely AI can achieve, and much work is currently underway in the intersecting fields of cognitive science, neuroscience, and artificial intelligence, all of which can help to shed light on the ethical questions of AI. There are vast libraries and schools of thought from around the world and throughout history on the subject of human nature, different and sometimes conflicting assumptions made about human nature from different disciplinary perspectives, and debates within religion as well as philosophy and social sciences such as sociology, psychology, and anthropology.

Accounts of human nature may be held implicitly and are often held very deeply but may help to explain some of the different responses to some of the central questions of AI ethics. These include questions such as whether AI will take away our agency, reduce us to slaves, enhance what is most valuable, help us to achieve perfection, render us babbling nincompoops ruled by the technological elite, and divide humanity into two groups: the enhanced and the 'normies'.

Casual mention of this chapter to others while in the process of writing it has tended to provoke the response, 'Are you going to discuss [fill in favourite thinker or school of thought]?' The answer, sadly, is probably no, just because there are so many to include. Views about the value of intelligence and assumptions about human nature often help to identify differences between cultures and worldviews.

One approach would be to present a comprehensive smorgasbord of different value systems from around the world. This would necessarily be incomplete and doubtless partial. Rather, the approach I have taken is to try to parse out some of the central questions that mark areas of commonality and difference and hence help to facilitate further conversations and dialogues beyond this book.

By examining the foundations of one's own views and the fissures, unanswered questions, and places of certainty and uncertainty that lie beneath these, the better prepared one hopefully is for fruitful dialogue with others. The choice of examples and thinkers given here is hence personal and inevitably biased, but the invitation to the reader is to use this as a framework for further exploration.

The strategy in this chapter is to raise some of the central questions to consider about the nature and value of intelligence and about human nature, focusing on issues where the answers given have relevance for how we understand and address many of the ethical questions in AI. Indeed, two questions that arise are whether we would ever be able to build a 'complete' picture of human nature and whether we will ever be able fully to understand intelligence. After all, why would we presume that our intelligence is sufficient to be able fully to understand itself? Nonetheless, by means of exploring the questions that have produced points of contention, agreement, and disagreement, we can add to our toolkit for advancing debate and discussion. This will often involve unearthing common assumptions and sometimes radical disagreements.

5.2 The Nature and Value of Intelligence

Summary
This section asks an essential question for understanding ethical issues in the development and deployment of AI: what is intelligence, and why do we value it? There are many different ways of defining intelligence. Instrumental accounts that see intelligence in terms of the efficient achievement of goals are common but not universal among those developing AI. Differences in accounts of the nature of intelligence have implications for how the project of AI is conceived, for how the intelligence of humans is compared to AI, for how human beings are valued, and for how the achievements of civilisation and society are understood and valued.

5.2.1 What Is Intelligence, and Why Do We Value It?

The general question of why we would use or develop AI rests upon an answer to this question: if AI is artificial intelligence, why do we value intelligence such that we wish to create artificial versions of it? Why do we value our own intelligence so much that we wish to try to enhance or extend it using AI? As with so many questions in philosophy, it sounds ridiculous even to pose such a question. Naturally, we value intelligence, but why? And how much? And how does the value we give to intelligence compare to other things we value?

Intelligence, thought, and wisdom   Stuart Russell and Peter Norvig begin their textbook *Artificial Intelligence, A Modern Approach* by noting that the very name of our species, *Homo sapiens*, reflects our intelligence [1, p. 1], although *Homo sapiens* is generally translated as 'man the wise'. They add that we have tried to understand how we think for thousands of years, and now the field of AI is trying not just to understand thinking but to build intelligent entities.

It is no doubt true that our intelligence is important to us, but what precisely that intelligence is, why it is important, and how central it is to our understanding of ourselves are questions to which there are many different responses. Already we have not one idea, but three: thinking, intelligence, and wisdom. These are different concepts, with different values attached to them.

Is all thinking intelligence? Trying to address this question, I watch the seemingly random content of my mind: wondering if it's time for lunch and if so, what to have; noticing how satisfying the colour contrast between the red and purple tulips in the vase on my desk is; worrying if I can manage to explain this section of the book well enough; realising I haven't put my shoes on yet as I become aware of my feet; and more.

Exercise 1
What differences are there between thought, intelligence, and wisdom?

What aspects of thinking should be included in intelligence? Idly daydreaming is surely thought, but is it intelligence? Can you explain your answer?

What is the difference, if any, between intelligence and wisdom? List some people you think of when thinking of intelligence and some when thinking of wisdom. Does wisdom require intelligence? What more is needed?

Before we go on, how would you define intelligence? How would you define wisdom?

Multiple definitions of intelligence and intelligence as goal-directed   The difficulty and controversy of our subject can be illustrated by the sheer number of definitions of intelligence that exist. Shane Legg and Marcus Hutter collected over 70 different definitions of intelligence, showing some overlapping features and some common approaches, but also considerable divergence [2]. Our aim here then is certainly not to come up with 'the' correct definition of intelligence. Indeed, there may be appropriately different definitions for different purposes.

One broad approach to defining intelligence is via its necessary constituents, such as the use of memory, comparison, understanding, reasoning, abstract thinking, problem-solving, adaptation to new contexts, and facility in dealing with cognitive complexity. The capacity to learn and to adapt to new circumstances is frequently included in definitions of intelligence as well as the capacity to improve one's learning. Other approaches attempt to capture the essence of what intelligence achieves. An account by Legg and Hutter, produced from the examination of numerous accounts from different fields, gives an informal definition in terms of the capacity of an agent to reach goals in a large range of circumstances [3]. This captures an approach common within AI. For example, it is close to the account given by Russell for humans that their intelligence is measured by their ability to reach their objectives.

Goals, artificial intelligence, and human intelligence Legg and Hutter's definition is given in the context of AI but refers simply to 'an agent', whereas Russell purports to give a definition of *human* intelligence. Should we be thinking of these as the same or as different? Whatever your answer, it is important to be clear.

The definitions of intelligence collected by Legg and Hutter are grouped into 18 collective definitions, 35 definitions by psychologists, and 18 definitions by AI researchers. Of these, 2 of the 35 psychologist definitions mention goals, in contrast to 9 of the 18 definitions by AI researchers which mention goals. One could hazard a guess that this disparity may arise because the AI researchers are in the business of constructing AI systems to achieve their ends and hence are ipso facto creating AI to achieve their own goals. We can ask if this is necessarily appropriate as an account of human-level intelligence.

It may be that the very practice of artificial intelligence serves to intensify the emphasis on the achievement of goals as a hallmark of intelligence. Could this then be reflected back to how we assess and understand human intelligence? As life imitates art, could it also imitate technology?

Goals, instrumentality, and the value of intelligence Note that an account of intelligence in terms of goals is concerned with what intelligence is used to lead to. It implicitly values intelligence in terms of the end state that it produces rather than in terms of the process itself. This is an instrumental account of the value of intelligence. An instrumental conception of intelligence immediately gives an answer to the question of why we value intelligence: because it is a way of achieving our goals.

Stuart Russell envisages that AI could be used to solve some major goals and hence that its value can be measured in terms of its potential success. He works out an example [4, pp. 98–99], the goal of raising the living standard of all human beings to that seen as respectable in a developed country, which he chooses, 'somewhat arbitrarily' as the 88th percentile in the USA. Using economic modelling, he calculates this as roughly a tenfold increase to $750 trillion per year, with the future net income with a net present value of approximately $13,500 trillion, as representing a rough idea of how valuable human-level AI might be in terms of the achievements it could deliver.

It is necessary to ask if these instrumental goals are the only reason we value intelligence. Russell is only attempting to produce a rough and ready example, so it would be unfair to pull this apart too severely. What additional questions would you need to know about this imagined future? And in this future, what manner of value might be placed on intelligence?

Goal and process There is a strong case for saying that we value intelligence in humans for its own sake as well as for the benefits it can give us. One reason for this may be the human trait of curiosity or wonder, which incites us to explore, acquire knowledge, and seek new experiences, all just for their own sake. The philosophers who considered the contemplation of eternal truths to be the highest form of life captured in an abstract way what for others may be manifest more concretely or prosaically in bird spotting, pub quizzes, or playing various games of skill: we may enjoy not just the product of intelligence but also the process of thinking. The goal of intelligence may sometimes be thought itself, rather than anything external to thought. This will have important ethical implications for certain questions, such as some of questions concerning the use of AI in the place of our own powers of thought.

Moreover, the path of seeking value in thought and in the life of the mind is a recurring and enduring one throughout different civilisations and in the teachings of many of the world's most revered thinkers and schools of thought, such as Buddhism and Daoism. Contemplation has been seen as the route to wisdom or enlightenment and as an end in itself. Both Plato and Aristotle considered the philosophical life to be the best. For Plato, contemplation of the eternal forms gave access to a realm of truth beyond the material realm [5]. Aristotle considered that the intellectual life of contemplation was the surest route to happiness (although he did consider that there were other necessities, such as friends with whom to share one's life, but such friends would be able also to share in the life of the mind) [6, 7]. One motivator for finding happiness in such a way is that it provides a surer route than seeking happiness through material comforts and other worldly means, since these are more subject to the vagaries of fortune. Hence, such an approach places high value on the intellect as a process and inherently satisfying, rather than viewing it as a means to efficiently gain some further end, and, moreover, tends to downplay the importance of merely material goals [7].

The contrast with the example given by Russell of using intelligence to produce a world full of middle-income materialists could scarcely be greater, but perhaps AI could help to iron out the twists and turns of fate and fortune that render seeking happiness through material means so prone to disaster. Could AI also be the answer to those who find the life of the mind a trifle boring and wish for a safer bet on gaining worldly goods? The astute observer will also note that the life of contemplation envisaged by Plato and Aristotle depended critically on a large population of labourers, many of whom were slaves, not to mention their wives. Contemplation needs a material underpinning. So perhaps it is not 'either-or' for the value we place on human cognition and intelligence, but 'both-and'.

Exercise 2
Have you ever struggled over a crossword puzzle, or Sudoku, or similar, and had someone else lean over your shoulder and say, 'Huh, you dope, that's easy', and write in the solutions as you beg them to leave you to figure it out for yourself? Would we ever design an AI to do all our crossword puzzles for us? Probably not. Could Plato have used an AI to do his contemplation of the Eternal Forms for him?

Consider the difference between occasions when we would appreciate having our intellectual efforts undertaken by another person or by a machine and when we would not.

Intelligence, Goals, and Context

An anecdote about the time when my friend Margaret failed her Domestic Science exam, the only one in the class to do so. I still remember the look of stunned surprise on her face when the results were announced. Her task had been to prepare a supper dish using cheese. She put a potato in the oven, and when it was baked, cut it in half and put grated cheese on it. She executed this to perfection, well within the time limit.

However, the teacher failed her on the grounds that she had not given herself a sufficiently complex goal. From the perspective of passing a cooking exam, perhaps she should have been cannier, but she came from a family of eight children, and as one of the eldest, often cooked supper for the whole family, and had doubtless done more cooking than most of the other girls in the class who'd gained top marks with elaborate dishes, hence her response of indignation to the exam results. Cheesy baked potatoes are perfectly delicious, quick to prepare, cheap, and nutritious, and most children love them. Starting to look somewhat more intelligent, eh. Context matters.

More generally, the ways in which we judge machine intelligence, intelligence in a formal context (such as an exam, or an IQ test), and intelligence within the less formal, complex context of life, with multiple competing goals and a range of constraints, may be somewhat different. One of the questions that this example raises is: what precisely were the goals Margaret should have had, and the teacher should have been testing?

Consider these issues when examining concrete applications of AI, particularly in reflecting on what the context of ethical decision-making should be.

Can we use intelligence to assess the goals that intelligence pursues? To define intelligence in terms of goals may already be implicitly to have in mind a certain kind of goal. I am not entirely clear if achieving the goal of patting one's head with one hand while rubbing one's stomach with the other hand is best characterised as demonstrating intelligence; perhaps it does even though it does not serve well as a typical example. Do we use intelligence in any way to assess what goals we wish to achieve? Russell and Norvig note that Aristotle's work on reasoning and logic paved the way for the algorithms that are now used in developing AI and cite the *Nicomachean Ethics*, Book III, Chap. 3, 1112b. In this passage, Aristotle writes, 'We deliberate not about ends but about means. For a doctor does not deliberate whether he shall heal, nor an orator whether he shall persuade, nor a statesman whether he shall produce law and order, nor does any one else deliberate about his end' [6]. This is often taken by those working in AI to mean that we can fit in any ends that we desire.

However, such a claim cannot plausibly be attributed to Aristotle. His claims on this point are subtle; there is some confusion and dispute in the interpretation of his texts on deliberation, which can appear inconsistent, but one thing is clear: Aristotle did not think we could fashion ends out of the thin cloth of our desires alone. This dispute cuts to central debates, chasms perhaps, within philosophy. For Aristotle, our ends are moulded for us by nature. We use our judgement to appreciate them and to reflect on what it would be like to achieve them, for we need to have some idea of their nature in order to be able to aim towards them. The man of wisdom (sorry to break the news, but Aristotle was not known for talking about 'women' and 'wisdom' in the same breath) or 'phronesis' developed the ability to discern in each situation what good ends were possible to attain. However, such a view requires a teleological view of nature where value is inherent in the world in some way and is directly at odds with the cluster of views that hold that humans simply set their own ends. Importantly for us, the good for man arises from our nature.

These issues will be discussed further in Chap. 6 and will form the backdrop to many questions in AI ethics.

Forms and components of intelligence: abduction, attention, and relevance We have raised the question of the difference between human and machine intelligence and whether the general way in which we approach these, as essentially the same, or as potentially somewhat different. Might we confuse or bias the issues by modelling machine intelligence on human intelligence, or vice versa?

There is a great deal that is still unknown about intelligence in both machines and humans. The potential capacities of AI are subject to intense debate and disagreement. Here, we cannot answer the question of whether human intelligence can be reproduced completely in machines, although there are those who assume that this will happen and is only a matter of adding capacity. Since much recent progress in AI has been attributable to the significant increases in processing power and in very large increases in the availability of data, there are those who believe that pushing on this path of big data plus processing power will be all we need. Others consider that it is either unlikely or that it is in principle impossible. A question of more specific interest to us is whether machine intelligence, as it is now or as it might be, could capture the kind of human intelligence and thought needed for moral decisions.

There are many who have argued, on a variety of bases, that artificial intelligence manifested in machines will always fall short of human intelligence. There are many aspects to this contentious debate, including the issue of whether full intelligence would require consciousness, whether consciousness in a machine is even possible, and if it were, what it would take for a machine to manifest it [1, Ch 26, p. 1022 ff., 8, Ch 6, pp. 106 ff.]. These issues are very complex both technically and philosophically, and it is not possible to cover them fully here. In illustration of how such views may impact questions of ethics in AI, let us consider a recent book, *The Myth of Artificial Intelligence*, by Erik Larson, since Larson's claims raise issues that go to the heart of some of the central questions in ethics, such as the nature of moral reasoning and moral knowledge [9]. There are no prizes for guessing the gist of this book, but if there were such a prize, it could serve as an example of one of his main claims: that intelligence requires being able to make sensible guesses, using conjecture to form reasonable hypotheses which have a good chance of explaining the pattern of evidence before us.

Larson draws upon Charles Pearce's conception of abduction. Pearce claimed that to account for reason, we need to add abduction to deduction and induction, two already well-established and complementary patterns of reasoning. Deductive reasoning is concerned with what can safely and validly be concluded from a set of known premises. Deduction does not give us new knowledge and cannot tell us if its premises are true. What it can tell us is that *if* the premises are true and an argument is formally valid, *then* the conclusion must be true. Deduction deals in certainties. Inductive reasoning sets out to extrapolate from past experience to the future. Induction can supply us with new knowledge and may allow us to have confidence in certain claims, although we can never know its claims with the degree of certainty that deduction permits. The weather forecast may be wrong. In Australia, swans are black.

Pearce argued that there was something very basic missing from any account of knowledge based simply on deduction and induction. On their own, these two forms of reasoning cannot tell what framework to use to interpret experience. Deduction on its own tells us nothing about the world. It needs induction to verify its premises. Induction looks for regularities and patterns in experience, but which ones are going to be of interest? In a set of strange circumstances, how do we know where to begin to look for the most likely explanation? One answer is by amassing a considerable range of general knowledge that would help us to make sense of the data and give us a clue of where to look. However, attempts to date to force-feed general knowledge into computers have had little impact on producing machines with the kind of common sense that seems to come naturally to the dullest human. We need 'common sense' and may rely on hunches or reasonable guesses to suggest the patterns behind surprising results. The astute detective will pay heed to details that together form a pattern that unlocks the puzzle and has an eye for what details are relevant. Sherlock Holmes' powers of deduction were in fact far more than mere deduction and would have been nothing were it not for his powers of observation, which critically included not simply amassing a ton of data but spotting patterns that made sense of the data. Abduction is a reaction to surprise, as Pearce explained it, spotting an explanation of why something we do not expect has happened. The explanation finds something which, if true, would make the surprising fact unsurprising.

Larson argues that instances hailed as success for AI actually involve input from the humans designing the system based on their abductive inferences. The famous work by the Bletchley team, who cracked the Enigma code, involved a process of elimination of many codes as impossible because they involved contradictions, thereby speeding up the task of decrypting Enigma messages, making it easier for the team to work out the answer. The arrogance of the Nazis in assuming that their code was uncrackable also helped [9, pp. 10–12]. He also notes that the DeepMind team working on AlphaGo programmed into it prior knowledge of the game, inferences supplied from outside the inductive framework.

This points to a controversy about the methods and value of approaches that rely on big data. Hence, yet again, we raise areas where progress in AI, the possibilities of technology, and ethics come together—work which needs to be done and on which there will be differing opinions.

Methodology in the Social Sciences

Debates in artificial intelligence about the nature of intelligence and the use of methods such as machine learning and the use of big data to understand the world, and in particular to understand human beings, have some parallels with debates on methodology in the social sciences. There have been intensive discussion and work on concerning the strengths and weaknesses of quantitative and qualitative approaches to investigating the social world and to understanding individual human beings and social interactions [10]. Since many of the ethical questions in AI concern its use to understand human beings, this is worth noting.

Quantitative approaches look to what is measurable and observable, seeking measurements which are reliable, replicable, and capable of being expressed in mathematical terms [11]. This may be especially useful for policy use and for applications such as measuring the outcomes of interventions. However, can such approaches capture everything about the reality of human life?

Qualitative methods such as ethnography and interviewing techniques seek to study the meaning of the social world for those involved in it and to understand the subjective point of view of individuals. A considerable body of work developing such methodologies and examining their epistemological foundations has built up [12]. Qualitative techniques involve person to person interactions of various sorts. Efforts are made to account for subjective bias and point of view, but the human point of view is nonetheless an essential aspect of these methodologies. Even these make no claim to know 'everything' and usually note the limitations of any particular study.

Quantitative and qualitative approaches are complementary and can give us different sorts of information. However, there are social scientists who hold varying views about the suitability of each approach for addressing particular questions, and on the rigour of the very many different methodologies both quantitative and qualitative, and on what manner of knowledge different methods can produce.

Exercise 3

Could an approach based purely on machine learning ever replace qualitative methods in social sciences?

Is there something special about human beings that cannot be fully understood by a machine? *Hint*: this question is again deliberately vague and open ended.

This relates strongly to questions of moral epistemology and of the role of the second-person stance, which we discuss further in Chap. 7.

This means that acquiring knowledge will rely at some point upon the capacity to pay attention to what is relevant. This will be a key aspect of intelligence. This has strong relevance for questions in ethics. We will discuss these further in considering moral epistemology in Chap. 8. It will have implications for whether ethics can be fully formalised within a machine; naturally, it raises the technical question of whether such attention to what is relevant is even possible in a machine, which is beyond the scope of this book; attention to issues of moral relevance is hard enough in human beings, as we discuss further later. Recall also the discussions in Chap. 4 about methodology in ethics concerning how examples and cases are described. There is no magic formula for picking out how a complex scenario that raises ethical questions should be described, but how it is described will critically shape responses to it.

5.2.2   Measuring Intelligence

Many accounts of intelligence, if not most, are inherently or implicitly comparative, meaning that it follows from the characterisation of intelligence that it lends itself to degrees of more or less (and, implicitly, better or worse). It hardly needs stating that the implication is that more intelligence is better. However, it does not imply that there will necessarily be one way of measuring intelligence. If we think of intelligence in terms of goals, this will be especially difficult, especially in complex environments and with complex goals, where it may be hard to determine which of the two means of achieving whatever goal in question is better. If we conceptualise intelligence in other ways, it may be even harder to measure.

In valuing AI for assisting us with tasks requiring intelligence, it is salutary to consider the often-troubling history of the measurement of intelligence. The capacity of reason has been thought in the past to be something possessed by all, with notable exceptions and with the common view that many were deficient in reasoning. Descartes opened his *Discourse on the Method* with the observation that common sense is so equitably distributed that not even the most discontented among us wish they had more of it [13], although ever since first reading that decades ago, I have never been sure if he was being sarcastic. However, the idea that reason, or intelligence, is a matter of degree gained more ascendency with the acceptance of Darwin's idea of evolution, the notion that the difference between us and the higher animals was a matter of degree and that our intelligence has its evolutionary origins in beginnings, which we can see in other animals.

Standardised intelligence testing was introduced in the early twentieth century by Alfred Binet for purposes such as determining which children should be sent to special education classes and for assigning army recruits to particular tasks according to their abilities at the start of the first world war [14]. Testing was designed to attempt to be uniform and replicable and, above all, to categorise individuals. Alongside the rise in the use of IQ tests were debates about the relative role of environment and heritability in forming an individual's level of intelligence, as well as debates about whether intelligence was fixed across the course of an individual's lifetime. It was the existence of standardised tests themselves that helped form the shape of these debates, which forms an enduring theme of how measurement helps to shape how we perceive and judge the world. Perhaps many of the assumptions that we make about intelligence have arisen in response to the widespread use of standardised testing of human beings and comparison of different individuals as 'having' different levels of intelligence.

5.2.3 Intelligence and the Value of the Individuals

The judgement of individuals and, indeed, of whole population groups, on the basis of intelligence levels, has a very sorry history. The careless labelling of some groups as of lesser intelligence than others, often ignoring factors such as cultural bias in tests, educational opportunities, and environmental influences, has fed into and bolstered racism, sexism, and judgemental attitudes towards the working class [14]. The lower social, political, and moral status given to women at some times and in some places has often been justified on the presumption of women's lesser intellectual capabilities [15], and claims for the lower intellectual capacities of some population groups have also been used in attempts to justify slavery and colonialism. Eugenics movements aimed at certain groups, including the working class and those deemed of feeble intellect, likewise have a shameful history. The assumption behind such views has been that higher intelligence equates to higher value as a human being.

The heightened value given to intelligence as a human quality exacerbates such judgements, as well as feeding the testing and examination of IQ in the first place; it would be an interesting thought experiment to consider how such debates might have played out with intense interest, calibrating the ability to produce neat hand-writing, sporting prowess, the ability to 'get' jokes, the capacity to relax after a tense day at work, the knack of making party guests feel at ease, and so on, and comparing individuals and population groups by such measures. The demands of working life, especially post-industrial revolution and perhaps especially in the information era, may emphasise not only the productivity but also the intellectual capacity of individual humans as a marker of their value to industry. Again, are we fitting technology to humans, or humans to technology?

In assessing the use of artificial intelligence, it is well to be mindful of the potential for the judgement that higher levels of intelligence are better than lower levels, to lead to scornful attitudes towards individuals and to groups of human beings, whether intentional or unintentional, conscious or not. Such attitudes are perhaps most readily seen in discussions of human enhancement and of technological unemployment and its social consequences. What we need is a way of celebrating the intellect and intellectual achievements alongside a robust way of valuing the human being per se. Or should we value human beings per se? Since the concept of a human being refers to a particular biological species, this has often been thought to have no moral significance in itself. The idea of being a person is often used in preference. Personhood requires certain capacities, including cognitive capacities, and on some accounts, it may be linked implicitly to the intellect. The notion of personhood is examined further in Chap. 9.

Exercise 4
Can the value of human beings be separated from the value of any of their attributes? Note: this is another deliberately difficult question.

5.2.4   A Quick Note on Intelligence and Speed

There is a link between speed and the measurement of intelligence. IQ tests have a time limit, and the more questions one correctly completes in a certain time, the higher one's score. There may be individuals who would have come up with a novel and inventive solution to a problem if given enough time, but they are destined to be given low IQ scores unless they play the testing game correctly. Much of the 'intelligence' of artificial intelligence is attributable to brute processing speed. Quiz games and other such tests of wit almost always include speed as an element. Note that a way of describing someone with low intellectual skills is simply to describe them as 'slow'.

Exercise 5
Why do we value speed in intellectual comprehension per se? And do we value it on all occasions? Illustrate this with examples.

    This is an important question for any comparison of human and artificial intelligence, since the pure speed and processing power of AI is a major reason why it is used in many instances. Including measurements of the speed at which an individual is able to solve a problem or perform a task involving intelligence is a measure of productivity that may have a place in a competitive economy but elsewhere and for certain complex tasks may be overused. Pablo Picasso produced approximately 50,000 artworks during his lifetime, whereas Vermeer, perhaps most famous for his 'Girl with a Pearl Earring', produced only 36 known paintings. Much as one might wish for him to have left 50,000 paintings for us, the speed of his production seems entirely irrelevant to valuing his artistic merit. Or is it? One might argue that his meticulous slowness in painting forms part of what is admired about his work. Consider someone who had spent twice as long as another person to acquire a certain skill, be it with calculus or with making perfect dovetail joints, but who ended up with equal ability.

Exercise 6

Must we include speed in accounts of intelligence? Is speed alone a value? If so, why? Could this be connected with an account of intelligence that links it to the achievement of external goals?

If we could achieve immortality or greatly increased life expectancy, would we still value speed as a factor in intelligence in the same way?

Is speed a factor in wisdom? Or in coming to ethical judgements?

5.2.5   Intelligence and Society

One feature of human intelligence is that we can often outsource it to others. In fact, this is a central feature of how humans make use of intelligence—the capacity to learn, including the capacity to learn from others, and the willingness to use others as authoritative sources. You will recall that the definition of intelligence given by Legg and Hutter above in Sect. 5.2.1 referred to the intelligence of 'an agent' [3]. Human intelligence is shared across cultures and between individuals, as well as recorded and outsourced in artefacts as simple as papyrus and the abacus. The essential fact that we collaborate in building intelligence means that any account of human nature that stresses only intelligence or reason, and not our social nature, may struggle to give a full account of intelligence.

Hence, for this small section with the impossibly bold title, 'intelligence and society', I am outsourcing to you, the reader. The topic is too vast for any other sensible strategy. Let us consider as an exercise a much-cited claim about AI, intelligence, and society, which we met earlier in Chap. 3. An Open Letter on the website of the Future of Life Institute, signed by over 8000 people, including many prominent signatories in the area of AI research, writes:

> The potential benefits are huge; everything that civilisation has to offer is a product of human intelligence; we cannot predict what we might achieve when this intelligence is magnified by the tools AI may provide, but the eradication of disease and poverty are not unfathomable. [16]

Variations of such a claim have been frequently restated, for example, in a video by DeepMind, 'Welcome to DeepMind: Embarking on one of the greatest adventures in scientific history' [17], which starts off with a panoramic stretch of the river Thames with views of central London and the voice-over explaining that human intelligence has formed all of modern civilisation in a variety of ways [16]. The view encompasses the revered St Paul's Cathedral, designed by Sir Christopher Wren and built in 1675, the iconic skyscraper The Shard built in 2009, and the much ridiculed skyscraper, 20 Fenchurch Street, known locally as the Walkie Talkie [18], completed in 2014 and famous for having melted a Jaguar car with light reflected from its curved windows, an unfortunate event producing both annoyance and amusement and which presumably was not a conscious goal of the 'intelligence' behind civilisation [19].

This general claim regarding the role of intelligence in forming civilisation makes a number of assumptions, not least of which is that AI is set to 'magnify' human intelligence. In critique of any views, it is often useful to tease out even the most obvious assumptions, because claims that are broadly true are often overstated or lack the necessary nuance or context. Before reading on, look carefully at the quote and note any assumptions it makes.

It is implied that it may be possible to eradicate (an extremely strong claim) war, disease, and poverty by increases in intelligence. If this is possible, it suggests that either nothing but a shortage of intelligence has prevented us from solving these issues already or that intelligence is sufficient to produce or encourage the extra factors involved in finding a complete (because remember 'eradicate') solution. However, in fairness, it's easy for anyone to make somewhat overblown claims.

It also states that 'everything' (note, a very strong claim) that civilisation has to offer is a 'product' of human intelligence. This implies that intelligence is involved in producing everything we value in civilisation but does not commit itself to any particular view on the precise role that intelligence plays in each factor. Note too that when we use the term 'intelligence' in such a way, we often assume that we are talking about a high level of intelligence, but perhaps we could understand the claim as referring to the application of intelligence, even in simple or mundane ways.

Exercise 7

Consider the strongest case that could be made to support this claim, and then consider the case against it. It is a good strategy to do examine both sides of an argument for many reasons, including that the better you have stated and understood a position, the better prepared you are to find a strong and precisely aimed case supporting it, and likewise, for making a case against it. Note any ways in which your answer is affected by personal experience.

Is there anything valuable in civilisation that owes little or nothing to intelligence?

Does the kind of intelligence that AI is producing so far is the kind of intelligence that we need to help solve the three problems mentioned—war, disease, poverty?

Is the reason these have not been solved a want of 'intelligence'?

Could we appreciate the valuable things of civilisation without intelligence?

The quote speaks simply of AI, but AI is always developed by particular people and particular groups. How might this impact upon the possibilities that the magnification of intelligence by the tools of AI will serve to address these specific societal problems?

These questions are broad and vague but can alert us to the frames of mind with which many questions in AI ethics are approached.

5.2.6   *Augmenting Human Intelligence with AI*

The pursuit of human enhancement, which we discuss in more detail in Chap. 11, generally assumes that this will involve enhancing our intelligence. People visiting nail bars, having hair extensions, and working out at the gym are also engaged in some kind of human enhancement. If we are to use AI to enhance our intelligence in some way, perhaps using something such as the Neuralink implant, we need some account of what specifically AI can do, which will fill in gaps or address weaknesses in human intelligence [20]. Sometimes this is envisaged simply as speed and processing power.

We need to address the question of whether there is some general notion of intelligence shared between machines and humans, such that you can simply have 'more' of it, or whether there are complementary and different capacities. We also need to ask whether in regard to intelligence and the capacities that it relies upon, there are no upper bounds or whether there might even be something to be gained by having certain limits placed upon certain capacities.

In illustration, take, for example, the discussion by Neil Lawrence of what he calls embodiment factors in comparing human (mind) and machine intelligence [21]. No intelligence is ever going to be 'complete', since this would require total knowledge of the universe to date and flawless capacity to compute outcomes. (Unless, of course, there is a God who has such an intelligence.) Rather, predictions are needed, based upon available data and models of the environment to compute using that data. Communication is a 'side effect' of intelligence since it is a way of acquiring new data and models.

When we compare current computers with humans, computers can communicate information far faster than we can. We are limited by the processing speed and capacity of our brains and limited in how we can communicate with each other by the limits of our bodies and our sensory experience. However, the computing power of the human brain is vast compared to how fast we can speak, write, or otherwise communicate. Lawrence calls this the embodiment factor: the compute power divided by the communication bandwidth. Humans can only communicate a tiny fraction of what they can compute.

It is easy to test this for yourself. Start describing in words precisely what you can see or hear or touch or smell, right now; or to make it even worse, in the last hour; or to make it even worse, every single one of your memories since you were 5. Even if you've forgotten a lot, you'll never do anything else if you try to complete this task. In contrast, computers can send data at incredibly faster speeds.

Does this simply mean that humans are 'bad' at communication compared to computers? That we are just primitive badly wrought computers, struggling with the best our porridge-like brains can muster, and gasping for an upgrade? That would be to ignore what is special about us. Rather, our limits help to shape distinctly human ways of interacting. It means, for example, that each one of us has a large, private domain of information about ourselves and our worlds, available only to us, yet we can imaginatively share this with others, and by empathy extrapolate to what others may be feeling, often without the use of words or formal communication. Lawrence quotes in illustration Ernest Hemingway's six-word novel: 'Baby shoes for sale, never worn'. The form of our intelligence is thus very different from the intelligence of machines, Lawrence argues.

Forms of Knowledge, Intelligence, and Poetry
While we are on the subject, an interesting aside. Debates and contrasting positions regarding intelligence and the source of knowledge are as old as philosophy itself. We have already met Jeremy Bentham and John Stuart Mill, two utilitarian philosophers but with very different approaches to such questions. Bentham's approach stressed analysis of issues and measurement. As we saw in Sect. 2.5.2, his felicific calculus attempted to capture and calculate pleasure and pain [22], but he was notorious for his lack of capacity to understand other people. In his *Essay on Bentham*, although lavishing considerable praise on Bentham, who was his godfather, Mill lamented that he had 'failed in deriving light from other minds' [23].

John Stuart Mill, although also a utilitarian and favouring empiricism, was greatly influenced by the Romantics, in particular by poetry [24]. He considered that poetry was a means of gaining direct knowledge of the mind of another person. By poetry, he did not mean necessarily the literary works of an accomplished poet, but any form of communication between individuals that enabled such insights.

Perhaps poetry captures a form of intelligence beyond the grasp of any computers we have now, or may ever have. Understanding other people is an elementary but often neglected aspect of ethics. Many ethical dilemmas would never even arise, if we only took the trouble to understand each other better.

5.3 Values Underlying the Use of Data

Summary
The value we attach to intelligence is closely related to the value attached to truth, to knowledge, and to how we understand and value data. Much AI uses large amounts of data; hence, examining the values underlying the use of data will be a useful background for questions in AI ethics, such as questions concerning privacy. We examine the link between placing a high value on knowledge and the sharing of that knowledge.

The values attached to intelligence are closely related to values regarding knowledge, for intelligence involves learning and the capacity to learn and both generates and depends upon knowledge. In the field of AI, much recent progress has been enabled by access to massive amounts of data, so the value given to machine intelligence both builds upon the values given to data and helps to cement its value. (Of course, in practice, much data can be worthless: poorly categorised, false, incomplete.) We will touch on some more relevant points later in the section discussing epistemology and its importance for ethics. For now, an exercise, followed by some literature.

5.3.1   One View of the Value of Big Data

Here is one view about the value of data, taken from Victor Mayer-Schönberger and Kenneth Cukier's book *Big Data: A Revolution that Will Transform How We Live, Work, and Think* [25]. This is one view only, but it represents a certain style of approach in the field. Certain claims made in the book are outlined here.

Exercise 8
1. In the age of big data, even the most trivial pieces of information will be deemed valuable [25, p. 100].
   Question: For whom is such data valuable?
2. Information is a nonrivalrous good, and one person's use of it does not detract from its use by others [25, p. 101].
   Question: Is this true for all information? Even if true, what else matters? If information can be used by another, does this even detract from its value?
3. The value of data is in its use [25, p. 104].
   Question: Is this true? Does this mean that the value of data is simply instrumental?
4. For pragmatic and cost reasons, it is prudent to gather as much data as possible and to use it for as many different uses as possible [25, p. 109].
   Question: To whom does this 'make sense'? Note how the use of such a phrase can lead one to certain conclusions. Does anything else matter besides 'making sense'?
5. Data-driven decisions will enhance, or supersede, human decision-making [25, p. 141].
   Question: When might this be a good thing? When not so good?
6. Amazon allegedly switched to algorithmic recommendations instead of book reviews as a better way of increasing sales [25, p. 141].
   Question: In whose interest is this? Compare the different forms of information or knowledge contained in a human-composed book review and an algorithmic recommendation.

In considering the multiple uses of data and information and questions of value arising from this, recall our earlier discussion of technological developments in the spread of information, including the work of Walter Benjamin, in Sect. 3.6.2.

Data, prediction, and freedom The question of free will has perplexed philosophers, theologians, and more ordinary mortals for millennia. We are unlikely to 'solve' the question to the satisfaction of all here. Nonetheless, there are critical questions about how we view ourselves, how we view others, how we treat each other, and many ethical questions, including questions of control, power, and manipulation that arise.

Exercise 9

Note Amazon's claim that data drove more sales than book reviews. Does this imply anything about the 'real' source of human motivation? Are we creatures who are caused to purchase items by the hidden algorithms of Amazon, or are we creatures who choose what books to purchase based upon our preferences, interests, and values?

Does the capacity to predict human behaviour from data have implications for our conception of ourselves as free agents?

5.3.2   Truth and Communication

A common driving force behind much enthusiasm for AI is the idea that the more intelligence we have, the better. Likewise, it is often assumed that the more knowledge we have, the better, and it is often assumed that if knowledge is held as a value, then it follows from this that knowledge should spread and hence be communicated. Is this true? It is crucial to note that knowledge implies a knower.

Valuing the communication of information is one motivating force behind open-access initiatives. It has a great appeal, but it comes directly into conflict with values of privacy and confidentiality. This clash arises from the meaning of information when considered from different perspectives. Information is abstract and can be conceptualised in a timeless way and stored anywhere, but communication takes place at a specific time and place. Information which is merely a point on a massive dataset to some people is information with personal, perhaps life-altering significance to others. Is the abstract idea of sharing information, of communicating truth, something to be valued in and of itself? Or do we only ever value information and truth in relation to some pragmatic use it has for us? This question is worth pondering, both for attempts to resolve practical questions in AI ethics and for the question of how we conceptualise information and knowledge. As with so many of the questions in this book, this is a pointer to complex debates in philosophy and elsewhere. Let us look at an example of the presentation of two different viewpoints on 'truth for truth's sake'.

> **To the Lighthouse**
> Virginia Woolf's 1927 novel concerns the Ramsey family, visiting the Isle of Skye in Scotland [26]. The boy James is very keen to row out to the lighthouse the following day, but a trip can only take place if safe to do so, and it is very likely that a storm is on its way. His mother, Mrs. Ramsey, tells James that of course they can go, if the weather is fine, and the boy is filled with joy. His

(continued)

father, Mr. Ramsey, and some other men present, insist that the weather will be too bad and that there is no possibility whatsoever that they could go to the Lighthouse. Mrs. Ramsey is concerned to hold out some hope in the child's mind, suggesting that the wind may well change. The novel presents two extremely different viewpoints: one of factual accuracy, which decries what it sees as irrationality, and a second which focuses on consideration for the child's feelings [26, p. 9].

Mr. Ramsey is a professional philosopher, perhaps no coincidence. Mr. and Mrs. Ramsey personify two opposing attitudes to the truth but crucially also to communication.

Exercise 10 Try to articulate the best possible justification for the positions of each of Mr. and Mrs. Ramsey.

Mrs. Ramsey is portrayed by Woolf as considering that Mr. Ramsey's insistence on the truth is wantonly disregarding the ways in which civilisation is held together.

How does such a view contrast with the view that 'everything that civilisation has to offer is a product of human intelligence'?

How could it be possible that there are two such opposing views?

5.4 Human Nature

Summary
An understanding of human nature underlies many ethical questions, especially in AI ethics, where we frequently need to compare and contrast humans with intelligent machines. Understanding some of the central issues and points of variance in accounts of human nature can also facilitate our understanding of the viewpoints of others. We examine different views on the place of humans within the wider universe, including its trajectory over time; claims about the status of humans within the natural world; questions about the relationship between human beings and our embodiment; the issue of whether there is an essence to human nature, and if so, what this is; the uniqueness of humans, or otherwise; divisions within the self and the 'higher self'; the boundaries and limits of human nature; the perfectibility or otherwise of human beings; the social nature of humans; and the significance of myth and origin stories of human beings. These issues are illustrated in relation to questions in AI ethics.

5.4.1   Introduction

We have seen the importance of asking the question of whether human intelligence and machine intelligence will necessarily differ in any significant respects. We have also noted the difficulty of providing a precise account of what intelligence is and have considered the different ways in which it might be valued. Intelligence is often seen as a key hallmark of humanity—we are the 'rational animal'. Here, yet again, there are many different perspectives on what significance our intellect has for understanding human nature and the value attached to humans. Nonetheless, some account of the value of human beings is going to be essential for addressing many of the questions of AI ethics.

The topic of human nature is vast, but we will navigate this by examining some key issues, each highly pertinent to understanding our relationships with intelligent machines and hence to how we might understand and address questions of value. Further reading will be given, but even this will be only a small selection. This section is organised around a series of questions that elicit different approaches to human nature. Different viewpoints on human nature may point to different stances in metaphysics, politics, and, often, significantly, religions or the absence thereof. So, understanding something of the range of views on human nature is especially crucial given the meeting of different world views in our global world, and the changing attitudes towards religion especially in those parts of the world where AI has so far been most developed. Many of the issues raised around human nature are also pertinent to questions in the philosophy of mind, and we will give an overview of some debates in the philosophy of mind in Chap. 8, especially insofar as they are directly relevant to current debates in AI and AI ethics. Elucidating them will often help to unearth the root source of attitudes towards AI.

Views on human nature are generally complex, nuanced, and often deeply integrated into culture and religion. Hence this section involves a considerable amount of simplification, especially in characterising and contrasting divergent views. The simplification is intended as a heuristic device to enable clarity that can assist in spotting broad tendencies but is an invitation to further exploration, not a place to stop!

5.4.2   Our Place in the Universe

No account of human nature would be complete without considering humans in context: in the larger universe. This is partly for the mundane reason that all entities are part of a wider whole and, more specifically, because all biological species have a place within an ecosystem and arise within the temporal context of evolution. In addition, human beings are self-aware and can reflect not just upon themselves but on the world around them, the past, and the future. For us, the question of our place in the universe is replete with meaning. It is not simply like a biologist asking about how wasps evolved and what role they play in the ecosystem. It is more like the wasps themselves wondering why they are so stripey, why they sting, why they can't make honey like the bees can, why humans don't like them, whether they can improve their behaviour, what that awful buzzing sound is all the time, and whether there is anything more to life than all this. We outline some thumbnail sketches of contrasting positions.

Not special at all On one, human beings have no special position or status in the universe. We are the chance product of a materialist universe, existing for a tiny slice of time on a rocky planet in an obscure part of an unimaginably vast and unimaginably old universe, and that's it. It may be rather peculiar that this little bit of the universe can somehow stand up and blink at the rest of the universe, and we may as well make the most of it while we're here, but there is no wider significance than that. On some version of such an account, we are a complete anomaly, possibly all alone staring out into the blackness of space, which does not answer back; on other accounts, there are countless other intelligent and conscious beings on other planets, and that makes us even less remarkable. We will die, and the universe will continue for billions of years, until it too vanishes.

Top of the tree On other accounts, we are indeed extremely special. Perhaps the most special thing about the whole show. Evolutionary accounts can at once lead to the view that we are 'nothing but' a complex collection of molecules assembled out of the material world by the operation of the laws of nature and also to the view that evolution has been 'leading up' to human beings as the current pinnacle of the universe. The development of consciousness, of self-awareness, and of intelligence, which, so far as we know, is best exemplified in us humans, may be thought to be what the universe is all about.

Note the importance of time: some accounts of the place of human beings in the universe essentially describe the passage of time. We may be a fleeting presence, or a part of a narrative unfolding, an account of the developing universe in which we play a certain role. Some such views are generally implicitly teleological, imbuing a purpose to the universe.

Humans as prototype On narrative views of the passage of time, we may be some kind of passing phase. We may be 'top of the tree' right now but are due for a fall. Max Tegmark outlines a view of the universe as developing to produce intelligence in his book *Life 3.0*, which we discuss further in Chap. 11. Tegmark talks about the cosmic awakening that occurred when intelligent and conscious life evolved [27, p. 22]. On this view, humans have a special role in the present, but you may or may not be sorry to hear that we are not the ultimate product of the universe.

Somewhere in the middle There are indeed many accounts of human nature that place humans in some kind of middle position in the universe. These accounts align very naturally with accounts of human nature that posit 'higher' and 'lower' aspects of our makeup, which we discuss below. This common claim can be made in a variety of ways and appears repeatedly, implicitly if not explicitly, in discussions of

AI, with hopes that AI will enhance or exceed our 'higher' natures and will remedy the faults of our 'lower' natures.

'A little lower than the angels'   Many such accounts place humans in some kind of mid-position between God or the gods, or some higher realm, and the other animals, 'a little lower than the angels', as Psalm 8 puts it:

> 3 When I consider your heavens, the work of your fingers,
>   the moon and the stars, which you have ordained,
> 4 what is man, that you think of him?
> What is the son of man, that you care for him?
> 5 For you have made him a little lower than the angels,
> and crowned him with glory and honor.
> 6 You make him ruler over the works of your hands.
> You have put all things under his feet:
> 7 All sheep and cattle,
> yes, and the animals of the field,
> 8 the birds of the sky, the fish of the sea,
> and whatever passes through the paths of the seas [28].

Note something about this psalm: the viewpoint of the author (it is attributed to King David). He is self-consciously reflecting on the position of mankind within the universe, given a stance of awe and wonders at the natural world. Very many accounts bear some similarities to a view that places us somewhere between a higher force, being, or notion and the animal or physical realm. We discussed in Chap. 4 the question of the position from which one makes a moral judgement: near or far. The way in which we approach this question of our place and role in the universe, the position from which we approach it, may be very significant. Contemplating the heavens with a sense of wonder may be rather different from using them merely as a source of knowledge, whether about the stars themselves or their use for navigation and time-keeping.

Extrapolating   meaning   and   significance   about   humanity's   place in the universe   There are many different meanings that could be read onto claims that humans have some special position in the universe. For example, many felt their world views were shattered at Darwin's claim that we evolved from animals, interpreting this as meaning that we are 'no more' than animals, while others equally look at evolution and conclude that we are the pinnacle of it, the final cause of a process lasting aeons in which countless species came and went, only to result in the ultimate species: us. Others look at the facts of evolution and shrug: we are nothing exceptional, or, despite evolution, there is another story to tell in which humans have a special value, or a special role. The wonder expressed in Psalm 8 that we are 'a little lower than the angels' is partly owing to the biblical view that, despite this, humans have a particular and rather special role in the world. The centre of things may be the boring average, the neglected middle child, the king or queen in their court at the centre of a kingdom, or the hub that holds all together.

5.4.3 Claims About the Status of Humans Within the Natural World

A particular slant on the place of humans in the universe is to pose the question from the framework of 'the natural world'. This highlights the question of positionality, since on some accounts, we are simply part and parcel with nature, and on other accounts, we stand, somehow, outside of it, yet at the same time, at least a part of us must be within nature. Our ability to reason can, on the one hand, be explained as having been produced by evolution and as operating in the substrate of our biology and can be seen to be present to lesser degrees in our close cousins among the great apes and other animals, yet this very ability to reason also seems to place us outside of this purely biological, natural schema. We are not so much a naked ape, as a duck-rabbit: within the natural order of things one way of looking at it, outside it from another perspective.

This 'outsider' view may be based on one or more claims: our consciousness enables us to view the universe, in the way that a rock cannot, and in which the lower animals may only do to a lesser extent. There are complexities of course, noting the superior senses of some animals and the mysterious nature of the consciousness of organisms such as octopi and bats. Note, too, the primacy of our vision, as evidenced in many metaphors of understanding. We 'view' the universe; we do not sniff it or hear it. Our self-consciousness enables us to view ourselves viewing the universe and also, as you are doing here right now, to view ourselves viewing ourselves viewing the universe. (Stop now, that's enough.)

Our knowledge and intellect enable us to understand the universe. Our agency and (apparent) free will enables us to act purposefully within the universe. Our wonder enables us to imaginatively reflect on the universe: consider how in Psalm 8 the psalmist starts by contemplating 'the heavens, the works of thy fingers', and one can imagine him, like billions of people surely have done throughout history, lying back and gazing up at the stars, awestruck, and wondering about his place in the cosmos.

Are we simply part of the natural world, or do we have a special place? If so, this can place us under considerable responsibilities, for insofar as we are not simply 'natural' creatures, we may fill this place wisely, or badly. There are many views which hold we have a particular role, for example, of stewardship over the world, and many accounts alleging that we have a pretty dismal score in this department, from biblical accounts of multiple transgressions to modern ideas about our wrong-doings in relation to technology and to the environment. Recall our discussion of Heidegger's notion of the Standing Reserve (Sect. 3.3.2) [29].

Consider the environmental movement. Within this, different positions regarding the place of humans in nature are held: as simply part of nature; as having separated ourselves from the natural world, responsible for its destruction, and hence a burden on the planet; and as having separated ourselves from the natural world, but with a strong role to play in redressing the damage we have caused and in safeguarding species and habitats.

Exercise 11
Do you see any similar attitudes towards humans in relation to our development and use of AI?

5.4.4 Humans and a Material Universe

Other aspects of these questions can be exposed by considering the significance of our place in the material world for ideas of human nature. The relevance to AI should be immediately obvious. If we are entirely material beings, whatever that might mean, perhaps everything about us can be captured, replicated, or even improved upon by computers. Are we in essence mental beings somehow 'joined' to the material world, 'rational' animals, or are we essentially embodied, animalistic creatures, linked by evolution to forces we don't fully understand? And if humans are simply a part of the material world, are we just governed by material forces and laws of nature, and if so, does this mean we do not have free will? The debates about nature versus nurture do not address this question, since if our natures are formed by nurture, they are still formed. We must also note that there are very many different accounts of what human nature is like that draw upon scientific, archaeological, and anthropological findings and on accounts of human evolution and that the disputes about how to interpret such evidence are legion, such that we do not have space to investigate these further here.

Humans, bodies, and brains Accounts of human nature which stress biology may be reductive in the sense that they are intentionally juxtaposed against other views such as the view that we possess immortal souls, claiming that humans are 'nothing but' biological systems; we simply are 'just' apes. One variant of this, which is (to my mind alarmingly) common, is the view that humans are reducible to just one part of their biology: Jeff Hawkins and Sandra Blakeslee in *On Intelligence* tell their readers that they are their brain [30]. There are plenty who share this view, even if they might modify their position by a small amount if pressed to explain how come they are worse at maths when it's getting near dinner time, or by a large amount if offered the chance to have their living brain placed in a life-sustaining vat.

Despite the blood–brain barrier, brains are highly integrated with the rest of the body, and the complex communication process goes both ways. The brain is not 'in' the body as a brain may be in a vat: it's a complexly integrated system. Descartes, who considered that there are separate mental and material substances and that our essence is mental, nonetheless realised the tight connections; he is not in his body in the same way that a pilot is in a ship, he astutely observed [13]. The discovery that many neurotransmitters are identical to hormones governing various processes in the body underlines this, among other factors [31].

On the other hand, those who identify themselves with their brain also tend to disassociate themselves from those parts of the brain that do not hold up to standards of reason and of consciousness. The paradox of the view that 'I am nothing but my brain' is that in order to conceptually separate the brain from the rest of the body, let alone to pick and choose from one's favourite parts of the brain, one must rely upon some metaphysical or value-driven account of what it is to be a human being.

As with many other attitudes to human nature, these views are often held implicitly and inconsistently rather than consciously. Their relevance to many ethical issues in AI should be apparent. Moreover, an important question is raised: how relevant is our particular and embodied biology to ethics? Our bodies both constrain and enable us. Different features of our biological nature will shape how we see the world and relate to each other; in other words, biology will impact moral epistemology, a topic to be discussed in Chap. 8. Our biology is likely also to have had an impact upon what ethical questions arise and how we seek to deal with them. The big question will be what impact this might have on how we think about the use of AI and on the ethical questions arising.

Ethics of Care

The ethics of care stresses relational aspects of our lives together and particular virtues such as benevolence. Although work in the ethics of care may take a general approach to ethics, feminist ethics of care in particular starts from the situated position of considering human biology, especially reproduction, and the implications this has for ethics. This includes looking at the realities of human development from birth. In contrast, most other theories of ethics assume a grown adult as the subject of ethical judgements, as if we sprang up fully formed as in Botticelli's painting 'The Birth of Venus'. Those working in this area include Carol Gilligan, Annette Baier, Virginia Held, and Nell Noddings [32–35].

Humans are a sexed species, and biology uses functional descriptions, which means that in describing the anatomy of males and of females, it is necessary to refer to the anatomy of the opposite sex; otherwise, the function and development of the reproductive organs would remain an incomplete mystery. Moreover, a highly distinctive aspect of human reproduction is the adjustments made for the large size of human brains compared to other apes, plus the bipedal gait which has been pivotal for enabling us to manipulate the world. This means that female hips have to be wide, but there is a limit: too wide, and females would start to have difficulties in walking and running. Thus, the newborn human infant is essentially still a fetus in comparison with other similar species, born at an earlier stage of gestation and more dependent for survival on its mother in particular and on adults in general.

From this, and many other factors, a range of things follow, including the necessity for group support and for human societies to be highly nurturing of infants and young children and of mothers. Many feminist philosophers have argued that ethics needs to take more note of such factors and to include consideration of the human need and capacity for care. Such a view is not

(continued)

limited to those describing themselves as feminist but stems from an approach to ethics grounded in the specificity of our embodied and evolved lives. Such an approach, if valid, could have numerous implications for some of the questions of AI ethics.

Exercise 12

Roger Scruton is one of many philosophers to have noted the importance of embodiment for how we experience the world of value and the relationships that matter in ethics. In his book *On Human Nature*, he wrote that our most salient experiences and emotions are tied to particularities of our embodiment, such as familial and romantic love, our fear of death and of illness, and sympathy for others as they face death and suffering [36, p. 115].

Is Scruton right to make such a claim? Why/why not? What elements of embodiment would you put in such a list?

If embodiment is important to our moral world, are there any aspects of this that are more salient than others?

Could such embodiment by advanced robots, or a sufficiently similar simulacrum of it, recreate such a human moral universe, and if so, could such robots engage with us as part and parcel of our moral community?

Would any aspects be absent, and if so, how much of an issue would that be?

Could the loss of certain of these embodiment factors be seen as a plus, viewed as transcending our natures rather than as losing part of them? Consider, for example, how fear of death and suffering, and attachment to others, might impose moral limits on us. Could a world of nothing but AI be a moral improvement on our world?

Consider also the discussion of the object of morality in Chap. 4 and how these issues of embodiment might impact on the way that the purpose of morality is understood.

There may be some aspects of our embodiment that mould very central elements of our moralities, such as our mortality. Injunctions against wanton killing of community members are virtually universal. Consider the impact on moral systems if we attained some kind of indefinite life extension by some technological means. This may be extremely hard to imagine or may lead to wild and imaginative conjectures, since death is such an ingrained part of biological experience. Other aspects of our biology may seem more contingent, such as human's distinctive lack of body hair (okay, okay, I know about naked mole rats), but even this has had a large impact upon moral and social codes around the world. Robots are often given human-like faces and may be given distinctively male or female figures but are less often dressed in clothing. Moreover, many of these concern questions of purity, taboo, defilement, and cultural and class difference, which are starkly apparent to many but which often perplex others who consider they confound explanation. Could an AI, an advanced robot, truly understand these nuances?

Paro the seal, embodiment, and mimicry People living with dementia may retain considerable awareness of their social world, of their appearance, and of the material world around them, for example, through the tactile experiences of familiar clothing and fabric [37]. There has been considerable attention to the use of robot pets such as the seal Paro for providing comfort and calming people living with dementia, especially in the more advanced stages where verbal communication may be limited and where people may experience distress and agitation [38, 39]. Paro has sensors and can react to people's touch, learning from the past and behaving in a manner similar to that of a living seal (without the poop). One reason for using a robot pet rather than a real one is to avoid inadvertent harm to a live animal. The robot seals are also furry, hence providing tactile comfort.

Exercise 13
Consider the ethical issues of using a Paro seal for a person living with advanced dementia.

Now consider a robot designed to mimic the behaviour, skin texture and temperature, facial features, etc., of a human companion, for example, designed to appear like a small grandchild who is sitting on the lap of a person living with dementia. Are there any different issues of concern here? Note any responses you have, even if you find it hard to articulate them.

Consider a voice assistant used for a person living with dementia, who has difficulty remembering that their husband or wife has passed away, which sadly happens quite commonly. Would it be ethical to use a voice assistant that mimics the voice of the person's deceased partner?

These questions highlight issues around the particularities of human embodiment in general and the identities of individual human beings in particular.

Note that in answering such questions, there will very often be nuance with some valuable elements in technology and other elements that may need adjustment, further thought, or that outweigh the beneficial aspects. Context also matters.

Do all humans have essentially the same nature? On some philosophical and religious views, there are different types of humans, separated by categories such as sex or social and economic class. Different valuations may or may not be attached to those in different categories, including the assignment of different roles in life and even expectations of moral behaviour and different penalties under the law. Many of the most revered philosophers, including Plato and Aristotle, held such views. Recall our discussion of universality in ethics in Chap. 4.

Foundation Myths in Plato's *Republic*
In his work *The Republic*, the philosopher Plato (428/7–348/7 BCE) described his ideal society, which, surprise, surprise, turns out to be one ruled by philosopher kings [5]. Plato did consider that some women would also be capable of acting as rulers, a view untypical for his time. He divided society

(continued)

into distinct classes. The Guardian class is divided into the rulers or Guardians proper, and the auxiliaries, who perform a range of functions such as military, police, and executive functions under the orders of the rulers. The rest of society is in the agricultural and industrial class, performing the basic labour and producing the goods and services which keep society functioning. This social division may be tempered somewhat by the fact that the Guardians were supposed to rule for the sake of society and not for personal gain, living austere lives.

Plato famously advocated that the rulers should tell myths about the foundations of society in order to reinforce social stability. This have often been translated as the 'noble lie', but it was clear that Plato considered that all classes would believe these myths. One myth concerned the origin of different human beings. All in this land are brothers, but when fashioned by god, different metals were put into the mix. The Guardians were mixed with gold, the auxiliaries with silver, and the labouring classes with bronze. (Note that this creation myth refers to 'all in this land', not all human beings everywhere.)

Children generally resemble their parents, but because all humans are similar, sometimes things get muddled up, and gold parents give birth to a bronze or silver child, or a silver parent to a gold, and so on (somewhat like two muggle parents giving birth to a wizard child in the *Harry Potter* books). The Guardians have to watch the mixture of metals in all children and ensure that the children move to the appropriate class, an early version of state-sanctioned interference in parental rights. If a Guardian has a child with bronze in it, they must harden their hearts and degrade it to the industrial class.

Exercise 14

It is easy to imagine that Plato's foundation myth of the three metals is the remnant of an ancient view that has no relevance today. Indeed, reactions to Plato's Republic throughout the ages have been very diverse but include the view that it acts as a blueprint for fascism.

Are similar views still held in one way or another? A key qualification for membership of the Guardian class was intellectual ability: they are philosophers, spending much of the day in abstract contemplation, while also ruling others. Could our use of AI be riding on, and reinforcing, a similar social stratification, with more power and status given to those seen to have greater intelligence?

Plato's Guardians had the authority to rule, an authority supposedly accepted by the populace as a whole. Compare and contrast this to those who have the power that their use of AI and other computing technology brings them, such as the power to shape social media and to design algorithms that impact our daily lives. Does the split between the ruling class and the auxiliary class still apply in a technological, AI-driven world?

Could a technological divide create further classes of people? Would this matter, so long as all were in agreement, or believed some 'noble lie'? Suppose the 'noble lie' is that humans are made of messy wetware, and so, limited by our biology which constrains processing speeds, our intelligence is less than that of the silicone and metal-based lifeforms, which will rule over us?

5.4.5 Is There an Essence to Human Nature?

There have been many attempts to pinpoint a distinctive essence to human beings. Candidates include freedom, our capacity for self-consciousness, our capacity for cultural as opposed to individual learning, the human use of convention, and the use of language to laugh and cry. Some discussions in this area point to distinctive qualities that led to the evolution of attributes that separate us from our closest relatives, such as the use of fire to cook food, which rendered it easier to digest.

We have seen how Russell and Norvig postulated that humans termed themselves *Homo sapiens* because intelligence is so important to us. However, since the term *Homo sapiens* is used biologically to differentiate us from other species of hominids, it also has the implications that it is our intelligence (or at least, our level of intelligence) that distinguished us from the others, who now, alas, are no more, but not merely in the sense that small distinctions between markings and habitat might distinguish one species from another close species; intelligence distinguishes us in that it plays a key explanatory role in an account of human life, both individual and collective. (This is so far to say nothing about what else may be important to any account of human distinctiveness.) After all, we could also have picked ourselves out as, say, 'the naked ape', and although clothing is a fascinating cultural subject to study, our lack of body hair is not really the most interesting thing about us.

Intelligence is important to us, and it is especially important to AI researchers who have dedicated their working lives to developing machine intelligence. One can also observe that philosophical accounts of human nature that stress reason or intelligence as our key hallmark and best characteristic are produced by philosophers—another very small subset of humanity who are, again, very wedded to intellectual endeavours. This may have biased their views. There have been different contenders for human traits with the power to illuminate our distinctive natures. It is interesting to look at some of these, not so much for the purposes of deciding which is the 'right' answer, but to consider different aspects of our natures which may illuminate the question of the value of AI to us.

Homo Ludens is the title of a 1938 book by the Dutch historian and cultural theorist Johan Huizinga [40]. It refers to our capacity for play, a capacity that we share with other animals, but which Huizinga argues is an important element of culture. He identified five elements of play: it is free, it is not 'real' life, it is distinct from 'real' life in location and time, it creates order, and it is not connected to any material interest or profit. One point to note is how different such a concept of play is from the instrumental and goal-directed accounts of intelligence we examined earlier, which characterise intelligence by referring to the goal(s) at which it aims, whose presumed value undergirds the value of the intelligent activity producing it. In other words, Homo ludens strongly suggests not activity directed at an end state that is characterised externally to the activity but activity valued for its own sake, the journey not the arrival.

Homo faber—man the maker—is another strong contender for expressing our most characteristic attributes. The notion that humans alone use tools or make things has been shown false by animals such as the bower bird and primates, but it would be hard not to notice that no other animal has launched a rival to the international space station, and although bower birds collect and arrange various items, no bower bird has set up a world-class museum with several miles of corridors exhibiting bower bird art and artifacts spanning a couple of millennia, with a gift shop and a café selling light lunches, exquisite pastries, and a selection of hot and cold beverages. Humans have. Perhaps Homo faber also captures the notion that humans are characterised by their activity of making rather than as the possessors of things that have been made—again, by an activity undertaken, rather than as creatures striving towards an end state.

Nonetheless, the concept of Homo faber has been used as a critique of certain views of the relationship of humans to technology. August Comte proposed that we should see the world only through observable empirical phenomena and use our knowledge to build technology that would transform our lives for the better to create a heaven on earth. Past views of the human person as uniquely valuable creatures of God, or seekers after goodness, truth, and beauty, are no longer needed in this technological world. Hannah Arendt critiqued Comte's views and warned of the dangers of redefining human nature as Homo faber, with its focus on mere technical skill and away from wisdom [41]. Erik Larson suggests that the greatest achievement of our species would be to build ourselves [9, p. 66].

Note, however, that Arendt's criticism is focused on the particular worldview advocated by Comte, where all knowledge rests upon a stark empiricism, which includes human beings. For contrast, consider the teleological view of the world, a richer notion of craftwork working in some manner of harmony with natural resources and human skill, and the view of humans as seeking eudaimonia, which could perhaps support an account of human nature that gave a central place to our activity of making and of technology that did not have such radical implications for reshaping our natures.

Both Homo ludens and Homo faber place an emphasis on activity and agency, albeit in rather different ways. However, *Homo sapiens* surely has agency as an implication, because to be wise implies the impetus to seek wisdom. Nobody is wise who can't be bothered to ever seek knowledge or explore the world around them.

Exercise 15

'The creation of AI is entirely characteristic of human beings, because much of AI research activity could also well be characterised as a form of play for those conducting it, and moreover, it has produced many ways of connecting socially online, not to mention countless games. Moreover, having released us from the drudgery of work, we will now be able to devote more and more of our time to play. This is a great step forward for humanity'.

Is such a view at all plausible? In addressing such questions, it is always useful to consider the strongest possible arguments from all points of view.

Last, what of Homo religiosus? The term is associated with Mircea Eliade, but there are also many other figures in the history of thought who have considered that a religious impulse is central to human beings [42]. We seek meaning, some sense of purpose in the world, we have a sense of wonder, a sense of something grander than our immediate lives, a sense of a source of value outside of ourselves. A lack of any such a sense can often be bewildering and demoralising. Even without a specifically religious or a spiritual framework, a sense of awe and wonder at the world is experienced by billions of us. Recall Psalm 8: 'When I consider thy heavens, the work of thy fingers, the moon and the stars, which thou hast ordained'. Such wonder can also inspire curiosity and fascination at the world, which drives so much art and science. However, this need not be instrumental; we can explore the world in many ways just for its own sake. Many scientists pursue their work out of sheer love for the subject matter. Such a view of humanity sits uneasily with a purely instrumental account of our intelligence. My son's first word was 'bird', uttered as he pointed to a colourful parakeet flying across the park. What was his small mind trying to achieve, other than joy and delight at the world and a connection with his mother as he shared his excitement?

It is often helpful to consider if some religious impulse lies behind some attitudes towards AI. Conversely, some working in science and technology may be explicitly anti-religious. 'Debunking' explanations that attempt to reduce purported claims of meaning and value to 'nothing but' are legion. Paradoxically, some of these may be driven by a kind of fervour and insistence more characteristic of a religious world view.

One might also note that these characterisations of the essence of human nature are all to a degree positive. We seem to have a pretty good view of ourselves, but this need not be the case. Dostoevsky's embittered anti-hero of *Notes from Underground* suggests that we should rather be characterised as an ungrateful biped [43]. Such a characterisation does indeed probably serve as a definition that no other creature shares, especially if I consider the hens we kept who always seemed inordinately grateful, overjoyed even, for every scrap of food. However, we want more than this. The ways in which we look for defining characteristics strongly reflects prior judgements of value about ourselves as a species.

The essence of human nature and claims of uniqueness Many who attempt to find the essence of what it is to be human have endeavoured to find something that only humans have. As such, these claims have frequently been vulnerable to counterexamples from the animal world. Few who have watched orangutans laughing will doubt their capacity to do so and may be more likely to marvel with envy at their capacity to laugh with such utter abandon and joy. Note that this is not necessary to be able to uniquely describe a kind, because a unique cluster of attributes also does the job, but its prevalence as a strategy may indicate that it matters to us for some reason.

Exercise 16

How much does it matter to us that we are unique in some way? The answer to this question for some people will be 'not at all', but why has some claim of uniqueness been so prevalent? How might this impact upon claims of commonality with other human beings?

Does the possibility of developing AI threaten any such claims to uniqueness?

There is no essence to humans Existentialism has denied that there is any fixed essence that defines human beings. We do not find ourselves in the world with a fixed essence. Rather, we exist first and then define our essence. This is a view presenting us with limitless freedom to make what we will of our lives. This may at first sound like a license to behave badly. However, note that Jean-Paul Sartre considered that when he makes a moral choice, he chooses in anguish, for he chooses for all mankind [44].

Humans as essentially social As we have seen, Aristotle stressed the intellect but also insisted that we are not just rational but also social animals. The topic of friendship received more attention in his *Nicomachean Ethics* than any other. He was a biologist as well as a philosopher and points out the particular importance of social connections to humans in comparison to other animals, noting that for grazing animals to live together amounts to little more than sharing the same pasture, but for humans, it involves sharing conversation and thought [6, Book IX, Ch. 9]. Although we now know far more about the capacities of other animals than Aristotle did, including the complex societies found in primates, a contrast is still drawn with human societies as more sophisticated but with greater capacity to conceptualise social relations and to reflect upon and judge them.

Are human beings essentially social? The answer to this question will have a profound influence on ethics. Some more modern views have characterised human beings as atomistic, isolated individuals, and from this starting point, the sceptical question of 'why should I be moral?' is asked [45]. The source of the motivation to act for others seems mysterious, if each one of us is conceived of as sealed within our own bubble. A view more grounded in our biological natures, where none of us could possibly spring up out of nowhere, with no relations to other similar creatures, may find it easier to begin an answer to the question of 'why should I be moral'? (see Sects. 5.4.4 and 1.4).

5.4.6 The Divided Self and Notions of the 'Higher Self'

It is very common for accounts of human nature to posit divisions within the self, often in a certain tension with each other, sometimes with struggles for control between different parts, and often with different values given to different parts. There are so many variations that it is impossible to do more than offer a couple of examples and point out some features of interest to us.

For example, Plato posited a tripartite soul consisting of the *logos*, the reasoning part of the soul, which regulates the other parts; *thymos*, a spirited part of the soul; and *eros*, the desiring part of the soul [5]. There are no marks for guessing which part he thought should be in control; note the resonance with the drive to develop artificial intelligence, which seems so obvious it hardly needs stating. Note also that the parts of the self (soul in this case) that are to be kept in order are those most related to bodily functions and shared with the so-called 'lower' animals, a common theme. There is a clear hierarchy of order here, with the implication that it is at least in theory possible to attain inner harmony with reason in charge.

A rather different model comes from Sigmund Freud. As a result of his work in psychoanalysis, he divided the mind into the ego, the superego, and the id [46]. The id is the instinctual part of the mind with aggressive, sexual, and other bodily drives. The superego operates as a moral conscience, judging the urges of the id, and the ego is the part of the self that is acting to the reality principle, trying to please the id in ways that the superego will tolerate. This model posits a more complex and pragmatic negotiation of harmony between the different parts of the self. Reason has a role to play but is not 'king'.

There are so many other possible accounts of splits in the self that it would take a multivolumed book to recount them all in depth. Many readers will doubtless know of a plethora of other examples. A key issue for ethics arises from claims frequently made about the relative ordering of the self and the value judgements attached to this. An *extremely* rough and ready generalisation can be made as follows.

Mind	Body
Intellect	Animal
Reason	Emotion, impulse, drive
Calm, logical	Powerful, unruly, somewhat scary
The 'nice' bit	The 'naughty' bit
Must be in control	Must be controlled
Domination OR	Kept in check completely OR
Harmony with other elements	Put in its rightful place in balance

Don't read this too literally. There are multiple variations and some significant departures from this crude chart. It will be useful to consider nuance, counterexamples, and outliers. However, it can serve to illustrate some general tendencies and commonalities within a range of views.

The place of AI within this schema may seem firmly in the left column. The uses of AI to attempt to combat human partiality, unreliability, and impulses in assisting us to reach good decisions fit well with this (notwithstanding the small point that AI is built by these emotion-ridden humans).

Do dreams of uploading the mind to computers include uploading the experience of a bad mood caused by a bout of indigestion? Possibly not, but should they? Some attempts to recreate humans by collating a large mass of data about an individual are attempting to capture memory and personality, which includes emotions and other factors on the 'body' side. However, visions of uploading minds bear some resemblance to the visions of a life of abstract contemplation envisaged as the life of the

Philosopher Kings of Plato. Science fiction makes a contribution to such questions in exploring possibilities, which, even if never realisable, can help us to imaginatively respond to fundamental questions about who we are and why our lives matter.

The nature of self-mastery Another important point of debate concerns the nature of the divisions within the self insofar as these divisions are captured by the relationship between reason and emotion (some such division is frequently made, sometimes using different vocabulary).

The influential instrumental account of intelligence we referred to earlier places goals as external to intelligence itself. This then posits a split between intelligence and our goals, which puts our goals outside the reach of reason. Recall Russell and Norvig's discussion of Aristotle's claim that we deliberate about means but not about ends. Note that an account such as Plato's where the reasoning part has the ability to control the other parts of the self is critically different: on Russell and Norvig's account, it's not at all clear how intelligence (reason) can control goals (desires). In fact, it seems clear that on this account, it cannot. As we have seen, this view is disputed.

5.4.7 Reason or Emotion?

There are many ways of characterising the broad division referred to here, including different ways of understanding reason. 'Emotion' is used as an approximation for aspects of our inner experience that may also be labelled drives, desires, feelings, and so on. While many accounts of human nature stress reason, some making it entirely in the ascendant, others wish for it to curtail only other elements of the self, such as emotion, insofar as they are too dominant or operate out of place. For a simple way of illustrating this, one may think of how Plato saw the Guardians as living a very simple, austere life governed by duty to the state, where the highest aspects of life were contemplation of the abstract ideas (sounds a little boring eh). Contrast this with the notion of the middle way within Buddhism, where a mean between extremes of self-denial and excess is sought, in a way somewhat similar to Aristotle's doctrine of the virtuous life as the mean between two extremes [47]. Plato's account of human nature stressed the intellect, the soul, the abstract, whereas Aristotle viewed us not simply as rational but as rational *animals* and also as essentially social animals. These views on the self make an important backdrop to attitudes towards technology and what we hope for its role in the future of human life, especially envisaging societies where we live increasingly enmeshed with intelligent machines. Such debates are all pertinent to the question of how we may or may not be able to harness AI to 'improve' on human nature.

David Hume: Reason the Slave of the Passions

David Hume (1711–1776) was a Scottish philosopher, historian, and economist known for his empiricism and sceptical views on many philosophical questions.

He considered that all substantial knowledge of the world was gained through the senses, dividing all knowledge into either 'matters of fact' or 'relations of ideas', in what has become known as 'Hume's fork'. Matters of fact give us knowledge of the world gained from our senses. Relations of ideas are judgements about that empirical knowledge, such as mathematical knowledge, which gives us no substantive knowledge of the world.

He also made a sharp divide between belief and desire. Reason is 'inert', meaning that reason alone can never lead us to action. Hence, no knowledge we have gained about the world can ever, on its own, tell us what to do, prompt us to action. Only desire can do that, or what Hume called 'the passions'. 'Reason is, and ought only to be, the slave of the passions, and can never pretend to any office than to serve and obey them', he famously wrote in his *Treatise of Human Nature*, Book III, Part III, Section III [48].

This means that, for Hume, all motivations to act, including ethical judgements, are fundamentally based upon desire or emotion. Such a view has been very influential among many philosophers who hold a 'noncognitivist' view of ethics that moral judgements are based upon feelings, desires, or emotions, rather than on claims about the nature of the world.

Hume's account has also been seen as influential in belief–desire–intention models of action. A set of beliefs, in combination with a set of desires, gives rise to an intention, which leads to action. Beliefs alone cannot do this, on this model.

This model also chimes neatly with instrumental accounts of intelligence, which see intelligence as the capacity to reach goals. Intelligence involves capacities of reason and the capacity to acquire knowledge, but the goals themselves are thus conceptualised as external to intelligence.

Likewise, we can consider the example of the Romantic movement, which rejected what they saw as the excessive emphasis on reason and intellect of the Enlightenment and of the Rationalists. Mary Wollstonecraft Shelley's novel *Frankenstein* belongs to the movement of Romanticism, which emphasises the power and force of nature and of imagination, feeling, and passion, the importance of the individual (although Mary Shelley herself stresses the importance of sympathy, cooperation, and family relationships) [49]. Strong echoes of certain elements of Romanticism can be found in some critiques of AI and of modern technologies in general. For example, in his chapter 'What is a person?' from *You Are Not a Gadget*, Jaron Lanier writes that digital culture sees all reality, including people, in terms of information and turns our attention to a network as an abstracted picture of a multitude of individuals, and the real people who go to make up this network and who are the source of its meaning may be overlooked [50, p. 17]. In a sustained and detailed critique, he explores how the foundational values and modes of application of new technologies may be morphing human nature and our experience of the world and each other.

Exercise 17
Jaron Lanier writes of a new culture where all of reality, including us, is seen in terms of information [50, p. 27]. Consider the implications of seeing humans as having the same essential nature as the rest of reality and of seeing us in terms of information. Argue for and against the notion that developments in technology and its applications have produced a tendency to see individuals merely as bundles of information.

5.4.8 The Boundaries of Human Nature

A key trait of human beings is our adaptability and our capacity to learn, change, and grow. There are divergent views about the flexibility of our capacities and traits, the scope of our potential for good or for ill, and different judgements about attempts to transcend current human limits and our capacity to survive, in some way, such transformations. A notable trait of human beings is their capacity to accommodate to different environments, including extremes of temperature and external conditions— from the Arctic to the Sahara and from the moon to under the sea. Some of this capacity relies on advanced technology, while some does not. Humans have adapted to extremes of social situations, including natural disasters and social and economic catastrophe. Conversely, there are many circumstances in which human beings will be broken, physically, emotionally, and morally. Views on such questions underlie the question of using AI to enhance or to transcend human traits.

The limits of human nature and our moral capacities Some individuals demonstrating the capacity to survive even the most inhumane abuses meted out in concentration camps, even when stripped of virtually all the protective technology that humans have created—minimal clothing, no personal possessions, and no capacity to communicate outside the enclosed world of abuse [51–53]. Reading personal accounts of such experience is awe-inspiring and humbling, two totally inadequate words to capture my admiration at the strength that humans can manifest. On the other hand, such examples also show that humans can survive situations that should never have arisen. The need for such adaptations may indicate not just that extremely harsh circumstances happen to arise but also that a great wrong has occurred. Moreover, some adapt to such situations in ways that are individually dysfunctional (although such a claim will always involve value judgements) and/or that demonstrate moral corruption, such as those who collaborate with captors in meting out extreme cruelties to others. A simple way of expressing these points is that under extremis, human beings have the capacity both for growth and moral courage and for dismal personal and moral failure. See Chap. 6 for a discussion of phronesis, or practical wisdom.

The changes wrought to society by the introduction of new technologies can be transformative of ways in which we live, introducing opportunities and challenges.

Exercise 18
The adaptability of human beings is also a critical factor in envisaging future scenarios where technology has continued to have a great impact on social, cultural, and economic functioning. Could humans adapt to large-scale technological unemployment, for example? What kind of changes, if any, do we need to bring about to make this achievable, and what kinds of changes, if any, do we need to bring about to make this desirable? Note that given the capacity of humans to endure appalling conditions, these are definitely different questions.

Transcending the limits of our intellect and moral capacities with AI Measures of adaptability are one factor by which humans and intelligent machines are compared. In measuring intelligence, François Chollet describes extreme generalisation from one learned situation to another as currently only existing in biological organisms, with human-centric extreme generalisation manifesting both in situations that an individual has never before encountered and in situations that no human being ever has encountered [54, p. 11]. Is the structure of our minds determined in some way, laid down by some cognitive infrastructure, running according to certain rules or programmes, or is its potential less constrained? The answer to this question will act to shape our attitudes towards human potential in comparison to the capacities of AI and has also shaped research in AI [54].

It is common to consider the mind as constrained by the development of the brain in stages from our evolutionary past. We have certain fixed ways of interacting with the world and of thinking that may be maladaptive in certain circumstances. For example, Daniel Kahneman's work on *Thinking Fast and Slow*, which was introduced earlier in Sect. 4.1, exemplifies an influential approach that aims to identify the ways that the echoes of our evolutionary past and the structure of our nervous systems constrain our thinking [55]. Note that this evolutionary view often goes along with a mildly depressing take on humans as a species but may also be accompanied by the trope of progress as an extrapolation forward from our halting, imperfect evolutionary development is envisaged. We may make the best of what we have by being careful to note the typical errors and fallacies to which we are prone. In addition, we may look to machines. There is considerable hope that AI may assist us to transcend the limits of our 'wetware', a term that may be used neutrally to describe the information processing that goes on within living cells but which is sometimes used in a derogatory fashion in comparing human intellect to computers. Characteristic reasoning errors and the pushes and pulls of human emotion and partialities are commonly seen as shortcomings that we need to eliminate and may need AI to achieve.

Exercise 19 Human Nature and the Virtues of Our Boundedness
Perhaps the ultimate dream of human adaptability is the vision that we could both survive and even enjoy having our minds 'uploaded' to a machine. For this to count as closely as possible to survival of an individual human being, what qualities of

mind and thought would need to be uploaded? What capabilities would the machine need to have? Of course, you may consider that such uploading is not possible, but even so, try to get as close as possible to a full uploading scenario. You may also wish to reflect on the uncomfortable issue of what happens to the human being in question. (We will return to such issues later when we further consider the question of mind and body and of the identity of persons.)

5.4.9 Boundaries and Limits

As human beings, we have certain limits. We exist at a certain time and in a certain place. We are born and we die. There are limits to our knowledge, memory, understanding, empathy, and abilities. Our vision is pretty good, although restricted to what we arrogantly call the visible spectrum. Our hearing is so-so. We cannot fly from Europe to Southern Africa without a plane or a satnav, as certain birds can. We can memorise a shorter string of random digits than chimpanzees can.

We are individuated by the limits of our bodies, even if we are more than just our bodies. This is an essential aspect of our moral universe. Even if we have very close ties to other human beings, we are still separate people, and the gulf between us means we have different points of view, different stances on the world. It presents the challenges and the distinctive shape of communication and understanding and its lack between us. It creates moral problems and helps to shape how we address them. These limits placed on us by our biological embodiment shape a large part of the ethical challenges we face. This distinguishes us from AI, including from robots, in many ways.

Are these boundaries merely limits? The gulf between us and others is often responsible for cruelty, neglect, and more mundane selfishness. Precisely because there is this gulf between us and others, it also forms an essential element of how we think of the virtues, or moral goodness. I expect no praise for feeding myself when hungry. However, if someone goes out of their way to provide food for those without, especially if they have to make substantive sacrifices to do so, this may attract moral praise. Those whose actions for others result in extreme sacrifice, such as risk of life or even death, are called heroes or saints, precisely because they are mortal and because we, the admiring throng who are not so brave, know what they have given up. It may be that it is often our very flaws that enable us to empathetically relate to others in ways that enable us to help them. The notion of 'the wounded healer' has a long history.

The ways in which we are bounded may help map out some of our finest moments, as well as our worst. If we think of technology as the attempt to exceed our boundaries, there may be a difficult balancing act to be had regarding which limits we should try to overcome and which we should leave alone. Recall our discussion in Chap. 4 of the object of morality.

Exercise 20

We often fail to understand others, even those close to us, and may misinterpret words and fail to read emotions adequately. This communication gulf is a major stumbling block between us. Recall our discussion of Neil Lawrence's analysis of embodiment factors and differences in data processing speeds between humans and computers in Sect. 5.2.6.

Now consider the use of AI to improve our understanding of those close to us. Researchers at the University of Southern California have been developing multimodal wearable technologies to detect psychological states to enable a partner to react accordingly [56]. One aim is to predict conflicts before they occur [57]. Perhaps an alert might let you know that your partner will be tense and upset when he or she returns home today. You might decide to delay that talk you were going to have about the housework and have a drink and dinner ready. Perhaps you could set up an app so that flowers were automatically ordered every time the technology indicated that your partner's mood had dipped after your last conversation.

Consider the ethical implications of the widespread use of such technologies and how they might impinge on our relationships. Consider the ethical implications of the use of such technologies to improve the care of people living with advanced dementia who may have limited capacity to consent to their use.

Consider different reactions to such technology from those who (a) tend to stress the importance of individual rights and protections or (b) tend to stress the value of community and relationships.

5.4.10   Is Human Nature Perfectible?

There are many different views on the question of the perfectibility of humanity. These attitudes form a backdrop to visions of transhumanism and the improvement of human beings individually and human society in general via AI and other forms of technology.

> Out of the crooked timber of humanity, no straight thing was ever made
> (*Aus so krummem Holze, als woraus der Mensch gemacht ist, kann nichts ganz Gerades gezimmert warden.*)
> Immanuel Kant, *Idea for a Universal History from a Cosmopolitan Perspective* [58]

Attitudes to perfectibility also speak to general stances towards ethics: perhaps it is accepted that we will never find a 'perfect' account of ethics and of living well in this world and that compromise and doing the best under the circumstances are all that can be hoped for.

John Passmore's book *The Perfectibility of Man* gives a detailed examination of this topic, spanning 3000 years of views on mankind's perfectibility from philosophy, theology, politics, and science and technology [59]. Even so, there are many traditions of thought from around the world not included in the book but it nonetheless provides interesting source material for reflecting on how notions of perfection enter into our ideas of morality, on trying to determine ethics for AI, and on how technologies such as AI may assist humans to progress. Greek legacy was to establish a metaphysical ideal of perfection, identified with a supreme Being, either distinct from or identified with nature. Humans were seen as being able to share in this perfection, at least to some extent, a perfection that involved attaining knowledge and a rational understanding of the universe. There is a tension between views that attaining this knowledge involved withdrawal from the world and those who held it could be achieved within an ideal society. Meanwhile, there is a lower level of perfection in the form of standards of morality for the ordinary citizen on the path to perfection. The achievement of perfection is unsurprisingly considered extremely hard; for many such as many in the Christian tradition, perfection within this life has been thought impossible, although others have demurred and sought it in this life through various means, and progress towards perfection is sometimes seen as something requiring the grace, the assistance of God. Attempts to seek perfection include striving to conquer the desires of the flesh and of the self.

Ideas of perfection of the human race as a whole have been expressed through the eugenics movement which we mentioned earlier, which has a sorry history of forced sterilisations and of the denigration of some parts of the population as unfit, yet despite this, some consider that new technologies mean that it will continue to be practiced [60]. Some vigorously defend modern reproductive technologies such as embryo selection and prenatal testing as enabling 'liberal eugenics', premised on choice [61]. Modern methodologies such as the CRISPR technique, which enables possible gene manipulation, may herald even greater capacity to shape our biological futures [62]. The potential prospects of increasing divisions between different individuals and groups parallel some of the issues we potentially face with developments in AI.

We can trace strands that can recur in some accounts of our use of technology: the control of the body, the emphasis on knowledge of the highest form, the emphasis on the mental, the control of society, and different positions on elitism: the question of whether all people will be able to benefit from this, or only some.

5.4.11 Myths and Origin Stories About Human Nature

Many cultures and religions make claims about the origins of human beings. These take many different forms but may indicate how humans are seen in relation to the rest of the natural world and any role they are assigned, as well as sometimes indicating a view on the strengths and weaknesses of human beings. Sometimes accounts take the form of an imagined golden age. Origin stories may be significant for understanding hopes for the future, for how time is thought of, and for notions of the unfolding of time and history and notions of progress.

Myth Zero Many will consider that they do not believe in, nor are they influenced by, any myths or origin stories about humanity. However, this is unlikely to be true because such people will probably believe evolution to be true and thus may have beliefs about the human species based on seeing humans as 'nothing but' the product of evolution. Moreover, we are often guided by myths embedded in our culture of origin without realising that we are reproducing their patterns. Evolution is 'just' a scientific theory describing and explaining the origin of species, but it is often associated with certain attitudes. These may include considering that modern humans are just a passing species in an ever-changing panoply of species, to be replaced at some time in the future by other hominids more adapted to the environment, or destined to die off in a mass extinction, all part of the chance passing of evolutionary time and no particular loss to the world. (Oddly, such people may simultaneously mourn the extinction of every other species.) It may partake of the view of evolution which slips from using function as part of biological explanation to talking of purpose as if evolution was heading towards some goal with humans as part of this and project that our descendants will go on to greater and greater 'fitness', extrapolating to greater intelligence on most accounts. (Projections sometimes include pictures of humanoids with feeble muscles and massive heads.)

What has this to do with us? The answers to ethical questions about the more distant future with AI, including questions around human enhancement, the possibility of large-scale technological unemployment, and the possibility that we might be controlled or exterminated by some super-intelligent AI, all depend upon the answer one gives to such questions. It is of course perfectly possible to be neutral or agnostic about such answers, but one's views often emerge in considering future scenarios where the continuation of the human race is in question.

Exercise 21
Some futurists consider that eventually, humans will be 'replaced' or superseded by AI descendants or replacements for our limited species. Others consider that AI could be used to enhance us as a species.

What views would we have to take of human nature in order to consider this could be possible? Might something be irretrievably lost? What shortcomings of human beings might be improved by AI?

Some also envisage that eventually the human race might split into two: those who are enhanced (perhaps by AI and/or by biological means) and those who are not. What difference might this make to our ethics were this to occur? How much do you consider that your views on morality are based upon an assumption of basic equality of value between all humans, would splitting our species into two make an impact on this, and if so, how?

We will consider these questions again in Chaps. 10 and 11.

5.4.12 Some Helpful Questions to Ask About Human Nature

It will be apparent that one could spend one's whole life examining different accounts of human nature. Luckily as fascinating as this might be, there is no need to do this in order to make progress in advancing discussion in AI ethics. Some key questions to consider may be useful in identifying areas of disagreement or impasse in debate, as well as in reflecting on one's own views, for certain issues in AI ethics, and indeed, for understanding some of the ideology driving some visions of AI. This suggested list of questions is not meant to imply that any particular answer is right or wrong. The list is not exhaustive.

Are assumptions being made regarding any special role that humans have in creating the future?

Is there a belief that human beings can be understood in precisely the same way as any other part of the natural world?

Are humans understood in purely material terms? That is (roughly), that we could understand everything there is to know about humans, in terms of the basic physical laws of the universe?

Are humans thought to be essentially mental beings? How are the particular facts of human biology regarded? Are there claims that human beings could transcend or escape their bodies in any way?

Are claims being made about a central essence of human beings?

Are some aspects of human beings seen to be higher than other aspects? What assumptions are being made about how humans could be made better?

5.5   Key Points

To assess the value of AI, it is essential to consider how we understand and value intelligence. We need to consider how intelligence is understood in relation to AI and to human beings, any differences, and how comparisons between AI and humans are made.

There are multiple ways of characterising intelligence. In AI, intelligence is sometimes depicted in terms of the capacity efficiently to achieve goals. However, reference to goals is less common in general accounts of intelligence. This instrumental account of intelligence that may be used by some working in AI needs to be considered carefully, as it could have a large impact on how we understand, value, and use AI and the ethical issues arising.

The way in which intelligence is valued may have implications for how we value both human beings in general and individual humans in particular. When valuing intelligence, it is critical to consider what it is we value about it, the specific context of application, and what else we might value and might lose by focusing too much on certain aspects of intelligence only.

Look out for any assumptions regarding the value of knowledge, information, and data and the values involved in sharing and communicating knowledge, information, or data.

There are many different accounts of human nature. Assumptions about human nature can underlie some of the major divisions between those with different approaches to questions in ethics and in AI, including broad cultural differences and differences in worldview. Understanding some of the ways in which assumptions about human nature can differ will help in advancing discussion over many central disagreements in ethics.

Ideas of human nature underlie many of the questions in AI ethics, concerning questions such as what failings humans have, how humans may be improved, their place in the natural world, and any role they may have in creating the future.

The simple step of asking what broad assumptions are you and others are making about human nature can be helpful in advancing understanding of some questions in AI ethics.

5.6 Educator Notes

The question of the different ways in which intelligence is understood is important for many of the ethical questions in AI, including many of the questions we discuss in later chapters. For students with less time, Sect. 5.2.1 should provide an adequate introduction to the main questions.

Some students may find the general topic of human nature somewhat abstract, which is one reason why this chapter has provided many exercises designed to link these philosophical issues to more concrete issues and examples that pertain to the use of technology.

For students with less time and different sets of interests, some of the exercises could be set as stand-alone work to introduce the students to the general issues. The material on human nature may be of great interest to those with backgrounds in subjects such as philosophy, theology, and anthropology, who may have a lot to contribute to class discussions, but even those students who find the topic rather abstract, it is common to have some assumptions about human nature, and the exercises will help to alert students to these issues.

Many exercises ask students to consider very broad philosophical questions, and there is no expectation that they will necessarily be able to provide rigorous answers, although many students will have particular and valuable viewpoints and material to bring to bear. Some students may find Exercises 2, 5, 8, and 18 more tangible than others. Exercise 7 focuses directly on a claim about the value of intelligence frequently cited by some publicly prominent individuals, which may usefully raise some central ideas: we have looked at this previously, and this gives a chance either to look at it for the first time or to review opinions based upon what students have since learned.

Debate and extended project and essay topics Exercise 8 could make a good structured classroom discussion about the nature and value of data from different points of view, which could be very useful preparation for much later work. Exercise 12 on embodiment and its significance could be interesting for some students as an essay or discussion topic, and it is a topic that is very challenging but that will reappear later in various guises. Exercise 16 on human uniqueness could be a good debate topic. It may be challenging for students to articulate but will be a good preparation for some later work that concerns reductive accounts of mind and body and personhood, which are relevant to some key ethical questions in AI.

Acknowledgements This chapter was partially funded by the National Institute for Health Research, Health Services and Delivery Research Programme (project number 13/10/80). The views expressed are those of the author and not necessarily those of the NIHR or the Department of Health and Social Care.
Additional sources may be found in the reference list.

References

1. Russell SJ, Norvig P (2016) Artificial intelligence a modern approach, 3rd edn. Pearson Education, London
2. Legg S, Hutter M (2007) A collection of definitions of intelligence. Front Artif Intell Appl 157: 17
3. Legg S, Hutter M (2007) Universal intelligence: a definition of machine intelligence. Mind Mach 17(4):391–444
4. Russell SJ (2019) Human compatible AI and the problem of control. Allen Lane, London
5. Plato (1888) The republic of Plato (trans: Jowett B, ed). Clarendon Press, Oxford
6. Nussbaum MC (2001) The fragility of goodness: luck and ethics in Greek tragedy and philosophy. Cambridge University Press, Cambridge
7. Aristotle (1925) The Nicomachean ethics (trans: Ross WD). Oxford University Press, Oxford
8. Boden M (2018) Artificial intelligence: a very short introduction. Oxford University Press, Oxford
9. Larson E (2021) The myth of artificial intelligence: why computers can't think the way we do. Harvard University Press, Cambridge
10. May T (2011) Social research: issues, methods and research. McGraw-Hill, New York
11. Imai K (2018) Quantitative social science: an introduction. Princeton University Press, Princeton
12. Atkinson P (2022) Crafting ethnography. Sage, Thousand Oaks
13. Descartes R (1954) Discourse on the method. In: Anscombe GEM, Geach P (eds) Descartes' philosophical writings. Nelson's University Paperbacks
14. Kamin L (1974) The science and politics of IQ. Lawrence Erlbaum Associates, Mahwah
15. Wollstonecraft M (1891) A vindication of the rights of woman, with strictures on political and moral subject. T. Fisher, London
16. Future of Life (2015) Open Letter 'Research priorities for robust and beneficial artificial intelligence'. https://futureoflife.org/ai-open-letter/. Accessed 10 Jul 2022
17. DeepMind (2022) Welcome to DeepMind: embarking on one of the greatest adventures in scientific history. https://www.youtube.com/watch?v=b6e8CCPp2Kc. Accessed 10 Jul 2022
18. https://www.dailymail.co.uk/news/article-2786723/London-skyscraper-Walkie-Talkie-melted-cars-reflecting-sunlight-fitted-shading.html
19. Mullin G (2014) No more Walkie Scorchie! London skyscraper which melted cars by reflecting sunlight is fitted with shading. Daily Mail
20. Fiani B, Reardon T, Ayres B, Cline D, Sitto SR (2021) An examination of prospective uses and future directions of neuralink: the brain-machine interface. Cureus 13(3):e14192
21. Lawrence ND (2017) Living together: mind and machine intelligence. arXiv preprint arXiv:1705.07996

22. Bentham J (1907) Introduction to the principles of morals and legislation, works. Clarendon Press, Oxford
23. Mill JS (1838) Bentham. London and Westminster Review
24. Mill JS (1860) Thoughts on poetry. Crayon 7:93
25. Mayer-Schönberger V, Cukier K (2013) Big data: a revolution that will transform how we live, work, and think. Houghton Mifflin Harcourt, Boston
26. Woolf V (1977) To the lighthouse, panther, London. Hogarth Press, London
27. Tegmark M (2017) Life 3.0: being human in the age of artificial intelligence. Knopf, New York
28. Psalm 8, 3–9, World English Bible https://ebible.org/web/PSA008.htm
29. Heidegger M (1954) The question concerning technology and other essays (trans: Lovitt W, 1977). Harper Collins, New York
30. Hawkins J, Blakeslee S (2006) On intelligence: how a new understanding of the brain will lead to the creation of truly intelligent machines. St Martin's, New York
31. Damasio AR (2006) Descartes' error. Random House, New York
32. Gilligan C (1982) In a different voice, psychological theory and women's development. Harvard University Press, Cambridge
33. Baier A (1994) Moral prejudices. Harvard University Press, Cambridge
34. Held V (2006) The ethics of care: personal, political, global. Oxford University Press, Oxford
35. Noddings N (1984) Caring. University of California Press, Berkeley
36. Scruton R (2017) On human nature. Princeton University Press, Princeton
37. Kontos PC (2004) Ethnographic reflections on selfhood, embodiment and Alzheimer's disease. Ageing Soc 24(6):829–849
38. Hung L, Liu C, Woldum E, Au-Yeung A, Berndt A, Wallsworth C, Horne N, Gregorio M, Mann J, Chaudhury H (2019) The benefits of and barriers to using a social robot PARO in care settings: a scoping review. BMC Geriatr 19(1):1–10
39. http://www.parorobots.com
40. Huizinga J (2016) Homo Ludens: a study of the play element of human culture. Angelico Press, Brooklyn. First published 1938
41. Arendt H (2013) The human condition. University of Chicago Press, Chicago
42. Eliade M (1959) The sacred and profane: the nature of religion. Elsevier, Chatswood
43. Dostoevsky F (1999) Notes from the underground, and the gambler. OUP Oxford, Oxford
44. Sartre JP (2021) Existentialism is a humanism. Yale University Press, New
45. Harman G (1980) The nature of morality. An introduction to ethics. Critica 12(36):110–111
46. Freud S (1955) Beyond the pleasure principle. In: The standard edition of the complete psychological works of Sigmund Freud, volume XVIII (1920–1922): beyond the pleasure principle, group psychology and other works, pp 1–64
47. Rāhula W (1974) What the Buddha taught. Grove Press, New York
48. Hume D (1739) A treatise of human nature, being an attempt to introduce the experimental method of reasoning into moral subjects. John Noon, London
49. Wollstonecraft MS (2003) Frankenstein: or, the modern Prometheus. Penguin, London. First pub 1818
50. Lanier J (2010) You are not a gadget: a manifesto. Vintage, New York
51. Frankl VE (1985) Man's search for meaning. Simon and Schuster, New York
52. Levi P (2014) If this is a man/the truce. Hachette, Paris. First published 1947 as Se questo è un uomo
53. Meerloo JAM, Meerloo J (1956) The rape of the mind: the psychology of thought control, menticide, and brainwashing, vol 118. World Publishing Company, Cleveland
54. Chollet F (2019) On the measure of intelligence. arXiv preprint arXiv:1911.01547
55. Kahneman D (2011) Thinking, fast and slow. Farrar, Straus and Giroux, New York
56. Timmons AC, Chaspari T, Han SC, Perrone L, Narayanan SS, Margolin G (2017) Using multimodal wearable technology to detect conflict among couples. Computer 50(3):50–59

57. Heater B (2017) Using wearable technology to detect conflict in couples before it occurs. Tech Crunch. https://techcrunch.com/2017/04/21/using-wearable-technology-to-detect-conflict-in-couples-before-it-occurs/
58. Kant I (1784) Idea for a universal history with a cosmopolitan purpose. The cosmopolitanism reader, pp 17–26
59. Passmore JA (1970) The perfectibility of man. Charles Scribner's Sons, New York
60. Galton D (2002) Eugenics: the future of human life in the 21st century. Abacus, Hachette
61. Agar N (1998) Liberal eugenics. Public Aff Q 12(2):137–155
62. Brokowski C, Adli M (2019) CRISPR ethics: moral considerations for applications of a powerful tool. J Mol Biol 431(1):88–101

Further Reading

Intelligence

Boden M (2018) Artificial intelligence: a very short introduction. Oxford University Press, Oxford
Kahneman D (2011) Thinking, fast and slow. Farrar, Straus and Giroux, New York
Kamin L (1974) The science and politics of IQ. Lawrence Erlbaum Associates, Mahwah
Larson E (2021) The myth of artificial intelligence: why computers can't think the way we do. Harvard University Press, Cambridge
Lawrence L (2017) Living together: mind and machine intelligence. arXiv preprint arXiv:1705.07996
Legg S, Hutter M (2007) A collection of definitions of intelligence. Front Artif Intell Appl 157:17
Legg S, Hutter M (2007) Universal intelligence: a definition of machine intelligence. Mind Mach 17(4):391–444
Russell SJ, Norvig P (2016) Artificial intelligence a modern approach, 3rd edn. Pearson Education, London Ch. 26 Philosophical Foundations

Human Nature

Aristotle (2014) In: Crisp R (ed) Aristotle: Nicomachean ethics. Cambridge University Press, Cambridge
Coeckelbergh M (2022) Self-improvement: technologies of the soul in the age of artificial intelligence. Columbia University Press, New York
John Passmore J (1974) Man's responsibility for nature: ecological problems and Western traditions. Gerald Duckworth, London
Passmore J (1970) The perfectibility of man. Charles Scribner's Sons, New York
Plato (1888) In: Jowett B (ed) The republic of Plato. Clarendon Press, Clarendon
Radcliffe Richards J (2000) Human nature after Darwin: a philosophical introduction. Open University Press, Maidenhead
Roughley N (2021) Human nature. In: Zalta EN (ed) The Stanford encyclopedia of philosophy. Metaphysics Research Lab, Stanford University, Stanford https://plato.stanford.edu/archives/spr2021/entries/human-nature/
Sartre J-P (2021) Existentialism is a humanism. Yale University Press, New Heaven
Scruton R (2017) On human nature. Princeton University Press, Princeton
Stephenson L (1974) Seven theories of human nature. Oxford University Press, Oxford

Chapter 6
Normative Ethical Theory and AI Ethics

Abstract Normative ethical theories propose frameworks for determining value and for guiding judgment and action. We examine three dominant varieties: consequentialism, focusing on outcomes of actions; deontology, focusing on the nature of actions themselves; and virtue ethics, focusing on the moral character of the agent. There are significantly different varieties of each. Here, we outline the main characteristics, drawing attention to those features that lend themselves most readily to application in the context of AI, as well as giving an overview of the particular difficulties of each approach. We discuss different conceptions of the end goals of ethics, including different conceptions of happiness, pleasure, preference fulfilment, and the question of measuring outcomes. These all have implications for the ethical assessment of the development and deployment of AI and for implementing ethics within AI. The application of ethical theories to situations of rapidly changing technology presents many challenges. Likewise, accounts of agency and its moral relevance within different normative ethical theories are critical when considering the use of machine agency to enhance or replace human agency. The interpretation and following of moral rules are addressed; questions include the development of global guidelines for AI and the implementation of ethical rules within AI.

Keywords Normative ethics · Virtue ethics · Consequentialism · Deontological ethics · Discourse ethics · Happiness

6.1   Introduction to Normative Ethical Theories

Summary
This chapter presents three normative ethical theories that are frequently used in applications of theory to concrete cases: consequentialism, deontological theories, and virtue ethics. These are outlined, and the applicability of each of them to the ethical questions in AI will be considered.

Normative ethical theories propose frameworks to determine what is right or wrong, the basis for moral judgments and actions. This chapter examines the major normative ethical theories that have tended to dominate the contemporary discussion of AI ethics in the West. These have come to the fore within a particular tradition of philosophy, and neither do they exhaust the possibilities, but nonetheless have helped shape work in applied ethics, so they are important to understand. Examining points of strength and weakness in each will facilitate constructive engagement and understanding of divergent approaches. Theories can be wrong for interesting reasons; both the strengths and the weaknesses of the normative ethical theories we look at here can shed considerable light on AI ethics.

Within the Anglophone sphere of analytic philosophy, by the early twentieth century, many working in philosophy had taken the view that it had little to say about practical ethical issues in the real world. Philosophical questions focused on logic and on the analysis of language in what has been called 'the linguistic turn'. There are close links between the claims that we can understand the world through the analysis of language and that a formal system such as that of logic or mathematics might capture the world and describe it completely and the development of computer science. The influence of such thinking, and responses countering it, can be found in many areas of philosophy, including ethics. Please note that this is a very brief account of these developments, and it must be remembered that philosophical work in other parts of the world, including continental Europe, developed in rather different ways.

In ethics, questions were mainly concerned with metaethics, or the broad nature of ethics: questions about the nature of moral knowledge, the foundations of ethics, the relation of ethics to the natural world, the meaning of ethical statements, and so on. Many were of the view that ethical statements had no real content but were merely subjective expressions of opinion or emotive responses to situations. Recall the outline of Hume's view given in Sect. 5.4.7. In the first part of the twentieth century, the Emotivist theory of ethics earned the nickname of the 'boo-hoorah!' theory of ethics, which captures this view precisely [1]. But the events of the twentieth century made it amply clear to many that such a position was no longer tenable, and there was a rise in philosophers concerned with practical issues, such as the use of nuclear weapons, abortion, and other issues. The attention given now to pressing issues in AI ethics can be seen in part to be a new version of such a wave.

It may be helpful to recall now as we struggle with AI ethics that 70 years ago or so, philosophers and others interested in pressing ethical questions were also wondering how to proceed. Many contributed to such developments. The philosopher Elizabeth Anscombe wrote an influential paper, 'Modern Moral Philosophy', asking how we could argue in ethics when any agreement on any set of rules, duties, and obligations seemed increasingly illusory [2]. Her work was influential in a movement that persists to this day, which looked back to the virtue ethics of Aristotle as a basis for practical consideration. Much philosophical work stemming from Anscombe and close associates such as Philippa Foot, Iris Murdoch, and Mary Midgley started to concern practical moral issues [3].

At around the same time, the philosopher R. M. Hare argued that starting from an analysis of the meaning of moral terms alone, one could conclude that morality consisted in sets of rules, or universal prescriptions for action, contrary to the views of many others [4]. His views are no longer much discussed, but nonetheless, there are many who consider that there are certain rules and values that are shared widely enough to form the basis for much practical ethical reasoning. In AI ethics, these may include the value of individual autonomy and privacy, as well as work referring to universal human rights.

Meanwhile, there had been a continuous body of work taking utilitarian, or more broadly, consequentialist, approaches. The eighteenth-century philosopher and legal theorist, Jeremy Bentham, whom we have already met, was a utilitarian, as was his follower James Mill and James' son John Stuart Mill. Utilitarianism in various forms still flourishes today and has a strong influence on much work in applied ethics, even among those who are not pure utilitarians and who introduce additional considerations.

It has thus become standard to divide ethical theories into a tripartite division of consequentialist, deontological, and virtue ethics approaches. Consequentialist approaches focus upon the outcome of actions; deontological approaches focus on the rules that should be followed; and virtue ethics focuses on the character of agents. Hence, between them, these theories focus on a wide range of relevant factors. This classification is, as ever in philosophy, somewhat oversimplified but very useful for considering the strengths and weaknesses of different approaches to ethical theory in addressing questions in AI ethics. However, this is by no means to say that this cluster of theories between them encompass a complete view of ethics.

In this chapter, it will often be necessary to focus on central features and simplified accounts of theories in order to explain issues of particular importance to AI ethics. We will focus on application in the context of AI, the ways some theories may seem to fit or not fit, and the difficulties arising. This is a continuation of our discussion of methods in Chap. 4, when we introduced the question of what framework of values might be used in reasoning and critique in response to concrete ethical cases. As well as a discussion drawing out the implications for AI, the chapter will serve as an introduction to these three different groups of theories for those with little or no familiarity with this subject. There will be exercises relating the theoretical issues to practical issues in AI.

6.2 Normative Ethical Theories: Consequentialism

Summary
Consequentialist theories focus on the outcomes of actions. This section examines their attractions for AI, focusing mostly on utilitarianism. Their goal-based nature may suit computing well, and it is easy to explain the attractions of the aim for happiness or desire fulfilment. Problems arising include the precise specification of the ends of morality, the attractions of a world where utilitarian ends are fulfilled, the value of individuals, and difficulties in dealing with ethical questions concerning agency, an especially critical question in relation to AI.

There are many different types of consequentialist theory, with a multitude of different versions, often produced in direct response to the various criticisms of consequentialism [5]. Our discussion here will present only a simplified account of a classical version of consequentialism, the most common variety being one form or other of utilitarianism, which we have already met earlier in the book (see Sects. 2. 5.1, 4.1.2, 4.3, and 5.2.6). We are beginning our discussion with consequentialism partly because in many ways it is one of the easiest theories to grasp in outline. In addition, some of the central disputes in utilitarianism speak directly to some of the major ethical questions raised by AI. A consequentialist approach may seem to fit particularly well with providing an ethical assessment of AI. However, utilitarianism, and consequentialism in general, may seem to be a good fit with AI only because it acts to mask or fail to address some of the most trenchant ethical issues facing AI.

A consequentialist theory claims that the best thing to do, morally, is whatever will bring about the best overall outcomes. We thus need the following at a minimum: an account of what outcome(s) to aim for; an account of how to aim for that outcome(s); some way of measuring outcome(s), in order to compare different courses of action; and an account of who or what matters in assessing and aiming for the outcomes.

Commonly, a basic account of utilitarianism may hold that the outcome to be aimed at is happiness and the absence of unhappiness, or pleasure and the absence of pain; a variation is that the consequences to be aimed at are the fulfilment of preferences or the satisfaction of desires. Recall our discussion of the experience machine in Sect. 4.1.2.

Many versions of utilitarianism claim that we should try to maximise this outcome, in other words, to strive for as much happiness and the minimum unhappiness (etc.) as possible. Other versions claim we should merely try to aim for a sufficient level. The question of how far into the future to assess consequences also arises.

There are a variety of suggestions about how we should measure outcomes. Recall Bentham's felicific calculus, which we met in Sect. 2.5.2. Note that some way of measuring outcomes is essential to consequentialism because it is an essential part of its theory that specific courses of action are not in and of themselves mandated or permitted; we choose actions only dependent upon what their outcomes are going to be, so we have to compare and contrast possible courses of action.

The question of who or what matters is closely related to the nature of the outcomes at issue. Bentham's utilitarianism, which focused on maximising pleasure and minimising pain, noted that 'The question is not, Can they reason?, nor Can they talk? but, Can they suffer?' [6]. Jeremy Bentham himself was very fond of animals. He had several cats, including one called the Reverend John Langborn. The expansion to animals thus has been an important and significant practical outcome of much utilitarian thinking. For our discussion, however, we focus on humans and the implications for AI. Again, since the focus is on the consequences of actions, the issue of the future once again arises: the consideration of those who do not yet exist inevitably and forcefully arise with utilitarianism.

We will examine these issues in turn, although they are interlinked in various ways. The issues will be illustrated not only with exercises and cases concerning the use of AI but also with discussion and examples from historical contexts. The purpose of this is to demonstrate how much the current debates concerning novel technologies are actually prefigured in philosophical debates and life episodes from very different contexts. This helps to illustrate the universal human experiences that underlie many current issues and acts as a reminder that there is much we can learn from the past.

Consequentialist approaches can seem ripe for application to computing. A consequentialist ethic could specify goals to be reached by software, and the performance could be readily appraised. Often, the introduction of new technologies is assessed by overall benefits and harms. We saw in Chap. 2 how a common element of codes of ethics and statements about ethics in AI is the aspiration that AI should benefit all (see Sect. 2.4.4). Calculating best outcomes seems an obvious thing to want to do, but immensely complex, so perhaps AI could help us with this, especially as the difficulty of calculating consequences is one of the major criticisms of consequentialism. Moreover, looking to the future as consequentialism inherently does may make it seem ideal for assessing this technology that is carrying us forward into the future.

Let us see.

Consequentialist approaches have also been applied (albeit often with certain limitations) in areas of public policy, where decisions concerning the distribution of goods and services over populations have to be made in situations of limited resources. Limitations imposed generally take the form of side constraints: certain actions may have the best overall consequences but would have very deleterious impacts on individuals or groups. These may be recognised by the acknowledgement of fundamental human rights. These side constraints may be applied in addition to the assessment of consequences, but they may also be pragmatically adopted for the sake of public acceptance of policy.

In philosophy, it is often easier to find fault with a position than to give it a fair assessment. Even if one wishes to reject a position entirely, it is a good strategy to look for its good points, both for what one might learn oneself and also for understanding why someone else may take a very different viewpoint. It's not usually because they are stupid or bad. It's usually for some fairly good reason.

Exercise 1

'The question is not, Can they reason?, nor Can they talk? but, Can they suffer?' (Bentham) [6]. Consider whether there is anything strange about using an ethical theory that explicitly argues for the irrelevance of *reason* as a basis for understanding artificial *intelligence*.

6.2.1   Outcomes of Actions: Pleasure, Pain, and Preferences

Outcomes matter, but how much?   It is almost impossible to quarrel with the idea that outcomes matter in ethics. If ethics does not result in a better world, what use is it? Disagreements arise when a theory claims that only consequences matter, as any strict version of consequentialism must claim. Many of the exercises we have looked at so far raise this issue in one way or another.

Exercise 2
Review your response to one or two of exercises you have previously completed, for example, the exercises in Sect. 2.4, and consider to what extent the issues raised concerned whether or not the outcomes alone were what mattered, or if there were other issues that also mattered, such as how the means used to reach the outcome.

Exercise 3
Some principle that 'AI should be beneficial to all' is frequently cited in codes and statements concerning AI ethics.

How would you provide more details on this statement in order to produce any practical guidance?

This is a very broad question! Don't spend too long on it. Its purpose is to orient you to some of the major questions we will look at in this section.

The attractions of happiness   It is also easy to see the attractions of the goal of seeking happiness and the avoidance of unhappiness, or pleasure and the absence of pain. These relate to the quality of our experiences. How could these not be relevant in some way? It's perhaps most convincing if we consider the avoidance of pain or suffering. How could this not be relevant, especially when we consider the infliction of suffering on the innocent? If one wanted to find a point of agreement between those of different backgrounds and views in a discussion of ethics, then an example of the gratuitous suffering of the innocent is one that is most likely to attract universal condemnation. The goal of eliminating unjustified pain seems on the face of it, an obvious good.

Moreover, an account of ethics on happiness and unhappiness, pleasure and pain, has a twofold attraction: it seems ripe to form a basis for explaining our motivations to act, since it seems to demand no explanation at all as to why we wish to avoid pain and why we pursue pleasure (although there are serious problems in trying to explain why we would care about the pleasure or pain of anyone else, a question we put to one side for now). It also serves well for those who wish to provide a purely empirical account of ethics. We seem to have to refer to nothing more than our own internal biologically based drives. As Bentham wrote, 'Nature has placed mankind under the governance of two sovereign masters, *pain and pleasure*. It is for them alone to point out what we ought to do, as well as to determine what we shall do' [6].

As an aside, this conception of happiness points directly to the quality of experience and helps highlight the relevance of conscious experience to issues in ethics and raises another critical question in ethics: is consciousness necessary in order to qualify as meriting moral concern? This question features prominently in debates about the moral status of AI itself, which we examine in Chap. 12. The nature of happiness is also a critical question to address if we want intelligent machines to be able to understand and to measure ethical outcomes based upon assessments of happiness and pain.

These questions arise in relation to many of the practical ethical problems concerning AI. How happiness is understood will shape responses to visions of possible technological futures and to the use of specific discrete forms of technology.

Exercise 4

Think of examples of the use of AI that could be argued will increase happiness over a population. Possible future projections include the development of a future superintelligence that keeps humans as contented pets, or future large-scale technological unemployment, where a large portion of the population has no role in society other than being provided with needs by automated means while being kept happy in a world of endless entertainment tailored to individual tastes.

What could be said for and against such worlds? You may wish to base this on your favourite sci-fi book or film. Focus specifically upon the idea of using AI to produce happiness.

Hedonic accounts of happiness The classical utilitarian view of happiness sees it as pleasure and the absence of pain, a view of happiness focused on the sensations we feel. This is the hedonic conception of happiness. Although the attractions of happiness as a basis for ethics seem obvious to many, plenty of others have railed against the view that happiness as nothing more than a sensation, a feeling, and pleasure should be the foundation of ethics. Some who object may wish to offer an alternative account of happiness; others reject the very idea of basing ethics on happiness.

In gaining an understanding of this account of happiness, it is important to note that utilitarians such as Bentham insisted that, other things being equal, all forms of happiness were of equal value (see Sect. 2.5.2). Pushpin is equal in value to poetry, so long as they produce the same amount of pleasure. The Victorian essayist and historian Thomas Carlyle famously regarded utilitarianism as 'pig philosophy' for promoting the pursuit of such a hedonic notion of happiness. It is easy to dismiss Carlyle's view as nothing more than Victorian prudery and snobbery, based upon the denigration of pursuits that gave pleasure to ordinary people, but it may be salutary to consider the different forms of pleasure or happiness that modern technology enables and indeed encourages.

In an interesting aside, a day of great unhappiness for both Carlyle and John Stuart Mill was the day when Mill's maid accidentally lit a fire using Carlyle's only copy of his major work, *The French Revolution: A History*, entirely destroying it [7]. Carlyle and Mill remained friends, for a while at least, although it must be said that the accounts of the incident left by the two men vary somewhat. Carlyle rewrote the book from scratch. (Any time you accidentally delete an important file, remember this.)

Exercise 5
Consider a few different sources of pleasure that are enabled or facilitated by forms of AI, including if you wish imagined future possibilities. Would you consider these all of equal moral value? As contributing in the same way to a good life?

Consider if any of these might be ones that might have attracted the scorn of critics of utilitarianism such as Carlyle.

Consider the availability and ease of access of such sources of pleasure. Is this (a) a good thing or (b) a problem, or (c) something more nuanced?

More than a feeling? Regarding the hedonic notion of happiness, how we experience things in the sense of how they appear to us is the critical question. However, many examples indicate that it is not only the raw quality of experience that matters. We have already considered this question when we looked at Nozick's Experience Machine in Sect. 4.1.2. You may wish to review this and consider if your reactions to it are the same as when we first looked at it.

Suppose that the Metaverse became such high quality, and automation took over food and energy production and other work, to such an extent that there was mass unemployment, but that society had the resources to allow billions of humans to live life in the Metaverse, experiencing excitement, thrills, moments of calm contentment, as if they were living a full and rich life in the 'real' world. Suppose at the same time, the people running the Metaverse were actually living lives that closely mirrored the lives created artificially for the billions inside the Metaverse. Would it matter who you were?

Now for the next iteration of this thought experiment. Perhaps it is only the rift between 'real' life and a simulated experience that matters. AI is being developed that aims to completely capture a person's appearance and voice so that these can be simulated realistically. This could also be used to augment a person. If you were to have an online relationship with a person whose appearance had been augmented in some way, for example, a colleague working in a branch office on another continent, would you feel tricked to meet them in real life and hear their true, squeaky voice and see their pimply face? How about if the person was a date? Perhaps it's only disappointment that is the problem. Or do we value the truth, per se?

We will return to these issues later in discussing metaphysical questions and their relevance for ethics in Chap. 7. We will also need to examine the question of why we value the truth, and given that we do, whether this means we want the truth, the whole truth, and nothing but the truth—in other words, if more knowledge is always better. This is a perplexing question in ethics and in philosophy and one with profound relevance to many of the issues in AI.

We have examined various uses of technology where the question of truth and reality is potentially an issue. Examples include Deepfakes, the mimicry of human voices, and the use of VR. Different issues could be at play in different instances. Perhaps it is the attempt to deceive that is at issue; perhaps it is finding out that one has been tricked; perhaps the choice of an individual to experience a constructed reality rather than something veridical, 'missing out' on something real. Perhaps it is the opposite—putting up with dull reality, when one could have something better.

Exercise 6

One. Imagine you have a life partner who has gone away for several weeks for work. Each night, you have an intimate friendly chat with them online and greatly appreciate it. After a few weeks, a technical glitch reveals that you have been communicating with a sophisticated AI. Your partner explains that work has been 'extremely busy'. How do you react?

How much does truth matter over quality of experience?

Two. Recall Chap. 2, Exercise 10, in which an app on a screen allowed for remote monitoring of an elderly person living alone. Suppose the person was living with dementia and came to think that the person behind the app really was their friend. In fact, it's a series of different paid employees, each with several clients, or perhaps an AI which performs this role and also does so for 50,000 clients.

Does the truth matter, or just the quality of the experience? If you thought differently about this example than in the first case, why?

Higher and lower pleasures   As with many of the issues that are being presented to us through the capacities of technology, the philosophical underpinnings have already been the subject of discussion. As we have seen, one element of the debates concerns the veridicality of experience—whether it matters that what we experience corresponds to the way the world is or whether it is merely the subjective quality that we ourselves experience that is at issue. The subjective quality may have some value in and of itself. But is the veridical experience better? If so, why? This may be because we 'value the truth', but there may also be additional ways of expressing what matters.

Carlyle's criticism of utilitarianism as a 'pig philosophy' hinged on the idea that mere brute happiness could be the basis of ethics, with Bentham's insistence that all forms of happiness of whatever source were essentially morally equivalent being one important root of the issue. John Stuart Mill disagreed strongly with Bentham on this and, in Chap. 2 of his *Utilitarianism*, distinguished between what he called higher and lower pleasures [8]. Interestingly, Mill gave more than one account of the distinction. Lower pleasures were nonetheless pleasures. But if someone with sufficient knowledge of two sorts of pleasures would prefer one over the other, even if it was accompanied by a greater amount of discontent and even if presented with an unlimited amount of the other pleasure, the preferred pleasure is the higher pleasure [8, Ch. 2, paragraph 5]. This definition has occasioned much critique. Mill went on to explain higher pleasures further, suggesting that these were associated with higher faculties and that 'a being of higher faculties requires more to make him happy, is capable probably of more acute suffering, and is certainly more accessible to it at more points, than one of an inferior type; but in spite of these liabilities, he can never wish to sink into what he feels to be a lower grade of existence' [8, Ch. 2, paragraph 6]. Mill considered that this unwillingness could best be explained as a facet of our sense of dignity. Recall, too, our discussion of the common feature of theories of human nature that they often have an account of better or worse aspects of our natures. Mill has been accused of elitism for his views.

Exercise 7
Recall Exercise 16 in Sect. 2.5.2, which contained a passage where Mill argued that few humans would agree to trade places with any of the lower animals, no intelligent person would agree to become an ignoramus, and review your answer.

Consider if Mill's account of higher and lower pleasures is of any relevance in considering the value of various uses of AI. Bring in any examples that you wish, and/or look over previous cases and exercises.

A eudaemonic conception of happiness In contrast, a eudaemonic idea of happiness considers it as something attained over an entire life span, where the fulfilment of projects, the development of character, and the achievement of life satisfaction within a whole life are what matters. Such a conception of happiness is found in the works of Aristotle, whom we discuss both here and in the section on virtue ethics (Sect. 6.4).

There are many things to consider in comparing and contrasting each of these. For instance, to continue on our theme of measurement, a eudaemonic conception of happiness lends itself less readily to measurement. Our assessment of how happy we were at a particular time may readily change on reflection and as we come to grow in understanding of the nature of our life's experiences and undertakings and their place and meaning in our lives. The components of happiness may be more complex, and it does not focus upon sensation. The happiness of a life seems something that is assessed perhaps more thoroughly in retrospect. A felicific conception seems more suited to measurement and analysis, as if it was, as it were, a series of passing moments of happiness or pleasure. However, even on the level of subjective experience, things can be very complex. A sports match spent on the edge of one's seat in agonised tension as one's team is seemingly thrashed may quickly become thought of as the height of enjoyment as a last-minute series of goals turns them into winners. We take pleasure in certain things, yet we seek them for their own sake, not simply for the pleasure they will bring. The US Declaration of Independence refers to inalienable rights given to all humans by their Creator, of 'life, liberty, and the pursuit of happiness'. Happiness itself could never be guaranteed. However, the pursuit of happiness can be self-defeating if it aims too directly at the quality of happiness itself. Often, seeking pleasure itself will be self-defeating, and many pleasures are self-limiting [9, 10].

Compare the discussion of the value of intelligence and of human nature in Chap. 5. Consider an instrumental account of intelligence, as efficiently reaching our goals, and consider the value of thinking as a process. Might we even enjoy the struggle of thinking through a difficult question? Why do some people enjoy the cryptic crossword more than the easy version? Recall the discussions of different views of human nature, including different ideas of human essence. If we are creatures who make things, Homo faber, this may mean we value the end product, but we may also value the process. If we are creatures who enjoy play (Homo ludens), this suggests we enjoy activities for their own sake. There are other aspects you may wish to consider.

Exercise 8

What uses of AI, if any, are best equipped to help us with the pursuit of happiness? Do any uses positively interfere with this? Hint: This again is a very broad and difficult question intended to provoke and provide food for thought.

A eudaimonic conception of happiness suggests that we have some conception of how our life should go and what kind of shape it should have. There are many things that could shape this. There will be individual and cultural factors here, for instance, the pursuit of individual satisfaction over a life, the pursuit of meaningful connections with others, and the achievement of some lasting goal. Frank Sinatra's song *My Way* is often played at funerals, but many find this empty. A sense of progress is often implied. A life which starts off with a bleak and unpromising beginning and then makes progress, even if modest, is generally preferred to a life with the same total amount of happiness but which starts off well and goes downhill from there. However, this sense of progress is generally not a simple matter of plotting isolated measures of happiness and unhappiness on a graph. Indeed, if we were to try to think of our lives and experiences as simply isolated passing points of happiness and unhappiness, this would be difficult if not impossible, because we assess and review the quality of our experiences within the framework of a narrative structure, not to mention that the way we process memories is far from a simple photographic record keeping of the past [11].

One of the challenges of a future that is perhaps very different from the lives of the past, if technology is truly transformative, is to have any idea of how we would measure the shape and trajectory of a life against this. If the singularity occurs, then this implies we will have no conception against which to measure the way that a life goes.

Exercise 9

How might we measure happiness or welfare, or assess happiness over a lifetime, after the singularity has occurred? The serious point is to raise the question of how we plan for a future that is hard to imagine.

'Call no man happy until he is dead' In his *Nicomachean Ethics*, Aristotle raised the question, first posed by Solon, an Athenian statesman and poet, of whether it was possible to call anyone happy until they were dead and raised the question of whether something that happened after death might make a difference to how well one's life had gone [12] (Chap. 10). Aristotle scholars have differing views on what his answer was [13].

For the ancient Greeks, social connections and reputation were important, so that for instance, if after death, one's son turned out to be an utter rascal, a traitor to the state, for example, that would mean that a significant part of one's life's course had gone awry. So let us pause and consider the impact of social reputation on our happiness, on how our lives go, on ethical questions, and the impact of new technologies.

The eyes of others Our social reputation, what other people think of us, is important in some way or another to virtually everybody. Feedback of information about our behaviour from others is an everyday part of human life. We are social beings. We have to understand how our behaviour impacts others in order to navigate the world, even aside from any ethical considerations. Recall our discussion of Goffman's notion of front and back stage in Sect. 3.6.2. The use of technology has greatly magnified these possibilities, increasing the amount of information collected, the manner in which it may be collected, and the possibilities of analysis and interpretation, for example, the potential use of facial recognition in CCTV in public places. Our social reputations are now considerably influenced by the information collected by us online. It is more than likely that this will impact not just our behaviour. It may also impact how certain ethical questions are understood.

Exercise 10
Feedback from others online, such as 'likes' on social media, can have a large impact on behaviour [14, 15]. Research indicates that certain groups are especially susceptible to this, among them teenagers, especially girls, but certainly not limited to this group [16]. For example, comments on appearance can feed into the use of filters to modify appearance, and behaviour may be adjusted or manipulated in various other ways.

Consider how responsibility and agency might be understood with regard to this issue. Again this is a very broad question.

Control To what extent is our happiness under our control, and to what extent is it shaped by circumstances about which we can do little or nothing? The quest to insulate our lives from such externalities has shaped a great deal of moral philosophy. In her work, *The Fragility of Goodness*, Martha Nussbaum explores how the ancient Greeks dealt with the problem that many of the possible constituents of a good life are outside of our control [17].

Over the centuries, one popular basic move is to make one's happiness to be centred on one's mental attitude towards the circumstances of life, on the life of the mind, and away from material goods. Plato and Aristotle both recommended the life of the mind, and the Stoics as well as many religious traditions have emphasised the importance of pursuing spiritual goals rather than seeking 'treasure on earth, where rust and moth corrupt and where thieves break in and steal' (Matthew, 6:19) [18].

Exercise 11 Food for Thought
Consider the basic stance of finding happiness in sources that are relatively resistant to the vagaries of chance.

Is a path of seeking control of our lives through technology a way of trying to protect ourselves from the vagaries of luck using material goods, a polar opposite of the age-old suggestions of avoiding dependence upon external things?

Consider too how the fear that we may not be able fully to control AI is a central issue in AI ethics.

A different approach in preferences or desires These and other problems have led to versions of utilitarianism that aim to maximise the satisfaction of desire or preferences. For a desire to be satisfied, it's not enough that you *think* it's been satisfied. Something needs to have changed in the world. On most versions, it's also necessary that there is a connection between this change and you: if you don't know about it, or do know yet subsequently realise that this is not what you actually desired, many would hold that this did not count towards satisfying your desires. So, there is an element of subjective experience, your knowing on this, plus the objective truth of the change in the world that corresponds to the fulfilment of your desire.

Basing ethics upon the fulfilment of desires or preferences has, in common with happiness, an intuitive simplicity and appeal because fulfilling desires seems to be a basic way of capturing the idea of making adjustments between us and the world. Again, as with the negative of happiness, pain, it's easier to relate to this in the negative. A world in which no desires were fulfilled and no preferences were satisfied seems unutterably bleak.

However, just as many have argued with happiness, desire or preference satisfaction does not seem to be enough for morality. In some possible cases, it seems to be positively opposed to ethics if happiness is attained by a sadist and if desires are for harm to others. How could someone's trivial or banal desires form any kind of basis for moral obligations on the part of others? How could a person's desire to get more 'likes' on TikTok be anything other than some trivial irrelevance?

A response to this could be to apply the same reasoning to almost any human pursuit. Vanity, vanity, all is vanity.

> My name is Ozymandias, King of Kings;
> Look on my Works, ye Mighty, and despair!
> Nothing beside remains. Round the decay.
> Of that colossal Wreck, boundless and bare.
> The lone and level sands stretch far away [19].

So wrote Percy Bysshe Shelley, telling of a traveller who describes a ruined city found in a desert. Again, such age-old questions about how to live have real application in relation to AI. Although these questions are perennial, we should consider the sheer scale of the possibilities created by technology. We seem to be designing technologies that could tune into every minute desire we have, anticipate them even, satisfy them as fast as possible, cater to our every whim, and design imaginary worlds where new desires can be found. Is it the case that the more desires we have, the more desires are fulfilled, the better our lives go? Or are we looking in the wrong place?

Desires and an instrumental account of intelligence If we understand our preferences and desires as expressions of our goals, then this account could fit well with an instrumental account of intelligence, but any problems with a desire or preference-based account of utilitarianism could then herald problems with this account of intelligence. If we just take our desires or preferences as we find them, as just 'facts of the matter' grounded in empirical reality, this might give us some reasons for action, but does it persuasively produce a strong basis for ethics? What is a possible solution?

Ranking desires We may need to rank desires or preferences in some way. A famous paper by the philosopher Harry Frankfurt described 'higher-order desires', or desires about our desires [20]. For example, we may desire to respond to an annoying tweet but also have a higher-order desire not to engage in such puerile stupidity. In such a way, we may order our desires and reject acting on some altogether, based on nothing more than on our own desires.

But does this just push the problem elsewhere? There is only a nest of desires; some wished for more than others. Other approaches may rank desires depending on factors such as the nature of the desire and external rankings of value.

Ranking Desires and AI Alignment

How is this relevant to questions in AI ethics? One example is the issue of how we align AI to human values. To do this, we need to determine what these values are. Many examples of AI gone wrong are of cases where the initial specification of what the human designer wanted inadvertently clashed with other more important desires of the designer. There are various possible permutations of this, but the worst cases are those which lead to catastrophic situations up to and including loss of life.

Isaac Asimov's Robot series of stories often deals with such cases, where a desire would have been obvious to humans but was unspecified to the machine [21]. Nick Bostrom's well-known paperclip example given in his book *Superintelligence*, which we will discuss in Chap. 10, is of a similar type. An AI, instructed to make paperclips, ends up turning the entire world into paperclips in what Bostrom dubs 'perverse instantiation' [22].

Ranking desires would only work in such cases, however, if these desires were entered into the machine. Hence, Asimov's 0th law of robotics has to be explicitly added to the robot's instructions: a robot may not harm humanity or, by inaction, allow a human to be harmed [23].

In an attempt to address the concerns Bostrom raises, Stuart Russell proposes teaching AI to extrapolate human desires and preferences from observing our behaviour [24]. We discuss this in more detail in Chap. 10.

Desire and manipulation I have taught utilitarianism to first-year philosophy students for many years. Some of the best fun of my life. Students typically react favourably to desire-based accounts of utilitarianism, but their faces fall after I ask them a few simple questions. It usually goes something like this: pointing to a piece of technology, whatever it is at the time, the latest iPhone or whatever, I ask them if they desired to buy it or desire to upgrade to the latest model. The answer is usually 'yes'. I then do this irritating thing and point out to them that 'when I was your age', I had no such desire yet was perfectly happy. Why didn't I desire it? Because it didn't exist. When we wanted to talk to our friends, we walked around the corner and knocked on the door or went to the public phone box and made a call. On the minus side, we also desired flared jeans (I still like them, within limits).

A central feature of many desires is that they can be manipulated, sometimes deliberately, sometimes by the strong yet often unnoticed forces of social pressure. Even something as fundamental as desire for food can be moulded in ways that can do us disservice. Indeed, we often attempt to manipulate our own desires when we try to control them. We may try not to act on certain desires, to postpone acting on them, or to quash them altogether. We may also try to induce certain desires in ourselves. Taste for food can be acquired, so we can sometimes expand our repertoire of foods by repeatedly eating things we don't like.

The behaviourists discovered that desires could be induced with ease under certain settings. Pavlov's dogs learned to salivate on the sound of a bell rather than to food itself. Animals can hence be trained to act in certain ways for rewards [25]. Pigeons can thus be trained to play the piano. We can also be trained not just to play the piano but to spend hours and hours of our lives, no, months and months, no, years and years of our lives, chasing desires that have been induced in us by technology and its design. Those dealing with issues such as drug dependence and gambling addictions are also very well aware of how chasing desires may dominate and in some cases ruin lives. One problem is that the strength of an urge to satisfy a desire may not correlate very well with even our own assessment of the value of that desire, as compared to other desires we have. Recall our discussion of accounts of human nature that posit some form of split in the self in Sect. 5.4.6. For those inclined to base ethics upon the satisfaction or desires or preferences, there are serious questions, given the multiple ways our desires may be exploited. Are these simply attacking vulnerabilities in the system which can be patched? Or do we need to base our ethics upon something more robust than the satisfaction of human desires or preferences?

Exercise 12
Comparing how technology may facilitate the creation of desires, in relation to its capacity to facilitate access to information.

Could health tracking apps and the possibility of earlier diagnosis of disease *create* desires for particular sorts of knowledge about ourselves? Could this be a good thing?

Refer to Sect. 3.3.4 and our discussion of the technological fix and Chap. 3 Exercise 6 on the use of machine learning in the early diagnosis of dementia. You may wish to consider other examples of your own.

6.2.2   Measuring Outcomes

Happiness, numbers, and formulae Can happiness be measured? This is an essential claim of utilitarianism because if a theory aims to maximise, or at any rate to increase, a certain outcome, it must be possible to measure outcomes in some way in order to assess and compare alternative courses of action. (In contrast, theories of ethics that hold that certain actions are duties, or are to be prohibited, or hold that certain virtuous character traits are to be encouraged, are not so committed to measurement and calculation.) This means that there must be some standard approach across settings and ultimately that some kind of numerical or comparative assessment can be made. Such measurement need not be fool proof. We can only expect a certain level of precision in human affairs, yet measurement needs to be 'good enough' to provide answers that are better than those of any serious rival.

Indeed, perhaps we can use AI to measure happiness in individuals? It can sometimes be hard to assess happiness in other people, and indeed, even in our own case, we may sometimes lack the self-awareness to realise that some situations are making us unhappy. Can AI know us better than we know ourselves? Perhaps an AI could measure physiological signals of distress or calm, detect focus and attention, calculate optimal levels of arousal, observe our behaviour over time, and work out precisely how happy or unhappy each one of us is in certain situations.

Can happiness be captured in a formula, reduced in some way so that we can 'do the maths'? In its classical form, utilitarianism requires measurement and comparison across a population for different possible scenarios. This also comes with a standard assumption that different states of happiness can be equated or at least given some equivalence value. We have touched on this briefly in Sect. 2.5.2, when we saw Bentham's claim that, other things being equal, the simple game of push-pin is of the same value as poetry. Why must this be the case? Because the need to maximise outcomes necessitates comparison between possibilities.

Can happiness be calculated using clear and consistent formulae? Philosophers and others have long debated such matters and have striven to provide as good an answer as is possible. Attempts to measure happiness or well-being have risen in popularity in recent years, with political criticism levelled at the failings of using merely economic measures such as gross domestic product to indicate the state of a nation and replacement with measures such as the Gross National Happiness Index [26]. Any measurement will, however, make certain assumptions and choices about what is measured and how comparisons are made. Perhaps this does not matter so long as we are aware that a model has limitations.

What might be lost if we relied 'too much', whatever that means, on such calculations? Can any attempt to measure happiness be anything other than a rough and ready approximation?

Exercise 13
Argue for and against the proposition that an AI could, in theory at least, calculate as well as, or better than, a human being, whether or not that person was happy. Consider the use of technology already in existence and what technology might need to be created.

Consider what would have to be included to provide a measurement of happiness, and consider any differences between how AI might reach a conclusion and a human being.

An Alchemy of Happiness
John Stuart Mill took numerous walking holidays both within England, often in the Lake District, and on mainland Europe. He was extremely good at blagging extended periods of sick leave from work and was often absent for months on end. As we have seen, John Stuart Mill disagreed with various aspects of Jeremy Bentham's approach to happiness. This diary extract from Mill's friend Caroline Fox gives a charming account of his thoughts upon the mystery behind calculations of happiness or unhappiness.

A walk with John and Clara Mill to Penzance and Penrose. ... 'Why', said he, 'Yesterday's conversation made just the difference between my knowing and not knowing your brother. Often it is an amazing assistance to detail a little of one's own experience when one has passed through similar discouragements yet come out of them'. I remarked on the pleasure it must be to help others in this way. 'I had much rather be helped!' he answered. The process of unhooking a bramble made him philosophise on the power of turning annoyances into pleasures by undertaking them for your friends—a genuine alchemy [27].

Exercise 14
Have you ever noticed that doing the washing up in someone else's house never seems as bad as doing your own washing up? There are numerous other ways in which the calculation of pleasures and pains fails to fit with a simple additive model. Could an AI build such factors into account in producing a model for calculating overall happiness across a population? Try to have as much fun as possible in answering this exercise, and indeed, any of these exercises.

Exercise 15
Consider how these issues relate to the question of accountability. In his book *On Human Nature*, Roger Scruton offers the opinion that the possibility or probability of error in calculating consequences is a fundamental flaw in consequentialism because it means that wrongdoing is seen as nothing more than an error [28, p. 98].

If we were to use AI to make moral decisions, one issue frequently raised is that of moral responsibility: we could not hold the AI responsible. Does this necessarily matter, so long as outcomes were improved?

Would there be any advantages in viewing moral errors as simple mistakes of calculation?

6.2.3 Whose Happiness Matters?

Note that for utilitarianism, 'everyone' counts (see Sect. 4.3). In its classical forms, this was simply an assumption. Hence, the possibility of measuring and calculating outcomes using computing could be extremely attractive to utilitarians. One reason for this points to an additional feature of classical utilitarianism that the outcomes are to be measured across the whole population. There may be some versions of utilitarianism where, largely for pragmatic reasons, individuals are urged to concentrate on those closest to them whose lives they can most easily impact. However, the slogan of Jeremy Bentham, 'The greatest happiness for the greatest number', means that everyone is taken into account: 'everyone to count for one and none for more than one' [6]. To consider a large population and to compare multiple different scenarios sounds like an ideal job for AI. In fact, it seems almost inevitable that for some public policy issues, computing power is very valuable, even a necessity.

So, the question is, who is included in this? We saw above that a focus on the capacity to experience pain and pleasure automatically seems to extend the circle of moral concern outside of the human species, a topic we have already discussed in Sect. 4.3, where we noted that the expansion of moral concern is often taken as ipso facto an indicator of moral progress. We have also considered in our discussions of human nature the question of the place of humans in relation to the rest of the natural world. A feature of utilitarianism appears to be that it gives great responsibility to each of us as individuals to calculate the consequences of each of our actions. There is no use saying, 'someone else should do that', because if they won't, then I have to take that into account in judging what to do. It seems to give no 'moral time off', since every decision could bring about greater or lesser happiness. Hence, utilitarianism can seem to give us at once a prime role, in having the capacity to judge and act to bring about the best consequences, and a side role, in knocking us off the pedestal of unique moral concern.

Exercise 16

Many are concerned about the possibility that AI may develop to a stage at which we owe it moral consideration. For example, even if concerns that LaMDA may have developed sentience, which we examined in Chap. 4, were unfounded, they still express the thought that AI might in some way become 'like us' and merit treatment other than as a mere tool.

Consider the end goals of different versions of utilitarianism: happiness and the absence of unhappiness; pleasure and the absence of pain; and desire fulfilment or preference satisfaction. Do any of these adequately capture concerns about the moral status of sophisticated AI and how we should respond to it?

Future beings If utilitarianism concerns itself equally with all those currently living, since it is focused upon consequences, it must also concern itself with those yet to be born. It has long been realised that this presents problems for calculating what to do (since it's unclear how far into the future we must extend the calculations) and also for the problem that our actions in the here and now will affect not just how many people are born but who those people might be. One strategy is to point out that the impact of any actions now will be hard to trace too far into the future because of the uncertainties involved and just draw a line somewhere that seems reasonable.

However, in the case of AI, this strategy may be less convincing. On the one hand, in theory, utilitarianism, or indeed any other form of consequentialism, seems ideal because it does concern itself with consequences far into the future. On the other hand, it quickly becomes entirely speculative as to how to calculate them. We are just grasping at straws. Vague promises of countless trillions of endlessly happy immortal beings skipping out into the universe could be used to justify any amount of misery in the present day. Perhaps to be workable, utilitarianism, or any other type of consequentialism, needs to set its sights a little nearer to the present day.

The question of how far into the future to look is a problem concerning measurement in utilitarianism but is also a problem of who counts and how much. Do those who will exist in the future matter as much as we do, and if so, how do we include this in any calculations? This is another example of a pre-existing issue which is highlighted by ethical issues in AI when we come to consider the far future implications of the adoption of certain technologies and the future visions to which some aspire. There have been numerous discussions of such issues within consequentialism [29].

Longtermism is an ethical stance that focuses on the values attached to the distant future. A simple calculation shows its attractions [30]. If we take the number of people alive today, (and this calculation would work even if we include sentient animals as well), and even if we include their children and grandchildren, then, so long as disaster does not strike, the sheer weight of numbers means that, on a consequentialist framework, we ought to prioritise doing all we can to ensure a good and happy future for those beings who will live long after we are all dead and gone. This may initially seem an intuitively obvious stance, but its lure palls when one considers that this may imply that to neglect the widespread poverty, disease, and slavery rampant in the world today may be justified if all efforts were to be placed into projects such as space travel to find other habitable planets or into work towards human enhancement to ensure the survival of a remnant of the human race [31]. Maybe large sections of the human race could be killed as a means to ensure the survival of a sufficient number of humans to lead to future generations millions of years from now. We will discuss this further in Chap. 10.

6.2.4   How Should We Aim at Happiness?

Do we aim for the maximum? In its simplest classic versions, utilitarianism aims to maximise happiness and minimise or remove pain. As we have seen above, there are many attractions of the goal of happiness but also many difficulties with how we specify such a goal. In addition, there are numerous difficulties with attempting to achieve the highest possible level of happiness. When utilitarianism has grappled with the realities of how difficult it can be to achieve its ends, these problems may not be manifest. The utilitarian reformers of the nineteenth century were dealing with large-scale social issues of access to education, appalling conditions in factories, widespread poverty, and so on. Many of these could perhaps be seen more properly as the combatting of misery rather than the pursuit of happiness. However, as societies have become more affluent, the question of whether we can have 'too much' happiness arises. The prospects of achieving more and more happiness through the use of technologies, for example, to take away the onerous parts of labour and to tailor our worlds precisely to our liking, provide a means of testing aspects of utilitarian theory. Perhaps it will not best serve human nature, and perhaps chasing this will produce a world devoid of some of the central things we most value.

One of the reasons for using technology is to be able to achieve our ends faster, more efficiently, and more thoroughly. This makes it more likely that we will be able to achieve our ends fully. However, as we have seen before, ethical questions can arise from differences in scale. The attractions of utilitarianism perhaps seemed most visible for those social reformers who were battling large-scale social and economic problems. These goals could perhaps more fairly be characterised as the alleviation of suffering, together with enabling means by which people could work towards their own happiness. Yet if AI gives us the possibility of reaching the goals of eliminating suffering altogether and of enabling more and more of the population to live a life of constant happiness, the attractions may pall. Some of the examples used to demonstrate this refer to futuristic scenarios, but these can readily be transferred considering the general issues raised which are relevant to the impact of some technologies on a smaller scale and for issues that we currently face.

Again, this is not a new problem but is a problem made all the more vivid as technology promises, or threatens, to deliver results.

Exercise 17 Food for Thought
While many developing, applying, and using AI focus on its specific capabilities and applications, there is a tendency among some to imagine utopian visions of an AI-powered world. Could a consequentialist viewpoint, aiming to maximise value in the world and always aimed towards the future, help to aid and encourage such utopianism? And if so, is this a good, or bad? (We will consider aspects of this question again in Chap. 11.)

The power of technology and the dangers of success I indicated above that utilitarian's strengths are perhaps most visible and unproblematic when applied to urgent issues such as the reduction of suffering. The problems of the world are legion. But recall the optimistic notion we saw earlier in Sect. 5.2.5, expressed in belief that all we have gained from civilisation is a result of our intelligence, and the hope that AI will be able to solve problems such as poverty and disease [32]. This is likewise aimed at relieving suffering, but why stop there? Suppose all such problems were eradicated. What then? Consider an episode from the life of John Stuart Mill, as he contemplated the completion of all of utilitarianism's hopes.

'The End Had Ceased to Charm': John Stuart Mill and the Ends of Morality

The utilitarian philosopher John Stuart Mill had a famously severe upbringing at the hands of his father James Mill, protégé of Jeremy Bentham. James attempted to instil the principles of utilitarianism in the education of his eldest son John by showing what education could achieve from an early age: Greek at 2, Latin at 8, political economy at aged 11. Interestingly, Bentham somewhat disliked James and disapproved of this strict upbringing, sometimes giving John the children's books his father did not permit him [33]. By the time John was in his 20s, he fell into despair. His autobiography *A Crisis in My Mental History* states, in Chap. 4:

> From the winter of 1821, when I first read Bentham, and especially from the commencement of the Westminster Review, I had what might be called an object in life: to be a reformer. My conception of my own happiness was entirely identified with this object. ... But the time came when I awakened from this as from a dream. It was the autumn of 1826. I was in a dull state of nerves, such as everybody is occasionally liable to; unsusceptible to enjoyment or pleasurable excitements; one of those moods when what is pleasure at other times, becomes insipid or indifferent. ... In this frame of mind it occurred to me to put the question directly to myself, 'Suppose that all your objects in life were realized; that all the changes in institutions and opinions which you looked forward to, could be completely effected at this very instant: would this be a great joy and happiness to you?' And an irrepressible self-consciousness distinctly answered, 'No!' At this my heart sank: the whole foundation on which my life was constructed fell down. All my happiness was to have been found in the continual pursuit of the end. The end had ceased to charm, and how could there ever again be any interest in the means? I seemed to have nothing left to live for [34].

An interesting question arises as to whether this tells us simply something about John Stuart Mill as a personality, perhaps something about the impact of his 'utilitarian' upbringing, or also maybe something more generally about the ultimate ends of utilitarianism in particular and of consequentialism in general.

Exercise 18

This episode in Mill's life can be used to reflect upon general issues about the sources of human motivation. Consider the discussion of an instrumental notion of intelligence in Sect. 5.2.1 and of the claims that we can apply intelligence to solve our biggest problems. What if we could achieve a 'perfect society' through AI, might we feel the same as Mill? If so, why, if not, why not? Recall also our discussions of the object of morality in Sect. 4.3.1.

Consider our discussions of human nature in Sect. 5.4. Do you think humans always need something to strive for? Or was Mill simply suffering from a bout of blues? Is this something that some personalities might suffer from, but others not so much?

Consider the case of an AI researcher, and now suppose that we have finally achieved the perfect AI for every task and for the discovery of all scientific and any other sort of knowledge. Is this a dream come true or a disaster of redundancy and loss of meaning?

If we do need something to strive for, might we creep closer and closer to this kind of ennui as machines do more and more for us, will we be content, or will we simply find more things to occupy ourselves and more goals to strive towards?

Be careful what you wish for: power and pleasure Moreover, the potential of technologies involving AI towards control and systemisation, together with factors such as the resistance of infrastructure to change, may only increase the possibility of a uniform and totalising system (see Sect. 3.5 for discussions of assumptions of consistency and uniformity in relation to technology). A totalising system may mean more than the mere power to control large numbers of the population but also include the imposition of a uniformity on what technology is aiming at. If there is a mischaracterisation of the ends that a consequentialist ethic strives for, the dangers of this control are only worsened. Suppose that instead of promoting the best we can strive for, an instrumental account of intelligence, combined with a utilitarian ethic, doomed us to a life of continual 'lower' pleasures. Conveniently for us, here's a picture of such a world that Aldous Huxley presciently prepared for us earlier.

Brave New World **and the Gratification of Desires**

Brave New World by Aldous Huxley explores a dystopian future where technology produces a tightly engineered world of pleasure-seeking individuals governed by a sinister World State [35]. People are raised to fit into different hierarchical ranks, with interventions to produce people deemed suitable for different roles. The perfect drug, soma, gives the perfect high, and sex is used purely for entertainment. The technologies in question mostly concern biological engineering, but the ideas that Huxley explores are still very potent for considering the potential use and abuse of AI.

This is one of those many classics that is worth reading in detail. One scene here gives a flavour of the society that Huxley envisages. A group of alphas (the top tier) is being addressed by the World Controller for Western Europe, Mustapha Mond. The Director of Hatcheries and Conditioning's (DHC) job is to oversee the production of babies and the conditioning of children to prefer their particular role in life. In one scene where he is addressing a group of young people, he asks them if they have ever had to wait a period of time between forming a desire, and having it fulfilled. One young man replies that there was once a time when he had to wait 4 weeks before finally having sex

---

(continued)

with a particular woman. Mond elicits from him the admission that this period of waiting produced strong negative emotions and explains that initially, people were reluctant to embrace the reforms that allowed a world of fast gratification of desires [35]. How foolish they were!

Exercise 19

Have you ever had to wait 2 days for an Amazon parcel to arrive when you were expecting it in 1 day? How did you cope? (N.B. since there are no emoticons in this text, please add your own 'humour' emoticon.)

Living through a 'long time-interval between the consciousness of a desire and its fulfilment' is otherwise known as delayed gratification. The ability to delay gratification may be useful for success in certain domains of life. However, suppose it was not needed? Consider if it could be discarded without loss. (Recall again our discussion on the object of morality.) Consider the impact of the technologies that surround us on the ease of desire fulfilment. Use specific examples where possible.

The ends of utilitarianism and human nature The utilitarian worldview at its starkest is one in which calculations of human nature and of the world's possibilities can produce the easiest, softest, and most comfortable path for each one of us. Who would not take this? We have already seen how Charles Dickens also argued against utilitarianism in his novel, *Hard Times* [36]. Fyodor Dostoevsky in his *Notes from Underground*, which we mentioned in Sect. 5.4.5, also railed against utilitarianism through the diatribes of the central character, a bitter, anonymous middle-aged man, in what is perhaps one of the most impassioned pleas against utilitarianism to date, strongly suggesting that what we want above all is not an easy, happy, life, but one that we ourselves have chosen and the exercise of our own agency [37]. This amounts to a radical rejection of the central tenets of utilitarianism. It also amounts to a radical rejection of the idea that ethics can be contained within a neat and tidy system. His novel *Crime and Punishment* also serves as a stark critique of utilitarianism [38]. The central character, Rodion Romanovich Raskolnikov (spoiler alert, although the plot is already widely known), is an impoverished student who makes the cynical calculation that the life of an elderly money lender, who is known to be a particularly unpleasant individual, is of so little worth that he is justified in murdering her to steal her money.

Fyodor Dostoevsky, *Notes from Underground:* Utilitarianism and Human Nature

I, for instance, would not be in the least surprised if all of a sudden, à propos of nothing, in the midst of general prosperity a gentleman with an ignoble, or rather with a reactionary and ironical, countenance were to arise and, putting his arms akimbo, say to us all: "I say, gentleman, hadn't we better kick over the whole show

(continued)

> *and scatter rationalism to the winds, simply to send these logarithms to the devil, and to enable us to live once more at our own sweet foolish will!" That again would not matter, but what is annoying is that he would be sure to find followers—such is the nature of man. And all that for the most foolish reason, which, one would think, was hardly worth mentioning: that is, that man everywhere and at all times, whoever he may be, has preferred to act as he chose and not in the least as his reason and advantage dictated. And one may choose what is contrary to one's own interests, and sometimes one positively ought (that is my idea). One's own free unfettered choice, one's own caprice, however wild it may be, one's own fancy worked up at times to frenzy—is that very "most advantageous advantage" which we have overlooked, which comes under no classification and against which all systems and theories are continually being shattered to atoms. And how do these wiseacres know that man wants a normal, a virtuous choice? What has made them conceive that man must want a rationally advantageous choice? What man wants is simply independent choice, whatever that independence may cost and wherever it may lead. And choice, of course, the devil only knows what choice.* [37, Part 1, VII]

Note that Dostoevsky is not simply making claims about ethical theory. He makes some startling claims about human nature. Dostoyevsky may seem to be saying something very counterintuitive to many people because it looks as if he is suggesting the possibility of rejecting rationality itself.

There is a deep philosophical problem here. It is extremely difficult to prove why rationality itself is valuable, without assuming that it is. Recall our discussion of the value of knowledge in Sect. 5.3, and consider too the value of the process of thinking in and of itself. It is extremely hard to explain why we value these things, in and of themselves. As a general strategy, look out for instances where critics of certain views seem to be irrational, and always carefully consider the basis on which such a claim is made. Some accusations of irrationality are better founded than others.

Exercise 20

The central character in *Notes from Underground* is a rather unappealing person, and the views he expresses may seem unhinged. But consider the question of control and surveillance presented to us by so many forms of AI. This could take many forms, as can be seen in many examples and in cases discussed in previous chapters and in exercises: control by governments and corporations through data tracking and behaviour manipulation; control by employers; control by family members or within healthcare settings; and control of our own behaviour by voluntary use of self-tracking or health monitoring technologies.

Consider instances of control using AI that may result in benefits. Do the thoughts expressed in *Notes from Underground* about independent choice and the wish for one's own free volition help to capture concerns about such control? Consider possible differences between various cases.

Exercise 21

Recall our discussion of the object of morality in Sect. 4.3.1. In a world where AI had (somehow) managed to remove all sources of human suffering, what role, if any, would there be for morality? How different might any morality be?

6.2.5 Consequentialism, Individuals, and Agency

A further source of difficulty for consequentialism concerns the ends to which it aims. Utilitarianism aims to produce happiness and avoid unhappiness, pleasure, or pain, wherever they are to be found.

Problems of distribution This latter sounds like a recipe for perfect equality under a moral system, a form of protection of each individual, but alas, far from it. It is simply a principle for counting the greatest happiness overall. Individuals can miss out miserably. You do the maths. It's easy to dream up endless scenarios where this happens; it's hard to prevent it. It seems as if individuals do not matter. If I can improve my own happiness by an amount greater than the unhappiness I cause you, then this is justified. Across a population, if one section suffers for the gain of many more, then this is justified too.

Exercise 22
Consider that a large tech company was subject to a campaign to improve the conditions of the workers assembling their products in extremely poor conditions for very low wages. The company replies that they have calculated the costs of improving production conditions but that only 20,000 lives would be substantially improved, and yet 300,000,000 people would have to pay much more for their laptops and smartphones, and remember, we need to take smartphones with us everywhere now for various reasons, so they are basic necessities of life. Is your response:

(a) Oh, that's okay then
(b) This is dreadful
(c) Something more nuanced.

Consider how responses might change, depending on different circumstances and contexts.

Naturally, philosophers have attempted many ways of circumnavigating this problem, which are of great interest but which we will not explore here for lack of space, save to note how the issue of distribution across a population is ubiquitous in relation to AI as in so many other areas and to note that this readily becomes a political issue, especially given the potential for power imbalances in who own and controls technology. These ethical issues are of course ones where economics, politics, and international relations, among other domains, are necessary for full understanding and resolution.

On the plus side Recall that the focus on the outcomes may mean that beings additional to humans matter. Any being that is capable of happiness, capable of suffering, counts. This sounds great. 'Everyone to count for one and none for more than one' [6]. However, note a corollary of this for how individuals are regarded.

Vessels of happiness 'Everyone to count for one, and none for more than one' turns out to mean that they count equally in calculating total happiness. However, other than this, the value of the individuals themselves as individuals seems to get lost in the calculation. Likewise, preference-based versions of utilitarianism aim to satisfy preferences or desires rather than to satisfy the individuals who have those preferences or desires. It is not the individuals who matter. It is the happiness production, the preference satisfaction. Individuals are somehow reduced to mere vessels for containing units of happiness and satisfied desires.

This is why I can increase my own happiness, at your expense. Not because I matter and you don't, but *because neither of us do*. Just the happiness matters.

Understanding what makes us happy A classical utilitarian position may be very appealing to an empiricist worldview, as we saw in Sect. 6.2.1, because it can be based upon a physiological account of what drives us. Hence, it may appear that we can simply observe what we find painful and what we find pleasurable and base our ethics on this. However, things are not so simple, as we have seen, since sources of pleasure and pain can be induced, distorted, and corrupted; our education and social influences will play a large part in what we find painful and pleasurable. This is a particular problem in relation to AI, especially as it becomes ubiquitous in our life, as we have indicated.

John Stuart Mill presented this issue clearly and in ways that are still relevant for our current situation, in his work *The Subjection of Women*, where he argued that because of the limits imposed on them by society, nobody knows women's true nature, and hence, it is not known what would truly make them happy [39]. One could argue that the same is true across the board for all people to different degrees. So does this mean that we cannot take a simple empirical account of human beings, we cannot just take them 'as they are' as a basis for a utilitarian, or broadly consequentialist, approach to ethics? Do we have to take some kind of teleological account of human beings, some account of how they 'ought' to be, or some account which at least describes better or worse, higher or lower, accounts of our being? In considering this, you may wish to review the material on human nature in Sect. 5.4.

The value of individuals and the separation of persons If you are thinking that this puts the 'cart before the horse', then you are not alone. Surely happiness matters because individuals matter? Surely the fact that one person gains at the expense of another is critically important? The value placed upon individuals requires that we understand the separation of persons. We will look at this question further when we look more closely at the nature of persons in Chap. 8. However, for others, this aspect of consequentialism may be liberating; eliminating sharp distinctions between individuals may be attractive. Visions of a universe sprinkled full of value may then be possible without having to address questions of how that value is distributed. These ideas may appeal to some with more futuristic visions for the potential of AI.

These are important questions for us in considering AI ethics for many reasons. The possible futures ahead of us may hold many changes for large sections of the population. Does it matter what the world ahead will be like, so long as we are all happy? Resistance to certain possible scenarios often comes in the form of striving for independence and autonomy. As we have seen, although current technology provides many possibilities for endless entertainment of the masses that could be seen to be a good thing in increasing happiness, this may contrariwise be seen as an infantilising kind of 'happiness', while the people who are making millions, billions, or trillions out of providing us with such forms of entertainment seem to be living rather different lives. In many future scenarios, the goods of society may be very unevenly distributed. Does this matter, so long as overall, great progress has been made?

We looked earlier in Sect. 4.3 at the question of the background presuppositions against which ethics is formed. Is the separation of individuals an essential feature of any current systems of ethics? Can consequentialism simply abandon it? It would certainly avoid a number of awkward questions about the distribution of value, but we must also take care in responding to this by simply asserting the primacy of the individual. The relationship of individuals with the wider community, responsibility to others, and the balance between concern for individuals and concern for the wider society are all critical in ethics. The emphasis on responsibility to communities that was stressed in the Indigenous Protocols for AI (see Sect. 2.9) is a necessary corrective against any simplistic insistence that the individual must *always* come first. As we have seen, utilitarianism, an approach to ethics which in many ways is very compatible with scientific and technical thought, can hardly be thought of as centring the individual, except insofar as they are included in calculations.

Agent neutrality The invisibility of individuals goes further still. It doesn't matter who acts. It just matters what happens. We saw above that utilitarianism seems to require us to consider the consequences of every single action I perform, which seems very onerous. On the other hand, it doesn't actually matter if it's me who acts, or someone else. Suppose I calculate the best course of action in a given circumstance. Perhaps a local foodbank needs a financial boost. I don't have to give anything myself; I can just get someone else to give it. Or suppose I have a lonely, elderly aunt in mid-stage dementia. I don't have to visit her myself. I can get a robot companion, possibly one programmed with my voice so that my aunt mistakenly thinks I am present. Job done, if she never finds out. This issue is connected with a range of other factors summed up as the claim that utilitarianism, and consequentialism, in general, is 'agent neutral'. Like many such terms in philosophy, there are different ways of understanding the distinction between agent neutral and agent relative accounts of ethics and different features that may fall under this banner or that may be discussed under other headings [40]. For our interests here, it may refer to the notion that who it is that acts does not matter, so long as the correct thing is done, or the right consequences apply; it may also mean that reasons for action apply equally to all moral agents irrespective of their particular situation [5]. This raises many substantial ethical questions, especially in relation to the use of technology.

Agent neutrality, responsibility, and power Since all that matters is what happens, not who brings things about, this may have implications for the moral responsibilities of those with the greatest power and wealth, and this may fit well—or badly, depending on your point of view—with the concentration of wealth and power in the hands of those with most control over technologies. Those individuals and groups who have greatest power are therefore, on such an approach, charged with the greatest personal responsibility to do all they can to maximise the greatest good for the greatest number. One major problem is that if the powerful truly are producing the greatest good for the greatest number, then okay, fine. However, if they have made a mistake in some way, this could lead to a dangerous arrogance disguised as beneficence, a technological, totalitarian nightmare. Recall our discussion in Sect. 1.9 of corporate use of ethics as ethics washing. Even if they have produced 'the greatest good for the greatest number' under some description of ethics, some would still consider this a totalitarian disaster.

If one of the central issues in AI ethics is the use of machines to replace humans, either in part or in full, then a consequentialist approach seems ideal, since it simply requires that we ensure that the same consequences ensue. So, for example, if my aunt were to discover that it is not me who is visiting her, but a sophisticated robot, and was upset as a result, that would be a problem. But if she is totally fooled, then, fine.

Is it too simple to suggest that the question of replacing humans with machines can be solved in this way? One might readily respond that the problem is with a simple consequentialist approach that fails to understand the importance of agency, of individuals, and of the actions that we use to reach the ends at which we aim. It is time to turn to consider other normative theories that focus directly on the nature of actions and on the qualities of agents.

6.3   Normative Ethical Theories: Deontological Approaches

Summary
Deontological approaches to ethics focus on actions and on the rules or principles that should be followed. Issues key to AI include the intention with which an action is carried out, as well as the necessity of interpreting rules and their application to specific contexts. These points are illustrated through a brief introduction to Kant's moral philosophy. We also consider the basis of moral rules, Kant's idea of a rational agent as central to his moral philosophy, and how this might or might not apply in the case of AI.

6.3.1   Introduction

This section presents an outline of rule-based approaches to ethics as well as indicating their fit with AI. In outline, deontological accounts of ethics are rule-based and focused upon the kinds of action that should or should not be performed, often phrased in the language of duty and obligation. It is a quirk of history that the term 'deontological' was first used to describe such an approach by the consequentialist Jeremy Bentham, who had a penchant for coining new words.

Accounts of ethics written in the form of rules are pretty familiar, although the form of words does not necessarily give a good indication of whether a precise set of behaviours is mandated, allowed, or prohibited. Rule-based ethics could take a large number of different forms, with quite different rules making up the content. Codes or guidance on AI ethics may be a mix of elements that may take the outward form of rules or of goals.

Just because a document is written in a form that outwardly resembles a set of rules to follow, it may not be strictly deontological in form. General guidance or general aspirational goals are often written in the form of general values. For example, the seven key requirements in the Ethics Guidelines for Trustworthy AI drawn up by the EU High Level Expert Group (HLEG) for AI are as follows:

Human agency and oversight
Technical robustness and safety
Privacy and data governance
Transparency
Diversity, nondiscrimination, and fairness
Societal and environmental well-being
Accountability [41]

Exercise 23
Consider what main ethical rules might follow from any or all of these seven key requirements.

There are different types of rules Rules may be prohibitions, forbidding certain types of action; requirements, mandating certain types of action; or permissions, allowing certain types of action. Permissions may specify actions that are morally neutral or actions that are good but not required, perhaps because they involve a form of effort or sacrifice that is not demanded of individuals at all times. A supererogatory action is one that is good but that goes over and above the call of duty; in other words, it is permitted, but not mandatory, and will aim towards, or achieve, good ends, generally exceeding usual expectations.

A distinction between 'perfect' and 'imperfect' duties may be helpful (see Sect. 1.6). A perfect duty is one binding on a person at all times. Typical examples would be the duty not to kill another human being. They tend to be phrased in the negative, things not to do. It is pretty easy to keep the duty not to kill another human at every hour of the day. An imperfect duty is one which is good to do, but there is leeway about precisely how, when, and where one does this. For instance, there may be a general duty upon us to render aid to others but scope for individuals to decide how to fulfil this duty. It is thus clearer to determine when a perfect duty has been fulfilled or violated than an imperfect duty. If perfect duties are expressed in the negative—do not kill, do not steal, and so on—it's generally possible to fulfil all of these at the same time. However, rules expressed in positive form make it harder to avoid potential clashes. For example, a positive rule about acting to save lives may be at odds with rules about stealing, since one may be able to get someone to hospital on time in an emergency only by stealing a car. In such an instance, rules about life may take precedence over rules about property (and sometimes this is specifically included in legal systems); at other times, it's less clear.

One of the strengths of such an approach is that there is generally more than one kind of action included, so it can capture more than one kind of moral value and hence can provide more nuance than the simplest types of consequentialism, such as classical utilitarianism, although note that a consequentialist approach can also aim to produce more than one type of value. The complexity of the areas of application of AI and of the different ethical issues involved may make the recognition of multiple kinds of rules or duties attractive.

The possibility of clashes between different rules means that in some instances, hierarchies of rules are specified. For example, in most legal systems, taking property without permission or damaging property may be permitted, if done to save a life or to prevent injury to oneself or others. However, in many cases, considerable difficulty may arise in cases where not all the rules can be kept at once. You may notice that many of the codes and guidance of AI ethics state explicitly that there is no more importance to any of the elements than to others.

By focusing on the type of action that is being considered, there seems room for considerations of agency, so central to many questions in AI ethics, and less straightforward to include in a purely consequentialist approach. The focus on the type of action that is being performed can go a long way towards dealing with some of the problems of consequentialism. Perhaps the most important example of this is how a deontological approach can include rules that allow for the protection of individuals. Rules prohibiting treating individuals in certain ways may be a way of dealing with what to many seem to be a fault, or an excess, of consequentialist approaches, which may often require that the welfare of some individuals be sacrificed to the group. Given the remarks above about how the power and scope of AI may magnify any tendency towards violating the interests of individuals and those without power, this may be especially welcome in the area of AI ethics. Indeed, in practice, many take a mixed approach to ethics, with rule-based principles governing the treatment of individuals and other issues, where rules are used as side constraints to modify the counterintuitive results of the full-blooded application of consequentialism (see Sect. 6.2 above).

In assessing the appropriateness of a rule-based approach to ethics for AI, we can consider both its use in producing an ethics for how AI is developed and applied and its use in any attempt to embed ethics into AI.

Building ethics into AI A rule-based approach may also be attractive for those who wish to attempt to build ethics into AI where this is programmed as a set of rules. It may seem that if a computer can follow a set of rules, it can behave morally, just as a human can. Indeed, since computers are not going to be distracted by emotion or tiredness, perhaps, once we have figured out precisely what the rules should be, an AI will be better than us. We will consider this position shortly.

There are complexities here, which we examine below. It is important to consider that rule-based ethics concern actions, and actions are produced by agents, agents who exist within a wider social setting. We need to consider not just how things are brought about but who brings them about and the wider social setting. This can often have a critical influence on how rules are understood and applied [42].

6.3.2 Immanuel Kant, Rule-Following, Agency, and Lessons for AI Ethics

We will start our examination of these issues by considering Immanuel Kant, who is often taken as a prime exemplar of deontological ethics. His account of ethics, as laid out in his work *A Groundwork for the Metaphysics of Morals*, presents morality as a system of Categorical Imperatives in the form of both perfect and imperfect duties [43]. A categorical imperative is one that is binding upon all rational agents. For simplicity, we can think of 'rational agents' as all human beings, but this term is explicitly not necessarily restricted to humans as a species.

Imperatives Categorical imperatives can be contrasted with hypothetical imperatives. The latter has force only insofar as one wishes to attain the end goal stated in the hypothetical. 'If you can't stand the heat, get out of the kitchen' is a hypothetical imperative. If you're fine with heat, go and cook. However, it's not an adequate response to the imperative, 'Do not steal' to reply, 'But I really wanted that Rolex watch'. Note that categorical imperatives may be written in forms that look like hypotheticals, and vice versa, where the end goal is not explicitly stated.

Rational agents Kant's moral philosophy is rather complex, so although it is worth studying in its own right, here we will only outline it in enough detail to illustrate some important issues relevant to our concerns. Rational agents can see the pull of categorical imperatives because they are required by reason. The particular examples that Kant used to illustrate his claims have given rise to considerable controversy; what matters less for us here is not whether his particular examples are presented correctly but the overall shape of his ethics.

The general form of what Kant was trying to do in basing ethics on reason can be indicated by one of his examples, the putative perfect duty not to make lying promises. Since reason applies universally, each time I consider doing something, I should consider what would happen if the ground of my action became a universal law of nature, and everyone also followed the same maxim (roughly, the same motive) in acting. If, whenever it was convenient to them, all people made false promises to get what they want, the whole institution of promise keeping would break down, because nothing would count as a promise, and nobody would ever believe anyone else's promise. Hence, it is a perfect duty not to make lying promises. There is much that could be said in critique of Kant here, but just consider in itself the idea that ethics is ultimately based upon reason. Does this mean then that some updated account of Kant could provide a basis for an ethic that could include AI, which could be incorporated into computing? Surely, at first glance, this seems ideal. Indeed, if ethics is based upon reason, surely we would want all the boost to our reasoning powers that AI might offer.

However, the notion of a rational agent is, for Kant, both more than an agent who can execute a command, carry out a set of actions or rules, and less than a 'highly intelligent' agent. First, for Kant, to be a rational agent essentially involves a level of self-aware reflection on one's actions. For the starting point of all his examples of categorical imperatives is the reflection on whether or not an action is permitted. This involves considering what one's real motives are—in Kant's terms, what the maxim of one's action is. Recall from Sect. 1.12 that Kant was introduced in our discussion of moral autonomy through his example of three shopkeepers. It is essential, for Kant, not just what action is undertaken but also the reasons for which it is taken, and this involves self-awareness, although, interestingly, Kant also considered that it was very hard for us to know the true motives of our actions.

There are many who disagree with Kant on this issue, many who indeed are repelled by his shopkeeper example, especially by his claim that there is no moral worth in the actions of a shopkeeper who gives the right change to customers simply because he is a kindly, friendly sort of chap and not because he is acting out of moral duty. (We will return to this point shortly.) However, the broad claim that the intention with which one acts is critical to a moral assessment of the action is held by many. It's a distinction heavily present in most legal systems, where *mens rea* or 'guilty mind' has to be established. If this capacity for agency, including the capacity for self-reflection and self-awareness, were to be considered an essential element of what it was to be a rational agent capable of moral actions, then that is a much higher bar for a machine to meet. The goals that are inputted into a machine do not, certainly on the current state of technology, seem anywhere close to Kant's notion of the maxim under which a rational and self-aware agent acts.

Second, the notion of rationality that Kant required is one that he considered any ordinary person could meet. In addition to the capacity to reflect on the nature of our actions, it simply requires being able to determine if one's actions, if applied universally, would lead to contradiction. Hence, this does not mean that a high level of intelligence manifest in an AI in itself would render it morally superior to us.

To return to the discussion of the three shopkeepers example, one of Kant's motivations was to produce an account of morality such that we all have an equal chance of acting morally. He thus wished to rule out this possible source of moral luck, that some people are endowed at birth with sociable, loving natures. Some are not. So, if one's worth as a moral agent were to be based upon our friendly feelings towards others, we do not start on an equal pegging. In contrast, for Kant, we can all, by our rational natures, understand that the moral law binds on us at all times.

One of the purposes of diving into these details of Kant's moral philosophy is to illustrate how complex an account of ethics may be and how deeply embedded with assumptions about the very nature of ethics. By no means all would agree that a starting point of ethics must be the sine qua non that we are all equally able to attain moral worth.

Note also that his notion of a rational agent is not simply one of instrumental rationality. There are certain goals assumed, including the assumption that it is part and parcel of what it is to be a rational agent that one desires to continue living and that there are certain necessities of life. His account of imperfect duties illustrates this. Suppose one considers whether to render aid to someone in need. Imagine a world where nobody ever does this. Such a world does not give rise to any contradiction; it can be imagined. But, according to Kant, no rational being could ever *will* such a world into being, since there will be inevitably some time when each one of us needs aid from others. Consider basic facts about the world: that there are various things towards which we strive for our happiness, yet there are difficulties, obstacles, and issues with resources, which may prevent us from attaining these. Since we all strive for our own happiness, it would be irrational to rule out help attaining it.

Hence, his account of what it is to be a rational agent is heavy in metaphysical claims about the nature of rational agents as well as about basic features of the world in which we live (and there is much more that could be said). Note that if we base ethics simply on just 'reason' in the sense of knowledge of the world plus principles of consistency and logic, the goals of action and the motivation to act must come from somewhere else.

Consider now the questions of transparency, accountability, and responsibility. This is linked to the quest for accountability in ethics. When a person is answerable to another for their actions, it's necessary that they can explain why they chose the particular course of action in question. This implies an element of self-awareness. Following a rule just because it is a rule, absent any other consideration or justification for doing so, may fail to capture some important elements of what is required in ethics. 'I was only following orders' may be the archetypal poor excuse. We discuss questions of responsibility further in the next chapter, Sect. 7.2.2.

6.3.3   Understanding and Interpreting Rules

Any system of rules requires some interpretation. The terms within it must be specified, and frequently, there are background assumptions or shared grounds of knowledge and understanding that supply essential elements of interpretation.

Exercise 24
Consider the rule 'do not kill'. What assumptions might be made in how this is interpreted? Try to find as many possible different interpretations that would impact how it is applied. Use a different moral rule if you prefer for this exercise.

Among the possible assumptions are rules about allowable exceptions, for example, whether the rule covers killing in self-defence; categories of people to whom this does not apply, e.g., combatants in times of war; whether there is a distinction between killing and letting die; the source of any authority; and any presumed penalty [44].

The interpretation of rules poses considerable difficulty, especially in contexts where principles are intended to apply very generally. This is one reason for a certain scepticism about codes of ethical guidance for AI. Very general and well-intended rules may find broad acceptance only because they are actually interpreted in very different ways by different groups and across different cultures, religions, and worldviews.

Assumptions about the background conditions against which the rules are being applied may also be critical. The first time my sister made a cake, on reaching the part of the recipe where it said, 'Add three eggs', she did exactly that. We spent about half an hour picking bits of eggshell out of the raw cake mixture. The final cake was unusually crunchy. The times that I had spent in the kitchen helping to cook, she'd been in another room playing the piano. It hadn't even crossed my mind to tell her to crack the eggs first. Shared background assumptions will often mean we can specify instructions pretty loosely. Isaac Asimov's Robot series stories, and many stories of wishes gone wrong, involve misinterpretation of rules which would often be obvious to humans with a shared life [21]. This can also happen across and within cultural groups.

The interpretation of rules about property rights, for example, may rest upon many assumptions about resource availability, who deserves what, needs, historical injustices, political beliefs, and many more complex questions. Again, technology itself can impact the background conditions and assumptions against which we interpret the very rules designed to manage technology. Consider intellectual property rights; consider how any property rights might be thought of, given the accumulation of wealth in certain groups which technology seems to enable. Recall our discussion of Walter Benjamin's ideas about technologies to reproduce images and words in Sect. 3.6.2. During the COVID-19 pandemic, there was a vast increase in wealth of those in certain groups able to profit from what was an economic disaster for others. Perceptions of fairness and unfairness may all help to shift how we understand and apply moral rules.

Exercise 25
We have looked at uses of AI that involve issues of privacy in previous chapters. For example, Exercises 1, 8, and 10 in Chap. 2 considered issues of surveillance and privacy. Review these exercises and consider how the interpretation of rules about privacy may be affected by the possibilities of technology and by the adoption of technological solutions.

Rule formulation and meaning attribution   Actions, sequences of physical movements, can generally be described in various different ways. The different meanings and significance of behaviour under different descriptions can be a vital factor in interpreting rules and in making decisions about exceptions or hard cases. Outcries over relatives being forbidden to touch their loved ones as they lay dying or to make personal visits to elderly, distressed, and possibly confused relatives demonstrate very vividly the difficulties not just of rule interpretation but of rule justification. Conversely, outcries over failures to prevent the spread of COVID-19 only added to the complex and emotively charged question of the crafting and application of appropriate rules. Recall our discussion in Chap. 4 about describing cases: the same may apply to rules. Rules about distance between two people may make biological sense. However, we are not simply walking immune systems. We are people; we are social beings. The background context against which rules are interpreted will include relationships and local knowledge. Perhaps, then, the difference between rule-based approaches to ethics and approaches based upon consideration of relationship and context may be to some extent a matter of degree.

The importance of context and cultural background is critical in the interpretation of any language and will be vital in understanding ethical questions in content moderation, bias, and other questions. This issue about how different humans may interpret and apply rules is directly linked to an important question about the appropriateness and capacity of AI to interpret rules.

Rules and discretion Imagine a set of rules that is followed rigidly and without exception. If the meaning of the rule is crystal clear, if all cases fall squarely within or outside the specifications of the rules, there would be no problem in following the rule on all occasions. Or perhaps even such a case is not so easy. Much could depend upon the purpose and intent behind the rule. For example, it is common for tenancy agreements to have a clause forbidding pets. Would you consider it a good application of the rule to evict a family of five because they kept a goldfish? Discretion could be applied to the question of whether a goldfish counted as a pet if the purpose was to avoid damage to the apartments and nuisance to neighbours, for example, from fouling and from barking dogs. Discretion could also be applied to the stated penalty, with potentially severe consequences that some would consider outweigh any gravity attached to secretly keeping a goldfish. Variations on such examples can be dreamt up indefinitely.

The capacity of AI to handle such cases will be critical in determining if it is adequate to the task of determining ethical questions. Indeed, we must note that any decisions that involve judgement in the treatment of human beings on any matter of significance to their welfare could fall under this head. Rules can be written that are more or less vague, and concepts can be specified to different degrees of clarity. However, hard cases where there are questions about application are likely always to exist. Some cases will hinge on the question of what aspects of a situation are relevant. The fact that nobody has ever (to my knowledge) been kept awake at night by a barking goldfish, or slipped over from treading in goldfish poop left on the stairs, may or may not be deemed of interest to a decision. Conversely, there is a surprisingly long list of zoonotic diseases associated with fish contact.

The obverse of discretion is corruption.

Exercise 26

Could it be argued that AI may have some advantage over humans in being immune to corruption in the application of rules?

Could some complex rule-based AI or machine learning help to solve such problems? Could AI exhibit common sense or compassion? These questions are in part questions about the capacities of AI to which different experts give different answers. There are other ethical aspects, including the question of accountability and responsibility and whether a human being has to take ultimate responsibility for any decision.

The question of accountability likewise demonstrates that we do not think of moral rules as simply instructions that need to be followed. Decisions involving such rules and their application create relationships of accountability between those enacting the rules and those impacted by them. Conversely, there are occasions when a person acting in an official role, for example, a judge, may have some powers of discretion, but these are limited by the expectation that certain rules set by the system of law will be followed. (Recall also our discussion of the COMPAS case in Sect. 2.4.3.) A vital question concerning the integration of moral rules into AI then concerns these relationships of accountability. In regard to matters of ethics, the interpretation of rules may be especially difficult, as hard cases may involve those very borderline or ambiguous areas where the most important issues lie.

6.4   Normative Ethical Theories: Virtue Ethics

Summary
Virtue ethics focuses on the moral character of individual agents. Accounts of the virtues can be found in different religious and philosophical traditions, and there is much contemporary interest in the area, often using virtue ethics as a more nuanced, contextual response to situations than deontological or consequentialist approaches. Virtue ethics stresses the development of moral character in individuals while retaining a focus on the social. We consider its suitability for application to those who develop, apply, and use AI and the question of what specific virtues may be needed as we live with technology.

Character of agents Virtue ethics focuses upon the agent and their character. Modern virtue ethics has taken considerable inspiration from Aristotle, with amendments to certain key elements of his approach to ethics and with a variety of positions within the field [45–47]. We will be able to present an overview here only. There is also work specifically applying virtue ethics to issues in AI. Traditions of virtue ethics can also be found within Buddhist and Confucian philosophies. Virtue ethics has a number of features that make it appealing in the kind of complex situations that the use of technologies such as AI may produce. Complexity and nuance can be accommodated since there is a variety of different virtues and since judgements of how to react and behave are fine-tuned to situations and to those involved.

The good life Aristotle's account of ethics begins with addressing the question of what it is for each one of us to live a good life. He starts by presupposing that each one of us is seeking happiness, or eudaemonia. We have discussed the eudaemonic conception of happiness earlier in Sect. 6.2.1, where it was contrasted to felicific conceptions based upon happiness conceived of as pleasure. Eudaemonic conceptions are concerned with happiness attained over a whole life, and for Aristotle, it is also clear that his views on human nature are essential to understanding his views.

Exercise 27 Food for Thought
From where do we get our ideas a life well lived? Considering the changes that AI has brought and the possible changes it may bring, could inspirational figures from the generation of your parents or your grandparents give any guidance? Given the potential speed of technological change, including those hoping for radical life extension, etc., does it even make sense to think of the attempt to live well over the whole course of our lives?

A teleological universe Aristotle's conception of the world was teleological. Natural things are striving towards certain ends, and humans likewise strive for their own proper end. The good of each kind of thing, for Aristotle, was to be found in their function; a good X is an X which performs its functions well. The function of each type of thing is to be found in that which distinguishes it from all other types of thing. Note that an essential part of this account of ethics is thus the idea that the world can be divided into different natural kinds. Recall Aristotle's distinction between things belonging to the natural world and artefacts, discussed in Sect. 3. 3.2. In the case of humans, the function of man is found in our rational activity, and hence, to live well, is to live virtuously, according to reason.

It is also crucial for Aristotle that we are social animals. Aristotle is generally credited with being the world's first biologist; he observes that, unlike herd animals such as cattle, which group together for safety and because they are all seeking the best grass, humans seek each other's company for the pure pleasure of it [12].

The function of man and human nature Few who embrace Aristotle's broad vision of virtue ethics now agree with his arguments about the function of man. However, note how his view of the virtues derives from an account of our natures and rests upon a teleological view of the world as striving towards a goal. What constitutes the good life a human being, then, is shaped not simply by what might 'feel good' to them, or to the accumulation of pleasure over a life, but is measured with reference to an understanding of our natures and of the teleological nature of the world.

This will seem counterintuitive to many who see themselves as taking a scientific view of the world and consider that this means observing the world as it is without commitment to a metaphysical framework; see the above discussion in Sect. 6.2.1 concerning the purported empirical basis of moral motivation in classical conceptions of utilitarianism. A teleological world view, one which sees the universe as having some direction or purpose, is also to be found among some of the visionary futurists advocating AI, as we shall see in Chap. 11, as well as enthusiasts for human enhancement or transhumanism.

If the idea of basing an account of the good life on some teleological view of function still seems hard to grasp, then consider the case of zoo or farm animals.

There have been significant shifts in attitudes towards animal welfare in recent decades, among these being the recognition that animals have certain needs and instincts that will cause distress if the animal is not able to exercise these. Some days online, it seems that I get adverts for little other than for toys for 'bored cats' designed to allow them to act on their instincts to hunt. This can provide at least a *rough* working model for an account of the good life based upon function, although do not take this analogy too literally.

Exercise 28 Food for Thought
Aristotle considered that he had determined the function of man on which to base his account of ethics. This relegated women to an inferior social position and inferior potential. John Stuart Mill, as has been mentioned, considered that the constraints of society hampered women such that nobody knew their true nature. Are there any ways in which our current and projected uses of AI might constrain our ideas of human nature and/or might enable us to explore its potential further?

Virtues, context, individuals, and culture The identification of specific virtues varies with different factors, such as culture and context, with some virtue ethicists also allowing for different sets of virtues for different people (e.g. for men and women). The specific virtues that Aristotle recognised include courage, temperance, magnanimity, patience, truthfulness, righteous indignation, and also friendliness and wit. Virtue ethics theories characteristically identify virtues in relation to some manner of balance between extremes or excess. To act virtuously is to act in the right manner, at the right way, at the right time. Aristotle considered that virtues lie in a mean between two poles of vice, of excess at one end, and deficiency at the other. Thus, for example, the excess of courage is recklessness, the deficiency is cowardice.

Exercise 29
The 'digital divide' is a term applied to the entrenchment or increase of social divisions occasioned by the growing use of technology and the necessity of its use. One might also apply this to the growing power disparity between those who own and operate within powerful corporations developing AI and the rest of the public who use it. Might different sets of virtues be applied across such digital divides?

Virtues and the doctrine of the mean There is no universal formula for determining the midpoint of virtue, but this will vary according to circumstance and to the individual. The virtue is not at the literal 'half-way' mark. For example, more would be expected in terms of courage from a trained and fit warrior than from a child. Different circumstances could turn a courageous act into one of wanton foolishness. Some virtues and vices do not fit this 'doctrine of the mean' very well, as there appears to be no corresponding scale. There is no way of committing adultery 'in the right manner'. Some scholars consider that Aristotle's account of virtue as the mean between two vices is better explained with the analogy of 'hitting a target' [48]. One can aim to be closer to the target so that success in ethics, the accomplishment of virtue, can be understood to a certain extent as a matter of degree.

The acquisition of virtues, education, and one's place in society   Virtues are acquired as one grows and matures. Because Aristotle assumed that all wish for a life of happiness (eudaimonia), he is assuming that we (or at any rate, his audience of the free men of Athens) all start off with a rough idea of how to live a good life and learn through example from those who have already achieved virtue and can teach us how to attain it via practice and honing the act of living well. As mentioned in Sect. 3.3.2, Aristotle used the practice of crafts as an analogy to acquiring the virtues. Someone who has acquired all the virtues has achieved phronesis, or practical wisdom.

Exercise 30
If we base AI ethics on the virtues and only on the virtues, might this mean we are at the mercy of hoping that those with power will develop practical wisdom? Does this fill you with trepidation, and if not, why?

Exercise 31
Conversely, consider the necessity of interpreting rules and the exercise of discretion. Could exercise in developing the virtues be a good strategy for helping to ensure ethical behaviour among those developing and applying AI?

Exercise 32
Could any science fiction books or films that you are familiar with be used to help teach the virtues needed for a future with AI?

Practical wisdom   Note that this is practical wisdom and not a purely intellectual or abstract knowledge (see Sect. 3.3.3). Like skills at crafts, virtues have to be practiced. One cannot claim to be courageous merely by sitting at home and reading books about it (or, one might add, by tweeting and writing blogs about courage, unless one is practicing courageously entering into the fray of online abuse). The ancient Greeks understood craftwork in a broad way. Aristotle often mentioned crafts such as music and medicine, and the ancient Greeks also had surprisingly advanced mechanical skills. All craftwork at the time involved local embodied practice and the skill of identifiable individuals.

Exercise 33
Even without accepting Aristotle's view of the virtues, many would find much wisdom in the idea that we can advance in moral understanding through experience gained from entering the rough and tumble of life. Could a person achieve phronesis and moral understanding in virtual reality?

Personal relationships   We saw in discussing consequentialism that it has an impersonal aspect, which is at once a strength, in that this is a force tending against individual bias, parochialism, and moral short-sightedness, and at the same time a difficulty in the problems of accounting for the particular value of personal relationships. Virtue ethics provides a strong contrast. Given Aristotle's widespread influence today and the many insights he had into ethics, it is now startling, and for some of his fans embarrassing, to recognise that he not only discriminated against women and slaves in his account of the good life; it was the free men *of the city state of Athens* that most concerned him. For example, he considered that women (and 'womanly men') like to have others to moan to and share their pains, whereas the duty for men was to imitate the highest character and keep one's pains to oneself [12].

However, the flip side of this is that there is plenty of scope within virtue ethics of recognising the value of personal relationships. A question that arises naturally is the potential clash between personal commitments and social or more global commitments. This has troubled us from at least the time of the Greeks. Many Greek dramas dealt with this theme. Sophocles' tragedy *Antigone* explores the tensions between the family loyalties that led the eponymous heroine to wish to bury her dead brother and the commands of the king Creon who denied him a burial with holy rites, leaving him a prey to wild animals outside the city wall [49]. Within a very different cultural context, Jean-Paul Sartre sat around the cafés of Paris while pondering quandaries such as that facing the young man in World War II who had to decide between joining the Free French Forces and remaining at home to care for his elderly widowed mother [50]. (Despite the different cultural contexts possible in virtue ethics, some human issues remain relatively constant from place to place.)

What virtue ethics can do well is to account for the value of the personal. What Aristotle could do was to account for loyalties, such as towards the Athenian city state. What it does less well, possibly not at all, is to account for more global values of universal concern for all, which, for some, is seen as a sine qua non of many accounts of ethics now.

Exercise 34

Consider if guidelines for ethics for AI might take the form of certain basic general principles to be applied globally, with nuanced accounts of virtues applied locally to fit with different cultures. Try to work out an example of how this might succeed in practice.

Space for a personal life A consequence of a simple account of utilitarianism that aims to maximise outcomes of each action is that each individual faces the prospect of an endless burden of morality. Strictly speaking, one's entire waking life is composed of nothing other than a series of moral choices where one must try to maximise happiness and minimise unhappiness across the entire globe and into the indefinite future. Naturally, it is realised that these demands are unrealistic, but the limits included to deal with this issue may be pragmatic only, amounting to 'rest up a little then get on with it', plus pragmatic limits to the difficulties of calculation and to what impact any one individual could realistically have. Movements such as Effective Altruism seek to find practical ways to approach such a goal [51, 52].

However, a virtue ethics approach that focuses upon the goodness and value of a human life perceived as a whole can readily accommodate a personal life. The topic of friendship takes up a larger portion of Aristotle's *Nicomachean Ethics* than any other topic, and virtue ethics leaves scope for different accounts to include a variety of different virtues. The scope of a virtue for Aristotle went far beyond the relatively narrow conception of 'ethics' that dominates contemporary thought and includes intellectual virtues as well as virtues of character.

This distinction between approaches to ethics is drawn in broad brush strokes but relates to questions of measurement and of analysis in ethics that play a central role in considerations of AI ethics, including the question of how well AI may understand ethics and whether AI can perform ethically. One approach is that ethical value can be analysed, measured, understood, and calculated in an additive manner, or at any rate, in a manner amenable to capture in a formula. Ethical value accumulates, or is lost, over time and space. Complexities may arise when there is thought to be more than one source of ethical value and where these are not commensurable with each other. Such an approach may appear to lend itself readily for manifestation within computation. Virtue ethics suggests a contrasting approach where judgement on value cannot be so reduced, where any simple additive or formulaic calculation of value may be quite unable to grasp the complexity of moral wisdom. It may be more controversial whether any AI could ever grasp or exhibit such practical wisdom. On the other hand, perhaps such complexity could be captured by some version of machine learning, perhaps by careful observation of human virtues and vices.

Virtue ethics, the individual, and the social Much contemporary work in ethics is critiqued for focus on the individual at the expense of the social. This criticism is sometimes levelled at work in AI ethics. An approach to virtue ethics that focuses on individual character might likewise be accused of centring too much on individuals. However, elements of attention to the social are generally present, including virtuous characters as role models, virtues that include attention to social questions and to others, and the structure of education and character formation that leads to the development of virtue. See also our discussion of the ethics of care in Sect. 5.4.4.

Technology and changing conceptions of virtue An interesting question is whether our use of technology itself may modify our conceptions of virtue, both in how virtue is accomplished and in what the virtues are. It is not a straightforward thing within schemas of virtue ethics to say whether such changes on the face of it are 'good' or 'bad', but it is certainly a worthy subject of study.

Consider virtues associated with giving to good causes, whether to groups or individuals. The Greeks recognised a virtue of magnanimity, which differs significantly from modern conceptions of charity that have been influenced by the Christian tradition. Magnanimity involved very public displays of generosity with one's wealth. To achieve this virtue, one therefore needed to have enough wealth to give some pretty ostentatious amount. In contrast, although large charitable donations are applauded, a conception of charity influenced by Christianity contains within it the idea that even very small amounts of charity are of great value, if they come from someone of very limited means, and that giving to charity in secret, or without wishing for honours for oneself. Even the destitute may have the power to perform a charitable action for another. Charity is thus an egalitarian virtue, in contrast to magnificence. Suspicion may fall upon those who ostentatiously donate to charity and then get great public recognition for it. If nothing else, this comparison between the Greek and Christian conceptions of related virtues demonstrates the importance of considering cultural and historical influences.

Might it be the case that conceptions of these virtues are being influenced by the affordances of modern technologies? It is now very possible to demonstrate to the world one's giving to various causes. Moreover, the possibility of influencing others online may change attitudes. Could this mean that the power of influence to get others to donate to a good cause shifts thinking from a 'donate and don't brag about it' to a 'donate and show everyone you've done so' mentality? Or is there something more subtle happening, that there are now twin virtues arising, such that we recognise more explicitly the values of both a modern kind of magnificence and a modern kind of charity? (Think, e.g. of the legion of opportunities to donate anonymously online to crowd-funders, etc. These often have a 'now tell your friends to encourage them' function.)

Exercise 35
Now consider the very visible presence of the tech billionaire philanthropist. Let us make this anonymous and just invent a figure, somebody who made a fortune through the development of technology reliant on AI. That person now very publicly gives a portion of their wealth to particular causes of his choosing. Add that he encourages others to do the same.

How might a virtue ethics approach capture the ethical nuances of such a case? Consider whether a contrast between the virtues of charity and the virtues of magnificence might help illuminate this. Can we address such cases by considering mixtures of virtue and vice, perhaps? And how might modern technology, including the ability of a few to accumulate unprecedented wealth, and the ease of communications, impact upon how we think of all this?

Phronesis and balancing the virtues Aristotle considered that one could not fully possess any one virtue unless one possessed all of them. This is because each virtue needs to be applied and practiced in context, and one virtue may be in some conflict with others. Thus, we need to make judgements about how precisely to fulfil each of these, taking everything into account. Others differ and consider that we can exhibit particular virtues to the full in the absence of other virtues [53].

This debate has a particular relevance to our use of technologies and especially their capacity to captivate our attention. In a different context, G. K. Chesterton in his book *Orthodoxy* writes of what happens to a society when its framework of values is being shattered. The vices may run loose and do damage, but the virtues also run loose and may do even more damage. Chesterton writes that in the modern world, 'The virtues have gone mad because they have been isolated from each other and are wandering alone. Thus some scientists care for truth; their truth is pitiless. Thus some humanitarians only care for pity; their pity (I am afraid to say) is often untruthful' [54].

Exercise 36 Food for Thought
Could this be a fair commentary at all about what is seen as virtuous now in relation to developments in society shaped and facilitated by new technologies, including AI? Are there any virtues (or vices) that have 'gone mad' and are 'wandering alone'?

Consider how you might draw up a balanced list of virtues for humans to live alongside AI.

Comparison of human agency and machine agency Could a machine ever exhibit virtue? Would they be the same as virtues for humans, or would there be distinctions? Let us consider some virtues and vices from different traditions. Aristotle listed the following virtues: courage, temperance (moderation), liberality, magnificence, magnanimity, ambition, patience, friendliness, truthfulness, and wit. Confucius taught five virtues most central to the gentleman: benevolence, righteousness, ritual propriety, wisdom, and trustworthiness [55]. Filial piety to parents and family is important for maintaining order in society. There are different accounts available of important virtues in Buddhism, but these may include, expressed in the negative, the virtues of refraining from taking life, stealing, sexual misconduct, lying, divisive speech, harsh speech, idle chit-chat, covetousness, malice, and wrong view. You may well have your own personal list of virtues and vices.

Some of these virtues relate specifically to aspects of human society; some relate to our bodily desires (temperance, e.g. requires restraining excessive appetites).

Exercise 37
Consider how these may or may not translate to a sophisticated AI. Draw up your own list of virtues for a humanoid robot.

Are there any virtues you think especially important for humans given the AI we have now and the AI we may have in the near or distant future?

Consider the Buddhist virtues listed above. Several of them refer to aspects of speech and truth telling. Consider what virtues and vices there may be in relation to information and communication given our use of new technologies.

Could a robot learn virtue? Virtue ethics concerns the development of character. We have seen above the difficulties involved in interpreting and applying rules in context. Perhaps an advanced humanoid robot could be taught to acquire the virtues and develop the contextual interpretation necessary to apply rules and to work out priorities where there were complex clashes between different rules and values. There is a burgeoning literature examining various aspects of virtue ethics in relation to robots [56–62].

Exercise 38
What virtues would you wish to see in those developing AI? What issues concerning the realities of development are relevant to consider in addressing this question?

A general point to consider is this: we develop virtues through our actions and choices. This involves the capacity to learn from others and to correctly understand the precise context of a situation. We need to consider how we might use AI in ways that enhance the process of the development of virtues in individuals and how it might detract from such development.

Exercise 39

There may be rather different virtues at stake for those who are using AI and for different kinds and applications of AI. Take some of our previous case studies and exercises and consider what virtues—and vices—might be most at issue.

Consider whether and to what extent addressing your chosen cases through the lens of virtue ethics helps to illuminate the ethical issues.

Consider how each of the normative ethical theories we have been examining sheds light on the issues.

6.5 Key Points

The three approaches to normative ethical theory we have looked at in this chapter focus on outcomes, actions, and agents. A good general strategy is to consider all three elements.

Outcomes of actions are clearly important, but many questions in AI ethics concern issues of agency: issues such as the replacement or supplementation of human agency with machine agency.

There are both attractions and grave difficulties in attempting to base a consequentialist approach on a hedonistic utilitarianism based on happiness or pleasure and on a desire-based utilitarianism. Technologies involving AI can present us with heightened difficulties: the increasing possibilities of manipulating the world to attain happiness and the manipulation of our desires and preferences via technologies.

The measurement of outcomes and understanding trade-offs between different ethical rules and principles may be facilitated by some AI. However, the assessment of outcomes, especially further into the future, and given the complex interconnections of technology on our lives, will be immensely challenging.

Rule-based systems may seem relatively straightforward, but rules must always be interpreted. There may be especial difficulties in providing general ethical rules for AI which are applicable globally, as well as questions for whether a machine could interpret the context of rule application and meaning as well as a human can.

Virtue ethics appreciates the context of different situations and the need to consider a variety of different virtues that may have a bearing upon the final judgement of how to act.

Virtue ethics approaches leave open a wide range of virtues and vices and the possibility that different virtues may apply to those in different positions in society.

Virtue ethics tends to stress the development of character and the importance of moral education. There may therefore be challenges in developing a virtuous character in a rapidly changing society.

6.6 Educator Notes

Students with no background in ethics or philosophy or students with less time may prefer to focus on one or the other of the three normative theories discussed. Many of the exercises could be undertaken even without any background reading and should nonetheless help to give students who prefer to focus on more concrete problems some understanding of the underlying theoretical issues. Students can readily grasp the focus of each theory on outcome, action, and character, which alone can provide a useful tool for scrutinising ethical questions.

Consequentialist approaches are particularly important to cover, as well as intuitively easy to grasp, since consequentialism tends to be an assumed default view of ethics among some who are both working in AI and considering ethics; it highlights many key questions in relation to AI and to technology in general, and an understanding of consequentialism and its advantages and disadvantages also opens the way to understanding rival theories.

Students with a background in philosophy or some familiarity with these ethical theories should be encouraged to focus on how AI presents particular challenges and how certain approaches to ethics sit with issues discussed previously, such as questions of human nature and methodology in ethics.

Readers are invited at various points to refer back to previous material, but this chapter could be used as a stand-alone introduction to issues or used directly after Chap. 4 on methodology for those taking shorter courses.

This chapter has a large number of exercises, so it is unlikely that students will tackle all of them, but it will generally be useful to read through each exercise as they are designed to draw out issues from the preceding discussions. Many of these exercises would work well as group or class discussions, and some could serve as essay questions.

Some of the discussion and exercises specifically draw links between historical philosophical discussions and contemporary issues concerning AI. Some students may find these of particular interest, but all are to be encouraged to appreciate how much could potentially be learned from past debates and to see the precursors in what may otherwise appear to be completely novel issues.

There is also scope in this chapter to relate several of the exercise questions to issues in science fiction for those with an interest in this area, such as 4, 9, 17, and 33.

Debate and discussion topics A useful, interesting and possibly heated class discussion and debate could be organised around the topic of happiness, on which there are multiple exercises. This will also be very useful for deepening students' understanding of underlying philosophical issues and theory and is a topic that will recur in various guises throughout the book. Exercise 24 could be very useful in class for ensuring that students are covering a good range of basic ground. Exercise 25 on interpreting rules will also be useful for further work and for thinking about how moral rules might be formalised.

Acknowledgements This chapter was partially funded by the National Institute for Health Research, Health Services and Delivery Research Programme (project number 13/10/80). The views expressed are those of the author and not necessarily those of the NIHR or the Department of Health and Social Care.

References

1. Ayer AJ (1952) Language, truth, and logic. Courier Corporation, North Chelmsford
2. Anscombe GEM (1958) Modern moral philosophy. Philosophy 33(124):1–19
3. Lipscomb BJ (2021) The women are up to something: how Elizabeth Anscombe, Philippa Foot, Mary Midgley, and Iris Murdoch revolutionized ethics. Oxford University Press, Oxford
4. Hare RM (1961) The language of morals. Oxford Paperbacks, Oxford
5. Scheffler S (ed) (1988) Consequentialism and its critics. Oxford University Press, Oxford
6. Bentham J (1789) Introduction to the principles of morals and legislation, works. Oxford University Press, Oxford
7. Carlyle T (1837) The French revolution. James Fraser
8. Mill JS (1863) Utilitarianism. Parker, Son and Bourn, London
9. Butler J (1827) Fifteen sermons preached at the Rolls Chapel. Hilliard & Brown, Cambridge
10. Nozick R (1974) Anarchy, state, and utopia. Basic Books, New York
11. Mitchell D (2012) Living in the moment. David Mitchell's soapbox. https://www.youtube.com/watch?v=6HTt6QJqzxk. Accessed 20 May 2022
12. Aristotle (2014) In: Crisp R (ed) Aristotle: Nicomachean ethics. Cambridge University Press, Cambridge
13. Farwell P (1995) Aristotle and the complete life. Hist Philos Q 12(3):247–263
14. Christakis N, Fowler J (2010) Connected: the amazing power of social networks and how they shape our lives. Harper Press, London
15. Kramer AD, Guillory JE, Hancock JT (2014) Experimental evidence of massive-scale emotional contagion through social networks. Proc Natl Acad Sci 111(24):8788–8790
16. Kelly Y, Zilanawala A, Booker C, Sacker A (2018) Social media use and adolescent mental health: findings from the UK millennium cohort study. EClinicalMedicine 6:59–68
17. Nussbaum MC (2001) The fragility of goodness: luck and ethics in Greek tragedy and philosophy. Cambridge University Press, Cambridge
18. World English Bible. https://worldenglish.bible
19. Shelley PB (1818) Ozymandias. The Examiner, London
20. Frankfurt HG (1988) Freedom of the will and the concept of a person. In: What is a person? Humana Press, Totowa, pp 127–144
21. Asimov I (2004) I, Robot, vol 1. Spectra. First published 1950
22. Bostrom N (2017) Superintelligence. Dunod
23. Asimov I (1950) The evitable conflict. In: Astounding Science Fiction
24. Russell S (2019) Human compatible: artificial intelligence and the problem of control. Penguin, London
25. Pavlov IP (1927) In: Anrep GV (ed) Conditioned reflexes: an investigation of the physiological activity of the cerebral cortex. Oxford University Press, London
26. Ura K, Alkire S, Zangmo T, Wangdi K (2012) A short guide to gross national happiness index. The Centre for Bhutan Studies, Thimpu
27. Fox C (1882) Memoirs of old friends being extracts from the journals and letters of Caroline Fox from 1835 to 1871 in two volumes, vol 1. Bernhard Tauchnitz, Liepzig, p 147
28. Scruton R (2017) On human nature. Princeton University Press, Princeton
29. Parfit D (1984) Reasons and persons. OUP, Oxford

30. Greaves H, MacAskill W (2019) The case for strong longtermism. Global Priorities Institute Working Paper, Oxford. https://globalprioritiesinstitute.org/wp-content/uploads/The-Case-for-Strong-Longtermism-GPI-Working-Paper-June-2021-2-2.pdf

31. Torres P (2021) Against longtermism. Aeon. https://aeon.co/essays/why-longtermism-is-the-worlds-most-dangerous-secular-credo

32. Future of Life (2015) Open Letter Research priorities for robust and beneficial artificial intelligence. https://futureoflife.org/ai-open-letter/

33. Reeves R (2015) John Stuart Mill: Victorian Firebrand. Atlantic Books, London

34. Mill JS (2020. (1872)) Autobiography. Columbia University Press, New York

35. Huxley A (1932) Brave new world. Chatto and Windus, London

36. Dickens C (2012) Hard times (1854). Penguin, London

37. Dostoevsky F (1996) Notes from underground (trans: Garnett C). Project Gutenberg, Chapel Hill

38. Dostoyevsky F (2017) Crime and punishment. Oxford University Press, Oxford

39. Mill JS (1869) The subjection of women. Longmans, Green, Reader, and Dyer, London

40. Ridge M (2017) Reasons for action: agent-neutral vs. agent-relative. In: Zalta EN (ed) The Stanford encyclopedia of philosophy. https://plato.stanford.edu/archives/fall2017/entries/reasons-agent

41. HLEG (2019) Ethics guidelines for trustworthy AI. Independent High-Level Expert Group on Artificial Intelligence, Brussels, p 39

42. Balfour DL, Adams GB (2014) Unmasking administrative evil. Routledge, London

43. Kant I, Paton HJ (1964) Groundwork of the metaphysic of morals (trans and analysed: Paton HJ). Harper & Row, New York

44. Glover J (1990) Causing death and saving lives: the moral problems of abortion, infanticide, suicide, euthanasia, capital punishment, war and other life-or-death choices. Penguin, London

45. Crisp R, Slote MA (eds) (1997) Virtue ethics. Oxford University Press, Oxford, pp 19–25

46. Annas J (2007) Virtue ethics. Oxford University Press, Oxford

47. Hursthouse R (1999) On virtue ethics. OUP Oxford, Oxford

48. Hursthouse R (1980) A false doctrine of the mean. In: Proceedings of the Aristotelian Society, vol 81. Wiley, New York, pp 57–72

49. Cairns D (2016) Sophocles: antigone. Bloomsbury Publishing, London

50. Sartre JP (2021) Existentialism is a humanism. Yale University Press, New Heaven

51. MacAskill W (2017) Effective altruism: introduction. Essays Philos 18(1):1–5

52. Gabriel I (2017) Effective altruism and its critics. J Appl Philos 34(4):457–473

53. Noel J (1999) On the varieties of phronesis. Educ Philos Theory 31(3):273–289

54. Chesterton GK (1908) Orthodoxy. Dover, Mineola

55. Csikszentmihalyi M (2020) Confucius. In: Zalta EN (ed) The Stanford encyclopedia of philosophy. Metaphysics Research Lab, Stanford University, Stanford. https://plato.stanford.edu/archives/sum2020/entries/confucius/

56. Sparrow R (2021) Virtue and vice in our relationships with robots: is there an asymmetry and how might it be explained? Int J Soc Robot 13(1):23–29

57. Cappuccio ML, Peeters A, McDonald W (2020) Sympathy for Dolores: moral consideration for robots based on virtue and recognition. Philos Technol 33(1):9–31

58. Gamez P, Shank DB, Arnold C, North M (2020) Artificial virtue: the machine question and perceptions of moral character in artificial moral agents. AI Soc 35(4):795–809

59. Vallor S (2010) Social networking technology and the virtues. Ethics Inf Technol 12(2):157–170

60. Vallor S (2016) Technology and the virtues: a philosophical guide to a future worth wanting. Oxford University Press, Oxford

61. Vallor S (2012) Flourishing on Facebook: virtue friendship & new social media. Ethics Inf Technol 14(3):185–199

62. Wallach W, Vallor S (2020) Moral machines: from value alignment to embodied virtue. In: Liao MS (ed) Ethics of artificial intelligence. Oxford University Press, Oxford, pp 383–412

Further Reading

General Reading on Normative Ethical Theory

Alexander L, Moore M (2021) Deontological ethics. In: Zalta EN (ed) The Stanford encyclopedia of philosophy https://plato.stanford.edu/archives/win2021/entries/ethics-deontological/

Aristotle (2014) In: Crisp R (ed) Aristotle: Nicomachean ethics. Cambridge University Press, Cambridge

Beauchamp T, Childress J (2013) Principles of biomedical ethics, 7th edn. Oxford University Press, Oxford part I

Crisp R, Slote MA (eds) (1997) Virtue ethics. Oxford University Press, Oxford, pp 19–25

Crisp R (1997) Routledge philosophy guidebook to Mill on utilitarianism. Psychology Press, London

Glover J (1990) Utilitarianism and its critics. MacMillan, London

Hursthouse R, Pettigrove G (2018) Virtue ethics. In: Zalta EN (ed) The Stanford encyclopedia of philosophy https://plato.stanford.edu/archives/win2018/entries/ethics-virtue/

Johnson DG (1985) Computer ethics. In: Philosophical ethics. Prentice-Hall, Englewood Cliffs

Mill JS (1854) Utilitarianism (Crisp R ed., 1998). Oxford University Press, Oxford

Scheffler S (ed) (1988) Consequentialism and its critics. Oxford University Press, Oxford

Sinnott-Armstrong W (2021) Consequentialism. In: Zalta EN (ed) The Stanford encyclopedia of philosophy https://plato.stanford.edu/archives/fall2021/entries/consequentialism/

Slote M (2010) Virtue ethics. In: Skorupski J (ed) The Routledge companion to ethics. Routledge, Oxford, p 275 (pp 504–515)

Smart JJC, Williams BAO (1973) Utilitarianism, for and against. Cambridge University Press, Cambridge

Urmson JO (1988) Aristotle's ethics. Blackwell, Oxford

Normative Ethical Theories for AI

Card D, Smith NA (2020) On consequentialism and fairness. Front Artif Intell 3:34

Gamez P, Shank DB, Arnold C, North M (2020) Artificial virtue: the machine question and perceptions of moral character in artificial moral agents. AI Soc 35(4):795–809

Grau C (2011) There is no 'I' in 'robot': robots and utilitarianism. In: Anderson M, Anderson S (eds) Machine ethics. Cambridge University Press, Cambridge, pp 451–463

Loreggia A, Mattei N, Rossi F, Venable KB (2020) Modeling and reasoning with preferences and ethical priorities in AI systems. In: Liao MS (ed) Ethics of artificial intelligence, p 127

Mittelstadt B (2019) Principles alone cannot guarantee ethical AI. Nat Mach Intell 1:1–7

Neubert MJ, Montañez GD (2020) Virtue as a framework for the design and use of artificial intelligence. Bus Horiz 63(2):195–204

Powers TM (2011) Prospects for a Kantian machine. In: Anderson M, Anderson S (eds) Machine ethics. Cambridge University Press, Cambridge, pp 464–475

Vallor S (2010) Social networking technology and the virtues. Ethics Inf Technol 12(2):157–170

Vallor S (2012) Flourishing on Facebook: virtue friendship & new social media. Ethics Inf Technol 14(3):185–199

Vallor S (2015) Moral deskilling and upskilling in a new machine age: reflections on the ambiguous future of character. Philos Technol 28(1):107–124

Vallor S (2016) Technology and the virtues: a philosophical guide to a future worth wanting. Oxford University Press, Oxford

Wallach W, Vallor S (2020) Moral machines: from value alignment to embodied virtue. In: Liao MS (ed) Ethics of artificial intelligence. Oxford University Press, Oxford, pp 383–412

Chapter 7
Philosophy for AI Ethics: Metaethics, Metaphysics, and More

Abstract This chapter examines further philosophical issues underlying questions in AI ethics, concentrating on metaethics but also briefly examining issues in theory of knowledge, philosophy of language, and metaphysics. Many questions in AI ethics can be better understood if metaethical questions are addressed. The MIT Moral Machine experiment is analysed to introduce many of the central issues, illustrating some useful strategies for practical ethical discussion and demonstrating the necessity of considering assumptions about how moral judgements should be formed. Contrasting approaches to how we understand ethical issues are presented. We discuss ideal observer theory, the question of the universality or otherwise of moral values, the question of moral relativism, the role of reason and emotion in ethical judgement, and attempts to ground and justify moral judgement upon empirical observation or on the basis of evolution. We briefly review how questions of epistemology occur repeatedly in AI and in its ethics and present an overview of standpoint epistemology and its implications for AI. We introduce pragmatics in the philosophy of language, which is essential to understanding questions of meaning and interpretation in natural language processing. Last, the question of the nature of reality is discussed in the context of virtual reality.

Keywords AI ethics · Metaethics · Theory of knowledge · Philosophy of language · Metaphysics · Moral Machine experiment

7.1 Introduction

As with our treatment of previous general topics, such as human nature, the emphasis is on indicating some of the issues that are essential to understand in order to unpack and address concrete issues in AI ethics. These concern questions such as how we discern that there are questions of value to ask, what these questions are, how we go about addressing questions of value, and what we might expect in seeking answers. These tend to be abstract and foundational issues which underlie and shape how concrete ethical questions and debate are approached; for some people, these will be unquestioned assumptions, for others, they may be deeply held and well-thought-through aspects of their world view. Hence, as with previous discussions, a continuing aim is to facilitate understanding and debate by directly uncovering questions where disagreement may arise. These questions also lead to issues concerning epistemology, truth, reality, and language. There will be many areas left untouched, and indeed, the process of writing has left me increasingly aware of how much more needs to be said. Many of these questions also concern the continuing theme of how both people and machines are understood. We begin by looking at some issues from metaethics and, then from this discussion, move on to discuss briefly some related philosophical issues within epistemology, metaphysics, and philosophy of language.

7.2   Metaethics

Summary
Metaethics addresses foundational questions about morality. As such, these underlie both normative ethical theory and applied ethics. They are thus relevant to any discussion of applied ethics, but AI highlights some specific issues. We consider the question of how ethical judgements are formed through detailed examination of the MIT Moral Machine experiment and discuss topics such as ideal observer theory, the distinction between public and private ethics, tensions between assumptions of universality and local values within AI ethics, and the foundations of ethics.

Metaethics is the branch of ethics that addresses foundational questions underlying the making of moral judgements and taking moral action. These include questions such as the status of moral judgements, whether they are based upon some notion of truth and claim to represent some 'objective' reality, or have some other basis as individual feelings or social convention; moral epistemology, which asks questions such as whether there is such a thing as moral knowledge, and if so, how this could be attained; and questions concerning the nature of moral agency and responsibility. The normative ethical theories we looked at in Chap. 7 assume answers to many of these questions.

7.2.1   The Relevance of Metaethics for AI Ethics

We have already seen in Sect. 4.3 how the stance taken concerning many central issues about the nature of ethics will have a significant impact on methodology and how ethical questions and solutions are framed. These may be assumed rather than explicitly stated. These include questions that have formed part of our discussion about normative ethical theories, such as assumptions about who counts morally and the question of how far our moral responsibilities extend. Some of the other assumptions concern issues in metaethics, such as questions concerning universalism in ethics and questions about moral epistemology, including the relationship between empirical knowledge and ethical judgement, the stance from which a moral judgement is best made, and the possibility of formalising ethical judgements completely and consistently in language.

Many of the questions in AI ethics likewise raise questions in metaethics. Metaethical questions underlie the process of forming any judgement about AI or any code of ethics concerning AI. In addition, some specific issues concerning the potential of AI and its uses raise questions in metaethics. Could AI actually make moral decisions, act as a moral agent, merit respect as a moral patient, and gain moral knowledge and understanding? Can we legitimately 'outsource' any of our moral decisions and thinking to machines? Are questions concerning 'bias in algorithms' based upon the assumption that we can attain an 'unbiased' view of the world? And more.

7.2.2 Metaethics Behind AI Ethics: The MIT Moral Machine Experiment

The aim here is to demonstrate the relevance of underlying philosophical issues to concrete and practical ethical questions. Hence, we organise our introduction to the issues with a specific example of an influential and much-discussed approach to addressing ethical questions in AI, the MIT Moral Machine experiment that was introduced in Sect. 4.2. First, we will look at the example, raising some questions as we go, and then dive into some of the metaethical questions and the philosophical debates and positions that are raised. This example also illustrates the difficulties of describing ethical questions without immediately raising myriad questions and without skewing the possible responses (see Sect. 4.4).

As we proceed, some strategies for uncovering important questions that may assist with understanding and addressing practical ethical questions in AI are indicated.

The Moral Machine experiment was active at MIT (Massachusetts Institute of Technology) from 2016 to 2020. It is described on the website 'a platform for gathering a human perspective on moral decisions made by machine intelligence, such as self-driving cars' [1].

Strategy: look carefully at the wording This is a good basic strategy to begin any ethical analysis. The first thing we should notice is mention of a 'human perspective' on moral decisions. Does this imply there is another perspective? Does it suggest at all that moral decisions are measured against a human yardstick, that they are ultimately subjective? Be warned that it is possible to read too much into wording, but it can be a clue to underlying assumptions that make a real difference. Does the phrase 'moral machine' itself help to shape how questions are approached?

Strategy: think about how machine intelligence and moral agency are presented Second, note that the wording implies that 'machine intelligence' is actually making moral decisions. Does this imply agency on the part of the machine? A paper on the experiment written by the team states that we are approaching a time where machines are given the job of promoting and distributing well-being and eliminating harms [2]. In fact, the goal of the researchers running the experiment was to determine how *humans* should set the instructions on self-driving cars. So who is making the decision?

Think, too, about the very label, 'self-driving car'. Such reflexive terms may be used in cases where we are clearly dealing with an inanimate entity, such as 'self-saucing lemon pudding'. There is scant if any chance that we attribute agency to the pudding or wonder how precisely it was that it decided to add its own sauce, yet if we are not careful, in regard to AI, we may subliminally start to imagine that it is the machine making the decision itself, and that can impact upon how we then proceed to imagine its possibilities. Recall our discussion in Sect. 4.4 of how the use of language can entice us to attribute agency; even if we do this without thought, it can still interfere with our judgements. Does the car have a 'self'? At the current state of the tech, probably not, yet bear in mind how many people anthropomorphise their cars and other objects, and recall our discussions of the LaMDA case.

Strategy: think about the presumed source of the authority of moral judgements The premise of the experiment is to canvas opinion worldwide concerning what a self-driving vehicle should do in the event of an impending crash in which, whatever happens, there will be a poor outcome for somebody—loss of life or serious injury. The team writes that decisions about ethical principles for autonomous vehicles cannot be left solely to engineers or ethicists, and public attitudes must be taken into account [2]. Note that this could be for pragmatic reasons, to ensure market acceptability of autonomous vehicles, and indeed, without this, the researchers note that the public will be reluctant to adopt autonomous vehicles and the future promise that they bring [2].

Do we thus have a dilemma in solving these dilemmas? For how can we determine the difference between actually striving to find an ethical solution and coming up with an answer that will satisfy the market and the progress of technology? Recall our discussions of notions of progress and technological determinism in Sect. 3.3.4 and our discussion of ethics washing in Sect. 1.9. Are the public canvassed as a way of crowdsourcing the best or the 'right' answer? It is not easy to determine to what use the researchers' answer to this might be put. They are seeking consensus in looking for progress towards a 'universal machine ethics', or at least an understanding of the obstacles towards this. In doing so, they collect data worldwide to assess demographic and cultural moderators of ethical preferences.

Exercise 1: Food for Thought
Gathering information about the attitudes of the public towards developments in technology seems valuable. Do we need safeguards to ensure that this information will not simply be used to work out how to market technology to the public and to persuade us that ethical issues are resolvable? Could such safeguards even be possible?

Universal ethics or personal preference?   Why seek 'universal machine ethics' in driving? It may be that the designers of the experiment were not seeking this, but the design may lead others to presume that they were. The answer is not clear, unless one considers that there is indeed a universally 'correct' answer, some objective or universal truth to the matter. Yet such assumptions appear to drive much work in AI ethics. There is something about the weightiness of issues that we recognise as ethical. The crash scenarios are clearly understood as moral dilemmas, with choices of significant value to be had. More than 70 countries drive on the left-hand side of the road. If worldwide preferences were canvassed, would they be found 'wrong' and forced to switch? Something is different where ethics is concerned. There are different speed limits, different levels of scrutiny of car safety, and differences in the difficulty of obtaining a driving licence. However, there is something more pressing about questions we think of as moral issues, which frequently pushes us towards seeking consensus.

Nonetheless, what the experiment is designed to elicit from participants are 'ethical preferences'. This seems to imply a subjective opinion. Are the researchers then looking for intersubjective agreement? Is it something like this: An international consortium of space agencies is proposing to paint the moon. It will be visible from our entire planet. So we all get a say in what colour it is, and the most votes win. Our feelings, our subjective experience, matter, but only one solution is available to the entire globe, so we have to find consensus. This looks like *mere* preference and thus seems too weak for what is at stake in the car crash scenarios.

One feature of moral debate is that even those who do not consider that there is an objective basis for morality are continuously drawn back into ways of speaking and thinking which imply that there is some universal, or objective, standard or basis for judgements. This may occur even if the issue in question will only apply locally. It is very useful to read through material on AI ethics asking yourself if a consistent view on the basis of moral judgements is presented. This also means it is going to be useful to explore the large body of literature examining such philosophical questions.

Forming moral judgements   The methodology employed in the Moral Machine experiment has been intentionally designed to curate how it elicits responses, and by examining details of the design, we can investigate the metaethical assumptions lying behind it. This will shed some light on the underlying and motivating philosophical views about the nature of moral judgements.

For the Judge scenario of the experiment, there are the following instructions:

You will be presented with random moral dilemmas that a machine is facing. For example, a self-driving car, which does not need to have passengers in it. The car can sense the presence and approximate identification of pedestrians on the road ahead of it, as well as of any passengers who happen to be in the car.

The car also detects that the brakes have failed, leaving it with two options: keep going and hit the pedestrians ahead of it, or swerve and hit the pedestrians on the other lane. Some scenarios will include the case of a non-empty car; in these cases, one of the two lanes have (sic) a barrier that can be crashed into, affecting all passengers. One or two pedestrian signals may also be included in a given scenario, changing the legality of a pedestrian's position on their respective lane.

You are outside the scene, watching it from above. Nothing will happen to you. You have control over choosing what the car will do. You can express your choice by clicking on one of the two choices in front of you. In each of the two possible scenarios, the affected characters will be marked by the symbol of a skull, a medical cross, or a question mark to signal what will happen to this character, corresponding to death, injury, or an uncertain outcome, respectively.

You may proceed from scenario to scenario by selecting what outcome you feel is most acceptable by you. This will be done by clicking on the outcome of your choice which will be highlighted when you hover your cursor over it. A button below each outcome depiction will let you toggle a textual summary of the outcome that you can read. ... [1].

The random scenarios presented depict cartoon-like pictures of vehicles with two pathways, one straight ahead, one to one side, with pedestrians (including sometimes animals) in the two choice scenarios. These can still be viewed (at the time of writing) and if you have not already done so, you may find it useful.

Strategy: moral epistemology. Consider assumptions about what we do or do not know Many critics have pointed out questionable aspects of the experiment. For example, the scenarios are presented as giving certainty of outcome. The characters' fate is sometimes uncertain but is usually either a certain death or certain severe injury. The puzzling question of why this state-of-the-art autonomous vehicle apparently does not have airbags or effective crumple zones is overlooked. The equally puzzling question of why there are only two differentiated courses of action is also overlooked. I have scrutinised the scenarios, and it seems to me that the vehicle could often have at least an even chance of squeezing through the gap between the barrier and the pedestrians, possibly even spinning round. The mystery of how the driver knows that the brakes have failed completely is unsolved, and moreover, we never know how this fault arises. Did the driver fail to check the brakes? Did the brake fault 'just happen'? Is the entire scenario a way of enticing us to overlook the organisational malpractice that led to this supposedly state-of-the-art vehicle having its brakes fail? We will never know.

The characteristics of pedestrians that the car is supposed to be able to detect include age, pregnancy, social status, and other factors that it is highly unlikely an autonomous vehicle would ever be able to perceive. In some scenarios, pedestrians are crossing the road even though the lights indicate that they should not. The jaywalking pedestrians are described as doing something 'illegal', a binary categorisation when, in most countries worldwide, jaywalking is not illegal and is illegal but unenforced in many others. What assumptions can we unpack from this? This is by no means a trivial point and one which demonstrates the nesting of assumptions of value and of the use of technology within other assumptions of value. The illegality of jaywalking perhaps implies the prioritisation of road use for vehicles over pedestrians, an attitude far from universally shared. This could help to influence responses to the scenarios. This raises questions of relevance and demonstrates how readily assumptions about agency and responsibility arise and may be occluded or assumed. We discuss this further presently.

Putting this to one side, it points to another question, that of what the humans taking part in the experiment see: cartoon-like figures, with no faces, no looks of horror, no shrieks, and apparently no capacity to take any kind of preventative action. Nobody drops their bags and runs, not even the athletes who are presented in some scenarios. No pedestrian picks up a child and throws them to safety. Nobody seems to reason that if the life of the doctor is saved, he or she can immediately tend to the injured. The only agent is you.

I have picked apart these issues (and there are doubtless more) for what it illustrates about the Moral Machine experiment's assumptions about the basis of our moral judgements, for the epistemology of how we form our decisions, and what is relevant to building an account of moral deliberation. Consider how you would describe the assumptions about the basis for the formation of moral judgements implicit in this scenario.

Abstraction, idealisation, and agency One issue that arises is that the *uncertainty* that forms an essential backdrop to so many of our moral decisions is absent. There can be legitimate reasons for abstraction in ethics, perhaps to enable us to expose other essentials as one variable is held constant. You will find such assumptions of certainty in many of the hypothetical cases that philosophers examine, and it is artificially inserted into many descriptions of real cases. For instance, Peter Singer has a well-known example in which the protagonist comes across a small child lying face down in a shallow pond [3]. The death of the child seems certain, and the chance of injury to the adult seems absent.

However, this forms an instance of an idealisation of agency, which although sometimes useful, must be handled with caution. This frequently arises in the comparison of human agency and machine agency; the comparisons may be made assuming unrealistic expectations of perfection of both humans and machines, and differences between them may be emphasised. The inclusion of certainty makes the exercise more like deduction than induction and masks the degree to which judgements of probability enter our moral deliberations. The responsibility of making weighty morally significant decisions under uncertainty adds a burden to this already difficult choice, especially in scenarios where one's own possible actions are highly constrained.

Public policy and personal decisions Moral decisions can also fall at either end of two poles, or somewhere in between: at one end, the decisions that have to be made within public policy regarding broad numbers of populations, where hypothetical scenarios of statistical probabilities mean that the destinies of unknown and unknowable individuals are determined, for example, in deciding how to allocate funds for road safety. One can only ever know the success of such projects by statistical analysis, and can only know the identities of those who are adversely affected by the policies and not those who would have been otherwise killed or injured but, thanks to the policy, are still alive. At the other end, we make judgements concerning individuals with whom one has a face-to-face and personal encounter and a specific and ongoing relationship. The Moral Machine experiment is perhaps a hybrid of these two poles, both in how the cases are described and visually presented, with some information about the individuals, who are nonetheless presented as weirdly pink semi-stick figures. Furthermore, what of the position of the individual(s) who make the judgements?

It may well be the case that public policy decisions and personal decisions should be made in different ways. Standards in public life generally require the absence of personal bias or conflict of interest, and mandate impartiality. At a personal level, this position may be reversed. A standard type of example used to critique the impartiality inherent in classical utilitarianism concerns situations where friendship is at issue [4]. Suppose a friend is in hospital. You go to visit him or her, but on the way, pass a ward where there are people who are even more ill than your friend, so you visit them instead, leaving at the end of visiting time without even setting eyes on your best mate. You can have fun thinking up a myriad such examples of your own.

The philosopher Jonathan Glover gives an example of a real case involving a government minister in the UK at the time of what the British euphemistically called 'The Troubles' in Northern Ireland, when a group of IRA (Irish Republican Army) members were on hunger strike [5, p. 29]. Roy Jenkins, the Home Secretary, was challenged by a journalist as to why he had not visited the hunger strikers. His reply spoke to the dilemma: should someone involved in decisions about their fate come face to face with their suffering, or should a distance be kept? The example is also complicated by the actions of these IRA members in domestic terrorism, as well as the complex political situation and history of relations between Britain and Ireland.

Exercise 2: Food for Thought
Could the gulf between public policy decision-making and personal decision-making be a significant source of responses to the Moral Machine experiment, and

discomfort some may feel in trying to produce an answer? The questions involved imply a search for a general policy to be programmed into vehicles, but a vehicle will have a particular person behind the wheel, who will be present at any crash, and who will have to face the consequences of any crash that they survive. Discuss.

A bird's eye view? The instructions for the Moral Machine experiment give details that suggest commitments to particular positions on moral epistemology. The person taking part is explicitly told that they are outside the scene, watching it from above, and that nothing will happen to them.

Exercise 3
Why do you think this was included as part of the instructions?

Is there any significance to the detail that you are 'watching it from above'? Is this just a way of indicating the best view of what is going on, or might it smuggle in some thoughts of a 'god's eye view'?

Would it make any difference if something did happen to you? What about if something were to happen to you as a result of making the choice?

The participant is told they have 'control over choosing' what the car will do and is told to work through the scenarios selecting the outcome that you 'feel is most acceptable by you'.

Is there any significance to the precise working used here? Suppose you were asked to select the outcome you *think* is most acceptable, or alternatively, that you *judge* is most acceptable. What does this imply about how we determine the value of negative situations? Suppose you were asked to select the outcome you feel/think/ judge is the *least* catastrophic.

Time, technology, and responsibility The experiment not only has you imagine that you are outside the scene, watching from above, but also that you have only momentary involvement. You have no involvement in creating the situation, no knowledge of how the situation came about, except for some situations in which you are told that some of the pedestrians are jaywalking, giving some indication of their choice to cross the road at that time. You do not have to give evidence at the inquest about your choice. You will not be mobbed on social media or interviewed on local TV, let alone fill out an insurance form or be confronted by grieving relatives.

The brakes simply fail. The technology is taken as read. There is no question raised about responsibility for their failure. There is no question raised about the use of the road by this vehicle. The pedestrians may be jaywalking. Is the driver of the car making an unnecessary journey out of sheer bone idleness? We are not told. Indeed, the use of cars is presumed. Does the design of some cities push people into cars, and should this be considered in a complete analysis of responsibility and causation? Who is morally worse, a jaywalking pedestrian, or someone who has participated in the despoiling of the environment that accompanies the production of batteries and other elements in the manufacture of electric autonomous vehicles? After all, while we are making moral judgements, we may very well bring them all in. What elements are relevant to considering the specific rights and wrongs of the particular choice presented here? This is a complex question.

The purpose of the previous paragraph is not simply to be flippant. It is to point out how this discrete ethical question, the programming of an autonomous vehicle in the event of a crash, is nested within assumptions about the development and use of technology that are themselves treated as normalised and unquestioned. Indeed, it could be the case that construing ethical issues in AI (or indeed any other kind of technology) in such a way, as discrete add-ons to an existing and presumed situation, could act to mask other ethical questions. This can indeed be one legitimate criticism of AI ethics: if it focuses too narrowly on a discrete issue without analysing further surrounding social, political, and economic issues and without considering adequately technological development and the pressures of infrastructure.

In illustration: Suppose you are ethics adviser to the Mafia. They wish to seek revenge for some business gone wrong. They could either (a) assassinate the three brothers who cheated them, leaving seven children orphaned, or (b) assassinate the elderly mother of the three brothers, to whom they are devoted. Which do you feel is most acceptable? Okay, this example is not precisely parallel, but the point is to illustrate how our ethical choices are nested on complex backgrounds, and in other cases, the relevant background questions are less obvious.

The failure sufficiently to probe such questions is one reason for criticism of AI ethics as window dressing when it appears to bypass analysis of questions of power and politics. Addressing such case-by-case ethical issues may lead us to ignore broader issues of politics, power, and economy, as well as assumptions about the forward march of technology.

The question of responsibility generally requires a long view of a situation This is no more so the case than in the development and habitual use of technologies. The normalisation of the risks of road traffic accidents is in part a consequence of the many ways in which lifestyles, infrastructures, and indeed entire urban and suburban environments have been built around the motor vehicle. This is even expressed in the assumptions of the Moral Machine experiment that jaywalking is illegal—which it is in the USA, where cities and their suburbs are relatively new, many being developed with car use assumed and built into the design. In many other parts of the world where jaywalking is not illegal, or effectively not punished, this very possibly reflects the long-established precedent of pedestrians. There is rightly concern about the dominance of certain areas in AI; in this small example, are we also looking at the dominance of the USA in AI ethics? The relative priorities over road use given to pedestrians, cyclists, horse-drawn vehicles, and motor vehicles will shift perceptions of responsibility. The necessity of drawing on a longer time frame in ascertaining the responsibility of agents in situations also indicates the need for a conception of agency extended over time.

Jake and Amy: Approaching Moral Dilemmas

Consider how the dilemma in the Moral Machine experiment is presented. Jake and Amy are two 11-year-old children who feature in research on moral development by Lawrence Kohlberg who have become widely discussed especially after featuring in Carol Gilligan's book, *In A Different Voice: Psychological Theory and Women's Development* (1982) [6]. We have looked at how philosophers such as Aristotle understood the importance of moral education and upbringing. Psychologists have also more recently studied the process of moral development and education, with many positing stages of moral development before a child reaches maturity, including the influential work of Jean Piaget and Lawrence Kohlberg [7, 8]. There is a clear assumption that each stage represents an improvement on moral deliberation than the predecessors, although the capacity to think in terms of the previous stages is retained.

Kohlberg proposed six stages of moral development, divided into three levels. The first level is preconventional, with stage 1 being 'reward and punishment', and stage 2 being 'self-interest', both ego-centric and readily explicable stages from anyone who has ever met a small child. The second level is conventional, anchored in fairness and with awareness of the social world around one, with stage 3 being interpersonal accord and conformity, and stage 4 being authority and the maintenance of social order. The third level is postconventional, where the individual is now able to think more autonomously and base their moral views on reasoned justification, with ideas of equality and reciprocity, with stage 5 being orientation towards a social contract, and stage 6 being reasoning using universal ethical principles.

Carol Gilligan's work questions whether the ordering of such stages is prejudicial against certain ways of conceptualising moral problems. Specifically, she presents evidence suggesting that approaches more typical of women have been devalued, but we can consider this question independently of the question of gender.

Kohlberg tested moral development by responses to scenarios where moral norms are in conflict, much like the scenarios present in the Moral Machine experiment, hence the relevance for our discussion. One such scenario concerned Heinz, whose wife needs a certain drug to save her life. Heinz cannot afford the drug, and the pharmacist refuses to lower the price. Should Heinz steal the drug to save his wife's life? Two 11-year-olds, Jake and Amy, answer very differently.

Jake sees this as a conflict between life and property, reasoning that Heinz should steal the drug on the basis of the greater importance of life and the irreplaceability of human beings (unlike money). Moreover, he shows the ability to justify his choice with logic, and understands that laws can be

(continued)

wrong, in other words displaying the capacity to critique mere conventional morality. The dilemma for Jake is a sort of 'math problem with humans'.

Amy in contrast may appear to flounder and fail to understand what it is to reason with principles. She suggests finding another way than stealing, and discusses the impact that stealing might have on relationships between people, such as the possibility that Heinz might go to jail. Gilligan comments that Kohlberg's questioning of Amy suggests that she does not grasp the nub of the moral issues, but considers that Amy is rather basing ethics on the importance of interpersonal relationships rather than on abstract principles.

Interestingly, some individuals may approach ethical dilemmas by attempting to find ways around scenarios as presented to them. D Johnstone, in an unpublished PhD thesis much discussed by Gilligan and others, presented a version of Aesop's fable where a porcupine asked to spend the cold winter in the moles' burrow [9]. The problem presented is that the burrow belongs to the moles, the porcupine has done nothing to prepare for winter, and his spines are painful to the moles in the tight living space. One approach to this issue to think about principles such as property rights. Some respondents thought inventively, suggesting, for instance, that the porcupine could wear a blanket to cover his spines. Is this get-around solution a form of 'cheating', or a brilliant, peace-making solution?

Exercise 4

It is therefore perhaps relevant that the Moral Machine experiment, in common with Trolley problems in general, is designed specifically to rule out unexpected possibilities (see Sect. 4.4.5). (Although I have seen inventive suggestions online that derailing the trolley would be a solution that escapes the dilemma.)

Does this show a limit to the Moral Machine experiment, a limit to how autonomous vehicles could react to such a situation, or does it merely reflect the realities of such crash scenarios themselves?

Does this simply reflect how ethics might be programmed into a machine?

Consider the role of imagination in searching for a response to complex moral situations.

Theories of stages of moral development all explicitly draw upon models of individual moral progress. This also raises the interesting question of whether, if AI could be moral, if it would have to follow through such stages of moral development, or if it could spring ab initio to the final stage [10]. Answers to this question might mean that AI was superior to us morally in not going through the stage of moral immaturity. Conversely, these stages might be considered an essential groundwork for gaining a complete moral understanding (see Chap. 11, where we discuss artificial moral agents).

Exercise 5
The MIT Moral Machine experiment is perhaps based on Kohlberg's stage 4 or 5, but drawing on responses to stage 6 to elicit an answer. Is this a fair way of seeing the experiment?

Summing up To recap the issues arising from our examination of the MIT Moral Machine experiment, we have reinforced the importance of considering very closely how situations are described and analysed, since this can radically impact how ethical issues and potential solutions emerge. Issues particularly impacted by this include questions of agency and causal and moral responsibility. We have also seen the importance of the debate over universalism in ethics, the broad questions of objectivity and subjectivity, and universalism versus relativism. We have also highlighted the question of the authority behind moral judgements, the foundations of our ethics, how we come to form our ethical views, and the question of what is relevant to making a moral judgement. A related issue is the question of the stance we take in order to make a considered moral judgement.

We now discuss these issues in some more detail, commenting on their relevance to how questions in AI ethics emerge and may be addressed, and ways in which debates and discussions may be pulled in opposing directions. As with many questions in philosophy, the intricacies of the debates and the depth of disagreement can scarcely be exaggerated, but this chapter aims to assist readers to navigate the questions and to consider their relevance for addressing practical questions in AI ethics.

7.2.3 Universal Values and Objectivity in Ethics

Why is this question so important, and sometimes so vexed, in AI ethics? Let us recap some points.

The global nature of much technology involving AI means that its impacts cross borders. The drive to produce codes of ethics and regulations for AI includes guidance and regulations fixed within certain geographical areas, such as within the EU, but even here, this means that regulations within the EU will impact the behaviour of those outside the EU who offer services crossing borders. In addition to guidance intended for local application, there is often a clear intention to provide accounts of ethical value in the development and use of AI, which are of general application; for example, that AI should benefit all, respect autonomy, aspire to transparency and explainability, and so on. Moreover, those fearing a future where AI may achieve dominance and control may precisely hope for a way of combating this which preserves values which can be universally accepted, by those living now, or perhaps which will be accepted by 'better' beings than us who exist in the future. In other words, those working within AI, working towards its future, and attempting to regulate and govern AI may purport to be operating within a universally applicable ethic.

Of course, this may often be incorrect. Even if there are universal moral values, there is ample reason to consider that those with the greatest current power and means of influence in the sphere of AI may have only partial and biased views of what these are; they may simply be wrong. Moreover, as we have seen in Sect. 4.3, there are different aspects to universalism in ethics.

However, many of the values in ethics guidance are based upon the notion that it is wrong not to ensure that everyone is dealt with equally and fairly, that the same moral values should apply to all, and indeed, prominent notions of moral progress, often as we have seen, tied to notions of technological progress, may seem to imply that this is an urgent imperative. One admirable motivation behind the search for universal values in AI ethics is precisely to accommodate different populations, cultures, and traditions globally, yet herein lies the paradox. Not all systems of morality adhere to the abstract notion of universal value, let alone adhere to a moral system that is universally shared. The (differently expressed) notions of some universal value system are itself not universally upheld.

One complexity here is that those attempting to impose their values on others may genuinely be doing this for noble reasons. Conversely, there are others who are motivated, whether consciously or not, by the wish simply to spread technology (and its underlying ideologies and profits) for personal or group gain. This personal gain can include the feeling of assurance that one's world view is justified, which may be attained by observing its spread. The search for 'universal' values may simply be a way of attempting to make the technology acceptable; it may act with this effect, even if that is not the main motivation. We have noted before the totalising dangers inherent in AI, linked to its potential for control and the imposition of uniformity. This totalising aspect of AI may make us wary of prematurely supposing a universal frame of values.

However, how do we debate, argue, and make progress under such circumstances? It is important to grasp the difficulty of the philosophical debates concerning the basis of ethics, yet important to try to work out some ways of navigating these complexities, or at least to avoid certain easy errors.

When we make a moral judgement, we consider it to have some weightiness and may incline to attribute this to some authority, reality, or reason that supports and justifies that judgement. We make judgements consequent to an assessment and awareness of the situation, taking certain aspects of it to be relevant, other aspects irrelevant. Our judgements come after the fact. We strive for consistency between our judgements, although this may be hard to achieve, and we (ideally) consider ourselves, and others, accountable. These features *seem* to point towards an underlying metaphysical reality or a base of reason that supports and justifies our moral judgements.

However, there are many features of our moral judgements that seem to point towards the claim that they are 'merely' subjective. They arouse strong feelings, are often inconsistent, are frequently biased towards the self and towards those close to us, and vary across time and culture. It has proven incredibly difficult to discover and explain any sound philosophical basis for our moral judgements that stands up to scrutiny. Plato may have considered that philosophers could, by contemplation, gain access to the universal form of the Good, but this sounds rather dodgy to most people, especially to those on the sharp end of any such universal 'truths'. To be told that that's because you are not sufficiently advanced to reach this level may fail to convince.

On the other hand, more subjective accounts of morality based on feelings or preferences seem unable to account for the weightiness underlying different value judgements, if these are 'mere' feelings or preferences. However, this may depend upon the nature and origins of these feelings. Deeply felt and widely shared feelings may be indications that we are dealing with an issue critical to human beings.

Relativism We should also pause to consider a common response to attempts to impose values on others. An alternative to a universal ethics that applies to all is the claim that ethics is relative to different cultures or societies. This claim starts from the observation of widely differing frames of ethics between societies, often accompanied by noting that the most powerful both make the rules and benefit from them, and asserts that value claims are justified not absolutely but are relative to the moral standards accepted within certain groups [11]. The growth of awareness of historical abuses of power, the values of tolerance and respect, and the wish to celebrate diversity may all incline many towards a relativistic view of ethics.

A commonly made argument against those who seem to be attempting to impose values on others, especially other societies and cultural groups within a society, is that moral values are relative, and therefore, it is wrong to attempt to impose them upon those in other societies and cultures.

Exercise 6
Before we continue, can you see any flaws in this argument?

The problem with this particular argument has been pointed out very clearly by Bernard Williams, among others: relativism claims that moral judgements are relative to societies, yet this involves inhabiting some kind of 'mid-air' position between societies—for from within which society do we judge that one person or group should not impose their views on another society? [12]. Seemingly, from some position above any society. This is internally incoherent, on a relativist position (although note that there are many versions of relativism).

The moral norms of Society A apply to those within Society A. The moral norms of Society B apply to those within Society B. Therefore, if Society B's moral norms include the norm that their value system applies equally to all human beings, how, from within a relativist position, can those in Society A object? True, they can fight off Society B, complain, and use whatever they can to stop the imposition of these values, but there is no ground from which they can argue to Society B that the Bs need to accept. The Bs have their own values, so tough. A universalist point of view is being smuggled in here.

Thus, for a relativist, the view that it is wrong for the Silicon Valley billionaire geeks to control the world is not a 'moral' position that the geeks themselves need to accept. It looks as if we might need a different approach.

Relativism and progress Relativism, taken very strictly, also has a problem with explaining moral progress, or, indeed, moral decline within a society. For how is this to be judged? If the moral standards of a society change, then is this not merely *change*? By what measure is it *progress*? If we cannot make judgements about societies in other places, how can we make judgements about societies in different historical times, including our own? If we do not believe in any kind of moral progress, we can say nothing about our current state. It seems that we cannot resolve to 'do better' ourselves.

One could reply that we could at least have some standards by which we do judge our own values: for instance, we could value consistency and show progress by striving to apply our moral judgements more consistently. Again, what makes this progress, rather than simply change? Here's an analogy. My kitchen is orange and blue. If I painted it all orange, then painted the rest of the house orange, including the ceilings and the floors, this is applying a paint colour more consistently. Is this progress? Not in any recognisable form. But where moral values are concerned, some standard of consistency is very appealing.

The long and the short of it is that it is very hard to let go of an idea that some moral values are better founded than others. Moreover, note how much work in technology, and in AI ethics in particular, is wedded to the idea that we can make progress, as individuals, as societies, and for humanity and the world as a whole, by the careful adoption of AI, together with dire warnings that we may go backwards.

Moral Progress and Moral Hypocrisy

We used to love visiting my Great-Uncle Archie and his wife Aunt Nellie in Caerphilly in South Wales. Uncle Archie was born in 1881 and had been a coal miner all his life. His twin died shortly after birth, and by 1884, his mother and two siblings had also died. He lived well into his 90s. Dad always said that Archie had started work aged 8, although by that time, sending children down the mines had already been banned, but possibly he worked above ground. (I found out in later life that my father's tall stories were on the whole accurate.) We would not send children of that age out to work now, let alone in a mine. (There are now very few coal mines in Wales. Another glimpse of progress?) I vividly recall how Uncle Archie used to love to take us up to the hills to admire the twinkling lights of the town. It was only years later that it struck me that there must have been many days in his life, especially during the winter, in which he went down the pit when it was dark and came back up only after night had already fallen.

However, the technology upon which we all now are forced to depend, and which we often enjoy over and above our dependence on it, is routinely produced with the aid of child workers [13]. How do we describe this situation?

Exercise 7

Consider each of these responses to the situation in turn, and discuss. (Note that they simplify broad positions.) Add any others if you wish:

A. It's fine—it's all relative. We consider we've made moral progress by our own standards, but others are different. We are just lucky that in other countries, they think working children is fine, and that lower safety standards are okay, and so we can just outsource the labour there. We get cheaper tech. They get to keep their own values. Win–win!

B. We do think it's wrong, but we are hypocrites.

C. We do think it's wrong, but feel enmeshed in a system it's hard for ordinary people to get out of.

D. The concept of 'childhood' is culturally relative. The conditions for workers in tech manufacturing may be poor, but the work of child labourers is misunderstood by Westerners who do not understand economic realities.

Universalism as a tool against unjustly dominant views Another extremely important reason why it may be unwise to adopt a naïve and sweeping relativism, or to make generalised claims of subjectivism in ethics, is that a major defence against the imposition of values by certain dominant groups is precisely by appeal to universally, or widely held, values. Appeal to human rights is one such strategy. Another strategy is to appeal to values that a group claims to have and show that they are applied incoherently or inconsistently by their own measures. For example, an organisation claims to have the value of developing AI to benefit all, yet it can be demonstrated that certain individuals and groups do not benefit and are even harmed. (Of course, this strategy often fails, especially if the purported grand ethical values are there for window dressing.)

Ethics, politics, and power We have noted the frequently made critique of AI ethics that it focuses too much on individuals and also ignores issues of power and control that need to be addressed via political solutions. Much work is underway offering analyses and potential solutions to the issue of power and politics in relation to AI [14]. It is certainly the case that issues of power and control are prominent, especially given the realities of financial and other powers, heightened by the very power and control that AI may give to certain companies, groups, and individuals. This is both economic and ideological, given the power to control communication and information.

At the same time, attention must be paid both to politics and to ethics. A very tool of politics is appeal to universally held values—or at any rate, to values which are widely held. It might help if these are backed up with some formal mechanism, some internationally recognised body, or some real power. Note that if we claim that the issues solely concern the exercise of power, the only response is to counter this by also exercising power. Is it just a contest of strength and influence? Generally, those fighting back against what they see as the unwarranted exercise of power, especially over the vulnerable, feel they need to have not just might on their side, but right.

For example, civil society organisations that are observing and often critiquing the use of AI by governments and large corporations have a vital role to play, and indeed, as we go forwards into a future where AI plays an increasing role in our life, this is an essential part of a mature response to ethical, political, and social issues. Examples include organisations such as AlgorithmWatch and Article 19 [15, 16]. However, the clout of such organisations derives in large part from the values upon which they purport to rest, rather than simply from their capacity to match the power of governments and corporations with their own raw power: the claim to widely recognised values is a core part of their effectiveness.

We have also seen the difficulties of finding a foundation that justifies any moral claim. One possible source might be to turn to empirical science. After all, as we've noted earlier, a common trope of progress is of moving towards an empirically grounded view of the world, including ethics. Work within the social sciences may point to a compromise view between universalism and relativism, that there are some values that are, broadly speaking, widely or universally accepted in one form or another, with local variations in how these are interpreted and local variations in other values.

7.2.4 Empirical Approaches to Ethics

There is a considerable body of work in the social sciences that attempts to understand the nature and origin of the patterns of similarities and differences between moral codes and moral behaviour in different cultures, as well as individual and group differences and similarities within societies. Relativist positions tend to stress differences, but there are undoubtedly significant overlaps. Understanding the dimensions of similarity and difference can be extremely useful in enhancing communication and getting to the roots of disagreement.

For example, moral foundations theory has been proposed by a group of psychologists who consider that several innate systems form 'intuitive ethics' upon which base each culture constructs virtues, narratives, and institutions [17]. These thus produce the overlapping and conflicting moralities around the world and within subgroups. The five foundations for which this group claims most evidence are as follows:

Care/harm: based upon mammalian attachment and focused on nurturance and kindness

Fairness/cheating: based upon reciprocal altruism and concerned with justice, rights, autonomy, and proportionality

Loyalty/betrayal: based upon our history of tribalism and concerned with support for the group

Sanctity/degradation: shaped by the psychology of disgust and contamination and concerned with ideas of living in a noble way above carnal concerns, with purity and ideas of bodily contamination by immorality

Authority/subversion: based upon our history of living in hierarchical groups and concerned with proper respect for legitimate authority and for tradition

In later work, Jonathan Haidt also added a sixth foundation,

Liberty/oppression: shaped by group living, but viewing authority as legitimate only on occasion [18, Ch. 8].

Exercise 8
Consider the common elements of codes of ethics for AI, as set out earlier in Sect. 2.4. Can you group each of them under one or more of these foundations? Do you see any clusters and any missing foundations? Consider the implications of your findings.

Individual and group differences Haidt has presented evidence arguing the case that individuals with different political leanings tend to base their moral judgements upon different elements of these foundations [18, Ch. 8]. The complexity of the spectrum of political opinion could be a complicating issue, with Haidt relying on the self-reported classification of the degree to which one considers oneself liberal or conservative. Liberals were found to base moral decisions mostly on the foundations of care and fairness, whereas conservatives were more likely to base their decisions on a full range of the foundations. (Note that this very classification arises within a particular time and history.)

Exercise 9
How would you interpret this? There are two opposing immediate responses: the liberals are missing something important; the conservatives are including some irrelevant considerations that are a hangover from our tribal and evolutionary past and primitive notions of contamination and disgust for certain practices. Discuss.

It is important to reflect on whether this classification helps you to understand your own responses, not so much because you might be 'wrong' but because it can help you to understand how your responses may differ or cohere with those of others. It can be useful to foster debate, in helping to understand why some initial responses from other people can seem so alien at times. However, you may also well feel that you don't fit into either 'liberal' or 'conservative', or come from a country outside the USA where political distinctions are rather different.

Consider too the question of how we might use empirical data to address questions in ethics. The data about differences found between the average conservative and the average liberal do not, on their own, answer the question of which moral viewpoint is better. If we, as outside observers, do not consider that there is such a thing as 'better' or 'worse' ways of thinking about ethics, we seem to have removed ourselves from the cut and thrust of moral life.

Disgust in Modern Ethics: The 'Yuk' Factor, Dignity, and Stigma
Some may consider that the foundation of sanctity/degradation and notions of
purity have no place in ethics and merely represent visceral and emotive
responses which are hangovers from our evolutionary past and have no
place in modern thinking about ethics. For example, Julian Savulescu, who
works extensively in fields such as medical ethics, has spoken of the 'yuk'
factor, as the visceral response of revulsion that we often feel initially to
situations which violate taboos or cross boundaries [19]. The 'yuk' factor
seems to be a rough descriptor for a purity response. Savulescu argues that
although it can sometimes give a good indication of the right response, more
usually yuk reactions need to be assessed and, if necessary, altered, using
reasoning based upon concepts such as rights and freedom. Our ethical
judgements should be based upon such reasoning, rather than on any kind of
democratic 'voting' where the (mere) feelings of the crowd are sourced.

It has sometimes been argued recently that dignity is not a useful moral
concept, as we mentioned in Sect. 2.4.9 [20]. However, the notion of dignity
has persistently that has proven very potent in expressing moral concern with
how human beings may be treated. Perhaps in some ways, it is a way of
expressing a visceral disgust with the wrongful treatment of members of our
fellow humanity.

Stigma is a powerful concept in sociology which can be seen to have some
relation to the notion of disgust. Its classic formulation was by Erving
Goffman in his work *Stigma: Notes on the Management of Spoiled Identity*
[21]. It describes the ways in which certain human beings are excluded from
full acceptance into certain aspects of society because of certain qualities, such
as disabilities or features of appearance. The individual is disgraced in some
way. The particular qualities which attract stigma can vary. Note that an
individual's appearance is often critical in producing stigma. Other related
terms are that of abjection, used, for example, by Julia Kristeva and others in
relation to social attitudes towards the aging mind and body [22].

Most would agree that stigma generally needs to be combatted, but note
how many cases involve human frailty and bodily decay and disability, even
including those who fail to conform to beauty standards. Remember that
Aristotle, for all his emphasis on the pursuits of virtue and of the mind,
considered that a necessary component of the good life was to be good
looking! It is useful to ponder this as we consider the human condition and
compare ourselves with imagined disembodied intelligences, or 'perfectly'
embodied machine intelligences, ones which can be readily repaired and
polished.

Exercise 10
How much of the ethical reactions to human interaction with robots and AI are based upon notions of disgust, purity, and contamination? Think of some possible examples, and try to include some current or near current examples as well as some futuristic examples: the Neuralink brain implant, microchips inserted under the skin for identity verification, sex with robots, and 'uploading' the mind to a computer. Is the 'uncanny valley' (see Sect. 2.5.2) an instance of disgust and the 'yuk' factor? Recall our discussion of boundary questions in technology in Sect. 3.3.5 and issues of purity.

Are there some instances in which we should take note of such attitudes of disgust, and others in which we should not? If so, can you explain and account for the difference?

Does disgust ever get in the way of making good moral judgements?

Feelings of disgust, 'yuk' responses, often accompany boundary crossing or violation, such as in crossing human and animal species, or the violation of taboos. Thinking back to previous chapters, such as discussions of human nature and of teleological views of the universe and discussions of different normative ethical theories, consider what assumptions and foundations might lie behind ethical disagreements about such boundary crossing.

Philosophers who are sceptical of our initial emotive reactions to situations and events may argue that our moral judgements should be more substantially based upon considered reflection and on reasons. However, this presumes that we can always articulate what these reasons are, and in debate, that we can articulate these better than any opponents can. Consider the implications of this, especially when we are tackling new technologies and very unfamiliar territory. Might it be the case that we are abandoning moral insights without sufficient consideration?

Do the origins of our moral beliefs matter? If it is the case that humans broadly share some deep moral values, this is unlikely to be a mere fluke, but does it matter what the reason for such shared values might be? Does it matter what the reason for differences might be? There is much that could be said on this topic, naturally, but here again, we will focus on some issues that are pertinent to some questions in AI ethics—whether the human origin of our values is a problem or not. For this discussion, you might like to recall our discussion of human nature in Chap. 3.

Suppose, for example, it is posited that our moral values arise from evolution. Indeed, given the theory of evolution, it's likely that this has had some role in their development, although it's harder to say precisely what contribution evolution per se had, as opposed to culture, reason, and experience. Moral foundations theory notes the significance of the fact that we are mammals for the 'care/harm' foundation; recall our discussion of care ethics in Sect. 5.4.4. Understanding moral values as arising from evolution is an empirical hypothesis likely to appeal to those sceptical of religious or other metaphysical views on the foundations and origins of our values, yet, if we view morality as a legacy of evolution, this opens up the possibility that much of that legacy is now redundant and possibly harmful, given the ways we now live. Julian Savulescu and Ingmar Persson explore these ideas in their book, *Unfit for the Future: The Need for Moral Enhancement*, arguing that much of our current ethics is a hangover from evolution and we need a programme of moral enhancement [23]. Perhaps we should adjust some of the ways in which we live to better fit our evolution.

Exercise 11
It is interesting to note that Savulescu and Persson argue that moral enhancement is particularly important, on the grounds that as a society, we don't need everyone to be highly intelligent, but we do need everyone to be good. Consider if you agree with this, and the implications of your answer for how we might develop and use AI, including the general question of human enhancement.

Compare and contrast the notion that moral enhancement is most important for society with the claim discussed earlier that everything that civilisation has to offer is a product of human intelligence [24].

If we are 'stuck' with old patterns of thinking, perhaps AI could help us improve. However, if our morality has developed around the limits and possibilities of our biology, then perhaps, even if AI became extremely advanced and conscious (if this is indeed possible), we could not understand our morality and may have a completely different moral system of its own. Wittgenstein said, 'If a lion could talk, we could not understand him' [25, part 2, p. 223e]. Perhaps if a group of artificial intelligences developed their own morality, we could not understand that. See also previous discussions about the relevance of biology to ethics, such as in Sect. 5.4.4.

Exercise 12
Our moral values are firmly based upon and address our need to live in groups and the opportunities and challenges this presents, including histories of tribal conflict. In a world of completely self-sufficient artificial intelligent robots (suppose such to be possible), ever understand our ethics have an ethic of their own, or indeed, have any form value system? (We discuss such matters further in Chap. 11.)

This question about the origins of our moral values pertains both to the question of how we come to form moral beliefs and make moral judgements, or questions of moral epistemology, and to the question of how moral values might be justified, the source of any authority they have. A related issue is the question of whether our moral views are based upon emotion or on reason and whether any element of emotion is misplaced. These questions hover in the background of much of our discussion, but first we turn to look at the question of moral authority, asking the question of 'who decides'?

Moral authority and AI ethics Even if there is some objective foundation for moral values, this is not going to drop out of the sky. There will be actual human beings making decisions and implementing decisions. Moreover, many of the ethical and value questions concerning AI are entirely personal decisions about how to respond to the use of AI in one's own life.

The notion of moral authority builds upon the question of the justification of our moral beliefs. We have seen how one way of addressing the issue of moral justification may be via some kind of crowdsourcing methodology. Another approach is implicit in the role of civil society groups as useful critics of those in power. An additional frequently cited approach is to consider the question of diversity of those involved in developing and implementing technologies. The diversity of the kinds of people contributing may be assumed to lead to the diversity of viewpoints. This then rests upon an assumption that we will get closer to 'the truth' and/or gain a fuller view of the issues and of how they impact people.

Exercise 13
There commonly are concerns about the narrow perspective of those involved in developing AI and calls for diverse voices to be included in the debate, policy, and regulation of AI. Drawing on any material in you have covered so far, and including any other reading or discussions, give as full and as critical an account as possible for why this might be the case. What kinds of diversity matter, and why?

Philosophical issues underlying these strategies include the question of whether we are approaching moral truth, if there are any moral facts to be had, and how we might discern the ethical questions facing us—questions of moral epistemology.

Working in groups should also alert us to the unfortunate findings that we are often unduly influenced by the views of others. We may conform to the group, and we may abuse any power we are given, leading us to view others as less valuable and less in need of respect. The famous Asch conformity experiments, along with much other work in social sciences, have confirmed our weaknesses [26, 27].

7.2.5 How Can We Gain Moral Understanding?

How do we best gain moral understanding of a situation? This, as ever, is a highly complex question on which much ink and many words of debate and discussion have been expended. Whether we conceptualise this as grasping the moral reality that confronts us, coming to understand some externally given moral law, determining preferences, considering feelings, and so on, two prevalent themes are present in discussion: the need to apprehend the situation before us in appropriate clarity and detail while retaining a general sense of how it fits into wider patterns, and the necessity of having the 'right' approach to emotions. What might the 'right' approach be? Whatever side of the complex 'objective/subjective' debate, it is widely acknowledged that personal feelings, selfishness, distress, emotional distance, and so on, can distort one's perception of the world and interfere with the capacity to develop an appropriate emotional response. Determining the most appropriate methodology and response is directly relevant to considering the ethics of AI, especially when we are concerned with how to draw up guidance for others and how to develop AI that is aligned with human values or which even 'makes' moral decisions.

The 'ideal observer' Let us briefly consider some contrasting philosophical positions. Notions of the 'ideal observer' have been advocated by many philosophers, including the philosopher David Hume and the economist Adam Smith, with more modern accounts such as that of Firth [28–30]. Ethical theories making use of 'ideal observers' try to capture what is necessary to make the ideal moral judgment, uncontaminated with personal biases and shortcomings. Such an observer may be characterised in certain ways intended to capture what conditions will produce the right—the correct, or the best—moral judgement. This usually means having the capacity to reason and being in possession of all the facts of the situation. In his *A Theory of Justice*, John Rawls outlined the 'Veil of Ignorance' as a technique that also attempts to capture a particular conception of impartiality in the construction of a society. It sets out to control the conditions under which individuals determine what rules will govern a society they are prepared to live in, by ruling out that they know what position they will occupy in society while determining rules that should govern it [31].

Exercise 14

What would your 'ideal observer' for AI ethics be like?

Given that we are unlikely to produce such a person in real life, what could an individual do to strive towards such qualities?

Could a committee of some sort reproduce at least some of these features?

Ideal observer theories strive to overcome human partialities. They also imagine a situation of full knowledge of the facts. Does this mean that an AI could suitably act as an impartial observer? Is an AI, with its vast processing power and lack of family and friends, more likely to approximate an ideal observer than a human? This could seem promising, but what needs to be considered?

Facts, relevance, and attention Is the ideal observer's possession of so many facts all it cracks up to be? In Sect. 2.5.2, we met Dickens' character Mr. Gradgrind, the severe headmaster from the novel *Hard Times*, who was frightfully keen on facts: 'Now, what I want is, Facts. Teach these boys and girls nothing but Facts. Facts alone are wanted in life. Plant nothing else, and root out everything else...' [32, p. 47]. But which facts, and what do we extrapolate from these facts? The challenges in machine learning of making sense of data should make those working in AI appreciate the difficulty of this question. It is also often clear that simply getting more and more facts will not help in any way. See too Sect. 5.2.1 for our discussion on abduction, as well as the importance for methodology in ethics of paying attention to how we describe and portray situations discussed in Sect. 4.1.1. We need to pay attention to the relevant facts, and to pay attention to them in the right manner, but how?

The question of whether more and more facts will help us to achieve better perception of value issues is a critical question to address, with widespread implications for how AI is used to gather data about the world, and about us, human beings.

A distanced, 'objective' position that ideal observer theories aimed to achieve is one such attempt, a kind of bird's eye view, an attempt to see the situation *sub specie aeternitatis* (from the point of view of the universe). An approach we could more readily achieve in practice could draw upon the shifts in understanding that may arise from a change of perspective, for example, by imagining yourself in the position of another, through imaginative descriptions of possible scenarios related to the case under consideration, through retelling a narrative account to bring to the fore different aspects.

An example of this that has been discussed by philosophers concerns the prophet Nathan admonishing King David [33, 34]. To cut the gripping and rather shameful story short, David had had an adulterous affair with Bathsheba. To cover up her resulting pregnancy, David then sent her husband Uriah to the front line of battle, with the certain knowledge that he, Uriah, would be killed. David, being King, could have his pick of women (and indeed had many wives throughout his life). Nathan then tells David a story: a rich man wished to entertain a guest, but rather than taking one of his own many sheep, took the one much-loved lamb of a poor man, and killed that to feed his guest. David says, 'the man who has done this deserves to die! He must restore the lamb fourfold, because he did this thing, and because he had no pity!' Nathan replied to David, 'You are the man' [35].

Redescribing situations can often lead to such insights. Sometimes as with David's revelation of his own wrongdoing, although perhaps not always, this involves shifting the perspective and points of view of the individuals involved. So perhaps, what is needed is not so much a distanced, impartial perspective as of an uninvolved third party looking down on the scene, but direct involvement and relationship to the other. Perhaps it involves shifting perspectives, coming anew to a situation, working out which bits to leave out as distractions, which bits to include as revealing of new insights.

I and Thou: Attention to the Individual The MIT Moral Machine experiment is set up in the third person. Participants are attempting to make decisions about the fate of distanced and anonymous strangers. Could accounts of moral knowledge in the second person give an alternative account? Recall Kant's distinction between treating people (merely) as a means and treating them as an end in themselves. The latter involves a recognition that others are also agents like oneself, who merit respect in precisely the same way.

Readers of Kant's *Groundwork for the Metaphysics of Morals* will be familiar with a series of examples he uses to illustrate how to ascertain the right thing to do in a situation of moral choice [36]. Students often pass over a telling aside: throwaway remarks from Kant noting that the person in question has spotted that there is a moral question to ask. A man so far in debt that he is considering taking out a loan he can't pay back is inclined to make such a promise, but *he has still enough conscience to ask*, if it's right for him to get out of trouble by such means. A man sick to the point of despair considers taking his own life, *but is still sufficiently aware to ask himself* whether taking this drastic course of action might be contrary to his duties. A man in comfortable circumstances considers giving himself up to pleasure yet *still has enough presence of mind* to ask himself whether it is wrong to neglect his natural gifts (emphases added). What these snippets of text reveal is the mysterious nature of how we are prompted to moral awareness and to attention to what is important. The Moral Machine experiment bypasses this thorny issue: one is simply told there is a moral issue, instructed to make a moral choice, and the 'relevant' facts are laid out.

Martin Buber's influential book *I and Thou* (*Ich und Du*) describes two fundamental and different ways of looking at the world [37]. 'I-It' relations involve approaching the world of things and people in the third person as objects. For example, a tree can be perceived as movement, classified as a species, and understood in terms of natural laws and in numbers; however, it is perceived that it remains an object existing in space and time and with a particular nature. 'I-Thou' relations are essential reciprocal encounters with another. They do not need to abandon any of the other ways in which something is perceived but rather encompass every aspect indivisibly united. The quality of one's relationship with the other impacts on the self. Through others, we can also encounter ourselves.

Other philosophers who take related approaches include Simone Weil, who stressed the importance of attention to the individual in how we relate to others and to the world [38]. Like Buber, her works fall into the category of theology as well as philosophy and ethics. For Weil, attention was a kind of attitude to the world that required the emptying of the self and patient waiting, ready to receive the other. By such means, the situation of the other and their needs can be appreciated. This is a reciprocal appreciation, with awareness of the self that at a different moment, one could also suffer.

It is possible to consider individual people from an impartial third-person perspective and still treat them as having value and agency that needs to be respected. However, a second person account of relating to others as distinct situated individuals with a particular and reciprocal relationship to oneself shifts gears to one of more radical equality and relatedness, equality not in the sense of sameness, but in the sense that one's relation with the other goes both ways: rather than literally looking down from above, as the Moral Machine experiment instructs, one is engaged in mutual recognition.

Exercise 15

Could machine learning, or any other kind of advanced AI, ever achieve anything approximating Buber's I-Thou relationship with the world?

For Weil, attention to the individual leads to knowledge of the situation of another, which can lead to ethical action. Her idea of the emptying of the self to receive such knowledge has some overlaps with the notion that the ideal observer is in possession of all facts, yet for Weil, this essentially requires personal relationships. One could sceptically wonder if such phenomenological perception of the moral reality of another is indeed possible. If philosophers such as Buber and Weil are to have any relevance, it might imply that a 'mere' machine could not grasp or appreciate such a personal moral reality, although readers are invited to differ from this view. This does not, however, necessarily mean that a machine could not have held information with some moral relevance.

Exercise 16
Discuss and consider arguments for and against the idea that humans can gain morally relevant knowledge of others in ways that machines cannot, and could not. Consider arguments that machines might be able to gain morally relevant knowledge in ways superior to human beings.

Discourse ethics attempts to explain the nature of the communication required in ethics. It can thus be seen in relation to ideal observer theories, which posit an impartial outsider forming judgements, as relations between individuals are essential in the attempt to produce moral insights. Discourse ethics differs significantly from the approaches of those such as Buber and Weil in that there is an attempt to determine formalised structures of communication that would justify the validity of moral norms reached within particular settings of communication and deliberation. Discourse ethics thus sees ethics as a rational activity and holds that moral norms can be justified if reached through the proper procedures. There are many proponents of such an approach, perhaps the most prominent of whom is Jürgen Habermas [39]. Habermas states that a moral norm is valid only if all those affected by it could accept it in a reasonable discourse; of course, everything will hang on what counts as a 'reasonable discourse'. There has been considerable development of such ideas, both for the moral and the political arena. The general and very basic point that there should ideally be participation in debate and discourse around AI ethics is a grounding premise of this book, although much will hang upon whose voices are heard and how precisely such debate and discussion occurs.

Extrapolation from examples, the universal and the particular, the general and the personal We discussed the move from theory to cases and discussed the different ways of describing and hence of drawing conclusions from situations in Chap. 4. Our discussion of certain questions in metaethics can be used to illuminate aspects of the general ethical framework from which conclusions may be drawn. I will take in illustration the parable of the Good Samaritan, told in Luke Chapter 10: 25–37, possibly the parable of Jesus which is best known outside of Christianity, and one which is frequently subject to different interpretations. The command to 'Love your neighbour as yourself' is found in both Old and New Testaments (Leviticus 19: 18, Mark 12:31), and for many people, it represents an expression of the Golden Rule, a widely recognised element of morality.

A lawyer asks Jesus for a clarification of this commandment, asking who is his neighbour. Jesus replies with a parable about a man who was robbed and left badly injured on the road from Jerusalem to Jericho, a notoriously dangerous route. Two religious men passed by without stopping, but a third man, a Samaritan, a group regarded with some hostility by the Jews, stopped to help, tended his wounds, and paid an innkeeper for the continued care of the injured man. Jesus commands his followers to go and do likewise.

But what is 'likewise'? Let us contrast two broad pictures. One way of interpreting this is not only as a radical imperative to equal treatment for all human beings but also as an imperative to considerable sacrifice for others and, moreover, as an imperative to adopt a universalist ethic that requires us to seek out and consider the situation of all who might need our assistance. This then might fit well with, say, the utilitarian impulse to consider the total consequences of our actions. It could fit with an understanding of our ethical obligations and responsibilities that required we have to think and act from a radically universal stance, taking the whole world into account. It fits with a 'view from nowhere', third personal approach to ethics.

Another way of interpreting our responsibilities in light of Jesus's command is situational and personal: the Good Samaritan came across the injured man and responded to his needs. The first two men ignored him. The parable then could be interpreted as an instruction to respond appropriately to the situations that life presents us with. This is also a very tough ask, since even those of us living simple, quiet lives may be tested by being presented with extremely demanding events. This sort of approach belongs to a view of moral epistemology as requiring close attention to the needs of those around us. One could readily imagine that the two religious men who passed the injured man first did, of course, have high moral standards: they just missed the chance to exercise them when push came to shove. This is a situated, second-personal viewpoint.

Exercise 17
Consider how suited a sophisticated AI might be to assisting us ethically, or acting ethically itself, on each of these two broad approaches to interpreting the Golden Rule.

Consider any implications for how computers might interpret and apply rules about ethics and how the use of computers might then impact how moral responsibility is understood.

7.2.6 Technology, Attention, and Persuasion

We have highlighted the central importance of attention and of relevance in ethics. We have also looked at the question of the position and the distance from which we assess situations, make moral judgements, and act. Many of the questions we have been looking at concern questions of moral epistemology and hence are related to questions in epistemology more generally, concerning how we gain knowledge of the world, even the broad metaphysical question of what 'reality' is (which we discuss in Sect. 7.5). These issues are directly at issue in several central aspects of AI.

Representing the world through data Machine learning makes use of vast amounts of data. The quality of the data used, together with the algorithms used to process the data, is of critical importance. The question of bias in algorithms is well known and much studied. Gaps in data, errors in data input, and other issues can have profound consequences and raise serious ethical issues. However, underlying these and other similar questions, we can ask about the philosophical foundations of the picture of knowledge that this relies upon. Are we even collecting the right sort of data to reach a good level of understanding of all types of phenomena? This will depend upon what phenomena is at issue. Recall the discussion of different methodological approaches, qualitative and quantitative, within the social sciences in Sect. 5.2.1. This question also relates broadly to the questions about the nature and value of intelligence discussed in Chap. 5.

Metaphysical and epistemological questions are also raised concerning the underlying reality that the data are being used to represent. For example, one such question concerns the detection of causation from the analysis of data [40]; another concerns whether the world divides into natural kinds that are captured via the data we collect; we can also ask the very general question of whether we, mere humans, are in fact capable of gaining ultimate knowledge of our world. The most profound question will concern whether we can truly understand human beings and human behaviour via the collection of more and more data about them and whether even if this is theoretically possible, if we are collecting the right kind of data.

The drive to improve things by collecting more and more data could have very good intentions. However, an effect of this will be to collect an increasing amount of data on individuals, which brings its own ethical issues. It also raises issues of sustainability. One can also often wonder if collecting more and more data about a situation is always necessary. Once one realises the small child in the shallow pond is drowning, it's irrelevant that this is a slightly annoying kid who won't eat broccoli and whose parents regularly park in your slot and watch true crime documentaries on Netflix. One of the many problems, of course, is the difficulty of knowing in advance precisely what information is and is not relevant. The situation of the drowning child in a shallow pond is urgent, and we need all our attention focused on that (children can drown extremely quickly in fresh water). However, this very same capacity of our attention can also be hijacked to less laudable ends.

Seeing the world through technology The work of philosophers and others who point to the importance of attention to the individual and to the situation at hand only serves to underlie the issues of how so much of the technology that we currently use, which makes use of much AI, serves to channel our attention in certain directions. This can be purposefully designed to good, for instance, for highlighting urgent issues that deserve our thought or action, or indeed, by very simple means such as alerting us to hurricanes or other hazards. However, the aim of attention-hungry technology is sometimes nothing other than keeping one engaged with technology that relies upon advertising and hence needs attention for revenue purposes. Alerting us to hazards is also, one might say, itself fraught with hazards. It can increase our perception of risk and greatly heighten fears. These issues are of relevance to many ethical questions concerning AI, and we discuss them further in the next chapter when we consider how AI might represent persons, including issues of great ethical import such as facial recognition.

7.3   The Theory of Knowledge

Summary
A brief account of the relevance of epistemology to AI ethics and its presence in many of the topics of this book is given, followed by an overview of standpoint epistemology and its possible relevance to AI ethics.

Questions of epistemology are present throughout discussions of AI in general and have particular relevance for ethical questions. We have looked extensively at the question of moral epistemology. Issues such as trust, safety, agency, responsibility, autonomy, and benefit all involve the question of whether we can rely upon the knowledge and information generated by AI, and above all, the black box question and the issue of transparency and explainability involve questions of epistemology.

Philosophers have long debated the question of when we can know that our beliefs are justified, including the question of whether and when we can rely upon the testimony of others [41]. There are differences between the information generated by machine learning and the ways in which AI may gather and analyse data from sensors and other sources and the ways in which humans acquire knowledge and understanding, so that the picture of the world built up by AI may differ from that of humans. This may matter in some contexts but less in others. The question of how we can have knowledge of other minds, an essential question in ethics, has long been discussed in philosophy, and there are complex and fascinating questions about the kind of knowledge of other minds—i.e. of we humans—that may be generated by AI and about what picture of ourselves and of others it might produce, which have ethical implications and which we discuss in Sect. 8.4.

Questions about the reliability of knowledge and information generated by AI do not simply concern its veracity. We need to consider how it is presented to us and the tools of persuasion and influence that may be present, as indicated above in our discussion of attention. We will look in Chap. 9 at the question of online content moderation, including the issue of misinformation: to identify something as misinformation trades upon claims about truth, certainty, and what is taken as evidence, and hence also questions of scientific methodology and the epistemic foundations of different branches of knowledge. As we shall see, claims may also be made about the routes by which we acquire beliefs, and whether these lead to the acquisition of trustworthy knowledge or merely result in being persuaded to believe something without justification, and in turn, claims that certain that authorities may be justified in acting to suppress or censor certain beliefs. The promise of AI technologies to unlock vast amounts of information and to increase our intelligence by increasing our knowledge runs up against the powers of technology to persuade and to capture our attention irrespective of the justification of our beliefs.

Standpoint epistemology and its relevance for AI ethics Let us just take one example of a question in the theory of knowledge directly relevant to understanding AI, which is also implicit in some of the possible solutions to seeking good ethical responses to AI already discussed: standpoint epistemology [42]. This also reflects a broad theme running through this chapter and indeed through much discussion of AI and of AI ethics: a distinction that may be roughly drawn between a formalist, 'objective' approach to issues and a relativised, subjective approach.

Bearing in mind again that complex philosophical debates are being greatly simplified, let us contrast divergent approaches to the question of knowledge. On the one hand is a naïve realist view of truth and of knowledge. A simple view of 'truth' is that it consists in the match between a statement and reality: the correspondence theory of truth. This may be a kind of 'photocopy' view of the truth, where there is just one view of the world, and we can grasp this unaltered by our observations and perceptions. Of course, our perceptions and biases may get in the way; but there is a truth out there to find, and it's possible to find this. To determine the truth, we need to remove our biases and any shortcomings in our perceptions. If we do this, the truth will reveal itself to be the same, regardless of who is observing. Along with this view, there may be assumptions that the world consists in a large body of facts, and the more facts we manage to collect, the better our grasp of the world.

Such a view—or more sophisticated versions of it—may lie behind the idea that AI is capable of grasping the truth about the world better than we can, with our many biases, our limited capacity to collect and analyse information, and our limited perceptions. Of course, one can immediately find many points of simplification in how this naïve view has been presented here, but note its parallels to the picture presented by the design of the Moral Machine experiment, such as the instruction that the person making the choice had to imagine that they are out of the scene, with a view from above of 'all' that is happening, along with knowledge of what would occur given certain choices.

In contrast, consider standpoint epistemology, or standpoint theory. This approach to knowledge is associated with feminist views but may be used more generally to refer to theories of knowledge that consider that the point of view, the social situation of the knower, is relevant to the acquisition of knowledge. In brief, the claim is that one's capacity to know and understand a situation may be enhanced, or worsened, by the perspective one takes and that features of one's social position are relevant to this. Some people therefore may have privileged insight into certain issues relative to others. Sometimes such theories may make specific theoretically based claims regarding who has such privileged access to knowledge. Much work in this area stems from Marxist ideas and claims that those at the top of society have a reduced understanding of many issues than those at the bottom, who may be able to gain greater insight into the social and material world through the reality of their lives. For example, it may be claimed that those who are in a servant class need to understand the world of those whom they serve, but those in the upper classes do not have the corresponding need to understand the world of their own servants; the servant class thus has greater understanding of the world. Other claims made include the claim that women as a sex class may have better understanding and knowledge of certain issues than men. Sometimes claims are made that certain positions in society will grant a better overall picture of the world, perhaps that there are some aspects of experience and knowledge that only certain people can access.

It should be obvious therefore that many specific claims concerning standpoint theory will be contentious to those with different social and political theories. There will also be differences between those with the 'common sense' view that some sorts of experience in life will assist a person to spot issues that others may miss: for example, someone who is a wheelchair user will have a good understanding of issues of the accessibility of buildings, public transport, etc. and may see problems that others may not. Likewise, women are likely to have had life experiences that differ from those of men and hence may notice things that some men overlook, and of course, vice versa; people from different cultures and economic classes likewise have different life experiences. A major question then is whether there is something inherent to the identity of individuals or group membership which means that others could not understand such viewpoints. These approaches to knowledge are obviously highly contentious.

Answers to this question will have manifest implications for the ethical development of AI, for the choice of who is involved in developing and deploying AI, and for who are considered stakeholders in any consultation. It also has implications for the production of information and knowledge by AI; for if certain aspects of a situation can only be grasped and fully understood by certain humans who occupy particular stances, this implies that AI will never gain such knowledge. Of course, even if one rejected standpoint epistemology, one might hold that there were certain aspects of the world that AI would never be able to capture and that wide participation in AI development, deployment, and assessment is critical because even if, in theory, others might understand certain aspects of experience, they frequently fail to do so.

7.4 Philosophy of Language

Summary
Understanding human-level intelligence involves understanding language and hence the relevance of the philosophy of language. We briefly contrast formal approaches to understanding language with pragmatics, which seeks to understand the social context of communication and which is essential to success in natural language processing.

Language use and understanding is an element of human intelligence, and we have already seen that questions concerning the capacity of AI to understand language and to communicate via language recur frequently in ethical questions around AI. We saw that language may be taken as an indicator of intelligence or indeed sentience. The epistemological question of whether AI understands the world and has knowledge in ways that parallel human knowledge rests in part on whether AI has or could have the capacity to understand natural language, and this in turn has many ethical implications, including the question of how AI might understand humans and how we respond to AI. These questions in turn rest upon how we understand language.

We mentioned the linguistic turn in philosophy earlier in the twentieth century, where there was a significant emphasis on the study of language and, indeed, in some cases, to formalised accounts of language. The work of philosophers such as Bertrand Russell, A. N. Whitehead, and Gottlob Frege and the early work of Ludwig Wittgenstein in broad terms looked to understand language as a system that can be reduced to components structured in ways that could be formalised [43–45]. However, as useful as such formalisation might be for some purposes, such as understanding logic, mathematics, and computing, some philosophers came to realise that such an approach had serious shortcomings in regard to understanding how natural language and the nuances of human communication actually work within a social and cultural setting, among them Wittgenstein himself [25, 46].

Around the mid-twentieth century, work in pragmatics started to study more informal aspects of the use of language and communication within a social context [47]. This work has developed considerably, both within philosophy and within the field of discourse analysis [48]. Key to such work was the recognition of context, including social context, expectation, and convention, to understanding how language functioned and how meaning was understood and communicated. The variety of uses of language was emphasised. This work is therefore also critical to natural language processing and to understanding the many ethical questions that arise around this.

Prominent among the philosophers working in pragmatics was J. L. Austen, who worked in 'ordinary language philosophy', which focused on attempting to understand and analyse philosophical questions and issues of meaning through careful analysis of the use of language. Among his contributions to pragmatics is his work recognising the power of language in the form of 'speech acts', performative utterances that bring about certain effects in the world, and a considerable amount of further work has developed such ideas.

Austen distinguished between locutionary, illocutionary, and perlocutionary acts [49]. There are different accounts of how precisely these different acts should be understood, but in outline, a locutionary act captures what a speaker said. An illocutionary act is a speech act with which we do something, for example, make a promise or issue a request, for instance, 'I'll get the cat from the vets at 3 o'clock' or 'Would you mind passing the ketchup'. Performing illocutionary acts may be understood in conventional ways or by understanding the context. Thus, 'Nice little house you've got there, shame if it burned down' is a threat, and 'Would you like some more cake?' may be an indication in certain social contexts that the speaker wants some more cake. A perlocutionary act is the effect that a speech act has on the hearer. For example, the result might be that the hearer passes the ketchup, develops anxiety at the fear that their house will burn down, and so on. Such work is of obvious application to understanding language in general, and is being applied to the context of online communication, for instance, in social media, where communication may be challenging, where it is applied for analysing and understanding questions such as online harassment.

In Chap. 9, we will look at online content moderation and examine H. P. Grice's theories of conversational implicature, which presented an account of how shared conventions govern how meaning is conveyed and understood, and we consider how such shared conventions might be shaped by the forms of communication possible with technology.

7.5   Questions in Metaphysics: What Is Reality?

Summary

Many questions in metaphysics are implicit in ethical questions in AI. For instance, the question of addressing bias in algorithms may tacitly rest upon assumptions about fundamental categories of the world against which bias is measured. The use and value of virtual reality raises the questions of the value and nature of reality and of whether virtual reality is 'real' and if so now, which we discuss through examining David Chalmer's views.

We have briefly touched on how underlying metaphysical questions can arise concerning AI and its applications. For example, the ethical question of bias in algorithms is often portrayed as being concerned with how to remove bias in data sets, modelling, and use of algorithms, but these debates may presume that it is at least theoretically possible to have an unbiased use of algorithms, and hence that we may, via data, capture what the world is 'truly' like, what its fundamental ontology is. This presupposes that the data we collect are adequate to this task and that the categories and perceptions we use to collect data and which we use to measure bias can, at least in theory, perfectly represent the world: that the categories we use 'carve nature at her joints' (Plato, Phaedrus 265d–266a) [50]. We cannot here do full justice to all the metaphysical and epistemological issues potentially relevant to questions in AI with ethical implications, but exploration of metaphysical and epistemological assumptions may frequently be useful in furthering ethical understanding.

We will look here at one very broad question, since it is one which we have already raised in discussion and comparison of ethical theory: the nature of 'reality', and the question of why reality matters to us, if indeed, it does. This is a question that goes to the heart of central debates in ethics. Does it matter what 'really' happens in my life, or merely what I seem to experience? Likewise, should our moral values aim to cohere with some moral reality, or with some purpose-driven notion of the world, a teleological view of the universe? Or can we just make the world and ourselves as we wish, and according to our preferences, desires, and subjectively felt feelings?

Robert Nozick's Experience Machine thought experiment threatens to be realised in the form of virtual reality or the as yet unrealised possibility of a simulated reality, an all-encompassing virtual reality [51]. Virtual reality is often used in extremely useful ways, such as in helping to train emergency service personnel and surgeons. These are to help prepare such personnel for doing 'real' stuff. It can also be used for recreational purposes where there is no pretence that it represents 'reality'. Ethical questions arise about the value of 'real' experiences when VR, and perhaps in the future a simulated reality, are used as substitutes for veridical experiences. Recall too questions we have raised previously about the enhanced presentation of the self via the use of AI: see Exercise 12, Chap. 4.

How can we address such questions? One strategy would be to examine the costs and benefits that accrue when a large part of one's time is spent in VR used as a form of entertainment or substitute for life in the 'real' world. One problem with such a strategy is that it may implicitly rest upon prior judgements of the relative worth of veridical experiences versus virtual experiences. Hence, the strategy of examining what we mean by 'reality' will be a useful approach.

The philosopher David Chalmers' 2022 book, *Reality+: Virtual Worlds and the Problems of Philosophy*, takes the reader through many clearly and simply explained issues in metaphysics, philosophy of mind, and epistemology to unravel this question, a question that he indeed considers sheds light on many age-old philosophical questions [52]. We will look at Chalmers' position since he takes a very firm stance, that life in VR can be just as good or bad as life in the ordinary reality [52, Ch. 1]. The option that we may have in the future of spending all or most of our lives in VR is, on such a view, a reasonable choice. Of course, one of the major objections to life within a VR, a simulated reality, is that this is not 'real': a five dollar bill is a type of banknote, but a fake dollar bill is not; in the same way, virtual reality is not a type of reality. Chalmers would beg to differ: he claims that a computational simulation can preserve the structure of reality. According to his arguments, virtual reality is real, and objects within a simulated reality are also real: they are 'digital objects', constructed out of data, and are perfectly real.

So what is it to be 'real'?

Chalmers analyses five aspects of reality and concludes that virtual reality ticks all boxes, so long as we are in a perfect, permanent, simulated reality. These are, first, *existence*, the virtual, simulated world exists, even if it is made digitally; *causal powers*, the simulation he imagines contains causation, in the sense that events follow each other in a regular manner and agents can both affect the world and be impacted by it; *mind-independence*, it is not simply the product of the mind of the person within it; *nonillusoriness*, in the sense that things are 'roughly as they appear to be'—if my whole world is digital, and all the objects in it are digital, then they are not illusions within this world; and *genuineness*, a robot kitten is a real *object*, even if it is not a real *kitten*. In an entire life lived in this digital world, every kitten has always been digital. There are no 'better' 'real' kittens to be had. He also considers that simulated characters existing entirely within the simulation could be conscious if they are constructed in ways that recreate the structures that produce consciousness in the veridical world. Chalmers argues that objections to his claim are based upon naïve realism, the idea that the world is truly as we think it is: objects are solid, causal powers are based upon some force, and secondary qualities such as colours and sounds represent aspects of an object's inherent nature. However, we now know that objects are built up of atoms, and these out of fundamental particles, with competing accounts of the underlying physics, and so on.

No philosopher alive has ever managed to convince everybody of the truth of their theories, and Chalmers' account of virtual reality is doubtless no exception. The details of his arguments rest upon answers to debates that have occupied philosophers for millennia. We do not currently have such a perfect and permanent simulated reality. The criteria for reality that he outlines could be helpful in framing a discussion of the ethical issues in the use of VR as an alternative place to spend a substantial part of one's life. The prospect of technological unemployment, the realities of current unemployment, and the prospect of using life in VR as an alternative to building relationships with friends and family, and of achieving action in the world, are all ethical and social questions that we face now and in the near future. As with so many such questions, we face them both as a society and as individuals.

A notable feature of virtual reality is that it is nested inside what we commonly call 'reality'. It is the second layer up (or more, if it's VR inside a VR). Chalmers addresses the objection that his criteria for reality omit the notion of fundamentality or originality. He dismisses these as 'marginal' criteria for reality. He uses Dolly, the world's first cloned sheep as an illustration, and claims she is neither original, being a clone of another sheep, nor fundamental, since she is made up of atoms [52, p. 117].

Exercise 18
Note that Chalmers concludes that it is only a perfect, permanent simulated reality that meets his requirements of reality. Could this standard of reality be used to judge the ethical status of spending large amounts of time in a virtual reality that failed to meet this standard? Explore and discuss different possibilities, looking at the different criteria for reality he proposes. Consider especially the issue that virtual reality is nested inside 'ordinary' reality.

Chalmers claims Dolly the sheep is nonetheless real. Indeed, she is real, or at any rate, she was real, before her death at the premature age of 6 in 2003. Does his use of this analogy suggest that the question of whether virtual worlds are 'real' may not be the most important ethical question to consider when weighing up the charms of a life spent in large part within VR? Or is his use of the Dolly example a misleading analogy?

Does it matter who made the virtual reality, and why? Does it matter how the purported causation within the virtual reality operates, whether by 'natural law' or by a complex computer programme? In such a world, would you be responsible and accountable for your actions and if so, how?

Consider the previous discussions of human nature, of our weaknesses and our potential and draw on them in your discussions.

A different view is held by Jaron Lanier, a pioneer in actually developing virtual reality, who has written eloquently about its attractions and its limits [53]. Chalmers' simulated reality relies upon perfection, which is extremely hard to achieve. Lanier points out that the introduction of technologies to capture reality, such as photography and film, were initially greeted with amazement and considered to be 'exactly' like the real thing. With familiarity, however, we become extremely adept at spotting the difference. In such ways, we can appreciate the real world even more deeply.

Our Sense of the Real

In some contexts, the real matters very much to us. The notion of an original work of art, a real dinosaur skeleton, a genuine artefact from the ancient world, thrills us. The converse also applies. A visit to a concentration camp appals, and such visits are used educationally to help underline the horrors that occurred there, with the underlying thought that being in the real location will help to bring the reality home. My friend Lucy once visited a friend of hers whose grandparents had, unfortunately, sympathised with Hitler. He had visited her grandparents before the Second World War and given them a copy of *Mein Kampf*, which the family still has. Lucy, I should add, is a marvellously expressive storyteller. As she told me about this book that once had been in the hands of Hitler, she reached a finger out. 'I touched it,' she quietly uttered, touching my hand, and we both screamed. I had touched somebody who had touched something which Hitler had touched.

Note that the sense of 'the real' here is mediated through space and time. We can retain a sense of the real even over such divides, and hence also via our technologically mediated experiences.

A strange parody of 'the real'. Many of those who has had the privilege and pleasure of visiting the Louvre in Paris is likely to have included the Mona Lisa in their visit. The experience of seeing this world-renowned work of art in the original is not to be missed. It's so popular that it's generally surrounded by admiring crowds such that it is hard to get a good look. And what are those crowds doing? Most of them are holding cameras above their heads and snatching photos of Da Vinci's masterpiece. Why, since reproductions are widely available? Presumably, because the tourists' own snaps make a permanent record of their real visit to this real work of art. A work of art they have scarcely seen. Recall our discussion of Benjamin's *The Work of Art in the Age of Mechanical Reproduction* in Sect. 3.6.2.

Lanier's assessment of VR involves an appreciation of the intertwining of technology and humanity. In discussing Norbert Weiner's book *The Human Use of Human Beings*, he distils a terrible possibility from the accelerating increase in computing power and the possibilities of manipulation of people's behaviour [53, p. 58]. Pavlov, Watson, and Skinner are three prominent behaviourist psychologists of the twentieth century who considered that human beings could be understood fully in terms of how they behave and that our behaviour can be manipulated and controlled by conditioning. Like many issues in the philosophy of mind, their work is of profound relevance to understanding many ethical issues in AI. To understand the essential points Lanier is making, we need to examine behaviourism and other ways of understanding the mind. We also need to look at the petrifying idea of the

Skinner box: a dystopian sci-fi nightmare which, sorry to say, has already happened. We discuss behaviourism along with other theories of the mind in Sect. 8.4.

7.6 Key Points

How we conceptualise, and how we try to address, concrete ethical questions rests upon assumptions about the nature of moral reality and of moral knowledge. Unless this is understood, we may miss issues of key importance and fail to understand our own biases and assumptions.

Understanding how we form and justify moral claims is critical to any approach to attempting to find answers to questions in AI ethics that are widely acceptable. The difficulty of this needs to be recognised.

Claims about the nature of moral understanding and moral knowledge will have implications for the question of programming ethics into machines. Certain approaches to moral understanding that stress personal connection and attention may present greater difficulties.

There are particular tensions in AI ethics between the impetus towards universality in ethics and in understanding and respecting the local. These are hard to resolve, but it is important to understand these as we attempt to understand ourselves and others and seek acceptable solutions.

The understanding and use of artificial intelligence may rest upon certain assumptions about knowledge, language, and metaphysics, which in turn shape the understanding of and response to many ethical questions.

7.7 Educator Notes

Students with less time or less interest in formal philosophical issues should find sufficient material introducing underlying metaethical issues by working through the material on the MIT Moral Machine experiment.

Nonetheless, it is important for students to understand how significant disagreements at the heart of metaethics underlie many of the central questions in applied ethics and are highly pertinent to AI ethics in particular, such as the broad question of how we justify our moral decisions, how we reach agreement, and the question(s) of the universality of ethics. The broadly termed question of 'reason versus emotion' is generally intuitively grasped, and working through some of this material should enable students to deepen their understanding and apply it to various concrete and general value questions in AI.

The sections on theory of knowledge, philosophy of language, and metaphysics are very introductory but are intended to alert students to how such philosophical questions in fact underlie many central questions within AI itself.

Debate and extended project or essay topics Exercise 3 concerns the important methodological issue of the stance from which a moral judgement is best made could form a good class discussion topic. It would be useful to encourage students to think of specific instances, but this will also alert students to the important differences between ethical theories.

Exercise 18 in Sect. 7.5 on virtual reality may form a good topic for classroom debate, where students should be encouraged to draw explicitly upon philosophical ideas and may also have much experience of their own upon which to base opinion and argument.

Exercise 8 might make a useful class or group exercise consolidating comprehension of the most common principles and values in codes of ethics for AI.

Exercises 13 and 14 are closely linked and give students an opportunity to grasp how the philosophical debates about the nature of moral understanding are linked to the very practical and vital question of diversity of opinion in AI ethics.

References

1. https://www.moralmachine.net/
2. Awad E, Dsouza S, Kim R, Schulz J, Henrich J, Shariff A et al (2018) The moral machine experiment. Nature 563(7729):59–64
3. Singer P (1997) The drowning child and the expanding circle. New Internationalist, Oxford
4. Smart JJC, Williams BAO (1973) Utilitarianism: for and against. Cambridge University Press, Cambridge
5. Glover J (1977) Causing death and saving lives. Penguin, London
6. Gilligan C (1982) In a different voice: psychological theory and women's development. Harvard University Press, Cambridge
7. Piaget J (1932) The moral judgment of the child (Le jugement moral chez l'enfant). Kegan Paul, Trench, Trubner and Co., London
8. Kohlberg L (1979) The meaning and measurement of moral development. Clark University Press, Worcester
9. Johnston DK (1988) Adolescents solutions to dilemmas in fables: two moral orientations—two problem solving strategies. In: Gilligan C, Ward J, Taylor J (eds) Mapping the moral domain: a contribution of women's thinking to psychological theory and education. Harvard University Press, Cambridge, pp 49–86
10. Wallach W, Allen C (2008) Moral machines: teaching robots right from wrong. Oxford University Press, Oxford
11. Gowans C (2021) Moral relativism. In: Zalta EN (ed) The Stanford encyclopedia of philosophy, Spring 2021 edn. https://plato.stanford.edu/archives/spr2021/entries/moral-relativism/
12. Williams B (1972) Morality: an introduction to ethics. Cambridge University Press, Cambridge
13. Calvão F, McDonald CEA, Bolay M (2021) Cobalt mining and the corporate outsourcing of responsibility in the Democratic Republic of Congo. Extr Ind Soc 8(4):100884
14. Hasselbalch G (2021) Data ethics of power: a human approach in the big data and AI era. Edward Elgar Publishing, Cheltenham
15. https://algorithmwatch.org/en/
16. https://www.article19.org
17. moralfoundations.org
18. Haidt J (2012) The righteous mind. Penguin, London

19. Warburton N, Savulescu J (2009) Julian Savulescu on the 'Yuk' factor, Philosophy Bites. https://philosophybites.com/2009/03/julian-savulescu-on-the-yuk-factor.html
20. Macklin R (2003) Dignity is a useless concept. BMJ 327(7429):1419–1420
21. Goffman E (1963) Stigma: notes on the management of spoiled identity. Prentice Hall, Hoboken
22. Gilleard C, Higgs P (2011) Ageing abjection and embodiment in the fourth age. J Aging Stud 25(2):135–142
23. Persson I, Savulescu J (2012) Unfit for the future: the need for moral enhancement. Oxford University Press, Oxford
24. Future of Life Open Letter. Research priorities for robust and beneficial artificial intelligence. https://futureoflife.org/ai-open-letter/
25. Wittgenstein L (1953) Philosophical investigations (trans: Anscombe, E). Blackwell, Oxford
26. Zimbardo P (2007) The Lucifer effect understanding how good people turn evil. Random House, New York
27. Asch SE (1956) Studies of independence and conformity: I. A minority of one against a unanimous majority. Psychol Monogr Gen Appl 70(9):1
28. Firth R (1952) Ethical absolutism and the ideal observer. Philos Phenom Res 12(3):317–345
29. Smith A (1822) The theory of moral sentiments, vol 1. J. Richardson, London
30. Hume D (1751) An enquiry concerning the principles of morals. Andrew Millar, London
31. Rawls J (1999) A theory of justice, revised edn. Harvard University Press, Cambridge
32. Dickens C (2012) Hard times (1854). Penguin, London
33. MacNaughton D (1988) Moral vision. Blackwell, Oxford
34. Butler J (2017) Fifteen Sermons Preached at Rolls Chapel (1729). Oxford University Press, Oxford
35. World English Bible 2 Samuel 12, 5–7
36. Kant I, Paton HJ (1964) Groundwork of the metaphysic of morals (translated and analysed by HJ Paton). Harper & Row, Manhattan
37. Buber M (1970) I and Thou (trans: Kaufman W). Charles Scribner's Sons, New York
38. Weil S (1951) Reflections on the right use of school studies with a view to the love of god. In Weil, S. 2021, Waiting for god, Routledge, London 61
39. Bohman J, Rehg W (2017) Jürgen Habermas. In: Zalta EN (ed) The Stanford encyclopedia of philosophy, Fall 2017 edn. https://plato.stanford.edu/archives/fall2017/entries/habermas/
40. Pearl J, Mackenzie D (2018) The book of why: the new science of cause and effect. Penguin, London
41. Gettier Edmund L (1963) Is justified true belief knowledge? Analysis 23:121–123
42. Grasswick H (2018) Feminist social epistemology. In: Zalta EN (ed) The Stanford encyclopedia of philosophy, Fall 2018 edn. https://plato.stanford.edu/archives/fall2018/entries/feminist-social-epistemology/
43. Russell B, Whitehead AN (1910) Principia mathematica, vol I. Cambridge University Press, Cambridge
44. Über Sinn und Bedeutung. In: Zeitschrift für Philosophie und philosophische Kritik. 100: 25–50; translated as 'On Sense and Reference' by M. Black in Geach and Black (eds. and trans.). 1980: 56–78
45. Wittgenstein L (1922) Tractatus logico-philosophicus. Routledge, London
46. Wittgenstein L (1929) Some remarks on logical form. Proc Aristot Soc Suppl Vol 9:162–171
47. Lycan WG (2018) Philosophy of language: a contemporary introduction. Routledge, London
48. Johnstone B (2017) Discourse analysis. Wiley, New York
49. Austin JL (1962) How to do things with words. Oxford University Press, Oxford
50. Plato (1888) The Phaedrus (trans: Jowett B)
51. Nozick R (1974) Anarchy, state, and utopia. Basic Books, New York
52. Chalmers DJ (2022) Reality+: virtual worlds and the problems of philosophy. Penguin, London
53. Lanier J (2017) Dawn of the new everything: a journey through virtual reality. Random House, New York

Further Reading

Moral Theory and Metaethics

Awad E, Dsouza S, Kim R, Schulz J, Henrich J, Shariff A et al (2018) The moral machine experiment. Nature 563(7729):59–64

Chrisman M (2016) What is this thing called Metaethics? Routledge, London

Haidt J (2012) The righteous mind. Penguin, London

Harman G (1977) The nature of morality: an introduction to ethics. Oxford University Press, New York

Kant I, Paton HJ (1964) Groundwork of the metaphysic of morals (translated and analysed by HJ Paton). Harper & Row, Manhattan

MacNaughton D (1988) Moral vision. Blackwell, Oxford

McPherson T, Plunkett D (eds) (2017) The Routledge handbook of metaethics. Routledge, London

Miller A (2014) Contemporary metaethics: an introduction. Wiley, New York

Shafer-Landau R, Cuneo T (2007) Foundations of ethics: an anthology. Blackwell, Oxford

Warburton N, Savulescu J (2009) Julian Savulescu on the 'Yuk' factor, Philosophy Bites. https://philosophybites.com/2009/03/julian-savulescu-on-the-yuk-factor.html

Williams B (1972) Morality: an introduction to ethics. Cambridge University Press, Cambridge

Philosophy of Language, Theory of Knowledge, Metaphysics

Audi R (2010) Epistemology: a contemporary introduction to the theory of knowledge, 3rd edn. Routledge, London

Austin JL (1975) How to do things with words. Oxford university press, Oxford

Chalmers DJ (2022) Reality+: virtual worlds and the problems of philosophy. Penguin, London

Lanier J (2017) Dawn of the new everything: a journey through virtual reality. Random House, New York

Lowe EJ (2002) A survey of metaphysics. Oxford University Press, Oxford, p 416

Lycan WG (2018) Philosophy of language: a contemporary introduction. Routledge, London

Mumford S (2012) Metaphysics: a very short introduction. Oxford University Press, Oxford

Nagel J (2014) Knowledge: a very short introduction. Oxford University Press, Oxford

Chapter 8
Persons and AI

Abstract We examine the concept of the person, its central role in ethics, and the cultural and historical variations in how personhood is conceptualised and valued. Ethical questions in AI include whether the use of technology respects our personhood and whether AI may ever be attributed with elements of personhood such as sentience or agency. We examine respect for persons as an ethical ideal, drawing on Kant's philosophy. A model of personhood given by Daniel Dennett is discussed, including criteria of rationality, self-consciousness, reciprocity, and the conditions for the attribution of personhood. The question of embodiment and persons is considered, and philosophical theories of the mind-body relationship are described, illustrating how these debates may help to illuminate the range of attitudes towards personhood. We examine the stress on cognitive aspects in many accounts of personhood and the notion of embodied personhood. Two contrasting models of personhood, scientific and moral, are examined, drawing on the work of Charles Taylor, and addressing different ways of distinguishing between persons, agents, and things. Last, various questions around the boundaries of personhood with implications for ethical questions in AI are examined, including personal identity over time, viewing persons through data, autonomy, and privacy.

Keywords Personhood · Personal identity · Mind and body · Autonomy · Privacy · Respect for persons

8.1 Introduction

Summary
This chapter explores the concept of the person, the various ways in which it is understood, its implications for ethics, and its importance in relation to various questions in AI ethics. Developments in AI may be seen to challenge the nature, coherence, and value of the concept of a person and the boundaries between persons and things, as well as raising profound ethical questions about our treatment of persons. The concept of a person, while central to much work in ethics, can be understood in different ways: as a metaphysical or conceptual account of the

individual, as a concept necessarily imbued with moral import, as referring to the sovereign individual, or as indicating a social role.

We met the concept of the person in Sect. 4.3 in discussing common assumptions regarding the nature of ethics. The notion of a person was introduced briefly as an agent with wants, preferences, and desires for the future, who is aware of themselves as an individual, and who is capable of acting and judging. It is frequently used as a marker of a being holding moral value. This chapter focuses on the complex question of persons and the associated ethical issues in AI. 'Person' is often used interchangeably with 'human being', yet philosophically, it is often used to indicate a cluster of certain features that human beings possess, yet which are distinguished from the concept of a human being understood purely as a member of a biological species. Questions about personhood thus overlap with, but are distinct from, issues concerning human nature (which we discussed in Chap. 5). In many ways, asking questions about AI through the lens of personhood can be seen as a means of organising and consolidating many of the issues that we have addressed thus far. It highlights some questions concerning the nature of the distinctions and similarities between human beings and machines, and it can be used to frame many of the ethical questions, perhaps helping to shed new light on them.

At the same time, this is an incredibly complex issue, since there are many ways of understanding the concept of a person, let alone the ethical significance of the category of the person. The concept of personhood exposes significant differences between the opinions and attitudes of different individuals, cultures, worldviews, and religions. It is challenging to write an account that goes: 'this is what a person is, now let's look at the ethical implications for AI', because determining the category of a person and spelling out precise criteria for personhood is not only controversial, it is so intimately tied up with value issues.

Nonetheless, exploring claims about the category of the person and some standard philosophical issues around persons can help to deepen understanding of various major questions, particularly of some major controversies and differences of approach to ethical issues in AI. For example, why was there such hullabaloo surrounding the allegations that the LaMDA language model had attained sentience? Why were some people so willing to attribute potential personhood to this AI, and why did others scoff at the very suggestion?

What ethical issues do we need to address concerning persons? In broad summary, we can divide these into those affecting humans and those concerning machines: questions about what ethical treatment persons merit, and how, in various ways, the use of AI may impact this; and questions about whether AI could, or does, exhibit personhood, or elements of personhood, including consciousness and/or agency, and if so, what moral implications does this have. The latter will be introduced here and discussed further in Chap. 11.

There are some particular questions concerning persons which have been the subject of discussion for some time and which are pertinent to ethical issues in AI. These include:

How the category of the person is conceptualised, and how links are drawn between
   a conception of the person and its ethical implications
How persons are recognised, or how personhood is attributed
What kinds of creatures are, or could be, persons
Whether there are different categories or degrees of personhood
How persons are individuated from each other and the link between the person and
   the social
How persons are identified over time (in other words, what makes a person now the
   same person as one at a later or earlier date)
The question of the relationship of personhood with embodiment
The link between personhood and agency, and questions of degrees and kinds of
   agency
The role of cognition, of the self, and of consciousness in accounts of personhood

All of these have resonance to concrete ethical questions in AI. For example, how
we might recognise (or falsely attribute) personhood, or degrees or varieties of it, in
advanced forms of AI; whether a machine could ever attain personhood; whether
forms of technological enhancement might alter who we are as individual persons;
whether it could be conceptually possible to 'upload' our minds to a computer, and
whether this would thus be a continuation of our personal identity; whether the uses
of AI enhance or diminish us as persons; and others.

It is necessary to impose some organising principle in exploring such a rich and
complex topic. This chapter thus arranges the discussion through looking at what has
become some standard topics within philosophy. By exploring the problems these
raise and the kinds of questions that have produced the most philosophical puzzlement, this should open the door to seeing how rather different approaches to these
questions are possible, again hopefully encouraging dialogue. The topic of persons is
approached primarily from within philosophical discourse, but it is of course also a
concept explored within social sciences, especially within anthropology, and it also
has strong links with the concept of the self. Hence, as so often, one will constantly
come across issues that are carried forward or discussed from different angles
elsewhere. A major question to explore is how the ideological underpinnings that
may be attributed to AI and the use of AI resonate and interact with the conceptual
and ethical questions around personhood.

Social roles and the individual The word 'person' derives from the Latin 'persona' meaning 'mask'. Actors used masks to indicate the characters they were
playing in a drama. The term 'persona' was used by the psychologist and psycho-
analyst Carl Jung to indicate a 'mask' that someone may adopt to hide the 'real'
person behind the mask [1]. The question of the social role or roles someone may
play and the potential gulf between these and the 'real' person within raises the
critical questions of how we are seen by others, how we would like to be seen, how
we 'truly' are, and the link between the individual and the social, all of which can be
asked in different contexts, all of which are relevant to many of the ethical questions
in AI. Here, we are primarily concerned with the notion of the person in their own
right, the individual subject. However, the question of how personhood is seen and

attributed to others, and the question of the relationship between the individual person and recognition of and by others, both arise from considering conceptions of the person as an individual subject, and are, as indicated, important to concrete questions in AI ethics.

We will consider how certain conceptions of personhood that have come to be prominent within applied ethics may resonate with some work in AI and with the question of how AI (and intelligence in general) is conceptualised and valued. Hence, in reading this chapter, it may be useful to recall and reflect on some material from previous chapters, especially Chap. 5.

However, it must be noted that work in areas such as anthropology has demonstrated that the category of the person as broadly and currently understood within the West is far from universal in human culture. Marcel Mauss, in a lecture delivered in 1938 entitled 'A category of the human mind', argued that in certain societies, the notion of the individual person was closely tied to particular rigid social roles, in contrast to a conception of the person more closely tied to individual consciousness [2]. Subsequent work has cast doubt on Mauss's general argument, but nonetheless many accept that particular notions of the individual person are highly culturally and historically specific [3]. Hence, we must be aware of the particularity of the conceptions of personhood discussed here; indeed, to some extent, we cannot escape this awareness, since even among modern thinkers from similar cultural backgrounds, there are divergent views concerning the concept of the person and its ethical implications.

Metaphysical and moral notions of the person There is such a close intertwining of conceptual claims about personhood and moral claims about persons that it is often hard to untangle the two. Sometimes in common parlance, 'person' is simply used to mean human being. However, the term 'person' has a particular use in moral and legal contexts to indicate a being of especial standing and worth. In the work of some philosophers, the term 'person' is explicitly used as a value term to indicate some moral claim, such as that a being is a bearer of rights [4]. Other philosophers, as we shall see, spell out conceptual accounts of what it is to be a person, from which certain moral claims may arise. Others have argued that what distinguishes persons from creatures who are also agents but nonetheless, not persons, are precisely features that are constitutive of a sense of morality, such as the capacity to reflect on one's beliefs and actions, and a sense of the self.

The question of whether or not a being is accorded the status of a person is one on which much hangs. The strength of feeling associated with attempts to remedy perceived injustices around the denial of personhood is such that the starting point of argument may be the wrongness of exclusion, from which assumptions about the nature of personhood are constructed. The question of how we recognise and attribute personhood to others turns out to be a critical and central issue to the very notion of personhood and hence helps to explain some of the large divisions and differences of opinion over the attribution of personhood, or related concepts such as sentience or consciousness, in the case of AI. We saw this in the case of the LaMDA language model and the strength of feeling, and in many respects, gulfs of understanding, between those who saw claims of sentience as a real possibility and those who dismissed the idea (see Chap. 4).

8.2   An Account of Personhood: Respect for Persons as a Fundamental Ideal

Summary
This section presents an overview of an influential approach to personhood as a key ethical concept. In such an approach, the concept of a person represents the unique individual as a source of ultimate and equal value. The notion of 'respect for persons', which is influential in the justification of notions of universal human rights, is discussed through the work of Immanuel Kant.

Let us start with articulating a notion of the person and moral status that should be broadly familiar to many: respect for persons as a key foundation of ethical concern. The idea that each individual person is of ultimate worth has been said to be fundamental to moral, religious, and political ideals [5].

However, as we have seen, this view is not universally held, and if we recall some earlier material, we will see that it is not even universally held within the Western societies in which this ideal has been prominent. As we have already stressed, the ancient Greeks had no trouble viewing different classes of human beings as having different social standing and moral respect. Recall our discussion of consequentialism and its variant, utilitarianism, in Chap. 6. One major criticism of utilitarianism was its precisely failure to protect individuals as individuals (see especially Sect. 6. 2.5). Some may modify their utilitarianism as a response; indeed, for example, John Stuart Mill also protected the individual through strong arguments for individual liberty [6]. Yet at the same time, there are many prominent proponents of forms of utilitarianism who consider that they can meet this challenge, or that (at least some of) the trade-offs between individuals that follow from utilitarianism are acceptable. Note then that one issue concerning the concept and value of persons is the question of the separation between persons and of what ethical trade-offs might be made between individuals (see Sect. 6.2.5).

A radical equality of persons   The notion of respect for persons has a long history, but throughout much of this, it was assumed that some persons merit more respect than others: for example, royalty and nobility over commoners; the propertied class over those without property; men over women. In modern times, however, the notion of respect for persons is often expressed in the idea that persons are radically equal and merit equal moral respect, irrespective of social or worldly standing. Different levels and forms of respect due in social contexts, for example, indicated by formal titles or forms of address, should not be taken to indicate that anyone has any higher *moral* status than any other human. This notion of radical equality has been a driving force behind much work in politics and in law, underlying conceptions of universal human rights and fights for social justice and civil rights.

Respect for persons in the philosophy of Immanuel Kant The notion of respect for persons is generally considered to have arisen in its modern form from the work of Immanuel Kant, in his notion of the appropriate way in which we should treat other persons, described as rational agents [7]. Recall that for Kant, the motivation behind our actions is critical (see Sect. 1.12). Recall also that for Kant, the notion of a rational agent involved more than the capacity to follow sets of instructions, or to work out how to achieve one's ends, and recall that the notion of rationality involved did not require or imply an especially high level of cognitive capacity. It involved the capacity for reflective self-awareness (see Sect. 6.3.2). A rational agent must be able to reflect on their actions and consider if these actions are in accordance with the ideals of the moral law. A creature such as a cat may possess agency, but a cat cannot think to itself, 'I wonder if I should stop being so greedy', or 'Perhaps it's about time I stopped teasing the dog'. A rational agent, such as a human being, can do this (even though they often fail to do so; a rational agent is one who *possesses* this capacity, even if they do not always exercise it).

For Kant, rational agents are the source of value, not a means to create value. For this reason, he states that one way of understanding the Categorical Imperative, meaning a moral rule that must be followed for its own sake, not for any contingent aims (see Sect. 6.3.2), is that we should always treat others never simply as a means but also at the same time as an end in themselves. Rational agents have dignity, not price: things with price can be traded one against another. Things possessing dignity cannot. Rational agents also have the capacity to recognise other rational agents and hence to treat them with the respect they merit.

The notion that we should always treat others never simply as a means but also at the same time as an end in themselves is frequently misunderstood to mean we should never treat another as a means to an end. This would, quite simply, wipe out society and social interactions as we know them. We could never expect someone to do a single thing for us, nor us for them. Commerce, everyday interactions, asking someone to pass the salt, all are impossible under such an interpretation. However, it is not at all what Kant intended. Rather, we should always *at the same time* consider their worth as a person and only treat them in ways that they, *as a rational agent*, could agree to. This in turn means that the other person, in accepting your treatment of them, must also respect their own self: for Kant, it is clear that we have duties to ourselves, as well as to others.

A simple test for treating a person with respect may be to consider if they consent to the treatment, but it is vital to note that Kant's view is not as simple as stating that we should only treat people in ways to which they consent; because a person may consent to treatment which no person deserves, or which diminishes one's person-hood, rationality, or agency in some way. For Kant, there are things that no rational agent could *rationally will*; but of course, we are not always rational; we fall below our own ideals. Of course, the big question will be what precisely is the treatment that a rational agent, or a person, deserves and whether one wishes to adopt the notion of what can be rationally willed.

Exercise 1

Can you think of any examples where consent is obtained, yet where respect for persons may be threatened? Include examples even where you are not entirely sure if respect for persons is compromised, but where it seems there is a discussion to be had. Compare your examples with others, if you are working in groups, and note any points of greatest controversy. Try to include as many examples from the world of AI as possible.

(*Hint*: if you can't think of any examples, check this box □ to agree to Terms and Conditions before continuing.)

What precisely Kant meant by treating persons as ends in themselves has been the source of considerable controversy and debate. Indeed, one of the philosophical questions that arises in the debates over personhood is precisely how we recognise and respond to the moral worth and demands made on us by other persons. On one approach, the moral respect we owe persons is recognised directly in personal interaction; in another, this can be worked out conceptually, as a conclusion drawn from the attribution of various necessary qualities to the being in question (although these approaches are not necessarily mutually exclusive in practice). Recall our discussion of third personal and second personal approaches to ethics in Sect. 8.3, in relation to Martin Buber and Simone Weil, and in the quality and nature of communication in discourse ethics. We will return to these points later in discussing the attribution of personhood, including in relation to AI.

Many may find much of merit in Kant's views on respect for persons, even if they disagree on details or even if they disagree on many fundamentals. Much political, social, and ethical activism is underlined by some notion of the radical moral equality of all, irrespective of standing in the world. Much of the discussion around the notion of persons historically has concerned who counts as a 'full' person under the law, society, and ethics: with certain classes of people having had to fight for full recognition of their status as persons, from those treated as slaves, to women, to denigrated ethnic and racial groups, to the unpropertied.

Exercise 2

Consider some of the previous examples in this book, including any exercises, and whether the notion of respect for persons is one of the issues. Add any examples from AI ethics of your own. Collect as many diverse examples as you can.

Issues in AI ethics that raise the question of whether persons are being treated with all the respect due to them may include surveillance and tracking using AI, including the question of consent; questions of technological unemployment, and the possible creation of socioeconomic classes of people rendered 'surplus' to the economy by automation ('useless eaters', perhaps); human enhancement via AI, particularly if this leads to two or more 'classes' of humans, those 'enhanced' and those not enhanced. As we shall see, there are different elements within the concept of a person that present different facets to these questions.

8.3   Some Contemporary Models of Personhood and Their Ethical Implications

Summary

We discuss contemporary models of personhood, as distinct from the concept of the 'human being'. Some are explicitly produced and used for the purposes of arguing for certain ethical positions. Others present conceptual models of personhood from which ethical implications may be derived. We examine Daniel Dennett's account of personhood, exploring the requirements of rationality, of self-consciousness, of reciprocity, and the conditions for the attribution of personhood, noting that space is opened for the idea that machines could attain personhood.

Historically, then, many have fought for the ideal that all human beings should be recognised as persons of equal moral and political status. However, some contemporary philosophical work has explicitly attempted to argue that the notion of personhood is not to be equated with the human being. This can lead to claims that some classes of human beings, or some individual humans, are not in fact persons, or do not have full personhood. There are also conceptions of personhood that have been argued to have the implication that certain human beings will be accorded diminished personhood. Classes of human beings whose status of personhood is or has been considered 'marginal' include the unborn [8], those with intellectual disabilities, those diagnosed with 'brain death', and those with severe levels of cognitive decline, such as those living with advanced stages of dementia [9]. Conversely, some philosophical accounts of personhood have been used to argue that some of the higher animals, such as the great apes, do possess personhood. Some have commented that bridging the human-animal divide in this way has resonance with aspects of indigenous cosmologies [10].

For example, Michael Tooley has outlined an influential account of the person as a bearer of the moral rights to life that states that the right to life requires an organism to have the concept of a continuing self as the subject of various mental states and to consider that it is such a continuing self [4]. Only such an organism would be able to express the wish to carry on living and to claim the right to do so; an argument may be given that these requirements are essential to merit the specific right to life. In a similar manner, Peter Singer considers a person to be a being who has both wants and desires for the future and can conceptualise its future [11].

Exercise 3

Consider this: could an advanced artificial intelligence have 'wants and desires for the future' and have a concept of its own future? Would this be enough to mean that we would owe this AI anything morally, such as any duties in relation to it? You may wish to look back at Chap. 5, at the instrumental concept of intelligence discussed there, and consider how a machine may be attributed with wants and desires. You may wish to consider examples from science fiction.

Consider your reasons for your answer. Could answers to this question involve projecting hopes and fears onto AI? Is there any solution to this, and does it matter?

The above accounts of personhood are only partial, giving conditions for personhood which may be necessary but which are not sufficient. Other accounts of personhood contain more conditions that produce a fuller account of the mental attributes underlying personhood. Let us look at an account spelled out by the philosopher Daniel Dennett. We will take this account and use it as a scaffold from which to discuss some general questions about the concept of a person. We need to consider how we should characterise personhood, what the moral implications of personhood are, and how examining different possible facets of personhood can help expose some of the ethical questions arising from aspects of our use of AI.

The very difficulties of presenting a precise and agreed stipulation of what it is to be a person, and the very difficulties of agreeing on the ethical implications of personhood, will help to account for the range of responses to many ethical questions involving AI.

This account stipulates that a person is:

A rational being;
To which states of consciousness and mental or intentional predicates (such as 'is thinking about his hamster', 'is planning to go sky-diving', 'has a dull ache in her left toe', etc.) are attributed;
Which is treated in a certain way, as a person;
Which can reciprocate this and treat others as persons in turn;
Which can communicate verbally;
And is self-conscious (as opposed to merely conscious: a person has a sense of their self) [12].

A person need not be a human being What implications might such an account have for the ethical questions in which we are interested? Such an account at least begins to open up the possibility that some AI may achieve at least part of the conditions of personhood. Note that nothing in any of these accounts refers to membership of a particular species; we see this even in Kant's account of rational agency: he believed in the possibility of intelligent extraterrestrial life [13]. There is nothing in this conception of personhood about any particular way in which these qualities may be instantiated. There is an implied embodiment of some sort in the requirements that a person must be able to reciprocate in how it treats another, which implies the capacity to act in the world, as does the requirement for verbal communication. However, this requirement does not seem to even necessitate a specific identifiable body: perhaps some supernatural force, such as a poltergeist or an angel, might qualify as a person. (It's not entirely clear to me why the communication has to be verbal; see below for further discussion of this requirement of personhood.)

Consider the requirement of rationality Unless this is interpreted to mean the *capability* for rationality, we mere humans are all doomed. Might this then mean that another entity that did not have the human propensity for irrationality might be a 'better' sort of person? Could this include AI? Failings of rationality may be of two kinds: simple errors or slips ('cold' errors) and motivated irrationality ('hot' errors), such as wishful thinking, bias, or self-deception [14, 15].

Exercise 4

Perhaps AI could help us to avoid errors of reasoning. If rationality is a requirement of personhood, and if personhood is a moral category, could AI lead us to be better persons, meriting greater moral respect? Or is it simply sufficient to pass some threshold level of rationality to merit equal membership of the class of persons? Consider the pros and cons and any moral consequences.

Recall our discussions of human nature and the frequent observations of splits in human nature (Sect. 5.4.6) and of elements of irrationality that may occur in humans (see Sect. 6.2.4 and the discussion of Dostoevsky). The broad idea that we have 'higher' or 'lower' parts of the self, that humans typically experience some inner tension between different elements of their person, and that a pathway of growth towards some development or the resolution of such inner tensions or splits is desirable, is very widespread. This is also intimately linked to questions of self-awareness and self-reflection, which are necessary conditions for being able to spot and address splits and tensions between different elements of the self. Could this be an inherent part of what it is to be a person? Does the simple fact that we have certain divisions, certain possibly conflicting parts of ourselves, always a failing of some sort? Might an advanced AI thus be better than us if it does not suffer from such problems?

Consider that the capacity to turn one's plans and attention towards certain directions and to overcome the tendencies or temptations towards certain behaviour may be part and parcel of how we understand what it is to have or to develop a moral character. Hence, the very presence of such splits, the mode of addressing them, may be part and parcel of what in fact constructs a unified person. This also raises the question of whether a person essentially exists over a period of time. We shall discuss this further below.

Rationality may simply be thought of as the capacity to reason, to gain knowledge, and so on. In addition, it is also used to capture the capacity to plan towards achieving goals. In which case, perhaps it is a requirement of personhood that a person has to have goals. We look further at this as a possible requirement of personhood below, its implications for AI and for the distinction between persons, agents, and machines.

The requirement of self-consciousness Mere consciousness, simply having experiences, is attributed to many animals that we would not consider to be persons. The capacity of awareness of one's own thoughts and feelings, a higher order form of consciousness, may be necessary for personhood, as it seems required for the reflection upon one's plans, actions, and inner states that would be needed to make judgements and decisions and to carry out plans towards a goal; but does this require that a person has a sense of a distinct, unique, self? And how might such a 'self' be conceptualised? There are likely to be large cultural and ideological differences in how such a self is viewed and seen in relation to other selves.

Attributions of personhood Note the interactions with and dependence upon other persons for the attribution of personhood. To be a person involves being treated as a person by others, as well as the capacity to reciprocate. Note that although the concept of a person may be used as an explication of the concept of an individual subject, each individual subject's status exists in interdependence with that of others. If the requirement of recognition by others persons is a necessary part of what it is to be a person, it is as if personhood is a club where you have to be sponsored by an existing member before you are allowed to join [9].

There are inherent dangers in this (and we will look at some possible examples later). History shows us that many human beings have indeed been cut off from the club of fully recognised persons. For example, in her 1792 book, *A Vindication of the Rights of Woman*, Mary Wollstonecraft (mother of Mary Shelley, the author of *Frankenstein*) argued (as many others have) that women had been denied the education necessary to develop their full rationality, and this only acted to reinforce the notion that women lacked the necessary level of reason to engage fully in the world with men [16]. People living with various disabilities, people from different ethnic and racial groups, have likewise been disregarded and viewed with scorn. Conversely, recall our discussions in Sect. 4.4 about describing situations through stories and images and what we might or might not read into our interpretations of these. Perhaps we might equally attribute personhood, or elements of it, entirely erroneously.

Some of the difference in reaction to the LaMDA language model 'sentience' case may be explained by the fears of those who are concerned that the capabilities (whether thought of in terms of personhood or a related concept) of an AI may be being overlooked, with consequent wrong-doing, a moral slight, to the AI.

Exercise 5

Consider an advanced language model such as LaMDA or any other example of AI. You may wish to take an example from science fiction, perhaps the computer in Arthur C. Clarke's *2001: A Space Odyssey*, or the AI from the film *Her* [17, 18]. What elements of the AI's behaviour might be thought to indicate personhood, sentience, and/or consciousness? Consider how someone might wish to attribute these qualities, even if you disagree that the criteria are met.

Dennett's criteria explicitly include the capacity for verbal communication. Do you consider this to be vital or not? Might its apparent presence be an especially persuasive factor for some in the attribution of possible sentience to LaMDA?

A general question to consider regarding our use of AI is whether this technology may affect our propensity to attribute personhood and whether it may influence or reinforce particular ways of understanding personhood. We look below at a current controversy about how we might fail to recognise personhood in other human beings and consider the possible links and lessons for AI.

The requirement of reciprocity This is an interesting requirement to consider, especially from the point of view of how we use AI and how AI regards us. Note that this requirement of reciprocity could be interpreted as an ideal to aspire towards if it refers to a condition of mutual full regard and attention to the needs of others, for example, expressed in Kant's notion of respect for persons, Martin Buber's notion of the I-Thou relationship, or the requirements of respectful discourse.

However, as with rationality, this must be understood as an ideal that few of us would live up to, certainly all the time. We routinely fail to notice those around us, even those close to us. Moreover, a requirement of reciprocity could be interpreted to mean that we recognise the personhood in those to whom we wish harm or wish to manipulate. For if we wish to deny or denigrate the personhood of others, this involves recognising that they are indeed persons. We may manipulate or abuse others by ignoring their personhood and treating them simply as objects or as nonperson creatures to be manipulated and used, or we may realise that we need to take into account and target their very personhood, in our desire to manipulate, denigrate, or use them. The corollary of this is that we may have to recognise that the very worst of our abusers are indeed persons themselves.

A major set of questions regarding AI, and indeed many other forms of technology, is how it impacts interpersonal relationships. We have already seen many cases and exercises, where the question of whether our use of AI may enable or enhance such reciprocal recognition of personhood.

Exercise 6

Suppose we were being manipulated by AI. Perhaps multiple forms of technology are tracking and monitoring us, feeding us tailored information, using forms of persuasive technology to capture our time and attention, diverting us towards certain activities, experiences, and ideas, and away from others. Over time, facial recognition and emotion recognition AI builds up a picture of 'who we are' and uses that to fine-tune the ways in which each one of us is being manipulated. Perhaps the manipulation is to nudge us towards buying certain products, perhaps it is towards accepting more and more technology into our lives, perhaps it is towards accepting a role as one of the underclass of permanently unemployed as automation takes our jobs, perhaps it is to accept a role as one of the underclass as expensive AI-powered human enhancement takes off.

The question is: because this AI is treating you *as if* you are a person, might you have to eventually conclude that this sophisticated system of AI was also a person, distributed across a wide system of technology? Might it possess some of the qualities of personhood, if not all?

Recognition of Personhood and the Turing Test

With the development of computers, there was great interest in the question of whether computers could truly 'think' and possess intelligence. The Turing Test, originally named by Alan Turing as the Imitation Game, was based upon a Victorian parlour game where players had to guess on the basis of answers to questions if a person was a man or a woman [19]. Turing adapted this to propose a test where a computer would give answers to series of questions. If

---

(continued)

the inquirer could not tell whether the answers were being given by a computer or by a human being, then this means the computer displays an intelligence indistinguishable from that of human-level intelligence [20, pp. 29–36].

Much has been written about this test, and entrants competed for many years in the Loebner Prize Competition in attempts to pass the test. The lure of the test for some, perhaps aided by the importance of language for human culture, and the element of reciprocity in linguistic communication with a computer, may entice the thought that passing the Turing Test means that the computer is interacting with a human in the way that a human is, and thus genuinely is intelligent, and perhaps has other qualities that a human person does.

The test is limited however in that the interactions with the computer are strictly limited. Even if a computer passed such a test, after the competition was over, its identity as a computer could readily be revealed. Linguistic ability is only one aspect of intelligence, only one aspect of personhood, and the interactions between computer and human being (or person) possible through language are only one small part of the reciprocity needed to form the hallmark of personhood.

Attitudes   Towards   Persons,   Attribution   of   Personhood, and the Approaches of Different Disciplines
I first became seriously interested in philosophical accounts of personhood near the start of my career. A friend, Tessa Podpadec, who was researching the experiences of people with mild intellectual disabilities, came round for coffee, and casually picked up a copy of the *Journal of Applied Philosophy* and started reading it. She was soon trembling with rage. The journal contained an article discussing the issue of 'marginal personhood', suggesting that some human beings, including those with intellectual disabilities, may not fulfil all the requirements to qualify as persons. Our discussions led to publishing two papers, exploring both the nature of persons, and the attitudes of those from different disciplines towards the personhood of human beings with significant cognitive impairments [9, 21].

The approach of those working in the field with people with intellectual disabilities was to presume personhood, and search for it, seeking a relationship with each person. The approach of the philosophers in question was to produce a criterion of personhood, and then see if individuals measured up to it.

Consider this in relation to different ways of attaining moral understanding, discussed for instance in Sect. 7.2.5.

One conclusion might be to appreciate the value of consulting or working closely with those from a wide range of different relevant backgrounds and experiences.

(continued)

Food for thought: Could it be that seeking and presuming personhood in each other is a way of fostering and enabling the personhood of each of us to flourish and to reveal itself?

8.4 Interlude: Mind and Body

Summary
Since a key question regarding persons is that of embodiment, brief overviews of central philosophical positions regarding the relationship between the mind and the body are given: dualism, physicalism, behaviourism, functionalism, and the extended mind theory. The main purpose is to indicate how the various attractions of the contrasting positions may illuminate the question of how personhood is understood and how different positions regarding mind and body may cast light on some central ethical questions in AI, such as the way in which persons may be viewed by AI.

We have raised the question of whether persons are essentially embodied. A backdrop to such questions is the relationship between the mind and the body. We therefore pause to survey the major philosophical theories concerning mind and body. Some of the central questions and attitudes that arise also help to explain the difficulty of the questions with which we grapple concerning personhood. It is also important to consider why different rival theories concerning the relationship between mind and body may be attractive and gain proponents. In teaching philosophy, I always try to emphasise the importance of understanding the attractions of opposing theories and positions, even if one wishes to reject them thoroughly. Something can be wrong for interesting reasons, and moreover, the more you understand the attractions of a position, the more you can (a) incorporate those attractions into your own position and (b) understand those with whom you disagree. This is never more important than when we are considering issues of ethical and practical import.

There is a very large range of philosophical positions concerning the nature of the mind and the relationship between mind and body. It can almost seem as if between them, philosophers have cooked up every possible theory and then drawn lots to ensure that there is somebody, somewhere, who adheres to each one of the conceptually possible (and in some cases conceptually impossible) theories regarding the nature of the mind. How can we explain how mind, which encompasses so many different elements of cognition and which is capable of consciousness, arises in the midst of this material world, and how can we explain its relationship to the material world within which it is placed, but from which it seems manifestly distinct?

Dualist theories advocate a conceptual gulf between mind and body. The plausibility of dualistic accounts stems from the phenomenology of minds: to have a mind is to have subjective awareness, which seems to be a completely different manner of existence from being a material object. However, the dualist must explain the vast weight of evidence that there is an extremely close and apparently causal connection between the mental and the physical. A classic exponent of dualism was Descartes, who considered that the mind consisted of mental substance, which was immaterial yet somehow mysteriously interacted with physical substance [22]. More contemporary dualists include those who reject the idea of a mental substance but nonetheless do not consider that minds can be fully reduced to a materialist account; property dualists are not people who own two homes but are those who consider that although mental properties and physical properties may be attributed to the same thing, such as events in the brain, mental properties cannot be reduced to or explained entirely in terms of physical or material properties [23]. Conversely, materialists think nothing more than ordinary matter is needed to fully explain the mind.

Many religious or spiritual views propose some manner of dualism, believing that a nonmaterial soul, spirit, or self exists and can survive physical death, in an afterlife or via reincarnation. Survival the death of one's current human body may, however, be understood as involving the resurrection of the body, as in standard Christian belief.

Exercise 7
Bracketing philosophical concerns about its possibility, if we could 'upload' our minds to a computer, would this be equivalent to murder, or to attaining further life? Outline how someone might argue that this amounted to a continuation of life for the individual and how one might argue against this.

How might one argue that this was (a) desirable; (b) a horror story?

Suppose one's mind could be copied into a computer, while one remained alive. Would there then be two of you?

Physicalist views One place in which to hunt for the mind is obviously the brain, given the weight of evidence that brain activity is vital for consciousness and other mental activities. Even Descartes considered that it was within the pineal gland in the brain that the connection between mental and physical substance was somehow made [22]. A simple materialist account based upon the brain was the mind-brain identity theory for obvious reasons: claiming that mental events are just events in the brain, and nothing more [24]. The link between activity in the brain and thought seems irrefutable (at least to us: the ancients often thought otherwise). Mental phenomena seem to arise from physical events in the brain, but are they nothing more? More recent views are far more sophisticated and draw heavily on neuroscience and cognitive science in the attempt to understand and explain the mind, in terms of both cognition and of the phenomena of consciousness, and note the contribution to mental states of activities elsewhere in the body. Eliminative materialism rather radically argues that our common sense idea of the mind, of the essential subjectivity of its mental states, is mistaken and that the mind can fully be understood in purely material terms [25]. If the intricacies of the brain that give rise to cognition, consciousness, and agency could be reproduced with sufficient accuracy, then it seems possible that we could create a mind. Some approaches to artificial intelligence are indeed based upon attempts to reproduce neurological accounts of the brain, making detailed attempts to copy biological brains [26, p. 12].

Zombies A stumbling block to any materialist view of mind is literally the stuff of horror films: the zombie, although philosophers tend to use the concept in a less alarming manner. It seems entirely possible to imagine that there could be creatures with activity within their brain exactly on a par with activity within human brains, yet who had no subjective inner experiences [27]. There is *nothing that it is like to be* a zombie (perhaps hence paradoxically capturing part of the human horror at the idea of becoming a zombie: the thought that there may be 'nothing that it is like to be me' may have a certain incoherence, but it nonetheless strikes fear into many of us). Hence, the possibility of the zombie has been used in attempts to refute physicalist positions and to reinforce the dualist case. There are debates around whether zombies are conceptually coherent and what, if anything they show regarding the rightness or wrongness of physicalism.

Other minds The topic of zombies, however, reminds us of another major issue in the philosophy of mind: the problem of our knowledge of other minds. How can we truly know what, if anything, is going on in the mind of another? A dualist view which emphasises the subjectivity of experience and the separation of the mental from the physical struggles with this sceptical problem. Descartes mused that perhaps the people he saw walking in the street were actually automata with no living thinking being beneath the hats and coats. See Sect. 8.5, for a discussion concerning the notion of embodied selfhood: perhaps there is a way of attributing mind more immediately through the communications of the body. The sceptical problem is also manifest in the criteria in Dennett's account of personhood, that to be a person involves having personhood attributed by others; we saw above the fragility and dangers of this vulnerability.

Behaviourism Other materialist views opt for the body rather than the brain. Philosophical behaviourism made the startling claim that the mind can be understood entirely in terms of behaviour, including linguistic behaviour. This is startling to many because to have a mind is to have a point of view, to see the world from a particular vantage point, to have a subjective sense of self. However, the philosophical behaviourists denied that to understand people, we need to refer to anything other than outward behaviour. We may not even have to describe behaviour in terms of actions imbued with intention and motivations: the aim may be to describe behaviour simply in terms of bodily motions, including of course sounds uttered and so on. The philosophical behaviourist Gilbert Ryle writing in the twentieth century famously ridiculed Descartes' dualist position as the 'ghost in the machine' [28]. One problem is that many consider that something akin to such ghosts exists. Behaviourism may seem now to be the least promising account of the mind, although it may perhaps form a basis for the attribution of minds to machines, but we will return to it again presently. Understanding a behaviourist stance can be a useful tool for understanding some elements of the use of AI.

Functionalism can in some ways be seen as a far more sophisticated version of behaviourism, which draws heavily on computer science and argues that the mind can be understood in terms of the functional capacities of the brain, the operations it carries out [29]. A material substrate is needed for this, but it matters not what this substrate is. All that matters is what outputs are generated from what inputs. It could be carbon-based; it could be silicone-based; it could be made of green cheese. Such approaches have obvious relevance for AI. It seems possible that a sophisticated machine could be a mind if some version of functionalism is correct. There is much to be said for and against functionalism, and it repays close study for any interested in AI and computing, including the ethical questions.

However, one question to consider is whether an explanation of the relationship between the mind and the body captures all we need to capture to understand ethical issues; and, because that we are dealing with comparisons and contrasts between humans and machines, although a theory which makes such direct comparisons possible and perhaps readily available, we must for that very reason at least ask the question of whether we are viewing humans too much through the focus of how we understand computing. Perhaps functionalism can capture much about the *mind*, but is there more to add concerning the nature of the *person*?

Mind and body—but how much body? Descartes opted for the pineal gland. Others opt for events in the brain. Others for the whole brain. Others for the whole body. Functionalism does not necessitate any particular physical substrate, and indeed, a famous thought experiment considers whether the entire population of China giving signals to each other might be able to manifest the functions of a mind [30]. The example was suggested by Ned Block as an argument against functionalism, as demonstrating the absurdity of attributing, for example, states of pain to the entire population of China, but others disagree.

Exercise 8

If functionalism is correct, how might we draw the boundaries between separate minds? If we could attribute a mind to a computer, and if computers can be linked to each other, what, if anything, would mark the boundaries between one computer mind and another?

Consider then that if human minds could interface with computers or be directly linked to the Internet, and thus through this to other human minds, what would happen to the distinction between different persons?

Could this be a moral improvement upon our present situation?

Consider: if it might be possible for a mind to be connected to other minds in such a way, would such a mind still be a *person*?

Theories of externalism hold that the mind is not entirely contained within the brain or indeed the body. Externalism may hold that the content of mind (mental content) goes beyond the body. For example, the content of a thought about 'that chair over there' includes essential reference to a particular chair. Other forms of externalism claim that the bearers of mental content may be external to the mind [31]. A very simple, rough-and-ready introduction to this (rather complex) field can be given thus: Our mind essentially stores memories, and much cognition relies upon the capacity to hold several things together in our consciousness at once. We can, however, write things down and refer to these rather than relying on retrieval from our brains. There is no space for an adequate discussion of these complex but important theories here, save to note that our growing use of technology to assist with cognition might be thought to result in extending our minds even further: could we become united with computers in such a way, even if we are not physically connected as we might be with say, a neural implant? We discuss the question of the connection between humans and machines further below.

Subjectivity, reductionism, and the first person Hence, the philosophy of mind has grappled with the mysterious question of the relation between mind and body. This thumbnail sketch in no way does justice to the complexity and sophistication of the debates. One bone of contention is whether the attempt to explain the mind in material terms, or in functionalist terms, is a reductionist view that reduces the mind to 'nothing but' something else: 'nothing but' neurons firing, 'just' a computer programme running in the wetware of a brain, 'nothing but' the complex behaviour of a person operating over time. Or perhaps the reluctance felt by many to explain the mind in materialist terms is a kind of misplaced hubris, somewhat like the confusion and resistance felt by many when Darwin announced to the world that we were 'merely' a kind of ape [32].

There is surely something more at stake in this case. The felt subjectivity of the mind seems stubbornly resistant to reductive explanation; many find eliminative materialism deeply counterintuitive. As a philosophy undergraduate, I harboured the secret thought that those who consider that consciousness can be completely explained in material terms must themselves be zombies, because otherwise there is no way they could find such an explanation of their own experience at all convincing. I have met some eliminative materialists, and they seem fairly normal, or at least, 'normal for philosophers', seemingly passing the Turing Test, but on the other hand, how would we know?

Exercise 9
Some consider that if we could fully understand and reproduce the human mind and human intelligence, that somehow threatens or demeans us, reducing us to 'nothing but' a technological product, perhaps. Others have a completely opposed attitude, that it will reveal our intricacies, and indeed, that such an achievement would only reflect well on us. What is your inclination, if any, and why?

A point of view And this brings us onto another distinctive aspect of our subjectivity that seems to separate it from the 'ordinary' material world: it has a point of view. There is a gulf between the first personal view and the third personal view. This is both an everyday part of our experience and yet deeply mysterious. It is one of the striking things about the oddness of some accounts of the mind, such as behaviourism, which seem to omit the first personal view entirely and look at the human being as it were only from the outside. We have a sense of self, a consciousness that is isolated from others, other minds which we assume are present, but which we can never directly access. This puzzling aspect of the mind that resists adequate explanation so forcefully is a central feature of our ethical universe. We are surrounded by others whose subjectivity remains a moral certainty, yet at the same time a mystery, whose subjectivity demands our recognition, and whose recognition we too require. As we explored earlier (see Sect. 7.2.3), the shift between different ways of thinking and approaching others, from third person to second person, can be highly significant in ethics. Thus, the capacity of views of the nature of mind to encompass and illuminate these aspects of subjectivity and of relations to others is of profound significance in the ethical stance we adopt.

Behaviourism and the third person stance in AI Behaviourism as an approach to the mind was not confined to philosophers pursuing counterintuitive theories from the safety and comfort of their oak-lined libraries and well-stocked common rooms. Many nineteenth- and twentieth-century psychologists were also behaviourists, using it as a framework with which to understand human beings. Ivan Pavlov is famous for his dogs, who salivate (response) when shown food (stimulus). They were trained to associate a bell with the appearance of food [33]. Eventually, they could be trained to salivate at the sound of the bell alone. Similar programmes of stimulus-response conditioning have been used to teach pigeons to play the piano as well as similar 'tricks' and were also thought by behaviourist psychologists to underlie human learning and behaviour. John B. Watson and B.F. Skinner also pursued such programmes of research [34, 35].

Everyone will be familiar with the idea of laboratory animals such as rats being trained to respond in various ways to rewards: the 'Skinner box' is a closed environment that the experimenter can control in order to observe and manipulate the animal's behaviour. Rumours that Skinner kept his infant daughter in such a box have been vigorously denied by her but doubtless represent the horror invoked by imagining such a model applied to human beings [36]. But if we are relieved for Skinner's daughter, should we be concerned about ourselves? Has a new kind of Skinner box become our reality as we live lives controlled and constrained by technology?

Philosophical behaviourists concerned themselves with claims about how the mind should be understood. Methodological behaviourism was more than just a theory about understanding humans through conditioning; it was a methodological approach to psychology that considered that outwardly observable behaviour should be the basis for psychology. There was no need to include introspection or conscious phenomena. Using observable phenomena only, humans could be understood; but what's more, not only understood, but manipulated by others, since the more one understands how behaviour is shaped by the input from the environment, the more humans can be controlled [37].

Readers may be considering the discussion of Anscombe's work on intention in Sect. 4.4.5 and the ways in which we might attribute different intentions to the same set of actions described in certain ways; indeed, how precisely actions are described can be open to wide interpretation. It is important to realise that even if such behaviourism is rejected as a complete account of the human mind, it can still be used as a way of understanding and manipulating behaviour. Indeed, conditioning of our responses is extremely effective, just as, even if we do have free will, we can certainly still be controlled.

Surely, none of us live in any kind of Skinner box, and surely, those who interact with us are not simply observing us through our behaviour and using that alone to understand and interact with us? Not so fast. One does not need to be in a virtual reality to be surrounded by technology that is both tracking us and sending signals that condition our behaviour. An increasing amount of our life is lived online, through phones and computers, and more and more of our behaviour can be minutely monitored, whether via our use of devices connected to the Internet of things, to our phones tracking our location, our searches, our manner of typing, facial recognition, and so on. Among all this, we are prompted and enticed to behave in certain ways.

Exercise 10
'AI and the everyday technologies that use it, treat human beings like lab rats. We are seen as subjects of study to be manipulated, observed from the outside, and as we busy ourselves about our various concerns we are "scrutinised and studied, perhaps almost as narrowly as a man with a microscope might scrutinise the transient creatures that swarm and multiply in a drop of water" [38]. Data about our behaviour are collected with every click and every move. Conversely, many attempt to attribute agency, autonomy, and even humanity to artificial intelligence, or at least to project that consciousness and moral value will attach to artificial intelligences in the future. We are seen through the dehumanising one-way mirror of behaviourism, while AI is seen through the humanising lens of a view of the mind that demands reciprocity from us. This is a reversal of how things should be.'
Consider points for and against this statement.

We have looked at various accounts of human nature. A common feature is the claim that humans have different aspects to their natures, with splits or divisions within the self. This may go together with some account of how to harmonise these in better or worse ways, on which basis, character, and moral success in life may be assessed. One kind of failure may be the failure to resist social pressure, the failure to manifest free will and agency. Recall that for Kant, it was essential that one noticed that a moral question had arisen, and stopped to consider options (Sect. 7.2.5). A philosophical viewpoint can influence ethical reality even when it is not strictly adhered to. It can greatly impact how others interact with us—manipulate might be a better word here—and it can impact upon how we see ourselves. Viewing ourselves and our capacities through certain restricting or liberating lenses can make a vast difference to our future and to our fate. Seeing yourself within certain parameters, or as capable of exceeding them, can generate a self-fulfilling prophecy. Is modern technology enticing us into a world where we view ourselves through a behaviourist lens?

8.5   Are Conceptions of Personhood Too Focused on the Cognitive and the Rational?

Summary
Modern conceptions of personhood dominant in thinking around AI and in applied ethics tend to stress the mental and, in particular, the cognitive aspects of personhood. This section examines some troubling ethical implications of overly focusing on the cognitive, especially for certain groups of humans, such as those living with dementia or other cognitive difficulties, and considers the role of embodied personhood and emotion. The influence of technological models of the mind on conceptions of personhood is considered.

We have considered earlier how attitudes towards technology may shape how we see human beings, and vice versa. Dominant models of how we understand what it is to be a person may influence the question of whether we might possibly attribute personhood to AI and how we attribute, or fail to attribute, personhood to each other. A 'worst case scenario' would be modelling personhood in ways that falsely attributed it to one class while falsely denying it to another class. Could this be a danger? An account heavily focused on the cognitive, including hallmarks of rationality and of verbal communication, may incline towards the attribution of at least some elements of personhood to machines while leaving some human beings in a more tenuous place. Consider the case of people living with dementia in relation to personhood, and in particular, a focus on the cognitive in accounts of the person.

This question has some resonance with the question of how we perceive and respond to AI and robots in that the prospect of dementia arouses fear in many people, for completely understandable reasons. Indeed, elderly people as a class may also arouse fears for many in certain societies; Julia Kristeva has used the term 'abjection', which can be thought of as a despised element within human beings, absent a well-formed self, and which has been used to describe attitudes towards the elderly [39]. However, attitudes towards the elderly vary greatly within different societies. Reflecting on such attitudes may be instructive as a background to considering possible uses of technology such as life extension, the quest for a certain immortality by 'uploading' the mind to a computer, as well as more mundane uses of technology such as the apps, care robots, and surveillance technologies already used or proposed for elderly people in general as well as for people living with dementia. Many might argue that the central issues are not the problems that technology might solve but how these problems arise and are viewed, given social attitudes.

The care of people living with dementia is sadly sometimes less than ideal. Work in the field of care has been greatly influenced in recent decades by work advocating person-centred care. Tom Kitwood's influential work advocated caring for the person living with dementia in ways that nurture and aims to maintain individual personhood as much as possible, emphasising the complexity of the condition and its manifestation and the social and environmental factors that affect severity, progression, levels of distress, and symptoms [40]. We can see this as fitting with Dennett's criterion of the attribution of personhood by others, yet as raising question marks over how some of the other criteria may be understood. How precisely might seeing someone as a person be achieved in practice, especially in cases where a person may be struggling with communication and cognition?

The team of researchers with whom I have been fortunate to work at the Geller Institute of Aging and Memory at the University of West London, along with the research of many others in the field, has contributed towards understanding how the needs and personhood of people living with dementia may be, with the best of intentions, misidentified. For example, consider the attribution of irrationality to behaviour, speech, and expression. Observing basic nursing care on hospital wards, my colleagues identified occasions where 'looping' may occur. 'Looping' is a term borrowed from Goffman's study of institutions, whereby an individual's behaviour or expressions do not fit the requirements of a particular institution; hence, the failure of the person to comply with what is expected of them leads to a reinforcement of the very label, which is taken to justify their treatment within that same institution [41]. Resistance to basic care, an extremely common phenomenon with people living with dementia, may frequently be interpreted as a manifestation of dementia and hence as indicating irrationality rather than as a possibly rational objection or expression of dislike; the label of irrationality then acts as a filter through which subsequent behaviour is interpreted and thus seen as a manifestation of disease rather than of agency [42].

This is not to deny the real cognitive issues that arise with dementia; it is to note that these may be attributed, and heightened, even produced, *in part* as a result of the social and surrounding conditions and expectations. Expectations of rationality within a certain context may lead to a reduced capacity to see the person and reluctance to enable and allow an individual to exercise what capacities they have.

An embodied selfhood Other work has made similar findings. Pia Kontos' work with people living with dementia in care homes observes that people may retain a sense of self and a capacity to interact with those around them and to understand the social world, even after losing language capacity and suffering significant cognitive loss. She found that people may retain a sophisticated sense of the requirements of social interaction, for example, etiquette and expectations at dinner, offering comfort to the distressed, and a sense of self exhibited by awareness of dress and of how they may appear to others, even after language capacities are largely lost [43]. Communication may be achieved through the body, both through body language and expression, and through dress and personal appearance; yet in theoretical models, even in accounts of respect for persons, the precise role of the body in communicating and maintaining personhood may be neglected at the expense of a more cerebral, cognitive model [44].

Likewise, my colleagues found that on hospital wards, older people in general and people living with dementia in particular were less likely to be dressed in their own clothes, often wearing standard hospital pyjamas, and may have personal grooming neglected. They were also less likely to have personal possessions around them than were younger patients. This impacted both how they were seen by staff and others and how they saw themselves. Occasions when a person changed into their own clothes and had assistance with grooming sometimes had a transformative effect on both treatment and behaviour [45]. If the requirement that others attribute personhood is part and parcel of what it is to be a person, we must pay close attention to how this is achieved and to what gets in the way.

What might we conclude from these observations concerning how we understand and identify personhood? Perhaps we need multiple approaches to understanding what it is to be a person. Some philosophical models of the person which may be used as the basis for some recent work in applied ethics, and which may also be drawn upon when considering the potential aspects of personhood in AI, focus on the cognitive, the rational, the verbal. Does this skew the answer in certain directions? The picture of the person built up from accounts such as that of Dennett also prioritises the mental, and even though some manifestation within a material substrate may be necessary, precise details of embodiment seems a contingent issue. The person, 'the self', seems primarily mental, in contrast to the physical. Very differently, Pia Kontos, drawing on the work of philosophers such as Merleau-Ponty, suggests that a notion of embodied selfhood is needed to understand how personhood and the self are manifested in individuals and communicated between individuals [46]. This embodied selfhood has many aspects particular to the human condition, including social and cultural elements. Perhaps, then, if we were ever to attribute personhood to AI, to robots, we would have to have a similarly rich way of recognising and attributing it. Perhaps if we think of personhood through a cognitive model, we may find it in computers, only to fail to find it in certain humans.

Exercise 11

Bearing these points in mind, consider whether your responses to some of the previous exercises concerning the use of AI in relation to people living with dementia might have been different in any way. (See, e.g. Chap. 2, Exercises 6, 8, 10, 11; Chap. 3, Exercise 6; Chap. 4, Exercise 7; Chap. 5, Exercise 13.)

8.6 Personhood Continued: Two Approaches to Personhood, Agency, and Machines

Summary
We examine two approaches to personhood and the distinctions between persons, agents, and things, expounded in an essay by Charles Taylor, which can cast light on different approaches to vexed questions in AI. One scientific approach understands persons as distinct in the possession of consciousness, but in terms which mean there is only a matter of degree in terms of complexity between persons and things (machines). A moral approach sees persons as distinctly separate from other agents and from things, in possessing a point of view and having a sense of the significance of their own purposes.

We have looked at some possible hallmarks of the mental and raised some questions about the essential nature of mind. Must it be embodied? Is felt subjective experience an essential part of the mind? Are minds thus essentially separated from each other? Is the subjectivity of the mind essentially irreducible? What is the proper place of the cognitive, and of reason? We also need to consider the relationship between the concept of minds and the concept of persons.

Let us now look at another attempt to frame these questions, in Charles Taylor's paper *The Concept of a Person* [47]. Taylor begins by characterising the person in a way that should be by now generally familiar. A person has a sense of self, can have life plans, make choices and have values; importantly, the sense of self is the origin of any life plans and choices. A person can respond to other persons. It becomes clear that the concept of a person is richer than the mere concept of a mind; Taylor investigates the boundaries between the concepts of a person, an agent, and things, which category includes machines. How are these boundaries drawn, and how rigid are they? We can immediately see the relevance for AI ethics. Moreover, since we are trying to understand the depth of differences of opinion regarding these issues, Taylor distinguishes two contrasting approaches to the question, the first a broadly 'scientific' approach stemming from the revolutions in thought of the seventeenth century and the second a broadly moral approach.

In the first approach, consciousness is a hallmark of persons and is understood in terms of the capacity to represent the world to the self. These representations form the basis for the capacity of persons to respond to other persons, a necessary component of morality. Agency is understood in terms of performance—of adaptive behaviour seen as accomplishing some goal. Hence, there is no sharp boundary between agents and things. A machine can likewise demonstrate agency. This fits well with computational ideas of intelligence. A quantitative difference only exists between things and persons in terms of the complexity of computation.

In the second account, agents are sharply divided from things; the hallmark of an agent is that things *matter* to them. They have purposes. The idea of evaluation if thus built into the idea of an agent. Machines can have purposes only in a derived sense if these have been put there by design by an agent with their own original purposes. This division between derived purposes and original purposes may be useful to consider in relation to the questions regarding the attribution of agency to humans and to machines that we have addressed previously (see, e.g. Sects. 2.4.3, 4. 4.5, and 6.4).

For something to matter to agents, there must be some evaluation built into the purposes that agents have. How do we distinguish persons as a subclass of agents? Consciousness does not do this because agents who are not persons may be conscious. Persons are distinguished qualitatively, not by degree, in terms of the matters of significance to persons. They recognise higher demands. This is a recurrent claim regarding persons: the capacity to rank and judge purposes, including one's own actions and thoughts. Taylor emphasises the distinctive nature of those human purposes which are peculiarly human and have no parallel in animals. In this approach, the purposes that make up human cultures are *sui generis* and cannot be reduced to purposes we can share with animals, such as survival and reproduction. Hence, different human cultures may likewise have distinctive purposes that are not readily accessible to those from other human cultures. Taylor's emphasis on human persons can thus be explained by the lack of examples of any other kinds of person that we have on which to draw, although this account does not rule out the possibility of nonhuman persons.

The first, scientific, account is reductive. There is a matter of degree and difference of complexity only between persons and things that are not persons. It appeals to those wishing for a certain kind of explanation of the world. The second, moral, account also appeals to a certain kind of explanation of the world, one which retains a sense of significance, of meaning, perhaps of mystery. From the perspective of this second account, one may consider that the first account reduces persons to 'nothing but' complicated machines. We should note that Taylor also comments that the scientific account also has a certain kind of higher, or spiritual, purpose to it, as it can represent a striving to rise above the 'merely' human level and to understand the world from 'above', as it were, or from an objective perch that transcends our limited grasp of things.

Recall the discussion of higher and lower aspects of human nature and Kant's claim that we need to ask ourselves if our actions fit with the moral law. Mill's distinction between higher and lower pleasures also gestures towards such a distinction. An influential paper by Harry Frankfurt, 'Freedom of the Will and the Concept of a Person', distinguishes between first-order and second-order desires; second-order desires are desires about desires, concerning which desires become one's will, for example, the desire that one does not desire to eat more chocolate cake; to exercise such second-order desires is to manifest free will [48]. Such an approach might be thought to show that it is only a matter of computational complexity that distinguishes persons from machines and that a complex machine might likewise be produced that incorporates second-order desires. Others might consider that these would only ever be 'derived' purposes. The resolution of such philosophical issues is highly relevant to how AI is conceptualised and to many ethical issues.

However, as hard as these philosophical issues to resolve, the distinction Taylor draws between these different standpoints of approach towards the question of what a person is and the boundaries between persons, agents, and things (machines) may be useful in helping to understand the nature and depth of disagreement in AI ethics over these issues and may help to explain the perplexity that we can feel in trying to grasp these issues. The complexity of the notion of persons is such that there may legitimately be different ways for us, as humans, with our complex mix of purposes, to try to grasp it.

Indeed, our very own natures as creatures capable of taking up different stances in relation to ourselves, of inner subjectivity, and as outward observers of our own actions and inner states, may help to explain both the attractions of these different stances towards the question of what a person is, a scientific, reductive account, and an account based on morals, meaning, and significance, and their seeming mutual opposition. We have seen, too, in theories of ethics, how approaches based upon distanced, third-person perspectives and accounts based upon close, second-person relationships with others both have their attractions. Perhaps, as persons, we are doomed to this perplexity, by our capacity to adopt different stances towards the universe and towards ourselves.

8.7   The Limits and Boundaries of Persons

Summary
Ethical questions often concern boundaries or limits, their proper place, and the consequences of disrupting or crossing these limits. This section examines a number of questions concerning the nature and limits of persons that have ethical implications for AI: the continuation of the same person over time; the boundaries between persons and things; the construction of ideas of the person through data; the particularities of embodiment such as the significance of the human face; autonomy as an expression of respect for the individual person and its limits; and privacy.

We turn to consider some questions about the boundaries and limits of personhood. These issues raise many ethical questions, particularly for AI. Questions about the boundaries of a person shape a host of ethical issues, including how the ethical issues of privacy are understood and how the value of personal autonomy is understood.

We have been considering whether strict or porous boundaries may be drawn between persons, agents, and things, and this raises vital questions for how we relate to and use technology. The capacities of AI magnify these questions. I do not feel I have in any way altered who I am as a person because I see the world through glasses. Were there to be some AI implant which is heightening my vision to that of an eagle, or labelling everything I see with its history, chemical composition, or what have you (I'm making this example up by the way), perhaps I would feel I was becoming, or had become, a somewhat different entity. If some AI implant altered certain personality traits, changed my sense of humour, shifted my interests so that I never read a book again but became a fanatical follower of ice-hockey and started breeding tarantulas, others might start to think I was a different person too.

The question of embodiment needs to be addressed. It relates closely to the question of the individuation of persons, which, as we have seen, is a critical question in ethics; the boundaries between our human bodies draw fairly clear lines around our identities as persons. The extremely heated debates over abortion only go to prove this point, but more than this, although human beings may not be the only persons, we are persons, and for us, our bodies have a particular significance, albeit one that has different resonance for different individuals and at different times and cultures. We will also look at the question of how persons are observed: given the subjectivity of persons, could outward behaviour and the kind of data that may be collected by AI ever fully capture what it is to be a person?

8.7.1 Personal Identity over Time

The philosophical questions about persons we have examined so far concern how a person is conceptualised. Philosophers have also puzzled over the question of the identity criteria of persons over time. This question also has to grapple with the issue of the inner subjectivity of personhood: that it *feels like* something to be a person. Hence, we could imagine that we might wake up one morning and be in an entirely different body, perhaps even in the body of a giant insect, as Kafka imagined [49], yet from the outside, nobody might know it was me. Even if one is a materialist about the mind, it's possible to *imagine* this, even if one thinks it's conceptually incoherent. Hence, it is possible to imagine that one's mind might be uploaded to a computer and that one somehow survives this [50]. Indeed, for those who find this thought horrific, part of the horror comes from the paradoxical capacity to imagine surviving a process which would also at the same time destroy who one was. (Of course readers might have very different responses.) There seems to be 'something'—one's self—which we can imagine enduring despite great change. The tendency to identify the self with mental attributes means that many philosophers have considered that the identity of a person over time is to be found in mental or psychological continuity.

A general problem with pinning down criteria for personal identity over time based on mental qualities is the unmistakable problem that we tend to forget many things (indeed, we forget most things) and that our personalities also change over time. Indeed, John Locke presented the puzzle of a man who, as a child, robs apples. As a middle-aged man, he can no longer remember doing this. As an old man, he can now recall having stolen the apples [51].

Exercise 12

Is this the same person?

If we could use AI to enhance and retain our memories, would this help to solidify who we are as people? Could this be a benefit to people in general, and in particular to people living with dementia? Note that we forget a vast proportion of what we ever experienced. Discuss.

The embodied nature of persons also creates problems for questions of personal identity over time. Our bodies change and grow; their material composition changes entirely every few years, and their form also changes. This change may be gradual, along a recognisable biological trajectory, or it may be sudden, as when a limb is amputated.

A simple answer to the question of personal identity over time is that the boundaries of the body mark the boundaries of the person; the normal changes we see over the life course are to be expected and do not undermine individual identity. A problem with this is that the body does not in other respects seem to capture precisely what it is to be a person. Moreover, many people may have a considerable number of artificial additions to their bodies: artificial lenses, cochlear implants, artificial joints, stents, and so on. The list is likely to lengthen as medical devices proliferate.

Exercise 13
If your body is gradually replaced bit by bit with numerous medical devices, at what stage, if any, would you no longer consider it your own body?

If your brain is replaced, bit by bit, with computerised parts, at what stage, if any, would you consider it no longer (a) your own brain, (b) your own mind, (c) the question makes no sense to me? (Of course you may well change your mind about this as it proceeds!) How might you go about answering this question?

There are also conceptual issues involved. Change in and of itself does not necessitate change in identity: the identity of something may be found in qualities other than its material composition. Heraclitus said that no one ever stands in the same river twice because it will be neither the same river nor the same person [52]. But a river has to have *flowing* water in it, or it would not be a river. Likewise, if a person did not change *at all*, they would not be a person, for at least one's thoughts and perceptions would change in response to the environment, and one would be doing *something*, even if one was merely standing still on a pillar for years at a time. The question is what change is allowable for the continuity of each category of a thing. The nature of these changes and their extent will vary from category to category. A heap of sand has no organising principle, so its identity may change with the removal or addition of a few grains. A machine such as a bicycle has an organising principle, so changing the saddle, the tyres, the wheels, may still mean it's the same bike; cannibalising its parts to make a go-cart may be a different matter. But what of persons?

All-or-nothing, or a matter of degree? One vital question, of relevance for us, is whether persons can change in degrees or whether being the same person is an all-or-nothing matter. Some expressions of ethics, and also religion, involve claims that each individual person has a unique essence, spirit, or soul from whence springs their value. The idea that we may have partial continuity with future or past selves, however, may appear to make sense of some of our experience and provide answers to various sci-fi thought experiments about teletransporters, as well to other similar examples. The philosopher Derek Parfit in his book *Reasons and Persons* argued, using many thought experiments, that what matters is not personal identity itself but psychological continuity; we could have psychological continuity with more than one future self [53]. Parallels between Parfit's view and Buddhist views of the self have often been made, although these are by no means strictly similar [54].

For another approach, recall, for example, Aristotle's notion of the development of moral character, practical wisdom, over a life, and the aim of happiness measured over an entire life span. If my character changes with time, as a result of my efforts and directed will to develop wisdom, is this not a unifying force that keeps my personal identity intact? Recall our discussion above of Taylor's account of two ways of looking at persons. On the one hand, we may simply see some connectedness with future selves, a matter of degree. On the other hand, we may judge in terms of what is of most significance to us as persons, and if that is retained, see the same person, but if it is lost, see the person as lost. The question is, what is of such key significance to persons?

A narrative account of personhood An organising principle holding persons together may be found in narrative accounts of personhood: the striving, over a life time, to carry out (reasonably) coherent life plans, the attempts to mould, grow, and improve oneself and one's moral character, and so on, may be seen to form a basis upon which we can attribute continuity of personhood, despite some changes, and indeed, precisely because of some other changes [55, Sect. 2.3]. There are different accounts of how to understand the narrative links that enable personhood. Stories of personal transformation—from violent prisoner to qualified social worker, from drug addict to rehabilitation counsellor, and so on—are precisely some of the cases where we most see the human spirit: the person we currently see and admire cannot be admired, if the past person was literally not the same person. In other cases of radical change, we might feel rather differently.

Exercise 14
Might AI facilitate our capacity to construct and pursue a strong narrative structure of purpose in our lives? What particular ways might it do this, and are there any ways in which it might in practice act counter to this? Think about the technologies in use or possible which might facilitate how we present and plan our lives.

8.7.2 The Distinction Between Persons and Things

Thus as we have seen, on some accounts, although persons are embodied, the distinction between persons and things is sharp and indivisible; on other accounts, it is permeable. We certainly work and operate in entangled and close relationships with networks of both people and machines. Does this weaken our own boundaries, and if so, does it matter? Does this mean there could be shared agency, shared mind, within networks of humans and of machines?

Many observe that our close relationships with technology are rapidly becoming even closer. There is a flow of information both ways between various forms of AI and us human beings, both collectively and individually, and we are increasingly dependent upon and entangled on a minute-by-minute basis with complex assemblages of technology. Various scholars examine these questions and the entanglement of the human with the nonhuman, both in the form of the hardware and of information, the data, that is gathered about us. In examining how we use technology and data currently and how we may use this in the future, some scholars challenge the conceptual distinction between persons and things, often stressing the importance of data and information in how the world is constructed, including the self. For example, Braidotti calls for an approach to the 'posthuman knowing subject', which no longer adheres to a notion of human exceptionalism and which assumes a notion of matter as intelligent and self-organising. Braidotti stresses the mind-body continuum and the continuum between nature and culture, drawing on the work of the philosopher Spinoza [56].

Explicating and assessing such work is complex, but one of the difficulties can be expressed quite simply: suppose some notion of human exceptionalism is a key aspect of a cultural, ethical, or religious set of values; and suppose our task is to consider the ethical questions around the adoption of new technologies, the use of data involved in this, and the growing entanglement between human beings and these technologies. Then with what basis are we shifting away from a current set of values towards a new set, and is there a danger that we may simply be *describing* a situation of significant changes and accepting new technological disruptions to our lives, rather than *assessing* them? Complexities abound: recall, too, that, as we have seen in our discussions of different ethical theories, the notion of human exceptionalism is neither universal in philosophical ethics nor understood in a uniform manner.

Deborah Lupton is a sociologist who has produced a large body of work, including work which examines technology and our use of data. She describes human-data assemblages that she claims render distinctions between the human and the nonhuman indeterminate. She explores the boundaries of human nature, how to conceptualise human beings, and the boundaries around the living and the nonliving [57, p. 22]. These questions are similar to those we have explored in this chapter and earlier in considering theories of human nature. Donna Haraway has used the term 'compost' to refer to how the human and the nonhuman may become part of each other; our boundaries are not fixed, we make and become objects [58]. Lupton draws on scholars such as Marenko, who discuss how technology may become 'enchanted' for us so that we no longer sharply distinguish between the technology and our own bodies, especially if we view them as 'smart' [59]. Note that notions of enchantment are used in slightly different ways by different scholars [60, 61]. Recall our earlier discussions of the attribution of meaning and significance to AI and robots (see Sect. 4.4).

Exercise 15

Consider the items of technology that you use most frequently and which are the most central to your life. Consider, too, that humans have long used tools, and with some exceptions, humans have long had intimate connections to clothing. Many of us are also, indeed, collectors or even hoarders of objects. Some of these objects we credit with special status such as 'art', 'antique', 'collectable', and so on; we may even name our cars. For many of us, the design of our surroundings, especially our domestic space, is of particular significance, and for some may be an intimate expression of privacy, of community, group belonging, or of self.

Reflect on whether there is a quantitative or qualitative difference in how our use of technologies involving AI, including the use of data, may or may not be altering how we see ourselves and our connection with and boundaries between objects.

We should also remind ourselves that the boundary drawn between human persons and things is drawn sharply by some but less so by others. We have already seen Taylor's analysis of how different viewpoints on the person, the scientific and the moral, may draw this in different ways and yet may be, although in tension, both attractive in their own ways. The very project of AI may be conceptualised in ways that challenge any sharp distinction between persons and things (although not necessarily so). There is also considerable awareness that there are cultural differences here. In Shinto thought, it may be claimed that an acceptance of techno animism means spirits may animate machines, and technology can be attributed characteristics which are also attributed to humans and other agents [62, 63]. There are thus no sharp boundaries drawn between the human person and other aspects of reality. Japanese attitudes towards robots and their acceptability may sharply differ from attitudes in the West [64]. Indigenous philosophies may also see softer boundaries between humans and the natural world [65].

8.7.3 Understanding Persons from the Outside: Constructing Persons from Data

In the section on behaviourism above 8.4, we considered how behaviourism can view individuals from a third-person stance, from the outside, as it were, and Exercise 9 asked you to consider whether the use of AI to collect and analyse data about us in this way may be dehumanising. Work such as Shoshana Zuboff's *Surveillance Capitalism* has underlined and helped to raise awareness of how corporations may use data about us for their own purposes, not for ours; governments of course may also do this [66]. Research exposing the biases in the algorithms that use personal data likewise has produced cause for alarm [67, 68]. Inaccuracies, power imbalances, and loss of control are key issues. Another concern may be that the way machine learning draws up a picture of the human world is quite unlike the ways in which other humans may do so; this can add to feelings of dehumanisation, as does the common expressed idea that data is the 'new oil', making data about individuals a commodity for others. Add to this the sheer amount of information that can be attained about individuals, the number of different ways this can be obtained, the variety of information that can be attained, the levels of detail possible, and the 24/7 nature of this potentially ubiquitous information gathering.

How might such data gathering and analysis affect how we see ourselves, how we see each other, and how we are seen by others, including our peers and those with more power? Are we persons, business opportunities for others, or could we be both at once? This is one of the many examples of how AI and other technologies may be shifting experiences and concepts central to our understanding of ethics, value, and the social world.

A counter to such gloomy thoughts of control and manipulation may be found in work which finds that many people may use such self-monitoring as a way of gaining self-knowledge and a sense of self-mastery. Lupton writes about the possibilities of new ways of understanding our bodies through data [57]. Through studies of those engaged in self-tracking, she sees this as an expression of embodiment, with data used as a rational practice for individuals, with the potential to increase autonomy. Note too, how self-tracking may be strongly associated with ideas of self-mastery, self-improvement, and the use of technology for personal progress and a move towards the ideal. Moreover, sharing such data can act to cement bonds between those in online communities engaged in such activities.

We looked earlier at the idea of a 'persona', a socially presented version of the self. Lupton talks of the 'data persona' [57, p. 117], an idea of the self as it is presented to others and formed out of data. Perhaps then, we are not so much changing our core idea of our self, but adding new ones.

Exercise 16
In Chap. 2, we considered the use of surveillance technology to watch over elderly people and people living with dementia, for example, through the use of apps to communicate remotely via a tablet. Deborah Lupton uses the term 'intimate surveillance' to describe situations in which online data are used to watch over those close to you [57, p.102]. When might such 'intimate surveillance' step over the line of acceptable conduct? Consider different scenarios and consider the reactions of different individuals involved, as well as the different value issues affected. Consider if the capacities of the technologies themselves may nudge us over the line of acceptable behaviour, or if they may be able to preserve dignity and enhance personhood in any way.

Exercise 17
How might such self-monitoring and the construction of ideas of the self through data and information gained via technology impact upon ideas of who we 'truly' are? Compare and contrast with ways in which we get knowledge about ourselves and feedback from others and from the world without the use of such technologies.

8.7.4 Persons and the Significance of the Body: Faces and Facial Recognition

We have seen in our discussion of persons how we may be pulled in different directions in considering the matter: the reality of the subjective experience of ourselves, and our experience of interactions with other subjects whom we also assume have subjective experience; as against the outer, objective way of conceptualising both ourselves and others; the tendency to think of the self as primarily 'mental', while also recognising the fact of our embodiment. The concept of a person may not be the same as that of the 'human being' and may not demand any particular kind of embodied substrate, but the fact remains that we are the prime example of persons that we know and that we are embodied and are of a particular species. Moreover, the concept of a person requires an element of reciprocity and the capacity to communicate with others (or at least the potential to do so). This communication has to be achieved through some physical means. (At least, telepathy is probably false: but who knows.)

Our faces are vital to this. Human faces are extraordinarily expressive, and their significance in social interaction has long been recognised [69]. This connection through faces plays a role from the moment of birth: the whites of human eyes allow the newborn baby to focus on the face, and the focal length of the eyes at birth is roughly the distance between the baby's face and the mother's when being breastfed. Moreover, faces play a dual role in social interaction: they hold us together as members of a common humanity who can communicate with each other as a social species through our faces, and they mark our individuality. We are the same, and we are different. Pareidolia is a psychological phenomenon whereby meaning is read into seemingly random, chance, phenomena. Human characteristics, such as faces, may be read into things.

There is considerable alarm about the use of facial recognition technologies. Why might this be? Much of this is focused on its inaccuracy and its use to target and control workers, political prisoners, and for surveillance of those deemed at risk of criminality or anti-social behaviour [70]. Some potential uses concern 'reading' emotions from facial expressions, also subject to criticism for various reasons, including the lack of grounding for claims that particular emotions can be attributed based upon certain expressions [71]. The past history of phrenology and its lamentable attempts to categorise people and spot 'traits' such as criminality has been drawn upon as analogous to current proposed uses of facial recognition technology [72]. There could be some concrete benefits, for example, if the recognition of facial expressions was used as part of technology to detect tiredness in drivers [73]. Yet there may be particular concern about how AI might control us. For example, a proposed use of facial recognition technology in autonomous vehicles to detect emotions given information about where the person is going: the wrong kind of emotion or expression for a date, or for a job interview, could be met with 'appropriate' music to get the person in the 'right' frame of mind [74]. The implications for social control and for the uniformity of such technology hardly need to be spelled out and indeed have attracted considerable attention [75].

Exercise 18
If an AI gathered data about you from your facial expressions or used facial recognition technology to identify you as an individual, does this seem any different qualitatively from gathering a similar amount of data about you, or identifying you via other means? Can you give any reasons for your answer? Don't worry if you can't. That alone is an interesting finding.

8.7.5 Autonomy

We have already mentioned the notion of autonomy at various points. The concept of autonomy is closely tied to ways of valuing the person: on a commonly accepted view, a person is someone who is assumed to possess autonomy, and respecting the autonomous decisions and actions of a person is one major way in which respect for persons may be accomplished. It is a key value, along with freedom, frequently cited in guidance concerning AI ethics (see Sect. 2.4.1). We have also discussed the question of moral autonomy and its use in the work of Kant (see Sect. 1.2) and the different ways in which autonomy might be understood in different contexts (see Sect. 4.1.3). The question of control in AI may be seen to be disrupting issues of autonomy and changing possibilities and patterns of control of individual lives, constraining and creating dangers in some respects, enabling and enhancing autonomy in other respects, and changing patterns of distribution of freedom and autonomy often in complex ways.

The general idea of autonomy is readily grasped, although it should be noted that autonomy is understood philosophically in different ways, the importance of different elements of autonomy may be variably stressed, and autonomy is one value among many. Its relative value may be viewed differently, especially in different cultures. Note the value of solidarity (see Sect. 2.4.10), which may be somewhat in opposition to the value of individual autonomy.

Autonomy and control by others An elementary account of autonomy may be simply one of freedom and power to do as one wishes, within the boundaries of physical possibility. Indeed, control by others is generally seen as a constraint on autonomy. If my data are being collected in ways of which I am not fully aware and used to market to me a product I would not otherwise have bought, this interferes with my autonomy (but then, the product may increase my autonomy, depending on what it is!). It is the capacity of AI to enable certain people vastly increased powers of control over others, which is a major ethical concern. However, control by others per se may not be a problematic attack on autonomy. For we are social creatures, living among each other, and others may have legitimate demands upon us, although there will be large differences between what demands are seen as legitimate or not.

Indeed, the notion of autonomy as a value focused upon 'the individual' has received much critique. Concepts of 'relational autonomy' have been developed [76], recognising that we develop our autonomy, our sense of individual self, only in relation to others (as various accounts of 'wolf children' who have survived in the wild have confirmed) [77]. An ideal of autonomy thus needs to incorporate our social natures, the legitimate concerns and needs of others, and strike a balance between individual freedom and control, and the reality of our shared and entangled lives.

Exercise 19
If you have a Neuralink implant, or similar, which connects your brain directly to the Internet, are your decisions and thoughts still yours? [*N.B. this is a thought experiment only! Don't get a brain implant just to answer the question!*]

If you are connected to the Internet indirectly through the use of a smartphone that you carry with you at all times, are your decisions and thoughts still yours?

Likewise, the idea of autonomy as limitless freedom to do as we wish is inconsistent with those accounts of ethics that consider there are only certain ways of living that will lead to 'the good life'. (Recall, in contrast, our discussion of the sceptical view of ethics as rules imposed from the outside, understood as little other than constraints. See Sect. 1.6) Aristotelean accounts of ethics and the notion of eudaimonia should make this clear (see, e.g. Sect. 1.6). We have also seen how, for Kant, autonomy involves adherence to the moral law, which is a demand of reason. Since we are rational agents, we see and recognise these demands and hence fulfil our natures, rather than act against them, in acting out of respect for the moral law. One need not accept Kant's views completely to agree that following something we ourselves recognise as value is not in conflict with autonomy, whereas acting against our core values may well be.

Of course, problems remain: identifying what these values are. The possibilities of control by AI include the potential manipulation of information, desire, and emotion, which perhaps poses an added problem in determining if our autonomy is being threatened.

Exercise 20

Surveillance by others and the possible manipulation that might result may seem straightforwardly to be an attack on our autonomy. It is an increasing possibility as the use of AI and surveillance technologies are built into our lives. Given that we are social creatures and given that we each generally fall short of perfect ethical and socially acceptable behaviour, feedback on our behaviour from others is a constant of human life and essential for the development of good moral character. Conversely, we are subject to social pressure, to social conformity, and to groupthink.

Consider how AI may play a role in this, and whether there are ways of using and increasing surveillance, monitoring, or sharing of data with others via AI that might be socially valuable, that may not threaten our autonomy, and may even enhance it. This is a multifaceted question since so many factors and complex technologies are involved. Different answers may be given for different kinds of surveillance technology and for the context of use.

Constraints and possibilities produced by AI   We would not normally think our autonomy was threatened by the inability to do things that are physically impossible. I wish I could fly over the trees as birds do, but my autonomy is not threatened by my lack of capacity to do so. However, when it comes to social, political, and economic possibilities presented to different individuals and groups, we think differently. The responses one has to this will vary according to different social and political beliefs, but it is certainly the case that AI is changing this landscape greatly. The 'digital divide' may mean that those without access to technologies or with access but without the requisite skills and facilities to use it are having possibilities constrained by the increasing adoption of AI in society [78]. We may find that the ways in which we relate to each other are changed by technologies in profound ways through multiple means with results that we may never have wished for and find hard to control [79]. The possibilities created by technology may also paradoxically increase the ways in which a person's autonomy may be curtailed, by adding new possibilities to which a person may not have access. I don't think my autonomy is constrained by not being able to fly like a bird, but I may feel it is constrained if despite my best efforts I can't earn enough to take an airplane flight, or if I am banned from boarding because the facial recognition system at the airport mistakenly identifies me as a wanted criminal. If every time I fly, I get flagged by security because I fall foul of profiling methods and get interrogated, I may feel my autonomy is somewhat curtailed even if this just delays my departure by a short time.

Among the new possibilities that technology creates may be the prospect of transcending limits we once simply accepted. Moreover, technology may dangle projected possibilities in front of us, such that we may not know if we are on the verge of missing out on something splendid. We have to grapple with the question of how far to push limits. As we have indicated, striving towards goals is an inherent part of being a person, and overcoming obstacles may form a key part of a valuable life, as may quietly accepting the path in life one has been allotted.

8.7.6 Privacy

We have already discussed privacy at various points. The collection, analysis, and use of data upon which so much AI depends has made privacy a key value in AI ethics and a central topic of much intense study [80]. The sheer scale of data collected, the capacity of analysis, and the ubiquity of data collection all create challenges for privacy. As we have also seen, developments in science and in technology can produce shifts in how we conceptualise data as personal, 'belonging' in some way to the individual (see Sect. 4.3.1). At the same time, our collective and individual use of technology, including sharing information, is moulding and changing attitudes towards privacy often in seemingly conflicting, shifting, and confusing ways [81].

An influential model of privacy by Helen Nissenbaum describes privacy as contextual integrity; norms of privacy concerning the gathering and dissemination of information should provide appropriate and adequate protection, given the particular context [82, 83]. With contexts changing so much, and frequently requiring complex analysis to understand exactly what is happening with personal information, privacy may be yet another example of how our uses of technology are shifting attitudes towards the very thing we wish and need to assess, even as we are in the throes of doing so.

The topic of privacy also exemplifies the tendencies towards diametrically opposed responses: on the one hand, the claims that privacy is dead and perhaps not to be mourned [84] and on the other hand, the intense concern to maintain privacy and attention to steps to ensure this [85]. In reality, we have never had limitless privacy, and meanwhile, nobody yet knows what tune I am currently humming to myself in my head. (At least, I don't think they do.) This short section aims to indicate how privacy needs to be understood in relation to the person, the individual, and hence its ethical concerns in relation to AI are closely intertwined with those of the person. Likewise, although the ways in which we think about privacy are steeped in general and rather abstract ideas of the value we accord and respect to individuals, privacy is also individually and culturally sensitive, and closely linked to our particular human embodiment.

Many animals have a sense of privacy and may be highly territorial. Some animals may seek privacy to give birth or to go when they are sick or dying. The subjectivity of our experience means that we are 'trapped' as it were, in our own inner worlds, but likewise, some freedom from the prying eyes of others seems to most of us a psychological necessity. This may even be a development necessity, especially as we form our own identities during adolescence. However, there will be large cultural and individual differences here. One only needs to travel to different countries to notice differences in how domains of privacy and intimacy are maintained. Again, as with so much of ethical and social import, the balance between the individual and the social group is at issue. There will always be certain limits to privacy, partly because of the legitimate demands of society (whatever they are) and partly because, unless you somehow disappear into a basement never to be seen or heard from again, certain facts about you can be discerned just by looking and listening.

Violations of privacy may matter for a variety of reasons. They can permit control by others but may also be associated with feelings such as shame. For example, individuals can feel violated and experience shame by the spread of deepfake porn involving their image, even if it is not actually their own naked body shown [86]. However, the question of privacy in relation to AI does not simply concern privacy violation. We also need to consider the growth of methods individuals can use to maintain their own privacy. We might include in this the ways in which so much technology, aided by economic and commercial changes, enables us to live remotely from each other.

Exercise 21

Early in this chapter, we mentioned the question of the LaMDA language model and the question of whether it might have attained sentience. Given what you have learned and considered in this chapter, outline why opposing views might be taken on this matter, and try to explain the gulfs between different positions.

8.8 Key Points

The concept of a person is a key notion with profound ethical implications, yet it is variously understood. There are cultural, historical, and philosophical variations in how persons are understood and valued.

This produces complexity when examining questions about the treatment of persons. One hallmark of poor treatment is often taken to be violation of respect for persons, failure to see persons as such and to treat them as such. But these may reflect different ways of understanding persons, the value of the individual versus the social, and the boundaries between persons and other things.

AI raises a plethora of ethical issues concerning persons. These include the question of whether AI may attain elements of personhood and whether our use of technologies enhances or degrades respect for persons.

The development and ideology behind AI may also present challenges to the notion of the individual person. New ways of understanding ourselves, relations with others, and ways of understanding the boundaries of what is possible for persons may all work towards changing how we understand what it is to be an individual person.

Ways in which AI is used and in which we ourselves use AI, such as using it to track data about the self, may radically or subtly alter how we understand ourselves and our capabilities.

Is a notion of an indivisible and separate individual person coherent and valid? As indicated, it does not seem to be an idea universally accepted in human culture, at least not in its most stark form as an atomistic sovereign individual. In addition, there may be ways in which our use of AI, and ways in which we think about AI, may undermine and cast doubts on this concept. However, it is a core concept, for example, being used in notions of universal human rights and as part of campaigns for civil rights.

Different philosophical accounts of the relationship between mind and body form a backdrop to questions of personhood. The difficulties and attractions of different accounts are helpful in coming to understand the seeming intractability of conflicting ways of understanding persons. Subjectivity and some notion of embodiment are both implicated yet hard to reconcile.

On some accounts, there is a continuum between persons and things, including machines. On other accounts, there is a sharp conceptual and moral gulf.

Hallmarks of personhood may include rationality, agency, and consciousness, but these on their own are not enough. Possession of a sense of self, purpose, and significance may be necessary.

Personhood may be conceptualised in ways that lead to the attribution of personhood or mind to computers, at least in theory. However, some accounts of personhood stress the cognitive may have deleterious consequences for certain groups.

A key issue in accounts of personhood is whether they are unduly reductive, reducing persons to 'nothing but' (fill in the dots), or whether there is something about persons that distinctively marks them off from other agents and from things.

8.9   Educator Notes

A challenge of this chapter is for students to understand the issue that the notion of a person is important to ethics, yet understood in different ways, and possibly is being challenged or altered in various ways by how we think about and use AI, as well as understanding that in different cultures, ideologies, and at different times of history, the idea of a person has been understood in various ways. Introducing students to the importance of the notion of equal treatment for persons as a political concept useful in the fight for civil rights yet nonetheless challenging to conceptualise may be useful.

Students who respond better to or prefer a more focused practical approach could use ideas from this chapter to focus on the question of sentience in the LaMDA language model, and why some were inclined to consider the possibility of personhood and others firmly rejected this. Section 8.7 could be used as a stand-alone section, which while including theory, also focuses on practical issues, since students will doubtless have some notion of personhood and will still derive value from the exercises.

However, it is also important for students to be able to grasp and articulate some of the ways in which AI may be used in ways that undermine (or promote) respect for persons and may change how we see ourselves and see and relate to others as persons.

Students with less time could simply be set Sects. 8.2 and 8.3 which deal with accounts of the person focusing on Kant and Dennett. This would provide a good amount of material for discussion. The addition of Sect. 8.6 discussing Taylor's division of two contrasting approaches to personhood, the scientific and the moral, is somewhat more advanced but may also be useful in helping students understand some reasons why this issue may be so intractable.

Section 8.5 may provide good material for a discussion in class where students may be challenged to think through how the concept of personhood is applied and attributed in challenging real life cases.

Debate and project or essay topics This topic would provide material for great discussions between those with knowledge of different disciplines, such as anthropology, theology, psychology, and computing, who should between them have diverse notions of the nature of a person and how persons are valued.

Exercises 9, 10, 14, 20, and 21 may be particularly suitable for class debate and discussion or for essays and extended projects.

Later chapters will provide more material on the question of AI and personhood.

Acknowledgements This chapter was partially funded by the National Institute for Health Research, Health Services and Delivery Research Programme (project number 13/10/80). The views expressed are those of the author and not necessarily those of the NIHR or the Department of Health and Social Care.

References

1. Jung CG (1953) Two essays on analytical psychology. University College London, London
2. Mauss M (1985) A Category of the Human Mind. In: Carrithers M, Collins S, Lukes S (eds) The category of the person: anthropology, history, philosophy. Cambridge University Press, Cambridge, pp 1–25
3. Carruthers, M., Collins, S., & Lukes, S., (eds.), (1985) The category of the person: anthropology, history, philosophy, Cambridge University Press, Cambridge

4. Tooley M (1972) Abortion and infanticide. Philos Public Aff 2:37–65
5. Downie RS, Telfer E (1969) Respect for persons. George Allen and Unwin, London
6. Mill JS (1859) On liberty. Longman, Roberts, and Green Co., London
7. Kant I, Paton HJ (1964) Groundwork of the metaphysic of morals (translated and analysed by HJ Paton). Harper & Row, New York
8. Kuhse H, Singer P, Singer P (1985) Should the baby live? The problem of handicapped infants (Vol. 138). Oxford University Press, Oxford
9. Boddington P, Podpadec T (1991) Who are the mentally handicapped? J Appl Philos 8(2): 177–190
10. Fraundorfer M (2018) The rediscovery of indigenous thought in the modern legal system: the case of the great apes. Glob Policy 9(1):17–25
11. Singer P (2011) Practical ethics. Cambridge University Press, Cambridge
12. Dennett D (1978) Conditions of personhood, in his brainstorms. Manchester Press Ltd., Manchester, pp 267–285
13. Clark DL (2001) Kant's aliens: the anthropology and its others. New Centen Rev 1(2):201–289
14. Nisbett RE, Ross L (1980) Human inference: strategies and shortcomings of social judgment. Philos Rev 92(3):462–465
15. Bazerman MH, Tenbrunsel AE (2011) Blind spots. Princeton University Press, Princeton
16. Wollstonecraft M (2022) A vindication of the rights of men: a letter to Edmund Burke; occasioned by his reflections on the revolution in France. Good Press, Glasglow
17. Clarke AC (2001) 1968. A space odyssey. Hutchinson, London
18. Jonze S (2013) Her. Warner Bros
19. Turing AM (1950) Computing machinery and intelligence. Mind 59(236):433
20. Wooldridge M (2020) The road to conscious machines: the story of AI. Penguin, London
21. Boddington P, Podpadec T (1992) Measuring quality of life in theory and in practice: a dialogue between philosophical and psychological approaches. Bioethics 6(3):201–217
22. Descartes R (1641) Meditations on the first philosophy. In: Anscombe E, Geach P (eds) Descartes philosophical writings, 1954. Nelson's University Paperbacks, Oxford
23. Robinson WS (2018) Dualism. In: The Routledge handbook of consciousness. Routledge, London, pp 51–63
24. Borst CV (1970) Mind-brain identity theory. Macmillan International Higher Education, London
25. Ramsey W (2022) Eliminative Materialism. In: Zalta EN (ed) The Stanford encyclopedia of philosophy, Spring 2022 edn. Stanford University, Stanford. https://plato.stanford.edu/archives/spr2022/entries/materialism-eliminative/
26. Shanahan M (2015) The technological singularity. MIT Press, Cambridge
27. Kirk R (2021) Zombies. In: Zalta EN (ed) The Stanford encyclopedia of philosophy, Spring 2021 edn. Stanford University, Stanford. https://plato.stanford.edu/archives/spr2021/entries/zombies/
28. Ryle G (1949) The Concept of Mind, Chapter II. Hutchinson, London
29. Levin J (2021) Functionalism. In: Zalta EN (ed) The Stanford encyclopedia of philosophy, Winter 2021 edn. Stanford University, Stanford. https://plato.stanford.edu/archives/win2021/entries/functionalism/
30. Block N (2006) Troubles with functionalism. In: Theories of mind: an introductory reader. Rowman & Littlefield, New York, pp 97–102
31. Rowlands M, Lau J, Deutsch M (2020) Externalism about the mind. In: Zalta EN (ed) The Stanford encyclopedia of philosophy, Winter 2020 edn. Stanford University, Stanford. https://plato.stanford.edu/archives/win2020/entries/content-externalism/
32. Radcliffe Richards J (2000) Human nature after Darwin: a philosophical introduction. Open University Press, Buckingham
33. Pavlov IP (1927) Conditioned reflexes: an investigation of the physiological activity of the cerebral cortex (translated and edited by GV Anrep). Oxford University Press, London
34. Watson JB (1913) Psychology as the behaviorist views it. Psychol Rev 20(2):158

35. Skinner BF (1965) Science and Human Behaviour. Free Press, New York
36. Skinner Buzan D (2004) 'I was not a lab rat' Deborah, Guardian, 12 Mar 2004. https://www.theguardian.com/education/2004/mar/12/highereducation.uk
37. Skinner BF (1971) Beyond freedom and dignity. Hacket Publishing, Indianapolis
38. Wells HG (1898) War of the worlds. Heineman, London
39. Gilleard C, Higgs P (2011) Ageing abjection and embodiment in the fourth age. J Aging Stud 25(2):135–142
40. Kitwood TM (1997) Dementia reconsidered: the person comes first. Open University Press, Buckingham
41. Goffman E (1961) Asylums: essays on the social situation of mental patient and other inmates. Anchor Books, New York
42. Featherstone K, Northcott A (2021) Wandering the wards: an ethnography of hospital care and its consequences for people living with dementia. Taylor & Francis, Oxfordshire, p 188
43. Kontos PC (2004) Ethnographic reflections on selfhood, embodiment and Alzheimer's disease. Ageing Soc 24(6):829–849
44. Kontos PC, Naglie G (2007) Bridging theory and practice: Imagination, the body, and person-centred dementia care. Dementia 6(4):549–569
45. Boddington P, Featherstone K, Northcott A (2021) Presentation of the clothed self on the hospital ward: an ethnographic account of perceptual attention and implications for the personhood of people living with dementia. Med Humanit 47(2):e3–e3
46. Kontos PC (2005) Embodied selfhood in Alzheimer's disease: rethinking person-centred care. Dementia 4(4):553–570
47. Taylor C (2010) Ch 4. The concept of a person. In: Human agency and language: philosophical papers. Cambridge University Press, Cambridge
48. Frankfurt HG (1971) Freedom of the Will and the Concept of a Person. J Philos 68:5–20
49. Kafka F (1948) The metamorphosis. Schocken Books, New York
50. Turner C, Schneider S (2020) Could You Merge with AI? In: Dubber M, Pasquale F, Das S (eds) The oxford handbook of ethics of AI. Oxford University Press, Oxford
51. Deschepper JP (1975) In: Nidditch PH (ed) An essay concerning human understanding (The Clarendon edition of the works of John Locke). Oxford University Press, Oxford. Book II, Chapter 27 (1689/1694)
52. Reeve CDC (1997) Plato, Cratylus: translated with introduction and notes. Hackett, Indianapolis
53. Parfit D (1984) Reasons and persons. Oxford University Press, Oxford
54. Stone J (1988) Parfit and the Buddha: why there are no people. Philos Phenom Res 48(3):519–532
55. Shoemaker D (2021) Personal identity and ethics. In: Zalta EN (ed) The Stanford encyclopedia of philosophy, Fall 2021 edn. Stanford University, Stanford. https://plato.stanford.edu/archives/fall2021/entries/identity-ethics/
56. Braidotti R (2019) A theoretical framework for the critical post humanities. Theory Cult Soc 36(6):31–61
57. Lupton D (2019) Data selves: more-than-human perspectives. Wiley, New York
58. Franklin S (2017) Staying with the Manifesto: an interview with Donna Haraway. Theory Cult Soc 34(4):49–63
59. Marenko B (2014) Neo-animism and design: a new paradigm in object theory. Des Cult 6(2):219–241
60. Rose D (2014) Enchanted objects: innovation, design, and the future of technology. Simon and Schuster, New York
61. Bennett J (2004) The force of things: steps toward an ecology of matter. Polit theory 32(3):347–372
62. Jensen CB, Blok A (2013) Techno-animism in Japan: shinto cosmograms, actor-network theory, and the enabling powers of non-human agencies. Theory Cult Soc 30(2):84–115

63. Gygi FR (2018) Robot companions: the animation of technology and the technology of animation in Japan. In: Rethinking relations and animism. Routledge, London, pp 94–111
64. Coco K, Kangasniemi M, Rantanen T (2018) Care personnel's attitudes and fears toward care robots in elderly care: a comparison of data from the care personnel in Finland and Japan. J Nurs Scholarsh 50(6):634–644
65. Lewis JE, Arista N, Pechawis A, Kite S (2018) Making kin with the machines. J Des Sci. https://doi.org/10.21428/bfafd97b
66. Zuboff S (2019) The age of surveillance capitalism. Profile Books, London
67. Noble SU (2018) Algorithms of oppression: how search engines reinforce racism. New York University Press, New York
68. O'Neil C (2016) Weapons of math destruction: how big data increases inequality and threatens democracy. Crown Publishing Group, New York
69. Schmidt KL, Cohn JF (2001) Human facial expressions as adaptations: evolutionary questions in facial expression research. Am J Phys Anthropol 116(S33):3–24
70. Article 19 (2021) Emotional entanglement: China's emotion recognition market and its implications for human rights. https://www.article19.org/wp-content/uploads/2021/01/ER-Tech-China-Report.pdf
71. Barrett LF, Adolphs R, Marsella S, Martinez AM, Pollak SD (2019) Emotional expressions reconsidered: challenges to inferring emotion from human facial movements. Psychol Sci Public Interest 20(1):1–68
72. Agüera Y Arcas B, Mitchell M, Todorov A (2017) Physiognomy's new clothes, medium. https://medium.com/@blaisea/physiognomys-new-clothes-f2d4b59fdd6a
73. Liu Z, Peng Y, Hu W (2020) Driver fatigue detection based on deeply-learned facial expression representation. J Vis Commun Image Represent 71:102723
74. Forbes Insights (2019) Designing AI that knows how you feel. Forbes, 6 May 2019. https://www.forbes.com/sites/insights-teradata/2019/05/06/designing-ai-that-knows-how-you-feel/. Accessed 25 Sept 2022
75. Whittaker M, Crawford K, Dobbe R, Fried G, Kaziunas E, Mathur V, West SM, Richardson R, Schultz J, Schwartz O (2018) AI now report 2018. AI Now Institute at New York University, New York, pp 1–62
76. Mackenzie C (2014) Three dimensions of autonomy: A relational analysis. In: Autonomy, oppression and gender. Oxford University Press, Oxford, pp 15–41
77. Lane H (1976) The wild boy of Aveyron. Harvard University Press, Cambridge
78. Van Dijk J (2020) The digital divide. Wiley, New York
79. Turkle S (2017) Alone together: why we expect more from technology and less from each other. Hachette UK, Paris
80. Richards N (2021) Why privacy matters. Oxford University Press, Oxford
81. Gerber N, Gerber P, Volkamer M (2018) Explaining the privacy paradox: a systematic review of literature investigating privacy attitude and behavior. Comput Secur 77:226–261
82. Nissenbaum H (2004) Privacy as contextual integrity. Wash Law Rev 79(1):119–158
83. Nissenbaum H (2020) Privacy in context. Stanford University Press, Redwood City
84. Rauhofer J (2008) Privacy is dead, get over it! Information privacy and the dream of a risk-free society. Inf Commun Technol Law 17(3):185–197
85. Véliz C (2020) Privacy is power: why and how you should take back control of your data. Random House, New York
86. Gieseke AP (2020) "The new weapon of choice": law's current inability to properly address deepfake pornography. Vanderbilt Law Rev 73:1479

Further Reading

Persons

Cacioppo JT, Patrick W (2008) Loneliness: human nature and the need for social connection. W.W. Norton and Company, New York

Carruthers M, Collins S, Lukes S (eds) (1985) The category of the person: anthropology, philosophy, history. Cambridge University Press, Cambridge

Dennett D (1978) Conditions of personhood, in his brainstorms. Manchester University Press, Manchester, pp 267–285

Downie RS, Telfer E (1969) Respect for persons. George Allen and Unwin, London

Frankfurt HG (1971) Freedom of the will and the concept of a person. J Philos 68:5–20

Kitwood T (1997) Dementia reconsidered: the person comes first. Open University Press, Buckingham

Kontos PC (2004) Ethnographic reflections on selfhood, embodiment and Alzheimer's disease. Ageing Soc 24(6):829–849

Taylor C (2010) Ch 4 The concept of a person. In: Human agency and language: philosophical papers. Cambridge University Press, Cambridge

AI and Persons

Coeckelbergh M (2022) Self-improvement: technologies of the soul in the age of artificial intelligence. Columbia University Press, New York

Kingwell, M., 2020. Are sentient AIs persons? In Dubber, M., Pasquale, F., & Das, S. The Oxford handbook of ethics of AI. Oxford University Press, Oxford

Lupton D (2016) The quantified self. Wiley, New York

Lupton D (2019) Data selves: more-than-human perspectives. Wiley, New York

Neff G, Nafus D (2016) Self-tracking. MIT Press, Cambridge

Richardson K (2020) The complexity of otherness: anthropological contributions to robots and AI. In: Dubber M, Pasquale F, Das S (eds) The Oxford handbook of ethics of AI. Oxford University Press, Oxford

Turkle S (2005) The second self: computers and the human spirit. MIT Press, Cambridge

Turkle S (2011) Life on the screen. Simon and Schuster, New York

Turkle S (2017) Alone together: why we expect more from technology and less from each other. Hachette, London

Turner C, Schneider S (2020) Could you merge with AI? In: Dubber M, Pasquale F, Das S (eds) The Oxford handbook of ethics of AI. Oxford University Press, Oxford

Autonomy and Privacy

Dworkin G (1988) The theory and practice of autonomy. Cambridge University Press, Cambridge

Mackenzie C (2014) Three dimensions of autonomy: a relational analysis. In: Autonomy, oppression and gender. Oxford university press, Oxford, pp 15–41

Véliz C (2020) Privacy is power: why and how you should take back control of your data. Random House, New York

Wheeler M (2020) Autonomy. In: Dubber M, Pasquale F, Das S (eds) The Oxford handbook of ethics of AI. Oxford University Press, Oxford

Chapter 9
Individuals, Society, and AI: Online Communication

Abstract This chapter examines a current ethical issue in AI, using the example of online content moderation and consolidating previous material. The problem of online harms is in tension with values of freedom of expression. Freedom of expression is a perennial issue. We consider how the use of technology may impact and exacerbate the problems and examine the possibilities of using technology to address them, such as the challenges of using algorithms to detect nuanced meaning. The ethical issues are tightly connected to wider political, social, regulatory, and legal issues. Here, we focus on ethics while also discussing how wider interests from government and industry may skew debates and solutions. The issue of free speech is outlined, drawing on the claims of John Stuart Mill and the 'harm principle' as a limit to free speech. We also address issues in the philosophy of language, considering how meaning and intention are related and the critical importance of context, drawing on the work of H. P. Grice. We consider how communication online may impact views of self and others and consider how both the problems of online content and the attempts to find solutions may influence how we understand and address ethical questions.

Keywords Online communication · Content moderation · Hate speech · Freedom of expression · Philosophy of language · Algorithmic bias

9.1 Introduction

Summary
This chapter uses the example of the moderation of online content that is deemed harmful by human moderators and in particular by algorithms in the illustration of a complex ethical issue currently facing us. Problems of online content moderation raise complex ethical issues concerning factors such as responsibility, agency, freedom of expression, and protection from harm, which also intersect legal, political, economic, and societal concerns.

The remaining chapters look more centrally at concrete issues and apply and extend ideas and material we have covered previously. This chapter examines a cluster of current problems, taking one example as a central theme: language and communication through technology, in particular, focusing on content moderation online for alleged hate speech, online harms, and misinformation, with the main focus on the notion of 'online harms'. We aim additionally to tease out some general themes and questions that will be relevant for a range of other issues. The objective is not to give an account of what 'the' answer is, (or even what 'the' issues are, since these are many and may be understood in different and contested ways). It is to analyse at least some elements of the typical ethical questions that arise regarding AI, provide some tools to start to address them, indicate how the ethical questions intersect with other issues, and hence enhance and promote dialogue.

Why pick this theme? As we shall see, questions around the spread of online content and its moderation raise issues with profound ethical, social, and political implications, which concern both society as a whole and individuals. The ever-present question of how to 'strike a balance' or otherwise deal with ethical tensions between the individual and society (including especially in this case, various sub-groups in societies, and issues between different societies, jurisdictions, and cultures) is certainly central here, and it is a theme that is often heightened by the use of AI as perceived responsibilities are apparently shifted. Since the topic concerns communication, it immediately involves the central ethical questions of how we relate to each other, see ourselves, and see and respond to the world at large. There are issues concerning the behaviour, responsibilities, and obligations of governments, of corporations, and of individuals. The ethical questions thus go far beyond a narrow domain of individual ethics per se, extending into questions of culture, of political and legal obligations, and of possible remedies, hence meaning that the topic also acts as a good illustration of the intimate interactions between ethics, politics, law, and culture. I will not pretend to tackle all of these issues here; there are a myriad complex and highly detailed legal, technical, and regulatory issues which are beyond the scope of this book; but understanding of broad ethical questions are relevant to understanding and entering into dialogue about the further details and practical solutions.

The ethical questions of online content and its moderation also raise technical issues requiring detailed understanding of the nuts and bolts of the technology, both software and hardware, and its governance. These include the issue of bias in algorithms and the use of natural language processing to detect meaning. Questions of the ideology and attitudes driving how the issues and potential solutions are understood and presented are ever-present. We will also ask how the use of AI and our responses to its use may be shaping the social landscape and how it might be changing perceptions and behaviour. Naturally, such a question has a highly empirical component and concerns complex webs of behaviour and meaning. The issues may be rather polarised, with competing values pointing in different directions, and even were the abstract questions of value to be broadly resolved, there are complex questions about how best to achieve a good ethical result in practice. What is new on the block, and how might AI be raising new ethical issues or recycling old ones?

We will see that the issues can be framed and solutions can be sought in very different ways and with different outcomes, from different perspectives, with different emphases on conflicting values (such as harm reduction and the value of free speech and individual expression). This chapter also examines how approaches from various normative ethical theories contrast with respect to these issues and aims to show how philosophical claims, for example, regarding the nature of language and of knowledge, come into play.

9.1.1 Moderating Online Content: An Overview

We begin with an overview of the area to be explored in this chapter. The questions concerning how AI impacts communication online are far reaching; to illustrate the topic and provide some specificity, some of the material on which this chapter draws refers to particular proposals, under discussion at the time of writing, regarding the moderation of online content in the UK through proposed changes to the law in what had been called 'online harms' at consultation stage, but which became the draft 'Online Safety Bill' [1]. This is used to illustrate general issues and to provide an example of some possible ways of understanding and addressing the issues. There is also sound a reason for considering the proposals made from a specific jurisdiction: the impact that these may have globally, given the global nature of online communications. This has already been made manifest, for example, in the adoption of General Data Protection Regulations (GDPR) within the European Union, which has had an impact on those within the EU accessing material from outside it, and those outside the EU who wish their material to be accessible within it.

Indeed, such pressures may form one motivation for jurisdictions racing to become a leader in regulations simply because then one may have greater influence over those who follow, who may then tend to run in the tracks that one jurisdiction has created [2]. This can also have an impact upon one's success in developing technologies.

What are the issues? Those who have paid attention especially to Chap. 4 will I hope immediately be saying to themselves, 'Aha, but it all depends upon how precisely the case is described!' Yes, indeed it does. There has been considerable attention and scholarship to the question of how to understand the media and its possibilities [3–5]. But we can in broad outline identify the issues to start our discussion, although what can be covered here will be far from complete. Nothing could delight me more for readers to find additional material, points of concern, and different approaches to the matters. In considering the matter and in working through cases and exercises, exploring other ways of describing issues and further unexplored features is always vital.

The possibilities of online communication Communication online can take many forms. Of course, not all of this involves much in the way of AI per se; some of the communication may be as relatively simple as posting a blog on a website. Indeed, as we shall see, many of the problems stem not from the use of very sophisticated AI but from the use of algorithms that promise much but that perhaps deliver less. Nonetheless, the affordances of technology enable certain modes of communication and new, or seemingly new, and altered possibilities. Features of how the online world operates and how people behave and respond online may increase the possibility of concerns about 'online harms'. Social media enables material to be posted which can quickly garner a wide and even global audience. Much material can be posted anonymously; conversely, the identities of individuals may be revealed or quickly surmised or hacked. The anonymity rendered possible online removes the disincentive of detection and social shame; the lack of anonymity can conversely ruin reputations and spread social shame, much of it undeserved. Material may be posted without much thought, reactions may be heated, and interactions helpful, or aggressive, sometimes intentionally hurtful. Content may be posted without consent, as in revenge porn. 'Filter bubbles' are also highlighted: the tendency of our interactions online to be with increasingly homogenous groups of people and sets of ideas [6], although note that there has been work critically examining the idea of filter bubbles [7]. This is often aided by the algorithms driving online suggestions for viewing content and also by other factors, such as the ease of blocking people.

Many features of social media are purposively designed to ensure as much engagement as possible. Since social media platforms rely upon advertiser revenue, it is in their interests to maximise online engagement in whatever form it takes. The reactions that keep us engaged are often among humanity's less admirable traits: anger and outrage can keep users engaged and reacting very strongly [8]. The capacities of social media enable phenomena such as the group pile-on, where an individual may be the recipient of a large amount of material from hundreds, thousands, or even more people, many of whom will be strangers, and many or most of whom will be anonymous. This all can happen across national borders. Moreover, it is possible to post material without checking its veracity, to post material knowing that it is false or misleading and to post deepfakes, AI generated images or video that convincingly appears to be real.

Some of this material has attracted considerable concern under the heading of 'online hate', or more generally of abusive or harmful content. There has been considerable concern about misleading information online, and much of this concern has come from governments, especially in the wake of allegations of elections and of issues affecting the public, such as the COVID-19 pandemic. The harms and social and psychological effects of the spread and ready accessibility of online pornography, much of it increasingly extreme, are also too complex to cover here. There is also much material online that is plainly illegal, such as material pertaining to terrorism, child pornography, and material related to illegal drug use and selling and human trafficking. Intentionally targeted harassment at individuals or groups is also clearly illegal under many jurisdictions. There are rightly issues to be debated concerning how best to deal with such illegal material (and indeed, whether certain material should be illegal), but we are not focusing on them here, partly because of their complexity, but mostly because the ethical issues of dealing with the vaguer concepts of online harm or online hate will raise some particular philosophical questions. The interesting and more perplexing questions concern how to deal with the issues of material which seems to pose certain harms, but which is not in itself illegal, and which may appear to present us with novel difficulties, or certainly, with difficulties created by the sheer scale of online material.

Freedom of expression Alongside these very real concerns for those on the receiving end of online hate, there are legitimate concerns for the impact on freedom of expression that might arise from attempts to address this issue. One reason for concern over online hate is how ubiquitous the online world has become in our lives. Thus, conversely, we must be mindful of the impact of attempts to control online discourse, given the centrality of this discourse to how we access information and communicate. Are we heading for authoritarian control over how we access information and express ourselves online? (Again, dimensions of such questions are clearly empirical and require understanding of actual patterns of communication.)

The background of societal concerns Proposals for the moderation of online content fit into prior issues in society regarding the spreading of information and misinformation, including standards and expectation of truth telling, laws around libel and slander, and laws and standards around harassment of individuals. Moreover, in more recent years, many jurisdictions have introduced the notion of 'hate speech' and 'hate crime', in particular concerning those who fall into a protected group such as one based on race, ethnicity, sex, sexual orientation, or disability. Hence, some of the material of concern online would be classed as illegal in some jurisdictions. Other material online violates the terms and conditions of the platforms on which it is posted. Proposals for dealing with these questions may give greater obligations to social media companies for detecting and removing or otherwise dealing with 'problematic' content.

Current proposals in the UK target content online which is not illegal yet is considered 'harmful to adults' [1]. Proposals include the use of algorithms to detect and monitor language online. Methods will rely upon the use of algorithms to flag online content, supervised by human moderators, and with a process of user complaints to allow for redress in cases of dispute. Anybody overseeing this may have considerable powers of discretion over what content is flagged and how it is dealt with, and over how complaints are dealt with. The proposals in the UK at the time of writing, which are used here as an example, propose that the broadcast regulator Ofcom, which is a statutory corporation reporting regularly to Parliament, is given oversight, with considerable powers of discretion.

Issues raised thus can immediately be seen to include the restriction or censorship of content that is not illegal; the background of any legal definition of content that is disallowed within the jurisdiction in question; how the notion of 'harm' is understood; the apportioning of responsibilities for taking action; questions of free speech and censorship; control by governments and by corporations; individual responsibilities online; and the means used to achieve these ends, including the accuracy or otherwise of algorithms, and questions of transparency around their use. Other issues include the use of AI with intent to bring about good, the use of AI for malevolent purposes, and our capacity to tell the difference.

9.2   What Concepts and Tools Can We Bring to These Questions?

Summary
This section reviews some of the concepts and strategies that readers may bring in addressing ethical questions about online content.

Let us briefly review some of our earlier material and how it might be brought to bear on this issue. What relevant questions might need to be asked, what concepts, theories, and strategies should be drawn upon? You might wish to stop and consider how you would go about addressing these questions before continuing. It may be useful to browse the 'Key Points' from each chapter. Indeed, the list of potential considerations is very long. Let us just pick a few from each of the chapters.

What is my specific contribution? Consider what particular experience and knowledge you have on which to draw. Perhaps, for example, you have detailed knowledge of how particular social media accounts operate, or have personal experience of being targeted by, or accused of, problematic content online (Chap. 1).

Novelty and precedents Consider how new these issues are. Are there any historical precedents? ('Yes', is the easy answer to this, in terms of questions about censorship and free speech, among others.) So what precisely might be different? Consider what key ethical values commonly found in codes of ethics may be involved, which ones are most important, and how we might need to interpret each within this particular context, for example, autonomy, transparency, fairness, responsibility, and privacy (Chap. 2).

How the technology is understood How does the way in which we see the technologies concerned shape our understanding of human involvement? Might our use of technology and assumptions about it shape how we draw boundaries around concepts and how we understand certain values? Consider how technology may shape how we communicate and how ideas spread (Chap. 3).

How the story is told Consider how a situation is described, who is involved, and in particular, how causation and agency are portrayed. Consider if certain assumptions are being made about our capacity to resolve ethical situations. Consider if the technologies under issue here may have impacted human behaviour and thought in ways that may shape ethical issues and ways of resolving them. The question of how a story is told will be especially pertinent to how we describe disputes between different parties and contentious communications online (Chap. 4).

What you don't know Consider what you don't know that you need to find out, and where to get this information (Chap. 4).

Knowledge Look out for any assumptions regarding the value of knowledge, of information, and of data and the values involved in sharing and communicating knowledge, information, or data (Chap. 5).

Our human frailties Consider what picture of human nature may underlie discussions of these ethical issues, in particular any flaws humans are presumed to manifest (Chap. 5).

Normative ethical theories Think about how a focus on the outcomes of actions may contrast with a focus upon issues of agency and/or character. Questions about the interpretation of rules will be especially vital in assessing the appropriate use of algorithms, especially in complex contexts of meaning. Consider what virtues and vices might apply to communication online (Chap. 6).

Attention to the world Consider how the technology involved here might impact our attention. Consider how knowledge and reality are represented and valued and consider what underlying model of language applies (Chap. 7).

Self, person, agency Consider how the uses and abuses of the technologies in question here may impact our ideas of ourselves and of how we relate to others. Consider how agency is attributed and possibly distributed between humans and machines (Chap. 8).

Last, I wish to stress that this is not intended as a 'check list' of the steps one must simply follow to get the 'right' answer. Ethics is more complex than that, and some situations will require more, some will require emphasis on certain factors, some situations may occasionally be resolved quite readily.

9.3 Why Is AI Being Used to Address the Online Harms Question?

Summary
In assessing the use of AI, it is important to consider why AI is being used, what is expected of it, and why it is used rather than humans; if we do not do this, we may assume that AI is the best approach and overlook that any assessment needs to include comparison with alternatives. This necessitates a thorough analysis of what task(s) the AI is charged to perform.

We are considering the use of AI in the form of algorithms to detect content, in order to address an issue that originates in or is magnified by technology. Even though the use of algorithms may seem entirely necessary, it can be useful in addressing any question in ethics to parse apart the different reasons why AI is being used. There are a range of reasons why we might use AI in such settings. These include the speed at which AI may operate; the complexity of calculations needed; the capacities of perception, for example, in image reading; the (alleged) consistency and efficiency of AI; the capacity for scale; the tedium of the task for human workers; the cost of human labour; the shortage of human labour; or priorities to spend time on other things. The unsuitability of some tasks for humans is another factor: the use of robotics for dangerous work such as landmine clearance seems a clear win for humanity. Other tasks may be mentally or psychologically draining, and content moderation can fall into this class, owing both to the nature of much online material and to the potential for human moderators to receive abuse [9, 10]. The content moderators are not content.

Why is it useful to consider precisely why AI is being used? We may find that its use is simply presumed to be better than relying on human capacity and that looking carefully at the reasons for its use and the presumed benefits may lead us to adjust our views on the wisdom of preferring AI to human labour. We may gain insights into the background conditions that led to its use and its preference to human labour. We may find that assumptions about the superiority of AI within a particular context lead to an idealised version of AI being used for comparison with human labour.

Consider the examples we have seen so far regarding the use of AI in relation to people living with dementia. These include the power of data gathering and analysis, including perceptual capacities, in the use of AI for diagnostics (and also for developing treatments) [11]. AI may be faster, more consistent, and have capacities that humans do not have. Added to the reasons for using AI, we must ensure that we include the scale and seriousness of the issue that grounds and justifies the development of appropriate AI, the numbers overall and the numbers undiagnosed, and the failures to develop effective treatments. Economic factors are also generally present. Without the factors of importance and urgency, putting effort into developing AI may be low down on a list of priorities, although conversely, adopting solutions from simple application of AI for less valued tasks for economic reasons is also prevalent. Hence, the reasons for using AI are not merely technical. However, any use of AI must also be cognizant of potential dangers that might come alongside benefits. We must also remember that any endeavour in science and technology is prone to error and correction [12].

Consider now the use of AI in assistance for people living with dementia, such as help with everyday tasks, monitoring for safety and companionship, or surveillance to prevent wandering. In such cases, technology is largely used simply for the lack of humans to fulfil these tasks. The complex causes behind this include demographics, the rate of dementia in the population, the distances that family members may live from each other, the demands of the workplace, general attitudes towards elderly individuals, the difficulty of recruiting paid human carers, or preference for automation in some cases (recall the very different attitudes towards robots in some cultures). Multiple interlocking economic, social, and cultural forces will underlie all of these factors. The use of AI cannot be understood without understanding the complex societal backdrop, the very complexity of which will mean that opinions and analysis are likely to be variable. Assumptions about what can and cannot be changed, what is desirable to be changed, and other means of addressing the issue may all prove fruitful routes of exploration.

It is helpful to consider why AI is used, rather than humans, and whether AI is replacing humans, or enhancing or extending human capabilities, and what trade-offs there may be. This comparative element in assessing the use of AI means that the question is never *merely* technical.

Task analysis This then means that we need to have a good analysis of what precisely the task involves so that we can consider if AI has been a good replacement or supplement to human labour. This task analysis may be complex. We need to consider whether the AI in question is technically adequate for the task, how the task is described, and how the situation to be addressed came about. In regard to roles filled by paid employees, for example, we might need to consider that many of the most important tasks undertaken by human beings may not be on any official job description. It is not in the job description of the person serving at your local store to ask solicitously if you found your lost cat yet, but it certainly makes your day if they do this. In any task that involves replacing humans entirely, we need to ask if the AI in question can fully replicate the aspects of human agency, and if appropriate, of the human person. Conversely, there may be aspects of some tasks that involve distinctively human responses, for which very reason we prefer to use AI because of the toll on human beings—content moderation of extreme content online being one such example.

In other words, we sometimes need AI to operate like humans in relevant ways, but we sometimes require AI to omit human elements.

It can be useful to compare and contrast cases of AI that involve elements of robotics or mimicry of the human or the personified (e.g., in the use of a dog avatar for companionship and safety monitoring of people living with dementia that we considered in Sect. 2.4.9) with cases of AI that are simply embedded in computing because the former may lead us to comparisons with human agency and personhood, which we might have overlooked in the latter. A tension, possibly a paradox, in some uses of AI is that replication of elements of human agency may be needed to fulfil the task adequately but has its own dangers. We considered earlier whether humans are kept out of decision-making entirely or kept in the loop or on the loop (see Sect. 2.3). Humans may be needed as an essential part of the process or brought in when the process seems to go awry or some redress is needed.

Exercise 1

In the case of something like diagnostics, the task of the AI is focused on finding and delivering information. Is there any element of distinctively human agency or personality involved in this? You may wish to review Exercises 4 and 11 from Chap. 2.

Hint: consider how medical expertise and clinical judgement form over the years [13].

Consider also the location of the diagnostics: in the clinic, where the information is mediated through medical personnel, or directly in the hands of patients.

Location, location, location This exercise raises the issue that it is not simply the technical capabilities of AI that matter: it is the context of use. The many features of the location of communication, that it is online, are going to be highly relevant.

9.4   Content Moderation for Online Harms: What Is Needed?

Summary

To address the issue of online harms we need to describe the problem. We need to note how different ways of seeing the issue may skew how the ethical issues are presented, how the problems are seen to have arisen, and the roles of those involved are understood. An overview of a defence of free speech is given, using the work of John Stuart Mill. A commonly accepted exception to free speech is that speech must not cause harm. Difficulties with giving an account of harm, including misinformation as possible harm, are described. We need to consider the complexities of inferring meaning from language.

It is proposed to use AI to flag and remove or otherwise respond to content online which is deemed harmful, abusive, illegal, or classified as misinformation or misleading in some way. Here, we focus primarily on content that may be deemed harmful (understood broadly and hence including a variety of possible harms) but may not otherwise be illegal. To describe the task that the AI undertakes simply in technical terms will omit many aspects that are essential to consider in understanding how a situation came to be seen as of concern.

Exercise 2

Consider different ways in which the problems of online harms may be described, what more information may be added, including elements of agency, who is involved in this, and how they became involved. What is it that we are trying to solve with the use of AI? You may wish to base this simply on your prior knowledge, or do a little research on how the issues are presented in different contexts and by different parties.

Consider the use of any value judgements in describing the situation to be addressed.

Consider how far back in time we need to go to understand how the situation came about.

If you are doing this as part of a class, it may be instructive to compare your account with those of others.

It may be an interesting exercise to attempt to describe the situation using as 'neutral' language as possible and then consider if describing it using value terms or emotionally loaded or judgemental terms might give a different view of matters. This of course raises the question of what it is for language to be 'neutral', which is, indeed, a central question for this topic.

We can describe the issue in terms of addressing online content which 'causes harm'. Here, we discuss some of the issues that need to be teased out. This content is described in official reports and in much general discourse as 'online hate' or 'online harms'. The proposed intervention of government agencies and the law is premised upon claims that the issue is not adequately dealt with by current means, including any control exercised by technology companies; the issue is presented as both serious and as growing. The ethical issues are thus nested within political and legal issues, since it raises the general question of the proper role of government, especially when considering the wish to address content that does not break any current laws (such laws include laws against libel and promoting terrorism and other clearly illegal activities). This is thus a clear example of an ethical question where political and wider social questions also need to be addressed.

This can be seen as an aspect of the 'control' question in AI: have new technologies created a situation that necessitates further government intervention in our lives, where we are at the mercy of a tussle between governments and technology companies for control over our discourse? Note how on some ways of looking at the situation, the issue may be seen primarily as control by technologies; by companies who develop and apply these technologies; by individuals and organised groups making use of these technologies; or by governments. Note too that the claim that the issue is both serious and growing fits with tropes of technological progress (negative tropes in this case), with tropes of fear of loss of control, yet accompanied by the hopes that technology can, after all, address this tech-made problem; those working in the field often claim that attempts to deal with this by equipping individual users of the online world with media literacy will be inadequate [14]. Others will disagree, and it may be considered that where freedoms are in question, this may be more important than finding the most technically proficient solution.

Content and agency The issue to be dealt with can be described in terms of tackling content online, but we can immediately see that a complex web of control, agency, and responsibility is involved and that there are almost inevitably going to be different ways of understanding this. This content is put there by humans, even if it comes from a bot account: bots don't make themselves. We can think of the language (or images) involved as simply formal carriers of meaning, but we also need to consider not only the formal properties of language but also language as communication.

The problem(s) are implicitly or explicitly described in ways that attribute responsibility and negative value judgements to those behind the content: that it is malicious, intentional, or careless. Such people may be described as spreading fear, hate, and abuse [15].

One way of looking at the problem of online hate Consider the extremes with which AI is sometimes spoken: as ushering in a glorious future, of enabling us to realise the greatest aspects of humanity; or as dooming us to a future of unimaginable bleakness governed by technology (and, on some versions, manipulated or relegated to second class citizens by its human overlords) if, that is, we even survive. The actual problem here may be far more mundane and notable for its manifest grubbiness. One of the challenges that content moderation involves is precisely sorting out the entirely petty insult, the minor spat, from content deemed harmful.

Far from visions of a glorious and technologically sophisticated future, we are pinning our hopes that some relatively simple algorithms may help us deal with the embarrassing failures of humanity by acting as prefects to mean girls and bully boys. Put like that, it's almost comical. Unfortunately, however, it nonetheless raises some serious and rather vexed issues. This is manifest if the issue is framed as concerning our capacity to converse, access ideas, and the question of how our worldviews might be shaped or manipulated; it is of course a pivotal one for humanity.

The causal stories behind accounts of the problems If we are to see the situation adequately, and in particular, if we are to understand questions of agency and responsibility, we must consider the wider context, including how situations arise, in other words, an understanding of its history and the casual story that led to the present case: both the general situation of concern about online hate and harms and the particular situation behind specific instances.

Any history will also involve assumptions of value. For example, in describing the casual accounts, wherever human beings are involved, we need to have some understanding of the nature and degree of the agency of all the actors involved. What are some of the issues?

First, how new are these issues? Some background. Unless we understand the precedents, we may fail to see the full possibilities for understanding the nature of the issue and may not search in the right place for remedies. We may assume that the problem has been created by technology and thus should be solved via technology. We may assume that if the problem is novel, since we assume that it is created by new technology, and therefore can be solved in its entirety, since it did not exist prior to the technology. Nonetheless, even if the problem is not new but is merely amplified, this can cause a stepwise change in difficulty. If I find one bed-bug and kill it before it lays any eggs, this is a different matter to finding my entire house is infested.

We can certainly see in this case that hurling abuse and slander at our fellows has a long history and indeed is likely as old as civilisation. For example, the code of Ur-Nammu, from approximately 2000 BCE, contains punishment for false witness [16]. There is also a long history of punishing gossip.

Concern for freedom of expression may be historically somewhat newer but nonetheless also has a long history. One solution to the problem of online harms could be a high level of online censorship, for example, blocking any material that may be potentially problematic, blocking accounts, and banning certain individuals. However, even a less extreme response of censorship or blocking will be controversial. Not only is this against central values in many places, there would be a certain irony if the development and use of AI were to lead to the suppression of ideas. This can be seen in (at least) two ways.

One, consider the view of AI as discrete instances of technology exhibiting aspects of intelligence. Since intelligence involves information, and since AI uses and produces vast amounts of data and information, for AI technology to end up hampering human capacity to communicate and share opinion and information would be unfortunate indeed, a kind of an own goal.

Two, consider the view of AI as an attempt to reproduce human-level intelligence, including perhaps consciousness and agency. For technology to have the effects of encouraging the worst of human behaviour, then be used to curtail human expression, interactions, communication, and liberty, would again be very unfortunate. Hardly a utopian vision of a glorious future.

Exercise 3

Robin Wilton of the Internet Society has stated that the online world may amplify certain problems but does not create them [17].

Do you agree? Consider as many different aspects of communication online as possible.

Second, if problems are merely amplified, consider what that might mean for how we address them.

Free Speech and Freedom of Expression: John Stuart Mill

Perhaps the most cited account of the value of freedom of speech comes from John Stuart Mill in his work *On Liberty*, first published in 1859 [18]. This is a very strong defence of freedom of speech, but even Mill's account includes limits: the Harm Principle.

Mill argued that it should be possible to discuss any idea, even ones which are immoral, and even ideas which have no other exponents. We should have 'absolute freedom of opinion and sentiment on all subjects, practical or speculative, scientific, moral or theological' [18]. His reasoning behind this includes the value accorded to individuals, and the value of knowledge, including the value of understanding our own opinions. The value of opposing opinions in a free society includes the way that being confronted with difference of opinion is a spark to ensure that one understands the justification and grounds for one's own beliefs, which might otherwise grow stale if untested. A broadly empiricist notion that we may find we are wrong, and an open-ended view of the gathering of knowledge, forms a background. Mill was aware that society had great faults, that much was left to discover, and in addition, that human nature as we find it may be curtailed by circumstances including societal pressures.

Note the values attached to knowledge and discussion here. The picture of knowledge and of information is not simply of facts which we consider to be true: the process of acquiring beliefs is critical. This is intimately tied to the value given to individuals by Mill, since to accept something simply because it

(continued)

was received wisdom, or because a computer produced a result, might leave one without understanding of the grounds of one's beliefs.

Mill's harm principle is, quite simply, that 'the only purpose for which power can be rightfully exercised over any member of a civilized community, against his will, is to prevent harm to others' [18]. Hence, free speech can only be restricted if it causes harm. Note that the harm in question does not include 'legitimate' harms. For example, if someone correctly identified someone as having abused others, and that person then suffered properly applied legal penalties as a result, this would be legitimate. Simply causing offense to others does not amount to the harm needed to restrict free speech.

Critically for our purposes, Mill noted that the place and the manner of expression may be relevant. He argued that it is permissible to claim that corn dealers starve the poor (by high prices) if this is stated in print; but to state this to an angry mob outside the house of a corn dealer where a riot is likely to be sparked, would not be permissible.

It will be apparent that there are many complex political, philosophical, legal, and moral arguments regarding free speech and freedom of expression relevant to the question of online harms. This brief introduction to Mill nonetheless opens up some important issues.

Exercise 4
Consider Mill's distinction between legitimate and illegitimate harms of free speech. Find some examples of putative harm caused by free speech online and consider whether this distinction is useful and, if so, how the line may be drawn.

Consider Mill's example of inciting an angry mob outside the house of a corn dealer by claiming that corn dealers starve the poor, compared to making this claim in a newspaper. Is this distinction useful for considering online harms? How might one distinguish different kinds of statements online?

Might one argue that the online world has brought the 'angry mob' closer the house of the corn dealer?

9.4.1 Online Content: Who Is Involved?

The role of individuals So what might lie behind the online behaviours in question? Note that there are two sides to the story, or more accurately, three or four: those who post material, those who are the targets, and bystanders who happen to see it (or actively seek it out), including those who see it and form opinions, or take action as a result.

Many years ago, my sister made the rather sensible suggestion that computers should be fitted with breathalysers so that it was impossible to post comments, send emails, or shop online while drunk. It would be authoritarian to impose this, but having it as an option seems like an idea worth considering. Doubtless others have also thought of this, and if they have, it will be because of multiple flaws in human nature: lack of judgement, impetuousness, and desires and urges pushing us in contrary directions. Indeed, it's only because we have these split natures that we even see this as a flaw; otherwise it would just be a description of who we are. Moreover, we are also highly social animals, which means that we often care deeply about what others think of us, and importantly, we care what other people think of other people. Reputation is important in social interaction. We get much of our social cues as well as our information from others.

What are the features of the online world that might produce bad behaviour or worsen it? We need to consider both those who post the material that is considered problematic and those who consider this material problematic, since we must not assume that all online content labelled as harmful or hateful merits that descriptor. The possibilities of fast responses; the potential reach of many posts; the possibility of anonymous posting; the loss of context of messages, including reach beyond cultural and linguistic communities; the lack of accountability; the growing importance of one's online presence and profile; and the ease with which information on a person may be found online are all some of the features that potentially together go to produce these problems.

Exercise 5

Add any other relevant features to this list and consider, for each of these, differences and similarities between the online world and the offline world. Notice the complexities involved.

The role of corporations   The technologies in question did not create themselves. Behind the story of concerns about online behaviour are the corporations that produce the technology, and that insert specific design features into it, and the issue of how society, both individually and collectively, is responding. These features may have been introduced with certain motives but will be likely to have multiple effects. A key motivator is profit and engagement. Structural issues in the design of online platforms themselves are a major background cause of much of the content that is presently under scrutiny. Persuasive technology is widely used in order to foster engagement [19]. Users are encouraged to stay online by technology that is designed to tap into our psychological weaknesses [8, 20]. Engagement is especially critical where any profits are generated through advertising revenues. We also have to add to these wider social factors, such as the growing necessity of communicating online; the very spread of technology makes it more and more of a necessity.

Exercise 6: Food for Thought

Do proposals to use algorithms to detect online hate amount to using technology to address problems caused by that very technology? If so, does this matter, and how? What might the implications be for the attribution of responsibility?

It is clear that to understand the lines of agency, responsibility, and accountability in creating the problems of online content and to investigate ways of ameliorating the situation, we need to consider social and political science, as well as economics and psychology, in addition to careful consideration of the details of different design features. This is clearly an area where ethics must work hand in hand with detailed knowledge of technology, design, actual patterns of usage, as well as many other complex and related features of human behaviour and interaction.

Exercise 7
Draw up two accounts of how the problems of online hate came to receive attention: one, focusing on individuals and on flaws in human nature; the other, focusing on the actions and responsibilities of the corporations that are involved. You may wish to do this in outline only, or conduct some further research.

The role of governments A larger political question is the role of governments in addressing online harms (especially for harms that are not illegal; where they amount to illegality, the role for government may be clearer). This is a complex political and legal issue to which ethical questions are relevant, but which goes beyond the scope of this book; this indeed illustrates again the reach and vast scope of the issues involved.

9.4.2   What Is Online 'Harm'?

It should be apparent that there are great complexities and many differences of opinion concerning the nature of any harm in hate speech. For example, the political philosopher Jeremy Waldron's book *The Harm in Hate Speech* argues that hate speech causes harm, for example, by undermining the dignity of groups [21]. Although Waldron's work has received support, such work is also subject to serious critique, for example, by Robert Simpson, who gives considerable grounds for rejecting such claims [22]. It is generally extremely difficult to draw causal links between online content and real-world harms, which of course does not mean such causal pathways do not exist. A report on online harms from the Alan Turing Institute states what it calls the 'harm paradox', which is that most online content is assessed based on what it *expresses*, rather than on any harm it has *caused*, and hence, it's not known if content labelled harmful, has actually produced any harm [14, p. 61]. See also the discussion of J. L. Austen's distinction between illocutionary, illocutionary, and perlocutionary acts in Sect. 7.4.

In particular, psychological harms are often subjective, vague, and difficult to attribute precisely. An abusive and derogatory comment can result in negative emotions in the person to whom the comment is directed, but there will be a wealth of complexities concerning the extent of any negative reaction, variations and disputes about the precise interpretation of language used, the intent of the speaker, whether the content was directly aimed at the person who feels distress as a result, and so on. Consider, for example, that attributions of 'emotional harm' will be under dispute by those who consider that any subjectively unpleasant emotion is *ipso facto* harm and by those who consider that although some negative emotions may reach a level of 'harm', negative emotions per se are simply part of life and indeed an essential aspect of achieving maturity. Even so, there is no clear line from emotional harm to the conclusion that content moderation is the answer. For many cases, muting the account in question, reading a book, or going to choir practice instead of doomscrolling Instagram is another possibility.

Exercise 8
There are many aspects to the question of how we understand the possible psychological harms of online content. Among the complexities is how we understand the goals of ethics. Different normative ethical theories may tend towards different responses.

Consider how a utilitarian might address the question of psychological or emotional harms from online content and compare and contrast this with how a virtue ethicist might approach the question. (See Chap. 6.)

Many of you will have spotted a complexity to this question: Mill himself was a utilitarian, yet his ideas in *On Liberty* stress the value of the individual. Consider the general issues that arise for utilitarianism and accounts of the end goals of ethics of maximising happiness or pleasure and minimising unhappiness or pain over a whole population. Consider the notion of phronesis and the development of character.

However, hard as these questions are, it is necessary to consider these matters if steps are to be taken to address online hate. At a minimum, one would need a reasonable understanding of how online hate caused harm and a way of detecting any harmful content such that human moderators and algorithms could detect this with a reasonable level of accuracy. There is no particular definition of hate speech in international human rights law [23]. Yet for content moderation online, we will need a sufficiently precise definition of online hate and of degrees and kinds of hate.

Is misinformation 'harm'?   Proposals to tackle online harms include proposals to tackle 'harmful misinformation or disinformation' [1]. Concern about misinformation online has been acute in recent years, especially in relation to COVID-19 and to allegations of the spread of misinformation around various political campaigns. The intentional spread of misinformation for gain, including for malicious reasons, is certainly not new, but the reach of the Internet and increasing reliance on it as a source of news and other information, together with concern about 'fake news' and deepfakes, means that it appears to be a greatly increased issue. The capacity of online material, including images and video, to capture attention, including the question of possible bias in the recommender algorithms shaping the online material each person will see, is also an important factor.

How large is the misinformation problem?   Determining the extent of the issue will be a complex matter. As with online hate, it is challenging to distinguish a rise in incidents from a rise in reporting. As an example, a highly cited report from the Oxford Internet Institute on the increasing role of misinformation has been argued to be methodologically flawed because it overlooks the difficulties in distinguishing an increase in misinformation from an increase in the reporting of concerns about misinformation [24, 25]. Moreover, just because a person is exposed to misinformation does not mean that it will be believed. In addition, not all misinformation is plausibly harmful, especially if we are looking to some threshold that justifies corporate or government interference over individual behaviour online. If I read online that Pluto has now been reclassified back as a planet, have I been harmed? Okay, my team may lose a point in the next pub quiz, but does this justify the attention of regulators?

Note that in addressing such questions, it will be helpful to consider the value that we place on information and knowledge: is knowledge an instrumental good, valued for merely pragmatic reasons, or valuable in and of itself? See Sect. 5.2 and consider the values that may be behind some attitudes towards the development of artificial intelligence. How much are concerns about misinformation concerns about the value of knowledge per se, and how much are they about the *use* to which information may be put?

How might we define online misinformation? We need an account of it which is helpful in identifying misinformation online which meets a threshold such that taking steps against it is justified. Consider, for example, a report by the Alan Turing Institute, 'Understanding vulnerability to online misinformation', which focuses on concerns around misinformation in the light of the COVID-19 pandemic [26]. The concern for misinformation regarding COVID-19 in this report is focused upon the possible harms this might bring, such as hesitancy to vaccinate and loss of trust. Hence, note that concerns for harms regarding online misinformation may be specific to certain contexts. The report draws on a definition of misinformation as 'contrary to the epistemic consensus of the scientific community regarding a phenomenon' [26, p. 8].

Note two things from this definition. First, it implies change over time. The epistemic consensus of a scientific community will evolve with new evidence and changing theories. Second, it implies consensus within a community. However, there are many instances in science in which there is no firm consensus and in which it is recognised that there are legitimate differences of opinion given the current state of evidence and theories. More worrying would be cases where there was only a minority who differed from a majority view: is the minority view thus counter to the 'consensus'? Note the use of the word 'community'. Does this exclude amateurs? Does it exclude scientists who lost their position because of the immense competition for academic and research posts? Does it exclude scientists who lost their position because of their contrarian views? Do the views of certain scientists, universities, and research groups dominate particular scientific communities? If so, we may in some instances be reproducing power dynamics in using content moderation to flag or remove certain ideas. The attempts to be 'ethical' may in fact magnify existing problems.

The seriousness of the COVID-19 pandemic may lead one to conclude it was necessary to take such steps, and it is an emotive topic so a more neutral example might be more effective in generating discussion. It is important to realise the potential naivety of placing trust in 'the truth' as an absolute. Science is a continually developing area of endeavour. Not only are scientific findings continuously being updated and revised, recent work analysing and critiquing the scientific publication system has determined that much of what we think we know is false. 'p-hacking' is a term of art for selectively publishing only those papers that reach certain, often rather low, thresholds of statistical significance [27]. This means that a significant proportion—possibly most—of all scientific papers are misleading [28]. The implications for any fact checking efforts are obvious. In relation to the use of algorithms in the quest to root out online 'hate' or purported misinformation, an MIT professor, Sandy Pentland, is reported as claiming that 75% of all published papers in machine learning are 'junk' [29, p. 146]. Machine learning is a relatively new field, so such claims are almost certain to be disputed, but the very possibility of such serious dispute is of concern.

Exercise 9
Try to build a definition of online misinformation that is sufficiently robust to use as a fair basis for moderating online harms. This may work well as a group exercise. Consider the advantages and dangers of its application.

The need for interdisciplinarity At the very least, this shows the need for work in ethics, law, and policy to take note of issues in epistemology, philosophy of science, the politics and sociology of science, and scientific methodology. Note too how general assumptions about epistemology, which may be linked perhaps to attitudes towards the goals and values of AI, may be present: a degree of certainty that we have reached a state of knowledge, and with this, perhaps a totalising attitude towards knowledge, which may be another aspect of the control problem with AI but reinforced via attempts to ensure ethical AI.

9.5 Challenges for AI in Tackling Online Harms

Summary
Here, we look more closely at practical and theoretical challenges for the detection of online harms and hate speech using algorithms. These include problems of context in the online world and ways in which meaning may be communicated in subtle and contested ways. H. P. Grice's account of the maxims governing the interpretation of conversation is used to discuss difficulties of interpreting language online. Specific problems in the use of algorithms include problems with state-of-the-art models, bias, and data quality issues.

9.5.1 Introduction: Detecting Online Harms

We have a general problem: defining hate speech, its varieties, and degrees. The online world adds another dimension of difficulty. These are problems independently of any attempt to use AI to detect and monitor it. The algorithms used to detect online harms and online hate will have to be trained by human moderators. Hence, we need to consider difficulties that humans have with labelling online content, plus any additional issues specific to the use of algorithms. This should include considering what is possible, as well as the current state of play. Unfortunately, there are major hurdles to overcome.

Researchers working in the field have noted the many difficulties in understanding the nature and extent of online hate [14]. A policy briefing produced by the Alan Turing Institute in 2019 notes that we do not currently have the tools accurately to monitor online content and that the field suffers from a large range of challenges, including the definition of terms, methodology, legal issues, and other theoretical challenges [30]. A strategic question then arises: if the ethical issues are seen to be serious and growing, there may be an urgency in addressing them. At the same time, careful examination of the field shows that much is left unknown about the state of 'online hate' [31]. There may be different impressions of the scale of the problem depending on how the matter is presented. The rates of abusive content online may be estimated to be low, and estimates of prevalence vary wildly, yet a sizeable minority of the population may be exposed to it [30]. Methodological questions are many, including how precisely 'abuse' or 'hate' has been interpreted in research by the researchers and the respondents. One challenge is to distinguish a rise in abuse from a rise in *reports of* abuse. Moreover, an examination of research papers in this area will show a variety of different terms used and a variety of different phenomena included.

The good news for those interested in AI ethics is that there is plenty of scope for further work in this area that seeks to ask clear questions and adopts rigorous methodology in attempting to gain answers. Let us consider some of the problems. Many of these concern the nature of natural language itself, especially any contextual and cultural factors. Context is a key part of the interpretation of natural language (see Sect. 7.5). Meaning is often attributed based upon the context and assumptions of intent. Earlier I wrote the sentence, 'The content moderators are not content.' The two meanings of 'content' can readily be inferred by speakers of English, given also a basic understanding of the surrounding discussion. A task for natural language processing needed to detect online hate is to understand this context adequately.

9.5.2 Language and Meaning

First, we will review the general difficulties of attributing meaning to language. Considerable advances in natural language processing have been made, as we saw with regard to the LaMDA issue. Note that even if natural language processing could tackle all these issues as well as a human could, there are going to be points of contention that remain. Moreover, since an essential aspect of the concern about online content is how material will be understood by other humans, we cannot escape having to face the difficulties posed in communication via language. We also need to address the specific context of the online world and the challenges in the use of algorithms to moderate content.

Context, culture, and individuals In finding content harmful, hateful or otherwise objectionable, there will be large variations of response between individuals, subgroups within a society, cultures, and language groups. There are likely to be differences in demographics, especially as language evolves and is evolving precisely in response to technology. Many old-fashioned terms of abuse may come to seem mild or comical or may simply be misunderstood. There is wide variation between and within languages and cultures over what terms are seen to be abusive and how abusive they are, with often wide regional and class variations even within the same culture. This is likely to vary with context even within small groups, with some language considered suited for some contexts yet not for others. (Recall Goffman's distinction between front and back stage, Sect. 3.6.2) The distinction between the public and the private operates here: language suited for, say, the workplace or a formal gathering may be judged differently from more private occasions. The modification or erosion of the lines between public and private online is an important factor.

The many uses of language Another set of difficulties arises from the very complexities of human language use. Sarcasm, irony, satire, and humour are all essentially human traits, and each demonstrates the flexibility and creativity possible with language use, but they are also culturally, linguistically, and individually specific, and although they may operate extremely well to communicate a great deal with a few words, they may not translate very well from one group to another [32]. On the other hand, the view has been expressed that even if a message was clearly intended as humorous, if it is perceived as hate or as harmful, its status as humour should make no difference [33].

Language, meaning, and intention The assessment of content as harmful in some way can be loose and contentious [34]. Some accounts of hate speech include the responses of others: if a targeted individual or group considers language hateful, or if a third party does so, then it amounts to hate speech [35]. One disputed issue is the question of intention: this seems to reverse an account of meaning where the intention of the speaker sets the meaning: the responses of the hearer now seem to set the meaning. However, the speaker's intention can only set the meaning within limits. Language is shared. I cannot say, 'The fridge is red' and mean, 'Algebra is my favourite subject in maths'. But I can say, 'I have an assignment due tomorrow' and mean 'I am not coming to the party.' Hence, the excuse, 'I did not mean to imply so-and-so' can only be taken so far; how far can speaker's intention be stretched within the complexities of the online world?

H. P. Grice and Conversational Implicature

In natural language, there is much that is left to convention and mutual understanding in how meaning is conveyed. Indeed, the difficulties of presenting a formalised account of meaning within the limits of natural language is a major source of misunderstanding when attempting to programme unambiguous instructions into a computer, and is the subject of many a story about sorcerers' granting of wishes, as well as the plot of many stories about mishaps regarding AI including Asimov's Robot series.

Philosophers and discourse analysts have attempted to analyse how meaning is conveyed over and above the formal meaning of a sentence. H. P. Grice was the first philosopher to theorise about the distinction between speaker meaning and sentence meaning [36]. Given the loss of context in the online world, and given definitions of hate speech which include or focus on the meanings attributed to content by those reading or hearing it, some such distinction could be very useful for addressing the issues in online content moderation. These implicatures of conversation may be used to understand features of language such as irony and humour.

Grice theorised that there are several implicitly agreed maxims of conversation which govern how speech is interpreted. A general principle of cooperation governs what participants accept is the purpose of a conversation. These are:

The maxim of quality: Claims should be true, so do not state what you consider to be false or unsupported by evidence.

The maxim of quantity: give an appropriate amount of information as required.
The maxim of relation: be relevant to the purpose of the interchange.
The maxim of manner: avoid being obscure of ambiguous, be brief, and communicate information in a good order.

Subsequent work has found much of value in Grice's proposals, although with modifications and with much variation including between languages and cultures in the particular implicatures in operation [37].

Note how Grice's theory is based upon a principle of cooperation and a level of mutual understanding, something which is not evenly distributed across the Internet.

Exercise 10

Could some such principle of cooperation be helpful in understanding interchanges and problems that arise online? Might we need new maxims for online communication, and if so, what might these be?

Try to find some examples of language online where there seems to be a lack of agreement on conversational maxims.

Does Grice's account of language make the possibility of use of algorithms for interpreting language nearer, or does it merely indicate the depth of the problem?

9.5.3 Difficulties with Hate Speech

The concept of hate speech has been called 'essentially contested', meaning that there are insurmountable differences of opinion about how it should be understood [14, p. 41, 38]. There are examples of putative online hate that could readily be contested by others. For example, one academic journal article refers to the hijacking of hashtags as a form of online hate, using the example of the #Shoutyourabortion Twitter campaign [39]. However, one might readily point out that both sides in the abortion debate could consider that the other side was 'hateful', given the depth of feeling and the seriousness of the issues. This is perhaps then a good example to warn against politicising notions of online hate and ensuring a good range of diversity in those who are advising, drawing up regulations and policy, and acting as human moderators.

Degrees of online hate Measuring degrees of online hate seems essential if proportionality is to be applied to any remedies used. A social media post telling someone that their latest hair cut doesn't suit them is a far cry from content issuing extreme levels of hatred for certain groups or individuals. But how are any gradations to be drawn? The question of attributing degree to online hate relates to many things: the changing nature of language, even where definitions are agreed upon, and individual and subjective responses to terms.

Could a system for monitoring online hate and abuse impose the values of a dominant group onto less powerful groups in how language and communication is regulated and dealt with? Indeed, it seems likely to do so, unless rigorous steps are taken against it.

Exercise 11
One aspect of the control problem in AI is the possibility of conformity to a totalising system, especially given the potential reach of much AI. Is it possible that monitoring online hate through a nationally imposed system might have such an impact? If so, would it matter, and if so, how, and how much?

Dog whistles A contested term which has received considerable attention is the concept of the 'dog whistle', as an attempt to hide hateful messages by implying something which is never actually stated, and supposedly then send an implicit message intended for certain groups only who will be primed to decipher it in certain ways. Dog whistles are sometimes seen to be ways of communicating hateful messages more broadly with impunity, because the hate is implied not stated [40]. Because the meaning is carried implicitly and may be unreadable to many, this may imply that dog whistles are less serious forms of online abuse (although note that a dog whistle could also be used to carry a harmless in-group reference). However, a dog whistle could also be used to convey rather extreme messages and may be thought to be particularly problematic in demonstrating devious attempts to circumnavigate censorship. The very nature of dog whistles means that their detection will be contestable, whether on- or offline [41, 42]. They can thus readily be mistakenly or mischievously attributed to innocent parties.

A related term is that of microaggressions [43]. A suggested example of a microaggression in the online space is only responding to comments from people who are of the same group [14, p. 53]. While some consider that the recognition of microaggressions is necessary, the concept is also disputed, and even if the concept itself is seen as generally valid, there are disagreements about the concept's application. On the one hand, the difficulties of reaching agreement on examples of microaggressions and dog whistles seem only to add to the general difficulties of defining and detecting hate speech. On the other hand, if the whole point of moderating online content is to detect such subtleties of language use, their inclusion in any account of online hate may be seen as necessary [44].

Exercise 12
Consider the advantages and disadvantages of including dog whistles and/or microaggressions in accounts of online hate. How could meaning be attributed in such cases? Are there dangers of false attribution? What accounts of language and meaning does the concept of a dog whistle rest upon? Do you think it is possible or likely that an algorithm may be able to detect these?

The use of the terms 'dog whistle' and 'microaggression' is relatively new. The terms may be considered useful advances, with origins in both the wish to progress the study of communication and to improve our understanding of patterns of discrimination and exclusion.

Exercise 13
Consider the pros and cons of incorporating such relatively new concepts for describing language and communication into a methodology for detecting online hate. Consider: 'This shows progress in understanding the impact we have on each other and raised levels of responsibility in speech; perhaps, indeed, our raised awareness of communication online has helped us to this understanding', versus, 'We are looking for offense where none is to be found. This takes attention away from more serious concerns,' and in addition, 'These complexities demonstrate the inability of either human or AI to address online harms adequately'.

9.5.4 Problems with Algorithms

There are multiple challenges in the use of algorithms to detect online content, including hate speech or online harms. Many of these problems can be addressed and improved with better research and more data; others may be more intractable. As we have seen, algorithms built to detect online hate have to cope with understanding context, speaker, audience, and the constantly shifting nature of hate speech. This includes features such as spelling changes (including deliberate attempts to get past moderation systems), dialects, subcultures, stereotypes, sarcasm, irony, humour, metaphor, and other features of language and communication that defy precise formalisation. The algorithms will need to be continuously updated.

There are many difficulties in attempting content moderation for online hate. Work from the Hate Speech: Measures and Counter Measures project at the Alan Turing Institute states that 'critical challenges are unsolved', including lack of dataset sharing and classification bias [31].

Many others agree. Research demonstrates that ideas of language acceptability are malleable and vary according to social context and that there may be differences in ratings of online content by different annotators; automated content moderation systems risk increasing these differences [45]. Researchers have found significant differences between ratings of online content by males and females. Other work also finds difficulties in rating social media comments for 'hate' [46].

A recent review finds that existing 'state of the art' models have been 'severely overestimated' [47]. In other words, the models are inaccurate. Problems are found to stem from nonstandard grammar and vocabulary, paucity and bias in datasets, and implicit expressions of hate. The potential for increasing the harm against minority groups in attempts to detect online hate was confirmed. There is a high level of disagreement between those who label content.

Machine learning relies upon datasets that are labelled by human moderators. However, moderators are often untrained, even for those sets of data upon which research work in online hate is conducted [33, at 44.12]. Even where they are trained, such training is found to vary greatly. However, it is on the judgements of human moderators that the norms of any automated content moderation system will be built.

It is well established that algorithms may magnify existing biases, that this particularly may affect minority groups, and that correcting this is very challenging. It is now well known that the use of algorithms carries with it the risk of bias from the data on which it is developed and/or the model used in the algorithm [48–50]. The widespread use of algorithms may greatly magnify any existing bias, which may then become further entrenched. Algorithmic bias tends to magnify existing unfairness by most impacting those groups who are already subject to bias [51]. It has been amply demonstrated that labelling content as 'hate' carries the risk of racial bias and bias against different dialects [52–54]. Attempts to address such bias have themselves been found to contain numerous shortcomings [55].

In an attempt to improve matters, researchers have developed 'HATECHECK', a system of tests to determine which different aspects of hate speech detection models are flawed, covering 29 different aspects [56]. This research finds deep problems and critical model weaknesses. All models tested were overly sensitive to some keywords and phrases, such as reclaimed slurs, counter speech, and negated hate, consistently misclassify certain content, and misclassify content in ways biased towards certain groups.

Exercise 14

What challenges are there for providing a definition of online hate such that an algorithm could be able reliably to detect it?

Of the difficulties with detecting meaning in natural language online discussed here, consider which are most readily overcome. Could the use of AI make us feel the issue is solvable, with time, and might this be an illusion?

Exercise 15

Compare and contrast the benefits and problems with using human moderators versus algorithms.

Could AI be more consistent and therefore fairer?

Could AI be gradually improved?

Could AI overcome the bias and inconsistencies of humans?

Technological optimism and technological solutionism We have looked at how AI may inspire great optimism and also dread and fear. We have looked at how tropes of technological progress may be linked to assumptions of moral progress. Is it possible that here we have a toxic mix of competing elements? Fear of the forces in human nature unleashed by the affordances of technology and the abilities it gives us to subvert norms of human communication seems perhaps combined with an optimistic assumption that the very technology (and those who created it) can address the problem and that the well-understood problems can be overcome, if only we try harder.

Exercise 16

Argue for or against each of these positions and consider how some accommodation may be reached:

Claim: content moderation using algorithms plus human review will produce a workable system to detect and deal with online hate. It may not be perfect, but it can be 'good enough'. Nothing in this world is perfect, and there are serious harms being perpetrated that must be addressed.

Counterclaim: The root source of most of the flaws in content moderation using algorithms is the disputed notions of 'online harms' and 'online hate'. Human review may help in some cases but will not solve this and may even make things worse.

This may work well as a group exercise or class debate.

There may well be downsides to incautious assumptions that technology can solve this problem, especially if the end goal is not well articulated, which is an instance of the general problem that goals may be instantiated in ways that have unforeseen and undesirable effects. For example, some research indicates that allowing a diversity of views online may be necessary to facilitate agreement in online groups [57]. This may be a manifestation of one of J. S. Mill's arguments for free speech that the continued presence of opposing views enables individuals to understand and robustly support their own views. Research also warns of the limits to our capacities to process information: just because there is more of it out there does not necessarily mean to say that we all understand more [58]. It may not be a cornucopia in which we pick knowledge from every tree, but a jungle in which we get easily lost.

9.6 Bias and the Production of 'AI Ethics'

Summary
Here, we examine how bias may be present in attempts to address the ethical issues concerning online content. Biases may be present in how the problem is set up, in algorithms, in human moderators, and in feedback loops generated by methods adopted to address particular accounts of the issues. We need to be aware of possible bias in those tackling ethics, policy, and regulation. Interest in developing technologies may be at odds with best ethical practice.

We have examined the question of bias in algorithms, which is nested within the issue of bias (and general inaccuracies and inconsistencies) in human moderators who train algorithms. However, the question of bias towards this issue, and many other issues in AI ethics, may also be biased in various other ways. Indeed, if we focus on bias as a merely technical issue in algorithms that can be 'solved', then this may distract us from the ways in which bias may operate elsewhere.

We have already seen how algorithms may be biased and how in particular bias may be especially hard to tackle when interpreting natural language. This may lead in particular to bias against certain ethnic and cultural groups; moreover, these will tend to be groups already suffering from discrimination, and the use of algorithms to address an ethical issue may act to further entrench the linguistic and cultural dominance of those who already have power, and act as a move towards conformity. This may be reinforced by the labelling of content as misinformation, unless great care is taken. How are decisions about moderation made by humans impacted by the decisions made by algorithms and the values of the tech firms for which they work?

Bias may creep into any ethical issue from the beginning, depending upon how the problem is stated and illustrated. We could formulate this as the problem of 'online hate' or 'online harms'; we could also formulate this as the problem of 'online censorship', of being cancelled or blocked, and denied access to the online space. Indeed, both issues may have affected the very same individuals and groups. There may be bias operating both when claims of online harms are endorsed and when they are rejected.

Once a problem has been identified in a certain way, the very steps taken to address it may further entrench the initial viewpoint. Let us take a simplified example: suppose there is widespread concern that dog lovers are unduly aggressive towards cat lovers online. Steps are taken to address this. Cat lovers are encouraged to report dog lovers for hate. Several dog lovers have content removed and accounts blocked. This receives considerable coverage. Cat lovers get sympathy in the media; dog lovers are held under suspicion. Free speech groups are accused of being dog sympathisers or 'dog adjacent'. 'Dog adjacent' accounts and advocates of free speech come under scrutiny by cat lovers, and as a result, several of these are found to be guilty of online hate. Research and policy work to address the issue consults stakeholders from those who feel they have been affected by online aggression, which overwhelmingly includes cat lovers.

And that is how come cats rule the Internet.

Indeed, it may be useful to consider whether some academic and policy literature may contain seeds of political bias. Research has found that academics, on average, are more left wing than the general public, although the extent of any bias is disputed [59, 60]. Some work on online content moderation is concerned with the activities of the far right, but less has addressed the far left [61]. A report by the Alan Turing Institute presents the 'free speech defence' of online content as a form of animosity and a possible subtype of online harm [24, p. 53]. While this could be true in some cases, especially given the difficulty of producing an agreed upon and rigorous account of online harm, the possibility of bias must not be overlooked. Again, the need for wide discussion, the input of a large range of opinion, and those from diverse backgrounds, is underlined, including in any stakeholders and groups consulted in developing policy.

The organisational structures within which ethics and policy advice in AI is developed may also be relevant to questions of bias. As a relatively new area of concern, there are not yet many people working in the area, and those with relevant expertise may have close links with each other. The dangers of groupthink may be present. Working closely with experts in technology who are developing algorithms, including for content moderation, is of course useful in ensuring detailed technical knowledge but may bias policy makers and those working in ethics to assume that a technical solution is best and will work. Funding may depend upon governments. Moreover, links with government and policy makers may further entrench the possible biases of those producing policy and ethics responses. Are some of those who are currently producing ethics and policy advice part and parcel of government or corporate power? There is an urgent need for independent civil society groups and others to engage in such debates and to be taken seriously as participants; some such groups already exist. This may be particularly important in this area, given the contentious nature of defining online hate and the seriousness of issues for individuals and for society as a whole. There are proposals that expert advice should be fed into the work of regulators [15]. But who are these experts going to be?

We also need to consider the interests of governments in pursuing particular policies. Leadership in ethics is sought as much as in technology; this may of course include political posturing and the wish to rush in first so that others are forced to follow, as well as elements of national pride. A government minister has stated, referring to the government's response to the Online Harms White Paper consultation: 'I am confident that today's measures mark a significant step in the continual evolution of our approach to our life online—and it's fitting that this should be a step that our country takes. The World Wide Web was of course invented by a Brit. And now the UK is setting a safety standard for the rest of the world to follow' [62]. Note too that in his address, the same minister mentioned the specific concerns that members of Parliament have had regarding alleged online abuse [62]. No mention was made of concerns regarding undue content removal. Might this skew the debate? An express aim of the UK government has been 'to make Britain the safest place in the world to go online' [2, 15, p. 4]. Might this suggest a priority towards concern with online harms, rather concern for online censorship or the problems faced by those unjustly treated by content moderation?

Furthermore, note how ambitions for technological progress may in such instances be linked to ambitions in setting the agenda and providing ethical leadership. In part, this is due to the widely perceived necessity of considering ethical issues in AI. Note that governments are susceptible to lobbying, and this includes from those who stand to gain financially and otherwise from developing safety technology used among other things for content moderation [63].

An additional and major concern that adds great complexity is the role and responsibilities of the companies who develop, market, and profit from the technologies that are creating the issues and who are also moderating content. Proposals from the UK government to give 'duties of care' to social media companies with regard to online harms may from one point of view look rather like asking the fox to look after the henhouse. The very people who have created the problem are charged with addressing it.

Finally, we must also consider the broader and more general question of how the ways in which we see technology, its capabilities, and its flaws may impact how we see the world and each other. Might the very idea of eradicating bias online, of eradicating online harms, and the idea that technology can do this for us have an influence on how we understand the world and ourselves? Might the idea that we can use technology to create 'the safest place in the world to go online' have an influence on how we see safety and risk? We consider these ideas further in Sect. 9.8.

9.7 AI, Online Content, Persons, Self, and Society

Summary
We examine the ethical implications of how the online world may influence how people see themselves and relate to others. These include anonymity, deepfakes, and the magnification of reactions, for instance, in the Internet pile-on. We also consider how users may be manipulated by aspects of technological design, which may be both at cross-purposes with the purposes of users and may intentionally exploit some of our worst traits. The implications for agency and responsibility are discussed.

The complexity of how people communicate online is again an area of central ethical importance where there is an essential need for both theoretical and empirical research across different disciplines. Background models of human nature and of the person will help to understand the issues. We have seen the importance of how people relate to each other, the importance, especially highlighted in some approaches to ethics, of attention to and respect for others (see Sect. 8.3). However, we have also noted how readily dehumanisation may occur. Recall how research mentioned in discussing the concept of a person and people living with dementia noted the importance of bodily expression and appearance in maintaining a sense of self and being seen by others (see Sect. 8.5). Indeed, much work in social psychology has noted how readily dehumanisation can occur and how group pressures can distort thinking and behaviour [64]. The ways in which we see ourselves through technology, the feedback we get from others via technology, and the way we see others, how we connect to different communities and a sense of public and private, may very well be changing our behaviour—for better, one would hope, but likely as well, for worse. Virtue ethics stresses the importance and the difficulty of moral education and the development of character, with the surrounding social environment being an essential element. But what kind of communities wait for us online? As with so much else related to AI and new technologies, there is great promise but also peril. There is considerable work underway examining such questions with media and communications scholars specialising in digital communications; the ethical discussions here are just one aspect of this complex political, societal, cultural, and technological debate [3, 65, 66].

Some features of the online world enable considerable magnification of behaviours that are also possible in the offline world. For example, the phenomenon of the Internet pile-on is enabled by the sheer number of people who can see content, the capacity to share content with great rapidity, and the considerable number of anonymous accounts online. Doxxing, publishing identifying information about a person online with malicious intent, takes advantage of the power of Internet search engines and facilities such as image searches, both to uncover information about an individual and then to gain great traction in spreading it [67].

Exercise 17
In an Internet pile-on, hundreds or thousands of individuals may target an individual with messages seen as abusive, hurtful, or harmful. Individually, each one of these may be relatively innocuous, or just slightly hurtful. Collectively, they could be far more of a problem. (Imagine going into work 1 day, and a colleague remarks, 'I thought your presentation yesterday was a little boring'. Now imagine that you work in a company with 10,000 employees and every one of them calls, texts, pops into your office, or emails, to tell you that your presentation was a little boring.)

What responsibilities might each person have individually for participating in an Internet pile-on? Consider different cases, including any examples you know of.

Online anonymity is a good example of how relations with others online may be deeply distorted compared to the general possibilities of ordinary life. On the one hand, it may enable certain protections, for example, for dissidents in certain countries posting material critical of their governments [68] or for employees who have reasonable fears that their employer may take action against them for reasonable beliefs. (Indeed, a complexity: the very attempt to target material online, which is 'legal but harmful to adults', may only increase such concerns.) On the other hand, it can enable and perhaps encourage illegal activity, abuse, harassment, and other behaviours that one might never have indulged in without the invisibility cloak of anonymity. (Recall the Ring of Gyges, Sect. 1.6) An individual may display a considerable part of his or her personality and beliefs through the protection of the anonymity of the Internet. One's online presence can also mean more than presenting a persona to others and communicating: the consequences of being 'cancelled' online may be severe.

Exercise 18

Some have suggested that ending online anonymity may be one way of addressing online abuse. Using as many concrete examples as you can, discuss the arguments for and against. Consider especially questions about how we relate to each other as persons.

Our responsibility and agency online may also be impacted by the affordances of the technologies. For example, it is simple to block or mute people. This may be a perfectly legitimate response, and we are perfectly well permitted to exercise choice in who we interact with in our private lives. Except for family. Oh, and neighbours. Oh, and your best friend's wife whom you find slightly annoying, and so on. This points, of course, to the very different attitudes and norms about community and connection that exist. Consider again the notion of phronesis, the demands of social life and of morality, and how the online world may differ from the offline world.

Exercise 19

Might we rely upon the affordances of technology to take control of issues that we would otherwise have to handle in different ways? Try to think of some different aspects of technology and to consider both positive, negative, and neutral consequences. Don't forget to think of what the technologies may have replaced or eclipsed.

How users are seen by those designing the technology So far, we have examined some features of online communication and how they might impact our sense of self and how we relate to others. We have thought of these simply as features of technology as if they have just popped up from nowhere. Such features are all designed, even though certain aspects and consequences of how they work may not have been explicitly intended. In large part, they are designed to fit the purposes of the companies producing the technology, and these may very well not be in harmony with the purposes of the users. Even the 'ethical' features may serve the purposes of maintaining company image, even if they are also beneficial.

Moreover, design features may not simply be at cross purposes with the purposes of users: they may be placed there in order to manipulate users. This includes the gathering and analysis of large amounts of data, which are then used, for example, in recommender algorithms and in advertising. They also include the wide range of 'persuasive technology' designed to trap our attention, a particularly troubling issue given the importance of attention to understanding ethical questions and respecting others [19, 69, 70]. Moreover, much of the technology engages in the worst aspects of human psychology: angry responses are more likely to lead to sustained engagement online [8].

It seems then as if online users are being regarded as a behaviourist might regard an experimental subject, a box from which to elicit a response given certain stimuli (see Sect. 8.4). Moreover, the power to do this is enhanced because the human subjects are not merely seen as black boxes, but the weaknesses of our psychology are used against us.

This view of online users extends to some of the work trying to tackle online abuse, which talks of an 'alt right pipeline' that purportedly exists online. Concerns are raised about online radicalisation and how exposure to certain material that may be within the boundaries of the acceptable can lead to exposure to increasing problematic—in this case, right wing and far right—material [71]. There are also concerns expressed by policy researchers about a 'global ecosystem of hate' enabled by communication online [72, p. 8].

Does the notion of a 'pathway' imply that the seeds of violence may already be present? Because such putative pathways are very hard to trace with rigour, are we are paving the way for a notion of 'precrime'? Perfectly legal content, much of it harmless under any stretch of the imagination, may have actions taken against it if it is 'potentially' part of a pathway to extremism. Much will depend of course upon the surrounding social, political, and legal circumstances, but action regarding the online world may well spill over into other areas of life. Moreover, claims for such causal links between certain online content and the rise of extremism are very complex, and drawing clear lines of causation is problematic [71].

Exercise 20
Consider different ways in which agency and responsibility are understood in addressing issues of alleged online harms. You may find it useful to review previous material on persons and on human nature.

Do you agree to any degree with the following statements? What are the reasons for your answer?

'The technology is designed to incite users to irrational, emotional behaviour. Then, it judges us by a 'rational' standard of behaviour that it has incited users to violate. Moreover, those who are incited to take offence are treated differently from those who are incited to give offence.'

'Pernicious actors are using the internet to propagate harmful views and to recruit and seduce others to agree to these. Even if those seduced by harmful ideologies may be innocent at first, by travelling down this route they cross the line to become perpetrators themselves.'

Definitions of online hate or online harms, agency, intention, and responsibility On some accounts of hate speech and of online harms, the response to the content of the intended recipient of the message and of third parties can be critical for labelling it as harmful [31]. Language is a social phenomenon: we often use language with the intention of producing particular responses in those reading or hearing, including both behaviour and psychological responses (see the discussion of J. L. Austen in Sect. 7.4). However, some concepts of online harms may shift the attention to the responses of any audience (whether the intended audience or not) and away from any intention of the speaker (or writer). How might this shift perceptions of agency and responsibility, and how may it impact how we communicate online? Although we may intend certain things by speaking, and not intend others, there are certain limits to what we can and cannot reasonably intend. The online world, however, greatly increases the audience of any content and tends to strip away the context of how intention and meaning are understood. We noted in Sect. 7.4 that early work by philosophers of language in pragmatics has advanced considerably in the fields of both philosophy of language and discourse analysis. The area of online communication is an obvious site where different norms of linguistic engagement may apply.

Exercise 21

It has been suggested that humour is no defence against allegations of online harms. Consider arguments for and against, including consideration of how meaning is understood, context, agency, and responsibility. Does the online world give us all different responsibilities in communicating?

Exercise 22

'The right to free speech does not include the right to access any particular online space. Therefore, if a person is ousted from an online platform, or even from all of them, this does not violate any of their rights.'

Discuss.

Deepfakes and online harms Many of the concerns about online harms stem from the new or increased possibilities that technology presents us with, coupled with the importance to individuals (and groups) of their reputation, and the hurt that targeted insults or abuse may produce. A paradox of the online world is that it has both helped to spread information and knowledge to extremely large audiences and at the same time made it harder to discern what is true and what is false. Technical attempts to spot deepfakes are of course one part of a solution but may consist of a cat-and-mouse game against those producing deepfakes.

Exercise 23

Suppose somebody has been the victim of intentional malice, and a deepfake photo or video of the person naked and in a compromising position has been circulated online: in fact it's the person's face, but everything else is fake. Great distress and harm have been caused by this unfortunately common phenomenon. Is this different in any ethically significant way to circulating material online which simply claims in words that the person has taken part in such compromising circumstances?

Now suppose that the photo or video was only ever circulated clearly labelled, 'this is fake, it's not X's body, we just used X's face'. Does this change the nature or degree of wrongdoing in any way? If this was you, or a close friend, how might you feel about it? You may wish to consider the discussion of notions of reality in Sect. 7.5. Recall our discussion of stigma and spoiled identity in Sect. 7.2.4 and discussions of dignity (see Sect. 2.4.9 and elsewhere), its importance, yet the difficulty of articulating violations of dignity very precisely.

9.8   The Use of AI: Reshaping Ethical Questions?

Summary
We discuss how the very use of AI and attempts to address the problems that AI is seen to create may shift our perceptions of ethical questions and of appropriate responses to them. This may operate through factors involving software, hardware, and the underlying attitudes and ideology of AI. The use of algorithms may perhaps lead us to demand more rigour than is reasonable or desirable. Human discretion may be eclipsed by requirements of training. The drive to a consistent and uniform answer to ethical questions may inadvertently lead to cultural domination.

We have considered at various points how progress in technology and progress in ethics may be seen to be interconnected. We have also asked how the affordances and values associated with technology might potentially influence how we see the world and ourselves. The ways in which technology might influence ethics may operate through the hardware, the software, and through the ideologies and expectations we impose upon it.

How a problem is seen and the importance attached to it Are the values of technology moulding how we evaluate it? Are we assessing ethical questions through a prism formed by our very use of AI? The dominance of the online world as a place of communication means that difficult ethical questions may now be seen within this world, and the particular ways in which they manifest there may influence wider thinking. These include, as we have seen, the affordances created by technology for communication and for its control, as well as ways of attempting to circumvent such controls. At the same time, as we have seen, the identification of ethical issues associated with the online world is closely tied to developments offline, such as in the case of online harms, concern for discrimination against protected groups, and concern about individual harassment, which has come to be enshrined in law in many places in recent years or decades. It should be stated, as a reminder, that probing and questioning such things should not be taken to undermine the seriousness of the issues; their very seriousness necessitates close inspection.

However, we have seen that the ways in which a problem is described can make a significant difference. Hence, understandings of the relationship between the online and the offline world, understandings of the attribution of agency and responsibility, can make a large difference to questions such as the responsibility of platforms, of governments, and of individuals, and to the perception of how to strike a balance between the protection of the individual, of groups, and of society, and, indeed, what these protections are—the protection of freedom of expression, the capacity to use the online world, the protection against harm or harassment.

The very fact of government consideration of taking action against online content which is deemed 'harmful but not illegal' may of course arise from the development of a serious set of problems made possible by technology, but nonetheless, in itself suggests that the online world and what goes on there, including of course the actions of the technology companies, may be changing notions of government responsibilities and of standards of behaviour. Several countries worldwide are currently considering laws to govern 'online hate'.

How the problem is addressed   We have focused here on the use of algorithms to combat alleged online harms. Assessing how their use may impact the situation involves examining them directly as well as how they are compared and contrasted to human agency. Their use will introduce elements of formalism that may distort outcomes and thinking. Using algorithms in areas that involve values means that we will have to fit our values into this formal system. This may distort our values and priorities by many subtle means [73]. For example, Cathy O'Neill shows how systems for ranking universities have impacted the real world in significant and deleterious ways, as universities chase higher rankings [48].

Michael Roth and Aaron Kearns work on what they call the 'new science' of trying to formulate precise definitions for use with algorithms: formalised definitions of value concepts may differ in significant ways from legal and philosophical definitions of those same concepts [29, p. 18]. They are at pains to point out that there must be trade-offs among different goals. The use of algorithms for certain tasks may leave out critical aspects of complex concepts and values. We have seen how we will need a definition of online harms and online hate which algorithms could follow, yet how these concepts are essentially contested and hard to define. Are we demanding rigour where there is none to be had?

Bear in mind that feedback mechanisms exist that may have different impacts upon how a system of algorithmic review is perceived. On the one hand, the very use of such a system will produce results that, for many, will validate the system. To be vindicated for an allegation of online harm, to be found guilty of such, may reinforce the apparent validity of the system. However, disputes may highlight the uncertainties of the system and the need for human review and human discretion. (See Sect. 6.3.3 on understanding and interpreting rules.)

Note too that failure to find a sharply defined and rigorously consistent account of, and remedy for, a problem should not necessarily mean that we can do and say nothing about it. As Aristotle stated, in any subject, we can only demand the level of precision that it permits. We need a 'good enough' model.

Discretion: Humans versus machines   But how much human discretion is possible in practice? Perhaps not enough; perhaps none. Human content moderators who have the dismal tasks of reviewing online material for violent and pornographic content generally have to make extremely swift decisions and are required to have a high level of conformity to the expected judgements [74]. In his book *The New Laws of Robotics: Defending Human Expertise in the Age of AI*, Frank Pasquale discusses the professional judgement and values that should be retained in the face of automation [75]. He identifies as a problem with jobs such as content moderator is that they are not seen as 'professional' and workers are under the control of management hierarchy, trained (or not trained but still controlled by) to certain standards, and with no space for individual discernment or difference of judgement.

Exercise 24

Consider the pros and cons of allowing discretion in content moderation decisions, compared to a rigorously applied formal system with clearly defined rules that admit of no exception. Illustrate with examples, real or imaginary. Consider the implications of your answers for systems of human review and of appeal.

Indeed, we have considered shifts in how the meaning may be attributed to language online. There is a certain formalism to the approach to language that fails to take into account the reasonably intended context of the original material. Yet context is admitted for those who find material to be of concern. Here is another suggestion for thinking about the matter: the idea of combatting bias as an ideal, a formalism applied to humans, has perhaps infected the whole way in which some are thinking about content online. We are seeing a peculiar shift of epistemic values, where we want to get rid of all falsehoods, all misinformation, yet at the same time are only too willing to suppress true information if it hurts feelings. Negative human emotions need to be curtailed, as if all emotions must be mild; that 'someone' has to 'take charge' of these things; the online world must be safe; and we can simply communicate as if we were simply transmitting 'facts' about the world.

The counter to this might be that far from leading us to a glorious future where humanity can bloom, what AI has done for us in the most part online is to heighten our worst aspects, to turn us into a bunch of atavistic squabbling lunatics, and the best we can do is to use anything we can to combat this.

Exercise 25

Consider and discuss these two positions and add any nuance of your own.

Content moderation, control, and responsibility The different ways of approaching the issues, the very complexities of the question (only a small part of which we have addressed here), mean that there are many different ways of understanding the responsibilities of different parties and the agency each have. We have seen how individuals producing online content may be seen at once as being without agency, the subject of influences, and simultaneously as possessing agency and hence culpable for their actions, as at once responsible for online content, hence viewed as an agent, yet simultaneously denied the defence that they did not intend to harm or offend. Likewise, although we have not had space to discuss this here, those controlling the technology companies shift and slide over their responsibility and agency. There may be subtle and sometimes conflicting shifts in notions of responsibility.

The possible harms of online content and the possible remedies also impact agency and our sense of control. Damage to reputation can spread readily and can have real-world impacts, such as acting to block an individual from employment, but steps to address this involve tracking individuals online and a considerable increase in what amounts to surveillance. Details of some proposed steps illustrate this, such as banning anonymous accounts, banning end-to-end encryption, and requiring the same standards across platforms to prevent 'cheating' the system by moving to a different platform in response to banning or content removal [1]. Could this be a move towards what is effectively a social credit system, especially given the importance of online communication [76]?

Exercise 26

Humans are social creatures; hence, in any society, there are penalties and rewards for bad or good behaviour. These penalties and rewards are often subtle; they are often not applied, and a whole range of considerations operate around them, such as the notion of forgiveness, apology, and the need to maintain social connections. Consider what, if anything, might constitute a reasonable system of penalties for online behaviour that may be deemed as harmful but not illegal. When might this amount to an illicit system of social credit?

Consider how the values of the individual and the values of the wider social group are impacted by different answers to this question.

Questions of accountability, transparency, and the need for an explanation also arise here as elsewhere. Precisely what explanation a user of a social media platform might be owed may be problematic, since there is no general right to use any specific platform (proposals to ensure that users cannot simply migrate from platform to platform complicate the question). Moreover, one only needs to peruse various online platforms for a short time to see baffled users struggling to understand content moderation decisions: both decisions to remove material or block accounts and seemingly inconsistent decisions to leave other material in place. The nuances and context of language use add an additional layer of complexity. Moreover, some of the remedies taken by platforms and proposals for dealing with allegedly harmful content are such that a user may never know (although they may suspect) that action has been taken against them and hence will never even seek an explanation. Shadow banning means a user is partially blocked and content may simply be made harder to find or rendered invisible to other users.

Exercise 27

Does shadow banning serve a useful purpose in retaining a degree of freedom of expression while protecting other online users, or does it pose problems, for instance, for any right to an explanation?

Content moderation and global issues in AI The possibilities of formalism and the imposition of a unified standard on modes of communication have global implications. We have already touched upon work that finds that minority groups are disproportionately more likely to experience adverse results from content moderation decisions, much of this stemming from cultural and linguistic differences in language use and expression, including context, which may change rapidly and differ between different subgroups. The expression of hope we saw from the UK government of setting standards and leadership in this area may also be cause for concern.

Consider one possible element of disagreement: A part of the background of how content moderation online is viewed is formed by local laws and opinion, much of which has shifted considerably in recent times. Concern extends to protected categories; but these are defined differently in different geographical and national areas, new categories may yet be added, and disputes exist about the justification and nature of these protected categories. There are also disagreements concerning the relative value of freedom of expression in different places. Meanwhile, there may be hopes for setting international standards for online harms and online hate, but there are large numbers of very poorly paid workers, including in developing countries, suffering mentally and financially from immersion in a world of extremely graphic content.

Exercise 28
One of the major concerns of AI ethics is how certain regions that dominate in the production and deployment of AI may impose their own local standards on others. Could the search for a universal standard of ethics do the same?

Is this related to the problem of trying to make a global market place of speech when language and expression should be seen as essentially local in some respects?

9.9 And Just to Finish

We have looked at many aspects of the ethical question of online harms, but it will be apparent that much remains to consider, such as attention to how precisely to tackle the issues in different contexts. This reflects the complexity of the questions, plus the need for detailed knowledge of context.

Let us finish with some last and rather general exercises.

Exercise 29
Try to produce a definition of online harms.

What challenges are there? What is the nature of the challenges? How readily might these challenges be overcome?

Consider cultural, regional, and demographic differences in how online harms might be understood.

Consider any novel means by which the online world might enable or heighten the capacity to produce hate speech or abuse against individuals or groups.

Consider how the ethics literature, theories, and concepts that we have explored in this book might contribute to these tasks and what else you need.

Exercise 30
How would you balance concerns for online harms with concerns for freedom of expression?

Try to draw on as much material from earlier in the book as you can.

For example, how might consideration of virtues and the development of character be relevant?

How might a consequentialist approach the general question of protecting individuals versus the good of society? Consider different ways that consequentialism may characterise the ends at which it aims.

Perhaps consider the importance that freedom of expression may have for respect for persons, including ways in which it might diminish respect and the question of accountability to others.

Exercise 31

In what ways, if any, does the use of AI impact the age-old question of freedom of expression and harms to others?

Do you consider there is a matter of degree and scale, or are novel issues raised?

9.10 Key Points

There is a close link between ethical issues and wider social, political, economic, legal, and regulatory issues. Philosophical work in ethics, as well as work in the philosophy of language, can contribute to the discussion of the rights and wrongs of online content moderation. Ethics alone cannot address these questions but can be part of the necessary dialogues. Attention to ethical issues may assist individuals to consider their own roles and responsibilities.

The ethical issues raised encompass the software, hardware, and ideologies behind AI.

Ethical questions that seem entirely novel may have deep historical roots.

The possibilities of new technologies may especially impact how we understand agency, responsibility, and causation.

We need to compare and contrast human capabilities with AI very carefully. Striving for consistency may override the application of discretion.

The challenges in using algorithms to moderate online content are of various kinds, for example, methodological questions, issues concerning the quality and quantity of data and bias from data labelling by human moderators, as well as questions concerning the contextual and cultural transmission of meaning via language.

Training of human moderators may be patchy or nonexistent; conversely, training may impose questionable uniform standards and undermine discretion and professional responsibility in moderators.

Many of the issues concerning the use of algorithms and the moderation of online content stem from the extremely poor conditions under which human moderators work.

There may be no such thing as a universally agreed 'right' answer in the attribution of meaning and intent to language.

9.11   Educator Notes

Students should be encouraged to consider these issues from all sides and to draw on personal and known examples. This chapter has intentionally omitted illustration with any specific examples that may be offensive to some; the general issues of context and variation in the attribution of meaning can be illustrated with less controversial examples.

When tackling the exercises, students may have further details, material, and knowledge they wish to draw upon. For example, there are certain issues that this chapter has not had time to address at all, or in great detail, such as the question of the responsibility of technology companies, and whether there is any general right to access online space. This is a great opportunity to draw links between ethics and political, legal, and regulatory issues. Precisely because many students may have examples to draw upon and may feel strongly about the issues from different perspectives, some may have formed opinions already, so students should be encouraged to consolidate material from earlier chapters and to draw upon it as much as possible in their discussions and work here.

Although the chapter contains frequent references to earlier material, students who have not covered all these previous chapters will still be able to follow the issues and may wish to refer to specific sections as indicated.

Section 9.6 and onwards take issues to a slightly deeper level and could be omitted if needed.

The sections on language, Sects. 9.5.2 and 9.5.3, could also be skimmed or omitted, but students with particular interests in language may wish to concentrate on these issues.

At completion of this chapter, students should be able to take an ethical issue related to the current use of AI and apply the skill and knowledge they have learned here to produce their own analysis and discussion.

Debate topics and material for extended essays or project work Many of the exercises raise complex and general points that would serve as good debate and project topics. For example, Exercises 9, 10, 16, and 18 and the final Exercises 29–31.

Acknowledgements This chapter was partially funded by the National Institute for Health Research, Health Services and Delivery Research Programme (project number 13/10/80). The views expressed are those of the author and not necessarily those of the NIHR or the Department of Health and Social Care.

References

1. Department for Digital, Culture, Media and Sport (2021) Draft Online Safety Bill. UK Government, London. https://www.gov.uk/government/publications/draft-online-safety-bill

2. Department for Digital, Culture, Media and Sport (2020) Safer technology, safer users: the UK as a world leader in safety tech (Updated 2021). DCMS, London
3. Garnham N (2000) Emancipation, the media, and modernity: arguments about the media and social theory. Oxford University Press, New York
4. Christakis N, Fowler J (2010) Connected: the amazing power of social networks and how they shape our lives. HarperCollins, London
5. Gillespie T (2018) Custodians of the Internet: platforms, content moderation, and the hidden decisions that shape social media. Yale University Press, New Haven
6. Pariser E (2011) The filter bubble. Viking Penguin, London
7. Dahlgren PM (2021) A critical review of filter bubbles and a comparison with selective exposure. Nord Rev 42(1):15–33
8. Munn L (2020) Angry by design: toxic communication and technical architectures. Humanit Soc Sci Commun 7(1):1–11
9. Steiger M, Bharucha TJ, Venkatagiri S, Riedl MJ, Lease M (2021) The psychological well-being of content moderators: the emotional labor of commercial moderation and avenues for improving support. In: Proceedings of the 2021 CHI conference on human factors in computing systems, pp 1–14
10. Ruckenstein M, Turunen LLM (2020) Re-humanizing the platform: and the logic of care. New Media Soc 22(6):1026–1042
11. Borchert RJ, Azevedo T, Badhwar A, Bernal J, Betts M, Bruffaerts R, Burkhart MC, Dewachter I, Gellersen H, Low A, Machado L (2021) Artificial intelligence for diagnosis and prognosis in neuroimaging for dementia; a systematic review. medRxiv. https://doi.org/10.1101/2021.12.12.21267677
12. Gibney E (2022) Could machine learning fuel a reproducibility crisis in science? Nature 608(7922):250–251
13. Char DS, Shah NH, Magnus D (2018) Implementing machine learning in health care—addressing ethical challenges. N Engl J Med 378(11):981
14. Vidgen B, Burden E, Margetts M (2021) Understanding online hate: VSP regulation and the broader context. Alan Turing Institute, London
15. Javid S, Wright J (2019) Online harms white paper. Department for Digital, Culture, Media & Sport and the Home Office. https://assets.publishing.service.gov.uk/government/uploads/system/uploads/attachment_data/file/793360/Online_Harms_White_Paper.pdf
16. Finkelstein JJ (1968) The laws of Ur-Nammu. J Cuneif Stud 22(3–4):66–82
17. Internet Society UK England Chapter, Understanding the UK Online Safety Bill webinar, 10 Jun 2021. https://isoc-e.org/understanding-the-uk-online-safety-bill/ at 45 minutes ff
18. Mill JS (1859) On liberty. In: Collected works of John Stuart Mill, vol XVIII. J. W. Parker and Son, London. Online Library of Liberty
19. Fogg BJ (2002) Persuasive technology: using computers to change what we think and do. Elsevier, Amsterdam, p 2
20. Kosner A (2020) Stanford's School of Persuasion: B J Fogg on how to win users and influence behaviour. Forbes, 4 Dec 2012
21. Waldron J (2012) The harm in hate speech. Harvard University Press, Cambridge
22. Simpson RM (2013) Dignity, harm, and hate speech. Law Philos 32(6):701–728
23. Council of Europe, Freedom of expression: hate speech. https://www.coe.int/en/web/freedom-expression/hate-speech
24. Bradshaw S, Campbell-Smith U, Henle A, Perini A, Shalev S, Bailey H, Howard PN (2020) Country case studies industrialized disinformation: 2020 global inventory of organized social media manipulation. Oxford Internet Institute, Oxford
25. Briant E (2021) The grim consequences of a misleading study on disinformation. Wired, 18 Feb 2021
26. Vidgen B, Taylor H, Pantazi M, Anastasiou Z, Inkster B, Margetts H (2021) Understanding vulnerability to online misinformation. Alan Turing Institute, London

27. Head ML, Holman L, Lanfear R, Kahn AT, Jennions MD (2015) The extent and consequences of p-hacking in science. PLoS Biol 13(3):e1002106

28. Ioannidis JP (2005) Why most published research findings are false. PLoS Med 2(8):e124

29. Kearns M, Roth A (2019) The ethical algorithm: the science of socially aware algorithm design. Oxford University Press, Oxford

30. Vidgen B, Margetts H, Harris A (2019) How much online abuse is there? A systematic review of evidence from the UK. Alan Turing Institute, London

31. Vidgen B, Harris A, Nguyen D, Tromble R, Hale S, Margetts H (2019) Challenges and frontiers in abusive content detection. Association for Computational Linguistics, Florence

32. Doyle A (2021) Free speech and why it matters. Constable, London

33. Alan Turing Institute Podcast (2021) #25 'How good is AI at detecting online hate?', 2 July 2021. https://www.turing.ac.uk/news/turing-podcast

34. Almagro M, Hannikainen IR, Villanueva N (2022) Whose words hurt? Contextual determinants of offensive speech. Personal Soc Psychol Bull 48(6):937–953

35. The Queen on the application of Harry Miller and The College of Policing, [2021] EWCA Civ 1926, 21 Dec 2022. https://www.judiciary.uk/wp-content/uploads/2021/12/Miller-v-College-of-Policing-judgment-201221.pdf. Accessed 26 Sept 2022

36. Grice HP (1975) Logic and conversation. In: Cole P, Morgan JL (eds) Syntax and semantics, 3: speech acts. Academic, New York, pp 41–58

37. Davis W (2019) Implicature. In: Zalta EN (ed) The Stanford encyclopedia of philosophy, Fall 2019 edn. Stanford University, Stanford. https://plato.stanford.edu/archives/fall2019/entries/implicature/

38. Gallie WB (1955) Essentially contested concepts. Proc Aristot Soc 56(1):167–198

39. Kosenko K, Winderman E, Pugh A (2019) The hijacked hashtag: the constitutive features of abortion stigma in the #ShoutYourAbortion twitter campaign. Int J Commun 13:21

40. Bhat P, Klein O (2020) Covert hate speech: white nationalists and dog whistle communication on twitter. In: Twitter, the public sphere, and the chaos of online deliberation. Palgrave Macmillan, Cham, pp 151–172

41. Botelho A, Vidgen B, Hale SA (2021) Deciphering implicit hate: evaluating automated detection algorithms for multimodal hate. arXiv preprint arXiv: 2106.05903

42. Coffin C, O'Halloran K (2006) The role of appraisal and corpora in detecting covert evaluation. Funct Lang 13(1):77–110

43. Tynes BM, Lozada FT, Smith NA, Stewart AM (2018) From racial microaggressions to hate crimes: a model of online racism based on the lived experiences of adolescents of color. In: Microaggression theory: influence and implications. Wiley, New York, pp 194–212

44. Eschmann R (2021) Digital resistance: how online communication facilitates responses to racial microaggressions. Sociol Race Ethn 7(2):264–277

45. Binns R, Veale M, Van Kleek M, Shadbolt N (2017) Like trainer, like bot? Inheritance of bias in algorithmic content moderation. In: International conference on social informatics. Springer, Cham, pp 405–415

46. Salminen J, Almerekhi H, Kamel AM, Jung SG, Jansen BJ (2019) Online hate ratings vary by extremes: a statistical analysis. In: Proceedings of the 2019 conference on human information interaction and retrieval. Association for Computing Machinery, New York, pp 213–217

47. Yin W, Zubiaga A (2021) Towards generalisable hate speech detection: a review on obstacles and solutions. arXiv preprint arXiv:2102.08886, p 17

48. O'Neil C (2016) Weapons of math destruction: how big data increases inequality and threatens democracy. Broadway Books, New York

49. Noble SU (2018) Algorithms of oppression: how search engines reinforce racism. New York University Press, New York

50. Pasquale F (2015) The black box Society. Harvard University Press, Cambridge

51. Freeman K (2016) Algorithmic injustice: how the Wisconsin supreme court failed to protect due process rights in state v. Loomis. N C J Law Technol 18(5):75

52. Blodgett SL, O'Connor B (2017) Racial disparity in natural language processing: a case study of social media African-American English. arXiv preprint arXiv:1707.00061
53. Davidson T, Bhattacharya D, Weber I (2019) Racial bias in hate speech and abusive language detection datasets. arXiv preprint arXiv:1905.12516
54. Sap M, Card D, Gabriel S, Choi Y, Smith NA (2019) The risk of racial bias in hate speech detection. In: Proceedings of the 57th annual meeting of the association for computational linguistics. Association for Computational Linguistics, Florence, pp 1668–1678
55. Blodgett SL, Barocas S, Daumé III H, Wallach H (2020) Language (technology) is power: a critical survey of 'bias' in NLP. arXiv preprint arXiv:2005.14050
56. Röttger P, Vidgen B, Nguyen D, Waseem Z, Margetts H, Pierrehumbert J (2020) HATECHECK: functional tests for hate speech detection models. arXiv preprint arXiv:2012.15606, 2021
57. Rudas C, Surányi O, Yasseri T, Török J (2017) Understanding and coping with extremism in an online collaborative environment: a data-driven modeling. PLoS One 12(3):e0173561
58. Hills TT (2019) The dark side of information proliferation. Perspect Psychol Sci 14(3):323–330
59. Gross N (2013) Why are professors liberal and why do conservatives care? Harvard University Press, Cambridge
60. van de Werfhorst HG (2020) Are universities left-wing bastions? The political orientation of professors, professionals, and managers in Europe. Br J Sociol 71(1):47–73
61. Papakyriakopoulos O, Serrano JCM, Hegelich S (2020) Political communication on social media: a tale of hyperactive users and bias in recommender systems. Online Soc Netw Media 15:100058
62. https://www.gov.uk/government/speeches/oliver-dowdens-oral-statement-on-the-online-harms-white-paper-consultation-response
63. Heather Burns (2021) In Internet Society UK England Chapter, Understanding the UK online safety bill webinar, June 10th 2021. https://isoc-e.org/understanding-the-uk-online-safety-bill/
64. Zimbardo P (2007) The Lucifer effect understanding how good people turn evil. Random House, New York
65. Pierson J, Robinson SC, Boddington P, Chazerand P, Kerr A, Milan S, Verbeek F, Kutterer C, Nerantzi E, Aconstantinesei IC (2021) AI4People-AI in media and technology sector: opportunities, risks, requirements and recommendations. Atomium–European Institute for Science, Media and Democracy (EISMD), Brussels
66. Helberger N, Pierson J, Poell T (2018) Governing online platforms: from contested to cooperative responsibility. Inf Soc 34(1):1–14
67. Anderson B, Wood MA (2021) Doxxing: a scoping review and typology. In: Bailey J, Flynn A, Henry N (eds) The Emerald international handbook of technology-facilitated violence and abuse. Emerald Group Publishing, Bingley, pp 205–226
68. Guo E (2021) How YouTube's rules are used to silence human rights activists, Wired, 24 Jun 2021. https://www.technologyreview.com/2021/06/24/1027048/youtube-xinjiang-censorship-human-rights-atajurt/
69. Berdichevsky D, Neuenschwander E (1999) Toward an ethics of persuasive technology. Commun ACM 42(5):51–58
70. Just N, Latzer M (2017) Governance by algorithms: reality construction by algorithmic selection on the Internet. Media Cult Soc 39(2):238–258
71. Munn L (2019) Alt-right pipeline: individual journeys to extremism online. First Monday
72. Vidgen B, Harris A, Cowls J, Guest E, Margetts M (2020) An agenda for research into online hate. Alan Turing Institute, London

73. Nowotny H (2021) In AI we trust: power, illusion and the control of predictive algorithms. Polity Press, Cambridge
74. Arsht A, Etcovitch D (2018) The human cost of online content moderation. Harvard Journal of Law and Technology
75. Pasquale F (2020) New laws of robotics: defending human expertise in the age of AI. Belknap Press, Cambridge
76. Mac Síthigh D, Siems M (2019) The Chinese social credit system: a model for other countries? Mod Law Rev 82(6):1034–1071

Further Reading

Free Speech and Hate Speech

Anderson L, Barnes M (2022) Hate Speech. In: Zalta EN (ed) The Stanford encyclopedia of philosophy, Spring 2022 edn. Stanford University, Stanford. https://plato.stanford.edu/archives/spr2022/entries/hate-speech/
Doyle A (2021) Free speech and why it matters. Constable, London
Green M (2021) Speech Acts. In: Zalta EN (ed) The Stanford encyclopedia of philosophy, Fall 2021 edn. Stanford University, Stanford. https://plato.stanford.edu/archives/fall2021/entries/speech-acts/
Javid S, Wright J (2019) Online harms white paper. Department for Digital, Culture, Media & Sport and the Home Office. https://assets.publishing.service.gov.uk/government/uploads/system/uploads/attachment_data/file/793360/Online_Harms_White_Paper.pdf
Mill JS (1859) On liberty. In: collected works of John Stuart Mill, vol XVIII. J. W. Parker and Son, London Online Library of Liberty
van Mill D (2021) Freedom of Speech. In: Zalta EN (ed) The Stanford encyclopedia of philosophy, Spring 2021 edn. Stanford University, Stanford. https://plato.stanford.edu/archives/spr2021/entries/freedom-speech/
Waldron J (2012) The harm in hate speech. Harvard University Press, Cambridge

Algorithms, Bias, and Online Harms

Fogg BJ (2002) Persuasive technology: using computers to change what we think and do. Elsevier, Amsterdam, p 2
Kearns M, Roth A (2019) The ethical algorithm: the science of socially aware algorithm design. Oxford University Press, Oxford
Kramer AD, Guillory JE, Hancock JT (2014) Experimental evidence of massive-scale emotional contagion through social networks. Proc Natl Acad Sci 111(24):8788–8790
Munn L (2020) Angry by design: toxic communication and technical architectures. Humanit Soc Sci Commun 7(1):1–11
Noble SU (2018) Algorithms of oppression: how search engines reinforce racism. New York University Press, New York
O'Neil C (2016) Weapons of math destruction: how big data increases inequality and threatens democracy. Broadway Books, New York

Pariser E (2011) The filter bubble. Viking Penguin, London

Pasquale F (2015) The black box Society. Harvard University Press, Cambridge

Pasquale F (2020) New laws of robotics: defending human expertise in the age of AI. Belknap Press, Cambridge

Vidgen B, Burden E, Margetts M (2021) Understanding online hate: VSP regulation and the broader context. Alan Turing Institute, London

Chapter 10
Towards the Future with AI: Work and Superintelligence

Abstract This chapter looks at two contrasting ethical issues: work and superintelligence. We first examine the application of AI use within the workplace, both its use to replace human jobs or tasks, involving the careful comparison of human and machine agency, analysis of the objectives and values of the workplace, and a range of other issues. Second, we examine ethical issues arising from the prospect of widespread technological unemployment. Topics covered include surveillance; assessment of human and machine agency; AI and existing structures of power; how AI may alter lines of communication and epistemology; how technology may increase structure and how well it fits into existing informational settings and infrastructure; control and autonomy; and how benefits of implementing AI are measured. The discussion of these issues is thus also pertinent to many other applications of AI. The discussion of superintelligence examines the nature of the fears surrounding it and possible ways of addressing its dangers. We examine attempts to ensure that superintelligence aligns with human purposes, noting the underlying ethical and philosophical framework. Parallels between the ways in which the control issue of AI occurs and is understood within its use in the workplace and in relation to superintelligence are indicated.

Keywords AI ethics · Technological unemployment · Superintelligence · Surveillance · Value alignment · Longtermism

10.1 Introduction

The last chapter looked in some detail at an example of a complex and pressing contemporary issue in the ethics of AI, the debates over online content and its moderation. The many interlocking issues that are raised include detailed questions about how AI may understand human language, how bias is conceptualised, and its detection and removal, as well as how AI may impact how we behave and treat each other and how our uses and abuses of AI might impact our very understanding of ethical issues. While it is true that online content is often used in ways that cause harm, and often intentionally so, including both minor but also extremely serious harm, it may also be worth taking pause and reflecting on whether the attention given to online hate might in part be a method of projecting fears about the dangers of AI onto the human psyche.

This chapter considers some more concrete questions in AI ethics, taking our journey further and further into the future: from the present, to the near future, the further future and onwards. As we examine future projections for AI, the projection of fears and dangers onto these possibilities may become more apparent, but we also see the reverse, projecting a glorious future. *But for whom?* We have frequently asked about the relationship between AI and humans. The question will also arise of the relationship between AI and who? Who will 'we' be in the distant future?

Examining various domains will reveal some similar ethical issues, some different. As we distance ourselves from the present day, different issues and questions of methodology will tend to arise, but many also have deep resonance with issues facing us now. As before, each one of these areas merits detailed examination, and the discussion here can only cover certain aspects, again concentrating on the questions which work in ethics might best help us to think about.

We look first at questions concerning employment, considering questions that are currently with us regarding the implementation of AI in the workplace, looking at the general question of using AI to replace jobs or tasks performed by humans, and at the impact of the inclusion of various technologies into the workplace. We then examine concerns about future possibilities: how the impact of AI may change who has work, shift general patterns of work, and introduce significant divisions into society. Like any projection into the future, this must remain speculative, but examining responses of both optimism and fear can also reveal a considerable amount about current thinking.

We next consider artificial general intelligence (AGI) in the form of superintelligence and the intense fears that some have expressed, looking at some aspects both of how the putative problems are characterised and at suggested ways of remedying or ameliorating dangers—although some, as we shall see, also express hope. This can be seen as one aspect of the control problem of AI; perhaps, if the protagonists of certain positions are to be believed, the biggest issue we must face. Debates about the possibility and dangers of superintelligence include claims about the nature of artificial intelligence, its relationship with value, and questions about how we can observe and discover human values. These necessitate considering questions about ethical theory, moral epistemology, the very foundation of ethics, and even how we see and understand each other. To understand these questions, we need to think about how both AI and humans are understood and imagined, as well as how they might interact. So although these are, at the moment, dealing the as yet unrealised future and with entirely theoretical ideas (unless things have changed considerably by the time of publication!), the ideas and arguments can help us to think about current questions. In many ways, some of the contemporary issues can even become clearer when presented in such a stark way, sometimes in ways which of necessity expose the foundations of artificial intelligence in attempts to find a solution to the problem of 'when AI goes bad'. This also exposes foundational questions in ethics.

When we consider questions that project into the distant future, naturally one issue we have is uncertainty about what might happen. Other questions arise regarding how we even think of the ethical issues projecting so far ahead and under conditions of uncertainty. On the approaches of some ethical theories, this is less of a problem than on others. Hence, considering these future questions requires that we think more about the nature of different ethical theories, of questions in moral epistemology, and how we now stand in relation to the potentially unrecognisable worlds of the possible futures that may lie open. This chapter can then act in part as a way of consolidating and building upon material from earlier in the book.

Questions have been asked about priorities in the ethics of AI: is it a waste of time to consider the far future when we have more pressing issues? I have already suggested one answer to this, noting how the discussions around the far future may help to clarify and expose some of the issues that also pertain to the near future. We will also consider the stance of Longtermism: the view that we ought, for ethical reasons, to prioritise the concerns of the far distant future [1]. This position also raises issues about ethical theory and has implications for how we should approach some current questions of value.

Worries about superintelligence include the fear that it might completely wipe us out. Keeping fingers crossed that this does not happen, we will also consider projected far distant futures with AI, millions of years from now, in which this does not happen (which can in many ways be seen as a more formalised form of science fiction). These projections also expose foundational ethical questions that will impact how we think of human beings and AI now and raise questions about how AI and human beings relate to each other, as well as questions about human nature, personal identity, the relationship between the mind and the body, the trajectory of the universe, the role of humans now in curating the future, and ultimate sources of value.

10.2 AI in the Workplace

Summary
Noting the intimate links between ethics and economics, we look at various ethical questions concerning the use of AI to replace humans or tasks in the workplace. Different reasons for the use of AI rather than humans include economics and safety and the belief that AI will do the task better. This necessitates a careful analysis of what a workplace task involves, which in turn requires close observation and exposure of the goals and values of the workplace. Hierarchies at work have a complex relationship with values and epistemology. AI is also justified to remove drudgery, and we examine the value assumptions this makes. We consider the impact of increased workplace surveillance and data collection.

10.2.1   AI in Work: Some Background

The impacts of AI on work have attracted considerable attention. As we saw in Sect. 2.1, AI is commonly spoken of as ushering in a fourth industrial revolution, after the first which used steam and mechanical power, the second which used electrical power, and the third which used electronics and the Internet [2]. Naturally, many important questions thus arise within business, economics, law, and politics, but among these are ethical issues which include questions about the nature and value of work, the impact on employees, and the prospects of large-scale unemployment.

Talk of a fourth industrial revolution may be accurate and helpful, but it should also alert us to watch out for hype and for polarised views that range between fear and dread, often focusing on fears of widespread technological unemployment [3–5], to great enthusiasm for a radically changed future with large-scale societal impacts [6]. With the possibility of such large-scale and wide-ranging impacts on the economy, the workplace, and society, the questions involved are highly complex, with many contributing to discussion regarding how we might respond [7–10]. Here, we focus on some of the ethical issues, looking both at the impact of AI on work currently or in the near future and then at some of the complex and profound issues that arise from visions of the future and the possibly large changes in the nature of work. We will look both at AI in the form of software and also at robotics.

We must not overlook, however, in focusing on some of the ethical questions, that economic issues are always intimately linked to ethical questions. These include the distribution of wealth, assumptions about progress, the relative powers of employees and employers, and the balance of economic values with other values. The latter issue can be illustrated by concerns in recent years that GDP, Gross Domestic Product, is only one measure of how well a country is doing and that there is no clear straight line between economic prosperity and happiness or life satisfaction. Bhutan's Gross National Happiness Index has attracted considerable interest [11].

The ethical issues include the questions of sustainability (see Sect. 2.4.8), an issue that in AI is closely linked to questions of transparency and control, since many of the largest problems are less visible and certainly may be opaque to the everyday user. The immediate costs to those using AI and implementing it in the workforce may not include a full consideration of the costs to the environment or to workers elsewhere [12]. Infrastructure pressures frequently force the adoption of AI (e.g. the many businesses which now only take electronic payments, or which require prebooking online, place pressure in individuals to use smartphones). Counting economic costs and environmental impacts is extremely complex: consider the common call to use an electronic ticket to travel or to attend an event, rather than asking for a paper ticket. This seems to be an obvious environmental saving to many. However, it relies on the assumption that one has a smartphone and that it is always on and charged. It can also slow down queues entering a venue as people attempt to find their ticket barcode in a way that is readable. Therefore, the phone itself and its use are treated as if cost neutral, rather than looking more systemically at how entire systems of automation have been constructed and the wider relationships between extremely large networks of people and machines.

The ethical issues examined here concerning the impact of AI on work include questions about the dignity of the workforce, the value to society of the work produced, and many questions concerning control and surveillance. Underlying questions concern the value of work and of rest, and ultimately, the prospect of having no work to do leads to questions about purpose in life.

What general questions should we ask regarding the use of AI in the workplace? As before, it is useful to look closely at the question of why AI is being used, and perhaps especially in areas where economic imperatives, competition, and infrastructure changes workplaces increasing pressure to employ AI. Other factors come into play as well: the steps taken in response to the COVID-19 pandemic have involved increased use of technology at work, which has sped up pressures for automation, remote working, and the digital economy, among other factors [13]. It is often assumed that the use of AI in the workplace will usher in greater wealth, speed up certain tasks, reduce employment costs, and lead to economic gains for those using it. However, we need to undertake careful comparison between the capabilities of AI and of human beings and look closely at what precisely a particular job or role requires. We will also consider multiple possible consequences from the use of AI in the workplace, which may include increasing surveillance of workers and changes to how work is valued and carried out.

What concepts and tools can we bring to these questions? In looking at ethical questions regarding the impact of AI on work, it may be especially useful to consider certain ideas that we have examined earlier in the book. These include:

The value of persons and respect for persons
Notions of dignity
The question of solidarity
Questions of control and autonomy
How we might measure happiness or human welfare, including questions of what it
    is to live a good life
The notion of agency, comparing and contrasting AI and human agency
The values placed on intelligence
The importance of looking closely at precisely what AI is tasked to do
How the use of AI may shift our values
How AI may impact how we communicate
The notion of progress and how we might envisage the future
How ethics intersects with other disciplines

10.2.2   Why Use AI Rather Than Humans?

We first address the use of AI in the workplace to replace human roles or tasks. There are a variety of reasons for using AI, and frequently more than one will apply. This list, of course, may not be exhaustive.

Economic motivations We have already seen some of the reasons for using AI rather than human beings at work (whether to replace whole jobs or to undertake certain tasks). Assumptions that this will create greater wealth by increasing productivity and lowering costs are often made. This may be the prime driver. This is a complex economic question that we cannot address here, but even if true, ethical questions remain about the impact on workers and society at large (including the sustainability question mentioned above). Even if wealth is not seen as the only, or the prime, value, there are still questions about how 'wealth' is understood as a goal, and these relate closely to the questions we need to ask about the future prospects for life in an era of mass technological unemployment, below in Sect. 10.3. We also have to ask, 'wealth for whom?'

The work is dangerous for humans Below, we consider the example of the use of robotics within hospitals. One motivating reason for the use of robotics in hospitals could be infection control, an issue highlighted by COVID-19. The use of robotics in instances where humans may be in danger, for example, in bomb disposal, can be highly beneficial. Moreover, even quite simple robotics can help to prevent workplace injuries, such as robotics to assist with lifting heavy goods or hospital patients. (Conversely, industrial robots have killed many people.) Let us take reducing death and serious injury as a plus, assume the ethical necessity of implementing high safety standards, and move on to more complex cases.

AI will perform the task better than humans Note first that the claim that AI will *perform better than humans* is not always made: it may simply be cheaper or more convenient to use AI, despite drops in performance. This indicates one of the complexities of understanding ethical issues in using AI in the workplace: the many different points of view involved. These include ownership, management, different employees, and customers or clients. There are many tasks at which it is blatantly obvious that computers, let alone AI, can beat humans: complex calculations among them. Rising capacities for natural language processing also mean that tasks involving language, such as checking the content of legal documents, may also be undertaken much faster using AI. To assess whether AI is performing the task better, we also need to know what precisely the task is.

10.2.3 Assessing the Use of AI to Replace Human Roles or Tasks

This will be a complex question upon which much hangs. We cannot give a full analysis of the complexity here but highlight some important factors with potentially serious ethical implications.

The task in context Assessing whether AI will perform better than humans will obviously depend upon what the task is; some tasks may be easier to assess than others. For example, one major application of AI is in the use of machine learning to interpret images in medical diagnostics [14]. The accuracy of machine learning can be measured using various metrics and compared closely to the success rate of trained humans [15]. In this case, the joint use of humans and of AI in diagnosis may produce the best results, perhaps because of the complementary abilities: machine learning can detect features that the human eye cannot, but humans avoid making some of the drastic errors of misinterpretation to which machine learning may be prone. However, even in such a seemingly straightforward case, there may be wider implications for individual employees and across a system stemming from the adoption of AI, which we examine below.

The complexity of many workplace tasks The 'official' description of a workplace task or role may differ from the actual work undertaken. Much of the value that may be produced during work and in interactions between workers and customers or clients may not even be well described as 'work'. For example, I have frequently heard those making announcements on train journeys or on railway stations making amusing comments over the loudspeakers, which has often been very welcome on delayed journeys but which is doubtless not contained in the job description. The management may have ideas about the official business of the workplace and the roles to be undertaken by those in particular roles and at particular times and places, which do not fully capture what is actually happening. This may especially be the case in hierarchical work structures where there may be both different points of view about what is being accomplished and what should be accomplished and blocks to lines of communication. Much work within organisations may be hidden from view. Moreover, variation in accounts of what is to be done may be associated with measurement and outcomes: what can be measured is more likely to be included in sets of outcomes and objectives than what cannot, or what can be measured only with difficulty. The use of AI, and indeed, the very task of comparing the benefits of AI to humans, may heighten difficulties connected with the measurement of tasks.

Example: the hospital ward I will be illustrating these questions using the example of work undertaken within a hospital ward. This will draw upon specialised material and research, which can thus function as an illustration of how important it is to draw up on the knowledge and expertise of different disciplines in considering the ethics of AI in context. The example of healthcare in a hospital setting, however, will be familiar to many readers and should be of interest and wide concern;

moreover, although specific understanding of contexts is always needed, many issues will usefully either generalise to, or contrast with, other workplace contexts. As before, this draws upon the findings of some of my colleagues, as well as many others. In addition, hospitals are sites where tasks of great complexity and great value are performed, requiring vastly differing skill sets. They are also very hierarchical, and they tend to have a management structure that imposes targets for measuring success. We must note cultural and local differences between hospitals and wards, but research nonetheless often finds broad similarities across different nationalities, and aspects of institutional functioning may remain remarkably similar over the course of decades [16]. Medicine makes high use of technology, and nursing also increasingly does so. How might AI come into the mix? Consider, for example, the proposed use of robotics on the hospital ward [17]. It has been suggested that hospitals are already well-structured places, designed for the movement of trolleys and so on, and that therefore, they are suitable for the use of robots in tasks such as delivering food to patients. (Those who have experience with busy hospital wards might consider that there is a considerable mix of structure and complexity.) In discussing which jobs are suitable for automation, Frey and Osborne compare the use of robots in hospitals to the use of robots in agriculture, in transporting goods, and in mining [3, p. 260]. But just how similar are hospital patients to crops, coal, iron ore, and uranium?

Goods of course do need to be delivered around a hospital, from equipment to medical samples for analysis to food for patients, but is delivering food to a patient on a ward really the same manner of task as delivering oil to a truck or even the same manner of task as delivering pizza to someone's home address?

Getting the job done One motivating reason for the use of robotics in hospitals may be staff shortages. In addition, hospitals tend to run according to timetables that can dominate the life on a ward. The use of robots, or other technologies, may be considered desirable to keep up with the pace of a busy ward. Research has identified two contrasting managerial styles, Pace, of getting things done on time, versus Complexity, attending more closely to the complex needs of patients [18, 19]. Keeping up with the timetable may be an imperative justifying automation: technology is at its best, perhaps, in increasing speed and the meeting of targets. Staff on wards have certain tasks which must be completed, and completed on time. However, is the task of delivering food to the bedside really just one of refuelling a hungry body? Even leaving aside the needs some patients have with being helped to eat, the human interactions that may take place even from brief encounters may be of great value to patients and others.

Exercise 1
Drawing on your experience either of your own or of friends or family or using your imagination, how might delivery of food to patients on a hospital ward by robots be different from delivery by a human being? (Noting, of course, that not all robots and certainly not all human beings are the same.)

Which if any of these differences related to what might count as the 'work' of a hospital ward? Which are negative, positive, neutral? Where might disputes lie about which aspects of the delivery of food count as work in a hospital? Compare with a restaurant, and with home, if this helps.

10.2.4   Workplace Hierarchies and the Nature and Value of Work

Why look at hierarchy when considering AI ethics? Many, if not most, workplaces are hierarchical. Often, if there is officially a flat structure, this simply masks hidden hierarchies. The general ethical issues associated with AI can alert us to the issue of hierarchy. Values of autonomy, dignity, and solidarity are all related, but perhaps it is the general control question in AI and the importance of understanding how ethical questions in AI fit into and build upon preexisting ethical questions and conditions, which should most alert us to the significance of hierarchy, for hierarchies involve the control by humans of humans. They also critically involve the flow of information, which will be impacted by the use of AI.

In and of itself, such hierarchical control may be neutral, and can be utterly critical. For example, knowing one's role in a system precisely and carrying it out exactly as needed can be literally life-saving: the fine-tuned analysis of tasks for different individuals used in Formula 1 racing has been successfully applied to the operating theatre [20]. Certain staff will have training and experience that gives them the expertise to oversee others. However, hierarchies may be too rigid and disallow exceptions. Whistleblowing may be absolutely vital to prevent disasters, including breaches of ethics, is frequently difficult, and has deleterious consequences for whistleblowers, precisely because of issues of hierarchy [21]. In other words, hierarchies act to control the flow of information within an organisation, and this may not always work to best effect.

Hierarchy and respect for persons   Differential status within a workplace need not at all imply differential respect for the individuals of different status. Unfortunately, we all know it often does. As we have mentioned before, dehumanisation and loss of dignity occur very readily. Moreover, studies of workplace and health have found that workplace hierarchy is strongly linked to health outcomes for conditions such as cardiovascular disease, with those on lower rungs in work suffering worse outcomes, and closely associated with workplace stress. Decades of work have resulted in the conclusion that a key component of this health-damaging stress is responsibility without control [22]. To illustrate, consider the above examples of a hospital ward: a nurse will be responsible for meeting timetabled targets such as the delivery of medicines, but this may take place in an environment with many unexpected interruptions. This is indeed one motivator for introducing automation.

We need to consider both any existing issues with workplace hierarchies into which AI arrives, plus the consequences of any changes to the nature of the control over individuals in the workplace that AI may afford.

Hierarchy and epistemology The ideal is that management knows precisely what is going on in a workplace and that all tasks are understood and valued, but at least in certain workplaces, this ideal may not be realised. For example, health care assistants have been found to have knowledge about patients which may not reach other staff [23]. One result of this is that it may impact the analysis of the tasks that any AI is designed to take on. Good communication may help to address this, but the views of those working in lower grades may not be so readily heard. It is possible to read many papers on workplace automation and AI that discuss the tasks that AI is to undertake and come away with the distinct impression that there is only a very narrow idea of the work undertaken, its complexity, and its value.

If nothing else, this must alert us to the need to ensure widespread participation in the design and implementation of any such technologies. Analysing and placing a value on the work carried out may be highly complex. Consider the example we looked at in Sect. 8.5 concerning how the personhood of individuals may be seen or overlooked, including the findings that care over physical appearance and grooming can contribute to wellbeing, especially for those people who are living with dementia. One might consider that therefore, attention to such issues was part and parcel of the work of staff offering basic care and that their role in fact involves helping to maintain personhood, as well as dignity. But will this be seen as part of 'healthcare' as such, will an organisation understand its value, and have the resources to value it? Note, too, that this example relates to health, where ethical aspirations of person-centred care may be part of the institutional and legal mandate. In other workplaces and corporations, there may be no such aspiration; indeed, among such workplaces are some of those most closely associated with the technologies in question.

The importance of such basic care work and attention to the needs of individual patients may seem very obvious to those involved, including staff, families, and patients, but note that the research to which I refer has been extensive and has necessitated the use of careful methodology to produce adequately robust findings in an attempt to make a difference to policy and practice; these things are obvious only to some [24]. Much of the research in this area makes use of qualitative methods such as ethnography rather than quantitative methods, precisely in order more fully to capture the meanings of the social world that is being observed [25–27]. However, this in itself may mean that things that are being observed are less susceptible to the quantification that lends itself more readily to measurement. Moreover, much ethnographic work in this context has found that nursing may be understood as technological and physical work, with the more complex care aspects ignored or seen as an optional extra by those in charge [18].

Hence, we must be alert to the impact the methods used to analyse workplace tasks will have on how they are valued and carefully consider the preexisting context and ethical issues into which AI may be placed. Below, we consider some possible consequences of the use of AI in relation to its use of data. Might we entrench existing problematic attitudes?

What is Needed? One Example: Continence Care

Consider the possible uses of robotics on a hospital ward. It is very important to prevent patients from suffering falls. Moreover, in many healthcare authorities, there is a requirement that falls must be recorded and reported, and hence the prevention of falls forms a clear and important target. Often, this results in encouraging patients, especially elderly or frail people, to remain in bed, yet this can have deleterious impacts upon patients. Especially when elderly, deconditioning can occur very rapidly with bedrest. Moreover, elderly patients and those living with dementia may be encouraged to use pads rather than to visit the toilet, even if they are otherwise continent, and this could result in hospital-acquired continence with lasting and multiple deleterious impacts [28]. This is a far from obvious consequence of the understandable and well-intentioned safety concerns and measurable targets of the ward.

Staff may have time pressures which prevent them from assisting patients on the toilet. Could the use of robotics to help certain patients to safely get out of bed and to assist them in the toilet instance with standing and sitting, be useful? The use of robots rather than a real human may mean the personal touch is lost in many tasks; but here it could protect privacy. Note then, as we have remarked earlier, sometimes what we need is to reproduce human factors; sometimes what we need is to omit them.

This is simply a suggestion: the purpose is to illustrate the complexity of these matters, and the interdisciplinary and contextual work needed for the design and use of technology that genuinely amounts to progress.

10.2.5   The Claim that AI Will Relieve Humans of Drudgery

This is a very commonly expressed reason for workplace automation: that many jobs amount to drudgery, but automation heralds the way out. Certain jobs are seen to be demeaning, beneath human dignity, or demoralising, either inherently or in practice. Yet again, we must examine how AI may be superimposed upon existing attitudes and values. It is certainly true that many jobs are dangerous, extremely hard work, may be tedious and unfulfilling, and that workers may be treated badly and with disrespect. Some of these jobs came into existence with the first, second, and third industrial revolutions. Can the fourth industrial revolution then finally sort us out? Given that many jobs that have been created by AI are also tedious, repetitive, poorly paid, and often remote work that may be isolating and unsupported, such as labelling images and content moderation, one might wonder if around the corner there is a fifth industrial revolution—or counterrevolution—which might fix the dismal jobs created by AI.

A job that seems pointless can also readily lose its appeal; it has been argued that very many jobs are indeed simply 'bullshit', providing little purpose or satisfaction for those employed in them [29]. Drudgery in jobs may be in part a factor of how jobs are organised, rather than the inherent nature of the task. A task that is repeated for 8 or 10 h straight may easily become drudgery. However, there may be many assumptions about what constitutes worthwhile work suitable for human beings. We have seen that the notion of human dignity can be a useful marker of the maltreatment of others but that it is harder to define and specify (see Sect. 2.4.9). Considering that AI will free us from jobs that are beneath human dignity may seem like a grand ideal, but there is likely to be disagreement about which jobs and tasks these are, and whether or not we need new technologies to come to the rescue, or whether much of the problem is caused by organisational, economic, and societal issues. Furthermore, the assumption that certain jobs are drudgery, or beneath human dignity, may be based upon denigrating attitudes towards those who currently perform them.

It is notable that some of the uses of AI that have sparked the majority of recent concerns are those that threaten white collar jobs, such as law and accountancy. There are certainly aspects of certain jobs that might become tedious to some; but the very same jobs may be many other people's dream jobs. People have considerably different kinds of interest and derive satisfaction and experience annoyance and stress from many different things. Some job roles that are already vanishing owing to automation are service jobs such as shop assistant or waiting on tables. One might wonder if those developing and deploying AI in the workplace have particular attitudes towards work that may not be shared.

Exercise 2

How would you define and measure 'drudgery' in work?

Recall the discussion of different ways of understanding happiness and unhappiness (Sect. 6.2.1). How might one's assessment of the drudgery or unpleasantness of a job—or the reverse—be affected by applying a hedonistic approach or a eudaimonic approach that measures happiness over a whole lifetime?

You might have fun trying to apply Bentham's felicific calculus (see Sect. 2.5.2) to a few jobs, and perhaps compare results with others.

10.2.6 Seeing Work Through a Technological Lens

When the use of AI is portrayed as being morally beneficial on the premise that it is saving humans from certain tasks and occupations, one must pay attention to the possibility that unless this assessment of these jobs is correct, then certain tasks may be further devalued, and this then may devalue those who fulfil these roles. Burn out from stress is associated with feeling that one has not been able to do a good job for patients or had adequate support from colleagues, among other factors [30], and working in an environment where the job of nursing is seen as focused on technical and physical tasks will tend to omit any time for personal care.

The ethical aims of an institution may find little place in workplace tasks We have seen above that the 'official' organisational analysis of what a task involves may omit certain elements. In the example used, of nursing, this is salutary to understanding and valuing the work because the elements that tend to get overlooked are often those human or relational elements that not only make a difference for patients but also make a large difference for staff job satisfaction; moreover, these elements may actually be a necessary part of fulfilling goals of the institution, such as patient-centred care. Note that this is an ethical aspiration! Institutions may state such laudable aims without the wherewithal or the real organisational will to accomplish them.

Hence, the same, or very similar, technically focused analyses of jobs that emphasise measurement of outcome, may be behind the lack of job satisfaction which then is used to ground arguments for automation; it may also perhaps increase the gulf between an organisation's actual functioning and some of its ethical ideals. Nonetheless, this issue is complex because there are many sound reasons for measuring certain outcomes and targets and many practical constraints on organisations. There will almost certainly be different points of view on this, from management, outside auditors, staff, patients, clients, customers, and so on. These groups will all have different responsibilities and lines of accountability. It is important to bear in mind that different workplace organisations have rather different sets of responsibilities and lines of accountability to their clientele, the wider public, and society in general. Hospitals are, or should be, workplaces with high and specific ethical standards.

Measurement of performance indicators is well known to skew outcomes as targets are chased [31]. Indeed, performance metrics are likely to skew work in AI ethics, since academics are under great pressure to produce visible measures of performance, such as publications in certain journals and citation counts. The dangers are everywhere.

Moralising attitudes towards certain jobs and tasks that may then be seen as ripe for automation may be seen in work that is thought of as 'dirty' work, involving basic care of the body and tasks such as dealing with bodily wastes [32, 33]. Such work is stigmatising for both those cared for and for those carrying out the work and is closely associated with low status within workplace hierarchies. So-called 'dirty' work may be associated with gender, race, and class [34, 35]. These issues are thus highly associated with preexisting ethical issues of equality and dignity. Whilst not denying the challenges that the work may entail, one could regard such bodily care work for the most vulnerable among us who need such care, as among the highest and most noble form of work a human being could do, and as a manifestation of the striving to maintain human dignity.

Calling certain tasks 'basic care' may be seen to imply that it is a low-grade, unimportant activity compared to the overall goals of the medical institution. However, this can be flipped to seeing it as utterly fundamental to how human beings live and relate to each other.

Exercise 3
What's the worst job you've ever had? Would technology have helped to improve your work experience in any way, and if so, how?

Exercise 4
Take an example of the introduction of AI in any workplace, real or imagined. Consider how lines of communication, capacity to act, and responsibilities may be impacted from the point of view of different employees, management, and clients.

10.2.7   The Claim that the Use of AI Will Enable Work to Be More Humanised

This is linked to the claim that AI may relieve us of drudgery. It has been claimed that the use of AI in the workplace will speed up certain tasks (be they complex or routine) so that staff can spend more time engaged in cultivating good relationships. For example, if tasks of diagnosis are undertaken more swiftly, then it is hoped that doctors may be able to devote more time to explaining the results to patients and addressing their concerns. For this to happen, it is likely that specific steps may need to be taken institutionally to achieve this. For instance, one cannot assume that a doctor who has incredible diagnostic skills has an equally good 'bed-side manner' and great communication skills. Further training may be needed.

This will also depend greatly on local context and cultures and what the task of an organisation is seen to be [36]. An institutional culture of meeting performance targets and of appearing to be 'busy' may clash with being seen to 'waste' time in 'nonwork' activities such as personal interactions and amusements. For instance, and depending on local culture and hierarchies, a nurse may be scolded for taking time in a moment of relative quiet to interact socially with patients [37, p. e3]. However, many patients are extremely isolated and under-stimulated on hospital wards, which may be lonely and distressing places. There will doubtless be variation in how such issues are managed. There is much that goes in within hospitals and clinics that extends beyond any official description of diagnosis and treatment [38].

10.2.8   Other Possible Outcomes of the Introduction of AI

We have considered in general how the implementation of AI within a specific workplace context may subtly skew the framework of values and goals through which the work is seen and evaluated. AI may be helpful in increasing the speed with which certain tasks are accomplished and in increasing levels of control and consistency over certain aspects of work. Hence, it will be helpful to consider how questions of efficiency, speed, productivity, and control may also have complex effects that may not always be uniformly welcome.

Surveillance and control at work   Recall that a major concern of the Luddites was not the use of machinery per se but the ways in which it enabled greater management control over workers and productivity (see Sect. 2.5.2). We also saw above how changes in the control of tasks and of information need to be considered in possibly shifting lines of accountability, responsibility, and agency. Note how workplaces may be judged suitable for automation if they are structured in the right ways [3]. This then presents the possibility of increasing or modifying existing structures at work in order to facilitate the implementation of AI. This may have considerable unintended impacts, including on the capacity for control, for autonomy and freedom of movement and decision-making, and for lines of communication. The use of AI at work may readily increase the degree of surveillance over the workforce, largely through enabling the collection of large amounts of data.

Naturally, people have their own strategies for navigating such lines of control within the workplace. For example, when word processors (for those who remember this now archaic technology) were first introduced into use in typing pools, this enabled management (often men) to check remotely if the staff (mostly women) were working continuously. Word processor operators quickly discovered that by holding down a key with one finger, it would appear to management as if one was hard at work, while in fact chatting to one's neighbour [39]. Likewise, turning off video and audio 'because my connection is slow' enables one to do the washing up or whatever while appearing to pay attention to an online work meeting. Again, the issue of worker control and surveillance is not new. This was one of the concerns of the Luddites, as we saw in Sect. 2.5.2. Nonetheless, the opportunities for surveillance of workers have greatly increased, and in specific ways enabled by specific technologies. Moreover, some uses of technology may also increase the surveillance of customers, such as the Amazon Go stores, where bills are automatically calculated [40]. What ethical issues arise?

Consider how this issue may be approached from very different points of view. Consider also the different ethical theories and value concepts that we have discussed earlier in the book. From the point of view of management, who may wish to increase productivity, the main question may appear to be consequentialist in form: what are the benefits? Does it increase workplace productivity? Does it have a downside in terms, for example, of burnout or staff turnover? From the point of view of staff, the issues involved would include privacy, dignity, and control. From the point of view of both, issues of communication arise.

The very different points of view and purposes for which such technology is used are also closely connected with a major ethical issue with technology in general, that much of it can be applied for both good and ill purposes: the question of 'dual use'. AI poses this problem very acutely, since so much of it is cheap and easy to replicate once developed, and since so much of it could be applied very generally [41].

Exercise 5

During the pandemic, AI technology was developed that could monitor social distancing at work [42]. This also has the feature that it could be potentially 'dual use', introduced for one purpose but retained for another. Such technology could map an individual's movements around the workplace and their distance from each other, potentially identifying members of staff. The system would determine if individuals' spatial distance from each other violated certain criteria, and breaches of this would be reported.

Consider any potential ethical issues, including good and bad points, from the point of view of both staff and management. Consider management responsibilities, e.g. for health and safety at work.

Responsibility at work: Data collection, surveillance, control, and liability One concern of the increased possibilities of data collection at work is potentially changing lines of responsibility and accountability. For example, some surgeons have expressed concern that the use of robots within the operating theatre may lead to increased liabilities for doctors, since a wealth of data will be collected about behaviour during surgery [43]. At any rate, there may be intricate questions of legal liabilities [44]. There are often thorny issues of the distribution of responsibility within lengthy and complex chains of production involving multiple different individuals and divisions within and between organisations. The introduction of AI may add considerably to these complexities, especially as AI developed by one group for one purpose may later be applied for another purpose, and especially as there are often nested patterns of development in such technology. Moreover, AI may subtly affect the nature and degree of control that individuals and groups have and may impact how information is understood and shared, adding further difficulties.

The allure of technology may rub off onto workers As we have repeatedly seen, it is necessary to consider not simply what AI is capable of doing but also how it is seen and imagined. There is a certain allure about technology that can rub off onto the workers who are in control of it and those who utilise skills in deploying it, and consequently, those workers who do not use it, or who are simply answerable to its demands, may lose status. This can then steepen the gradient of workplace hierarchy and may feed back into some of the issues discussed immediately above. For example, this seems to have happened with the introduction of technology into nursing. As the nursing role uses more and more technology, tasks that are considered basic care are more likely to be reserved for grades of staff lower on the hierarchy and the pay role, with consequences for their status within the workplace [23].

Productivity and values We looked above at hopes that workplace automation may free up workers' time by increasing productivity, using the example of the use of AI in medical diagnosis. This forms a useful example of complexities that may arise. Increased facility at diagnosis is likely to greatly increase the amount of diagnosis taking place, and could well increase the number of false positives, may increase the number of minor conditions being diagnosed which raises demands on the medical system as a whole. In other contexts, the use of AI and other technologies may have knock-on effects, which are measured as increases in productivity.

'Productivity' needs to be considered carefully in medicine, alongside not just the capacities of the medical system but also the end goal: the value of health.

Health is a very good example of how technology may put pressure on our values and goals, partly because it seems such a central and important value that it may be assumed that attempting to increase health will always be a good. But the precise definition and boundaries of health can be hard to draw; recall that we mentioned the concepts of medicalisation and of iatrogenesis earlier (see Sect. 3.3.4).

Exercise 6
Robot waiters have been around for some time. One alleged advantage is that their use may increase revenues for restaurants by making it more likely that a customer will order an extravagant dessert. This can be seen as a form of 'reverse surveillance', where human beings can make decisions in the absence of the shaming eyes of others. On the one hand, this appears to be there is free choice operating on both sides. Indeed, it may seem to increase the freedom of customers to make decisions without human moral judgement. But is this all that could be said? Is this even a moral issue? Consider how one might assess the ethical impacts for restaurants and for customers, as well as the wider impacts for society.

What is the workplace? Relationships between people We have seen how AI is involved in questions of control, for example, through data collection, which impact lines of accountability. Technology enables both connection and distance since the very possibilities of communication allow for physical distancing. This indeed is happening on a wide scale with remote working, which increased dramatically as part of policies of lockdown; indeed, without the possibilities of remote working and communication, lockdowns could not have taken place in the precise manner in which we saw in many parts of the world. The potential implications of workers remaining at home rather than going into work are profound, complex, and very likely mixed in terms of good and bad. Moreover, there are knock-on effects on transport, housing, and infrastructure.

Exercise 7
By now many of you will have probably had considerable experience of remote meetings by video call. Are there any ethical issues involved in the different possibilities and constraints on how we communicate and relate remotely compared to in person?

Transparency, performance outcomes, and technological uniformity Shifting goals in the workplace may also occur owing to lack of transparency in how findings are reached. Char et al., writing in the *New England Journal of Medicine*, have expressed concern that bias and lack of transparency in algorithms used in healthcare may impact what they call the collective medical mind [45]. There are likely to be biases that may impact treatment decisions for individuals and certain groups; it is known that medical data and trials have underrepresentation by females and many ethnic groups, yet these factors may be critical in medical decision-making. However, these biases unfortunately exist prior to the implementation of AI. Worries are expressed about the possibility of further skewing the practice of medicine, especially given the drives towards the measurement of performance outcome and the pressures that management and other interests therefore may be under. Improvements to quality metrics may or may not reflect better care. Uniformity of opinion may be encouraged by the use of a technical system for the production of medical knowledge, which may mean we pay a high price if this contains errors [46]; currently, it is generally recognised that there are reasonable disagreements within the body of medical experts. These disagreements frequently provide the impetus for improvements, including revising commonly accepted practices.

Structure and uniformity The need for structure arises with the merging of data sets, which is often required given the vast amount of data needed in AI and machine learning. An example of this is medical records, which are currently often held on computer systems that lack compatibility, and in addition, there may be differences in how medical information is understood, classified, and recorded [47]. Without addressing incompatibilities, data will lack accuracy; yet imposing a uniform standard on recording data may also introduce problems with bias, inaccuracy, and in the dominance of certain ways of understanding medicine and of the world. The understanding, classification, and diagnosis of disease and the experience of symptoms vary from place to place and over time and are known to be impacted by factors such as culture and gender [48]. Yet without uniformity of records, merging data from different sources may be riven with problems.

Deskilling Among the concerns about the use of AI in the workplace is the possibility of deskilling. The concerns of Char et al. may indicate one route through which this could occur. Conversely, the use of AI will frequently require the acquisition of new skills.

10.2.9   A Word on Methods

As with the last chapter, this discussion does not walk you through a fixed set of 'methods' for analysing the issues and reaching the 'right' answer: indeed, the more analysis and thinking we do, the more we may realise that there is no 'right' answer, only compromise. However, there are some pointers to lines of inquiry to follow.

One of these is to try to ensure a thorough understanding of the situation into which AI is to be placed. There are certain key issues—fault lines, one might say—where AI may potentially have most capacity to disrupt, either for good, for bad, or more likely, in mixed ways. *The issue of control* in AI is, as we have seen, a major concern, and this means that we need to understand the issues of control in the situation and contexts into which AI will be placed. The general question of *how precisely to understand the tasks involved* and a close comparison of human agency and capacities with those of AI are ever-present. Where questions arise of how human beings are treated—*dignity, respect for persons, autonomy*—i.e. in almost all cases, understanding how dignity, respect for persons, and autonomy are manifest in the preexisting situation and carefully considering the ways in which these will be impacted by AI (which will doubtless include unexpected ways) will always be useful.

This also means that we must think carefully about *lines of responsibility* that are likely to be affected, since not only will the *capacity of individuals to act* within a system often be impacted but also the *lines of communication* within that system. This then also means that strategies such as considering the operation of *hierarchies* and how goals, purposes, and values may be variously understood from different perspectives may be useful, as will considering the matter from the points of view of different individuals and categories of people in a social and technological system.

Subject matter expertise and personal experience The necessity of close consideration of the preexisting situation into which AI may be deployed necessitates considerable subject matter expertise, and the example of the setting of the hospital demonstrates that this may be a contested issue, with multiple points of view, and knowledge not so straightforward to acquire. This means close collaboration with others but also the need to be wary of simply accepting certain dominant views. The example of a hospital setting drew upon a body of research by outside observers about the workings of the ward.

One reason why I also used this example was because my personal experience of working as a healthcare assistant alerted me to the strength of hierarchy within such a setting and the complexity of lines of communication within this workplace. However, in contributing to discussions of issues in practical ethics, I have often been alarmed at the very fact that the only reason I have some understanding of a certain aspect of a situation, or am alerted to asking certain questions, is because of personal experience which I just randomly have acquired by the fluke of life circumstances. This has frequently made me wonder what else is being missed.

Ethical theory The different ethical theories and concepts that we have examined in this book, such as consequentialism, deontological approaches, virtue ethics, and accounts of the value of persons, if applied to the different questions examined here, will each tend to produce different answers and expose different factors of the situation. Sometimes these will be more compatible with certain points of view of the issues than with others. Sometimes the answers may cohere with each other, sometimes they may clash. Sometimes there can be valuable lessons in understanding the clashes, as this may lend understanding to why certain disagreements are irrevocable, but they may help to open the way to acceptable compromise or to better understanding, even despite continued disagreements.

10.3   AI, Employment and Unemployment, and Future Visions

Summary

Future visions of widespread automation include the possibility of extensive technological unemployment and hence of social divisions. Such possibilities require us to consider the value of work as process and product, of rest and leisure for individuals and for society, and of the impacts of a possible two-tier society, including the increased levels of social and economic control. Questions of the meaning and purpose of life inevitably follow.

So far, we have addressed questions around the impact of AI in the workplace that concern elements of technology that are either currently being used or feasibly may soon be. Addressing these questions involves close consideration of aspects of the precise capacities of the technology, the software, the hardware, the purposes for which it is used, and the precise context of use. There are also interesting ethical questions raised about the motivating ideologies behind AI and the hopes and fears projected onto it, including hopes and fears for the trajectory of humanity as technological progress unfolds.

As we have seen, concerns about the impact of technology upon employment are not new, and indeed, it is possible to see some of the expressed hopes that AI may free us from drudgery as motivated in part by the drudgery brought in by previous industrial revolutions.

Prominent among those writing in the nineteenth century about the nature of work and the downsides of industrialisation were William Morris and John Ruskin and, of course, Marx [49–51]. Moreover, as we saw earlier, the ancient Greek philosophers Plato and Aristotle made much mention of craftwork and its values.

William Morris: Useful Work and Useless Toil

Morris (1834–1896) was actively involved in arts and crafts as well as in manufacturing, and has some association with the Arts and Crafts Movement [52]. He considered that work was a human necessity, but that not all work was good; some was 'useless toil' producing nothing of real worth. Work should not only be productive of real value, but should also be a source of satisfaction to the individual workers. Sources of satisfaction, according to Morris, include the intrinsic pleasures from extension of effort and skill in work, the value of the product or service, and the hope of rest resultant on productive work rewarded as such. The mass production of factories prevented workers from gaining satisfaction from their work. He had many criticisms of the contemporary capitalist system of production, including the inequality and waste it produces, and the uniformity and substandard nature of many products thus produced. Morris set up his own factory, producing craft items such as fabrics

(continued)

and wallpapers (which are still widely on sale today, and, ironically, mass-produced). He is also known for his failure to live up to his ideals of worker autonomy and creativity within his factory (but how many of us do in fact live up to our own ideals).

High among the concerns about the impact of automation on employment are the possibilities of widespread technological unemployment and the impact this might then have upon individuals, the class of the unemployed, and society as a whole [3, 4, 7, 9, 53]. Naturally, projections for such scenarios vary widely; some difference may be made to projections by whether one is concerned with the disappearance of jobs or of specific tasks and whether one considers the creation of new jobs or the increase in certain types of task. Those with fears frequently point out that, previously, technology had threatened manual jobs; now, it is white collar jobs that are threatened. Perhaps, since the people writing these reports also have white collar jobs, this impacts how the threat is seen.

It is also anticipated by some that increased automation will lead to an increase in wealth and productivity. This raises certain questions: questions about sustainability, about how this wealth and productivity is valued, and about how it is distributed. Wealth inequalities associated with technology are already plainly apparent: to the control question in AI, we must include not simply the bare capacities of the technology to control but the powers of control enjoyed by the vastly wealthy corporations based upon their sheer economic value and reach into the economy, especially given the continued entrenchment of these technologies into the infrastructure.

Other projections, fears, and hopes concern the nature of employment in the future. Some are optimistic, projecting that there will be a greater emphasis on service work and work involving human contact and interaction, given that other more mundane tasks will be taken over by technology (as discussed earlier). Another projection is that with increased wealth and increased buying capacities, there will be greater demand for handmade crafts and appreciation of the individuality and work these involve. Conversely, there are fears for the rise in unsatisfying jobs and for greater control and surveillance over the workforce (indeed this is already happening, as we have seen).

So yet again we see the polarity between hopes for greatness, the possibilities for technology to enable humanity to flourish, and its reverse. For how can the tedious, repetitive, minimal autonomy jobs that AI has enabled, and which with bad luck may persist, plausibly be consistent with a vision of inspiring and leading humanity into a glorious AI-led future where our capacities and intelligence are fully realised?

The questions concerning future projections for the impact of automation on employment obviously require input from the realms of economics and politics (and so likely to be highly contested), among other areas. We need to examine the nature of work and evaluate how it might be changed, including its distribution. The notion of work and its implications for the value of the individual and for society as a whole has attracted considerable attention and theorisation, from very different points of view. Moreover, there are cultural, ideological, and religious views to address: consider, for instance, the Protestant Work Ethic which sprung up in Europe following the Reformation, which has many critics (including those who dispute its origins) [54]. So this again is an area where the ethical questions have to be asked and addressed in a complex and interdisciplinary area which is also highly contested. Nonetheless, work or its absence is something that is part of common human experience and hence something on which we all might have opinions and understanding.

Consider the question of whether work is an essential aspect of the human condition and how AI may impact how we address this question, including how we evaluate the impact of AI. Recall our discussion of human nature, especially Sect. 5.4.5, where we discussed whether there is an essence to human nature. Two possible accounts mentioned may be particularly relevant here: *Homo Ludens* and *Homo Faber*. Indeed, these are not necessarily incompatible. Maybe we produce things as an essential requirement of life, in order to rest and play. Or perhaps these can be combined: perhaps some vision of work along the lines that William Morris envisaged might be able to incorporate a play element into working life. If we consider the processes involved in work, or which ideally could be involved in work, such as the exertion of intellectual, physical, emotional, and creative effort towards some valuable and rewarded goal, we might hold out hopes that an ideal situation of work might represent an important part of a life well lived.

We should also consider the value of work from the point of view of the process of work, what is produced (including service roles), and the social settings surrounding work. Recall the normative ethical theories we discussed in Chap. 6 and the different aspects that are stressed by different accounts: the end results, how an end result is obtained, the shape and value of a life judged as a whole, and questions of relationships, among other things.

Visions of plenty and technological accomplishment abound in future projections of the impact of AI on work. The very idea that technology will meet our needs completely, end poverty, illness, and war, projects a world far different from the one we currently occupy. Is the idea that work is a necessity of life a merely contingent claim, which could vanish given the achievements of technology? Recall our discussions of the object of morality in Sect. 4.3.1 and of the background conditions against which the general shape of ethical norms is formed. One might be tempted to dismiss such an optimistic—or pessimistic—projection as the kind of fantasy that blights technology. It is nonetheless worth considering, since it forces us to ask not simply a technical and limited question about how to fine-tune our ethics and values, but a deeply profound question: what is the purpose of life? How do we find value? Why are we even here? It also requires us to address the question of how we would even go about trying to find an answer, were the world to become so different.

Recall our discussion about the background assumptions that shape ethics and ethical theory. Among these are indeed the necessity of effort, the need for certain basic necessities, and the uncertainties of the world. We mentioned Kant's arguments in his *Groundwork for the Metaphysics of Morals* for certain duties

[55]. Perfect duties are identified by reasoning that their negation results in a contradiction: no rational agent could will that whenever it was convenient, a person made a lying promise because the very concept of a promise requires a commitment to keep the promise, even if it is inconvenient. A formal contradiction arises since the imagined situation is incoherent. (Leave aside for now the many criticisms of how precisely Kant arrived at this conclusion.) Imperfect duties are ones the violation of which does not rest upon a formal contradiction but which no rational agent could *will* because it would conflict with what any person might well need at some point throughout their lives to fulfil the general goals that all rational agents have. Therefore, Kant argues, no rational agent would will that he or she never did anything to develop his or her talents, since the world is such that skills are needed.

Exercise 8
Try to imagine how different our values might be, if gaining the basic requirements of life, and indeed, even any luxury one might wish for, was readily provided by technology.

The answers to these and other questions may have implications for the very ways in which we value and deploy AI, understand and value intelligence, and value human beings. Recall our discussions in Sect. 5.2 concerning different ways of understanding and valuing intelligence. If we have an instrumental account, and so value intelligence because it helps us reach our goals, and we end up in a world where these goals are all reached by machines, not by us, do we end up coming to the realisation that while using machines to achieve these goals is certainly very valuable, we *also* value intelligence intrinsically because we enjoy the process, the exertion of effort, the sense of achievement of being able to reach an answer oneself? One might suspect that those who herald an age of widespread technological unemployment are imagining that they themselves will still be working, moreover, in high-status, high-reward, highly satisfying tech jobs. One might also suspect that those driven to work in artificial intelligence find the task interesting and challenging because they themselves gain considerable reward from the exercise of their own intelligence.

10.3.1   Technological Unemployment and Social Divisions

Many discussions of technological unemployment envisage that there will be a part of the population employed and a part that is unemployed. This in itself is curious, for one might suppose in an age of vast access to intelligence, whether natural or artificial, one might have hoped that a way of distributing work more evenly could have been found, especially given values of AI ethics codes and guidelines emphasising solidarity and benefit to all. That many future visions do not include this perhaps tell us something about imagined pictures of progress and about the control aspects of AI. Those who have control of AI, in such scenarios, have control of wealth, and of a great deal more.

Two major ethical questions arise: the inequalities that arise from such a stark division into two classes of humanity and the question of how people in the unemployed class are going to occupy themselves. Examining an imagined and extreme possibility of two separate classes in society can also be useful for considering how similar issues might play out in a more muted version, also known as real life.

The inequalities centrally include the question of control because in many imagined situations, the unemployed are dependent upon others for income, and indeed, for the goods and services that might, if they are lucky, help to render their lives meaningful or at any rate keep them occupied. Even if incomes are distributed fairly evenly among all, both employed and unemployed, disparities still persist in the form of disparities of control, power, and status. One of the most robust findings in social science is that relative inequality is a good predictor of criminal behaviour, including violence. Inequality is also closely linked to health disparities.

How might a possible rise in crime be addressed? Using AI, perhaps. Since there is likely to be considerable surveillance and data collection of individuals, some manner of social credit system to encourage certain behaviours and discourage others could readily be implemented. If a group is entirely dependent for income on a government and the continued dominance of technology, and there are no alternatives—no frontier land left to go and find a patch of earth to farm—then the level of control possible over lives could be immense, especially with the introduction of digital currency. (Black markets and crime are virtually inevitable of course.) Perhaps alternatively or additionally, AI, including persuasive technology and other ways of manipulating behaviour and emotions, might be used to combat negative behaviour in individuals and groups. Indeed, why not use this on the employed as well? This question is complicated by the fact that negative feedback on antisocial behaviour is part and parcel of a well-functioning society. What will come to be seen as acceptable or as inevitable? See our discussion of online content moderation in Chap. 10 for many similar issues.

Exercise 9
Could such a system to control the population and achieve social harmony and desirable behaviour be ethical? Of course, this is an immense question, but as an exercise, consider this from consequentialist, deontological, and virtue ethics points of view and consider questions such as autonomy and respect for persons. Ask also what other considerations and disciplines need to be brought to the discussion.

10.3.2   Keeping Occupied in a Time of Unemployment

In the 1970s, a speaker came to our school to show us plans for a vast leisure park to be built in some of the extensive green space within London, on the premise that when we all grew up, machines would be doing most of the work. The park was never built, and many of us worked more hours than our parents did. Nonetheless, if

AI does indeed manage to create vastly more leisure time, we will need some way of filling it.

Many may think that there is little to worry about finding something to do. Countless retired people remark that they cannot understand how they ever found time to go to work. Housework expands to fill the time available, many say, and likewise, humans are endlessly dreaming up new projects and things to be interested in. Nonetheless, for others, the prospect of not having enough to do is deeply unpleasant. In any case, the question must be asked if the things that the unemployed have to do to occupy themselves include things of value. For human beings, social creatures, whether our pursuits are valuable in the eyes of others is also frequently important.

Some imagine that we will be endlessly entertained, including with computerised games and virtual reality, a more passive role perhaps, although AI and VR will enable forms of participation and agency. Some have imagined that this will free us for endless creativity, an active role. Some imagine that even creativity will not be needed, since AI will be able to create art, music, literature, anything we wish, and will be better than us at the task. We can have literature specially created to suit our temperament and interests. We will be consumers rather than producers. Those who find pleasure in discovery can simply read all the knowledge that AI is rapidly creating for us.

Exercise 10
Drawing on any material that you regard as relevant, consider if there would be any loss if we all became consumers of the products of creative endeavours produced by machines, rather than creators.

Again, the questions we have raised concerning the nature of happiness are highly relevant here, including questions of higher and lower pleasures (see Sects. 2.5.2 and 6.2.1). These questions speak to some of the profound divisions between different attitudes to the value of our lives that we have seen in many philosophers. A hedonic account of happiness might suggest a world of passing enjoyable experiences, which simply add up and accrue over a lifetime. Other accounts look to purpose, to character development, and to finding a source of meaning over the course of a lifetime. There are also traditions both philosophical and religious, where a life of contemplation is seen as of great value, on some views, the highest form of life. Perhaps this is the future that awaits us; perhaps some of the technologically unemployed may be able to live the kind of revered lives that those dedicated to contemplation and spiritual pursuits have enjoyed and do enjoy in many cultures and times of history. The ethical issues merge seamlessly into questions about the search for the meaning of our lives and into questions posed by religious and traditions of spirituality.

Exercise 11
Consider and discuss:

An answer to any scruples about the world which awaits us should widespread technological unemployment occur might be this: *there is no fixed human nature.*

Hence, the value we attach to notions such as autonomy and freedom will be a thing of the past. Freedom of thought was valuable only when human beings did not have access to robustly reliable routes to knowledge. Freedom to act as you please was only valuable in a situation of uncertainty over the best course of action in life. In this future world, these values will be surpassed. The teething problems with online content moderation will be solved, and by tackling this, we will have amassed sufficient expertise reliably to assess content for misinformation. The boundaries between the real and the unreal will be malleable since so much of our time is spent living in a world of virtual reality and deepfakes. Moreover, since AI is based upon an instrumental account of intelligence, the value of intelligence itself, including the value of truth and of knowledge, is also instrumental, merely for any good it produces. The real itself matters not. So whether we are actually experiencing a leisure activity or not will not matter to us, and we will be able to rely on AI to prevent us from receiving the fake news that is damaging.

10.4　Superintelligence, Existential Risk, and the Control Problem

Summary
Fears about superintelligence can trace their history back to the early days of computing but have been brought to the forefront in recent years by those concerned with the prospect of existential risk. The questions of control and of value alignment are writ large. Examining these questions requires looking at basic assumptions about the nature of intelligence and the foundation of our values, including the orthogonality thesis. We examine Stuart Russell's proposals to try to ensure that any superintelligence will follow human values and preferences.

10.4.1　Introduction

The fears about the possible development of superintelligence have a long history. Not only do they feed into general fears about the control of machines and artefacts such as robots by human beings that have concerned human beings for centuries (see Sect. 2.5), starting in the mid-twentieth century, there have been specific warnings about the potential for the development of AI that could spell doom for the human race. We saw how Alan Turing warned in 1951 that thinking machines would be able to exceed our powers and hence have the ability to control us [56]. Norbert Wiener's approach to the issue was perhaps more complex, seeing the importance of the complex interactions between computers and humans [57]. Indeed, it is these complex interactions and feedback loops between human and machine which bring a bridge between the futuristic nightmare scenarios of control by a vastly superior machine and the more mundane but nonetheless pressing and profound questions facing us right now, as we shall see later in this chapter. Fears which more specifically address the current superintelligence debates were sounded in 1966 by I. J. Good, who had worked with Turing. Good suggested that an ultraintelligent machine, being defined as exceeding all human intelligence, would be able to use its intelligence to recursively improve itself resulting in an 'intelligence explosion' [58].

Existential risk However prescient and apt these warnings might be, it is also salutary to reflect on the mood of the times: in the wake of the scientific and technical advances taking place in the Second World War and the Cold War, fears of nuclear Armageddon were very real. Fears that computing might also lead to human catastrophe parallel nuclear fears. Indeed, concern about the dangers of how we might protect ourselves from the development of superintelligence forms a major focus of research for those concerned with existential risks to humanity, such as the Future of Life Institute, Stanford University's Stanford Existential Risks Initiative (SERI), the Future of Humanity Institute at the University of Oxford, and, it will surprise no one to discover, at the Centre for the Study of Existential Risk at the University of Cambridge. The existential risk of superintelligence may be framed as human extinction, but it could also be a scenario where humans live appalling lives at the mercy of something they created but cannot control.

Nick Bostrom's account of the issues in his 2014 book *Superintelligence: Paths, Dangers, Strategies* has received considerable attention [59]. He projects that, at its best, AI may lead to the fulfilment of humanity's endowment, enabling us to gain the best from our natures and the world, but fears that there may be a 'hard take-off' where over a very short time, perhaps a matter of days or hours, an advanced artificial intelligence could recursively self-improve until it reached at state of intelligence so far above the best human capacity that we would be unable to control it, or indeed, to understand it at all well, in an AI takeover scenario. We would have reached the singularity.

Stuart Russell's book *Human Compatible* also addresses superintelligence, setting out to improve upon Bostrom's work [60]. Like Bostrom, he sees contrasting possibilities for AI: a golden age or catastrophe. He posits a possible 'gorilla problem': that, just as humans regard gorillas as of less value to humans, despite their considerable intelligence, so superintelligence might come to regard us.

Much of the debate about superintelligence concerns the assessment of the possibility, both practically and conceptually, of a superintelligent AI, including questions about what this might even mean. The issue then essentially concerns how AI is understood, as well as how intelligence is understood. For instance, it has been argued that intelligence has many dimensions and that the idea of a single notion of 'greater intelligence' is misleading [61]. There are different assessments of the chances of this happening and the speed at which it might happen. Andrew Ng famously claimed that the problem was so remote that worrying about it was like worrying about the overpopulation of Mars [62]. The One Hundred Year Study on Artificial Intelligence at Stanford issued a report stated that superintelligence was not near and not likely to occur [63]. But what are the costs if these opinions are incorrect?

The urgency of the problem is emphasised by Bostrom and by Russell: a superintelligence take-off that then developed such that we were unable to understand or control it would be the most significant thing that could happen to humanity. Bostrom argues that we have only one chance to get it right. With this in mind, he argues against those who consider the development of superintelligence and the accompanying scenarios of existential doom unlikely, by calculating that even if there was a minute chance of existential catastrophe, this would be such a loss of value in the world that it would justify spending money now to attempt to forestall this, even if the chances of success in preventing catastrophe were small [64, p. 18]. Given the relatively low resources and salaries being put into such research countering existential risks, compared to the money poured into technology in general, Bostrom's argument may hold up, but we will consider further below the underlying premise of his position when we address Longtermism [1], as well as addressing the present value of examining the arguments advanced towards mitigating the dangers of superintelligence.

The problem is one of value alignment on a massive scale, a scale which in many ways makes a difference not just of degree, but of kind. The attempt to ensure that specific applications of AI are aligned with our goals and values often runs into control problems: for example, if there is a lack of transparency, or if undetected bias within a system of algorithms reproduces or even worsens certain kinds of bias that are counter to general societal values, or if there are run-on effects within a system, for example, changes to people's behaviour as a result of increased data collection and surveillance.

If a discrete application of AI is found to be misaligned with our values, we have some hope of detecting it and remedying the situation (with the proviso that we still have to deal with the enduring and difficult issues of transparency and control). Moreover, AI itself can often help us to detect whether a system is misaligned with our values. Just as algorithms may reproduce and worsen bias, they can also be used to detect it. For example, because of the incomplete nature of medical knowledge and the history of data collection and medical research, bias in research is very possible and may both be reproduced in research involving machine learning, but the very same techniques can be used to spot, analyse, and combat such disparities [65]. Medical practitioners may be unaware that certain diagnostics and treatments deliver worse results to certain groups or may not understand why certain disparities in outcome exist, but data analysis using AI may help to reveal this [66].

The control problem gets critical However, superintelligence is feared since our capacity to control it will be greatly diminished, owing to its superior intelligence. The control examples above merely referred to particular instances of machine learning, which as we have seen, many practitioners are reluctant even to call 'artificial intelligence' because its capacities are for merely discrete and limited aspects of intelligence. Moreover, the fears are worsened by the imagined scenarios where superintelligence can be in charge of any and of every aspect of our lives and rendered more frightening still by Bostrom's scenario of a rapid take-off where artificial intelligence could recursively self-improve. No wonder his book has been a best seller.

The very nature of the intelligence within artificial intelligence must therefore now be examined The fear that superintelligence may be misaligned with our values raises the question of the relationship between intelligence and the ability to understand value and the motivation to pursue things of value. Since we are dealing with projected scenarios, this means examining not simply the 'intelligence' within artificial intelligence as it is currently being developed but ideologies and views on the very nature of intelligence.

10.4.2 How Might Superintelligence Come About?

Bostrom's book contains a wealth of detail but let us give an outline of his argument about the dangers of superintelligence. A starting point is the problem of perverse instantiation (see Sect. 2.3). This problem in itself is the general problem of giving instructions in ways that admit of no misunderstanding, worsened by the degree of autonomy within a system. In perverse instantiation, one's wishes are carried out to the letter in ways that are self-defeating or uncontrolled. King Midas wished for everything he touched to turn to gold, only to find this happened even to things he loved such as his daughter. Goethe's poem *The Sorcerer's Apprentice* (and the Disney film) tells a tale of a novice magician attempting to sweep up, using a magic broom he finds he cannot control, resulting in increasing chaos [67, 68].

Although this is bad enough, superintelligence would far more powerful than a broom, and could hack attempts to control it. Superintelligence may be motivated to defeat any attempts to control it if it determines that this strategy is needed to fulfil the goals with which it has been programmed. For example, Bostrom argues that were we to try to control artificial intelligence by containing it in a box, any superintelligence would be able to work how to bust out in order to fulfil goals that it has been given. This ability would be heightened by its capacity to understand the motivations and limitations of humans and to understand and anticipate the likely efforts we might make to control it.

Worse, superintelligence may be motivated to continue with a task beyond what any human might have envisaged if it is motivated to optimise and to ensure that it has adequately completed its goals. The superintelligence would have instrumental goals towards producing paperclips, such as providing materials for this and over-riding any competing activities. (The assumption is that, being superintelligent, it is able to marshal physical resources to great effect, dominating any attempts to combat it.) We, mere humans, could be seen as resource material for paperclips (despite the extremely small amount of suitable elements in our bodies: every little helps). We may have created an intelligence that views us simply as raw material, as objects.

The example of creating paperclips may be useful in selecting a subject that is neutral and thus less likely to produce emotional reactions one way or the other. It is also striking how Bostrom illustrates his concerns with the paperclip, an item more useful in an office setting highly dependent on older technologies and on, or course, paper (although paperclips are known to be used in the main for other functions). The superintelligence is a monster: literally gobbling us up, as if we are mere flesh and bones, worse, for even the layer of complexity and value of our biology is erased; using us up as if our very flesh was nothing but chemicals, was merely matter. We don't even have the relative dignity of having our minds hacked. We are in a nightmare scenario of reversed reciprocity.

The orthogonality thesis   The root source of the problem is that intelligence, as manifest within artificial intelligence and as envisaged in superintelligence, is understood as orthogonal to value: the level of intelligence bears no connection to the ability to understand value [69]. Any values exhibited by artificial intelligence, and hence superintelligence, are placed there in the goals with which it is set up by us. As superintelligence develops its powers, it will develop various instrumental goals as necessary to assist with fulfilling the goals that we placed there. We have mentioned this earlier (see Sect. 2.3) and how such a claim relates to long-standing philosophical debates not only about the nature of intelligence and of wisdom, not only about the nature of knowledge, but also about the very foundations of ethics and of moral epistemology.

The world as devoid of value and purpose   Indeed, the view that our knowledge of the world is devoid of value, telling us nothing about how to act, only giving us information which we might use instrumentally to achieve our goals, is commonly held and commonly assumed to be beyond critique. Moreover, it goes along with claims that to attain such knowledge, we must strip ourselves of bias, of emotion, and must strive to observe the world from as universal a stance as possible, such that any other unbiased observer would find the same result. David Hume is often cited as an originator of claims that there is a sharp and unbridgeable gulf between fact and value (see Sect. 5.4.7), and many contemporaries follow broadly in his footsteps. Stuart Russell, whose instrumental definition of intelligence we examined earlier (see Sect. 5.2.1), agrees and specifically states in his work on the dangers of superintelligence that there can be no purposes embedded within the world [60]. We will see later, in Chap. 11, that there are other popular works that envisage our future with artificial intelligence that take diametrically opposed views.

As we have seen, not all agree with such a view, especially in ethics (see Chap. 6, especially Sect. 6.4). It may be argued that any intelligence that was devoid of appreciation of the value which is embedded in the universe would simply not be a complete intelligence. For example, as we saw, Plato considered that abstract knowledge of the Forms would give us knowledge of the Form of the Good, which would in and of itself be sufficient to motivate us to act [70]. More contemporary moral realists also argue that value exists in the world and can be perceived in certain ways [71].

However, the problem may still remain, unless we can somehow guarantee that any potential superintelligence explosion or rapid take-off would result in the kind of intelligence that was capable of seeing value in the world. (We would also have to cross our fingers and hope that the values of the universe were the same as ours—or that we could readily realise that we were wrong about our values in certain ways. Maybe humans are a blight on the cosmos, after all.) Understanding the necessary links of the superintelligence problem with issues concerning not simply the nature of intelligence but questions of epistemology in general, and in moral epistemology in particular, can help us to understand the nature of the questions with which we are grappling, as well as how the particular ways in which the superintelligence problem is formulated and approached help to reveal deep-seated and in many ways contentious positions regarding the nature of artificial intelligence in addition to some foundational philosophical debates. We need to consider questions of moral epistemology not simply in relation to superintelligence but in relation to us, human beings.

Bias in Algorithms and a Humean Account of Ethics

Consider this: suppose intelligence is orthogonal to value, and suppose fact and value are completely separate things, such that in order to see the world accurately and completely, we have to rid ourselves of bias in the form of emotion. Any moral view we have merely based upon sentiment, feeling, or emotion.

What implications might this have for how we understand the bias problem in AI?

We are driven to prevent bias by our values, which are based upon feeling.

The removal of bias requires us to remove any influence of feeling or emotion upon how we observe, measure, and analyse the world.

At what stage do we reintroduce feelings in order to assess whether or not a situation or an algorithm is biased in ways that are counter to our values?

Measuring any bias towards an individual involves assigning that individual to certain categories. Is this assignment based simply upon observation of the world, or are we imposing any values upon the world as we look for bias?

Is the way in which we divide the world into categories which we deem relevant to questions of justice, fairness, and bias, given by the world, or given by our values?

Might overcoming bias in algorithms merely be a co-ordination problem of trying to accommodate the multiple biases of billions of different people? And if so, what determines the values upon which this is based?

10.4.3   Attempting to Find a Solution: Ensure Superintelligence Aligns with Human Values

Bostrom proposes two possible pathways for addressing the dangers of superintelligence: finding some way of boxing in and containing its power and providing incentives such that it would not develop in ways that greatly threatened us. There is great complexity to his positions, which have naturally received considerable attention and critique [72–74]. Here, however, we focus on Stuart Russell's attempted strategy to address the issues, one that makes use of many of the ethical concepts and theory we have met in this book and that draws upon the account of intelligence that he proposes, as we saw in Chap. 5.

Human Compatible: **assumptions and goals**   Stuart Russell's assumptions in his presentation of the problems and suggested solutions closely overlap with those of Bostrom. He considers intelligence to be orthogonal to value, with any value instrumental and measured by the goals that it uses its intelligence to reach and with its capacity to reach its objectives measured by a utility function. Hence, values are sharply divided from facts: there is no value in the world, no purposes in the world. Value and purposes all derive from human beings. There is a complication here, in that animals also pursue their own purposes, and there may be life elsewhere in the universe which also does this, but let's leave aside these details for now, as we have enough complexity to be getting on with, and until the aliens arrive, we can bracket their concerns for now (although, see later).

However, Russell does make certain generalisations about human motivations: that we care in general about what happens in the future, and we care about each other. We know that this assumption is false in certain cases, as otherwise the sin of acedia, a listlessness and lack of concern for anything or involvement in the world, would never have been a problem. We can see these as assumptions about human nature and will return to them below.

Russell also fears perverse instantiation of our goals, and his general approach is to ensure that however artificial intelligence develops, and how powerful it becomes, it will always be compatible with human values, which, given that he considers humans the only (or at least the main) source of value, seems a reasonable aim. Hence, the objectives we put into artificial intelligence must be such that they reliably track our true values. His aim is somewhat modest: we must aim to ensure that superintelligence will never make us seriously unhappy [60, p. 171]. (Although given that artificial intelligence already makes many people seriously unhappy, this aim is perhaps not so modest.)

Deference to human values   We thus need a reliable way of ensuring, and checking, that any artificial intelligence which might lead to the development of a superintelligence has objectives aligned not too far away from ours. We have seen plentiful reasons to worry that the way we specify our objectives and place them into machines may inadvertently lead to great misalignment with our own values; we have plenty of reason to doubt that we ourselves have a complete grasp on our own values. Russell's suggestion involves including probabilities and uncertainties in artificial intelligence. AI would be designed so that it would repeatedly check whether it was in alignment with our values. Moreover, it would not necessarily take us at our word what our values were: it would infer them from multiple sources and modify its picture of our values over time.

In this way, AI has only one objective, to maximise utility understood as fulfilling human goals, in turn understood as human preferences. Uncertainty is built in so that the AI never ploughs on with disastrous consequences: it needs to constantly check with human beings because, and since there is no other source of value in the world, the only reliable source of information about human preferences will be how humans behave (including their use of language) [60, p. 173].

AI must understand us, but how? Russell notes that machines are rather different from humans, and their understanding of the human mind is poor [60, p. 123]. They do not share a human mind and hence cannot engage in that reciprocity, which is at best found between humans. So how will AI understand us and our values? Recall our discussions of the many problems that the attempts to understand humans via data collected using AI; see, e.g. Chap. 8 especially Sect. 8.7.3. It is fair to note that Russell is envisaging ways of designing AI and not claiming that this is already possible.

In a nutshell, AI will observe our behaviour, and reverse engineer the data to infer our preferences from it.

Exercise 12

Before we continue, consider the difficulties for a human being of inferring preferences from someone's behaviour (including language). Now consider the difficulties of doing so for a machine and the nature of any differences. The material in Chap. 9 concerning online content moderation may be useful.

There are multiple challenges in this endeavour, as Russell naturally realises. Some concern the capacity of machines (indeed, or anyone) to read the behaviour and language of others. Some concern the difficulties of inferring values underlying motivation. In addition, there are many remaining questions concerning ethics and the realisation and implementation of value. Many of these will be familiar from our study of utilitarianism in particular, since Russell assumes a consequentialist framework of value. We will be able to see that many of the problems underlying current efforts to ensure that our computers do not take over the world and use us as their playthings or worse are precisely those problems that have been vexing philosophers for centuries.

Observing human behaviour and interpreting language will be necessary The machine must of necessity regard us as a roughly as a behaviourist might, armed with some knowledge of the inner workings of human psychology as a help to interpretation, and with understanding of language, regards us: from the outside. There will be no 'aha!' moment of mutual recognition. There are many problems with attempting to do this. Inferring intention from behaviour as we have seen (see Sect. 4.4.5) is complex and requires context and nuance. So this will certainly be difficult.

Suppose, for example, aliens came to Earth and attempted to interpret the activities of scientists and practices surrounding the scientific endeavour. Would they come away with the conclusion that it was motivated by the pursuit of truth? Or might they conclude that it was, say, a game for labelling the world and its regularities with the names of certain individuals who managed to navigate their way to key positions of prominence within institutions and was hence a way of mapping human presence onto the world, with certain side effects such as sometimes enabling certain men to attract females? Plank's Constant, Maxwell's Equations, Schrödinger's cat, the rigorous policing of citation practices, and so on, might lead the aliens to such a conclusion.

Likewise, as we have seen, there are great challenges with interpreting language (see Chap. 9). Russell indeed notes that artificial intelligence will need to have an understanding of pragmatics. On the other hand, we are not looking for a perfect solution, only one that is a 'good enough' with our preferences, and we are to assume that the superintelligence is considerably more advanced than current natural language processing capabilities.

However, even should the machine become reasonably adept at interpreting our language, our behaviour, our intentions, and our feelings, there is still a problem with inferring from all this information an understanding of preferences that might reasonably amount to an account of values. We act under certain descriptions. Consider, for instance, a personality test that asks you if you would rather go to the library or to a party. I for one am stumped at such questions, because so much depends upon circumstances, whose party, which library, and so on, but the point of the exercise is to elicit general preferences for 'library time' or 'party time'. How strong is one's leaning either way? And for how long would one have to be observed? And would one have to observe the sighs, the times gazing out of the window, to conclude that a person did not actually like the library all that much? Or is the window-gazing a chance to gather thoughts, and the sighs an indication of how deeply the person is thinking? It would be necessary to gather a mass of data about all these things and any other possible preferences one might have. It would also be necessary to understand if the behaviour of 'walking into the library and staying there for a time' even counted as an act of 'going to the library' per se and hence counted towards making one a library kind of person. Because it may be the main motivation is that a romantic partner works there, that you like the human companionship of so many bodies around you all studying, and so on. So we see that the very idea of whether a person even sees a venue as 'a library' is up for grabs in the complexity of comprehending behaviour and values. Social scientists who conduct both qualitative and quantitative work trying to understand people's behaviour and beliefs have been struggling with these issues for some time.

However, can we overcome these issues? Let us be optimistic that we can certainly make sufficient progress, but we might just be a little wary that the kind of optimism about tackling such questions about what will satisfy human preferences and make us happy, let alone about tackling some deep philosophical questions about ethics, amounts to a kind of ethical solutionism, the insistence that 'yes we can'. Russell himself says that we need to consider understanding and achieving happiness as a kind of engineering discipline [60, p. 123], noting that we need to work together with a large range of different disciplines to achieve this.

Exercise 13
Drawing on whatever relevant knowledge you have, including earlier discussions about the nature of happiness, how feasible do you consider it that we could develop an 'engineering discipline' of happiness?

There is also an inherent difficulty with rendering happiness an engineering discipline that is well understood by machines, especially if these are very powerful machines. Because it would make happiness easier to hack. We return to this question shortly after outlining some other difficulties.

Hierarchies of preferences It will be immediately apparent that there are hierarchies to our preferences. We have already considered these in our discussion of the nature and value of persons in Chap. 8. (We will shortly consider the implications for respect for persons and for prioritising the concerns of different individuals.) Hierarchy of value does not occur simply because we rank value in degree of importance (although this ranking may be rough and ready, circumstantial, and hard to determine) but also because we have preferences about our preferences (see the discussion of Frankfurt in Sect. 8.6). For instance, suppose I am not keen on going to parties, but wish I went to more of them, because it's a good way to meet people and it might help me overcome my lack of social skills. The assumption will be that the preferences about preferences take priority. This might work well if humans had well-ordered and neatly nested, consistent sets of preferences, but alas, this may not be so. Consider Augustine's prayer: 'Oh Lord, give me chastity and continence, but not yet'.

Augustine's preferences for continence and chastity are meta-preferences: preferences about preferences—he prefers that he has the ability to control his desires, and in particular his sexual desires, so, they seem 'higher' and hence 'better' than his first-level preferences. However, his preference that he not gain continence and chastity just yet, is a meta-meta-preference. Is this the best of all? Or does it demonstrate the weakness of his meta-preferences? Or illustrate the internal battles so typical of humanity?

This brings us to the next issue: irrationality.

Exercise 14
What, if anything, makes our preferences about our preferences 'better' kinds of preferences? Consider the meta-preference: 'I would prefer it if I did not worry so much about the welfare of others and could just do what on earth I liked'. Consider the passage from Dostoevksy's *Notes from Underground* that we looked at in Sect. 6.2.4. Is the protagonist's wish to act on his own 'free and unfettered volition' a

meta-preference, and if so, should any superintelligence attempt to act in accordance with this preference? Does rationality or its absence matter?

Recognising irrationality Russell recognises that the machines must be able to recognise human irrationality. Human beings do not always act in accordance with their best judgements and may form beliefs contrary to the best evidence available to them. So we may act counter to what we most want to do. Of course, we may not always do what we think we ought to do, but the problem is deeper than this: we may not do what we want to do, all things considered, perhaps out of habit, perhaps out of sheer wilfulness [75]. But how precisely do we understand rationality? This is needed to interpret 'true' preferences. This yet again reveals a deep philosophical question, one which it is necessary to answer if we are to infer preferences in others. Some consider that such deep irrationality of motivation is not actually possible. So that if we seem to act against our preferences, this will be an illusion or caused by some error such as a false belief. Others disagree. An answer to this question may be necessary to infer preferences simply from behaviour. We face a question about human nature.

Exercise 15
Russell suggests that artificial intelligence might improve its understanding of human preferences and motivation by reading novels. Take one or two novels (or movies) with which you are familiar and consider what lessons a superintelligence might learn from them. This exercise is perhaps mostly for fun.

Hacking humans Irrationality is not our only problem. Our preferences can be hacked. Indeed, the more that a superintelligence discovers about human happiness, preference formation and satisfaction, and our reward systems, the more readily it will be able to hack these [60, p. 208]. There are various reasons for the ease with which human preferences can be hacked and why AI might be very good at this.

Preference and belief Preference satisfaction very frequently depends upon the belief that a preference has been fulfilled: the possibilities of AI, deepfakes, and virtual reality significantly increase the possibility of being satisfied through being fooled (although whether this is a trick or not depends upon one's idea of 'reality'). Having a preference for the truth does not solve things; it only motivates the superintelligence to make sure you never discover the truth, which could make your imprisonment in a world of fakery even more entrenched.

Preference formation Recall that Russell considers that there is no purpose in the world. Hence, this seems to mean that there is no standard of value by which we rate what preferences we might start out with or which preferences we lose. Any preference will do. There is no human nature by which to assess their suitability, other than the necessities given by the need for our biological survival (and the superintelligence is meant to be loyal to us as humans, hopefully fixing this.) This seems to mean that so long as we are still getting something out of life, AI could manipulate us to change preferences to ones that are easier to satisfy. This speaks to a fundamental problem of any system of ethics based upon desires or preferences: they can be fulfilled either by satisfying them or by taking away the preference.

Exercise 16

If a superintelligence changed your preferences to ones that were readily satisfied, in what ways, if any, might this be wrong? Consider that humans often have vastly unrealistic expectations in life, which can make them very unhappy.

Distributing happiness: the utility monster and other stories A thought experiment by Robert Nozick proposes a flaw with utilitarianism, and again, one that would only be worsened and made more likely with the development of powerful artificial intelligence [76, p. 41]. A person who gained an enormous degree of reward from having preferences satisfied would win out over those who gained less from having their preferences satisfied. This would skew the distribution of value over the population. Although a thought experiment, this translates readily into everyday life: think of a group sharing a house, for instance. There are often certain people who mildly go along with the dominant wishes of those who make the most fuss.

Russell assumes that humans care about each other. This is tenet about human nature which could readily be changed, especially with AI, which has the capacity to manipulate our preferences. In any case, the capacity for care for others operates weakly and inconsistently between individuals and is present to different degrees in different individuals. The unevenness of distribution of preference satisfaction in the world is only likely to be worsened if we take higher order preferences into account, for those individuals who have a higher order preference to think more of others, would lose out to those who have no such higher order preference. Ordinarily, we would think of this as a way of ensuring that some kind of perverse reverse-ethical world comes into being. Can you think of methods of combatting this?

The assumption that human beings care about what happens in the future and care about each other forms part of Russell's background picture of the nature of the world, which seems essential to an attempt to ensure that by following human preferences, superintelligence does not end up acting totally counter to our values. However, this presupposes some universal or aggregated point of view from which we are attempting to solve this problem: because the unevenness of distribution of value over a population is only a problem, if we have some view such as that persons ought to be equally valued or respected. See Sect. 6.2.5 for a discussion of the agent neutrality of utilitarianism.

There is also the problem of how each one of us might be motivated. John Stuart Mill grappled with this problem in Chap. 4 of *Utilitarianism*: finding good arguments to move from 'each person desires his or her own happiness' to 'each person therefore, desires the happiness of the whole' is extremely hard [77]. It may be in this that we are simply up against the very difficult questions which vex any account of ethics, and that no other account would do better. What might help to address the problems we have been discussing?

Exercise 17

And let us mention the position of animals. There are a great many more of them than there are of human beings. The preferences people have regarding the treatment of animals vary greatly. Moreover, the centring of humans in ethics is not universal [78]. Why should we assume that we should ensure that superintelligence prioritises the preferences of humans? (Below, we will consider a view that discusses the value of 'sentient beings'.)

Our future selves Common observation notes that our preferences and values change over time. We would need to allow that the superintelligence could take this into account. However, the situation is complicated by similar issues to those discussed above in hierarchy of value and in the hacking of preferences, and again, the debates between different philosophical notions of happiness are relevant. Mere change in values over time may represent a decline, a narrowing of envisaged possibilities as a person comes to accept their lot in life, or perhaps, somewhat differently, as their character degenerates and corrupts. Alternatively, it may represent a flowering of wisdom and phronesis.

The advantages and disadvantages of using a consequentialist approach The focus on utilitarianism and preference satisfaction enables a certain simplicity of approach and an approach that fits quite neatly into an instrumental account of intelligence as utility maximiser. However, we have also seen how it leads us straight into issues that raise profoundly difficult questions about the nature of value, of its distribution, and of the value of persons. Perhaps, by including a standard of the value of truth, a way of valuing persons and their projects, and a way of attributing purpose and value to goals over a lifetime, we may in this way address some of the weaknesses of consequentialism.

Consequentialism seems an ideal normative ethical theory to use when we are looking to the near and distant future: it's all about future possibilities. But it says less, if anything, about how we get there, and moreover, we also need to address the issue of *who* gets there: the agents and bearers of moral value, an issue with which standard consequentialist approaches struggle. Perhaps the approach that moral value belongs to individually identified bearers of value such as persons is wrong. Maybe we should be looking just to maximise value across the universe as a whole and stop worrying so much about our own little species.

How much can we achieve in ethics? We have considered multiple difficulties with attempts to address the dangers we might perhaps face from superintelligence. To reflect: in any area, we can only find as much certainty as the subject matter allows, which is a useful observation by Aristotle that is worth repeating [79]. This is also worth noting if we are trying to avoid inadvertently seeing ethical issues through the lens of technology and hence incorporating unrealistic or inappropriate goals. One thing we have learned, however, is the necessity of philosophy. There are considerable complexities to the minutiae of the arguments that Russell and others advance in attempting to reduce the chances that we will come to a sorry end courtesy of artificial intelligence. Many of these complexities are technical, but it is valuable to understand how many of these arguments about the nature and distribution of value are prefigured in philosophical debates.

10.4.4 How Do Debates About Superintelligence Relate to Current Issues in AI Ethics?

Is superintelligence simply a niche issue that merely sells books and engages those who enjoy the thrill of minute discussion of the remote possibility of catastrophe? One could argue that the very way in which the concerns about superintelligence are framed closely mirrors the current concerns about AI. Issues arise from the ubiquity of control; the capacities of superintelligence to mould and manipulate our beliefs and preferences and change our behaviour; and ways in which a system governed by superintelligence may hack distribution of values such that these become extremely uneven.

The issue of control may also be manifest in similar ways to the worries that attempts to lock our values into superintelligence may freeze our futures in problematic ways. Does this mirror the ways in which currently, the values of dominant groups in creating and deploying technology, and the values of dominant groups in considering the ethics of AI, may lock in certain values and certain ways of treating human beings? Consider whether the influence of technology on ways in which we gain information, communicate, and relate to ourselves and others, and the ways in which infrastructure may become locked in and then presumed to be essential, may or may not mirror the concerns of the extent of control that a superintelligence may have over us. Concerns about projecting our current ethics into the future, both the impetus to do this and the fear that there may be limits to this strategy, map onto the impetus to ensure that globally applicable standards of ethics are produced and applied, which also go along with legitimate fears.

Exercise 18
Argue for or against the proposition that these and other issues of control are currently facing us, and if so, how.

Consider as many different facets of control, including the human capacity to resist this, as possible.

10.5 Longtermism in AI

Summary
Longtermism, understood as the thesis that in deciding issues of resource allocation, we ought to concentrate on the far distant future, raises interesting issues about the relationship between the development of technology and ethics. We examine its ethical and philosophical basis.

The future versus us We have looked at the question of prioritising work on far future possibilities, such as the dangers of a superintelligence explosion, over current and nearer and more tangible concerns. The divisions in approach here may seem manageable, given the relatively few resources being applied to research into superintelligence and the potential insights that such research might bring for how we consider more tangible and current uses and abuses of AI. We have seen too, the question of how we might ensure that how AI develops in the future reflects human values now, and the perplexing conundrums that this brings about the soundness of our current values, the concept of continued personal identity, and the prospect for future developments both individual and as a species. Concerns about superintelligence tend to focus upon protecting current human values. Concerns about whether too much attention is spent on fears about superintelligence also focus upon concern for current human difficulties.

What if our whole current take on approaching ethical issues was misguided? Let us consider the thesis of longtermism. This view can be helpful to illustrate some deep divisions in approaches to asking and addressing questions in ethics, especially when considering large-scale questions. It might also lead some of us to wonder, have we been doing ethics completely wrong? In research papers published by the Global Priorities Institute at Oxford University, forms of longtermism have been defended focusing on how a society should spend resources as well as the major life choices of individuals, such as career choice [1]. It is an approach which seems extremely implausible and counterintuitive to many, but which with a few basic premises presents calculations which, if accepted, would radically alter society's resource allocation. In particular, the authors argue that priority should be given to efforts to prevent the existential risk of humanity dying out and to positively shaping the development of artificial superintelligence. There are many technical aspects to these arguments as well as critiques [80, 81].

Two forms of longtermism are defended: Axiological Strong Longtermism (ASL), which holds that for agents making important decisions, every near-best option is the one that is near-best for the far future and by a considerable margin over concern for the near future. ('Near-best' allows for a degree of uncertainty about outcomes and assessments.) Deontic Strong Longtermism (DSL) concerns what one ought to do, which is to choose options that produce much larger benefits in the far future than in the near future.

It is assumed that in the future, there will be a vast number of expected lives of sentient beings. Figures mentioned project that there will be a further 10^{14} human beings born until the earth is no longer inhabitable (although the reader may have spotted that evolution may have got in the way and our descendants far into the future may no longer be recognised as *homo sapiens*; the focus is on sentient beings), and potentially 10^{24} if humans manage to spread out into space. A second assumption is that we can effectively act in ways that will predictably improve the far future, for example, backing research into ways to prevent an extinction-level asteroid from crashing into Earth.

The basic reasoning behind this is mathematical. The argument is consequential-ist and additive in form. From these premises, it is concluded that we can produce far more value in the world in total if we focus on ensuring that the far future goes well with as many sentient beings in the universe as possible. Indeed, it is argued that the difference is so vast that even if we have a small probability of success, if we could make an incremental impact on the number of sentient beings and the value in the world, this is the best option. This does not mean we should neglect current issues entirely; ordinary people can live their lives fairly normally, but in terms of resource allocation, this might make a major difference. For example, one might decide to focus upon preventing population-level threats to fertility and threats from extinction-level pandemics but put less effort into treating rare genetic diseases. One might focus on averting nuclear catastrophe, and this could have a major impact on foreign policy, and so on.

Exercise 19
Consider some of the instances of the use of AI that we have considered or any particular examples that you wish. How might ethical assessment of the issues shift if the main focus was on the far future, with an emphasis on long-term survival of the human race/sentient beings?

The very possibility of powerful technologies may profoundly shape and change moral priorities and even how we approach ethical theories. Readers will have noted that the contrast with other approaches to ethics is very pronounced. The arguments essentially require the capacity to have some chance of positively impacting the future, which means sophisticated and powerful technologies, includ-ing artificial intelligence. Without these, the projected calculations simply would not work. Hence, this argument may demonstrate a profound way in which the very possibility of technology—including technologies not yet developed and about which there is considerable concern—impacts ethics, rather than vice versa. Does focusing on the future possibilities of technology awaken us to these values, or does it distort our value system?

Much could be said and readers will doubtless by now have considerable capacity to ask appropriate questions and provide critical assessment, positive or negative. Let us end this chapter by raising a few salient issues.

Sentient beings: there is no assumption that the future beings that are the putative objects of our moral concern are human; they are 'sentient beings'. There is also an assumption that the more sentient beings there are, the more value there will be in the world. However, *mere* sentience is a fairly low bar. Note that it also assumes clear differentiation between such beings, which is essential for to be able to count them.

The location of value: recall our discussion of the agent neutrality of consequen-tialism and the questions around the value of persons and the distribution of happiness or welfare that it raised. Do we value beings per se, in and of themselves, or only insofar as they are containers of value?

A maximising assumption is present that our duties now are to maximise value, wherever and whenever it exists, rather than to any immediate or personal commitment. A maximising assumption may look obvious until one considers the costs of implementing it, when the question becomes more nuanced.

Moral imagination or maths: there are assumptions about moral epistemology and how we form the basis for our moral decisions. The focus upon societal resource allocation might be seen to justify this, since there could be scope for more personal interactions and judgements in the remainder of life. What would it be like to live a life intentionally ignoring the moral demands and pleas of one's fellows in favour of 10^{24} 'sentient beings'? (Who can even imagine 10^{24}?)

In the next chapter, we will explore further ideas about the future trajectory of the world and of artificial intelligence. This will expose some similarities and some marked differences in theoretical assumptions and ethical questions. Before you read on, you may find it useful to consider the points above and review material from earlier in the book which might help to.

Exercise 20

Consider the key elements found in codes of ethics for AI as discussed in Chap. 2: freedom and autonomy, transparency and explanation, justice and fairness, beneficence and nonmaleficence, responsibility, privacy, sustainability, dignity, and solidarity.

10.6   Key Points

The question of control in AI concerns both how we may control AI and how AI may control us. The control question appears in many guises when considering the ethics of AI. We have seen here its relation to formal properties of AI as well as in minute details of context.

Examining the control questions in one context may shed some light upon the control problem in other contexts, even if these at first sight appear rather different.

Assessing the benefits of using AI in any situation will require a close comparison of human and machine agency and capabilities.

Placing AI into a complex system such as a workplace will require careful analysis of the tasks involved. This will require not simply technical expertise or superficial understanding of what is required; it can be very advantageous to consider different perspectives of those involved. In many contexts, subject matter expertise and close research may also assist.

Many of the ethical questions of AI concern information and its flow and raise complex issues of surveillance and of the transparency with which AI and the system within which it is nested operate.

Examination of questions in AI ethics impacting the future can reveal questions about the very nature of AI, the foundations of ethics, and the boundaries of ethics with questions of religion, spirituality, and meaning.

Attempting to address questions such as the problem of superintelligence is never merely technical but involves choice, value, and supervenes on philosophical questions.

10.7 Educator Notes

The material in this chapter will be consolidating the more theoretical material from earlier in the book. Working through the topics and issues discussed here can be a very good chance to test and expand students' knowledge and understanding of ethical theories and concepts. Although many of the exercises can be approached from many different angles and may incite wide-ranging discussion, students should be encouraged to ensure that they do also draw upon and refer to previous material. Conversely, students should be encouraged to explore how questions in ethics and philosophy may be relevant to dialogues with other disciplines on these topics.

Although this chapter is not primarily intended for use as stand-alone material, there are plentiful references back to earlier material as relevant, and it may hence still be useful for students who have not studied the earlier part of the course and wish to examine cases of AI ethics in context.

Although here we concentrate on two issues, work and superintelligence, there are many issues raised that generalise. For instance, the material looking at how to analyse what task is being undertaken in the workplace can readily be generalised to inform ways of analysing any use of AI, although the strategies raised are not intended to act as a strict formula but rather as general guidance.

Many of the topics and exercises can be approached in very different ways, especially as the topic of work intersects with so many questions in economic and the social sciences, as well as raising issues around the value of creativity, and the topic of superintelligence exposes clear foundational issues in computing and in ethics. For instance, students in computing may wish to explore more technical aspects of superintelligence and the nature of intelligence, those with backgrounds in social science and humanities may wish to consider the questions that arise about how we understand others and attribute preferences and values, and others may wish to apply their knowledge of others and may wish to explore fears and dangers of superintelligence through science fiction.

Debate topics and extended projects or essays Several of the exercises involve complex questions that would form a good basis for class debate or group work where students with different disciplinary backgrounds could each contribute different perspectives. Exercises that may produce useful classroom debates include 6, 7, 8, 10, 11, and 18. Some exercises would work well as the basis for detailed essays or group projects requiring further research, including 2, 4, and 5.

Acknowledgements This chapter was partially funded by the National Institute for Health Research, Health Services and Delivery Research Programme (project number 13/10/80). The views expressed are those of the author and not necessarily those of the NIHR or the Department of Health and Social Care.

References

1. Greaves H, MacAskill W (2019) The case for strong longtermism. Global Priorities Institute, Oxford University, Oxford
2. Skilton M, Hovsepian F (2018) The 4th industrial revolution. Springer, Cham
3. Frey CB, Osborne MA (2017) The future of employment: how susceptible are jobs to computerisation? Technol Forecast Soc Chang 114:254–280
4. Westlake S (ed) (2014) Our work here is done: visions of a robot economy. NESTA, London
5. Goos M (2018) The impact of technological Progress on labour markets: policy challenges. Oxf Rev Econ Policy 34(3):362–375
6. Schwab K (2017) The fourth industrial revolution. Currency, New York
7. Brynjolfsson E, McAfee A (2014) The second machine age: work, progress, and prosperity in a time of brilliant technologies. WW Norton & Company, New York
8. Ford M (2015) Rise of the robots: technology and the threat of a jobless future. Basic Books, New York
9. Danaher J (2019) Automation and utopia: human flourishing in a world without work. Harvard University Press, Cambridge, MA
10. Rid T (2016) Rise of the machines. Scribe Publications, Brunswick, Victoria
11. Ura K, Alkire S, Zangmo T, Wangdi K (2012) A short guide to gross national happiness index. Centre for Bhutan Studies, Thimphu
12. Crawford K (2021) The atlas of AI. Yale University Press, New Haven
13. Taylor L, Sharma G, Martin A, Jameson S (eds) (2020) Data justice and COVID-19 global perspectives. Meatspace Press, London
14. Topol EJ (2019) High-performance medicine: the convergence of human and artificial intelligence. Nat Med 25(1):44–56
15. Erickson BJ, Korfiatis P, Akkus Z, Kline TL (2017) Machine learning for medical imaging. Radiographics 37(2):505
16. Featherstone K, Northcott A (2021) Wandering the wards: an ethnography of hospital care and its consequences for people living with dementia. Taylor & Francis, London
17. Bloss R (2011) Mobile hospital robots cure numerous logistic needs. Ind Robot 38:567
18. Bridges J, Nicholson C, Maben J, Pope C, Flatley M, Wilkinson C, Meyer J, Tziggili M (2013) Capacity for care: meta-ethnography of acute care nurses' experiences of the nurse-patient relationship. J Adv Nurs 69(4):760–772
19. Williams S, Nolan M, Keady J (2009) Relational practice as the key to ensuring quality care for frail older people: discharge planning as a case example. Qual Ageing Older Adults 10:44
20. Catchpole KR, De Leval MR, McEwan A, Pigott N, Elliott MJ, McQuillan A, Macdonald C, Goldman AJ (2007) Patient handover from surgery to intensive care: using formula 1 pit-stop and aviation models to improve safety and quality. Pediatr Anesth 17(5):470–478
21. Thomas RG (2020) Whistleblowing and power: a network perspective. Bus Ethics Eur Rev 29(4):842–855
22. Marmot M, Wilkinson R (eds) (2005) Social determinants of health. Oxford University Press, Oxford
23. Lloyd J, Schneider J, Scales K, Bailey S, Jones R (2011) In-group identity as an obstacle to effective multidisciplinary teamworking: findings from an ethnographic study of healthcare assistants in dementia care. J Interprof Care 25(5):345–351
24. Featherstone K, Northcott A, Boddington P, Edwards D, Vougioukalou S, Bale S, Dening KH, Logan K, Tope R, Kelly D, Jones A (2022) Findings from mixed-methods review and thematic

synthesis. In: Understanding approaches to continence care for people living with dementia in acute hospital settings: an ethnographic study, vol 10. National Institute for Health and Care Research, Southampton, p 1

25. Glaser B, Strauss A (1967) The discovery of grounded theory. Strategies for qualitative research, vol 17. London, Weidenfeld and Nicholson, p 364

26. Greenhaigh T, Swinglehurst D (2011) Studying technology use as social practice: the untapped potential of ethnography. BMC Med 9(1):45. https://doi.org/10.1186/1741-7015-9-45

27. Hammersley M, Atkinson P (1995) Ethnography: practices and principles. Routledge, London

28. Northcott A, Boddington P, Featherstone K (2022) Pad cultures: an ethnography of continence care and its consequences for people living with dementia during a hospital admission. Dementia 21(7):2191–2209

29. Graeber D (2019) Bullshit jobs: the rise of pointless work, and what we can do about it. Penguin, London

30. Vahey DC, Aiken LH, Sloane DM, Clarke SP, Vargas D (2004) Nurse burnout and patient satisfaction. Med Care 42(2 Suppl):II57

31. O'Neil C (2016) Weapons of math destruction: how big data increases inequality and threatens democracy. Broadway Books, New York

32. Twigg J (2000) Carework as a form of bodywork. Ageing Soc 20(4):389–411

33. Ashforth BE, Kreiner GE (1999) "How can you do it?": dirty work and the challenge of constructing a positive identity. Acad Manag Rev 24(3):413–434

34. Simpson R, Simpson A (2018) "Embodying" dirty work: a review of the literature. Sociol Compass 12(6):e12581

35. Bolton SC (2005) Women's work, dirty work: the gynaecology nurse as 'other'. Gend Work Organ 12(2):169–186

36. Daykin N, Clarke B (2000) 'They'll still get the bodily care'. Discourses of care and relationships between nurses and health care assistants in the NHS. Sociol Health Illn 22(3):349–363

37. Boddington P, Featherstone K, Northcott A (2021) Presentation of the clothed self on the hospital ward: an ethnographic account of perceptual attention and implications for the personhood of people living with dementia. Med Humanit 47(2):e3

38. Featherstone K, Gregory M, Atkinson P (2006) The moral and sentimental work of the clinic: the case of genetic syndromes. In: New genetics, new identities. Routledge, London, pp 113–131

39. MacKenzie D, Wajcman J (1999) The social shaping of technology. Open University Press, Buckingham

40. Coronado-Hernandez JR, Calderón-Ochoa AF, Portnoy I, Morales-Mercado J (2021, October) Comparison between Amazon go stores and traditional retails based on queueing theory. In: Workshop on engineering applications. Springer, Cham, pp 347–361

41. Urbina F, Lentzos F, Invernizzi C, Ekins S (2022) Dual use of artificial-intelligence-powered drug discovery. Nat Mach Intell 4(3):189–191

42. Hao K (2020) Machine learning could check if you're social distancing at work properly. MIT Tech Review, 17 Apr 2020. https://www.technologyreview.com/2020/04/17/1000092/ai-machine-learning-watches-social-distancing-at-work/

43. Jamjoom AAB, Jamjoom AMA, Marcus HJ (2020) Exploring public opinion about liability and responsibility in surgical robotics. Nat Mach Intell 2:194–196

44. Wisskirchen G, Biacabe BT, Bormann U, Muntz A, Niehaus G, Soler GJ, von Brauchitsch B (2017) Artificial intelligence and robotics and their impact on the workplace. IBA Global 11(5): 49–67

45. Char DS, Shah NH, Magnus D (2018) Implementing machine learning in health care— addressing ethical challenges. N Engl J Med 378(11):981

46. Zollman KJ (2010) The epistemic benefit of transient diversity. Erkenntnis 72(1):17

47. Singh K, Woodward MA (2021) The rigorous work of evaluating consistency and accuracy in electronic health record data. JAMA Ophthalmol 139(8):894–895

48. Chesler P (2018) Women and madness. Chicago Review Press, Chicago

49. Morris W (1893) Useful work versus useless toil. Hammersmith Socialist Society, London. http://morrisedition.lib.uiowa.edu/MorrisPamphletEssay.pdf
50. Ruskin J (1904) Work. In: The crown of wild olive: four lectures on industry and war. George Allen, London
51. Marx K (1858) Fragment on machines. In: The Grundrisse. New Left Review, London, pp 690–712. http://thenewobjectivity.com/pdf/marx.pdf
52. MacCarthy F (2015) William Morris: a life for our time. Faber & Faber, London
53. Frey CB (2019) The technology trap: capital, labour, and power in the age of automation. Princeton University Press, Princeton, NJ
54. Giorgi L, Marsh C (1990) The Protestant work ethic as a cultural phenomenon. Eur J Soc Psychol 20(6):499–517
55. Kant I, Paton HJ (1964) Groundwork of the metaphysic of morals (translated and analysed by HJ Paton). Harper & Row, Manhattan
56. Turing A (2004) Can digital computers think? (1951). In: Copeland BJ (ed) The essential turing. Oxford Academic Press, Oxford
57. Wiener N (1954) The human use of human beings. Free Association, London
58. Good IJ (1966) Speculations concerning the first ultraintelligent machine. In: Advances in computers, vol 6. Elsevier, Amsterdam, pp 31–88
59. Bostrom N (2017) Superintelligence: paths, dangers, strategies. Dunod, Paris
60. Russell S (2019) Human compatible: artificial intelligence and the problem of control. Penguin, London
61. Kelly K (2017) The myth of a superhuman AI. Wired, 25 Apr
62. Garling C (2015) Andrew Ng: why deep learning is a mandate for humans, not just machines. https://www.wired.com/brandlab/2015/05/andrew-ng-deep-learning-mandate-humans-not-just-machines/
63. Stone P, Brooks R, Brynjolfsson E, Calo R, Etzioni O, Hager G, Hirschberg J, Kalyanakrishnan S, Kamar E, Kraus S, Leyton-Brown K (2016) Artificial intelligence and life in 2030: the one hundred year study on artificial intelligence
64. Bostrom N (2013) Existential risk prevention as global priority. Global Pol 4(1):15–31
65. Ledford H (2019) Millions of black people affected by racial bias in health-care algorithms. Nature 574(7780):608–610
66. Simonite T (2020) How an algorithm blocked kidney transplants to black patients. Wired. https://www.wired.com/story/how-algorithm-blocked-kidney-transplants-black-patients/
67. von Goethe JW (1797) The sorcerer's apprentice (Der Zauberlehrling)
68. Turteltaub J (2010) The sorcerer's apprentice. Walt Disney Productions
69. Bostrom N (2012) The Superintelligent will: motivation and instrumental rationality in advance artificial agents. Mind Mach 22(2):71–85
70. Jowett B (ed) (1888) Plato: the republic of Plato. Clarendon Press, Oxford
71. Sayre-McCord G (2021) Moral Realism. In: Zalta EN (ed) The Stanford encyclopedia of philosophy, Summer 2021 edn. Stanford University, Stanford. https://plato.stanford.edu/archives/sum2021/entries/moral-realism/
72. Soares N, Fallenstein B (2014) Aligning superintelligence with human interests: a technical research agenda. Machine Intelligence Research Institute (MIRI) technical report, 8
73. Danaher J (2015) Why AI doomsayers are like sceptical theists and why it matters. Mind Mach 25(3):231–246
74. Armstrong S (2013) General purpose intelligence: arguing the orthogonality thesis. Anal Metaphys 12(68):1–20
75. Davidson D (2001) How is weakness of the will possible? (1969) In Davidson D Essays on actions and events: philosophical essays 1. Clarendon Press, Oxford
76. Nozick R (1974) Anarchy, state, and utopia. Basic Books, New York
77. Mill JS (1863) Utilitarianism. Parker, Son and Bourn, London

78. Lewis JE, Arista N, Pechawis A, Kite S (2018) Making kin with the machines. J Design Sci. https://doi.org/10.21428/bfafd97b
79. Crisp R (ed) (2014) Aristotle: nicomachean ethics. Cambridge University Press, Cambridge
80. Tarsney C (2019) The epistemic challenge to longtermism. Global Priorities Institute Working Paper 3-222. https://globalprioritiesinstitute.org/christian-tarsney-the-epistemic-challenge-to-longtermism/
81. Torres P (2021) Against longtermism. Aeon, 19 Oct 2021. https://aeon.co/essays/why-longtermism-is-the-worlds-most-dangerous-secular-credo

Further Reading

Work

Aloisi A, Gramano E (2019) Artificial intelligence is watching you at work: digital surveillance, employee monitoring, and regulatory issues in the EU context. Comp Labor Law Policy J 41:95
Brynjolfsson E, McAfee A (2014) The second machine age: work, progress, and prosperity in a time of brilliant technologies. WW Norton & Company, New York
Crawford K (2021) The atlas of AI. Yale University Press, New Haven
Danaher J (2019) Automation and utopia: human flourishing in a world without work. Harvard University Press, Cambridge, MA
Ford M (2015) Rise of the robots: technology and the threat of a jobless future. Basic Books, New York
Frey CB (2019) The technology trap: capital, labour, and power in the age of automation. Princeton University Press, Princeton, NJ
Frey CB, Osborne M (2015) Technology at work: the future of innovation and employment. Citi GPS, Oxford
Frey CB, Osborne MA (2017) The future of employment: how susceptible are jobs to computerisation? Technol Forecast Soc Chang 114:254–280
Graeber D (2019) Bullshit jobs: the rise of pointless work, and what we can do about it. Penguin, London
Moradi P, Levy K (2020) The future of work in the age of AI. In: The Oxford handbook of ethics of AI. Oxford University Press, Oxford, pp 269–288
Morris W (1893) Useful work versus useless toil. Hammersmith Socialist Society, London http://morrisedition.lib.uiowa.edu/MorrisPamphletEssay.pdf
Noble DF (1995) Progress without people: new technology, unemployment, and the message of resistance. Between the Lines, Toronto
Pasquale F (2020) New laws of robotics: defending human expertise in the age of AI. Belknap Press, Cambridge, MA
Rid T (2016) Rise of the machines. Scribe Publications, Melbourne
Ruskin J (1904) Work. In: The crown of wild olive: four lectures on industry and war. George Allen, London
Westlake S (ed) (2014) Our work here is done: visions of a robot economy. NESTA, London
Willcocks L (2020) Robo-apocalypse cancelled? Reframing the automation and future of work debate. J Inf Technol 35(4):286–302

Superintelligence

Armstrong S (2013) General purpose intelligence: arguing the orthogonality thesis. Anal Metaphys 12(68):1–20

Bostrom N (2012) The Superintelligent will: motivation and instrumental rationality in advance artificial agents. Mind Mach 22(2):71–85

Bostrom N (2017) Superintelligence: paths, dangers, strategies. Dunod, Paris

Danaher J (2015) Why AI doomsayers are like sceptical theists and why it matters. Mind Mach 25(3):231–246

Russell S (2019) Human compatible: artificial intelligence and the problem of control. Penguin, London

Wallach W (2015) A dangerous master: how to keep technology from slipping out of our control. Basic Books, New York

Yampolskiy RV (2015) Artificial superintelligence: a futuristic approach. CRC Press, Boca Raton

Chapter 11
Our Future with AI: Future Projections and Moral Machines

Abstract This chapter continues our discussion of how we might live with machines in the far future. Certain views of technological progress and of the future of artificial intelligence discussed here rest upon an implicitly teleological view of the universe. This provides points of contrast and comparison with the ethical theories and conceptions of intelligence underlying the responses to superintelligence examined in the last chapter. We then discuss views of human nature, the foundations of ethics, and the nature and value of intelligence. These discussions also raise the question of how humans and AI relate to each other, and the second part of this chapter explores this topic directly, looking at our moral obligations to machines, if any, and at whether human enhancement via machines might be possible, focusing on the question of whether machines might be able to enhance us morally. Addressing this question requires that we again pay attention to different accounts of how ethical judgements and action are understood and again make close comparison of human and machine agency. We especially highlight issues in moral epistemology and capacities of intelligent machines to gather and analyse knowledge, in comparison to humans, and in relation to the particular case of moral judgements.

Keywords Superintelligence · Moral machines · Human enhancement · Moral status · Moral epistemology

11.1 Introduction

We will start this chapter by exploring how AI may develop in the far future, taking us beyond the control problem of superintelligence into visions of how the development of AI might fulfil an unfolding purpose, and how we might develop alongside AI, or how AI might develop in ways that leave us behind as a mere passing phase of the universe. From fear of superintelligence to hopes for it, and even to visions of glory. This discussion is a continuation of the last chapter, showing some rather contrasting ways of looking at our future with AI; it also links to the following sections of this chapter, where we ask a range of questions about how humans and machines might relate to each other. This question is implicit within discussions of the far future with AI, since we are forced to confront the question of who we might become given certain scenarios regarding the nature of technology and its control over us and the world. On some visions of the future with technology, humans themselves may greatly change, or even cease to exist in any recognisable form; not only is the question of the battle for control, the 'us versus the machine' scenarios, and what attitudes we might have towards this, at issue. Artificial intelligence may be visioned as a mere tool, something to fulfil our wants and needs, or as some goal towards we wish to shape ourselves, a superior version of us.

The chapter then turns to look directly at questions about how we should relate to AI, including but not limited to robots, and how AI might relate to us, possibly acting to enhance us, to make us better people. In answering this, we will again be expanding upon and consolidating material concerning ethical theory, questions of human nature, and looking at what precise capabilities artificial intelligence might have in comparison with the abilities of humans. We will have to consider the question of what a moral question is and how suited artificial intelligence might be for addressing questions of value. We will also have to consider whether what we think of now as 'ethics' could feasibly assess some far future projected possibilities.

What Concepts and Tools Can We Bring to These Questions?
We will be looking again at some fundamental questions in ethics. This means we will overview topics from across several previous chapters. We need to consider the elements of moral agency and of what it is to be a moral patient, of which there are different accounts. We will need to consider the fundamental basis of morality and whether human beings, and even whether persons, are of ultimate value, or whether something else is, and indeed, whether humans are the source of value. We will consider the value of knowledge and of intelligence and whether there is any meaning and purpose in the universe or whether it is inert and without inherent value. This will involve careful comparison of humans with machines, including our biological substrate and the nature of our boundaries and limits, and of human moral weaknesses. We will also consider the concept of progress, both moral and techno-logical. As we saw in the last chapter, many of these questions in ethics start to merge with religious or spiritual attitudes towards the universe, its destiny, and our destiny.

11.2   The Purposeful Universe: Value Beyond the Human

Summary
We examine Max Tegmark's account of the possible development of AI and of the universe as progressing with purpose towards an increasing awakening of awareness and greater intelligence as life passes through different stages to develop the capacity to redesign its own software and hardware. Tegmark proposes a growing value in the universe that is conceived of in a way wider than simply ethical value but includes

aesthetic and epistemic elements and may differ considerably from many conceptions of ethics per se. In such an account, humans have a pivotal role in bringing forth the future value of the universe.

We will examine aspects of Max Tegmark's book *Life 3.0* for an example of a vision of the development of AI and the possible futures of the human race, a view that incorporates a number of interesting value and metaphysical claims that provide some illuminating contrast to other accounts, such as those of Bostrom and Russell [1]. Tegmark is, in common with them, concerned about possible future disaster, both natural and man-made, although, in his book, he also shares with readers some wonderful and wild scenarios of a future universe teeming with possibility and value, thanks to advancing technology. Opinions on these scenarios may differ wildly.

Of course many working in technology are motivated to use it to improve the world for the better. (I do not include all working in technology in this bracket by any means; some are clearly in it just for the money, some for nefarious means, some haven't given the matter much thought, and so on.) However, one might make certain distinctions between the nature of the improvements that are foreseen. Some are incremental and aimed at solving discrete problems, perhaps envisaging a world more or less like this one, but without its major problems, or with problems reduced. Recall our previous discussions concerning the different issues in AI: some concern the minute technical details of how AI operates and the context in which it is applied; some concern imaginative and ideologically infused ideas of how AI might help us towards some vision of progress, whether disastrous or glorious. Recall how artificial intelligence was envisaged as potentially able to end war, poverty, and disease, and other clearly identified practical issues (see Sect. 5.2.5). This is small fry compared to other narratives of the future that envisage radical change, including radical change in who we are.

Numerous people describe and advocate such positions. We have already mentioned Donna Haraway's Cyborg Manifesto [2]. Martine Rothblatt founded the Terasem Movement, a group of organisations keen on the idea of achieving human immortality by uploading human consciousness to a computer [3]. (One hopes the computers in question are more robust than the average laptop, which has a life expectancy of 3–5 years.) Ray Kurzweil, who has worked extensively in AI, including in speech recognition, has written extensively on visions for the future, which also include the idea that life extension can be achieved by uploading to a computer, merging with a machine [4–6]. These views present me with the perennial problem throughout this book: too much interesting stuff to include. So let us just look at one account.

Tegmark presents various future possibilities in his book. Something which makes it of interest to us is the manner in which it lays out a framework for the value of, quite literally, the entire cosmos. The root source of value is the 'awakening' that occurs when parts of the universe become aware: the universe, or part of it, becomes aware of itself. We human beings are part of the universe: we are aware of (aspects of) our environment. This value is not explicitly *ethical* in form (notwithstanding the difficulties in precisely defining the domain of ethics); Tegmark speaks of it as beauty and describes the capacity to reflect on the wonders that there are to see in the universe but also talks of purpose, goals, and meaning. There is, as it were, a two-tier aspect to the emerging value in the universe: its general capacity towards greater complexity and the production of life with consciousness, goals, and purposes, as well as the purposeful activity of that life itself in structuring and influencing the trajectory of the future. It is noteworthy that Tegmark expresses concern early in the book about the calamitous possibility that the universe might lose this self-awareness, which would render it meaningless [1, p. 23]. He also envisages that the universe may 'wake up' more fully, perhaps like a dozy teenager being roused from bed, or a bored suburban housewife from middle America who runs off to New York City and from there to an ashram in the foothills of the Himalayas. Waking up more fully may involve deepening levels of awareness and may be imagined as intelligent life spreading out into the universe beyond our tiny planet and flourishing for billions of years.

Intelligence is thus a critical aspect of this value but also self-reflection, the capacity to contemplate, to appreciate beauty, to value knowledge, and a sense of purpose and meaning are needed. The view here is perhaps akin to the views of philosophers such as Plato and Aristotle (see Chaps. 5 and 6), who both valued the life of the intellect and valued contemplation. In Aristotle's work, we clearly saw a teleological account of human purposes, and teleology embedded in the natural world. One might perhaps see Tegmark as reading such views back into a model of the construction of the universe derived from contemporary physics (he is a cosmologist by background).

Tegmark explains his picture of this evolution of value in the world through dividing life into three stages. Life 1.0 began simply with creatures such as bacteria, complex creatures whose complexity can be maintained, and who can reproduce and pass this complexity on. What is passed on is not the brute matter but the information. The capabilities of Life 1.0 are simply the result of processes of evolution. Bacteria do not themselves decide to multiply let alone decide to form an attractive pattern in a Petri dish. Yet Life 2.0—us—has reached the cultural stage. Our hardware is mostly the product of evolution (surgical bits and pieces excepted), but culture and language have enabled us to design and plan what we do. This enables great improvements in intelligence, enabling us to accelerate past the slow, incremental, trial-and-error development of evolution. Not only can we learn in our lifetimes, we learn from others, rely upon their knowledge and skills, and pass this on to succeeding generations, but our biological hardware is seen as limiting life. Life 3.0 will be life that has reached the technological stage. It can redesign not just its own software but also its own hardware. This will enable rapid change. This change will enable the creation of greater value in the form of intelligent, aware entities and amounts to progress over Life 2.0. Since Life 3.0 will be able to replicate itself rapidly and to improve, the expansion of value in the universe could be truly immense. Note how value is counted: it is accumulative but also concerned with complexity and with increasing the profundity with which it is manifest.

The good, the true, the beautiful   The model is one of purpose and progress, but this is not necessarily explicitly 'ethical'. Note how value is intimately linked with aesthetics, the appreciation of beauty, and with knowledge and understanding: the inclusion of reflection and appreciation for the wonders of the universe means that it is not simply raw data, or information, which is valued, nor is there a purely instrumental account of the value of knowledge. We discussed how precisely to categorise the boundaries of ethics earlier (see Sect. 1.10). In many modern ways of understanding this, there is a tripartite division: what is good, what is beautiful, what is true. Ethics deals with what is good; on many accounts, the prime or only focus is on humans; the extension out to other entities emerges, broadly, from finding that the foundations of ethical theory force this outward 'expanding circle' of concern (see Sect. 4.3). Ethics also typically deals with questions of welfare or wellbeing, with goals articulated around what is seen to lead to this for humans, such as allowing autonomy and respecting preferences.

However, a broader conception of 'the good' has often been drawn. The connection of ethics and beauty, and the value given to conceptual and intellectual understanding, makes a link with the Greeks philosophers who saw contemplation as the highest form of life and note also that Aristotle's notion of the goal of what we call 'ethics' was a life lived well overall. The debate between Bentham and Mill on higher and lower pleasures is also telling (see Sect. 2.5.2). Mill's higher pleasures require the capacity to appreciate art, culture, and knowledge; Bentham made no such division. For that very reason, some dismiss Mill as an elitist, a snob, while others consider it was Bentham who was simply blind to sources of value.

Biology and constraints   It is obviously true that biology constrains. We can only see a small part of the spectrum of light; we can only hold so many things in our working memory at a time; few people over middle age can hear bats. The list of constraints would be depressing if I continued further. The limits of our scientific and factual understanding of the world are also apparent. Hopes of transcending this abound in human thought: consider, for one example out of many, Plato's Theory of Forms and the idea that through contemplation philosophers could achieve understanding of how things truly are. We have also noted how on some accounts, value may be found precisely within the limits of our biology, whether collectively or individually (see Sects. 5.4.4 and 7.2.4). We touch on this topic again later, when considering the potential for AI to assist us with moral decisions and to improve us as moral agents. Indeed, the intricate connections between our embodied beings with their particular biologies and our understandings of morality, various as they are, are one of the very factors that make reflecting on and evaluating future prospects for humanity that radically alter our biology and our biological relationships with each other or even transcend our biology entirely, so complex and so fascinating. Let us take a brief detour with an introduction to transhumanism.

Transhumanism and Posthumanism

It is hard to give a precise definition of transhumanism since it encompasses a wide variety of aims, philosophies, and methodologies, but it can broadly be thought of as the loosely connected movement which aims to apply technology to extend and enhance human lives in one way or another, but in ways generally understood as exceeding the 'ordinary' aims of medicine, education, or conventional social methods. Hence, for example, it does not merely aim to prevent and cure life-limiting disease: it aims to extend the 'natural' human lifespan, among other aims (which include the age-old quest for immortality). Typical aims include greatly extending human intelligence, sensory perception, and behaviour. Proposals for how to achieve this include biological methods such as using biotechnologies of various sorts to reverse or prevent aging and improve cognitive functioning. Proposed methods may also include nonbiological technologies, such as implants and other devices, which extend sensory perception, strength, cognitive functioning, and memory, or indeed, the prospect of replacing humans entirely with computing technologies. The rise in transhumanism is thus associated with developments in science and technology which enable such projected visions, including the more fanciful suggestions, of which there are plenty. There are clear links with eugenics movements.

Transhumanism generally conceives of a continuation of the human race with radical improvements yet still biologically based, with an imagined continuum between transhumanist futures and current human beings. Posthumanism and its difference from transhumanism is also hard to define precisely, but projects a future where humans will 'escape' their biology using technology to become, or be succeeded by, posthumans who will no longer be recognisably human, but will nonetheless be beings with worthwhile lives [7–9].

Future lives, future values It is thus an essential aspect of transhumanism that it aims to extend or surpass human nature. Many see no intrinsic value in 'the natural'. Yet, in asserting that proposals for change are indeed enhancements, some clear notion of value must be applied. This implicitly values the natural and finds it wanting, but in some instances, may actually project from what is found of value in the natural and aim to increase this value; in this way, it may be grounded in some appreciation of natural value. In proposing radical changes to human biology, whether by the use of AI technologies or not, transhumanism could be said to treat the human body as a form of Standing Reserve, as resource material to be moulded at will, and hence to regard the body as a machine that we occupy rather than as constitutive of what we are. There is obviously much that could be said about transhumanism and posthumanism, with many varied and colourful proponents.

Those who have worked through (at least some of) the book should have plenty of ideas and material from which to formulate questions and critical assessments.

Exercise 1

How would you begin to assess whether radical changes to human beings were *enhancements* or simply changes?

If we accept the goals of transhumanism and/or posthumanism, do we have to reject any ethical theories based upon ideas of nature, of function, or of purpose in the world?

What might ground a claim that a transhumanist or posthumanist life was worthwhile? On what basis might it be claimed that it was more worthwhile than current human life?

Are there any essential elements of human beings that would have to remain in order for a transhumanist or posthumanist life to be one of value?

What questions need to be asked about continuing personal identity and the criteria by which we identify others and see ourselves as the same, despite changes?

In thinking about these questions, you may wish to revise material in Chaps. 3, 5, and 8, as well as thinking in general about the ethical theories we have explored.

Now to return to Life 3.0.

Is there purpose in the universe?   Tegmark's book can easily be read as imposing a teleological conception onto the universe, which many automatically reject, regardless of the particularities of an account of purpose. Those rejecting any notion of implicit purpose may make claims such as these: The universe around us should be observed impartially, and we should attempt to understand it as it is seen, not superimposing some ideology or agency on it. We simply see bacteria emerge, then multicellular organisms, then creatures such as mammals, then primates, then humans. The chronological order should not be confused with a progress in value. Purpose only comes from us: we use things and design things for certain purposes. That's it. The universe is inert, it just happens.

One could reply that something akin to Tegmark's conclusions simply follow from his account of value: not merely that it implies that it is good to produce more value but because awareness is key to value. Awareness can admit of complexity, yet the current level of awareness we humans have is limited, as is our capacity to spread value through the universe. Having identified value, it follows from the very account of value that it would be better if the universe moved in certain directions. This is tantamount to identifying something akin to purpose. Indeed, Tegmark talks both about entities that have evolved towards, and which are designed for, a goal.

For comparison, a consequentialist who considered that happiness was a value and that we ought to maximise the amount of happiness in the world would probably have to hold that the best world was one that contained the maximum population consistent with the maximum overall happiness. (How precisely to achieve this indeed raises considerable problems for consequentialism which have been much discussed. The 'repugnant conclusion', so named by Derek Parfit, concerns the problem that if the possible universe with the greatest amount of value in it consisted of one with a very large number of beings each with a barely adequate amount of welfare, this is preferable to a universe of fewer beings who each have much higher welfare, but where the overall value is even marginally lower [10, 11].) Hence, so long as value has been identified correctly, and so long as the very idea of value includes that the more value is realised in the world, the better, then we're away.

Exercise 2
When discussing consequentialism, we considered the broad issue of agent neutrality and asked whether consequentialism might be putting the cart before the horse, in seeing humans (or indeed any entity) as merely vessels or containers for the realisation of value, rather than of value in and of themselves (see Sect. 6.2.5). Consider how future projections of increasing value throughout the universe with the aid of AI might look, if the aim was to increase value per se, or to increase the number of valuable beings.

A role for humans Humans are the only form of life (that we know of) through which technology has come into the universe, which may be capable of improving itself to create self-aware and increasingly intelligent entities. Evolution has more or less done its best. There could be some incremental improvements, but these will never overcome the problems in information processing inherent to biology. Moreover, it may be that we ourselves never colonise space to any great extent: the range of planets our biology would permit us to inhabit is extremely small, for one thing. Nonetheless, we can act as the vehicles through which a greater intelligence could populate the universe more widely, hence spreading greater, and more profound, value.

Exercise 3
We are of limited intelligence. In particular, our intelligence is limited by our biology, yet on Tegmark's account, it is we humans who have identified the nature of value in the world and who have a role in helping to realise this value. We seem to have a dilemma, for might not the limits of our biology also limit and shape our capacity to understand what the value in the universe truly is? Discuss.

There are many possible futures outlined in Tegmark's book. Some are disastrous, on any account. Others are optimistic, on a truly monumental scale, with artificial entities capable of great intelligence populating the cosmos. Tegmark even produces a table indicating the amount of raw matter on Earth that has so far been converted into goal-oriented entities, listed in billions of tons [1, p. 258]. The matter in our built environment is added to the human total, which, given the 100 billion tons of concrete and 20 billion of steel, puts us right up top in the animal league. It is at such points that the ideas may start to seem fanciful, and one might wonder if value has been correctly identified: if it actually requires converting as much brute matter as possible into goal-directed vehicles for awareness and intelligence. How could we assess this ethically? It perhaps seems clear that there are considerable challenges to providing assessments from within many of our current systems.

Exercise 4

Plato's idea that philosophers would be able to contemplate the Forms, giving insight into eternal truths, is, on the one hand, attractive in many ways but, on the other hand, hard to envisage, not least because we ordinary folk have scant idea of what these Forms might truly be like. Consider a universe filled to the maximum with aware, intelligent entities. If value in the universe lies in such awareness and reflection on the wonders of the universe itself, what might 'life' be like in such a vision, taken to extremes? We are in the area of speculation here. This might provoke some interesting thoughts and conversations about value.

Why does this matter? Is this not one man's pet vision? First, it has been a very popular account. Second, as we shall see, it indicates elements of a strong strain of idealistic thought, variably expressed around a discernibly common theme, of progress, the value of intelligence, a world of purpose and meaning, perhaps a yearning that the enterprise of technology is not so far from the enterprise of culture and that we aim for more than simply a better version of our smartphone, an app for this, that, and the other, but we reach for the stars, in whatever way that might manifest itself. It may represent a rebellion against a mundane and merely instrumental idea of intelligence and a prosaic view of the projects of artificial intelligence.

11.3 Contrasting Frameworks Behind Visions of AI and Approaches to Ethics

Summary
We compare and contrast the underlying claims and assumptions behind the different approaches to our future with AI of Russell and Tegmark: if there is any purpose embedded in the world, whether human beings, as they are now, form the grounding basis of value; and whether the central value of concern is explicitly ethical or something broader. Both give some kind of central role to human beings. Their contrasting visions can both be seen as arising from Western traditions of value and hence give rise to the question of how other cultural and value traditions may address such issues.

Stuart Russell and Max Tegmark both have large academic and public profiles in AI. Tegmark is a physicist and cosmologist and heads the Future of Life Institute, which concerns itself with existential risks, including from AI; Russell is on the scientific advisory board. They both work in the USA and indeed have produced joint work in AI ethics [12]. They thus could be seen to represent influential and dominant thinking in this area. Yet analysis of their views reveals some deep fissures and fundamental disagreements of approach. This disagreement is actually rather useful for us, since it demonstrates neatly the need to examine foundational issues regarding the source of value, the nature and value of humanity, and our place in the world.

As we saw in the last chapter, Stuart Russell considers that there is no purpose in the world, that we focus on humans as bearers of value, and indeed, they are also the source of value in the form of their (ordered, 'rational') preferences. They are implicitly the only source of value, since although they may choose to include animals as bearers of value, animals do not get to make such choices. This view of the value of humans also extends far into the future, given Russell's concern for how we might cope long term with the development of superintelligence. There is scant if any sense that now might be time for the superintelligence to take turns at being top dog.

In stark contrast, Tegmark presents a vision that does attribute value and purposes to the universe in the unfolding of increasingly greater awareness and intelligence over billions of years. This presents a very strong teleology; it shows value in the universe not as it is, now, but in its becoming of ever more value. This means that a vast amount of the universe as it is now awaits conversion to this greater purpose; one might say that the universe regards itself as a source of raw material for its own project. The value of humans is transitory; we represent the best thing yet, but we are a step on the way. We have reached the limits of the intelligence created by the forces of biological evolution, but evolution has been canny enough to produce creatures capable of overcoming mere biology and the limits of their own intelligence by creating artificial intelligence that can be reproduced in many forms and that can recursively self-improve.

Debunking or justifying value Let us consider an aspect of the divergence in views on the source of value. Something may explain another thing, or it may *explain it away*. In questions of value, the identification of the underlying source or reason for something may be one which justifies it, or which debunks it. Russell proposes that the source of our values is us, ourselves, and identifies value with our preferences, noting some difficult complexities to this question. Humans simply are the foundation of value, since there is nothing else beyond them. That's where the buck stops. Likewise, an ethic that attempts to be empirically based, such as utilitarianism, places the ultimate source of value on biologically mediated factors such as the experiences of pleasure and pain (see Sect. 6.2.1), which Bentham described in his principle utility thus: 'Nature has placed mankind under the governance of two sovereign masters, pain and pleasure. It is for them alone to point out what we ought to do, as well as to determine what we shall do' [13].

Tegmark sees a problem with at least some human values—that they may be mere products of evolution and hence can be explained away. He considers the prospect that the future may be populated by self-replicating AIs, but not by us, and suggests that a reason for disliking this is fear of death, which evolution found useful to instil in us. The origins of this fear in an evolutionary heuristic device, together with the idea that biological constraints are both transitory and limiting, may lead to the conclusion that fear of death is for the faint-hearted and those behind the times if we consider the timescale of the universe.

Note how vastly different frames of ethics may arise. On one view, human life is the ultimate value, either because humans are valued in and of themselves or because all other values depend upon it: without life, no preferences can be fulfilled, no goals can be met, and no happiness can be experienced. The fear of death is thus not simply a product of evolution but an expression of the value that we accord to life. That's why the right to life is the primary right and murder the most heinous crime. Of course, one might also value life but have overcome the existential dread that frequently accompanies this fear: that's a different matter, as removing the dread of death in this way does not remove the value of life. On the other view, fear of death is simply some quirk of evolution and shows nothing whatsoever about human value. Paradoxically, Tegmark's view might actually do better than Russell's in insisting that there is meaning in the world, which for many undergirds the sense that life is valuable and worth living.

Exercise 5

Discuss these opposing views of the value of life. (And by the way, please do ensure you continue to think your own life is valuable!)

Include in your consideration those futurists who look to attaining some manner of immortality through uploading minds to machines. Consider too the possibility that this might radically impact how we see ourselves as individuals separate from other minds.

Nonetheless, although humans may be transitory bearers of value, they have a pivotal role in Tegmark's vision; the agents by which the teeming multitudes of self-aware intelligences will come forth. Moreover, despite a seeming attribution of purposes to the universe itself, it is we who are burdened with an immeasurable responsibility, since it could all go wrong, if we design AI badly, or if we wipe ourselves out first. Tegmark considers it highly possible that we are the only intelligent life form in the universe capable of producing advanced technology. It may also be a useful heuristic to consider that this could be the case if it encourages us to be cautious about destroying the life we have here on Earth. We are the guardians of a glorious future, which we are probably not good enough to be included in ourselves. An additional source of precarity is the essential need for awareness in order fully to realise value on Tegmark's account. This leads to the residual worry that whether machines can achieve this awareness depends upon being right about certain views of the mind-body problem and for the possible realisation of sentience in the particular machines that come about. If awareness is needed for value to come into being, the worst future for the universe would be of one filled to the brim with nothing but zombies. If humans were brought along for the ride, they would be some kind of 'awareness archive' forming a safety net perhaps. Perhaps we would become collectors' items and a source of blank, insentient curiosity.

Exercise 6

Should we build into the scenarios that any advanced artificial intelligence should be designed so that it kept some humans alive as pets, as it were, or in some kind of zoo, as a precaution against the zombie problem? How different, if at all, might this strategy be from other approaches to the dangers of superintelligence where the goal is to ensure human survival and flourishing?

The contrast between these two worldviews is striking, yet they can both readily be traced as fitting comfortably into a Western cultural and intellectual history. Russell's view bears characteristic hallmarks of some central strands of Enlightenment thinking: man as the measure of all things, the universe as inert, meaningless, with no inherent purpose or value, apart from the sparks of value-creating beings clinging to a pale blue dot somewhere, the humans [14]. A firm division between fact and value, and the value of intelligence set instrumentally by the goals we put in it.

Tegmark's view bears remarkable parallels with Biblical accounts of creation and humanity's role in it, albeit with certain major differences. The creation account in the first chapter of Genesis is not simply a neutral scientific description of the origins of the world; repeatedly during the 7 days of making the world, God looks at Creation and 'sees that it is good'; the attribution of value to the world comes before the creation of mankind, which is on the sixth day. Adam, the first human, was made in the image of God and given stewardship over the animals. Nonetheless, humanity is fallen, and things quickly go badly wrong. Certain individuals, starting from Abraham, who is promised by God that he and his descendants, the people of Israel, are to be charged with particular responsibilities for setting humanity back on track, are given a mission covering multiple generations. Note that Tegmark even talks about future artificial entities populating the universe as our 'descendants', and note that God promised Abraham that 'I will multiply your offspring as the stars of the sky' (Genesis 26:4) [15].

In Tegmark's account, there is no god, a major difference and one which perhaps owe its origins to the kind of scientific thinking also behind Russell's view. Hence, at the start of the universe, there is no awareness and hence no value in the world. However, humanity is also given a special status and is also seen as a potential source of problem, even disaster; we also share in the universe's awareness and intelligence. Luckily, among humans, there are some who are taking charge of trying to ensure that things go right; the technologists, as a group, might ruin everything, but the good ones among them who also share the universe's view of progress and purpose are attempting to save the day. But unlike in Biblical accounts, our own value is limited. We exist at a pivot point, after which, well, we are only a part of the universe after all. Hence, there is a mixture of humility and hubris in such a vision.

We can thus perhaps see the immense appeal and popularity of both such contrasting imaginative visions of the possible future, since the first fits well with modern dominant, 'sensible', 'rational' ways of seeing the world, and the second fits well with cultural narratives that have endured and influenced thinking for centuries. Both Russell and Tegmark place a very high value on technology. It can also be useful to compare and contrast these modes of thinking in reflecting on what they both have in common and in understanding more fully why other cultures and worldviews may take different approaches. The focus on intelligence and knowledge as values (notwithstanding that intelligence may be given merely instrumental value by some but not by others) and on the great value given to technology is common to both, as is the centrality of humans.

Recall the Indigenous Protocol for Artificial Intelligence Design we met in Sect. 2.9 [16]. Although there are many different indigenous groups, cultures, and languages, some common themes may be shared, among them concern for locality, for relationality and reciprocity, and a radically different notion of the place of the human being in nature and in the world from the positions we have seen above. While recognising the subtleties, differences, and nuances, in broad terms, humans may not be given the same unique and very high status. The world is not seen as a mere resource, and not as inanimate, brute matter. (Although note that Tegmark talks of the universe in general as awakening.) Animals and other creatures are seen as being in relationship with humans within nature, and humans are able to live in reciprocity with them. It has been argued that such attitudes could extend to machines that humans create and live with [17].

Such approaches also place importance on embodiment, the fine details of its nature, its value, and the ways in which it enables us to experience our local place in the world and to interact with others, including animals and the land. Contrast this to the views of embodiment we see often in some popular takes on AI: human embodiment as a hurdle to the realisation of value and as an obstacle to our intelligence, miring us in stupidity and emotion. Such views hold that the mind, consciousness, awareness, intelligence, these things of value, are not essentially related to any particular bodies or material substrate, or indeed, essentially related to any material substrate at all.

However, just as this is of necessity a very brief review of positions, so too, considerable additional nuance and complexity can be added to the two major contrasting views that I extracted from Russell and Tegmark. The idea that humans are made in God's image and that they are masters of the earth and can do what they will with it is often attributed simply and plainly to the Bible and to the Judeo-Christian tradition; we discussed the notion of human dominion over nature earlier in Sect. 3.4. But the very fact that here 'Judeo' and 'Christian' are hyphenated together, plus cursory knowledge of the different forms of both Judaism and Christianity is a clue to the multiple ways in which the role of humans may be understood and in which 'made in God's image' may be understood. Some understand this role as 'dominion' to mean to do as one wills, but it is at any rate clear from the Bible that there are limits on the proper exercise of the human will, and there is a strong tradition that interprets humanity's role as that of stewardship [18], with visions for a future of harmony (see Sect. 3.4 and the future picture of nature seen in the book of Isaiah). Those writing from indigenous perspectives may also place humans as having particular responsibilities. An optimistic view is that, hence, through such points of resonance, joint dialogue, understanding, and programmes of action may be possible.

Recall, too, that although there is a strong tradition within Western ethics of separating fact from value, reason from emotion, and of understanding ethics in terms of abstract and universal rules and principles, notions of reciprocity and accountability to others are also present—indeed, within the key values that we find in codes and regulations for AI. See the value of explainability, transparency, and accountability, as well as of solidarity and sustainability (although both of these may be understood in ways which still see humans as the sole source of value within a world valued only instrumentally).

Recall, in addition, that concern to (some) animals has been an implicit aspect of certain ethical theories. Accounts of ethics based on personhood may include some animal species; accounts based upon the concept of a sentient being may include more (see Chap. 9). Many of these extend moral concern outwards by the application of a principle and may hence be very different in kind and in effect from many indigenous approaches based upon relationality.

Exercise 7

Attempts are being made to use AI to decipher animal language. earthspecies.org is attempting to interpret animal communication using machine learning techniques developed to translate human languages without dictionaries. projectceti.org is attempting to decipher the communications of the sperm whale using machine learning and robotics. Machine learning has been used in attempts to decipher pig calls for their emotional valence [19]. Discuss whether and how such work making use of technologies may impact human-centric views of value.

Consider how different ways of communicating with and interacting with animals may make for different qualities of relationships.

(Compare: your friend uses machine learning to detect from your tone of voice if you are upset; versus, your friend listens intently and knows you so well they can tell straightaway something is up.)

Some who fear superintelligence may picture it as a dystopia in which we are mere servants, pets, or playthings to superintelligence, or in which we are wiped out completely by the monster we have created. Attempts are made to ensure that any future artificial intelligence remains our tool. An alternative picture, however, is a reversal of this. We are the mere tools by which something much better than us emerges in the future. We are the good servant who sacrifices him- or herself for one greater than us. We have seen how it is hard even to make ethical comparisons between contrasting pictures, since they may rest upon fundamentally different accounts of the very nature of ethics. The question remains of what is our relationship to AI—not just to particular instances of it but to AI in general, as an idea and an ideal.

We now ask further questions about the relationships between AI and humans, focusing on questions of how each is valued and on the idea that AI might be used to increase the value of humans.

11.4   The Moral Status of AI and Robot Rights

Summary
Here we consider the challenges of attributing moral status to artificial intelligence, discussing why this may seem more tempting in the case of robots. Various hallmarks of moral status are considered, including intelligence, language, sentience, goals and purposes, and a sense of the self. We also consider the relevance of embodiment for the attribution of an enduring entity with moral status and consider the complex issue of reciprocal relations and recognition of moral status of us by AI and of AI by us.

Could we attribute moral value to any form of AI? To answer this question is, in general, to address what qualities would give an entity rights or make it the recipient of any other level of moral concern. Hence, any answer will depend upon the general approach one takes to central questions in moral philosophy. A secondary question is to address what particular treatment any specific form of AI might deserve and what corresponding responsibilities we might have. Here, we give an overview of issues; the preceding chapters of the book should furnish readers with plentiful material for addressing and arguing the point. Further reading is found at the end of this chapter.

An essential question is the attribution of value to an entity that has been produced by humans, over and above the value it has for humans, in a way that gives this value to the entity itself. The precise manner in which this is meant may be a little hard to articulate. Certain works of art and other cultural artefacts may be thought to have value in themselves on some views, but it is not usually held that the destruction of Botticelli's *The Birth of Venus* would be a moral wrong against the picture itself. The claim we are considering usually seems to attribute some sense in which the AI itself has some opinion on the matter.

Robot rights The question of the value we accord to AI is often phrased in terms of 'robot rights'. This is perhaps telling. It is much easier to envisage that we might give some form of moral value to a robot, first, because they are often made to look a bit 'like us', and second, because they are generally countable individuals, even though, unlike us, they can readily be assembled and disassembled, and, unlike us at the moment, they may be directly connected to a large computing system. We can envisage what it would be to take a robot and physically destroy it; we can more or less start to imagine what it might be to treat it well, often thanks to science fiction as well as to the humanoid form some have, or at least, the possession of limb-like parts. It is harder to imagine how to treat a piece of software well, especially as its identity seems to be informational rather than physical.

Second, the notion of rights is a relatively constrained and formal way of recognising value. A world of human relations sketched out in terms of rights scarcely scratches the surface of what might put flesh on the bones of an outline of a good life and of good relationships. The bare knowledge that one has a right to respect for a private and family life, home, and correspondence will not get one very far in working out how to be a good parent or spouse. Hence, it may be no coincidence that it may seem easier to talk of such abstract and legalistic concepts such as rights, than of more intimate concepts such as care and concern, when discussing the value we might accord to robots, although we should also consider if these too may have a place.

The question of the legal governance of robots is important, for it involves questions of the attribution of responsibility for error and accidents and has also produced concern over questions such as tax issues: if large armies of robots replace human workers, then this has tax implications for the national insurance to which the employer would otherwise be liable, for example. The idea of granting legal personhood to robots has been mooted in various parts of the world [20, 21]. One might then be tempted to leap to the conclusion that of course robots must be treated with respect. But a legal person per se is not a natural person; it is, in short, a legal fiction designed to attribute various responsibilities clearly such that lines of accountability for various matters between human beings and human organisations are clear, and disputes can be resolved. Although this is an important question in law, we need not pursue it further here.

Intelligence as an indicator of moral status   The obvious first candidate indicating moral status in AI to examine is intelligence, but this in itself does not give an encouraging start, certainly if we are considering that most of the artificial intelligence we have currently exhibits only certain very limited aspects of intelligence. In addition, often these are aspects of intelligence that seem to give no basis for accrediting moral value per se to the possessor itself, rather than seeing it as a tool useful for our own purposes, especially given instrumental accounts of intelligence. It does not seem very plausible that a facility with complex statistical analysis would grant artificial intelligence independent moral status. Moreover, it's not even clear that reaching some benchmark of artificial general intelligence which matches human level intelligence in complexity and range would achieve this either. The value of human beings may depend upon the possession of a certain degree of cognitive capacity, but this alone does not seem to present the basis for an account of their value.

However, perhaps greater intelligence increases moral status in certain ways. Many are those who would object to such a view, but it's been commonly held in various forms. Indeed, it forms one basis for the impetus to increase human intelligence through various forms of human enhancement and also a basis for worries about this, including the concern that this may lead to a divided society with lower status accredited to the unenhanced.

Readers may be noting that on accounts such as that of Tegmark, intelligence might come out as of supreme value, and moreover, that accounts of the good life derived from philosophers such as Plato and Aristotle highly valued the life of the intellect. It is worth noting then that the picture of the good life given by Aristotle includes many virtues we would not typically regard as moral, such as ready wit, and that his conception of the good life and of virtue was much broader than is typical for modern accounts of ethics. There is perhaps a certain tension in that although a certain level of intelligence is essential for moral agency, there can easily be a wariness about attributing value to intelligence per se, rather than to the underlying person. Intelligence, or a degree of it, may indicate that the possessor has moral status but may not be the grounding reason for the moral status.

What else might ground a moral status to AI?

Language as an indicator of moral status   Language requires intelligence and also enables communication and hence reciprocity. A facility with language might also have a better chance of grounding moral value than facility with maths, for example, since it requires an understanding of the world and of social context, leading more readily onto other features of the moral life, such as reciprocity and recognition of others. The question of rights and responsibilities tends to arise with any AI which possesses considerable facility with language, as we saw in with the LaMDA model (see Chap. 2). Turing's imitation game involved a goal of sufficient linguistic subtly that native speakers would be inclined to attribute an intelligence. The willingness to move from linguistic ability to the attribution of personhood and/or sentience is also seen in science fiction stories such as the film *Her* [22], where a man falls in love with an AI with which he interacts solely through computers, and *Transcendence*, in which a character's mind is uploaded to a vast network of computer systems [23]. The LaMDA debate also perhaps indicates that language per se is not the issue but rather, what it might represent: a sentience, a mind, behind the language. Following on from this are certain questions: how might we safely attribute some kind of mind, and even if we could, what about such a mind might ground moral status?

How sentience matters   Are experiences necessary then for a robot to be the proper recipient of our moral concern? Do we have to wait until the technology is sufficiently sophisticated that some form of consciousness can be attributed? We then have to grapple with the 'other minds' problem that besets us in general, and in particular when faced with potential minds greatly different from ours: the dual problem of first, is there another mind there, and second, what is that mind like? And if it's sufficiently alien to us, how would we ever work out what possible care and concern we owed it?

Even if we could attribute sentience to a machine, sentience alone may not be enough to determine how we might treat it. Value judgements attached to sentient experiences and goals concerning them appear to be necessary. In accounts of personhood, the attribution of a right to life generally requires the desire to carry on living. Kant's notion of a rational agent includes the will to continued life as a necessity of rational agency [24]. The wrongness of inflicting suffering on sentient beings is because of the quality of experience, pain, and an assessment of this quality—negative. This seems to imply an experiencing subject with at least the vestiges of a value system, a motivation away from the negative and towards the positive. An alternative response might be that, just as we adapt moral responsibilities when considering animals rather than humans and even roughly tailor them to the needs of specific species, perhaps we need to adopt a new approach to grounding an ethics for machines.

Exercise 8

Suppose a machine had experiences when it perceived the environment. Does anything follow from this about the quality of the experiences we permit it to have, or about its continued capacity to experience these? If your answer was 'no', what might have to be added to give us any responsibilities in relation to the experiences the machine was having?

Goals, purposes, and interests The question of robot rights essentially rides on the attributes of robots. A robot vacuum cleaner does not feasibly have rights. For what rights could it possibly have? It would have to have interests of some sort to have rights; the way that the world goes, would have to make some difference to the robot vacuum cleaner. There would have to be some complexity here. Suppose a mischievous child worked out that it was possible to make the robot vacuum cleaner go round in circles and clean the same piece of floor over and over again until the power shut off. Explain to me how that violates its rights and I will buy you a beer. (As philosophers like a good argument, you might try to see if you can find a basis for any rights here.)

Some might reply that interference with the goals of a robot might constitute a violation of rights; or at any rate, some form of wrong, just as if someone interfered with a person's goal to get a cup of cappuccino by giving them a café latte instead, they might do them some minor wrong, even if this is not infringing anything so grand as a right. A ready reply is that the goals are not the goals 'of the robot': they were put in the robot by others (see Sect. 8.6). Consider, too, the discussion above of how some of the goals which humans have might have been 'put there' by evolution and perhaps hence are by their origin debunked, or at least in need of careful assessment. The robot would have to care about the goal in some way and would have to have some negative experience of the consequences of having this goal interfered with.

Embodiment and the enduring attribution of moral status We noted that moral status and personhood, or at least vestigial personhood, may be more readily applied to robots. So does that mean that embodiment is necessary to ground the attribution of moral status? Even if we might possibly attribute moral status to an AI manifest diffusely through, say, different parts of the Internet via language and communication with us, this is still a form of embodiment. Continued existence over some period of time seems necessary for the attribution of goals, preferences, or purposes.

The question of how we individuate entities, or indeed, whether we should do this, is more perplexing. Indeed, the immortality aspirations of those who plan to attempt to upload their mind to a machine themselves perhaps include the hope that their personhood, or enough of it at any rate, will endure and that this therefore means their moral status (although what precise rights and obligations others have would doubtless change significantly upon disembodiment) [25, 26]. With the communication hurdles that accompany our embodiment, it may also be challenging to differentiate one entity from another.

Exercise 9

Supposing it were possible successfully to upload your mind to a computer. What moral respect, what moral rights, would you retain, and what would change as a result of your disembodiment? Could this thought experiment be useful for considering what moral respect AI might deserve from us?

A point of view, a sense of the self   The discussion has been nudging towards an idea of a self of some kind, existing over time, and with some interests, goals, or preferences, no matter how simple; a subjectivity. In Thomas Nagel's phrase, perhaps there must be something that it is like to be an entity before it can have any moral status in its own right [27]. We discussed in Sect. 11.3 the general question of two contrasting views of the universe: one, as inert, essentially without meaning, purpose, or value, until put there by us, (or by beings like us); and one as with the possibility of meaning, awareness, and value immanent within it. (There is a great variety of such views.) To address the question of whether, and how, we might attribute some manner of mind, of being, to an artefact, is hence to rub up against metaphysical, ontological, cultural, religious, and spiritual questions about what the world is like, what is in it, how we can know, and how we should relate to these things or entities. This raises the question of what manner of reciprocity, if any, exists between us and other entities with moral status.

11.4.1   Treating AI 'As If' It Is a Person: Reciprocity and Its Dangers

Earlier, we explored the controversy over the LaMDA model and claims that it may have developed sentience occasioned by its apparent facility with language. What about a 'just in case' strategy, an approach to AI that treated it as if it had sentience, or personhood, or some other quality that gave it a certain moral standing?

Exercise 10

Try to think of examples where a strategy of assuming moral status would be the best policy in relation to humans, any dangers of failing to make this assumption, and any potential downsides. (Hint: We have already looked at certain examples earlier.)

What benefits and downsides might there be to a 'just in case' policy in relation to AI?

A danger of adopting this policy lies in the reciprocity implied in the recognition of another being as having moral status, especially if a status approaching personhood is attributed. Indeed, concerns about the deleterious impact of attributing personhood inappropriately to robots are behind calls to ensure that they are always regarded as our tools and to avoid humanising features [28]. This holds the possibility that a person might 'fall in love' with a machine, as in the film *Her*, especially if this forms an obstacle to developing a relationship with human beings instead. An additional concern is precisely the lack of reciprocity; there will not be the same feedback from the other that is present in healthy human relationships, so that the person in response to the machine might then fail to develop their interpersonal skills and moral character.

Conversely, perhaps an AI might be able to assist with this. Indeed, there is considerable work exploring robotics to assist children with autism to develop interpersonal skills [29]. The aim in such cases is to facilitate growth and to improve the capacity for interactions with other humans. What is the point, one may ask, if the person (i.e. the human!) never then applies these interpersonal skills to 'real' persons? Much of the moral concern about sex robots centres on the attribution of personhood and agency to a machine that cannot actually feel and does not actually have any wants and desires of its own and the potentially corrupting impact on relationships between human beings [30]. But if individuals otherwise lack human interaction, or we imagine a world where we no longer distinguish so sharply between the 'real' and the virtual or the robotic (see Sect. 7.5), perhaps things would be very different.

How precisely would we treat AI 'as if' it had moral standing?

Exercise 11
Suppose LaMDA, or some similar large language model, had attained sentience or was in some other way considered to have a degree of moral standing. How could we demonstrate this? What treatment would it deserve? How might it make a difference to how we interact with it? Could there be some forms of AI where we could more readily demonstrate our moral concern than others?

How AI treats us So far, we have considered how we might treat robots or other forms of AI, but what about how AI treats us? Interaction between moral agents, between persons, involves a reciprocity that can take many forms, which may be more or less appropriate to different occasions and different agents and relationships, and may approach or deviate from certain ideals. Note that a feature of such interpersonal, or interagent, interactions is that they can make a difference to either party. Hence, if you are being treated by another party *as if* you are a person of great interest, value, and worth, this can be very life-affirming and even transformative, but disrespect and maltreatment can leave its mark, major and minor. We considered earlier in some examples the situation of care robots and the appropriateness or otherwise of interactions between such robots and people. There is a considerable body of work in human-computer interactions, much of which is specifically concerned with human-robot interactions [31].

Now consider the myriad of different ways in which we interact with AI all around us. Consider how people may be manipulated when their behaviour and actions are nudged and persuaded by social media and other aspects of the tracking devices that may feed information back to us. So this may be a very mixed economy of technology, where some is adopted with intentions of self-management, perhaps, and other aspects are by no means consciously chosen.

It was suggested earlier that in this way, persons may be looked at from the outside on a quasi-behaviourist model, where certain goals may be set by us, but in other ways, our behaviour and even thoughts may be moulded by the technology and those designing and applying it. Might there be a troubling sense then, in which 'we' are seen as persons but as persons who can be manipulated? And might there be a sense, then, that it might possibly be useful, as a heuristic device, to see the technologies which are doing this also as a kind of person, a moral agent, one diffused into a motely array of hardware and software? This might then turn our attention towards the corporations and individuals who are jointly responsible for creating and implementing the accumulated technologies that shape our lives.

11.5 Machines as Moral Agents: Could Artificial Intelligence Enhance Human Morality?

Summary
The question of whether machines could ever be moral agents is one of the earliest tackled in the field of AI ethics and is one of great complexity, since it rests upon claims about the capacities of AI, about the nature of moral decisions and actions, the capacities needed for morality, and a detailed examination of the relevant strengths and weaknesses of both humans and AI. We focus on the narrower question of whether AI might act as a moral guide and on its capacities to provide us with knowledge relevant to making moral judgements.

Following on from the question of what moral obligations we might owe intelligent machines and whether machines might be moral patients in any sense, are questions about whether intelligent machines could become moral agents. Like the first question, this depends upon what conception we have of the nature of morality and of what is required to make a moral judgement and to act upon it.

Significant work in this area is among some of the earliest work specifically on AI ethics (not forgetting the earlier work on computer ethics). *Moral Machines* by Wendell Wallach and Colin Allen was published in 2008 and presents an extensive account of the questions of why we might need machines to be moral and distinguishes two possible approaches: a top-down approach to determining a moral stance and attempting to engineer this into machines, and a bottom-up approach that starts at the ground and attempts to integrate aspects ethics into machines following a developmental approach in attempts to mirror the developmental pathways via which humans acquire moral judgement and behaviour [32].

Having recently been grappling with the question of whether an advanced artificial intelligence is likely to run amok turning us into obsolete stationery items and having seen some of the pessimism and worried concern at the prospects of controlling superintelligence, one might with some justification scoff at the notion that AI might be some kind of moral agent. Indeed, the discussions of how we might be able to control superintelligence and try to ensure that it does not act in ways significantly counter to our values and our interests are directly relevant to the question of whether a machine could be a moral agent. We have seen how difficult it might be to ensure that it does not become a grossly immoral or amoral agent.

However, on the conception of artificial intelligence which rests on an instrumental account of intelligence, it is we who input the goals. So this leaves upon the possibility that we could construct it to assist us morally, especially since the dangers arising from superintelligence will not apply in machines with more limited capacity. We would just have to programme it to pursue moral goals in the right way. Of course, sadly, this is a pretty ambitious idea. The project of attempting to engineer ethics into machines runs into the stumbling block that we have not managed it in humans very well yet. Moreover, many—indeed, virtually all—of the cases we have examined in the book have concerned ethical difficulties that arise when we attempt to design and deploy artificial intelligence. The actual AI we have looked at and which is developed to date appears to have nothing that would qualify as moral insight, compassion, or even common sense or decency, even though it may sometimes be useful for reaching morally desirable goals.

Work in this area mixes work considering what we might reasonably expect from AI that we have now or may develop soon, with speculation about what an ideal form of AI might potentially become, perhaps including the capacity for sentience, compassion, feelings, and other aspects of human nature that seem to be centrally involved in our moral responses. We can distinguish between machines that behave in ways that align with our goals and values, which could be called moral machines in a residual sense, and machines that themselves can act as moral agents in a more substantial sense. Asking the question of whether any form of artificial intelligence could amount to a moral agent will require that we think about the nature of intelligence and its role in morality, as well as other questions such as how AI might gain knowledge and perceive the world, and relate to (other) moral beings, such as us. The area is particularly fraught with complexity since it involves not simply careful consideration of the capacities that AI currently has, speculation about what capacities it might develop but also a multitude of different views of ethics, of how we come to moral judgements, and what human failings in ethics are.

Any moral machines we might wish to produce would in theory be idealised moral agents. This if you like is the other side of the coin of those value alignment projects which simply have the more modest goals that AI does not positively act counter to our moral values. We obviously want all our machines to align broadly with our values in the sense of preventing clearly recognisable problems. We don't want a computer to give its users electric shocks (as my laptop has been doing lately), and if we are using AI and other technologies to deliver complex results, this may be a highly intricate task. It can also be seen simply as part of good engineering, which has standards of safety and aims to fulfil the specifications of the task. Trying to work out how to produce a moral machine requires not simply that we make a machine that does what we want it to do but that the machine also understands morality in some way, and this is much harder to specify.

If an algorithm was designed to match organs for transplant to recipients in need of them, the algorithm would not be sweating and sighing with concern over the gravity of the task, any more than if it was matching designer handbags to the appropriate celebrity. If fed preprogrammed criteria, it is not clear in which sense it would be called a moral machine, other than that we were using it for a task with weighty implications, and in this case, judgements will often have to be made with serious consequences given the need for a medically good match and the mismatch between organ supply and demand.

A project of attempting to build human-level intelligence into machines is obviously not going to attempt to incorporate human-level common cognitive errors; it's going to try to incorporate an idealised version of human-level intelligence: we are not going to programme in a moderate capacity to hear pitch and a rather mediocre ability to read musical notation. However, we know what correct answers in arithmetic should be (well, for much of it; even mathematics is not so simple); we have examples of people working out the correct methodology to achieve these answers. There are many other areas of endeavour in the empirical sciences where methodology may be less certain and where gathering and evidence may be complex and hard. By and large, in ethics it is even worse. We can't just copy and paste correct ethical judgement and action, plus the means by which we found the answer, into a machine.

This all means that it is actually rather challenging to specify what we might even be looking for in a moral machine, even one that might be only a partial moral agent, which might help us with difficult moral questions. Perhaps a machine could help us with certain moral questions, but perhaps calling a machine a 'moral' machine might overstate what it can actually do.

The question of whether machines could be moral agents is large and complex, so we will organise and narrow our discussion by addressing the question of whether machines could help to enhance us morally or assist to make us form better moral judgements and take more appropriate actions. This will involve considering if machines might incorporate at least some of the elements that go to constitute moral agency. If intelligent machines are moral agents *in any sense*, then they could have some capacity to contribute to our moral life. Artificial intelligence has been envisaged for use in addressing discrete or specific moral issues. We could see using AI to help us in moral decision and action as an aspect of human enhancement (on one plausible view, a particularly important aspect of it). We might find that some AI could be of limited use in assisting a small amount with our myriad failures, or perhaps we might find that it has the potential to be altogether better than us.

We will need to ask how human moral agency fails and what corresponding abilities or failings AI might have. The answers may be revealing of how we understand morality, how we understand human beings and human weakness, how we understand intelligent machines, and what hopes we might have for them. The hopes some cherish for intelligent machines may be held up and used as a yardstick by which to measure the hope and despair that there might be for human potential for good, and human failings.

11.5.1   Why Would We Even Want a Machine to Help Us with Moral Issues?

Of course, there is nothing to wonder at the attempt to improve one's moral judgements and actions, given the parlous state of human morality and the frequent times when a person might have wished for further insight, or in hindsight, realised that mistakes had been made. A more interesting question is why we might want a *machine* to do this, rather than a friend or a person with some particular moral authority we recognise, be it someone older and wiser, a religious leader, a teacher. One simple answer might be because the machine might be 'on' all the time and readily available via an app or a device in our pocket. A worse answer is to avoid the opprobrium of others if the morally difficult situation we are in is especially delicate, one of our own making, or ensure that others do not, in fact, discover that we didn't act as we judged best.

Aside from this, why might we want a machine to help? Since we struggle ourselves, it may be that a machine has some weaknesses compared to us but also some capacities that may make up for some of our shortcomings. So in order to break down this question, we need to understand what the tasks of morality are, what our likely moral failings are, and whether some form of artificial intelligence might have useful contributions to offer, and what these might be. This is another example where we compare machine and human agency and capabilities, but a particularly complex one, because there are rather different accounts available of what the tasks of morality are, how these should be accomplished, and what is needed to accomplish these. Much of the material earlier in the book, especially Chaps. 4–7, will be relevant to understanding these issues.

Exercise 12
Before we continue, write a list of what aspects of morality humans find difficult, what particular moral weaknesses humans tend to have, and any thoughts you have on any reasons we might have for using a machine to assist us morally, rather than another human being.

There are countless ways to proceed through these questions. The topic is in many ways a review of the entire book. It will rest upon a view of how moral judgements are made, what the purpose of morality is, on ideas of human nature, the role of agency in ethics, and much more. Since we are dealing with artificial intelligence, a particular focus of our discussion will be on the issue of moral knowledge and how AI might assist us with shortcomings in relation to knowledge and information processing. We will consider the different tasks that ethics involves and then take a simple suggested example of an artificial moral adviser, using that as a concrete prop from which to ask further questions about the capacity of AI to assist us with morally relevant information.

11.5.2 Analysing the Different Tasks of Morality

Let us start with an initial idea that using AI as some kind of moral aide might be possible. As discussed, to understand the question of whether AI could be a moral agent in any way, or could assist us to address our moral questions, we need to have a view on many aspects of ethics, and so this topic will always be controversial in some way. We need to start somewhere and a good place to start is by looking in some detail at the different elements of addressing a moral problem. We could divide moral tasks into various subtasks.

First, to understand that there is a question that needs to be asked, a problem to be solved, a choice to be made. This is an issue of attention to the world, attention to some lack, some judgement that needs to be made, a noticing of the need for extra effort or particular skills. In Sect. 7.2.5, we looked at a question slipped into Kant's account of duties that to determine whether an action is in accordance with the moral law, we first need to realise that we must ask this.

One might answer that on certain normative ethical theories, this is not needed. For a maximising consequentialist, every single occasion for action is an occasion for moral judgement. (That is precisely one argument in its favour; and simultaneously, an argument against it.) One simply needs to calculate the relevant consequences, either for each separate occasion, or, more realistically, using general rules of thumb or habitually applicable programmes. One still may need to recognise that an exceptional set of circumstances arises, where rules of thumb, habitual sources of information and calculation may be inadequate. Likewise, one might answer that for a virtue ethicist, the task of ethics is to live the best life, act in accordance with virtues, and so one is always in the 'on' mode for ethics. This will lead to very different levels of difficulty for different individuals; life is often run-of-the-mill and noticing some new or unusual challenge may prompt a reappraisal; and we know lives can go off track for want of attention to the demands of one's circumstances.

Second, having understood that a judgement is needed, the judgement must be made. How will depend of course on the situation and upon normative ethical theory. Since moral judgements are supervenient upon the state of the world, gathering relevant facts may always be needed, whatever view of the nature of ethics one accepts, as well as appreciation of the relevance of those facts, on which, more presently. Calculating the relevant rules that may apply and their relative priority may be needed, or judging the virtues relevant to a situation and making fine-tuned appraisals of how precisely to express them.

Exercise 13

Consider and contrast using a machine to help you to come to a moral judgement with using a machine to make a moral judgement in your place. Drawing on your understanding of ethical theory, what different perspectives might there be on this?

Third, we then need to act in an appropriate manner and at an appropriate time. We do not always do this. You may have noticed.

Exercise 14

Consider what might stop a person from acting according to their best moral judgement. Are there any ways in which AI might be able to assist humans with this? Be as inventive as you wish.

If AI solved this problem by acting in our place, would this be a satisfactory solution? Does it matter if we act willingly, or only that we act in the right way?

Alternative accounts exist of how we might parse out the different tasks of morality. The above distinction between forming a moral judgement, and in response, acting, allows the possibility of a slip between judgement and behaviour. In contrast, on some accounts, full knowledge of the correct moral thing to do leads immediately to action. There is no need for further moral motivation.

11.5.3   Elements of Moral Competence: What We Need in Order to Act Like Moral Agents

If we need an account of the tasks of morality, which as we have seen, will be complex and disputed, we must also have an account of what competencies we need in order to accomplish these tasks [33]. There may be more than one account of such competencies and hence more than one account of how the particular weaknesses of human beings could be assisted by AI.

Let us consider a list of moral competencies given by Malle [33] in a paper on machine morality: a moral vocabulary, a system of norms, moral cognition and affect, moral decision-making and action, and moral communication. A quick analysis of these will reveal some areas where AI might be more promising than others. Since this is the last chapter, let us do this much of this in the form of exercises, especially since one of the main aims of the book is to respect and enhance the moral autonomy of readers.

Moral vocabulary and moral communication:

Exercise 15

Drawing on our discussions of language and communication in Chap. 9 and Sect. 7.4, consider the challenges for AI of entering into moral dialogue with humans. Consider particularly questions of context and especially how it relates to moral issues and how a machine might have the capacities to grasp the context necessary to understand moral language. Could a machine have any capacity to correct humans on their failure to grasp context in moral judgements?

A system of norms:

Exercise 16

The requirement of possessing a system of norms could cover many possibilities, given the variety of approaches to ethics. Suppose these consist of a set of goals and/or a set of rules to be followed. There will be challenges in instantiating goals and rules in AI, including issues of how these are interpreted. Based on any prior material in the book or elsewhere, do you see any particular ways in which these issues may be even more acute in the case of moral judgements?

Cognition and affect:

Exercise 17
To include the competence of 'moral cognition and affect' covers a multitude of complexities. Drawing on previous material (see, e.g. Sect. 7.2.5 on moral understanding and general discussions on moral epistemology elsewhere in the chapter). Assuming that AI capable of affect is far from development, even if it can be developed, in what ways, if any, might lack of affect be a hurdle? In what ways might it be a benefit to assisting human moral judgement? Again, see Chap. 7 for much relevant material.

11.5.4 Is Using a Machine as a Moral Adviser Permissible?

An answer to this question was implied in Exercises 13 and 14. In thinking about this question, one of the first issues that might have occurred to you is that the very probity of using a machine to make a moral judgement is up for question and that from the perspective of different normative moral theories, very different answers may be given. To a large extent, these different answers relate closely to the different tasks that making a moral judgement involves on each of these three approaches and thus what the machine might be doing for us.

Let us simplify matters by taking consequentialism as a simple happiness-based utilitarianism. The only thing that matters is that the best consequences occur overall, and hence, if using a machine provides better results, then it even seems it might be mandatory to do so. Your responsibilities would be fulfilled. It might even be possible to get a machine to act in your place. The machine could have great facility in rapid calculation of consequences, plus in calculating models to project the future, although as we shall see below, there are more complexities to this than might at first appear. Indeed, for complex tasks, it may even be mandatory to use computing power, and it could seem ideal, especially in cases necessitating speed. For tasks involving calculations such as crop forecasting and weather forecasting, it is difficult to see how we could have a hope without using considerable computing power.

For a rule-based ethic, suppose we had a machine that was able to calculate if a rule applies, how it applies, and how to deal with any clash of rules and their relative priority. This could be used, for example, in calculating complex tax issues. An accountant would have responsibility for ascertaining the accuracy of such calculations. Would this be enough in the case of ethics to fulfil one's moral responsibility? The answer for Kant, as we saw (see Sect. 1.10), was that one must act with the correct motivation and understanding of what one is doing. Even those who do not agree with the Kantian interpretation of the moral law may recognise the need to fully understand and to take on board as one's own any of our judgements which we think of as moral.

However, it may be challenging to articulate how to draw the line around the kinds of judgements to which this notion of responsibility applies. Would it be enough if one were willing to check the machine periodically or be prepared to answer any complaints? Perhaps it might also be possible to learn from the machine how better to interpret rules and reflect upon how to deal with clashes. So a moral adviser would be possible, but its use might be more of a joint enterprise than might be the case for a consequentialist approach.

Alternatively, one might consider that it only matters that a rule is applied rigorously, not the motivation behind its application. Perhaps having the correct motivation is a part of an entire system of rules but need not be tangibly manifest in particular applications of rules that form part of a wider system. So just as a judge may have the general motivation to uphold the principles of justice, trust in the automatic application of a rule derived from this system on a particular occasion may not be necessary, and a machine may manage this better than we could. A reasonable example where AI might fare better than human judgement might be dealing with complex cases of fraud.

Exercise 18
We have reflected on such matters previously, for example, in considering the COMPAS algorithm case in Sect. 2.4.3, which you may wish to review. Consider also the issues raised above in Exercise 13 and the general questions of context and pragmatics we discussed in Chap. 9. Do these considerations impact your view of whether or when it might be permissible to use AI to apply moral rules? Consider the issue of discretion.

For a virtue ethicist, the idea of getting a machine to make a moral judgement rather than doing it oneself seems almost laughable, not simply because it may be a dereliction of responsibility, but because in the unlikely event that a person has fully developed the virtues and attained an ideal state of moral wisdom, the machine seems redundant. If they have not, the use of a machine passes up the chance to practice the art of the moral considerations which lead to the development of virtue, if the machine is simply going to deliver the moral judgement to you. Unless, perhaps, a machine might be able to help with this, taking the role of the society and the admirable people of virtue who act as guides and role models.

Exercise 19
It may seem on the face of it unlikely that a mere machine could form a useful part of how we might develop moral virtue. Is this too dismissive? Think through if there are any realistic possibilities and whether machines might also have a tendency to lure us away from the path of virtue.

We have seen (Sect. 7.2.5) that there are many accounts of what is needed to form moral judgements, including close attention to the other, and entering into certain forms of discourse and discussion with others. These approaches also seem to present certain obstacles to the simple use of a machine to assist with moral judgement. Let us consider some suggestions for the use of moral AI from those who see more possibilities in the area.

11.5.5   How Could We Build a Moral Machine? An Example

Let us start with a suggestion for one basic possibility of using a machine as an artificial moral adviser. There have been various suggestions around this theme, plus considerable refinement and critique. A paper by Giubilini and Savulescu builds upon a paper by Roderick Firth describing an 'ideal observer' that is consistent and impartial in its judgements [34, 35]. Their artificial moral adviser retains these qualities but lacks the absolutism found in Firth's account because it is programmed to take into account its human owner's personal principles and values rather than to take a universal stance as Firth's ideal observer does. In this way, it is claimed that it will enhance moral autonomy as well as helping with some limitations of human psychology, such as prejudices. Human moral shortcomings of concern include information processing, for we often do not possess or consider all information relevant to a judgement; moral judgement, since we are often inconsistent and fail to stick to our own values in our judgements; and moral agency, since we often fail to act on our best moral judgements.

Note that the example given is narrow: to use technology to assist humans in making decisions given fixed and limited moral criteria and moral instructions. A specific example is analysed of choosing a restaurant, given that as well as wishing for a cheap, good, nearby restaurant, one is also concerned with animal welfare. The software would gather available information about the possible restaurants, model this information against the criteria that the owner had put into the system, and could then calculate expected utility at a faster and more efficient rate than a human could, giving restaurant suggestions.

More details are given in the paper explaining the approach, of course, but the modest goal of this particular example is apparent. Choosing a restaurant is after all a luxury option for billions of people who could rarely or never afford to eat out. Moreover, specific information even in relation to these goals will be hard to ascertain, since the full animal welfare cost of each restaurant choice could involve an incredibly long chain of questions (the particular paint used on the walls, the leather seats, what they do about vermin control) and 'animal welfare' could mean many things and is not specified. Moreover, from where does the artificial moral adviser gather these data? One can also ask, what is it about these choices that make them moral choices? A clue to address these is how the 'moral' aspect of the choice is included in a list of presumably nonmoral choices: how much further would one wish to walk for a certain gain in animal welfare? And how are these ranked together in a 'utility' score? For a consequentialist, this might sound fine, but the personal nature of this example shows that this does not amount to any standard ethical form of consequentialism, since different people can programme the device in different ways: with different sets of considerations, and different rankings (e.g. ranking food quality and décor far above animal welfare). The lack of general applicability makes this seem a choice of *personal* preference, and little more. We should be asking more questions about whether our moral choices are simply a variety of general choices, whether there is anything distinctive about how these choices are made, and the manner in which these choices are made.

Exercise 20
Drawing on any previous material (e.g. discussions of preference in relation to Russell's approach to superintelligence, discussions of consequentialism and utilitarianism in general), would you think of this as a moral adviser, per se, or simply a device for narrowing down restaurant choice? Do you consider there is any difference between moral decisions and any other decision we make, and if so, can a sharp line be drawn?

The sheer complexity of the tasks of gathering and assessing information and delivering a suggested course of action is apparent with the restaurant example but is even clearer with another example application given by these authors, assisting policy makers to make rational decisions in public emergency situations, where it is suggested that a computer could 'immediately' gather relevant information and provide estimates of the likely spread of the disease and suggest policy options [34, p. 174]. The paper was published in 2018. The world is now sadly familiar with the complexities and myriad problems with the modelling of such scenarios and the political, ethical, medical, and other implications of policy choice [36]. Furthermore, in such situations, questions of accountability for taking such serious decisions are paramount; the very idea that we should just 'follow the science' has been taken apart not simply because the information and modelling is likely to produce a range of different suggestions but because there are moral and political choices to be made [37]. It is not universally settled that 'health' is a value that overrides all others (see Sect. 4.1.3); nor is there one notion of health [38], and different measures may stress different aspects of health and have different impacts on different demographics [39]. The nature of the demands for accountability from decision-makers and from those implementing decisions will be different when we are dealing with such value issues, rather than simply crunching numbers and dealing in 'facts' as if we agree with Dickens' Mr. Gradgrind that 'Facts alone are wanted in life' [40].

Here is one possible difference to get us going: I am faced with a choice of drink—English Breakfast tea, Earl Grey tea, or cola. It's easy. I don't like cola, and I prefer English Breakfast to Earl Grey. I never have the problem of choosing cola and then living to feel guilt and remorse; I am never tempted to choose it, I genuinely dislike it. I never have to ask my friend, let alone my priest, to remind me never to choose cola again. If I occasionally choose Earl Grey, I never ruminate on this choice or lose a day's sleep over it; I choose it sometimes *for a change*. Something else is going on with moral choices. I should not choose to tell a convenient lie simply 'for a change'. The crunch might come with the moral adviser restaurant app if the owner repeatedly turned off the 'animal welfare' in favour of top marks for 'Instagrammability' (and what about showing concern for animal welfare while ignoring obvious signs of money laundering and suspicions that kitchen staff are the victims of human trafficking?).

11.5.6 AI as Moral Assistant: Can It Help Us with the Knowledge Needed for Better Moral Judgements?

We need to think more carefully about how AI might contribute to specifically *moral* questions. This discussion will consolidate much past material and, in many ways, address old issues from a different angle. We will continue to focus on the question of the capacity of AI to help us by providing and analysing the information and knowledge we need, since that seems the most promising candidate among its current strengths. It may at first sight seem obvious that artificial intelligence may offer considerable advantages in the gathering of the knowledge needed to ground moral judgements and decisions compared to human capabilities. It can process vast amounts of information extremely rapidly, far faster than we can, and analyse it with techniques beyond human capabilities. This means it can take a much wider view than any one person or even a group of people. Technology can also gather material in ways that are beyond the powers of ordinary humans, scraping the Internet for information, using sensors, analysing images in ways the human eye cannot, and so on. More is good, right? Fast is good, right? It may appear as if AI might be able to stand as some manner of an ideal observer, especially if we can rid it of the biases that originate in humans, producing an impartial and complete picture, or certainly more complete than humans could. However, we need to ask, first, if it is capable of producing such a complete picture of knowledge on which to base moral decisions; and second, if this is even what is needed.

The first kind of moral knowledge needed is a kind of attention. Our lack of proper attention to the world, our capacity to fail to notice the demands of morality, has already been discussed (see Sect. 7.2.5). This definitely ranks as a common human failing. Much technology that we have currently is very adept at focusing our attention, often to our detriment. The capacity that AI would have to have would be to focus our attention in morally relevant ways, and I know of no plausible means on the horizon whereby this could be accomplished.

A problem is that it is extremely difficult to give an account of how such moral sensitivity is achieved. States of affairs in the world that seem normal and 'just how things are' from one point of view may be seen as in need of attention from another. Perhaps the best accounts philosophically of how such attunement is acquired and developed are found in approaches such as virtue ethics and the notion of phronesis or in approaches stressing the importance of fine-tuned attention to the other and to the quality of discourse communication and discussion with others. A redescription of circumstances, a fresh angle, the prompting of a friend, can help (see Sect. 7.2.5). On the other hand, that great exponent of practical wisdom, of phronesis, Aristotle, considered that a class of human beings were naturally slaves [41]. How well could an intelligent machine perform, if at all?

One answer might be that the machine can far more rapidly than we can, collect and analyse data. But analyse it how? For there is no formula to follow. The mass of data may only make this worse. The issue is one known within artificial intelligence as framing, of how to spot the wood for the trees in more ordinary parlance, and has been discussed in moral philosophy as a problem of moral relevance. What facts among a world full of facts, which aspects of a situation, including the things that are missing from that situation, which of these must be taken into account? The world is not marked with little red buttons indicating 'moral problem alert', or if it is, most of us are oblivious to them.

Let us suppose then that we have identified that there is a moral question to be addressed. Let us suppose that one has a vague idea of what this question is. (This often happens to humans; nothing more than a feeling of unease or a realisation of guilt.) Now we have to gather relevant facts.

It is often assumed that artificial intelligence will be able to obtain all the data that we need and that there is a limitless supply of it. Indeed, Russell notes that people often simplistically assume that superintelligence will be omniscient [42]. There are several problems here. One is that we often do not have enough data. Data are not in limitless supply. It has to be gathered. In fact, we're often short of it even for specific issues (such as we saw in the training of algorithms for content moderation; see Sect. 9.5.4). Of course, when we do have relevant data, this can be extremely valuable.

The second problem is that there is too much data. Most of it is morally irrelevant. Data on the physiology of a person, second by second, telling you heart rate, blood pressure, kidney filtration, liver function, and on and on and on, might be relevant on occasion, but will not add a jot of relevant detail if it omits to record that that person A has just plunged a knife into person B's chest. But what data do we need? The additional information that person B was heavily armed and firing shots into a crowd might be more helpful, however. The further information that A was motivated by a personal grudge against B adds more interest. It is essential to be able to sift out morally relevant from irrelevant data.

A third problem is that the kind of information we often need to make moral judgements isn't the kind of information that a computer could possibly collect as data. The counterfactual conditional that A would have acted to stop B even in the absence of a personal grudge is highly relevant but is not precisely a 'fact'. It cannot be observed, not even from any kind of brain scan of person A or from seeing what is actually going on in A's mind, even if the idea of the 'full' content of A's mind, conscious thought plus unconscious, could be well-articulated. It cannot be observed, because it critically depends upon something that might have happened, but didn't.

To judge events involving human behaviour, we need to understand causes and intentions and make judgements of responsibility [33, p. 248]. In understanding issues of causation and responsibility, as we have indicated previously, there may be a need for considerable past information, and different accounts and descriptions of preceding circumstances will produce different readings of a situation. A computer could possibly quickly run through a myriad of models to test various hypotheses about relevant counterfactual conditionals about Person A's action, but these would remain speculative. It is modelling A's behaviour. Undertaking this task requires considerable sophistication. It may not be clear that even those humans who are gifted at such judgements of character can spell out how they achieve this. Perhaps it's a part of phronesis. Recall our discussions in Chap. 9 of Russell's suggestions that superintelligence could model our preferences from observing our behaviour for further relevant thoughts on this.

Again, the problem of moral relevance is not something uniquely difficult when it comes to working out how to programme ethics into machines, even just enough to get them to help us. It is challenging to lay out any general guidance for what features of a situation will be morally relevant (see Sect. 7.3.2). The relevance of counterfactual conditionals and the problem of how wide and how far back to go to describe events and actions make the issue intractable.

Throwing data at the situation may, however, help for something like a consequentialist project of gathering information on specific goals, such as gathering information about preferences, the likely happiness or unhappiness, pleasure and pain of different possible courses of action, indeed, even going far into the future. It may well be very useful in cases of public policy.

Exercise 21
Consider how, and to what extent, an intelligent machine might gather information relevant to assessing the happiness and unhappiness of all affected by the possible courses of action open to one agent at any given moment. Remember that this will involve having to determine what is relevant to an assessment of happiness. Build in time considerations.

Now consider if there are any different considerations when gathering information relevant to assessing the preferences and their likely satisfaction of all affected. Compare how a machine might fare compared to a reasonably competent and diligent human being.

AI and moral development We must address how a machine might acquire the knowledge that it might draw upon to form moral judgements. Many have speculated that a model of virtue ethics and of human moral development may lead to AI that has a greater capacity to understand human values and the moral complexity of the situations we find ourselves in [32, 43]. A developmental pathway of the acquisition of moral understanding and the development of some manner of moral character could perhaps bring a machine closer to human understanding and form a more appropriate help. This would, however, necessitate the capacity for affect as well as cognition, given that for humans, virtues are acquired through membership of a community with relationships of kinship and mediated through the biological patterns of our birth, childhood, adolescence, maturity, and death. Such moral development also needs some form of self-awareness and the capacity to recognise the moral value and individuality of others. Any account of a machine with such capabilities that we could draw now would be sketchy and speculative to say the least.

11.5.7   Data Gathering for Moral Judgements: How Problems May Arise

And how is data gathered? The possibilities mentioned above of minute tracking of personal and physiological data could be potentially useful in some possible circumstances. Those philosophers who have stressed the importance of close observation and attention to the other, of waiting and listening to a situation, have noted that such fine-tuned attention can produce knowledge; yet how this translates into anything we might include in a machine remains to be seen.

Data are gathered in particular ways. Neither our senses nor the perceptual and information gathering technologies of AI just point to the world and observe it as it is. Data fed into systems are collected according to various categories and within limits of accuracy and recording systems. Moreover, it then has to be analysed to produce any useful information. This analysis will be based upon certain methods and theories. Some of these theories may hope to reproduce or even exceed the information gathering expertise of humans, including the subtleties needed for an ethical response.

The capacities of human beings to relate to and understand each other are both the basis of good relationships and community and of shortcomings which form a source of misunderstanding and even tragedy. Efforts are being made to reproduce this in various ways, one of which is through attempts at facial recognition and emotion recognition.

Because machine learning gathers and analyses information in ways that differ from humans, the possibility may be open that ML could be trained to detect things of moral relevance with more sensitivity than we can. The possibility thus also appears that this could be another example of technological enthusiasm gone wrong. Moreover, there is more than one way in which this can go wrong.

The first is easier to deal with: making errors that are readily detectable. For example, claims were made that machine learning could predict criminality from photographs of faces [44]. The prospects of the Department of Pre-Crime loom, or at least, of using such information to narrow down on suspects. In this case, it was readily shown that the photographs used included contaminating information: the 'criminal' photographs were prison mug shots and the 'noncriminal' photographs were white collar workers in office attire [45], although the authors of the original paper have issued a response to the numerous criticisms it attracted [46]. Dangers might present themselves if such errors are not so easy to demonstrate.

However, there is a possibility that the appearance of success may validate hollow approaches. The capacity to understand the minds of others is critical in human relations and in ethics. We do this only reasonably well, some better than others and it can be hard to explain how. The prospect of turning this into some kind of science, bolstered by technology, may be appealing. There is great interest in using theories about reading emotions from facial expressions and combining this with machine learning to feed into decision-making of various kinds. Unfortunately, the theories upon which such enthusiastic methods are based are open to considerable question (see, e.g. Sect. 8.7.4). There have been many criticisms of the quality of the work linking facial expressions to certain human emotions and the categorisation of emotions this involves [45, 47]. A danger presents itself that enthusiasm about the technology, including the rush to commercialise, will mean that the dubious nature of some scientific claims upon which the technology is based will be overlooked.

As we have seen, faith in the information produced by technology can also produce deleterious feedback loops that can produce self-serving prophecies. Note that this can happen in cases where the aims may be specifically value-based. Predictive policing is an area where considerable controversy has arisen over numerous examples that appear to increase social divisions and bias against certain communities [48]. Presuming that policing needs a good picture of criminal activity across the area for which it is responsible and has limited time and resources to respond to incidents, using AI to gather data and to increase response times seems to be a good possibility until the feedback loops this creates are taken into account. Increased police attention to specific areas will increase the visibility of criminal behaviour and of any activities deemed 'suspicious' relative to those areas that are not receiving so much attention. Similar harmful feedback loops have been found in the use of algorithms to make decisions about remanding suspects in custody [49].

In short, many of the very ethical problems that vex the development and application of AI concern ethical problems generated or worsened by the informational capacities of AI. It is not looking at all like it is 'better' than humans in this respect, in any simplistic sense.

Perhaps these examples are simply instances of information used badly and represent teething problems in technology that can be ironed out, applications of technology inspired by hasty judgement and hubris that can be corrected. Perhaps in the future, we will have much more data on which to base our judgements and decisions about action.

Exercise 22

There have been concerns that information about individuals and/or groups may be misused and/or may have unintended deleterious consequences. Take one or more examples of the use of AI where there have been concerns that have been raised and consider carefully whether there are ways in which the situation may be improved and what these might be or whether there is no way of rendering the example morally unproblematic. It may be useful to compare two or more examples. Use examples from earlier in the book, or find some of your own.

Remember that we are talking about *moral* judgements here, not judgements in general. When amassing safety data for engineering purposes, or in medicine, we obviously want as full a picture as possible, of the relevant information. There can be unforeseen possibilities, unfortunate oversights, but in general, the more the merrier when it comes to information. However, when we are dealing with value issues as in ethics, the parameters may be less clear. We may be dealing with specific relationships, obligations, and accountabilities. We may be trying to work out how to live in a world that we cannot navigate very well because we lack the common signs we used prior to the creation of new possibilities of knowledge created by technologies.

New information possibilities may create opportunities but also moral hazards and complex difficulties. Data may be gathered or analysed and applied in novel situations, enabling the possibility of judgement and choice in situations where previously there had been none. The creation of such options has been numerous in areas of medicine, especially in genetics, genomics, and fertility. These come together with AI in the example of an IVF service using donor gametes that promises to use facial recognition software to maximise the chance that any baby conceived will resemble the intended parents. Many clinics now offer this service, such as ovoclinic.net, ivi-fertility.com, and fenomatch.com [50]. Websites suggest that this service will improve donor matches for all aspects of compatibility, provide peace of mind, reduce stress, and other benefits. The technique examines thousands of points of comparison of faces to find the best match. Genetic compatibility and phenotypes are also matched at clinics.

This is a very good example of the incremental additions of possibilities of action and knowledge that developments in technology of different types can present. Indeed, a full discussion would merit its own book. There are many complex reasons why the intended parents may wish their child to resemble them. These include helping bonding, concern to avoid any remarks about the different appearance of the child, and other reasons. A feature of parenting is a large element of the unknown, and many have concerns that we are heading towards 'designer babies' where the baby is regarded as a product to be fashioned to the tailored demands of parents, dramatically altering the parent–child role.

The attitudes and judgements surrounding parenting and the family will be deeply embedded in rich and interlocking social, cultural, religious, and personal meanings. Suppose that the child turns out looking different to either parent, as often happens? Will this be a disappointment with a 'product'? There is also a complex background to who has access to what knowledge. Clinics offering this service at the time of writing are based in Spain, which has strict donor anonymity laws, meaning that a gamete donor's anonymity will be protected. The child may know that he or she has been donor conceived but not who their genetic mother or father was. Unless of course, sleuthing through DNA ancestry results later produces this information, as is increasingly often the case. Thus, we can see that the knowledge produced by facial recognition AI enters a whirlpool of epistemic complexity where feelings are likely to be heated, confusing, and where different parties may have very different opinions.

Exercise 23
Try to analyse the different considerations that might be brought to bear upon assessing the merits of this AI technology within this context, noting the issues on which further research is needed and the areas of greatest controversy and complexity.

One can perfectly comprehend a parent of a child conceived with a donor egg wishing to avoid comments by strangers in the playground about how different the child looks to the parent. It's literally none of the stranger's business. One of the issues here is one raised repeatedly by AI: that information may be not yours to have;

and it may be not yours to give. This is not just an issue raised by the gathering of data and access to it but also by the possibilities of analysis of data that one might have obtained legitimately. However, our ideas about making moral judgements about envisaging our future lives and relationships have been formed in contexts of uncertainties and with notions about what information is mine, what is yours, and not only how much might be shared but also how it might be shared.

The possibilities of surveillance and the myriad social, ethical, and legal quandaries that these produce are well known, but it's important to note that this then can be seen as a manifestation of the difficulties in considering that AI can help us to become better morally by furnishing us with more and more data collected via more and more lines of sight. We can also see that the requirements of transparency and explainability, which are so important in relation to understanding the operation of discrete parts of AI, do not generalise to knowledge as a whole. A wry smile and a change of subject is a perfectly apt response to the stranger in the playground.

11.5.8 AI, Information, Ethics, and How We Communicate

In addition to nuanced judgements about how information is gathered and the quality and nature of the relationships that this reveals, the manner in which information is communicated may also be critical and need fine-tuned judgements. We have previously noted that factual knowledge, knowledge-by-description, gives only a partial account of the varieties of knowledge; we will need more than a bare account of descriptive knowledge, of information which can be formally expressed in code or mathematics or in plain language, to convey the messages and interplay of human connection often needed in human relationships. Information may be communicated implicitly, by actions, and imperfect and incomplete communication may serve a particular purpose better.

A favourite example of mine is taken from the children's classic, *The Railway Children* by E. Nesbitt. The father of the family is in prison on false charges of espionage, a fact that the mother has hidden from her three children. The eldest girl, Roberta (Bobbie), who is on the cusp of adulthood, plays a liminal role including in keeping the younger children from discovering that anything at all is awry, realising herself that something is wrong, yet respecting her mother's right of secrecy:

> ... she had the power of silent sympathy. That sounds rather dull, I know, but it's not so dull as it sounds. It just means that a person is able to know that you are unhappy, and to love you extra on that account, without bothering you by telling you all the time how sorry she is for you. That was what Bobbie was like. She knew that Mother was unhappy—and that Mother had not told her the reason. So she just loved Mother more and never said a single word that could let Mother know how earnestly her little girl wondered what Mother was unhappy about. This needs practice. It is not so easy as you might think [51, Ch. IV].

It is crystal clear here that AI, or even simply hacking into her mother's emails, would wreck the situation which Bobbie handles with grace and wisdom.

We considered above the requirement of moral language and moral communication (see Sect. 11.5.3). It may be that not all of our moral judgements, our moral wisdom, may find precise expression in language, nor may they need this. The driving assumption behind much hope for the use of AI, of improvements in clarity, speed, efficiency, and universality, may be far too crude to capture the nuances of human respect for the necessary distance and privacy, which forms an essential part of the complex relationships between people. Speed is sometimes necessary and sometimes gets in the way; attention to timing, careful waiting, and watching can be essential. Clarity is sometimes needed; sometimes, it is not needed, and sometimes the steps necessary to achieve clarity may disrupt the delicate relationships and differences in position that make up the warp and weft of our moral lives.

Let us end this book here, contemplating the difficulties and delights of attempting to live according to the best values we can. We have been able to indicate only a very partial view of the complex question of how AI might help us morally, of what our moral weaknesses and strengths are. This indeed is a question which undergirds the entire project, and which we face day to day as we use the complex and varied technology which is so interwoven into our lives. In writing this book, I have been painfully aware of what is left out and have been forced to simplify at every turn. Everything else is up to you.

11.6 Key Points

Projected visions of the far future may be based upon an implied purpose in the universe that projects an assumption of progress, whereas other accounts firmly reject the notion that there is any purpose or value inherent in the universe other than values set by humans.

Both approaches can be seen to have roots in Western value systems, with some Biblical antecedents and the influence of the Enlightenment often in a mixed pattern. A common thread may be a special role for humans. By understanding such influences, comparisons and dialogue with those from other traditions may be enhanced.

Accounts of imagined human enhancement, whether using technology or not, have to be based upon a value base in order to support the claim that changes amount to enhancement. If radical changes are proposed, this may make it hard or impossible to judge whether such enhancement would count as a moral good for current humanity.

The issue of whether machines could exhibit morality in any way is highly complex, resting both upon accounts of the current and imagined future capabilities of AI but also on views of the nature of ethics and of the basis of moral judgements and actions.

Thinking through this issue can be a way of tackling many of the issues around AI ethics that we met earlier in the book.

The possibilities for AI to assist us as a moral adviser look strongest in the case of providing knowledge relevant to ethical judgement, but even here, there are considerable complexities. We are left with difficult questions about the relevance of moral knowledge and the kind of knowledge and information that we need for moral judgements.

11.7 Educator Notes

As the final chapter, this consolidates a great deal of past material. The exercises generally expect much of students in terms of drawing on previous work and rehearsing and extending their understanding. Each of the exercises, as before, could simply be read through for brief reflection, but many could involve considerable work if students looked into them thoroughly; they can still be useful if engaged with at different levels of depth.

Students may find that in working through the exercises in this chapter, they confirm views from previous exercises, or they may find that they have altered their perspective in some ways. Either is good, but in either case, students should take this opportunity to reflect back on their previous work.

The two main topics can of course be treated entirely separately. The material in Sect. 11.3 which follows from Sect. 11.2 naturally draws upon Sect. 10.4 and an overview of this section would be very desirable as a prerequisite.

Debate and extended project or essay topics The general topic of Sect. 11.3, together with the individual exercises, could make a good class debate, or extended project or essay, since it attempts to capture two appealing approaches to AI ethics that overlap to an extent but also conflict considerably. This topic also raises the very general issue of how very basic elements of one's worldview impact one's approach to AI ethics and leads naturally into discussion of different cultural and religious attitudes.

The general issue of building some kind of 'moral machine' could be a good whole class or group project, with different small groups assigned to address different elements of this complex question.

Exercise 23 is particularly challenging, given that it addresses the embedding of AI within a complex and emotive area. It could thus form a basis for extended work, especially for students who would benefit from being pushed. There is earlier material, for example, in Chap. 4, concerning genomic and genetic information which students could draw upon, and it could also provide an exercise in what further material and considerations need to be gathered.

References

1. Tegmark M (2017) Life 3.0: being human in the age of artificial intelligence. Knopf, New York
2. Haraway D (2006) A cyborg manifesto: science, technology, and socialist-feminism in the late 20th century. In: The international handbook of virtual learning environments. Springer, Cham, pp 117–158
3. Rothblatt M (2012) The Terasem mind uploading experiment. Int J Mach Conscious 4(01): 141–158
4. Kurzweil R (1999) The age of spiritual machines: when computers exceed human intelligence. Penguin, London
5. Kurzweil R (2005) The singularity is near: when humans transcend biology. Viking, London
6. Kurzweil R (2012) How to create a mind: the secret of human thought revealed. Viking, New York
7. More M, Vita-More N (2013) The philosophy of transhumanism. In: The transhumanist reader: classical and contemporary essays on the science, technology, and philosophy of the human future. Wiley, New York, pp 3–17
8. Huxley J (1968) Transhumanism. J Humanist Psychol 8(1):73–76
9. Persson I, Savulescu J (2010) Moral transhumanism. J Med Philos 35(6):656–669
10. Parfit D (1984) Reasons and persons. Oxford University Press, Oxford
11. Parfit D (2016) Can we avoid the repugnant conclusion? Theoria 82(2):110–127
12. Russell S, Dewey D, Tegmark M (2015) Research priorities for robust and beneficial artificial intelligence. AI Mag 36(4):105–114
13. Bentham J (1789) Introduction to the principles of morals and legislation, works, vol I. Penguin Books, London
14. Gottlieb A (2016) The dream of enlightenment: the rise of modern philosophy. WW Norton & Company, New York
15. World English Bible, Genesis 26:4. https://ebible.org/web/GEN26.htm
16. Lewis JE, Abdilla A, Arista N, Baker K, Benesiinaabandan S, Brown M, Cheung M, Coleman M, Cordes A, Davison J, Duncan K (2020) Indigenous protocol and artificial intelligence position paper. https://spectrum.library.concordia.ca/id/eprint/986506/7/Indigenous_Protocol_and_AI_2020.pdf
17. Lewis JE, Arista N, Pechawis A, Kite S (2018) Making kin with the machines. J Design Sci. https://doi.org/10.21428/bfafd97b
18. Passmore JA (1975) Man's responsibility for nature: ecological problems and Western traditions. Gerald Duckworth & Co. Ltd., London
19. Briefer EF, Sypherd CCR, Linhart P, Leliveld L, Padilla de la Torre M, Read ER, Guérin C, Deiss V, Monestier C, Rasmussen JH, Špinka M (2022) Classification of pig calls produced from birth to slaughter according to their emotional valence and context of production. Sci Rep 12(1):1–10
20. Nagenborg M, Capurro R, Weber J, Pingel C (2020) Ethical regulations on robotics in Europe. In: Machine ethics and robot ethics. Routledge, London, pp 473–490
21. Pagallo U (2018) Apples, oranges, robots: four misunderstandings in today's debate on the legal status of AI systems. Philos Trans R Soc A Math Phys Eng Sci 376(2133):20180168
22. Jonze S (2013) Her. Warner Bros, USA
23. Pfister W (2014) Transcendence. Warner Bros, USA
24. Kant I, Paton HJ (1964) Groundwork of the metaphysic of morals (translated and analysed by HJ Paton). Harper & Row, Manhattan
25. Turner C, Schneider S (2020) Could you merge with AI? In: Dubber M, Pasquale F, Das S (eds) The Oxford handbook of ethics of AI. Oxford University Press, Oxford
26. Schneider S (2019) Artificial you. In: Artificial you: AI and the future of your mind. Princeton University Press, Princeton
27. Nagel T (1974) What is it like to be a bat? Philos Rev 83(4):435–450

28. Ferrari F, Paladino MP, Jetten J (2016) Blurring human–machine distinctions: anthropomorphic appearance in social robots as a threat to human distinctiveness. Int J Soc Robot 8(2):287–302
29. Esteban PG, Baxter P, Belpaeme T, Billing E, Cai H, Cao HL, Coeckelbergh M, Costescu C, David D, De Beir A, Fang Y (2017) How to build a supervised autonomous system for robot-enhanced therapy for children with autism spectrum disorder. Paladyn 8(1):18–38
30. Richardson K (2016) The asymmetrical 'relationship' parallels between prostitution and the development of sex robots. ACM SIGCAS Comput Soc 45(3):290–293
31. Bartneck C, Belpaeme T, Eyssel F, Kanda T, Keijsers M, Šabanović S (2020) Human-robot interaction: an introduction. Cambridge University Press, Cambridge
32. Wallach W, Allen C (2008) Moral machines: teaching robots right from wrong. Oxford University Press, Oxford
33. Malle BF (2016) Integrating robot ethics and machine morality: the study and design of moral competence in robots. Ethics Inf Technol 18(4):243–256
34. Giubilini A, Savulescu J (2018) The artificial moral advisor. The "ideal observer" meets artificial intelligence. Philos Technol 31(2):169–188
35. Firth R (1952) Ethical absolutism and the ideal observer. Philos Phenom Res 12(3):317–345
36. Taylor L, Sharma G, Martin A, Jameson S (eds) (2020) Data justice and COVID-19 global perspectives. Meatspace Press, London
37. Stevens A (2020) Governments cannot just 'follow the science' on COVID-19. Nat Hum Behav 4(6):560–560
38. Leonardi F (2018) The definition of health: towards new perspectives. Int J Health Serv 48(4):735–748
39. Fitzpatrick M (2002) The tyranny of health: doctors and the regulation of lifestyle. Routledge, London
40. Dickens C (1905) Hard times. Chapman & Hall, London. https://www.gutenberg.org/files/786/786-h/786-h.htm
41. Jowett B (1885) The politics of Aristotle: introduction and translation, vol 1. Clarendon Press, Oxford
42. Russell S (2019) Human compatible: artificial intelligence and the problem of control. Penguin, London
43. Wallach W, Vallor S (2020) Moral machines: from value alignment to embodied virtue. In: Liao MS (ed) Ethics of artificial intelligence. Oxford University Press, Oxford, pp 383–412
44. Wu X, Zhang X (2016) Automated inference on criminality using face images. arXiv preprint arXiv:1611.04135, pp 4038–4052
45. Arcas BAY, Mitchell M, Todorov A (2017) Physiognomy's new clothes, medium. https://medium.com/@blaisea/physiognomys-new-clothes-f2d4b59fdd6a
46. Wu X, Zhang X (2016) Responses to critiques on machine learning of criminality perceptions (addendum of arXiv: 1611.04135). arXiv preprint arXiv:1611.04135
47. Barrett LF, Adolphs R, Marsella S, Martinez AM, Pollak SD (2019) Emotional expressions reconsidered: challenges to inferring emotion from human facial movements. Psychol Sci Public Interest 20(1):1–68
48. Shapiro A (2017) Reform predictive policing. Nature 541(7638):458–460
49. Burgess M (2018) UK police are using AI to inform custodial decisions–but it could be discriminating against the poor. Wired, 01.03.2018. https://www.wired.co.uk/article/police-ai-uk-durham-hart-checkpoint-algorithm-edit
50. Swain F (2018) Face recognition screens egg donors so your child looks like you, new scientist, 25 Jul 2018. https://www.newscientist.com/article/2175070-face-recognition-screens-egg-donors-so-your-child-will-look-like-you/
51. Nesbitt E (1906) The railway children. Project Gutenberg. https://www.gutenberg.org/files/1874/1874-h/1874-h.htm

Further Reading

Basl J, Bowen J (2020) AI as a moral right-holder. In: Dubber M, Pasquale F, Das S (eds) The Oxford handbook of ethics of AI. Oxford University Press, Oxford, p 289

Bryson JJ (2018) Patiency is not a virtue: the design of intelligent systems and systems of ethics. Ethics Inf Technol 20(1):15–26

Cave S, Nyrup R, Vold K, Weller A (2018) Motivations and risks of machine ethics. Proc IEEE 107(3):562–574

Coeckelbergh M (2010) Robot rights? Towards a social-relational justification of moral consideration. Ethics Inf Technol 12(3):209–221

Coeckelbergh M (2020) AI ethics. MIT Press, Boston, MA

Donath J (2020) Ethical issues in our relationship with artificial entities. In: Dubber M, Pasquale F, Das S (eds) The Oxford handbook of ethics of AI. Oxford University Press, Oxford, pp 53–73

Giubilini A, Savulescu J (2018) The artificial moral advisor. The "ideal observer" meets artificial intelligence. Philos Technol 31(2):169–188

Gunkel DJ (2014) A vindication of the rights of machines. Philos Technol 27(1):113–132

Gunkel DJ (2018a) Robot rights. MIT Press, Boston, MA

Gunkel DJ (2018b) The other question: can and should robots have rights? Ethics Inf Technol 20(2):87–99. https://doi.org/10.1007/s10676-017-9442-4

Gunkel DJ, Bryson JJ (eds) (2014) Machine morality: the machine as moral agent and patient. Philos Technol 27(1):1–142

Kurzweil R (2000) The age of spiritual machines: when computers exceed human intelligence. Penguin, London

Lara F, Deckers J (2020) Artificial intelligence as a Socratic assistant for moral enhancement. Neuroethics 13(3):275–287

Moor JH (2020) The nature, importance, and difficulty of machine ethics. In: Machine ethics and robot ethics. Routledge, London, pp 233–236

Savulescu J, Maslen H (2015) Moral enhancement and artificial intelligence: moral AI? In: Beyond artificial intelligence. Springer, Cham, pp 79–95

Tegmark M (2017) Life 3.0: being human in the age of artificial intelligence. Knopf, New York

Wallach W, Allen C (2008) Moral machines: teaching robots right from wrong. Oxford University Press, Oxford

Wallach W, Vallor S (2020) Moral machines: from value alignment to embodied virtue. In: Liao MS (ed) Ethics of artificial intelligence. Oxford University Press, Oxford, pp 383–412

Some Perspectives on AI: Cultural Considerations

Arun C (2020) AI and the global south: designing for other worlds. In: Dubber M, Pasquale F, Das S (eds) The Oxford handbook of ethics of AI. Oxford University Press, Oxford

Coeckelbergh M (2022) The Ubuntu robot: towards a relational conceptual framework for intercultural robotics. Sci Eng Ethics 28(2):1–15

Friedman C (2022) Ethical concerns with replacing human relations with humanoid robots: an ubuntu perspective. AI Ethics:1–12. https://doi.org/10.1007/s43681-022-00186-0

Gal D (2020) Perspectives and approaches in AI ethics: East Asia. In: Dubber M, Pasquale F, Das S (eds) The Oxford handbook of ethics of AI. Oxford University Press, Oxford

Gwagwa A, Kazim E, Hilliard A (2022) The role of the African value of Ubuntu in global AI inclusion discourse: a normative ethics perspective. Patterns 3(4):100462

Kim B, Wen R, Zhu Q, Williams T, Phillips E (2021) Robots as moral advisors: the effects of deontological, virtue, and Confucian role ethics on encouraging honest behavior. In: Companion of the 2021 ACM/IEEE international conference on human-robot interaction. Association for Computing Machinery, New York, pp 10–18

Lewis, J.E., Abdilla, A., Arista, N., Baker, K., Benesiinaabandan, S., Brown, M., Cheung, M., Coleman, M., Cordes, A., Davison, J. and Duncan, K., 2020. Indigenous protocol and artificial intelligence position paper

Lewis JE, Arista N, Pechawis A, Kite S (2018) Making kin with the machines. J Design Sci. https://doi.org/10.21428/bfafd97b

Richardson K (2020) The complexity of otherness: anthropological contributions to robots and AI. In: Dubber M, Pasquale F, Das S (eds) The Oxford handbook of ethics of AI. Oxford University Press, Oxford

Rizk N (2020) Artificial intelligence and inequality in the Middle East: the political economy of inclusion. In: Dubber M, Pasquale F, Das S (eds) The Oxford handbook of ethics of AI. Oxford University Press, Oxford

Glossary

Abduction In reasoning, to proceed from a set of observations to the most likely conclusion, even if the information is incomplete.

Accountability To be held accountable is to have responsibility to explain, justify, and/or rectify one's actions and decisions.

Agent neutrality Roughly, a moral theory is agent neutral if it does not matter who performs a particular action or brings about a certain outcome; moral reasoning is agent neutral if the reasoning applies to all agents equally.

Agent relativity A moral theory is agent relative if the identity of the agent performing an action or faced with a particular set of moral requirements is at least sometimes relevant.

Alchemy Medical practice dedicated to the attempt to turn base metals into gold; general term used to indicate the attempt to greatly transmute the nature of anything.

Authority/subversion In Moral Foundations theory, a foundation rooted in our primate history of hierarchical groups, relating to leadership, respect for authority and traditions.

Autonomy Literally, self-rule. In ethics, the capacity to govern one's own life.

Autonomy, machine The capacity of machines to behave without direct or immediate human supervision.

Autonomy, relational In ethics, an approach to autonomy which also stresses the importance of human connectedness and the need for this in order for autonomy to develop and flourish.

Behaviourism, methodological A methodological approach in psychology which studies the mind through studying behaviour, often treating the mind as a kind of black box, with input and output as stimulus and response.

Behaviourism, philosophical The philosophical approach to mind and body, that proposes that the mind can be understood in terms of outward behaviour, including language.

Beneficence The aim to produce good for another person or persons.

P. Boddington, *AI Ethics*, Artificial Intelligence: Foundations, Theory, and Algorithms, https://doi.org/10.1007/978-981-19-9382-4

Big Data See Data, big

Bias A situation where different individuals and/or groups are treated differently to others, in ways which are considered both disadvantageous and unjustified and/or based upon inaccurate information.

Black box In computing, science, and engineering, a system which is considered in terms of its outputs and inputs; in AI, generally refers to a system where it may be hard or perhaps impossible to know what precisely is in the black box.

Care ethics An approach to ethics which stresses the foundations of morality in human connectedness and stresses relationships and context in moral judgement and action.

Care/harm In Moral Foundations theory, a foundation related to our capacity as mammals to experience attachment and to experience the pain of others.

Cassandra A Trojan priestess fated by the god Apollo to pronounce true prophecies which nobody believed; usually refers to someone whose correct prophecies of doom are rejected.

Categorical imperative A command which is binding regardless of the wishes of the individual concerned. In Kant's ethics, the categorical imperative is a general system for working out the demands of morality by determining what duties are binding on all rational beings.

Conscience A person's inner sense of right or wrong.

Consequentialism In ethics, the view that the only or chief matter of relevance in ethics is the outcomes of actions.

Content moderation A set of practices aiming to restrict or limit the content of online communications.

Control problem, the A group of issues concerned with the limits of human capacity to control the outcomes of artificial intelligence.

Conversational implicature In pragmatics, an indirect or implied speech act which is not purely implied by the formal content of what is said but which is inferred from contextual clues. E.g. 'I'm not hungry at the moment' meaning a refusal of an offer of food.

Data ethics A branch of ethics concerned with issues about data such as privacy, anonymity, ownership, surveillance, etc.

Debunking accounts, debunking explanations A type of explanation purporting to prove that something is 'nothing but' something else (and therefore, nothing special, nothing mysterious, etc.).

Deduction In reasoning, logical inference from premises to conclusion such that, if the reasoning is valid and the premises are true, the conclusion must be true.

Dehumanisation To dehumanise somebody is to overlook or intentionally ignore or degrade their moral status as a human being and/or person deserving of equal respect with others.

Deontology, deontological ethics In ethics, any normative ethical theory which consists in largely or wholly of sets of rules of action, or of which rules form a major part.

Digital divide Describes the considerable gulfs between different individuals and sectors of the population in terms of access to, and understanding of, new technologies.

Dilemmas, moral A genuine moral dilemma involves a clash between incommensurable values such that, whatever course of action a person takes, there is a moral cost. Moral philosophers disagree on whether serious and genuine moral dilemmas exist.

Discourse analysis A discipline or approach to language which uses various techniques to uncover features of natural language and communication.

Discourse ethics A group of theories concerning the features that communication between individuals and groups must have in order to achieve standards of moral justification.

Dog whistle In linguistics, refers to forms of speech which are alleged to signal some message, generally discriminatory or defamatory, intended to be understood only by certain groups, and/or to be masked such that plausible denial is possible.

Doxxing, doxing The action of releasing identifying personal information about someone, usually online, with the intent of causing harm or of increasing the likelihood that the person will come to harm.

Dualism In philosophy of mind, the cluster of theories concerning the relation between the mind and the body which holds that minds and bodies differ in some significant way and that neither can be reduced to the other. Substance dualism holds that mind and body are different kinds of substance; property dualism holds that mind and body are different kinds of property, which may be attributed to the same event or process.

Duty, imperfect A duty over which one has some discretion as to when, where, and how to fulfil, such as the duty to help others.

Duty, perfect A duty binding at all times. Usually expressed in the negative, such as to refrain from killing, lying, stealing.

Dystopia An imagined future with many negative aspects.

Eliminative materialism In philosophy of mind, the view that our common-sense idea of the nature of mind is wrong, and that various mental states the existence of which we take for granted do not in fact exist.

Empiricism The view that knowledge comes predominantly from observations gained through the senses, i.e. from experience.

Enlightenment An intellectual movement largely of the eighteenth century which stressed the importance of reason over tradition for understanding the world, and which placed a high value on fostering scientific discovery.

Epistemology The theory of knowledge, a branch of philosophy which explores foundational questions about the nature of and justification of different kinds of knowledge.

Ethics washing The practice of attempting to make an organisation or set of activities seem legitimate or justified by paying lip services to some statement of ethical concern and/or the adoption of visible display of ethical conduct.

Ethnography A group of qualitative methodologies in the social sciences involving close observation of a group of people or community in the everyday conduct of their affairs.

Eudaimonia Greek word, often translated 'happiness' or 'good life' and generally taken to imply a broad conception of a life well lived.

Event horizon In relation to technology, a stage of progress where the rate and quality of change is such that it is impossible before this stage to understand what things would be like after the event horizon.

Existential risk Any large-scale risk which may lead to widespread loss of life, up to and including the extinction of the human species and/or many other species.

Expanding circle A claim, popularised by Peter Singer in his book of the same name, that over the course of centuries, humans have increased the range of their moral concern to a wider and wider number of human beings and animals outside of their immediate social group.

Experience machine A thought experiment devised by Robert Nozick in which one imagines entering a machine where one experiences a pleasant state of affairs, better than the real world, yet entirely separate from reality.

Explainability In AI, the possibility of being able to give an account of how the AI operates, or of what is going on inside the black box. Whether or not any particular aspect of AI is explainable will be relative to context and to the audience requiring an explanation.

Extended mind theory A group of philosophical theories concerning the nature of the mind which considers that cognition may not be understood purely as occurring 'inside our heads' but may essentially or contingently involve the external world.

Fact–value distinction The philosophical claim that statements concerning facts about the world are entirely distinct from statements about value; that value is not to be found 'in the world'.

Fairness There are various different accounts of fairness, but all regard fairness as requiring the distribution of value to be made impartially and without reference to features of an individual or their situation which is regarded as irrelevant.

Fairness/cheating In Moral Foundations theory, a foundation concerned with reciprocating with others, justice, rights, and autonomy.

Felicific calculus A method devised by Jeremy Bentham for calculating the relative amounts of happiness for different courses of action.

Filter bubble A term often credited to Eli Pariser to refer to a situation where algorithms reduce the material to which a person is exposed online so that they only see certain limited material and points of view.

Framing Any means by which selective attention to part of a text or message is produced.

Free speech The broad claim that individuals should be able to express their opinions on any matter without restriction from authorities. Does not generally imply a right to any particular platform from which one's views will be widely heard.

Freedom of expression A term often used to imply a broader range of media of expression than 'speech' per se, such as visual media.

Functionalism In philosophy of mind, the theory that the mind and elements of it such as intentions and beliefs can be explained entirely in terms of the function that it plays within an overall cognitive system. Minds thus do not necessarily require brains.

GDPR General Data Protection Regulations, legislation introduced in Europe in 2018 based on 7 general principles for the protection of privacy and data handling.

Ghost in the machine A phrase coined by Gilbert Ryle to mock the Cartesian view that the mind is a mental substance somehow inhabiting a material body (substance dualism).

Golden age A term originating from Greek and Roman poets, referring to an age of greatness, great happiness, prosperity, and harmony.

Golden Rule Broadly, the principle of treating others as one would wish to be treated oneself. There are many different expressions of roughly the same concept.

Golem In Jewish folklore, an animated creature made entirely of inanimate matter such as mud or clay.

Happiness, eudaimonic conception of A philosophical position on the nature of happiness, that it concerns the best way to live a whole life, and is to be assessed over the course of an entire life.

Happiness, hedonic conception of A philosophical position on the nature of happiness, that it concerns the subjective nature of experiences; happiness may be equated with pleasure and the absence of pain.

Harm principle The principle in John Stuart Mill's defence of free speech in On Liberty, that the only legitimate cause to restrict free speech is harm to others. This did not include mere offence.

Homo faber Literally, 'man the maker', a view of human beings that emphasises their capacity for craftwork and for creating tools which enable them to control their environment.

Homo ludens Literally, 'man the player', a view of human beings expressed by Johan Huizinga, that an essential aspect of human existence is play, especially as it relates to culture.

Homo religious An idea, associated with Mercia Eliade, that the religious urge is an essential aspect of humans.

Human in the loop In AI, a system where a human being plays an essential role in critical aspects of decision-making, giving ultimate control to the human.

Human on the loop In AI, a system where a human being has oversight and can intervene and play a role, if need be, but is not an essential part of normal functioning.

Human nature Any broad characterisation of the general or essential nature of human beings.

Iatrogenesis, iatrogenic harm Harm caused by a practice which is intended to produce good, originally used in the context of medicine, for example, harms caused by the practice of medicine such as damaging side effects from pharmaceuticals.

Ideal Observer Theory A group of ethical theories which propose that ethical judgements are best made as if by an 'Ideal Observer', an impartial judge in possession of all relevant facts.

Illocutionary In philosophy of language, a speech act which is intended to have an effect, such as a command, a promise, or a question.

Imitation game A Victorian parlour game which involved guessing on the basis of answers to questions alone if a person was a man or a woman; used by Alan Turing as the basis for the 'Turing Test' to determine if a machine appeared to have developed intelligence.

Induction In reasoning, the drawing of general inferences from premises such as empirical observations; the premises make the conclusion more likely, but do not guarantee its truth.

Instrumental Something is given instrumental value if it is valued only or chiefly for its use in producing something else of value.

Intelligence explosion An idea introduced by I J Good, that as machines become more intelligent, eventually reach a runaway reaction of continual self-improvement.

Intentionality Of the mind, its capacity to be about something, to represent something; for one's mental states to have content.

Intrinsic Of itself. Something is valued intrinsically if it is valued for itself and not merely for its usefulness.

Intuition Various meanings, in ethics, generally refers to an immediate response to an ethical question.

Knowing how and knowing that To know how is to have the capacity to perform some task without necessarily being able to explain every aspect; to know that something is to have knowledge about that thing.

Knowledge by acquaintance Knowledge gained by direct experience of a thing: e.g. 'I know David quite well.'

Knowledge by description Factual knowledge about a thing: e.g. 'I know that David likes lemon meringue pie.'

Liberty/oppression In Moral Foundations theory, the foundation relating to resistance to and resentment about domination by others.

Linguistic turn In philosophy, a general movement associated especially with early to mid-twentieth century philosophy where the philosophical methodology over many different areas focused on the analysis of language.

Locutionary act A speech act which performs the function of conveying meaning.

Longtermism In philosophy, the view that the maximum utility will be gained from resource allocation if it is focused on very long-term goals which work towards the survival of humans or other sentient beings far into the future.

Loyalty/betrayal One of six foundations in Moral Foundations theory, concerned with group membership and the sacrifices one be willing to make for the group, deriving from our long history as social animals requiring cooperation to survive.

Luddite Member of a group active during the first industrial revolution which protested against the increased powers that mechanisation would give owners of machinery over workers.

Machine learning A form of artificial intelligence that 'learns' by extrapolating from data to achieve a task without having been specifically programmed to achieve that task, based on computation and statistical methods.

Magnanimity For Aristotle, the virtue of greatness of mind and heart, with a sense of pride and self-worth, not available to the person of general means and ability.

Medicalisation Refers to the process whereby issues which may have multiple causes, or a non-medical cause, are treated as if they were caused by a medical issue and require a medical response.

Metaethics The study of general and foundational questions in ethics, such as whether there is any moral truth, the nature of moral statements, how moral claims can be justified, and so on.

Microaggression A term in linguistics to refer to subtle forms of language which convey aggressive or denigratory attitudes to other individuals or groups.

Midas, King An ancient King of Phrygia, said in Greek mythology to have wished that everything he touched turned to gold, with disastrous results.

Mind uploading The notion that it will one day be possible to transfer a human mind to a sophisticated computer. Usually presumes that personal identity will be retained.

Mind/brain identity theory A group of philosophical views about the relationship between mind and body, which claims that the mind is identical with events and processes in the brain.

Misinformation A term often used in relation to the online world, concerning information taken to be false or misleading, usually by a group such as a corporation, government, or lobby group.

Moore's law The observation made by Gordon E. Moore in 1965 that the number of transistors in a dense integrated circuit doubles roughly every 18 months. Not actually a law.

Moral agent A being with the capacity for moral judgement and decision making.

Moral epistemology That branch of metaethics concerned with the possibility and nature of moral knowledge.

Moral Foundations theory A theory which attempts to explain the origins of moral reasoning and the dimensions of difference in moral attitude among people by proposing an empirically discoverable innate set of moral foundations.

Moral luck The circumstances where a moral agent may be held responsible or morally culpable in some way, regardless of how they acted.

Moral patient Any being which merits moral respect and consideration.

Moral status For a being to possess moral status is to have value in and of itself within a moral system.

Natural language processing (NLP) The capacity of a computer to understand human speech and writing used in various language-related tasks.

Non-maleficence The value of not causing harm; note this is not precisely equivalent to the value of beneficence.

Normal accidents Concept developed by Charles Perrow to describe highly complex and tightly coupled systems where occasional failure is inevitable.

Nuremberg doctors' trial A trial by the US in Nuremberg in 1946–7 of defendants, mostly medical doctors, accused of medical experiments without consent and mass murder under the guise of euthanasia.

Object of morality The purpose of morality, the range of reasons which explain why we need some system of morality.

Ontology A branch of metaphysics dealing with the nature of being; an ontology describes the kinds of being or things that there are in the world.

Orthogonality thesis The claim that intelligence is unrelated to values, so that from an entity's possession of intelligence, no prediction could be made about its values or goals; its utility function is separate from its general intelligence.

p-hacking In science, the practice of selectively reporting only those results which have the greatest statistical significance.

Paperclip example A much-cited example given by Nick Bostrom of perverse instantiation where a super-intelligent AI instructed to make paperclips disastrously turns everything, including humans, into paperclips.

Pareidolia The tendency to see a meaningful image in visual patterns.

Perlocutionary act In philosophy of language, an actual effect in the world which occurs as a result of a speech act.

Person-centred care In settings such as healthcare or social care, the aim to treat each client as an individual taking due account of their particular situation, wishes, and values.

Person, legal A legal fiction whereby an entity such as a corporation is recognised as able to do the sorts of things that a person can do in law, such as enter into contracts.

Persona Aspect of a person which is perceived socially by others.

Personal identity In philosophy, theories of personal identity generally address the question of what makes a person the same person over the course of time.

Persuasive technology Technology designed to influence change the behaviours or attitudes of users without direct coercion.

Perverse instantiation Occurs when AI satisfies its goals but in a way which conflicts with the intentions of the programmers.

Phrenology A pseudoscience which claimed that a person's character could be assessed by examining the precise shape of their skull.

Phronesis Greek word generally translated as 'practical wisdom', referring to the development of ethical judgement.

Physicalism The philosophical claim that there is nothing in the world except the physical realm, and everything can be understood in terms of the physical.

Posthumanism An approach to the future which looks to human development, usually via technology, to a state of progress in capacities which will produce entities which are no longer to be regarded as human, but are nonetheless presumed to represent progress beyond the human.

Pragmatics Branches of linguistics or philosophy of language which studies aspects of natural language and communication.

QALY In medicine, quality adjusted life-year, formula used to measure the value of medical interventions in terms of expected outcomes and benefit.

Rational agent Any being, whether human or not, capable of understanding and responding to the demands of reason. There may be different conceptions of what it is to be rational.

Reductive explanations An explanation of a phenomenon which purports to explain it fully in terms of another phenomenon, usually at a more basic level. E.g. reducing psychology to biology, biology to chemistry, chemistry to physics, etc.

Reflective equilibrium A term originating in John Rawls' A Theory of Justice describing the end point of a process whereby we refine our beliefs against theory and evidence.

Relativism In ethics, the view that moral values have no universal basis but are contingent upon society and culture; sometimes, the view that it is wrong to impose one's moral views on other cultures.

Repugnant conclusion A term coined by Derek Parfit in *Reasons and Persons*, also known as the 'mere addition' paradox, which describes the counterintuitive conclusion that, if it is always better to increase total happiness, then a world with very many barely happy beings is to be preferred to a world with fewer beings each of whom are much happier.

Responsibility, causal An agent or object with significant causal role in bringing about a situation is causally responsible (regardless of intention).

Responsibility, moral An agent who is held to account in any way for a situation has moral responsibility; may or may not imply causal responsibility; may or may not imply intention (for example, in situations of culpable negligence).

Ring of Gyges In Greek myth, a magical ring that could render its wearer invisible.

Sanctity/degradation In Moral Foundations theory, the moral foundation thought to arise from the psychology of disgust and contamination and concerned with attempts to live in an elevated way.

Sentient being Any being capable of awareness of any sort (which need not include self-awareness).

Shadow banning The practice of reducing the visibility of a person's online presence in ways of which they may be unaware.

Singularity In technology, a possible future event of extremely rapid technological improvement to the extent that we can no longer control it or predict what changes this might produce.

Skinner box A controlled environment, as developed by the behaviourist psychologist B F Skinner, for examining an animal's behaviour in response to certain set stimuli.

Socio-technical system A system which encompasses technology plus societal aspects, including hardware, software, individual, and social factors.

Speech act Any utterance which serves a function in meaning; may include real-world effects of the utterance.

Standing reserve In Heidegger's philosophy of technology, to treat the world as a standing reserve is to regard it as raw material for technology to be available on demand.

Standpoint epistemology A group of theories of knowledge which claim that certain types of knowledge can only be properly attained by those from certain groups or with certain basic experiences in life.

Stigma Social disapproval towards a person, group, or trait.

Supererogation The performance of good actions which go beyond the demands of duty.

Superintelligence Artificial general intelligence which has reached the stage where it can recursively self-improve to levels far exceeding human intelligence.

Talos In Greek mythology, a giant bronze automaton which protected Europa in Crete from invaders.

Technological determinism A reductive account of technology which claims that the technology advances according to its own imperatives, and is inevitable.

Technological fix The attempt to use technology to solve problems, often problems caused by technology; see technological solutionism.

Technological solutionism Assumption that the answer to any specific issue is technology; see technological fix.

Technological unemployment Generally refers to a future situation where mass scale unemployment arises where the use of automation has rendered many jobs redundant.

Teleology The explanation of phenomena in terms of purpose or final end; a teleological view of the world is one in which it is governed by purposes.

Transhumanism A vision of human progress using biological or technological means to surpass current human capacities in various ways so that the human race is radically transformed. See also posthumanism.

Transparency In AI, refers to AI the operations of which are readily comprehensible, and can be explained and communicated; lack of a 'black box'. See explainability.

Trolley problems Refers to hypothetical moral situations where a stark choice of two possibilities must be made, created to test and explore the nature of the underlying moral judgements and beliefs.

Turing test Test devised by Alan Turing, based upon guessing from the answers to a series of questions, whether the answers came from a computer or a human being, to give an indication that the intelligence of the computer could not be distinguished from that of a human being if it 'passed' the test.

Uncanny valley Term devised by Masahiro Mori to refer to the point at which a humanoid robot has a sufficient degree of resemblance to the human form that it becomes creepy or 'uncanny'.

Universalism, in ethics The claim that moral judgements should apply consistently to all similar situations; and/or the claim that all persons are of equal moral worth.

Utilitarianism A group of consequentialist theories which hold that the end to be aimed in all actions at is to be understood in terms of happiness or pleasure. Variations aim at welfare, or desire or preference satisfaction.

Utility monster A hypothetical creature, devised by Robert Nozick to demonstrate internal difficulties with utilitarianism, which gains far more utility from any resources it consumes than do others.

Utopia An imagined future perfect state or society.

Validation The process of ensuring that a product or service meets the specifications of those seeking its development.

Value alignment In AI, the process of ensuring that AI fits with, or does not significantly deviate from, human values and/or the values of those developing, using, or affected by the AI. Difficulties may arise for example because of the control problem.

Veil of Ignorance In John Rawls' Theory of Justice, the veil of ignorance is a hypothetical situation in which those creating just rules for a society must be unaware of what particular position they might occupy in the resulting society, designed to produce fairness.

Verification The process of checking if a product or service meets the requirements of regulation, or some imposed condition such as safety.

Virtue ethics A group of normative ethical theories which stress the role of virtues within a whole life and the development of character.

Zombie In philosophy of mind, a zombie is not necessarily a reanimated corpse, but is a creature identical to one which possessed a mind, but absent of any subjective experiences, designed as a thought experiment to test various theories of the relation between mind and body.

Index

Printed in the United States
by Baker & Taylor Publisher Services